PHILIP'S

G000292470

STREET ATLAS
Cambridgeshire

Cambridge, Huntingdon, March, Peterborough, St Neots, Wisbech

www.philips-maps.co.uk

First published in 2001 by

Philip's, a division of
Octopus Publishing Group Ltd
www.octopusbooks.co.uk
2-4 Heron Quays, London E14 4JP
An Hachette Livre UK Company
www.hachettelivre.co.uk

Third edition 2008
First impression 2008
AMCA

ISBN 978-0-540-09292-5 (spiral)

© Philip's 2008

Ordnance Survey®

This product includes mapping data licensed
from Ordnance Survey®, with the permission of
the Controller of Her Majesty's Stationery Office.
© Crown copyright 2008. All rights reserved.
Licence number 100011710

Data for the speed cameras provided by
PocketGPSWorld.com Ltd.

Ordnance Survey and the OS symbol are
registered trademarks of Ordnance Survey, the
national mapping agency of Great Britain

Post Office is a trade mark of Post Office Ltd
in the UK and other countries

Printed and bound in China by Toppan

Contents

II **Mobile safety cameras**

III **Key to map symbols**

IV **Key to map pages**

VI **Route planning**

X **Administrative and Postcode boundaries**

1 **Street maps** at 3½ inches to 1 mile

208 **Street maps** at 1¾ inches to 1 mile

239 **Street maps** at 3½ inches to 1 mile

246 **Street map of Cambridge city centre** at 7 inches to 1 mile

247 **Index** of towns, villages, streets, hospitals, industrial estates, railway stations, schools, shopping centres, universities and places of interest

Digital Data

The exceptionally high-quality mapping found in this atlas is available as digital data in TIFF format, which is easily convertible to other bitmapped (raster) image formats.

The index is also available in digital form as a standard database table. It contains all the details found in the printed index together with the National Grid reference for the map square in which each entry is named.

For further information and to discuss your requirements, please contact victoria.dawbarn@philips-maps.co.uk

On-line route planner

For detailed driving directions and estimated driving times visit our free route planner at www.philips-maps.co.uk

Mobile safety cameras

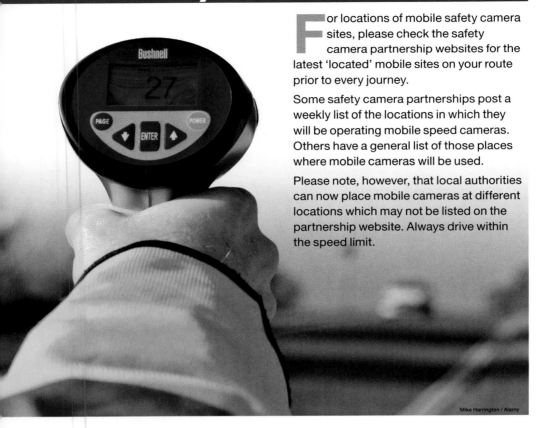

Mike Harrington / Alamy

For locations of mobile safety camera sites, please check the safety camera partnership websites for the latest 'located' mobile sites on your route prior to every journey.

Some safety camera partnerships post a weekly list of the locations in which they will be operating mobile speed cameras. Others have a general list of those places where mobile cameras will be used.

Please note, however, that local authorities can now place mobile cameras at different locations which may not be listed on the partnership website. Always drive within the speed limit.

Useful websites

Cambridgeshire Safety Camera Partnership
www.cambs.police.uk/camops/safetycameras

Hertfordshire Safety Camera Partnership
www.hertsdirect.org/envroads/roadstrans/rsu/driving/safetycameras

Further information
www.dvla.gov.uk
www.thinkroadsafety.gov.uk
www.dft.gov.uk
www.road-safe.org

Motorway with junction number	
Primary route – dual/single carriageway	
A road – dual/single carriageway	
B road – dual/single carriageway	
Minor road – dual/single carriageway	
Other minor road – dual/single carriageway	
Road under construction	
Tunnel, covered road	
Speed cameras - single, multiple	
Rural track, private road or narrow road in urban area	
Gate or obstruction to traffic (restrictions may not apply at all times or to all vehicles)	
Path, bridleway, byway open to all traffic, restricted byway	
Pedestrianised area	
Postcode boundaries	
County and unitary authority boundaries	
Railway, tunnel, railway under construction	
Tramway, tramway under construction	
Miniature railway	
Railway station	
Private railway station	
Metro station	
Tram stop, tram stop under construction	
Bus, coach station	

Walsall

South Shields

Ambulance station	
Coastguard station	
Fire station	
Police station	
Accident and Emergency entrance to hospital	
H **Hospital**	
+ **Place of worship**	
Information Centre (open all year)	
Shopping Centre	
P P&R **Parking, Park and Ride**	
PO **Post Office**	
Camping site, caravan site	
Golf course, picnic site	
Prim Sch **Important buildings, schools, colleges, universities and hospitals**	
Built up area	
Woods	
River Ouse **Tidal water, water name**	
Non-tidal water – lake, river, canal or stream	
Lock, weir, tunnel	
Church **Non-Roman antiquity**	
ROMAN FORT **Roman antiquity**	
87 237 **Adjoining page indicators and overlap bands** The colour of the arrow and the band indicates the scale of the adjoining or overlapping page (see scales below)	

Enlarged mapping only

Railway or bus station building	
Place of interest	
Parkland	

■ The small numbers around the edges of the maps identify the 1 kilometre National Grid lines ■ The dark grey border on the inside edge of some pages indicates that the mapping does not continue onto the adjacent page

Acad	**Academy**	Inst	**Institute**	Recn Gd	**Recreation Ground**
Allot Gdns	**Allotments**	Ct	**Law Court**		
Cemy	**Cemetery**	L Ctr	**Leisure Centre**	Resr	**Reservoir**
C Ctr	**Civic Centre**	LC	**Level Crossing**	Ret Pk	**Retail Park**
CH	**Club House**	Liby	**Library**	Sch	**School**
Coll	**College**	Mkt	**Market**	Sh Ctr	**Shopping Centre**
Crem	**Crematorium**	Meml	**Memorial**	TH	**Town Hall/House**
Ent	**Enterprise**	Mon	**Monument**	Trad Est	**Trading Estate**
Ex H	**Exhibition Hall**	Mus	**Museum**	Univ	**University**
Ind Est	**Industrial Estate**	Obsy	**Observatory**	W Twr	**Water Tower**
IRB Sta	**Inshore Rescue Boat Station**	Pal	**Royal Palace**	Wks	**Works**
		PH	**Public House**	YH	**Youth Hostel**

The scale of the maps on the pages numbered in blue is 5.52 cm to 1 km • 3½ inches to 1 mile • 1: 18103	0 ¼ ½ ¾ 1 mile 0 250 m 500 m 750 m 1 kilometre
The scale of the maps on pages numbered in green is 2.76 cm to 1 km • 1¾ inches to 1 mile • 1: 36206	0 ¼ ½ ¾ 1 mile 0 250m 500m 750m 1 kilometre
The scale of the maps on pages numbered in red is 11.04 cm to 1 km • 7 inches to 1 mile • 1: 9051	0 220 yards 440 yards 660 yards ½ mile 0 125m 250m 375m ½ kilometre

DY7

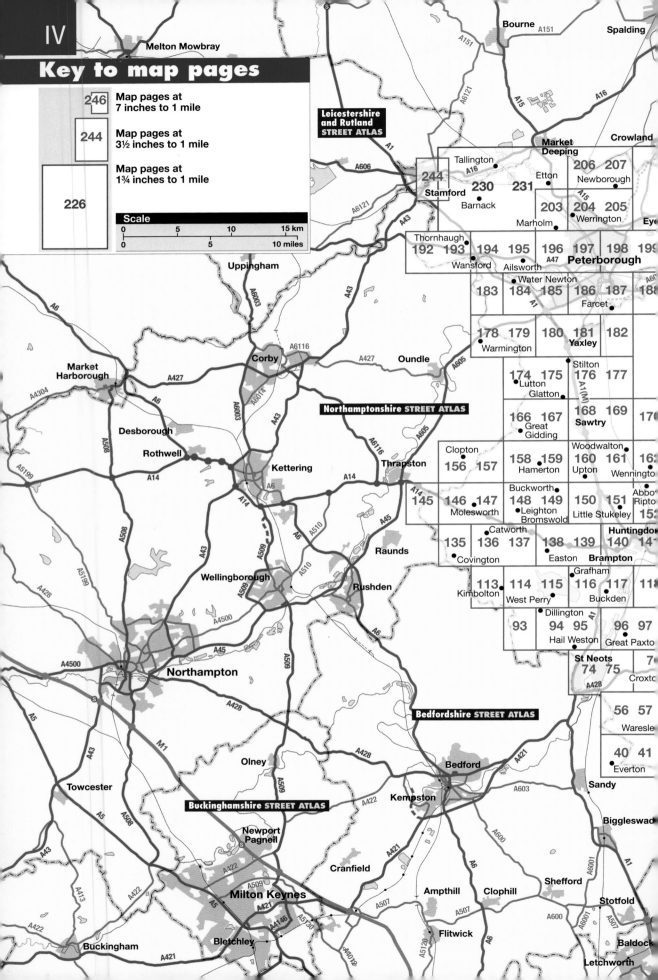

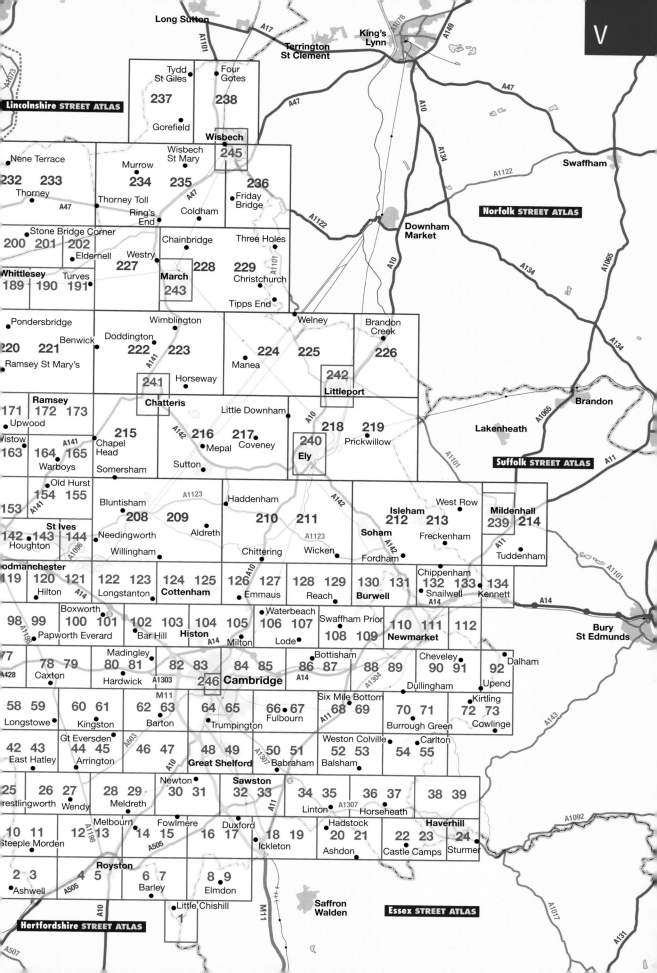

Scale

0   5   10 km

0   1   2   3   4   5   6 miles

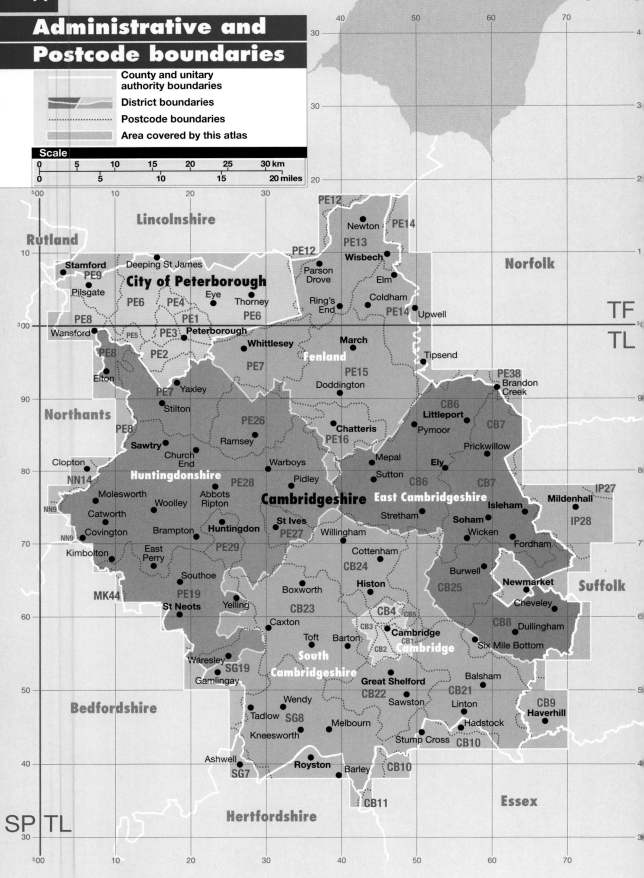

Administrative and Postcode boundaries

County and unitary authority boundaries

District boundaries

Postcode boundaries

Area covered by this atlas

Scale

0 5 10 15 20 25 30 km
0   5   10   15   20 miles

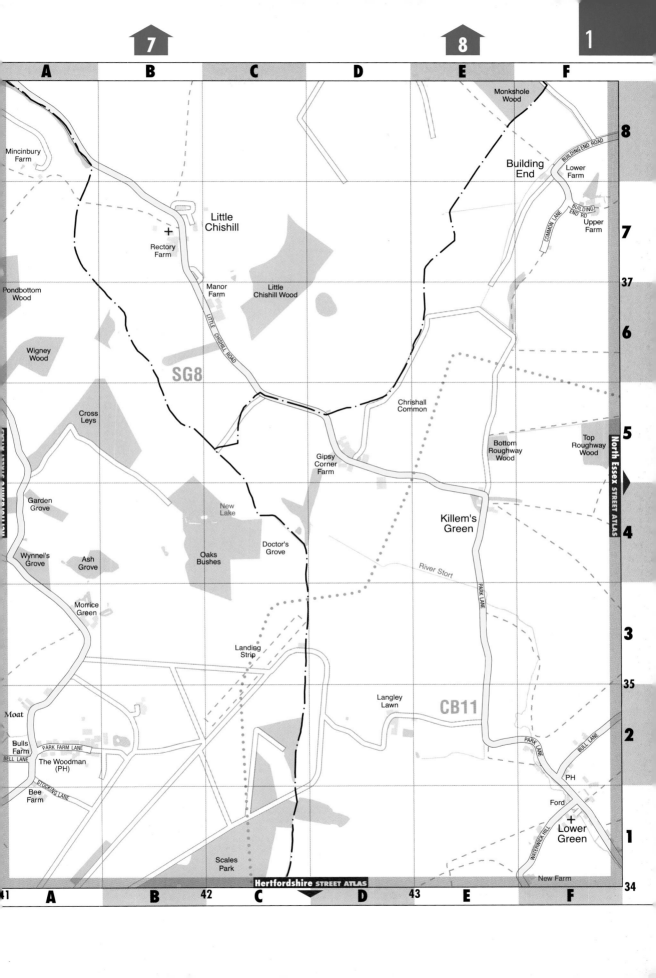

A   B   C   D   E   F

Monkshole Wood

Mincinbury Farm

Building End

BUILDING END ROAD

Lower Farm

8

Little Chishill

Rectory Farm

COMMON LANE

BUILDING END RD

Upper Farm

7

Pondbottom Wood

Manor Farm

Little Chishill Wood

37

LITTLE CHISHILL ROAD

6

Wigney Wood

SG8

Cross Leys

Chrishall Common

Bottom Roughway Wood

Top Roughway Wood

5

North Essex STREET ATLAS

Garden Grove

New Lake

Gipsy Corner Farm

Killem's Green

Wynnel's Grove

Ash Grove

Oaks Bushes

Doctor's Grove

River Stort

PARK LANE

4

Morrice Green

3

Landing Strip

35

Moat

Langley Lawn

CB11

PARK LANE

BULL LANE

Bulls Farm

PARK FARM LANE

BELL LANE

The Woodman (PH)

PH

2

STOCKING LANE

Ford

Bee Farm

Lower Green

WATERWICK HILL

1

Scales Park

New Farm

34

Hertfordshire STREET ATLAS

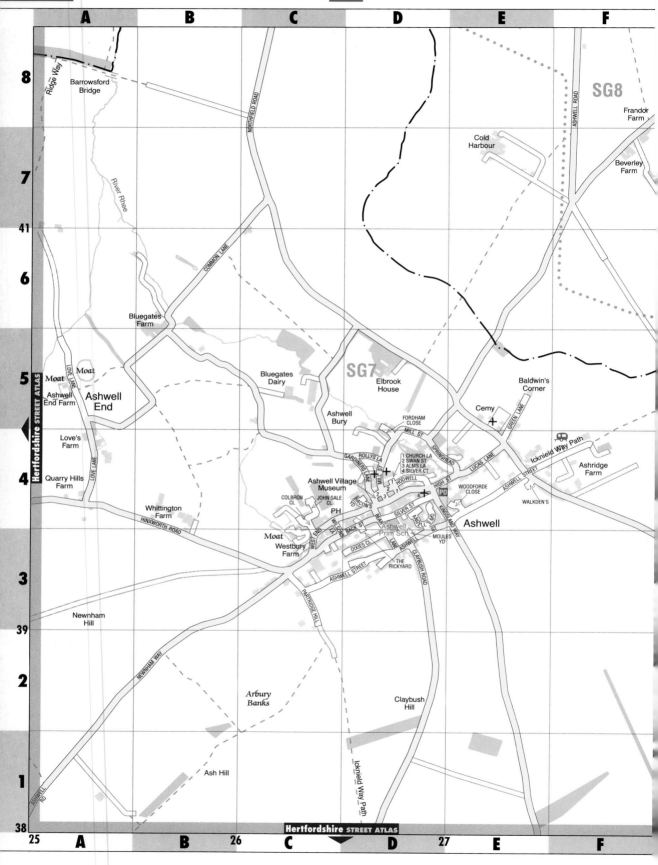

8

7

41

6

SG8

Ridge Way

Barrowsford
Bridge

Northfield Road

River Rhee

Cold
Harbour

Frandor
Farm

Beverley
Farm

Common Lane

Bluegates
Farm

SG7

Hertfordshire STREET ATLAS

5

Moat
Moat
Love Lane

Ashwell
End Farm

Ashwell
End

Love's
Farm

Love Lane

Quarry Hills
Farm

Bluegates
Dairy

Ashwell
Bury

Elbrook
House

FORDHAM
CLOSE

MILL ST

Cemy

SPRINGHEAD

Baldwin's
Corner

Green Lane

Icknield Way Path

Ashridge
Farm

4

1 CHURCH LA
2 SWAN ST
3 ALMS LA
4 SILVER CT

Whittington
Farm

HINXWORTH ROAD

COLBRON
CL

JOHN SALE
CL

PH

Ashwell Village
Museum

GARDINERS LANE

ROLLYS LA

BACON'S
YD

LUCAS LANE

HODWELL

HIGH ST

LUCAS LANE

WOODFORDE
CLOSE

PO

Ashwell

Ashwell STREET

WALKDEN'S

3

Moat

Westbury
Farm

WEST END

WILSON CL

BACK ST

DIXIES CL

Ashwell
Prim Sch

SILVER ST

MOULES
YD

CLAYBUSH ROAD

KINGS-END WAY

THE
RICKYARD

Ashwell STREET

PARTRIDGE HILL

39

Newnham
Hill

2

NEWNHAM WAY

Arbury
Banks

Claybush
Hill

Icknield Way Path

1

Ash Hill

ASHWELL RD

38

Steeple
Morden

Wyndmere
Farm

Gatley
End

Icknield Way Path

Upper
Gatley End

High
Farm

Flitton's Farm

Hill
Plantation

Morden
Grange
Farm

SG8

Chalk
Pit

Morden Grange
Plantation

Morden Grange
Plantation

Sunnymead
Farm

STATION ROAD

SUNNYMEAD OR 1
DAMSON WK 2
VILLAGE WAY 3
ORCHARD VW 4

Next
Odsey

Cheyneys
Lodge

Chain Walk

Tumulus

Redlands
Farm

SG7

Hill
Farm

Penny Loaf
Hill Plantation

PH

Icknield Way

A505

Ashwell &
Morden

Ashwell
Fields

Highley
Hill

Chain Walk

Odsey

70

Gallows Hill
(Tumulus)

A B C D E F

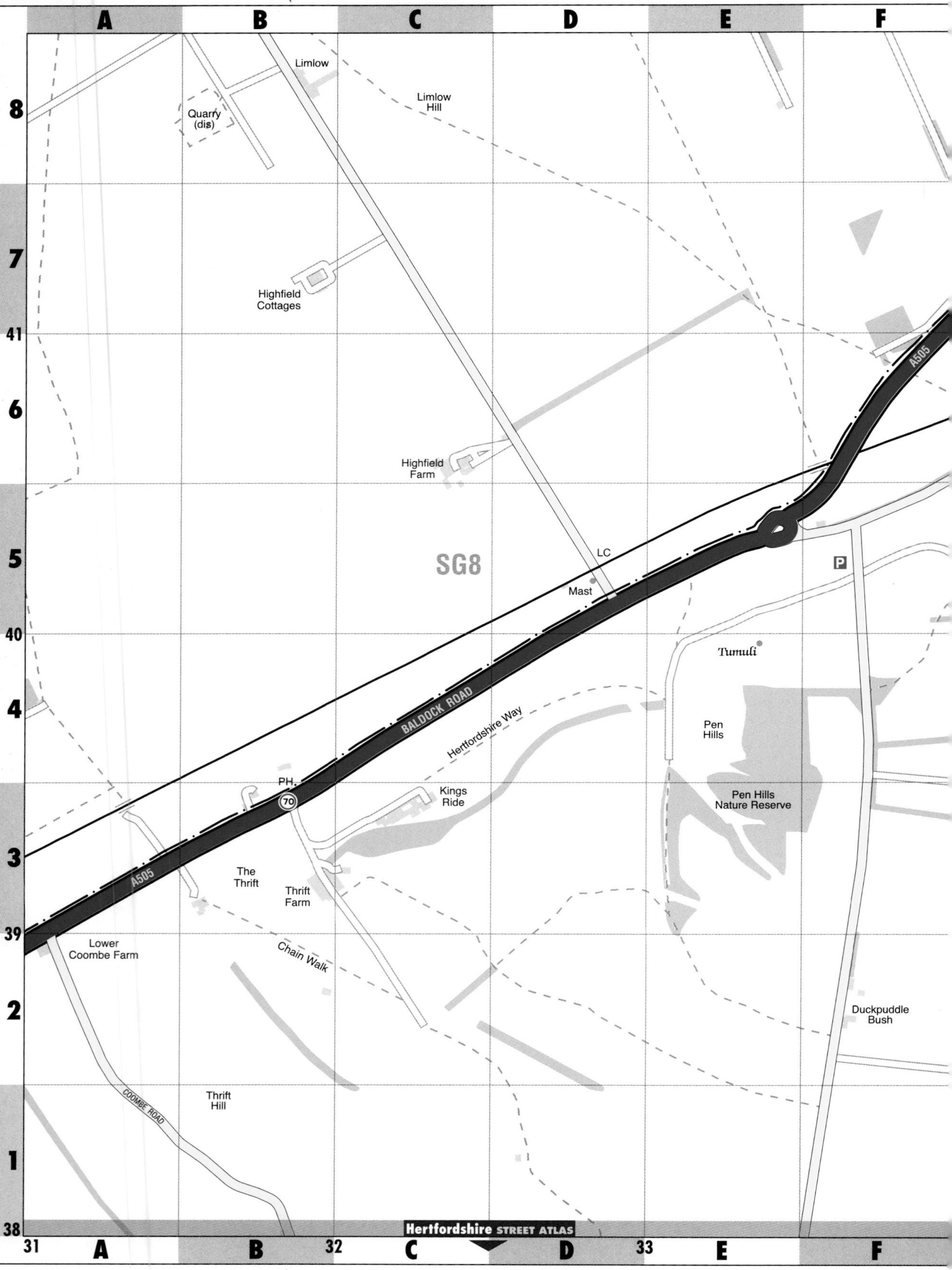

8

Limlow

Quarry
(dis)

Limlow
Hill

7

41

Highfield
Cottages

6

Highfield
Farm

SG8

5

LC

Mast

40

Tumuli

4

BALDOCK ROAD

Hertfordshire Way

Pen
Hills

Pen Hills
Nature Reserve

PH.

70

Kings
Ride

3

A505

The
Thrift

Thrift
Farm

39

Lower
Coombe Farm

Chain Walk

2

Duckpuddle
Bush

COOMBE ROAD

Thrift
Hill

1

38

31   A   B   32   C   D   33   E   F

A505

P

A   B   C   D   E   F

8

Heath Farm

Icknield Way Path

7

Hyde Hill Farm

Hillside Farm

Noon's Folly Farm

41

Mast

A505

NEWMARKET ROAD

Wardington Bottom

6

Burloes Plantation

Burloes Hall

Burloes Farm

5

Lowerfield

40

SG8

Cow Plantation

Poor's Land

4

B1039

Hillside Farm

New Stud Farm

Heath Farm

3

Whiteley Hill

ROYSTON R

BAKERS LANE

B1368

39

HIGH ST

2

Valley Cottage

Barley +

GREENBURY

CHANAPER CL

DR

HORSESHOE

TOMLING CL

Newsells Park Stud

THE MOUNT

CROSSWAYS

LONDON ROAD

SMITHS

END LANE

1

Newsells Farm

B1368

Horseshoe Farm

38

37   A   B   38   C   D   39   E   F

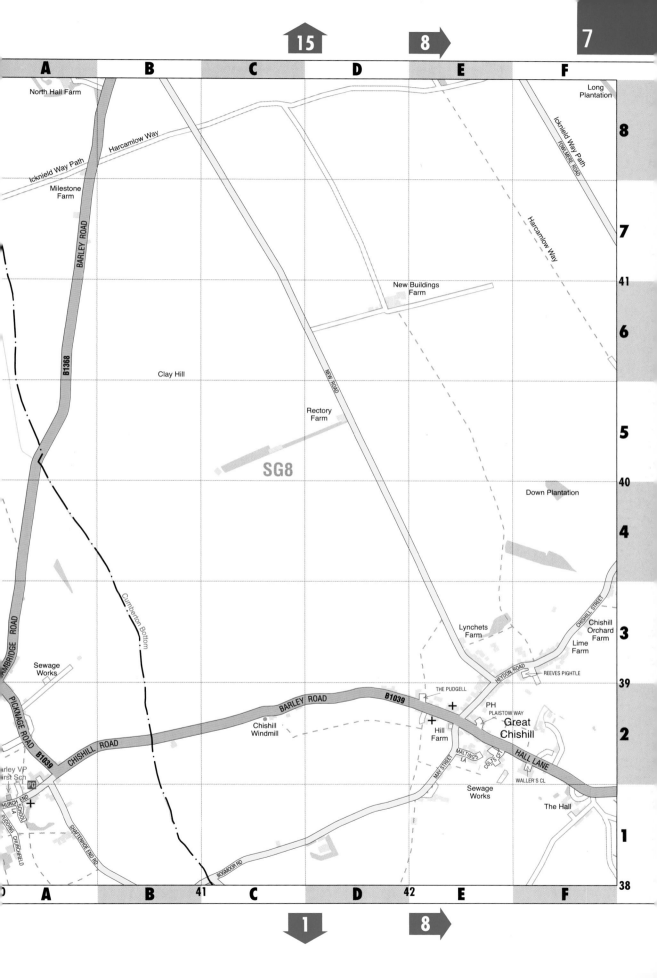

A   B   C   D   E   F

8   Long
     Plantation

     Anthonyhill   Anthony
     Plantation   Hill   Redlands   CB10

7
41

     *Strip
     Lynchets*
6   Reeve
     Hill
     Valley
     Plantation   Pightle
                                                                                    Farm

     Heydon
     Valley Farm   HERTFORD LANE

5   Heydon   MILL CAUSEWAY   Crawley
                   Lane   End
                   Farm   HEYDON LANE   Hillside   SG8   PINKENEYS
                                          Farm   *Earthwork*
40   HIGH   ENGLERIC   Moat   Castle
     CL   FLOWMERE RD   Grove

                                                                                          HEYDON LA
4   PH   Arrow   Wire
     CHRISHALL STREET   Plantation   Farm   CB11
     PO   Chrishall
     Woodgreen
     Animal Shelter   King's
                                Broad   PALMERS LANE   Park   Grove
                                Green Farm   Broad   Wood
                                               Green
                                               Chrishall   PH
3   Holy Trinity   BRICK   Park
                  Wisdom's   CE Prim Sch   ROW   Farm   Park Wood
                  Grove   HIGH STREET   Icknield Way Path
39   HOG'S LA
                                                      Parsonage   CHALKY LANE
                                                      Farm
2   Barnard's   *Moat*
     Wood
                                               HOLLOW ROAD   Glebe
                                                                           Farm
                                                           New   BURY LANE
                                                           Farm

1   B1039
                                          BUILDING
                                          END ROAD

38   Monkshole
           Wood   North Essex STREET ATLAS
     43   A   B   44   C   D   45   E   F

A B C D E F

CB10

Ickleton
Old Grange

GRANGE ROAD

Welches
Wood

Tumulus

Valance
Farm

8

7

Lodge
Farm

ROYSTON LANE

41

The
Poplars

6

North Essex STREET ATLAS

QUICKSET ROAD

New Jersey
Farm

Sewage
Works

5

40

CB11

Elmondbury

ICKLETON ROAD

ELM CL

HORSESHOE
CLOSE

HOLLOW ROAD

Strethall Hall
Farm

Strethall
Wood

Strethall

4

PH

Church
Farm

Elmdon

Round
Grove

Hill
Farm

KING'S LANE

FREEWOOD LANE

Mill Mound

Freewood
Farm

HOLLOW ROAD

Free
Wood

Ann's
Wood

3

Moat

Millfield
Plantation

39

Lofts
Hall

ESSEX HILL

Bradley
Grove

Bixett
Wood

2

Littlebury
Green

White
Coppice

THOMAS WK

Lee
Wood

Ash
Grove

Green
Farm

1

Elmdon
Lee

Wilford's
Wood

Beavers'
Wood

Teapond
Grove

38

A B 47 C D 48 E F

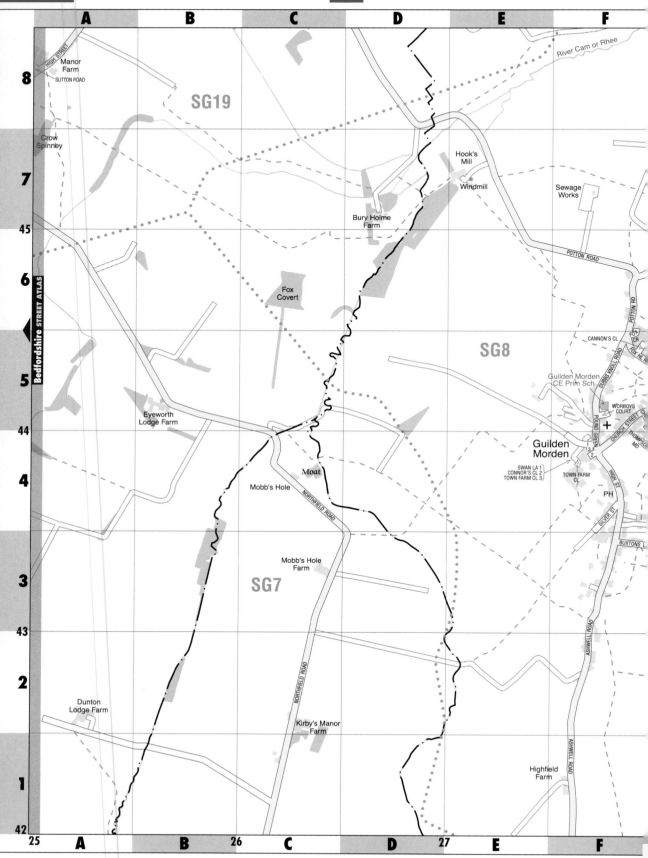

A B C D E F

8

SG19

Manor
Farm
HIGH STREET
SUTTON ROAD

Crow
Spinney

7

River Cam or Rhee

Hook's
Mill

Windmill

Sewage
Works

Bury Holme
Farm

POTTON ROAD

45

6

Bedfordshire STREET ATLAS

Fox
Covert

SG8

PD

POTTON RD

FOX HILL

CANNON'S CL

Guilden Morden
CE Prim Sch

DUBBS KNOLL ROAD

WORBOYS
COURT

5

Eyeworth
Lodge Farm

44

Moat

Mobb's Hole

NORTHFIELD ROAD

POUND GREEN

CHURCH STREET

THOMPSON
RD

Guilden
Morden

SWAN LA 1
CONNOR'S CL 2
TOWN FARM CL 3

TOWN FARM
CL

HIGH ST

4

Mobb's Hole
Farm

PH

SILVER ST

BUXTONS L

SG7

3

NORTHFIELD ROAD

43

ASHWELL ROAD

2

Dunton
Lodge Farm

Kirby's Manor
Farm

ASHWELL ROAD

Highfield
Farm

1

42

25 A B 26 C D 27 E F

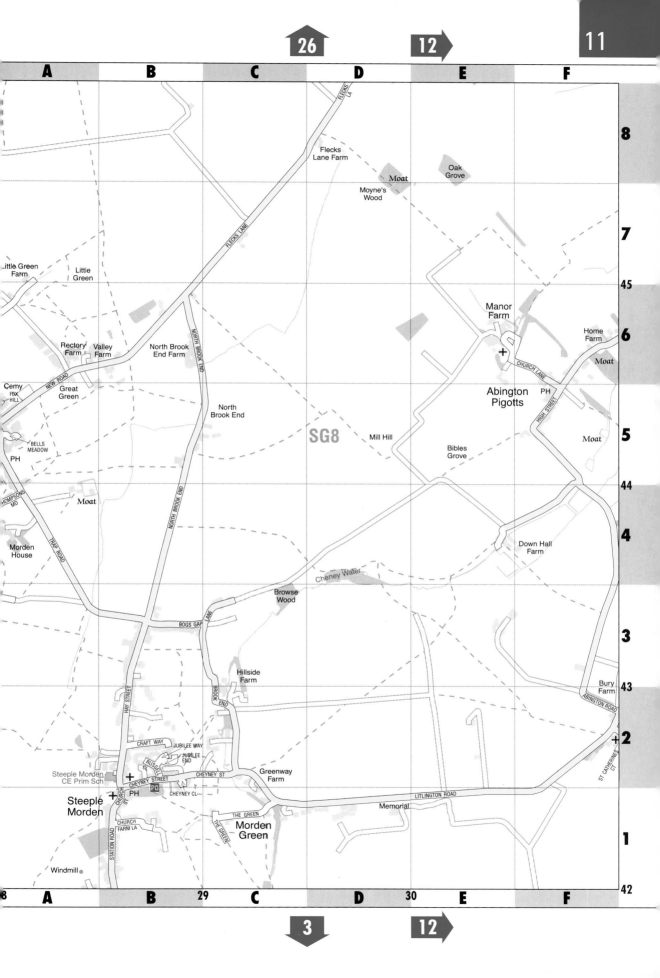

A   B   C   D   E   F

8

Mill River

DANGER AREA

Airfield
(dis)

Control Tower
Museum

Bassingbourn
Barracks

7
Boy
Bridge

FEN ROAD

OXFORD
CL

45
SAGGERS CL   GUISE LANE

Haygate
Farm

NORTH END

Bleak
Farm

Rectory
Farm

6

SG8

THE FILLANCE

WALNUT TREE
CL   PARK VW

Cemy

5

MILL LANE

PH

CHURCH
CL

PORTON VW

PARK CL

ELBOURN WY   C BOURN WAY
KEFFORD CL

Manor
Farm

PLAYSYD

SOUTH

THE LIMES

HIGH ST

WILLMOTT
WY

ELM TREE

44
POPLAR FARM CL

PO

Liby

KNUTSFORD ROAD

PH

PEPPER
CL

LAYNES
DRIVE

THE TANYARD

Ash
Plantation

BROOK ROAD

Bassingbourn

4

Bassingbourn
Prim Sch

Bassingbourn
Village Coll

Clear
Farm

SOUTH END

SPRING LANE

Sewage
Works

Low
Farm

Moat

BASSINGBOURN ROAD

Brook Orchard
Piggery

3

43
Bury
Farm

Cemetery

Darwin
Farm

CHAPEL
CL

PH

MEETING LA

NEW
CL

ABBOTTS
CL

2
SILVER ST   MIDDLE ST

PO

MALTING LA

CHURCH ST   SOUTH ST

Litlington

Icknield Way Path

ST CATHERINES
CT

ANVIL WY

COCKHALL CL

CHERRY TREE
CL

Sheen
Farm

ROYSTON ROAD

1

42
31   A   B   32   C   D   33   E   F

A B C D E F

8

Works
Foxfield Farm
THE GRANGE
BELL CL
HOWARD ROAD
ELM WAY
WHITECROFT ROAD
CHISWICK END
DARITS
HIGH STREET
Meldreth Prim Sch
FLAMBARDS PL
Meldreth
A10
THE MOOR
CH

7
Chiswick End
WOODLANDS DR
Meldreth
Valley Farm
STATION ROAD
THATCHER STANFORDS CL
Melbourn Village Coll
The Moor
Melbourn Science Park
CAMBRIDGE ROAD
Kingsway Golf Centre

45
St Johns Farm
STATION ROAD
McSplash Swimming Pool
Liby
VICARAGE CL
HIGH STREET
DICKASONS
MOAT LANE
LORDSHIP
CAMBRIDGE RD
HALE CL
HALE
PORTWAY
ARMINGFORD CRO
Solway Farm
Tostock Farm

6
Moat
MEADOW WY
COURTLOCK LA
BEETON W
NORGETTS LANE
SPENCER
DRURY LA
BARHAMS CT
RUSSELL WAY
BRAMLEY AVE
WORCESTER WAY
WORCESTER WY
East Farm
RISE
ROSE LANE
GRO CROSS LA
DOLPHIN LANE
MOAT LOCK LA
LITTLE LANE
ORCHARD RD
Melbourn Prim Sch
ORCHARD WY
PRIME
MEADCALF
OLSEN
JOHN ST
MPEY WY
FROG
HINKINS CL
FORDHAM WAY

5
Windpump
Windpump
Bury Lane Fruit Farm
Melda Farm
BURY LANE
Melbourn Bury
THE LAWNS
MEETING LA
CHAPEL
HIGH STREET
PO
ORCHARD RD
NEW RD
PALMER
MAPLE WAY
ELM WYWOOD AV
ASH GR
BEECHWOOD
CEDAR CL
WATER LANE
CLEAR CL
CLEAR CR
CARLTON RI
BEECHWOOD AV
CARLTON RI
VICTORIA WY
Melbourn
SG8

44
Moat
GREENBANKS
THE LAWNS
BACK LANE
BARROW
CHALKHILL
GREENGAGE
GREENGAGE CL
SAXON WAY
Works

4
A10
Long Barrow
Greenlow
NEW ROAD
Harcomlow Way
Icknield Way Path

3
43

2
Muncey's Farm
Summer House Farm

1
Goffers Knoll (Tumulus)
A505

42

37 A B 38 C D 39 E F

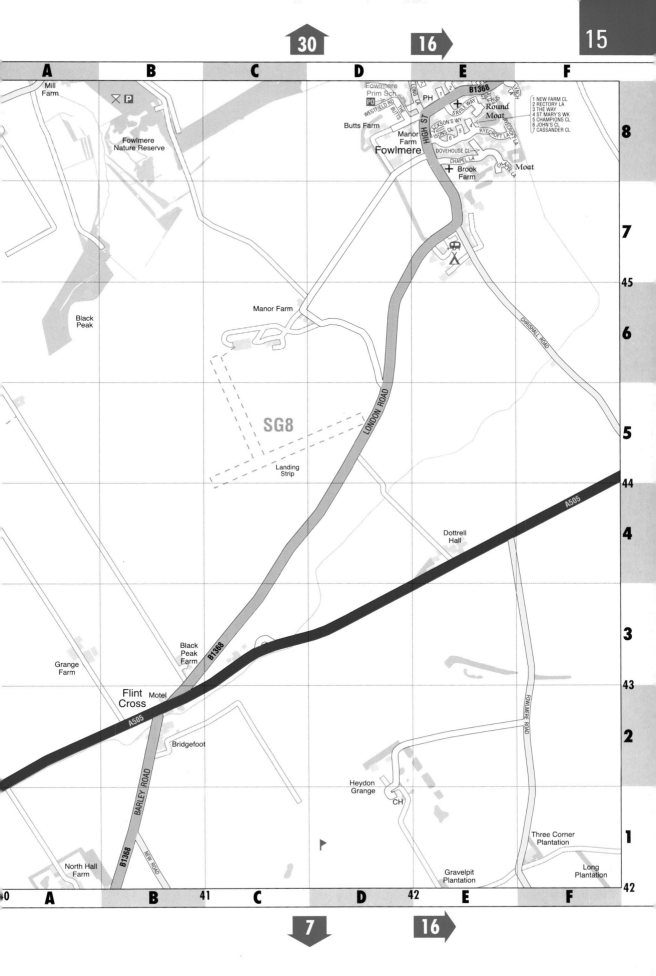

A B C D E F

Newditch
Plantation

GRAVEL PIT HILL

THURLOES WAY

A505

Long
Plantation

American
Air Museum

8

Gravelpit Hill
Plantation

The Royal Anglian
Regiment Museum

7

45

6

CB22

Heath Farm

Home
Plantation

Duxford
Grange House

5

CHRISHALL ROAD

A505

Duxford
Farm Cottages

44

Forty Acre
Plantation

4

SG8

Round
Plantation

3

43

Chrishall
Grange Cottages

2

Chrishall
Grange

Chrishall
Grange
Plantation

CB10

Laburnum
Plantation

1

42

43 A 44 B C 44 D 45 E F

A B C D E F

Gravelpit
Plantation

Duxford
Airfield

Maarnford
Farm

HUNTS ROAD

PETERS F

ST PETER'S ST

GRANGE RD

PH

MINTBURY

MARSH CL

HIGHFIELD
CL

PARSONAGE CL

THE BIGGEN

FISHER CL

RECTORY ROAD

CARTER

+ Moat

PO

Works

BLAKELAND HILL

HINXTON ROAD

Sewage
Works

(dis)

LC

LC

Duxford

Long
Plantation

CB22

ICKLETON ROAD

College
Farm

Barkers
Farm

GRANGE ROAD

45

6

Pepperton
Hill

Hinxton
Mill

5

DUXFORD ROAD

44

Mast

Abbey
Farm

4

ABBEY ST

COPLOE RD

MT1

3

43

Halfmoon
Plantation

CB10

Rectory
Farm

Hill
Cottage

Crossroad
Cottages

2

GRANGE ROAD

Engagement
Plantation

Long
Plantation

Ickleton
Grange

1

42

46 A B 47 C D 48 E F

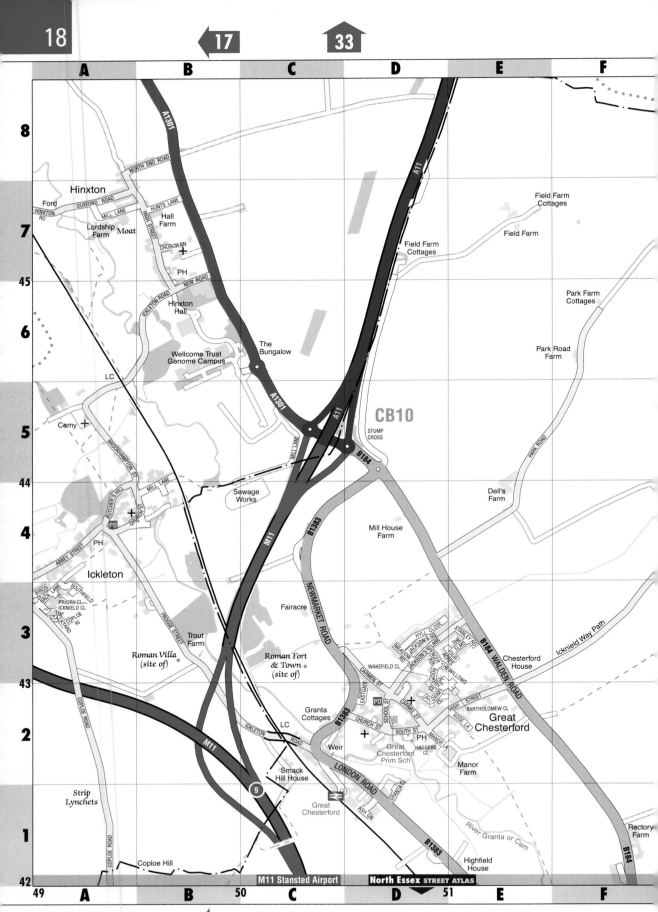

A1301
North End Road
Hinxton
Ford
Hinxton Rd
Duxford Road
Mill Lane
Hunts Lane
High Street
Hall Farm
Church Gn
PH
Lordship Farm
Moat
Ickleton Road
New Road
Hinxton Hall
Wellcome Trust Genome Campus
The Bungalow
LC
A1301
Cemy
Brookhampton St
Mill Lane
Butcher's Hill
Church St
PO
PH
Abbey Street
Ickleton
Birds Cl
Back Lane
Southfield
Priory Cl
Icknield Cl
The Stackyard
Icknield Ri
Frogge Street
Sewage Works
A11
CB10
STUMP CROSS
B184
Field Farm Cottages
Field Farm
Field Farm Cottages
Park Farm Cottages
Park Road Farm
Park Road
Dell's Farm
Mill House Farm
B1383
Newmarket Road
Fairacre
M11
Trout Farm
Roman Villa (site of)
Roman Fort & Town (site of)
Granta Cottages
LC
Ickleton Road
Weir
Smack Hill House
9
Strip Lynchets
Coploe Road
M11
Coploe Road
Coploe Hill
Hyll Close
Jackson's Sq
Jackson Spencer Rd
Meadow
Carmen St
Eastgate
PO
School St
Church St
Wakefield Cl
Carmel St
South St
Great Chesterford Prim Sch
Granta Cl
Ash Gn
London Road
Great Chesterford
B1383
High Street
Stanley Rd
The Elms
The Willows
Hookers Rd
Spring Cl
Bartholomew Cl
Rose La
PH
Haggers Cl
Manor La
Manor Farm
Chesterford House
B184 Walden Road
Icknield Way Path
River Granta or Cam
Highfield House
B184
Rectory Farm

A B C D E F

8

CB21

Hildersham
Wood

Mast

Park
Farm

7

45

Catley
Park

6

Icknield Way Path

Grumble
Hall

Crave
Hall Farm

CB10

5

44

Burtonwood
Farm

Burton
Wood

Great Chesterford
Common

4

COW LANE

Little
Paddocks

Icknield Way Path

3

Paddock
Wood

Park
Farm

43

Moat

Burntwood
End

Rynish
Plantation

Bassingbourne
Wood

2

Heathfield
Grove

Home
Farm

Fordham's
Grove

Fishpond
Plantation

Sewage
Works

Lady
Plantation

Ashwell's
Grove

Chesterford
Research Park

1

PETTS LANE

Emanuel
Wood

42

2   A   B   53   C   D   54   E   F

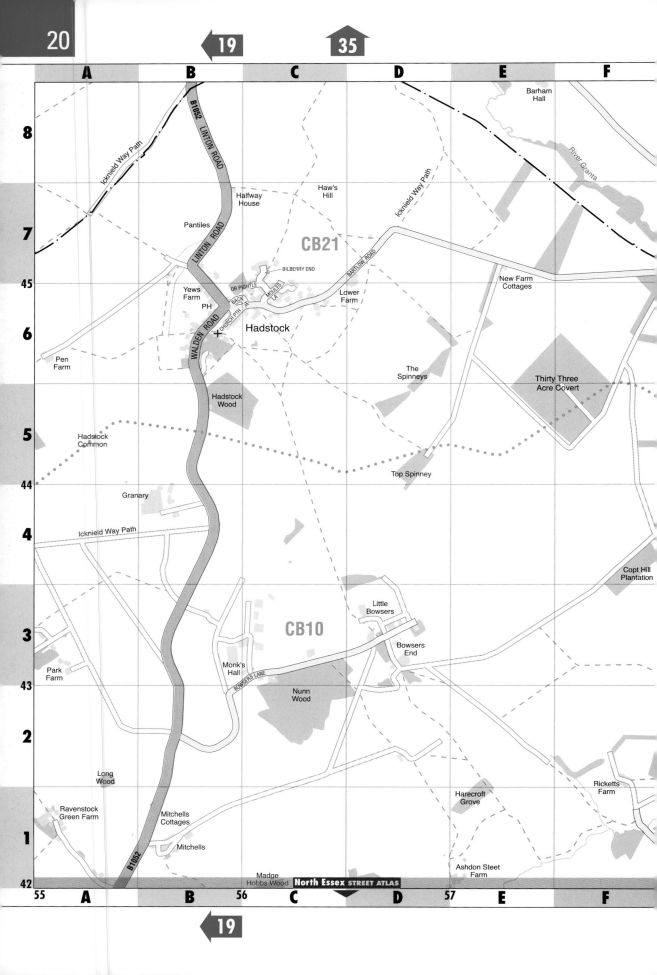

A B C D E F

8

B1052

LINTON ROAD

Icknield Way Path

Barham Hall

River Granta

7

Halfway House

Pantiles

LINTON ROAD

Haw's Hill

Icknield Way Path

CB21

45

BILBERRY END

OR PIGHTLE

BACK LA

MOULES LA

Lower Farm

BARTLOW ROAD

New Farm Cottages

Yews Farm

PH

CHURCH PTH

6

WALDEN ROAD

Hadstock

The Spinneys

Thirty Three Acre Covert

Pen Farm

Hadstock Wood

5

Hadstock Common

Top Spinney

44

Granary

Icknield Way Path

4

Copt Hill Plantation

Little Bowsers

3

CB10

Bowsers End

Park Farm

Monk's Hall

BOWSERS LANE

43

Nunn Wood

2

Long Wood

Ricketts Farm

Ravenstock Green Farm

Mitchells Cottages

Harecroft Grove

1

Mitchells

B1052

Madge Hobbs Wood

Ashdon Steet Farm

42

55 A B 56 C D 57 E F

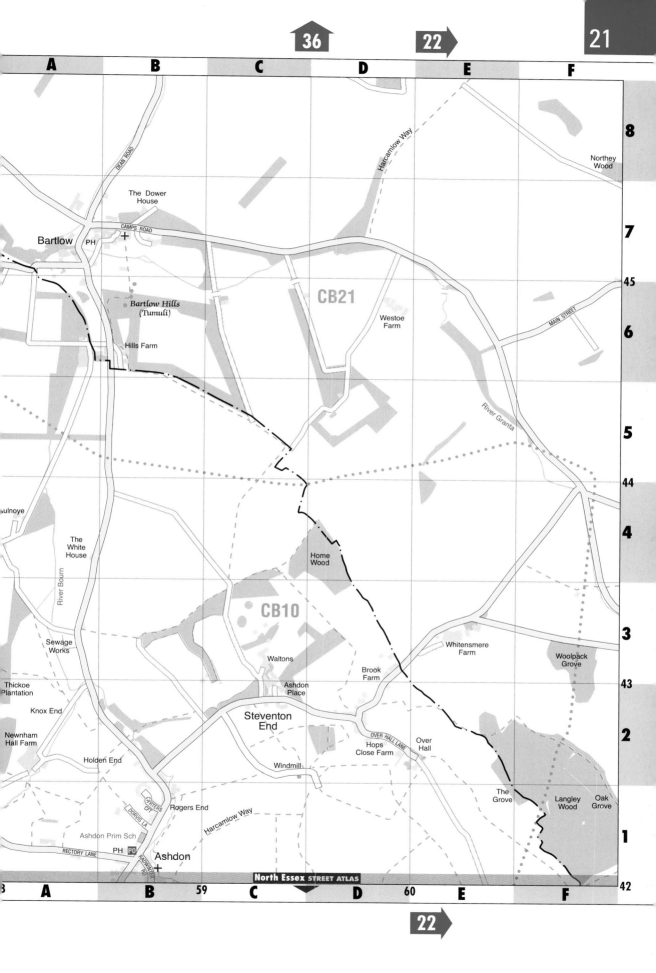

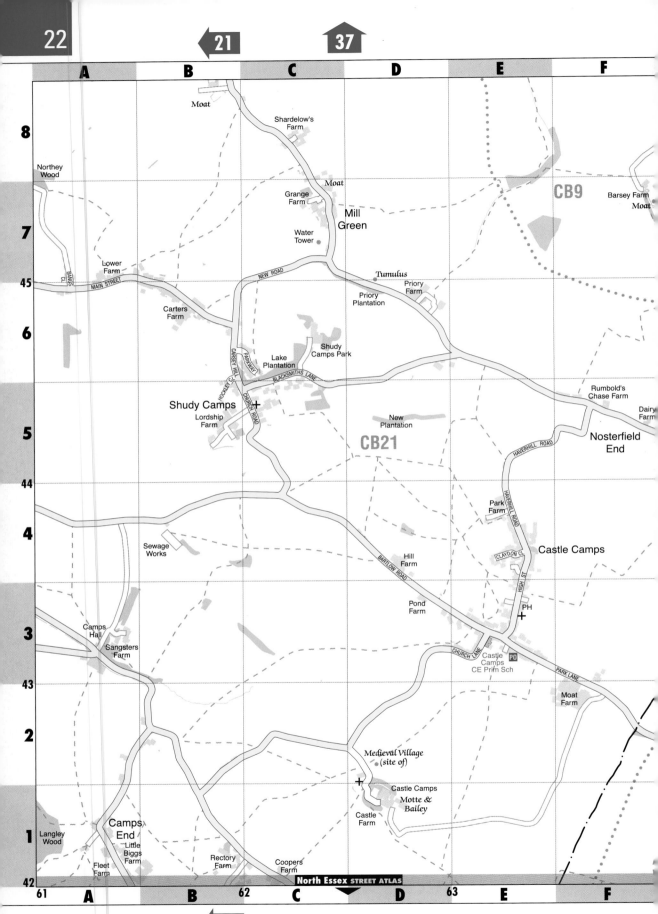

North Essex STREET ATLAS

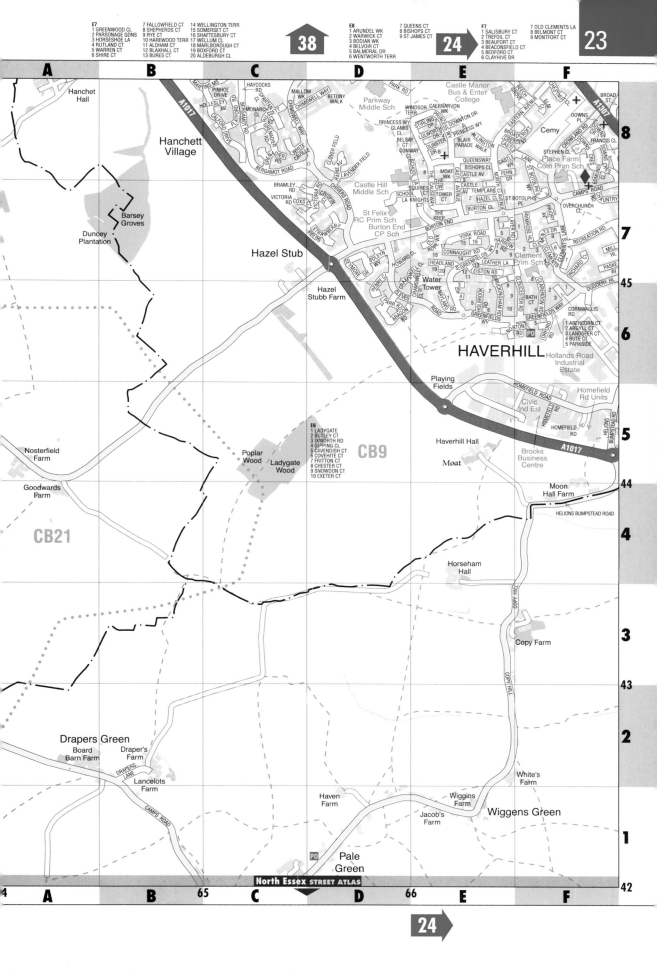

E7
1 GREENWOOD CL
2 PARSONAGE GDNS
3 HORSESHOE LA
4 RUTLAND CT
5 WARREN CT
6 SHIRE CT

7 FALLOWFIELD CT
8 SHEPHERDS CT
9 RYE CT
10 HAREWOOD TERR
11 ALDHAM CT
12 BLAXHALL CT
13 BURES CT

14 WELLINGTON TERR
15 SOMERSET CT
16 SHAFTESBURY CT
17 WELLUM CL
18 MARLBOROUGH CT
19 BOXFORD CT
20 ALDEBURGH CL

E8
1 ARUNDEL WK
2 WARWICK CT
3 BODIAN WK
4 BELVOIR CT
5 BALMORAL DR
6 WENTWORTH TERR

7 QUEENS CT
8 BISHOPS CT
9 ST JAMES CT

F7
1 SALISBURY CT
2 TREFOIL CT
3 BEAUFORT CT
4 BEACONSFIELD CT
5 BEDFORD CT
6 CLAYHIVE DR

7 OLD CLEMENTS LA
8 BELMONT CT
9 MONTFORT CT

E6
1 LADYGATE
2 BUTLEY CT
3 IXWORTH RD
4 GIPPING CL
5 CAVENDISH CT
6 COVEHITE CT
7 FRITTON CT
8 CHESTER CT
9 SNOWDON CT
10 EXETER CT

1 ABERCORN CT
2 ARGYLL CT
3 LANDSEER CT
4 BUTE CT
5 PARKSIDE

HAVERHILL

CB9

CB21

Hanchet Hall
Hanchett Village
Barsey Groves
Duncey Plantation
Nosterfield Farm
Goodwards Farm
Hazel Stub
Hazel Stubb Farm
Poplar Wood
Ladygate Wood
Castle Manor Bus & Enter College
Parkway Middle Sch
Castle Hill Middle Sch
St Felix RC Prim Sch
Burton End CP Sch
Water Tower
Clement Prim Sch
Place Farm Com Prim Sch
Cemy
Hollands Road Industrial Estate
Playing Fields
Civic Ind Est
Homefield Rd Units
Brocks Business Centre
Haverhill Hall
Moat
Moon Hall Farm
Horseham Hall
Copy Farm
Drapers Green
Board Barn Farm
Draper's Farm
Lancelots Farm
Haven Farm
Jacob's Farm
Wiggins Farm
White's Farm
Wiggens Green
Pale Green

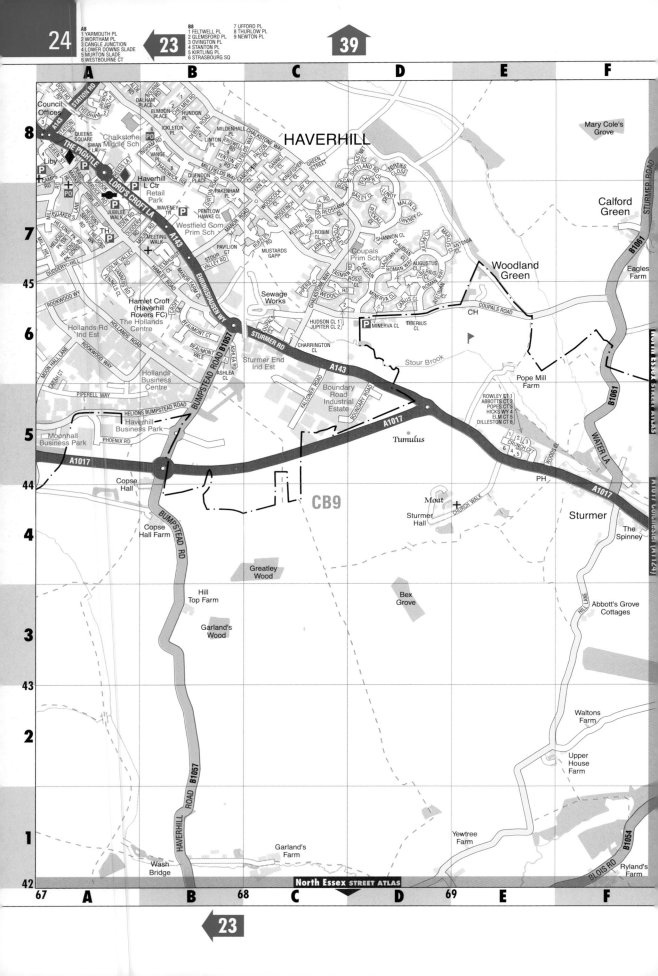

24

A8
1 YARMOUTH PL
2 WORTHAM PL
3 CANGLE JUNCTION
4 LOWER DOWNS SLADE
5 MURTON SLADE
6 WESTBOURNE CT

B8
1 FELTWELL PL
2 GLEMSFORD PL
3 OVINGTON PL
4 STANTON PL
5 KIRTLING PL
6 STRASBOURG SQ

7 UFFORD PL
8 THURLOW PL
9 NEWTON PL

23

39

HAVERHILL

Council Offices

Chalkstone Middle Sch

Mary Cole's Grove

Calford Green

Woodland Green

Haverhill Retail Park

Westfield Gdn Prim Sch

Eagles Farm

Hamlet Croft (Haverhill Rovers FC)

The Hollands Centre

Hollands Rd Ind Est

Sewage Works

Coupals Prim Sch

Coupals Road

Hollands Business Centre

Sturmer End Ind Est

Charrington Cl

Stour Brook

Pope Mill Farm

Piperell Way

Moonhall Business Park

Haverhill Business Park

Boundary Road Industrial Estate

ROWLEY CT 1
ABBOTTS CT 2
POPES CT 3
HICKS WY 4
ELM CT 5
DILLESTON CT 6

CRUNCH CFT

Copse Hall

Tumulus

Sturmer

The Spinney

Copse Hall Farm

Moat

Sturmer Hall

CB9

Church Walk

Abbott's Grove Cottages

Greatley Wood

Bex Grove

Hill Top Farm

Garland's Wood

Waltons Farm

Upper House Farm

Yewtree Farm

Garland's Farm

Wash Bridge

Ryland's Farm

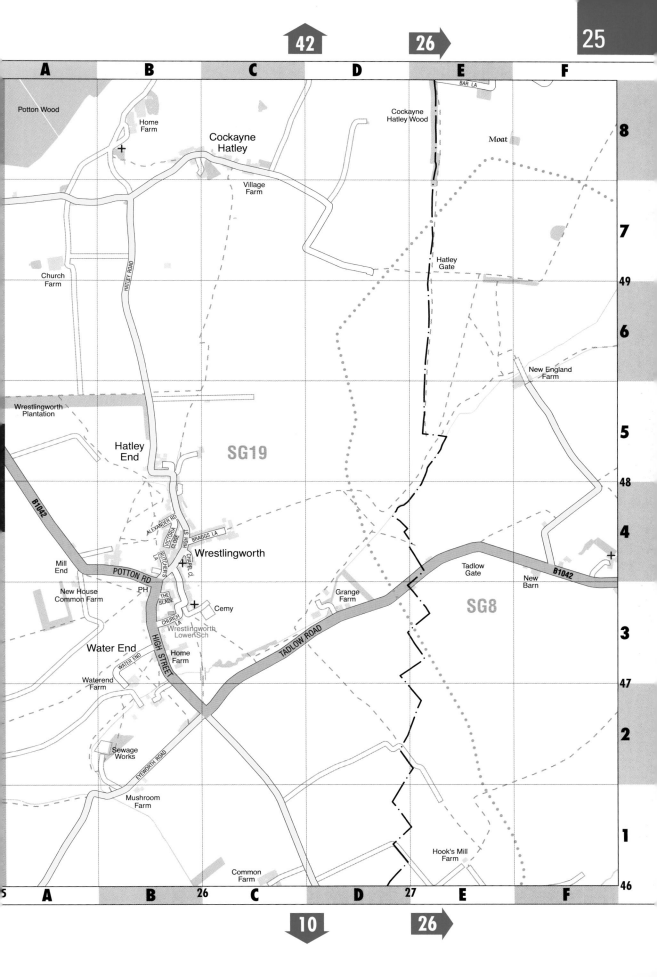

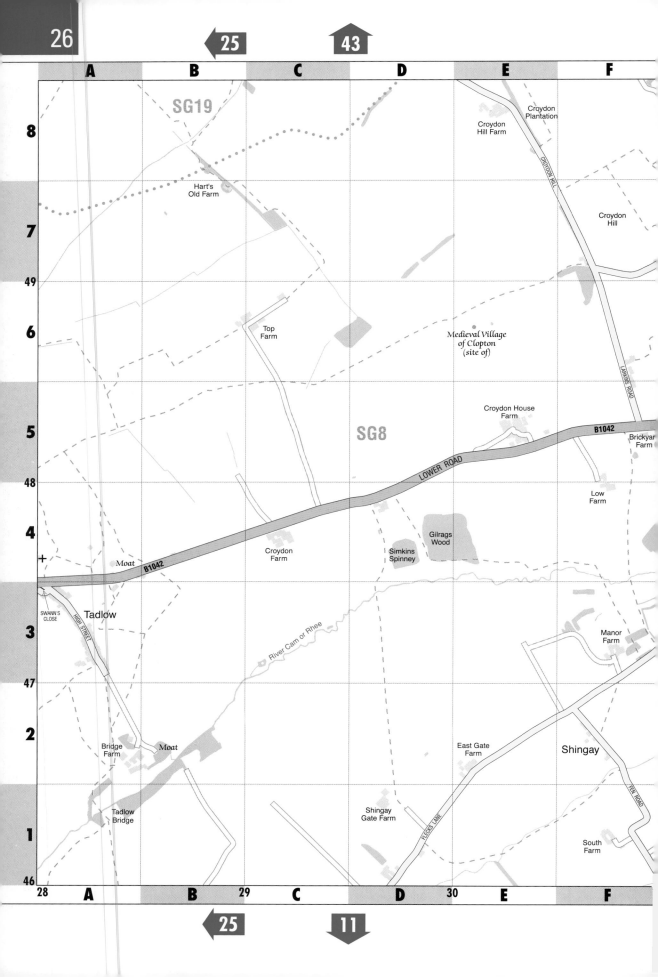

Map labels:

CHURCH LANE
Manor Farm
Medieval Village of Croydon (site of)
Sewage Works
CROYDON ROAD
Moat
PH
HIGH STREET
Croydon
Moat
Valley Farm
Croydon Old Farm
Lower Manor Farm
LOWER ROAD
B1042
River Cam or Rhee
SG8
Water Works
Lordship Spinney
Moat
MILL LANE
Church Farm
Moat
Wendy
Vine Farm
Moat
Site of Preceptory (Knights Hospitallers)
Moat
Moat
Whitelands Barn
Long's Lake
Fen Spinney
DANGER AREA
Airfield (dis)
Rouses Wood
Moat

A1198
ERMINE WAY
Sewage Works
Whitehall Farm
Eight Elms Farm
Harcamlow Way
Cambridge Road Farm
A603
CAMBRIDGE ROAD
CAMBRIDGE ROAD
WIMBRIDGE CT
Wimpole Lodge
Bridge Farm
Drug Farm
Arlington Bridge
Wimpole Avenue
North Road Farm
Road Farm
ERMINE WAY
A1198

Grid references (top): A B C D E F
Grid references (bottom): A B 32 C D 33 E F
Grid references (right): 8 7 49 6 48 5 4 47 3 2 1 46
Bottom left: 1

Arrows: 44, 28 (top); 12, 28 (bottom)

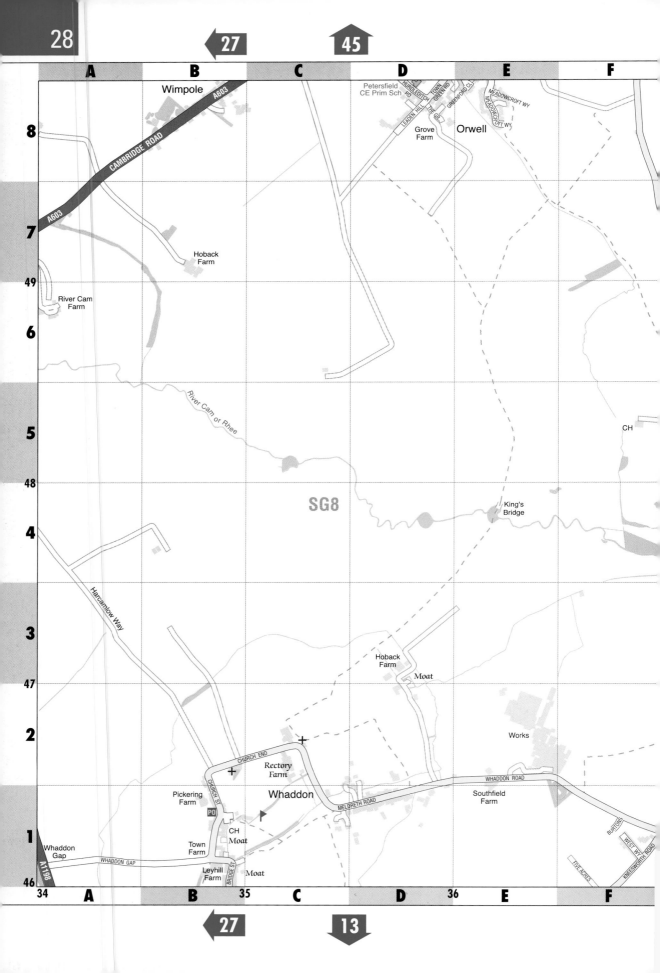

27
45

A **B** **C** **D** **E** **F**

Wimpole

Petersfield
CE Prim Sch

Orwell

8

CAMBRIDGE ROAD

A603

A603

7

Hoback
Farm

Grove
Farm

MEADOWCROFT WY

MEADOWCROFT WY

49

River Cam
Farm

6

River Cam or Rhee

CH

5

SG8

48

King's
Bridge

4

Harcamlow Way

3

Hoback
Farm

Moat

47

Works

2

Church End

Rectory
Farm

WHADDON ROAD

Pickering
Farm

Church St

Whaddon

MELDRETH ROAD

Southfield
Farm

PO

BURTONS

1

Whaddon
Gap

Town
Farm

CH
Moat

WEST WY

A1198

WHADDON GAP

Leyhill
Farm

Bridge St

Moat

FIVE ACRES

KNEESWORTH ROAD

46

34 **A** **B** **35** **C** **D** **36** **E** **F**

27
13

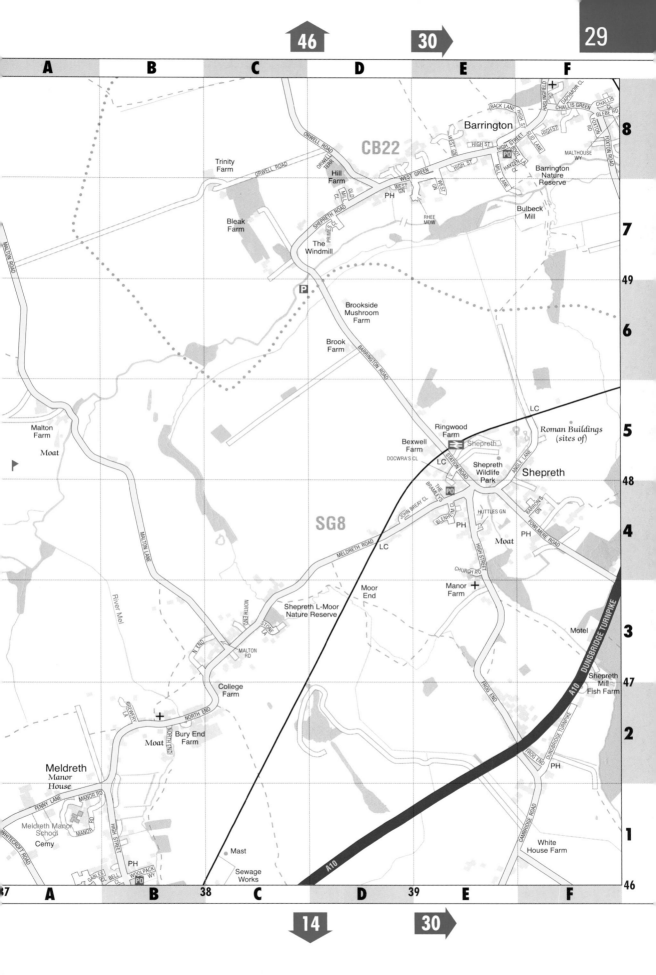

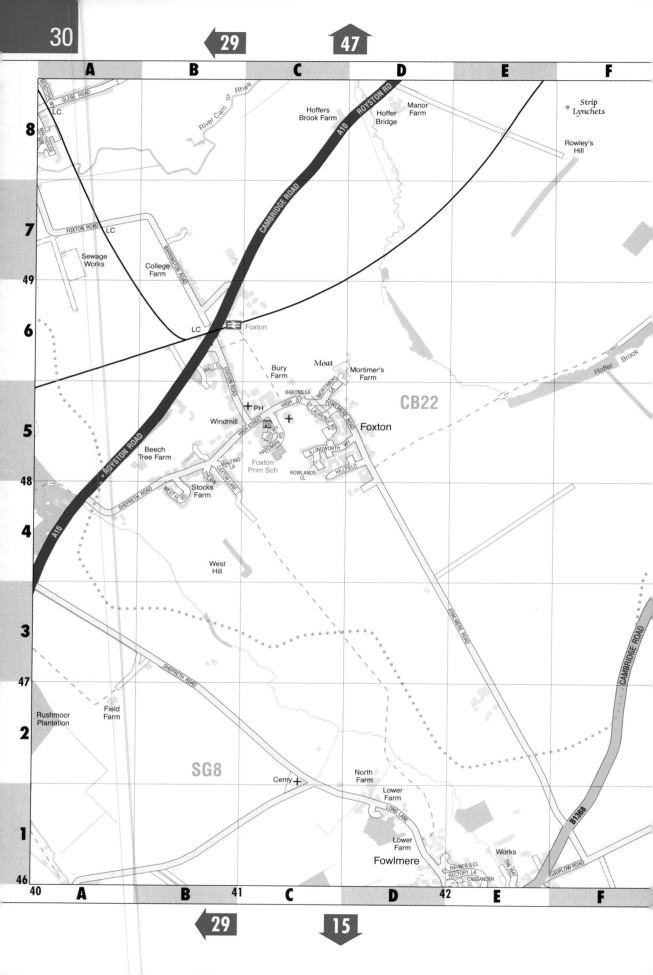

A   B   C   D   E   F

Newton Road
Newton Hill Poultry Farm
HARSTON ROAD
B1368 CAMBRIDGE ROAD
New Farm
Cockle Hill
M11
8

KIDMANS CL
COCKLE CL
CHTA LN
PH
Newton
7

COACH HOUSE CL
Top Farm
Newton Hall
Newton Manor
TOWN STREET
Whittlesford Road
Kidman's Plantation
New Farm
Reservoir

49

Foster's Farm
NEWTON ROAD
6

Hall Farm
FOWLMERE ROAD
CB22

Dairy Farm
Stanmoor Hall
Spinney Hill Farm
5

B1368
BROOK ROAD
48
M11
4

Fern Wood

Squires Plantation
3

Gate House Thriplow Farm
Thriplow CE Prim Sch
SG8
47

Thriplow Meadows Nature Reserve
SCHOOL LANE
PIGEONS CL
2

SHERALDS CFT
FOREMAN'S RD
LN
PO
THE BAULK
Thriplow
CHURCH STREET
FOWLMERE ROAD
PH

LODGE ROAD
Bassetts
Moat
Manor Farm
Granary
LOWER ST
MIDDLE ST
FARM LANE
CHURCH STREET
GRAVEL PIT HILL
Heathfield
KINGSWAY
HURDLES WAY
WHITEHALL CNS
KINGSWAY
PEPPERSLADE
WOBURN
LEDO ROAD
Duxford Camp
A505
Duxford Aircraft Mus (Imperial War Mus at Duxford)
1

Newditch Plantation

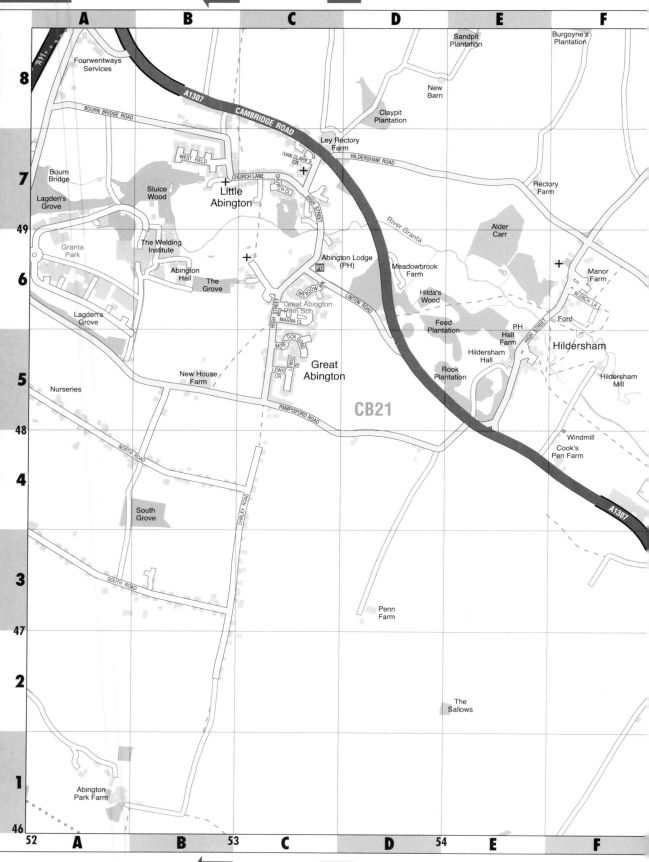

A   B   C   D   E   F

8

A11

Fourwentways
Services

A1307

BOURN BRIDGE ROAD

CAMBRIDGE ROAD

Sandpit
Plantation

Burgoyne's
Plantation

New
Barn

Claypit
Plantation

Ley Rectory
Farm

HILDERSHAM ROAD

7

Bourn
Bridge

WEST FIELD

IVAN CLARK'S
CR

CHURCH LANE

CHURCH CL

Rectory
Farm

Lagden's
Grove

Sluice
Wood

Little
Abington

HIGH STREET

River Granta

49

The Welding
Institute

Alder
Carr

Granta
Park

Abington Lodge
(PH)

Meadowbrook
Farm

Manor
Farm

6

Abington
Hall

The
Grove

P0

HIGH STREET

Great Abington
Prim Sch

MEADOW WK

LINTON ROAD

Hilda's
Wood

BLENCH LA

Lagden's
Grove

MAGNA CL

Feed
Plantation

PH

Ford

Hildersham

MOTT

LEWIS CL

LEWIS CR

TOCK GLNS

HIGH STREET

Hall
Farm

5

Nurseries

New House
Farm

Great
Abington

Hildersham
Hall

Hildersham
Mill

Rook
Plantation

PAMPISFORD ROAD

CB21

48

NORTH ROAD

Windmill

Cook's
Pen Farm

4

South
Grove

CHALKY ROAD

A1307

3

SOUTH ROAD

47

2

The
Sallows

1

Abington
Park Farm

46

52   A   B   53   C   D   54   E   F

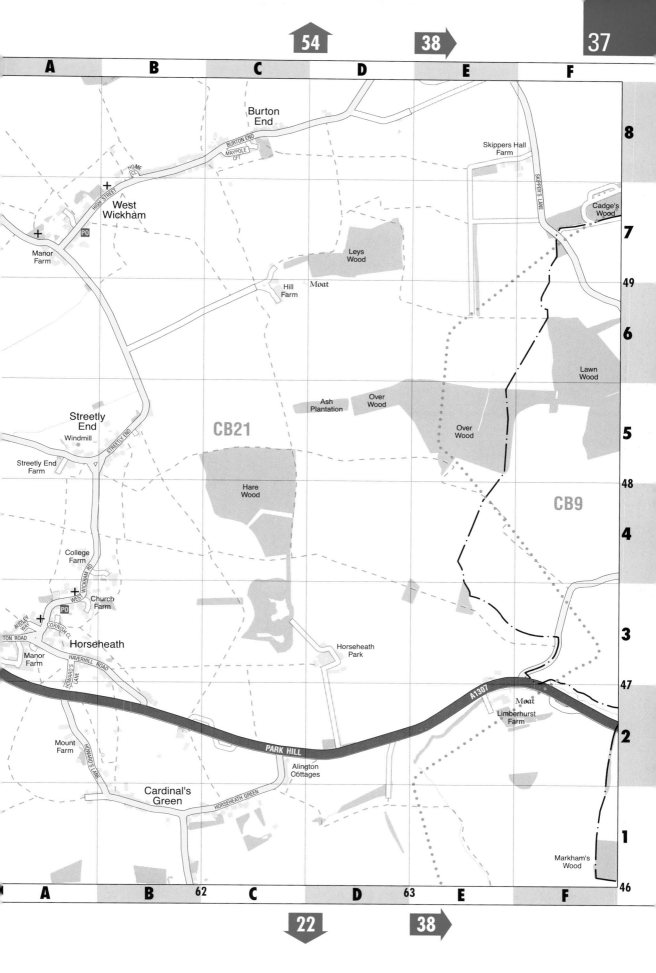

A B C D E F

8

Burton
End

Skippers Hall
Farm

BURTON END
MAYPOLE
CFT

HOME
CL

HIGH STREET

West Wickham

Cadge's
Wood

7

Manor
Farm

PO

49

Leys
Wood

SKIPPER'S LANE

Hill
Farm

Moat

6

Lawn
Wood

Streetly
End

Windmill

Ash
Plantation

Over
Wood

CB21

STREETLY END

Over
Wood

5

Streetly End
Farm

48

Hare
Wood

CB9

4

College
Farm

WEST WICKHAM RD

Church
Farm

PO

Horseheath
Park

AUDLEY WAY

CORNISH CL

3

TON ROAD

Horseheath

Manor
Farm

HAVERHILL ROAD

A1307

47

Moat

Limberhurst
Farm

HOWARD'S LANE

Mount
Farm

PARK HILL

2

Cardinal's
Green

Alington
Cottages

HORSEHEATH GREEN

Markham's
Wood

1

46

A 62 B C D 63 E F

Foxburrow Wood

Trundley Wood

Ganwick Wood

Hill Plantation

Nursery Plantation

Hill Farm

Hill Wood

Gravel Pit Plantation

Abbacy Wood

Jarvis Hill

B1061 WRATTING ROAD

THURLOW ROAD

Pelican House Farm

River Stour

Greenfields Farm

THE STREET

Moor Pasture Farm

WITHERSFIELD ROAD

CB9

Rook Tree Farm

Hall Farm

Stour Valley Path

Lion Meadow Plantation

Great Wratting

PH

SCHOOL ROAD

Wash Farm

MOOR PASTURE WAY

Factory

Old Haverhill Road

A143

B1061 HAVERHILL ROAD

Sports Ground

Little Wratting

Water Tower

HAVERHILL ROAD

Hilltop Farm

Hills Farm

ROWELL CL
ANN SUCKLING ROAD
COPELL IS CL
GOLDINGS CL
BOYTON CL

Boyton Hall

PH

BURLINGS
FALKLANDS RD
CROSS CL
FRYTH CL
HILL CR
COVERT CL
TRIPLING CL
ABBOTTS ROAD
CHAPPLE DRIVE

THE GLEBE
DEANS CL
DOVE HOUSE RD

WRATTING ROAD A143

BLADON WAY
BLENHEIM CL
CHURCHILL AVE

Samuel Ward Art & Tech College

ABINGTON PL
ALDE
BARTLOW PLACE

CHALKSTONE WAY

CHEDBURGH PLACE

Great Field Plantation

Moat

Great Wilsey Farm

49

48

47

46

8

7

6

5

4

3

2

1

68

69

24

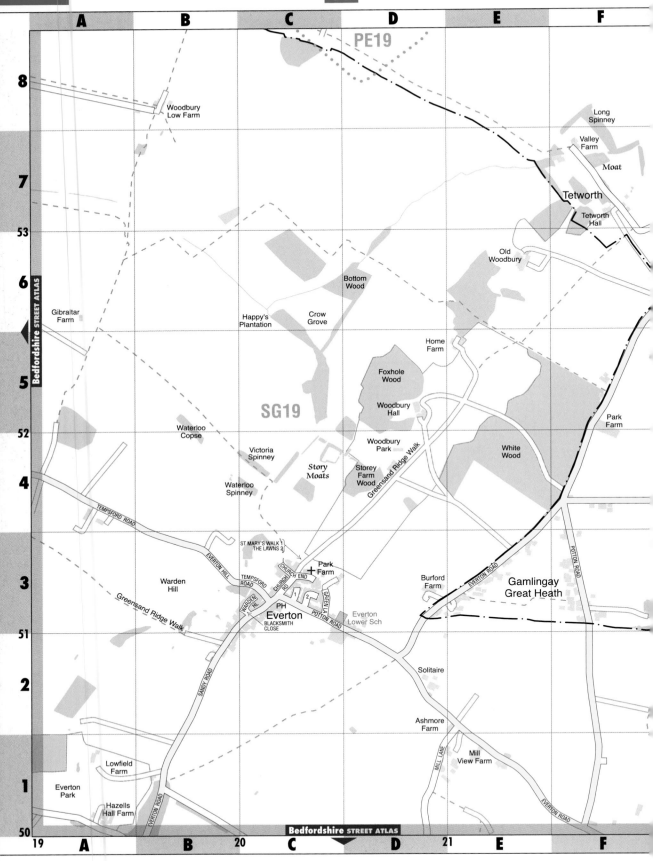

A B C D E F

8

7

53

6

5

52

4

3

51

2

1

50

19 A B 20 C D 21 E F

PE19

Woodbury
Low Farm

Long
Spinney

Valley
Farm

Moat

Tetworth

Tetworth
Hall

Old
Woodbury

Bottom
Wood

Gibraltar
Farm

Happy's
Plantation

Crow
Grove

Home
Farm

Foxhole
Wood

Woodbury
Hall

SG19

Waterloo
Copse

Victoria
Spinney

Woodbury
Park

Woodbury
Park

Story
Moats

Storey
Farm
Wood

White
Wood

Park
Farm

Greensand Ridge Walk

Waterloo
Spinney

TEMPSFORD ROAD

St Mary's Walk 1
THE LAWNS 3

Park
Farm

Warden
Hill

EVERTON HILL

TEMPSFORD
ROAD

CHURCH END

CHURCH RD

GREEN LA

Burford
Farm

Everton
Road

Gamlingay
Great Heath

POTTON ROAD

Greensand Ridge Walk

WARDEN HILL

PH
Everton

BLACKSMITH
CLOSE

POTTON ROAD

Everton
Lower Sch

Solitaire

SANDY ROAD

Ashmore
Farm

MILL LANE

Mill
View Farm

Lowfield
Farm

Everton
Park

EVERTON ROAD

Hazells
Hall Farm

EVERTON ROAD

Bedfordshire STREET ATLAS

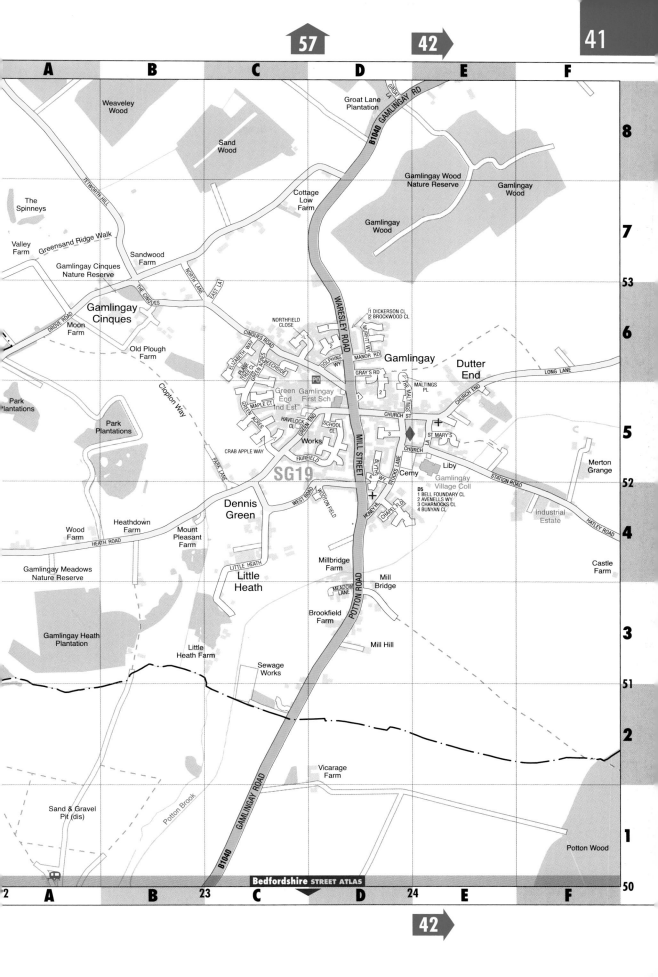

A B C D E F

8

Weaveley
Wood

Sand
Wood

Groat Lane
Plantation

GROAT LA

B1040 GAMLINGAY RD

Gamlingay Wood
Nature Reserve

Gamlingay
Wood

The
Spinneys

Cottage
Low
Farm

Gamlingay
Wood

7

Valley
Farm

Greensand Ridge Walk

TETWORTH HILL

Sandwood
Farm

NORTH LANE

EAST LA

53

Gamlingay Cinques
Nature Reserve

THE CINQUES

WARESLEY ROAD

1 DICKERSON CL
2 BROCKWOOD CL

6

DROVE ROAD

Gamlingay
Cinques

Moon
Farm

CINQUES ROAD

NORTHFIELD
CLOSE

1

2

MURITT WY

MANOR RD

Gamlingay

Dutter
End

LONG LANE

Old Plough
Farm

Clopton Way

ELIZABETH WAY

PLANE
TREE CL

GREEN ACRES

BEECHSIDE

DOLPHINS
WY

GRAY'S RD

2

THE MALTINGS

MALTINGS
PL

CHURCH END

Park
Plantations

GREEN MAPLE CT

Green
End
2nd Est

Gamlingay
First Sch

1

CHURCH ST

5

Park
Plantations

GREEN
ACRES

HAVELOCK
CL

GREEN END

SCHOOL
CL

Works

3

St Mary's

Liby

Merton
Grange

CRAB APPLE WAY

FAIRFIELD

BLYTHE
WY

STOCKS LANE

CHURCH

Cerny

STATION ROAD

52

SG19

WEST ROAD

WOXTON FIELD

Gamlingay
Village Coll

D5
1 BELL FOUNDARY CL
2 AVENELLS WY
3 CHARNOCKS CL
4 BUNYAN CL

Dennis
Green

PARK LANE

MILL STREET

MONEY LA

CHAPEL FLD

Industrial
Estate

HATLEY ROAD

4

Wood
Farm

Heathdown
Farm

HEATH ROAD

Mount
Pleasant
Farm

Millbridge
Farm

Mill
Bridge

Castle
Farm

Gamlingay Meadows
Nature Reserve

LITTLE HEATH

Little
Heath

MEADOW
LANE

POTTON ROAD

Brookfield
Farm

3

Gamlingay Heath
Plantation

Little
Heath Farm

Sewage
Works

Mill Hill

51

2

Potton Brook

GAMLINGAY ROAD

Vicarage
Farm

Sand & Gravel
Pit (dis)

B1040

Potton Wood

1

2 A 23 B C 24 D E F 50

41
58

SG19

Model Farm

B1046

Fuller's Hill Farm

FULLER'S HILL

Crooked Billet Farm

LONG LANE

Millbridge Brook

HATLEY ROAD

Castle Farm

Newlands Buildings

BAULK LANE

Church Farm

Dower House

BAR LANE

Hatley Park

Wood Farm

Cockayne Hatley Wood

BAR LANE

Potton Wood

BUFF LANE

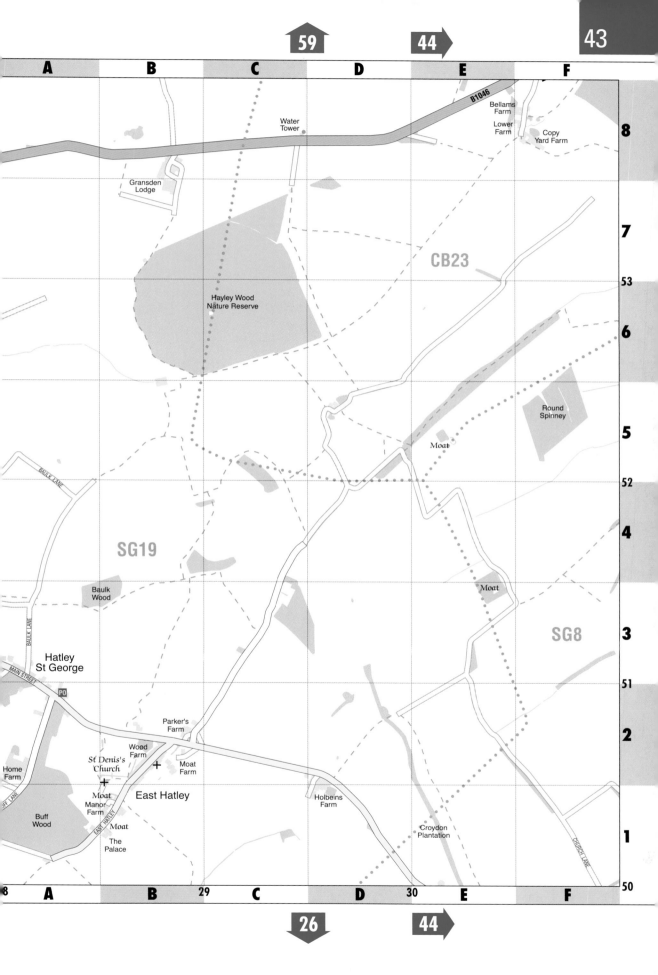

A B C D E F

B1046

Bellams Farm

Water Tower

Lower Farm

Copy Yard Farm

8

Gransden Lodge

7

CB23

53

6

Hayley Wood Nature Reserve

Round Spinney

5

Moat

52

BAULK LANE

4

SG19

Baulk Wood

Moat

SG8

3

51

Hatley St George

MAIN STREET

PO

Parker's Farm

2

BAULK LANE

Wood Farm

St Denis's Church

Home Farm

Moat Farm

East Hatley

Holbeins Farm

Moat Manor Farm

EAST HATLEY

Buff Wood

Moat

Croydon Plantation

CHURCH LANE

1

The Palace

8 A B 29 C D 30 E F 50

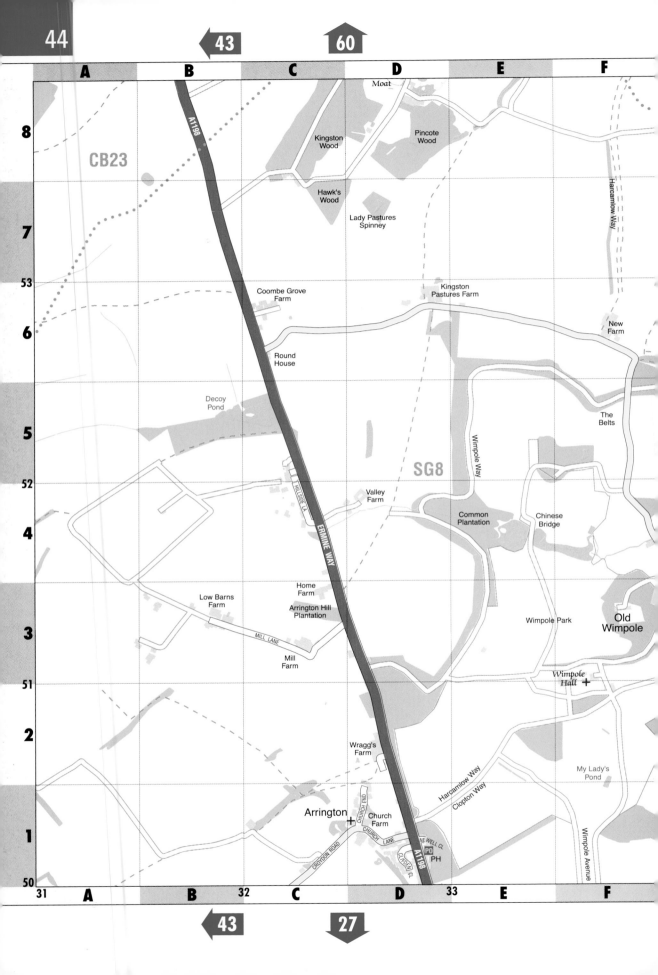

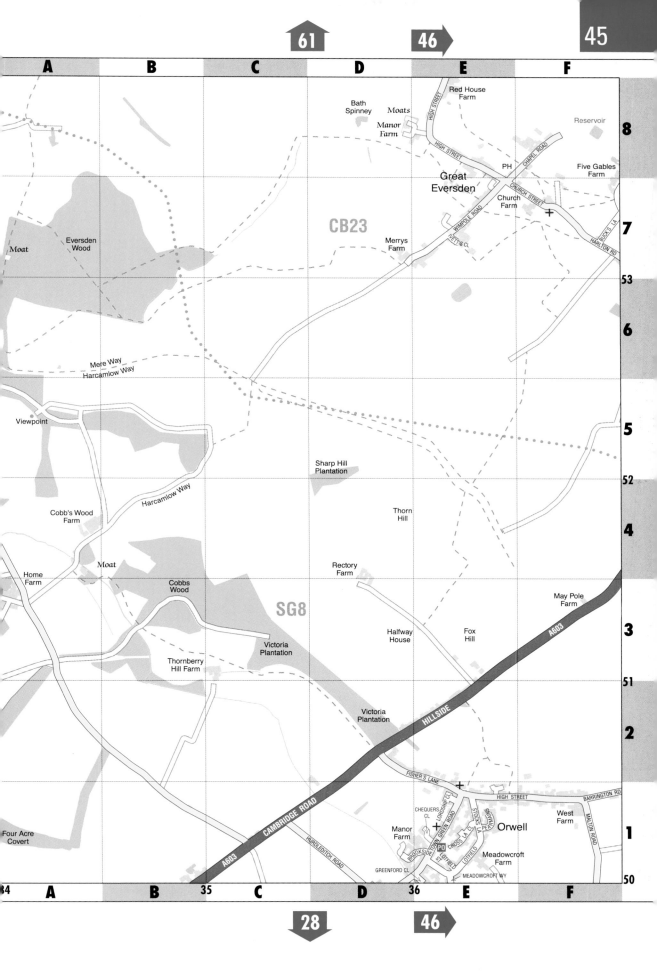

A B C D E F

8

7

53

6

5

52

4

3

51

2

51

50

37 A B 38 C D 39 E F

Travelling Telescope Lines

Radio Telescope

Radio Telescope

Travelling Telescope Lines

Mullard Radio Astronomy Observatory

A603

CAMBRIDGE ROAD

COMBERTON ROAD

WASHPIT LANE

WASHPIT LANE

CB23

Moats

Rectory Farm

Little Eversden

LOWFIELDS

LEETE'S LANE

CHURCH LA

FINCH'S FIELD

HIGH STREET

FINCH'S RD

WHEELER'S WY

WHEELER'S CL

Poultry Farm

PH

60

Butler's Spinney

Manorial Earthworks

Manor Farm

COACH DR

Harlton

HIGH STREET

EVERSDEN ROAD

PH

HASLINGFIELD ROAD

HARLTON ROAD

A603

Whole Way

SG8

Lime Quarry

Long Plantation

CB22

Hill Plantation

Cracknow Hill

Wilsmere Down Farm

Cement Works

LC

ORWELL ROAD

BARRINGTON ROAD

Lilac Farm

Moat

HASLINGFIELD ROAD

Church Farm

Barrington CE Prim Sch

A B C D E F

65 50

White Hill Farm
White Hill

Clarke's Hill

BABRAHAM ROAD

A1307

Heath Farm

8

The Uplands

Youth Wood

7

GRANHAM'S ROAD

HINTON WAY

Fox Hill

P

Magog Down

Earthwork
Granhams Farm Moat

Hillstead

Colin's Wood

Magog Wood

53

COPPICE AVENUE

THE ORCHARDS

Middlefield Farm

Little Trees Hill

GRANHAM'S CL

Mast
LC

DE FREVILLE RD

MACAULAY AV
MACAULAY AV

ORCHARD RD
MILLS VIEW

WHEELERS

HAVERHILL ROAD

6

A1307

HIGH GREEN

MARIS GN

POPLAR CL

BIRCH TREES
RD

CHASTON RD

GLEBE LANE

MULT CL

CB22

UNWELLS CL
SELWYN CL

HIGH STREET

SHELFORD PK

STATION RD

Shelford

MINGLE LANE

Cemy

Hill Farm

GOG MAGOG WAY

5

TUNWELLS LANE

ELM'S AV

LEEWAY AV

HAWTHORNE RD

DUKES

FINCH'S CL

BAR

52

ASHEN GN

P

Liby

SPINNEY DR

WOOLLANDS LANE

HEADLEY
GD

DOLPHIN WY

PRIAM'S WY

CHURCH STREET

COX'S CL

St ANDREW'S CL

Moat

BAR LA

Stapleford Com Prim Sch

GREENHILL CL

Stapleford

4

ROBINSON
CRANDAL WY
PEACOCKS
PCT

WOODLANDS RD

LONDON ROAD

GRANTA
TR

AYLESFORD WY

HEFFER CL

COLLIER WY

FORGE END

ANVIL
CL
CHERRY
TREE AV

WOODLANDS CL

ST SVENES

BURY RD

POPLAR WY

JOSCELYNES

Bury Farm

Sawston Bridge

River Granta

3

CAMBRIDGE ROAD

Bentfield Lodge

51

2

Cynamid Farm

Barns Farm

Sewage Works

Dernford Farm

CAMBRIDGE ROAD

Mast

BROADMEADOW

Deal Grove Moat

WAKELIN AV

Rectory Farm

A1301

Nine Wells Springs

WOODLAND ROAD

EDINBURGH

PRINCESS DRIVE

QUEENSWAY

DEAL GR

Hill Farm Cemy

1

50

46 A B 47 C D 48 E F

32 50

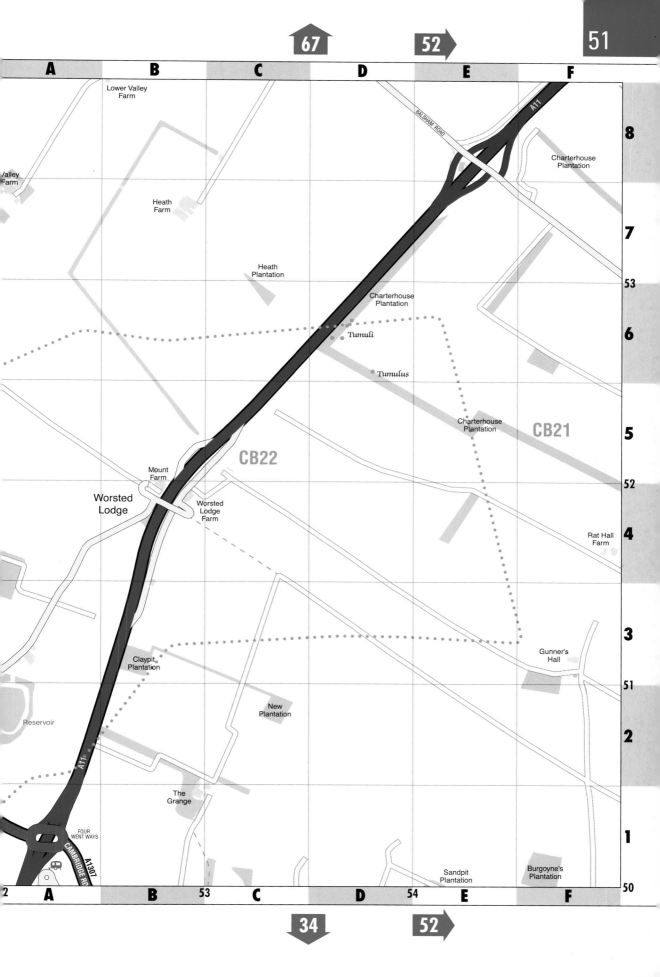

A B C D E F

8
7
53
6
5
52
4
3
51
2
1
50

Lower Valley Farm

Valley Farm

Heath Farm

Heath Plantation

BALSHAM ROAD

A11

Charterhouse Plantation

Charterhouse Plantation

Tumuli

Tumulus

Charterhouse Plantation

CB21

CB22

Mount Farm

Worsted Lodge

Worsted Lodge Farm

Rat Hall Farm

Gunner's Hall

Claypit Plantation

New Plantation

Reservoir

A11

The Grange

FOUR WENT WAYS

CAMBRIDGE RD

A1307

Sandpit Plantation

Burgoyne's Plantation

2 A B 53 C D 54 E F

A B C D E F

8

7

53

The Severals

6

Wadlow
Cottage

SIX MILE BOTTOM ROAD

Green End
Farm

B1052

BULL LANE

Playing
Field

West
Wratting
Hall

Hall
Wood

HONEY HILL

THE CAUSEWAY

West Wratting
Hall Park

CB21

West
Wratting

HIGH STREET

5

52

Harcamlow Way

Grange
Farm

B1052

HAYTER CL

SPICERS

PH

THE COMMON

Lordship
Farm

Moat

Scarletts
Farm

PADDOCK RD

Park
Farm

4

Harcamlow Way

SCARLETT'S LANE

WEST WRATTING RD

Oxcroft
Farm

3

Icknield Way Path

Smock
Mill

Mill
House

MILL ROAD

51

THE ROOKERY
THE ROOKERY

NINE CHIMNEYS LA

FIELD END

GOODWYFE AV

Plumian
Farm

B1052   HIGH STREET

CHURCH LA

The Meadow
Prim Sch

MAY'S AV

TRINITY CL

PO
SEFORD CL

PH

HAYCROFT

BARTONS

BURRELL WY

LINMAN WY

HORSESHOE CL

OLD HOUSE RD

DOLLS CL

Balsham

PRINCES CL

THE BRAMBLES

2

WOODHALL LANE

WEST WICKHAM ROAD

1

Wood
Hall

Balsham
Wood

50

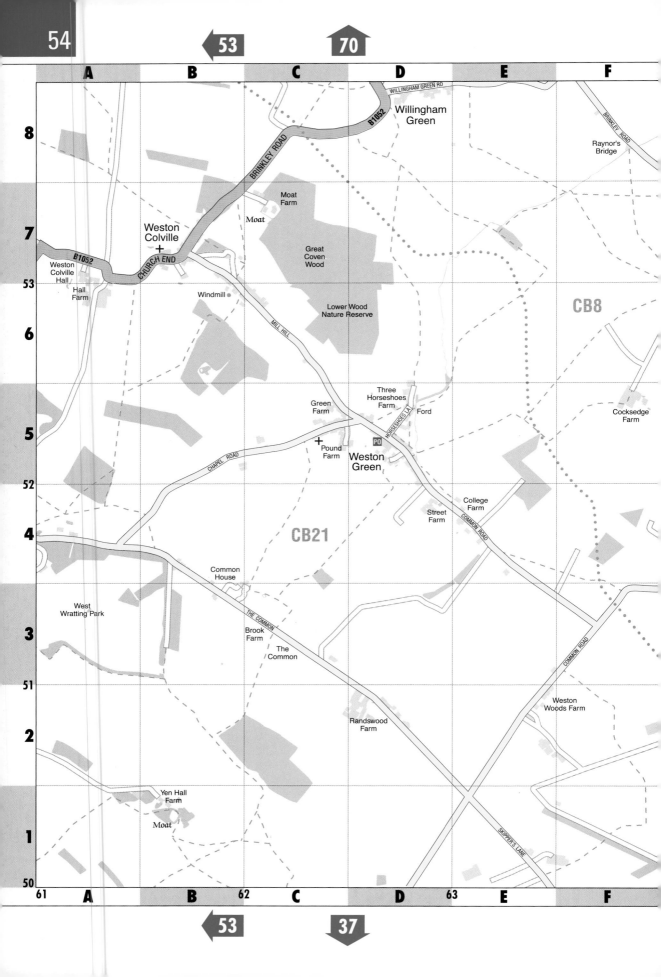

A B C D E F

8

7

53

6

5

52

4

3

51

2

1

50

Willingham Green Rd

B1052

Willingham Green

Brinkley Road

Raynor's Bridge

Moat Farm

Moat

Weston Colville

CHURCH END

B1052

Weston Colville Hall

Hall Farm

Windmill

MILL HILL

Great Coven Wood

Lower Wood Nature Reserve

CB8

Green Farm

Three Horseshoes Farm

HORSESHOES LA

Ford

Cocksedge Farm

CHAPEL ROAD

Pound Farm

PO

Weston Green

Street Farm

College Farm

COMMON ROAD

CB21

Common House

West Wratting Park

THE COMMON

Brook Farm

The Common

Randswood Farm

Weston Woods Farm

COMMON ROAD

Yen Hall Farm

Moat

SKIPPER'S LANE

A **B** **C** **D** **E** **F**

8

7

57

6

Jubilee
Plantation

Meadow
Plantation

Abbotsley Brook

Works

ST NEOTS ROAD

PE19

FIELD
CLOSE

1 HARDWICKE LANE
2 HIGH GREEN

Harbins
Farm

Rectory
Farm

Fen End

VICARAGE
FARM YARD

HOME FARM
CLOSE

HARBINS LA

Thorness
Farm

GRANSDEN ROAD

B1046

Southwood
Farm

PH

HIGH STREET

HIGH GN

LION
FARM CT

Fen End
Farm

Abbotsley
Bridge

BLACKSMITHS LA

TOP LA

GRANGE FARM
CLOSE

BLACKSMITHS
CLOSE

Abbotsley

5

Manor
Farm

56

PITSDEAN ROAD

Bullby
Hill

4

Langlands
Plantation

Lily
Hill

Ash
Plantation

Thistle Hill
Plantation

Lily Hill
Plantation

3

55

The
Spinney

SG19

Home
Farm

Manor
Farm

MANOR FARM ROAD

WEST CL

2

Mickle Hill
Plantation

Waresley

Waresley
Hall

B1040

Low
Farm

Waresley
Park

1

Weaveley
Wood

Great Lane
Plantation

GROAT LA

Woodfield
Farm

B1040 GAMLINGAY ROAD

54

57
77

57
42

A
B
C
D
E
F

BOURN ROAD
ROYSTON ROAD
A1198
Church Farm
ST PETER'S ST
TATES FIELD
Firs Farm
Vine Farm
8
Redwood Farm
Hardwicke Farm
GRANSDEN ROAD
7
57
Karting
6
A1198
ROYSTON ROAD
CB23
Common Farm
SG19
5
Home Farm
Home Wood
56
Cambridge Gliding Club
Ox Grove
Longstowe Park
Wilderness Spinney
Pond Plantation
Longstowe Hall
4
Gashouse Spinney
PARK LA
B1046
3
RUSHBROOK CLOSE
Longstowe
55
PH
PO
Middle Farm
HIGH STREET
2
Broad Close Spinney
1
(dis)
B1046
54

8
A
B
29
C
D
30
E
F

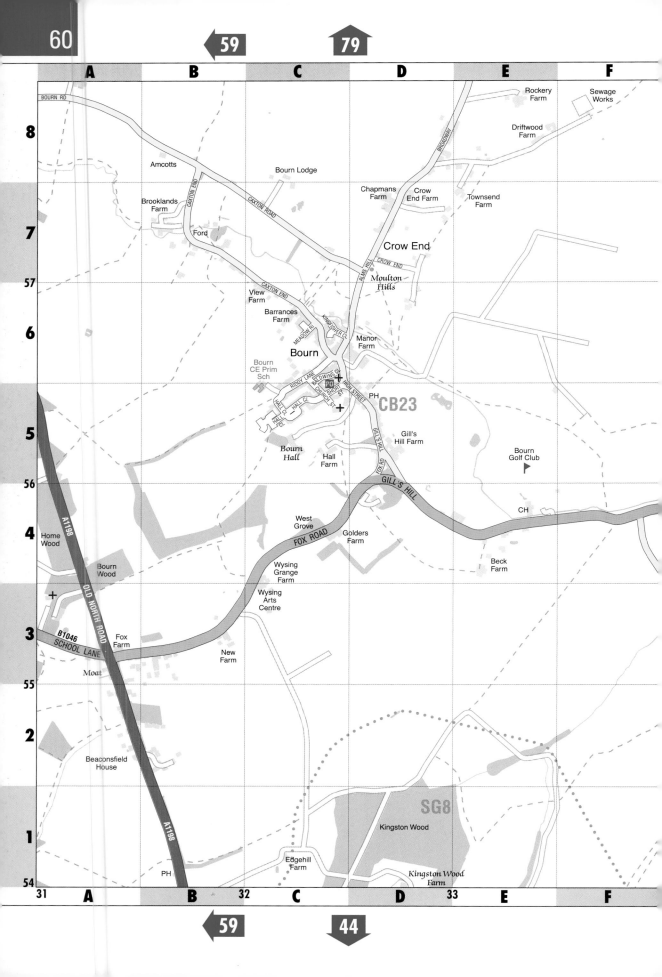

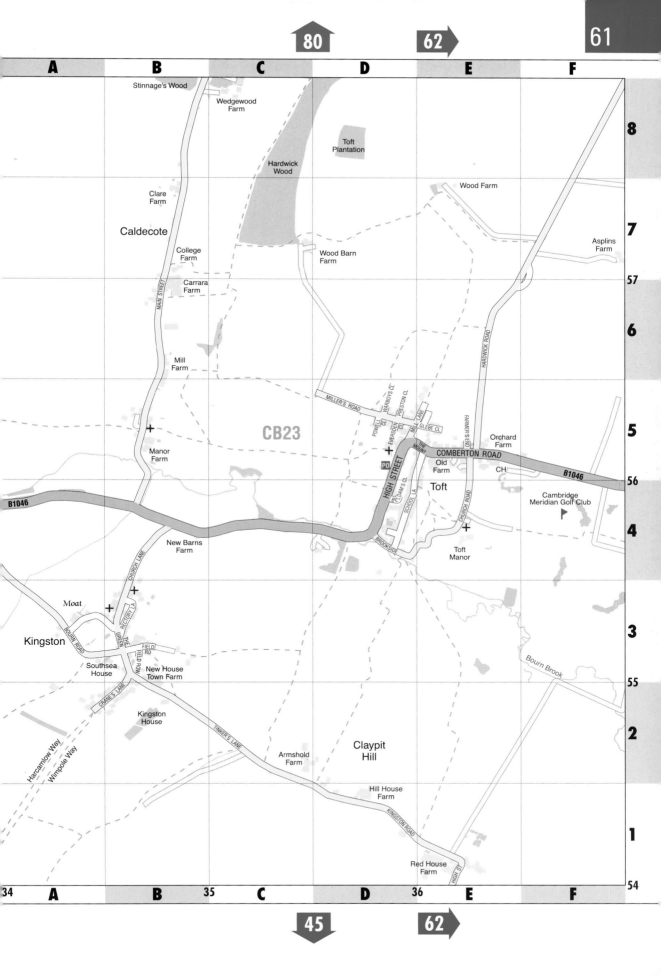

A **B** **C** **D** **E** **F**

8

7

BRANCH ROAD

Windale
Farm

Highfield Farm

57

GREEN END

FOX'S WAY

Moat

1 THE COVERT
2 MALLOWS CL

6

THE VALLEY

Green
End

Olde
Farm

Recn
Gd

Meridian
Prim Sch

THE OLD RECTORY

BARTON ROAD

Works

B1046

COMBERTON ROAD

Bennel
Farm

HINES LA

5

Home
Farm

WEST STREET

PH

Comberton

WOOTTEN SQ

BUSH CL

B1046

56

Comberton
Village Coll

Liby

KENTINGS

WESTLANDS

SCARRONS WAY

BARRONS
WY

BARRONS WAY

SOUTH STREET

SWAYNE'S LANE

Bakers
Farm

BARRONS WAY 1
NURSERY WAY 2
SOUTH LA 3
WESTCROFT 4

Manor
Farm

CB23

4

Church
Farm

Church
Farm

CHURCH LANE

ROYSTON LANE

3

Fox's Bridge
Farm

55

Westfield Farm

Fox's
Bridge

Lord's
Bridge

2

COMBERTON ROAD

Tumulus

A603

Radio Telescope

Radio
Telescope

Mast

CAMBRIDGE ROAD

Radio Telescope

Lords
Bridge Farm

1

54

37 **A** 38 **B** **C** **D** 39 **E** **F**

C7
1 THE CENACLE
2 NEWNHAM CFT ST
3 GRANTCHESTER ST
4 LAMMAS FIELD

63

83

F7
1 CLAREMONT
2 GEORGE PATEMAN CT
3 ABBEY COLL

For full street detail of the
highlighted area see page 246.

CAMBRIDGE

Newnham

Newnham Croft

Grantchester

Trumpington

Anstey Hall

CB3

CB2

CB1

CB22

Corpus Christi College Sports Ground

Mus of Classical Archaeology

Cambridge Rugby Football Ground

Pembroke College Sports Ground

St Catharine's College Sports Ground

Eight Acre Wood

Seven Acre Wood

Trumpington Hall Park

Trumpington Hall

Rupert Brooke Museum

Manor Farm

Moat

Byron's Pool

Weir

Brasley Bridge

Anstey Hall Farm

Grantchester Road Plantation

Glebe Farm

Superstore

Cambridge University Press

National Extension Coll

Rugby Club

Long Road Sixth Form Coll

University Botanic Garden

BBC TV & Radio

Hughes Hall

D3
1 LAMBOURN CL
2 SOUTHBROOKE CL
3 GAYTON CL
4 BEVERLEY WY

63

48

E7
1 BROOKSIDE LA
2 CORONATION MS
3 FRANCIS PG
4 ST ANTHONYS WK
5 CORONATION PL
6 ST ELIGIUS ST

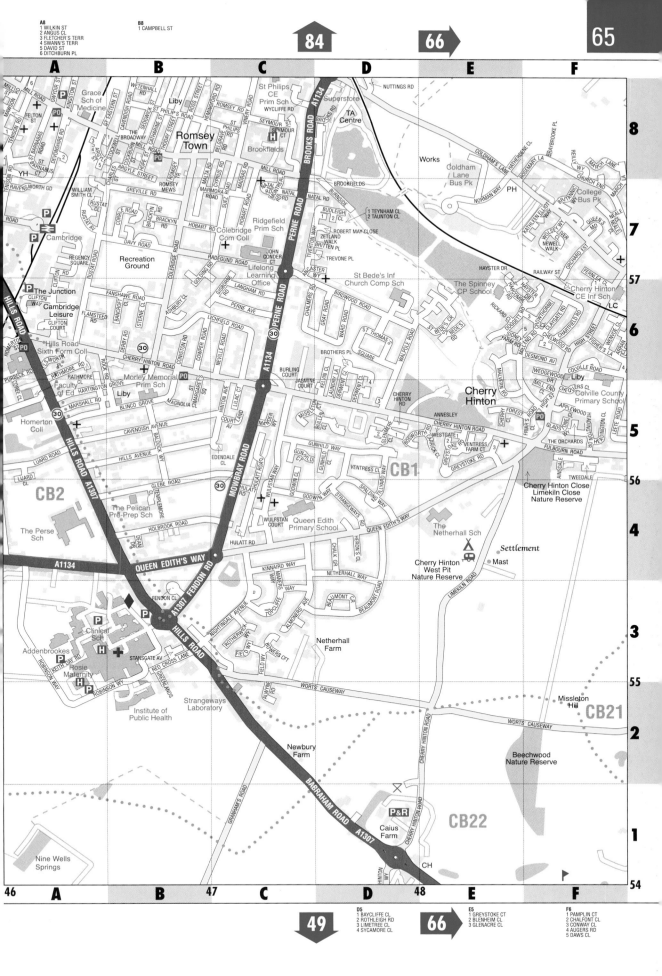

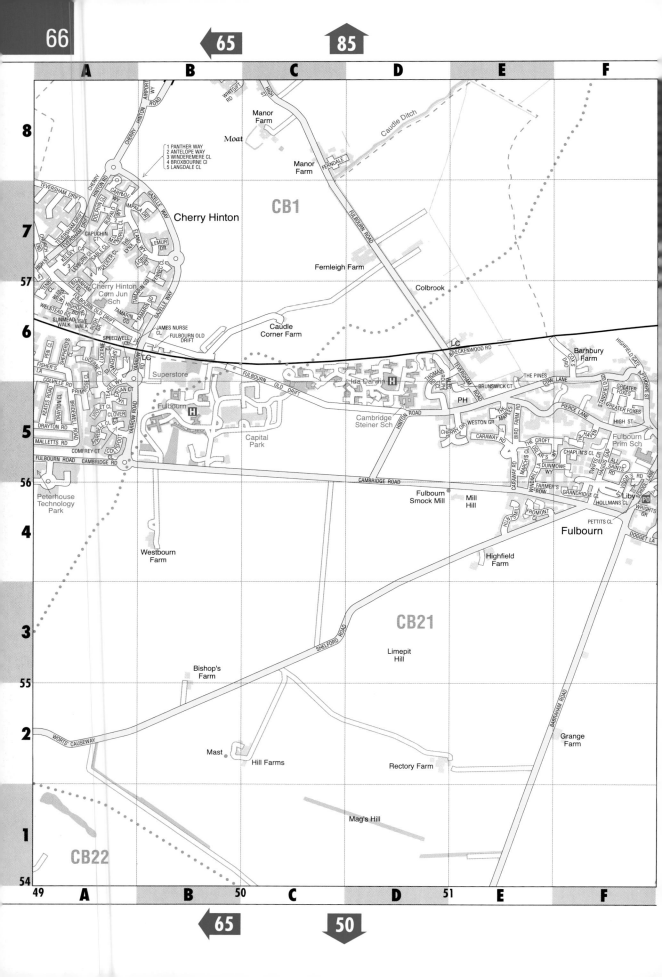

A   B   C   D   E   F

8

Great Wilbraham
CE Prim Sch

PO

Great
Wilbraham

THE LANES
ANGLE END
CHURCH RD
CHURCH ST

Queens
Farm

STATION ROAD

TOFT LANE
CHURCH CL
PH

Appleton
Plantation

THE SQUIRE'S FIELD

TOFT LA
HIGH STREET

7

Cole's
Bridge

WILBRAHAM ROAD

Herring's
House

Rookery
Farm

FROG END
MILL RD

Kennel
Farm

57

LC

Home
Farm

6

STATION ROAD

LANTHORN STILE
NORTHFIELD
BARLEYFIELDS
THE CHASE
RY
CHURCH LA

Moat

LC

5

Fulbourn
Manor
LUDLOW LA

HOME END
THE FOLDINGS

GEOFFREY BISHOP AVE

CB21

56

Mid Career
College

STONEBRIDGE LANE

Fulbourn
Nature Reserve

4

IMPETT'S LANE

SANDERS LA

Cemy

Fleam Dyke

3

BALSHAM ROAD

55

Works

Harcamlow Way

2

Fleam Dyke
Cottages

Mutlow Hill
(Tumulus)

New Shardelowes
Farm

1

A11

Lower Valley
Farm

54

52   A   B   53   C   D   54   E   F   54

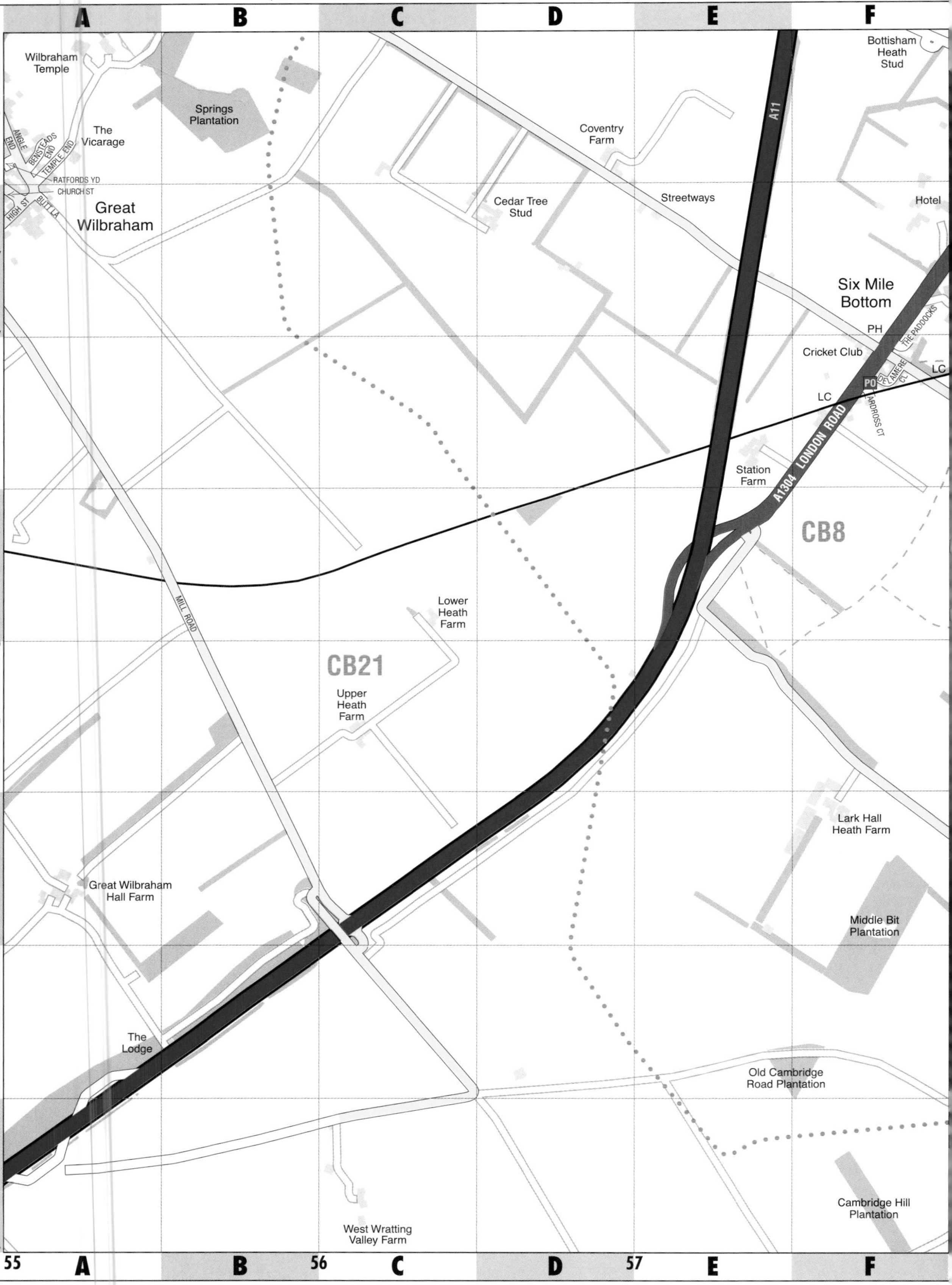

A **B** **C** **D** **E** **F**

Wilbraham Temple

8

Springs Plantation

Coventry Farm

The Vicarage

BERSTEADS END
ANGLE END
TEMPLE END
RATFORDS YD
CHURCH ST
HIGH ST
BUTT LA

Cedar Tree Stud

Streetways

A11

Bottisham Heath Stud

Great Wilbraham

Hotel

7

Six Mile Bottom

57

PH

Cricket Club

THE PADDOCKS

LC

LC

PO
CAIRDROSS CT
CT

6

Station Farm

A1304 LONDON ROAD

CB8

5

MILL ROAD

Lower Heath Farm

56

CB21

Upper Heath Farm

4

Lark Hall Heath Farm

3

Great Wilbraham Hall Farm

Middle Bit Plantation

55

2

The Lodge

Old Cambridge Road Plantation

1

West Wratting Valley Farm

Cambridge Hill Plantation

54

55 **A** **B** **56** **C** **D** **57** **E** **F**

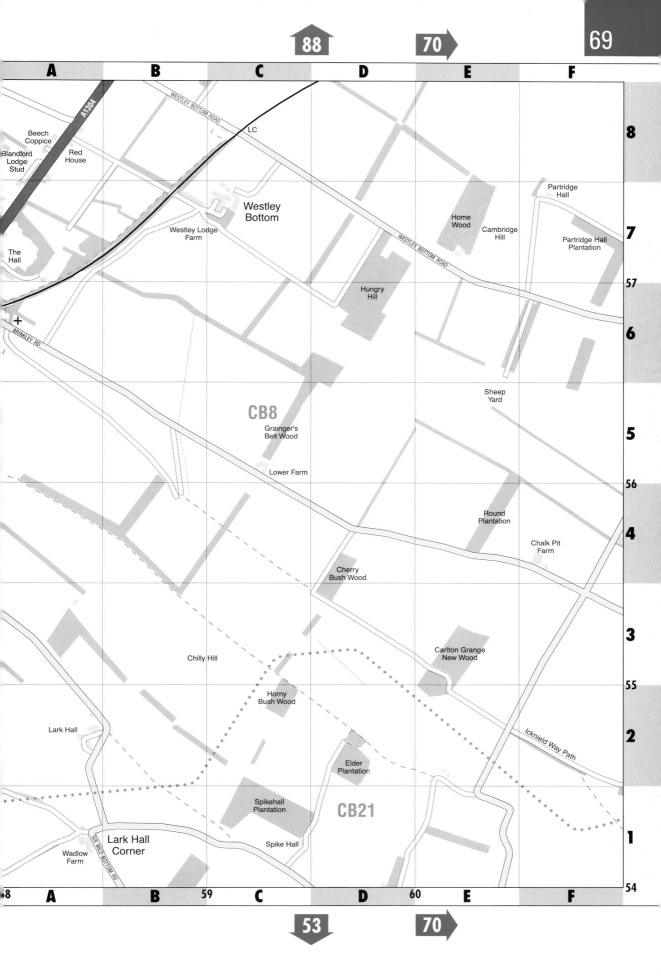

71
91

A B C D E F

8

Hall Farm

Chalkpit Plantation

Place Farm

Moat

Kirtling Towers

KIRTLING ROAD

Sixpenny Wood

7

Prince of Wales Wood

Park Cottage

Toilyard Plantation

57

Sewage Works

Lucy Wood

6

Ditton Park Wood

KIRTLING ROAD

Kirtling

THE STREET

Parsonage Farm

Oak Farm

HORN LANE

PH

CHAPEL LA

Jamies Wood

MILL ROAD

5

WOODDITTON ROAD

Yew Tree Farm

THE GREEN

PH

CB8

Mill End

56

PH

Batchelor's Hall Farm

4

Dianas Wood

Kirtling Green

MALTING END

Pratts Green Farm

Pear Tree Farm

BRADLEY ROAD

Whybrows Farm

Sascombe Vineyard

3

Great Widgham Wood

BRADLEY RD

55

Thrift Farm

2

Stour Valley Path

College Grove

Freedom Farm Stud

Bases Wood

1

Bradley Park Wood

54

71

BRADLEY RD

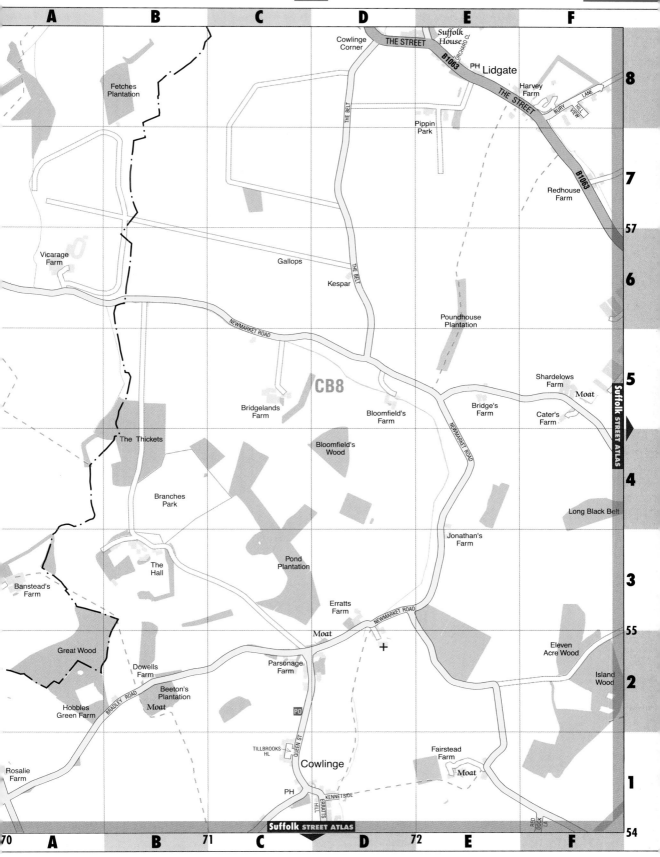

A B C D E F

8

7

57

6

5

4

55

3

2

1

54

Cowlinge Corner

THE STREET

Suffolk House

B1063

ORCHARD CL

PH Lidgate

THE STREET

BURY HILL

HILL VIEW

Harvey Farm

BURY LANE

Fetches Plantation

THE BELT

Pippin Park

B1063

Redhouse Farm

Vicarage Farm

Gallops

THE BELT

Kespar

Poundhouse Plantation

NEWMARKET ROAD

CB8

Shardelows Farm

Moat

Bridgelands Farm

Bloomfield's Farm

Bridge's Farm

Cater's Farm

The Thickets

Bloomfield's Wood

NEWMARKET ROAD

Long Black Belt

Branches Park

Jonathan's Farm

Banstead's Farm

The Hall

Pond Plantation

Errats Farm

NEWMARKET ROAD

Eleven Acre Wood

Great Wood

Moat

+

Island Wood

Dowells Farm

BRADLEY ROAD

Parsonage Farm

Beeton's Plantation

Moat

Hobbles Green Farm

PO

QUEEN ST

Rosalie Farm

TILLBROOKS HL

Cowlinge

Fairstead Farm

Moat

PH

KENNETSIDE

ERRATTS HILL

RED DOCK LA

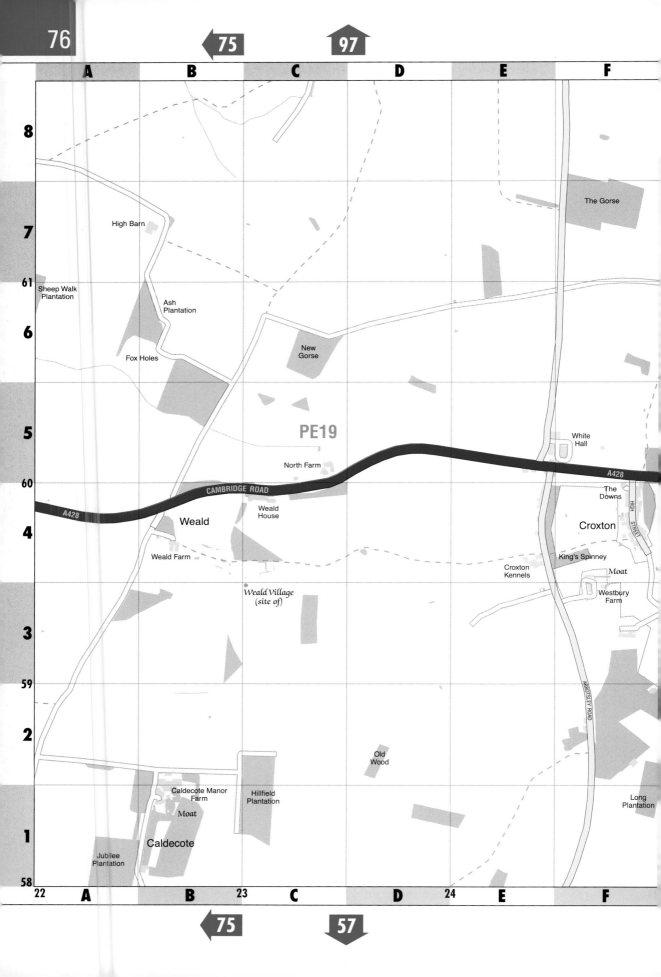

A B C D E F

8
7
61
6
5
60
4
59
2
3
1
58

22 A B 23 C D 24 E F

The Gorse

High Barn

Sheep Walk
Plantation

Ash
Plantation

Fox Holes

New
Gorse

PE19

White
Hall

A428

North Farm

CAMBRIDGE ROAD

A428

The
Downs

Weald
House

Weald

Croxton

Weald Farm

King's Spinney

Croxton
Kennels

Moat

HIGH STREET

Weald Village
(site of)

Westbury
Farm

Old
Wood

ABBOTSLEY ROAD

Caldecote Manor
Farm

Hillfield
Plantation

Long
Plantation

Moat

Caldecote

Jubilee
Plantation

A B C D E F

8

7

61

6

5

60

4

3

59

2

1

58

Papley Hollow

B1040

Moat

Papley Grove
Farm Cottages

Papley Grove
Farm

ST IVES ROAD

Orchard
Farm

Fairview
Farm

CAMBRIDGE ROAD
A428

B1040

North Lodge
Plantation

Pillar
Plantation

PE19

Privet and Gorse
Plantation

Oak
Plantation

Rectory

CAMBRIDGE ROAD
ST IVES RD

PH

St THOMAS

ST NEOTS ROAD

Broad Moor
Spinney

Moat

Eltisley

Croxton Park

Manor
Farm

B1040

Church
End

West
Farm

MEADOW
VIEW

Newton
Prim Sch

GREENFIELDS

Manor
Farm

Moat

CAXTON END

Moat

Turtlow
Plantation

POTTON END

Jesus
College
Farm

CAXTON DRIFT

Moat

Lodge
Plantation

Turtlow
Plantation

Eltisley Wood

South Lodge
Plantation

Church Hill
Plantation

South Lodge
Plantation

ELTISLEY ROAD

SG19

Safford's
Grove

Ash Spinney

B1040

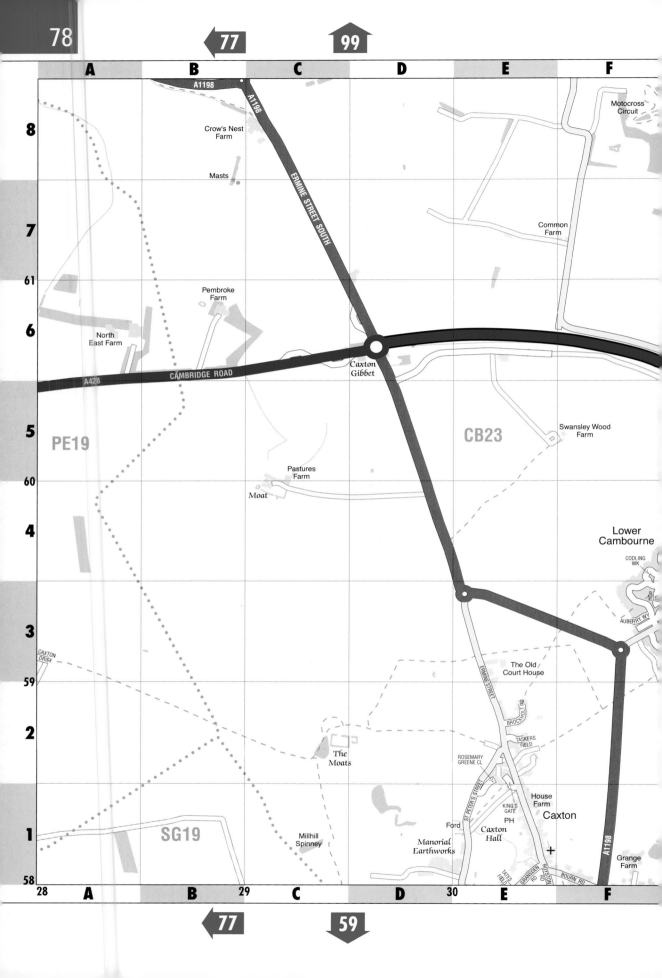

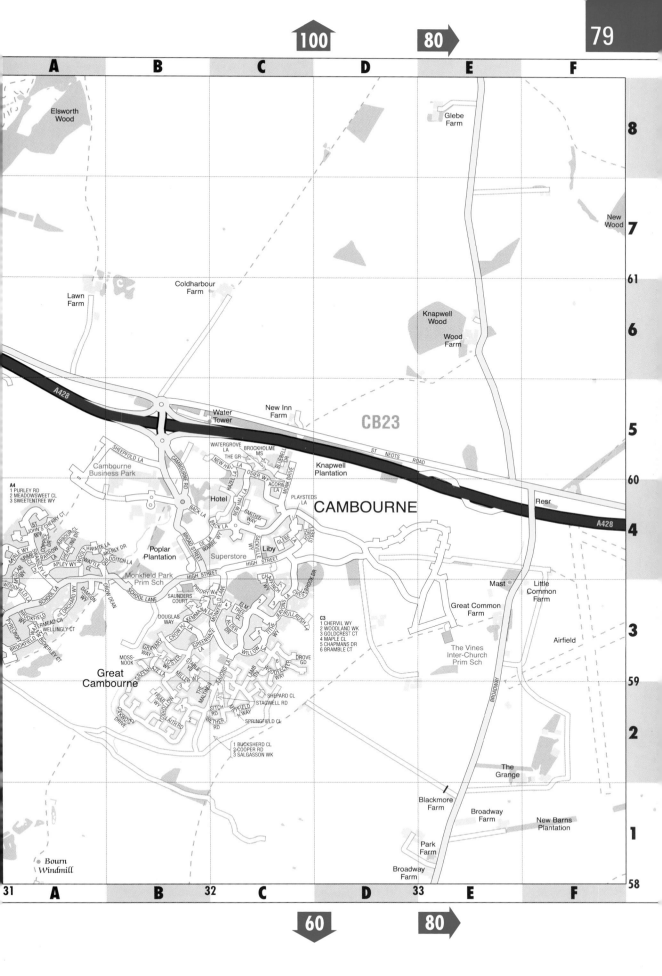

A **B** **C** **D** **E** **F**

8

Childerley

Black
Park

Battle
Gate

Childerley
Hall

Medieval Village of
Great Childerley
(site of)

Wood Walk
Spinney

Moat

New
Wood

Blackthorn
Spinney

7

61

Bird's Pastures
Farm

Weatherfield
Plantation

6

Double
Plantation

Honeyhill
Wood

CB23

5

Scotland
Farm

60

Two Pots
House Farm

40

ST NEOTS RD

A428

ST NEOTS ROAD

ST NEOTS ROAD

4

Childerley
Gate

HIGHFIELDS ROAD

LARK HALL DRIVE

3

Airfield

Works

THE WILLOWS

Highfield
Farm

APPLE
TREE CL

New Barns
Plantation

59

WEST DRIVE

Oak
Farm

DAMMS
PASTURES

Caldecote
Prim Sch

BOSSERT'S HIGHFIELDS ROAD

CLARE DR

Highfields

2

WT

HALL DRIVE

ROUND HO
CL

West Dr

SAMIAN CL

Bucket Hill
Plantation

GRAFTON
DRIVE

CLARE DR

MILL QUERN

ORCHID
FARE

EAST DRIVE

FURLONG
WAY

ROMAN
DRIFT

Caldecote

DEVONSHIRE MS

Harcamlow Way

Sewage
Works

COPEL CL

STRYMPOLE

BLYTHE
WY

GROVE WY

1

CAVENDISH
WY

STARGOOSE CL

DODRAL DEAN

GOOSE CROSS

MAIN ST

Mitchel's
Wood

Stinnage's
Wood

58

34

A **B** 35 **C** **D** 36 **E** **F**

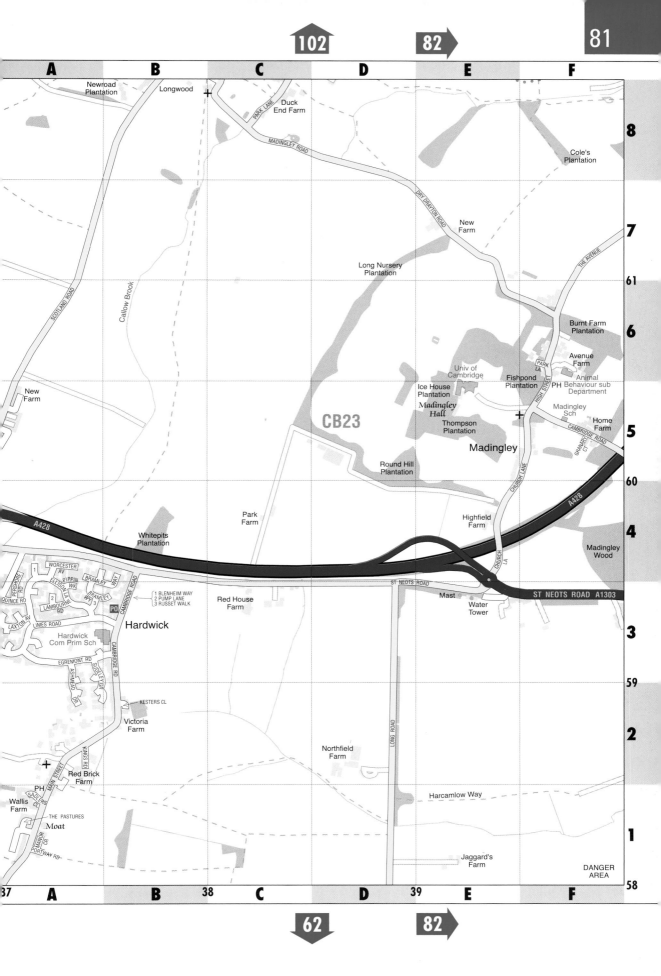

A B C D E F

8
7
61
6
5
60
4
3
59
2
1
58

Newroad Plantation
Longwood
Park Lane
Duck End Farm
MADINGLEY ROAD
DRY DRAYTON ROAD
Cole's Plantation
New Farm
THE AVENUE
Long Nursery Plantation
Burnt Farm Plantation
Avenue Farm
SCOTLAND ROAD
Callow Brook
Univ of Cambridge
PARK LA
Fishpond Plantation
PH
Animal Behaviour sub Department
HIGH STREET
Ice House Plantation
Madingley Hall
Madingley Sch
Home Farm
CB23
Thompson Plantation
CAMBRIDGE ROAD
New Farm
Madingley
GRANARY CT
Round Hill Plantation
CHURCH LANE
A428
60
Park Farm
Highfield Farm
Madingley Wood
A428
Whitepits Plantation
CHURCH LA
ST NEOTS ROAD
Mast
ST NEOTS ROAD A1303
WORCESTER AV
PIPPIN
BRAMLEY WAY
CAMBRIDGE ROAD
1 BLENHEIM WAY
2 PUMP LANE
3 RUSSET WALK
Red House Farm
Water Tower
PERSHORE RD
ELLISON LA
WK
BRAMLEY WAY
1
QUINCE RD
LAMBOURNE RD
2
PO
3
LAXTON AV
LIMES ROAD
Hardwick
Hardwick Com Prim Sch
EGREMONT RD
ASHMEAD DR
SUDELEY GR
KESTERS CL
LONG ROAD
QUINCE RD
ASHMEAD
KINGS RD
Victoria Farm
59
Northfield Farm
Red Brick Farm
PH
WALLIS FARM
SADLERS
THE PASTURES
MANOR CR
Moat
PORTWAY RD
Harcamlow Way
Jaggard's Farm
DANGER AREA

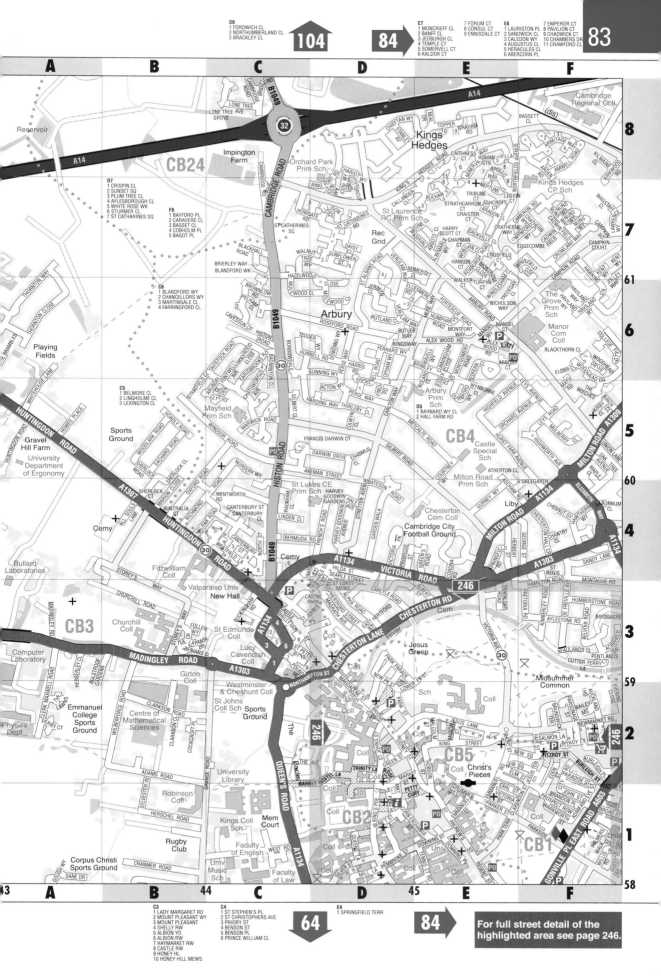

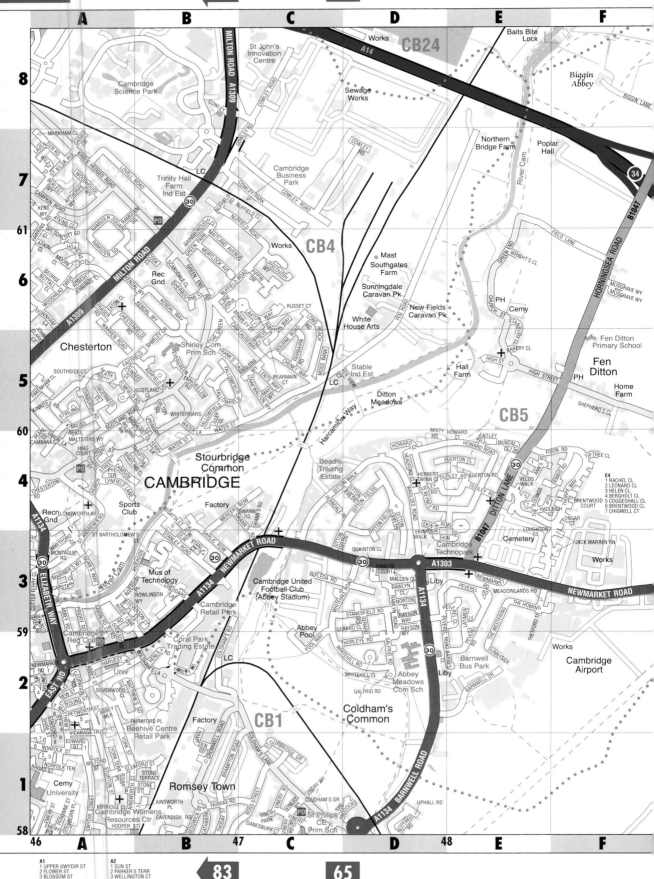

Grid references along top: A B C D E F
Grid references left side: 8 7 61 6 5 60 4 3 59 2 1 58
Grid references bottom: 46 A 47 B C 48 E F

Map labels:

Cambridge Science Park
St John's Innovation Centre
CB24
Works
A14
Baits Bite Lock
Biggin Abbey
BIGGIN LANE
Sewage Works
Northern Bridge Farm
Poplar Hall
34
MILTON ROAD A1309
COWLEY RD
Trinity Hall Farm Ind Est
30
Cambridge Business Park
COWLEY ROAD
Cambridge Retail Park
CB4
Works
Mast
Southgates Farm
Sunningdale Caravan Pk
New Fields Caravan Pk
River Cam
FIELD LANE
GREEN WRIGHT'S CL
HORNINGSEA ROAD B1047
MUSGRAVE WY
PH
Cemy
CHURCH ST
STANBURY
BAKERY CL
Fen Ditton Primary School
HIGH ST
Rec Gnd
RUSSET CT
White House Arts
Stable Ind Est
Hall Farm
HIGH STREET
PH
Fen Ditton
Home Farm
Chesterton
Shirley Com Prim Sch
Harcamlow Way
Ditton Meadows
SHEPHERD'S CL
CB5
Southside Ct
LC
Howard Road
30
FISON RD
TIP TREE CL
E4
1 RACHEL CL
2 LEONARD CL
3 HELEN CL
4 BERGHOLT CL
5 COGGESHALL CL
6 BRENTWOOD CL
7 CHIGWELL CT
Stourbridge Common
CAMBRIDGE
Beadle Trading Estate
Egerton Cl
Egerton Rd
Dudley Rd
Herbert Winn
VELDS WALK
Brentwood Court
THE HADLEIGH
THE RODINGS
ONGAR CT
Cemetery
Loughton CL
JACK WARREN GN
Works
Sports Club
Factory
St Bartholomew's Ct
Ditton Fields
Ditton Walk
Mercers Row
Swann's Rd
Cambridge Technopark
Recn Gnd
A1134
30
Mariner's Way
Montague Rd
Whytford
Longworth Av
River Cam
Mus of Technology
Regatta Ct
Stanley Road
NEWMARKET ROAD
A1134
30
RAWLYN COURT
A1303
NEWMARKET ROAD
Cambridge United Football Club (Abbey Stadium)
ELFLEDA RD
MALDEN CL
RAWLYN RD
Liby
PEVEREL RD
MEADOWLANDS RD
THE HOMING
Works
Cambridge Airport
ELIZABETH WAY
30
Cambridge Retail Park
Coral Park Trading Estate
LC
Abbey Pool
STANESFIELD RD
GERARD CL
HORLEYE RD
GALFRID RD
RAYSON WAY
Barnwell Bus Park
SUNNYSIDE
THE WESTRING
THETFORD TER
EAST RD
NEWMARKET
Univ
HARVEST
HENLEY RD
COLDHAMS RD
Cambridge
Abbey Meadows Com Sch
WHITEHILL CL
Liby
Barnwell Dr
Beehive Centre Retail Park
Factory
CB1
Coldham's Common
BARNWELL ROAD A1134
Cemy
University
Cambridge Womens Resources Ctr
HOOPER ST
Romsey Town
AINSWORTH PL
CAVENDISH RD
FAIRFAX RD
ROSS STREET
VINERY PARK
COLDHAM'S GR
PO
St Philips CE Prim Sch
THE PADDOCKS
UPHALL RD
NUTTINGS RD

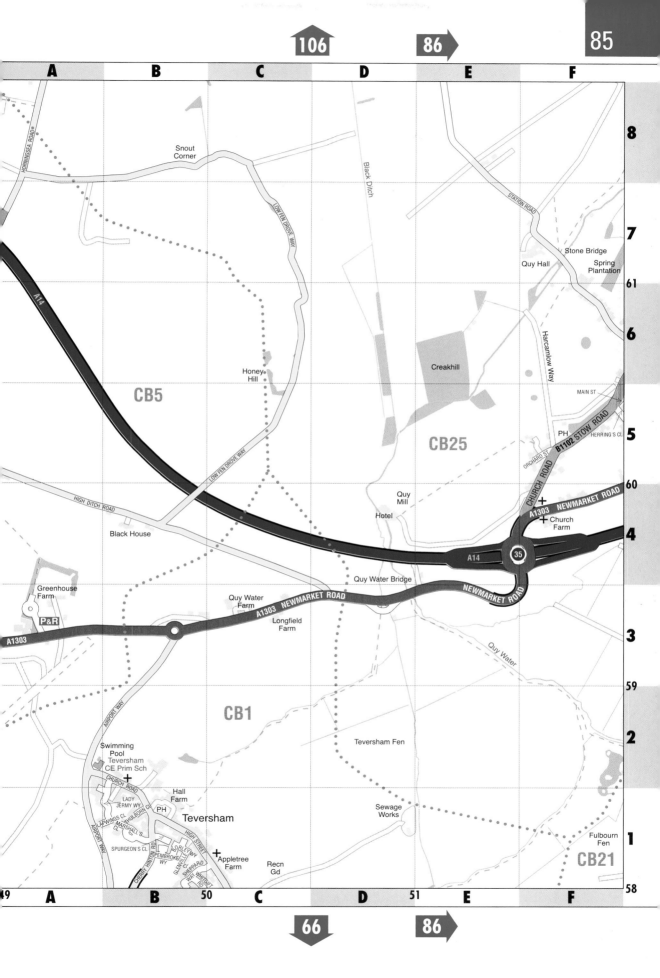

8
7
61
6
5
60
4
3
59
2
1
58

A   B   C   D   E   F

Middle Hill Plantations
SWAFFHAM HEATH ROAD

Park End

Stone Bridge Farm

Bottisham Hall

Stone Bridge

Howe Plantation

Bushmeadow Wood

CB25

Chalk Farm

The Grange

A1303

A1303

A14

Spring Hall

Heath Road

A14

CB8

A11

CB21

Council Farm

Bottisham Heath Stud

CB25

Beacon (Cesarewitch)

A14

70

New England
Farm

Memorial

The
National
Stud

Round Course

Egerton
Stud

Round Course

Egerton
House

New England
Stud

SWAFFHAM HEATH ROAD

A1303

A14

CB8

Lordship
Stud

36

A1303

Four Mile
Stable Farm

Mast

Tumulus

Lower Hare
Park Farm

Gran's
Plantation

Hare Park
Stud

Hare
Park

White
Wood

Hut Plantation

Allington
Hill Farm

Tumulus

Lower Hare
Park Farm

Lower
Farm

Bungalow
Farm

LC

A1304

Windmill

Bungalow
Hill

LONDON RD

WESTLEY
BOTTOM
RD

A B C D E F

8

Mertoun
Paddocks

Sixteen Acre
Plantation

Eight Acre
Plantation

WOODDITTON ROAD

Rockingham
Yard

Hadrian
Stud

7

Crockford's
Farm

DUCHESS' DRIVE

61

Derisley
Wood

Moat

Dalham Hall
Stud

Gateways

6

CB8

5

Icknield Way Path

Moorley
Plantation

60

Court
Barns
Farm

WOODDITTON ROAD

4

Stour Valley Path

North
Stud

Mill
Plantation

3

Stetchworth
Park

Stetchworth
Park Stud

Dane
Bottom

VICARAGE LANE

Woodditton

MAYPOLE LANE

CHURCH LANE

59

2

HIGH ST

THE ALLEY

Camois
Hall

Little
Ditton

PARSONAGE FARM LA

Parsonag
Farm

LITTLE DITTON

Stetchworth

COOPER'S CL

Camois
Hall Farm

1

JUBILEE CT

The Ellesmere
Centre

PO

Pickmore
Wood

Water
Tower

Ditton
Green

PH

DITTON GREEN

Woodditton
Stud

KIRTLING ROAD

58

64 A B 65 C D 66 E F

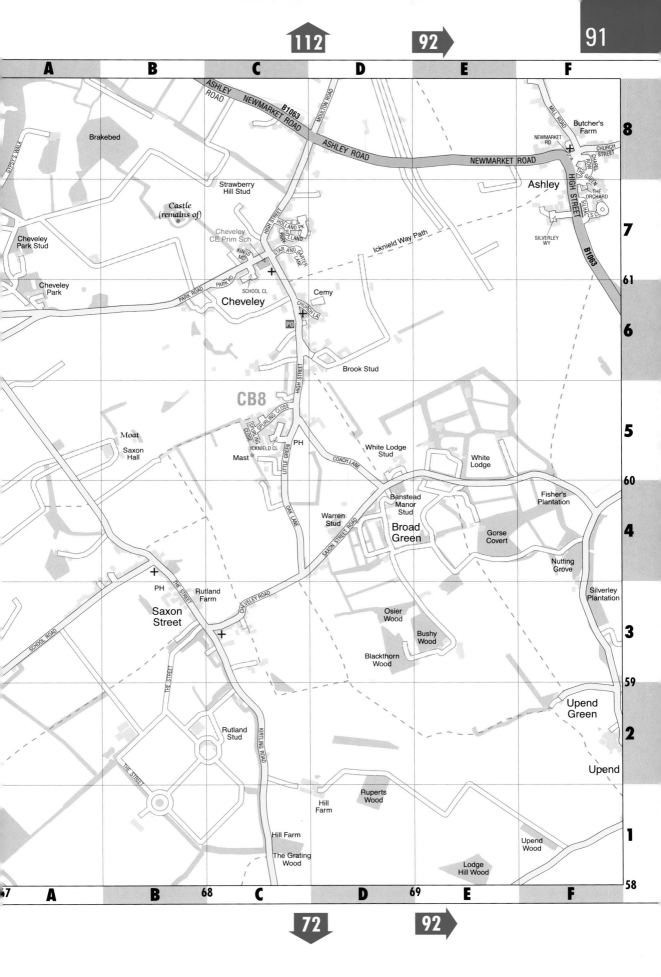

A B C D E F

ASHLEY ROAD
NEWMARKET ROAD
B1063
MOULTON ROAD
ASHLEY ROAD

MILL ROAD
Butcher's Farm
NEWMARKET RD

8

Brakebed

NEWMARKET ROAD

CHURCH STREET
CHAPEL ROW
THE GREEN
SILHAL LS CL

Strawberry Hill Stud

Ashley

THE ORCHARD

Castle (remains of)

HIGH STREET

HOLLAND PK
HOLLAND

HIGH STREET

Cheveley CE Prim Sch

SILVERLEY WY

B1063

7

Cheveley Park Stud

STAR AND GARTER LANE

KINGS MD

61

Cheveley Park

PARK ROAD
PARK RD

SCHOOL CL

Cheveley

CHURCH LA

Cemy

6

PO

HIGH STREET

Brook Stud

CB8

SPURLING CLOSE

White Lodge Stud

White Lodge

5

Moat

Saxon Hall

ICKNIELD CL
SPURLING CLOSE
LITTLE GREEN

PH

COACH LANE

Fisher's Plantation

60

Mast

Banstead Manor Stud

Gorse Covert

4

OAK LANE

Warren Stud

Broad Green

Nutting Grove

SAXON STREET ROAD

Silverley Plantation

PH
THE STREET

Rutland Farm

Osier Wood

3

Saxon Street

CHEVELEY ROAD

Bushy Wood

SCHOOL ROAD

Blackthorn Wood

59

Upend Green

KIRTLING ROAD

2

THE STREET

Rutland Stud

Upend

Hill Farm

Ruperts Wood

THE STREET

Upend Wood

1

Hill Farm

The Grating Wood

Lodge Hill Wood

58

Icknield Way Path

GYPSY'S WALK

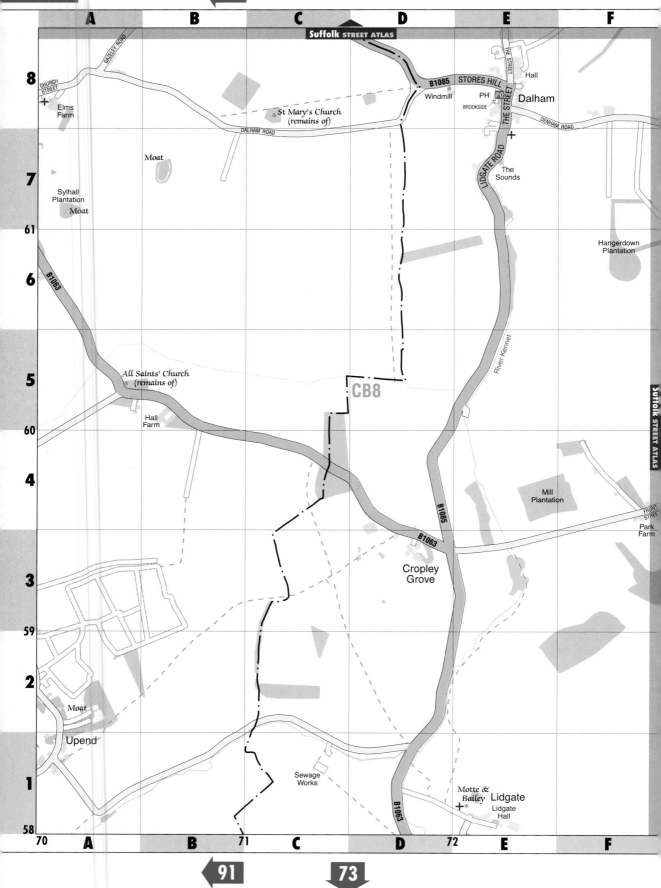

8

GAZELEY ROAD

CHURCH STREET

+ Elms Farm

Moat

St Mary's Church (remains of)

DALHAM ROAD

B1085

Windmill

STORES HILL

Hall

PH

PO

BROOKSIDE

Dalham

THE STREET

DENHAM ROAD

+

7

Moat

Sylhall Plantation

Moat

LIDGATE ROAD

The Sounds

Hangerdown Plantation

61

6

B1063

River Kennet

All Saints' Church (remains of)

5

CB8

60

Hall Farm

4

B1085

Mill Plantation

FRONT STREET

Park Farm

B1063

Cropley Grove

3

59

2

Moat

Upend

Sewage Works

1

B1063

Motte & Bailey

Lidgate

Lidgate Hall

+

58

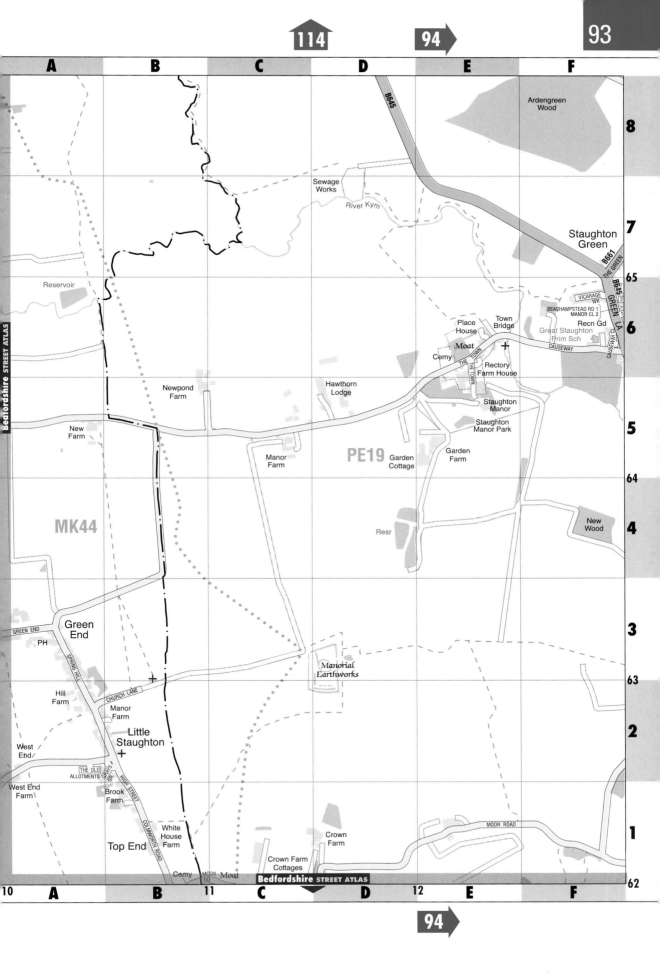

A   B   C   D   E   F

8

Ardengreen
Wood

River Kym

Sewage
Works

B645

7

Staughton
Green

65

Reservoir

B661   THE GREEN   B645   GREEN LA

VICARAGE
WK

BEACHAMPSTEAD RD 1
MANOR CL 2

Recn Gd

6

Place
House

Town
Bridge

Great Staughton
Prim Sch

Moat

CAUSEWAY

Cemy

Rectory
Farm House

Newpond
Farm

Hawthorn
Lodge

THE TOWN

Staughton
Manor

New
Farm

Manor
Farm

PE19

Garden
Cottage

Staughton
Manor Park

Garden
Farm

5

64

MK44

Resr

New
Wood

4

Green
End

GREEN END

Manorial
Earthworks

3

PH

63

SPRING HILL

CHURCH LANE

Hill
Farm

Manor
Farm

2

West
End

Little
Staughton

THE OLD
ALLOTMENTS

GRAYS

HIGH STREET

West End
Farm

Brook
Farm

White
House
Farm

MOOR ROAD

Crown
Farm

1

Top End

COLMWORTH ROAD

Cemy   MOOR
RD   Moat

Crown Farm
Cottages

62

A   B   C   D   E   F

8

Corner
Farm

Manor
Farm

Dillington

Dillington
Farm

HM Prison
Littlehey

PE28

Gaynes
Lodge Farm

Honey Hill
Plantation

THE GREEN

B661

Moat

7

PH

65

CAGE LANE

MANOR CL

BEACHAMPSTEAD

LYE CL

MOORY CFT CL

GREEN CL

SMITHS CL

ROAD

Great
Staughton

Three Shires Way

Midloe
Wood

6

B645

PO

THE HIGHWAY

Highway
Bridge

Staughton
Highway

River Kym

Meagre
Wood

5

PE19

64

4

B645

Rushey
Farm

Meagre
Farm

MOOR ROAD

3

Pastures
Farm

63

Reservoir

2

Wood
Farm

Mast

High
Wood

Huntingdon
Wood

1

Cherry
Orchard Farm

62

A B C D E F

Hangman's
Spinney

Diddington
Wood

PE28

Lodge
Farm

The
Vicarage

7

65

Common
Barn

Church
Farm

6

Midloe
Grange

RECTORY LANE

Moat

BELL LANE

PH

Southoe +

LEES LANE

TOWN OR
HIGH ST
HURLE CL

5

64

PE19

Manor
Farm

Earthwork

4

Little
Paxton Wood

Cock
Audley Farm

GREAT NORTH RD

3

63

Ford

Sewage
Works

GREAT NORTH RD

GT N RD
St JAMES RD
ELM CL
CFT FIELD
HALL
RAMPLEY
THE ROOKERY
MANOR
GROVE RD
MEADOW
HIGH ST
JUBILEE CL
PO
SYCAMRES
THE
LITTLE PAXTON LA
BYDAND
BEESON CL
PARK CR

2

A1

B1041

GREAT NORTH ROAD

Little
Paxton

HAYLE CL
CROWN CL
WESTON CL
MANOR WY
ORCHARD CL
Brookend
Farm
SPRING PL
ORCHARD CL
MANOR WY
FORD END
HIGH STREET
BARKER CL
POUND CL

Hail
Weston

KIMBOLTON RD
B645
GREEN LA
BIRD LA
+

PARK
PARK DRIVE
Little Paxton
Prim Sch
GORDON CL
PARK WY
PARK AV
BLOOMFIELD CL
RAMPLY CL
BOOTH WY
REYNOLDS DR
THE CROFTS
SIDAN
MILL LANE
SWEETING AV
WILLOW
RIVER CL

1

GREAT NORTH ROAD

62

16 A 17 B C D 18 E F

95
117

A B C D E F

8

Home Farm
Manor Farm
Diddington

7

Medieval Village (site of)

65

Boughton Village

6

Boughton Lodge Farm

Sand and Gravel Pit

5

Manor Farm

64

PE19

Great Paxton CE Prim Sch

MOUNT PLEASANT

CHURCH LA
RECTORY CL
MOUNT PLEASANT
LUDDINGTON CL

PO
TONGOOD WAY
GLEBE
BISHOPS WY

HIGH STREET
TONGOOD WY
MNT
LONDON LA
TRINITY CL 1
ST JOHNS MS 2
ADAM'S LANE

MEADOW WAY

Great Paxton

4

Paxton Pits Nature Reserve

Wray House

BROOKSIDE
RIVER LANE
DOVECOTE RD
Low Farm

3

Paxton Pits Nature Reserve

LAKEFIELD AV
NURSERY GD
PIPISTRELLE CL
HIGH STREET
DAVIS CL

63

LAKEFIELD AV
KINGFISHER CL
Visitor Centre P
PH
HAYLING AVE
VINTAGE RD
Pitt Farm
SCHOOL LANE
LAKESIDE CL
Little Paxton

Harley Industrial Park

2

BESON CL
GORDON CL
THE CROFTS

Ouse Valley Way

Paxton Hill

Paxton Hill House

1

B1043
HUNTINGDON ROAD

Sewage Works

62

19 A B 20 C D 21 E F

Ouse Valley Way
LC
PAXTON ROAD
B1043
HIGH STREET
Bullens Farm

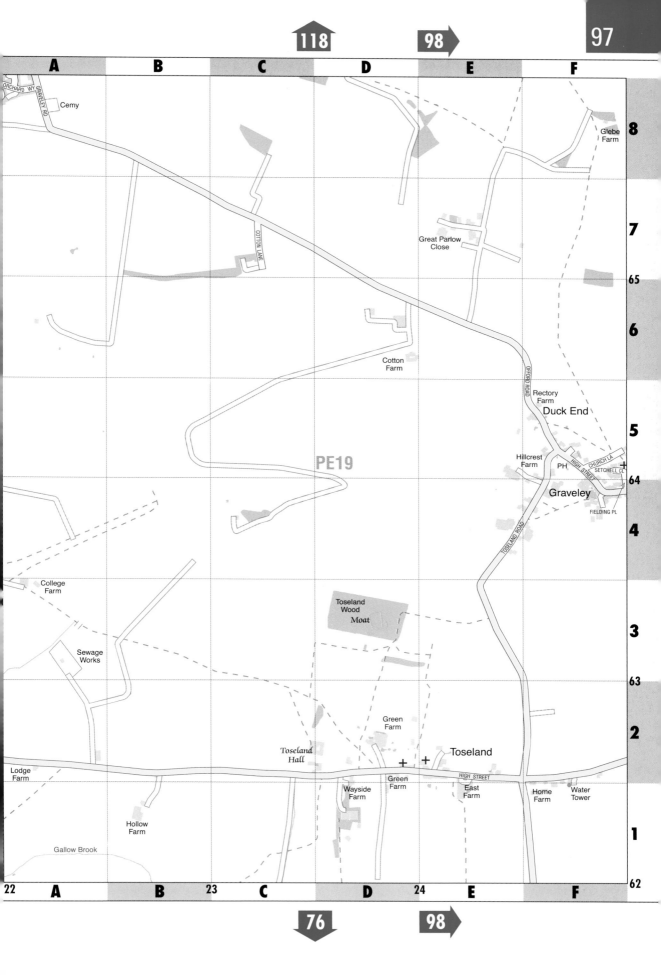

Cemy

Glebe Farm

8

Great Parlow Close

7

COTTON LANE

65

6

Cotton Farm

Rectory Farm

OFFORD ROAD

Duck End

5

PE19

Hillcrest Farm

PH

HIGH STREET

CHURCH LA

SETCHELL CL

64

Graveley

FIELDING PL

4

College Farm

Toseland Wood

Moat

TOSELAND ROAD

3

Sewage Works

63

Green Farm

2

Toseland Hall

Toseland

Lodge Farm

Green Farm

HIGH STREET

East Farm

Home Farm

Water Tower

Wayside Farm

Hollow Farm

1

Gallow Brook

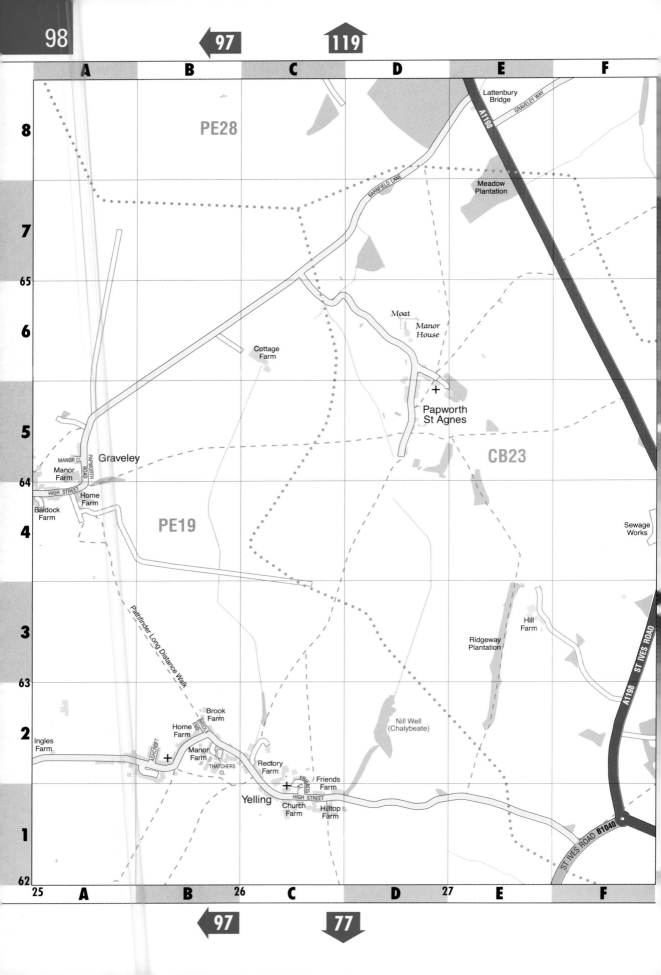

A   B   C   D   E   F

8

PE28

Lattenbury
Bridge

A1198

GRAVELEY WAY

Meadow
Plantation

7

BARNFIELD LANE

65

Moat

Manor
House

6

Cottage
Farm

Papworth
St Agnes

CB23

5

MANOR CL

PAPWORTH ROAD

Graveley

Manor
Farm

HIGH STREET

Home
Farm

64

Baldock
Farm

Sewage
Works

4

PE19

3

Pathfinder Long Distance Walk

Hill
Farm

Ridgeway
Plantation

ST IVES ROAD

63

A1198

Brook
Farm

2

Home
Farm

BRIDLE END

Ingles
Farm

ASHCROFT

Manor
Farm

THATCHERS
CL

Rectory
Farm

Nill Well
(Chalybeate)

FRIENDS

Friends
Farm

Yelling

Church
Farm

HIGH STREET

Hilltop
Farm

ST IVES ROAD B1040

1

B1040

62

25   A   B   26   C   D   27   E   F

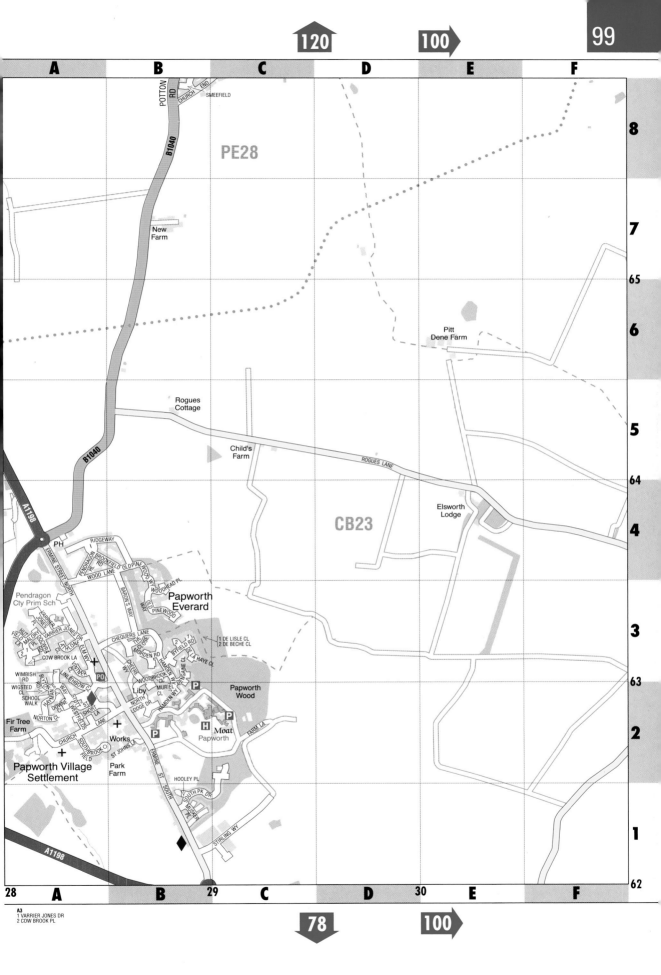

A   B   C   D   E   F

8

7

65

6

5

64

4

3

63

2

1

62

PE28

New Farm

Pitt Dene Farm

Rogues Cottage

Child's Farm

ROGUES LANE

CB23

Elsworth Lodge

B1040

POTTON RD

CHURCH END

SMEEFIELD

A1198

PH

RIDGEWAY

Pendragon Cty Prim Sch

Papworth Everard

1 DE LISLE CL
2 DE BECHE CL

Papworth Wood

PENDRAGON WL
BROOKFIELD RD
OLD PINE WOOD
WOODHEAD PL
BARON'S WAY
OLD PINEWOOD
WOOD LANE

VARRIER JONES DR
CHEQUERS LANE
THE FIRS
MORDEN RD
BYFIELD RD
HAYE CL

COW BROOK LA
VARRIER
ELM WY
HA'PENNY WY
CHEERE WY
ERMINE CL
MURIEL CL
WOODBROOK DR
PO

WIMBISH RD
WIGSTED CL
SCHOOL WALK
DOWNE CL
NORTON CL
HALL
MAY ST
WESTFIELD LANE
SHORT LA
ERMINE ST
NORTH LODGE DR
Liby

Fir Tree Farm

Papworth Village Settlement

CHURCH
SOUTHBROOK
St JOHNS LA
Works
Park Farm
HOOLEY PL
SOUTH PK DR
WHISKER PL
STIRLING WY
ERMINE ST SOUTH

Moat Papworth
H
P
P
P
P
FARM LA

HAMLEN WY

JONES DR
MALORY CL
FIELD CL
HUTTON CL

A3
1 VARRIER JONES DR
2 COW BROOK PL

99
121

Main Farm

Jack o' Thumbs Grove

Wash Bridge

ELSWORTH RD

Ebbs Gore Bridge

North Meadow Plantation

The Bungalow

MEADOW DRIFT

CB23

Windmill

Elsworth CE Prim Sch

Deers Farm

FARDELL'S LANE

Summerlin Farm

BOXWORTH ROAD

PADDOCK ROW

DUNNOCK LA

ROGER'S CL

Meadow Farm

Moat

PH

BROAD END

BOXWORTH RD

BROOK

ORCHARD

Elsworth

LOWDELL END

THE DRIFT

SMITH STREET

COTTRELL'S LANE

BROCKLEY ROAD

BROOK ST

PO

THE CAUSEWAY

CHURCH LA

ROGUES LANE

Avenue Farm

Rectory Farm

Overhall Spinney

Overhall Grove Nature Reserve

Mound

HIGH ST

Knapwell

HIGH STREET

The Red Well

Overhall Grove

Grange Farm

Manor Farm

Elsworth Wood

A B C D E F

8

7

65

6

5

64

4

63

3

2

1

62

HISTON ROAD

B1049

Jokers Wild Farm

Drove Moor

Beck Farm

COTTENHAM ROAD

Mill Lane Farm

Unwins Farm

BARROW CROFTS
COTTENHAM ROAD
ALSTEAD RD
GREENLEAS
NORMANTON WAY
FARMSTEAD CL
PARLOUR CL
MUNCEY WK
GARDEN WK
B1049
YOUNGMAN CL
CB24

CROFT CL
CLAY ST
WINDERS LANE
BURKETT WAY
OLD FARM CL
LOCKETTS
SWINDELLS
YOUNGMAN AVE
ORCHARD ROAD
DRAKE WAY
MILL LANE

Abbey Farm
ST ANDREW'S PK
BELTHILL
CLAY STREET
NARROW LANE
Histon & Impington Jun Sch
SPRING CL
PADDOCK CL

Histon Manor
Moat
CHURCH ST
WINDMILL
GLEBE WAY
Cemy
AMBROSE WAY
Manor Farm

PARK LANE
Liby
SCHOOL HILL
HIGH ST
LAWSON CL
THE GREEN
MILTON ROAD

MELVIN WAY
HARDING WAY
Histon
ST GEORGES CT
Green Gates Farm

MANOR PARK
AINGERS RD
STATION RD
PH
ST ANDREWS WAY

ST AUBYN'S CL
PARK AVENUE
SHIRLEY RD
MERTON RD
HOME CLOSE
JOYCE CL
BROOK CL
WATER LANE
IMPINGTON LANE
HEREWARD CL
ST GEORGES WAY
WOODWICK CL
Middlewhite Farm

MANOR PK
SOMERSET ROAD
WEST RD
BISHOP WAY
HEREWARD CLOSE
ROSELEA
CLAY CLOSE LANE
BURGOYNES FARM CL
DOCTOR'S CL

SAFFRON ROAD
NEW SCHOOL RD
HOM RD
NEW RD
BURGOYNE'S
PERCHERON CL

Factory
NEW SCHOOL RD
STATION RD
THE DOLE
Impington Sports Ctr

Park Farm
Histon & Impington Inf Sch
NEW
POPLAR RD
HENRY MORRIS
THE DOLE
PARK DR
Impington Village Coll

OAK TREE WAY
LOVE'S CL
S FARLANE CL
4
1 BRACKENBURY CL
2 DAVEY CL
3 PARR CL
4 SCHOOL LA

(dis)
KAY HITCH WAY
PIONEER CL
CHIVERS WAY
CHEQUERS RD
PO

VILLA ROAD
SOUTH ROAD
VILLA RD
NEW RD
MOWLAM CL
Impington
Field Steads Farm

BRIDGE RD
Glassworld Stadium (Histon FC)
CB4

COLLEGE RD
VILLA PL
THE CRES
PEPYS TR
LC
Windmill

MILL RD
CAMBRIDGE RD
CRESCENT ROAD
BURROS
THE COPPICE
B1049
Millfield Farm

HIGHFIELD RD
Hotel

43 44 45

A B C D E F

← 105   ▲ 127

A   B   C   D   E   F

8

Denny End
PEMBROKE AVE
WINFOLD CL
JUBILEE CL
WADDELOW
DENNY END
BANNOLD CT
CODY RD
FENLEIGH CL
BANNOLD
Midlode
Farm
LONG DROVE
Lock
Farm
Waterbeach
CP Sch
Liby
JOSIAH
CT
BANNOLD
ROAD
LC
BANNOLD
RD
Bottisham
Lock
WILES CL
PRIMROSE LA
PO
HIGH STREET
VICARAGE CL
CATTELL'S LA
BARKER
CHAPS
PARK CR
PIECES LA
SPURGEONS AV
HARTLEY
SOBERTON CL
Frolic
Farm

HARDING CL 1
POORSFIELD RD 2
SAKON WAY 3
MILL ROAD
GLEBE ROAD
GREEN SIDE
CHAPEL ST
WELLINGTON CL
JUBE
PIECES TR
WATERBEACH
Todds
Farm
Hall
Crest
Farm
BURGESS'S DROVE
Northfields
Farm
Hatley's
Farm
Vicarage
Farm

7
CAMBRIDGE ROAD
CORO NATION CL
CAMBRIDGE ROAD
DEN
GIBSON CL
CHAPEL
ST ANDREWS HILL
ROSEMARY RD
BURGESS
ROAD
ADAMS CT
LC
LUG FEN DROVEWAY

65
CAR DYKE ROAD
ST JOHN'S CL
STATION ROAD
PAYTON
LODE AV
WHITMORE WAY
LC
Waterbeach
CLAYHITHE ROAD

6
P

5
River Cam
CLAYHITHE ROAD
Clayhithe
Clayhithe
Farm
Queen's
Fen

64

CB25
Queens
Farm

4
Grange
Farm
Eye Hall
Farm

3
Roman Pottery
Kilns (site of)
CLAYHITHE ROAD
Harcamlow Way

63

2
Manor
Farm
DOCK LANE
ST JOHN'S
CHURCH
END
Northgate
Farm
Kings
Farm
PH
HIGH STREET
Stow cum Quy
Fen

1
ABBOTS W
PRIORY RD
Horningsea
PH
HORNINGSEA ROAD
Allicky
Farm
STATION RD

62
49   A   B   50   C   D   51   E   F

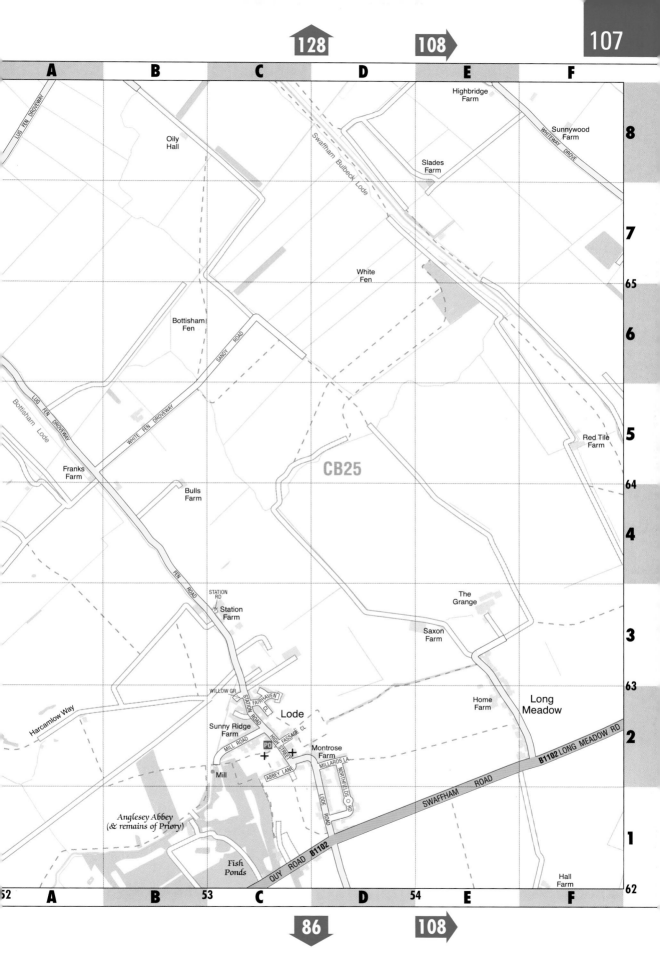

A   B   C   D   E   F

8

7

65

6

5

64

4

63

3

2

1

62

55   A   B   56   C   D   57   E   F

LITTLE FEN DROVE
BLACKBERRY DROVEWAY
BARSTON DROVE
DITCHFIELD

WHITEWAY DROVE

Adventurers'
Ground Farm

SWAFFHAM ROAD

ROGERS ROAD

BURWELL ROAD

B1102

CB25

Crow Hill
Plantation

Swaffham
Prior Park

STATION ROAD

Hall
Farm

Water
Tower

Swaffam Prior
Windmill

MILL HILL

Swaffham Prior
CE Prim Sch

HIGH STREET
PH

FAIRVIEW GR
LOWER END
CAGE HILL RD
GREEN HEAD RD
ADAMS RD
TOTHILL RD

HEATH ROAD

Speyside
Farm

FEN LANE

The
Coverts

Swaffham Prior
House

VICARAGE LANE
Cemy

Swaffham
Prior

Cowbridge
Farm

HIGH STREET

B1102

Sterling
Farm

Cow
Bridge

The Abbey

CADENHAM ROAD

Commercial End

COMMERCIAL END
ABBEY LANE
ARCHERS CL

MILL LA

Cadenham
Plantation

Cadenham
Farm

WHITE DROVEWAY

B1102

LONG MEADOW ROAD

STATION ROAD

Gutter
Bridge

Moat

Denny
Plantation

Lordship
Farm

GREEN

BANK ROAD

HEATH ROAD

MARYLAND AV

Downing
Farm

PH

Cemy
POUND WY

HIGH ST

HEATH ROAD

PO

Mitchell
Lodge Farm

DONKING CT

VICARAGE CL

QUARRY LANE

SWAFFHAM HEATH ROAD

Middle Hill
Plantations

Swaffham Bulbeck
CE Prim Sch

HIGH STREET

Swaffham
Bulbeck

Middle
Hill

A B C D E F

8

B1103 BURWELL ROAD

Orchard Farm

NEW RD

MILL LA

GEORGE GIBSON CLOSE

WINDMILL HILL

THE HIGHLANDS

PH

SAXON CL

A142

37

Studlands Park

QUEENS VIEW

OXFORD ST

SWAN LA

BEECH WOOD CL

GLANELY GDN

1 BROOKSIDE
2 CHURCH CL

A14

NIMBUS WAY

AUREOLE WK

HYPERION WAY

TUDOR RIDE

NIMBUS WAY

FORDHAM RD

Exning

Exning Prim Sch

PO

CHURCH ST

Exeter Stables

ROYAL PALACE CLOSE

TULYAR WALK

AUREOLE WALK

PERSIMMON WK

Harraton Stud

ST WENDREDS WAY

SWAN GR

NEW RIVER GN

DUCKS LANE

ST MARTINS CL

Cemy

CEMETERY HILL

HEATHERSETT CL

HYPERION WAY

PARKERS WALK

VINCENT CLOSE

AVENUE

Studland Ret Pk

7

LACEY'S LANE

FERGOMBRE

Brickfield Stud

BOLDEN CLOSE

BRICKFIELDS AVE

MILLER CLOSE

PETTINGO

Acorn Bsns Ctr

Newmarket Bsns Pk

OAKS DRIVE

The Oaks Bus Park Superstore

HEATH ROAD

B1103

Studlands Park Business Centre

Victoria Park

AVENUE

Minton Ent Pk

KINGFISHER DRIVE

SNAITH RD

65

Studlands Park Ind Estate

HAMMOND RD

LAUREATE SCHOOL RD

DOUG SMITH CL 1
GORDON RICHARDS CL 2
LESTER PIGGOTT WAY 3
MATT DAWSON CL 4

P

Playing Fields

St Felix CE VC Middle Sch

6

EXNING ROAD

Laureate Com Prim Sch

Factory

LAUREATE

LAUREATE GDNS

CRAVEN WAY

GUINEA'S

CROFT ROAD

DEPOT ROAD

CORSICAN

PINE CL

CARSON WALK

GREVILLE

STARKEY AVE 1

TOM JENNINGS CL 2

WESTON WY

MURLESS

Seven Springs

SCALTBACK CLOSE

FEILDEN WAY

ROSEBERY WAY

FIELDEN WY

ELIZABETH AVENUE

ELIZABETH PARADE

PO

B1103

Scaltback Middle Sch

CAMBRIDGE AVENUE

5

CB8

Hamilton Stud

HAMILTON ROAD

E5
1 ANDREW RD
2 BARTONS PL
3 COLLINGS PL
4 DURHAM WAY

CHURCHILL AVENUE

NORFOLK AVE

ELIZABETH AVE

FAIRHAVEN WAY

HALIFAX WAY

KING EDWARD VII RD

FIELD TO RD

ISLINGTON RD

LAMBTON AVENUE

HEASMAN

H

64

DERBY WY

BROCKFORT

ELVEDON

SEFTON WAY

LADY'S

LEADER'S WAY

SUFFOLK WAY

PHILIP'S ROAD

ST FABIANS CL

NORTH DR

SOUTH DR

Nmkt Leisure Ctr

TANNERSFIELD WAY

MILLBANK

FRESHFIELDS

EXNING ROAD

4

A14

Southfield Farm

Equine Pool

HAMILTON ROAD

PHILIP'S

DRINKWATER CL

EDINBURGH

WINDSOR

Playing Field

Newmarket Coll

1 BAHRAM CL
2 SOUTHFIELDS CL

ADASTRAL RD

KINGSWAY

Playing Field

ROWLEY DR

3

CB25

PRINCESS WY

CHARLES CL

MANDERSTON RD

PORTLAND HILL CL

Houldsworth Valley Prim Sch

VALLEY WAY

HAMILTON ROAD

PORTLAND GREEN

ROWLEY CT

THE ROWS

ROWLEY

DRIVE

HOULDSWORTH TERR

BRAZILIAN TERR

Newmarket Swimming Pool

CHURCHILL CT

LOWTHER ST

BLACK BEAR LANE

FALMOUTH AV

REGENTS CT

63

Newmarket Lawn Tennis Club

THE HAMILTONS

HAMILTON COURT

Government Offices

HIGH ST

FAIRLAWNS

Newmarket Heath

Cooper Memorial Fountain

40

Cemetery

FAIRLAWNS RD 1
HALLWYCK GDNS 2

B1061

2

BARBARA STRADBROKE AVENUE

F3
1 FALMOUTH ST
2 MARINO CT
3 Kings Theatre

DULLINGHAM ROAD

Beacon (Rowley Mile) Course

The Millennium Grandstand

Stour Valley Path

Cambridge Hill

1

Racecourses

Devil's Ditch

A1304

Wyck Hall Stud

B1061

62

61 A B 62 C D 63 E F

A14

A 8
B
C
D
E
F

British Racing
School

Woodland
End

Hatchfield
Farm

BURY ROAD A1304

The
Limekilns

B1506

7

Training
Ground

Oak
Wood

Woodland
Stud

B1506 · WELL BOTTOM

The
Flat

65

6

Bury Hill

Moulton
Paddocks

FALMOUTH
GDNS
BALATON PL

ST ALBANS
ARGENT
PL

WYNDHAM
WY
PAGET
PLACE

Balaton
Lodge

BURY RD

A4
1 ST GEORGE
2 ST ANDREW
3 ST ANTHONY
4 ST DAVID
5 ST DENYS
6 ST PATRICK
7 WILFRED SHERMAN CL
8 FERNELEY CRES

FORDHAM ROAD A142

MALCOLM
WAY

Warren
Place

5

NEWMARKET

Hotel

BURY ROAD

Long Hill

CB8

Warren
Towers

64

The
Severals

Gallops

Claypit
Plantation

Warren
Towers

SASSOON CL

St Louis RC
Prim Sch

Fairstead
House Sch

Superstore
The
Guineas
Sh Ctr

A1304

MOULTON ROAD

MOULTON ROAD

4

BAKERS
ROW
BARLINGS CT

EXETER

Munnings
CL

BAYES LANE

Warrenhill
Plantation

New Ground

B1103

ICEWELL
HILL

ROAD

FRED ARCHER WAY

A142

Jubilee Clock
Tower

3

Liby

HIGH STREET

OLD STATION ROAD

Warren Hill

Old
Hollow

P
CROWN
WK

SACKVILLE ST

All Saints CE
Prim Sch

HEATH ROAD

Meml
Hall

ROUS RD
LISBURN RD

PALACE ST

The Palace
House

FLATMAN
ST

CHEVELEY RD

Sidehill Stud

63

National
Horseracing
Museum

THE TERRACE

THE AVENUE

PARK AV

ALL SAINTS ROAD

GRANBY ST
VILLAGE

GREENFIELDS
HEATHBELL RD

ICKNEY RD

Mast

Tattersalls
Horse Sales

CARDIGAN
PLACE

WHITE
GATES

BOLEYN WALK 1
SEYMOUR CL 2

NEW CHEVELEY RD

B1063

B1063

2

Sale
Ring

STATION AP

GREEN RD

WARRINGTON ST

WILLOW CRES
CRICKET FIELD
RD

BARRY LYNHAM DR

ASHLEY ROAD

Newmarket

Newmarket
Town
FC

B1103

B2
1 MELTON CL
2 PEMBROKE CL
3 STAMFORD ST

THE DIP

CENTRE DRIVE

MOR MONT WY
SINGLASS
CL

Newlands
Stud

Icknield Way Path

WOODDITTON ROAD

Ditton Lodge
First Sch

Someries
Stud

Dunchurch
Lodge Stud

DUCHESS DRIVE

THE SHRUBBERIES

MEADOW LANE

Sandpit
Plantation

1

DITTON CL

GIRTON CL

Sixteen Acre
Plantation

Eight Acre
Plantation

62

64
A
B 65
C
D 66
E
F

A3
1 DRAPERY ROW
2 KINGSTON PASSAGE
3 WELLINGTON ST
4 JACK JARVIS CL
5 SUN LA
6 ST MARYS SQ
7 THE GUINEAS

B3
1 PARK COTTS
2 BARLEY CL
3 MALT CL

A B C D E F

8

Round
Plantation

WELL BOTTOM B1506

Chippenham
Hill

Lanwades
Stud

B1506

Lodge

7

Oak
Wood

Moulton
Paddocks
Stud

Folly Hill

CHIPPENHAM ROAD

65

Trinity Hall
Farm

B1085

KENNETT ROAD OR MOULTON ROAD

Moulton CE
Primary School

6

New
Farm

Folly
Farm

Moulton

SCHOOL RD

BENEFIELD RD

RIVERSIDE
WK

BURY LANE

GAZELEY RD

BRIDGE ST

PH

Bridge
Farm

NEWMARKET ROAD

MAYES
MD

PARK CL

BROOKSIDE

5

CB8

MILBURN DRO

LARK HILL

MALTINGS CL

MALTINGS CL

PO

THE STREET

CHURCH ROAD

LARK HILL

ST PETERS AVE

64

Glebe
House

ST PETERS CL

MOULTON ROAD

Moulton
Manor
Farm

DALHAM RD

B1085

SUFFOLK STREET ATLAS

4

Park House

Thrift
Covert

MOULTON ROAD

3

Ashley
Heath Stud

63

Trinity
Plantation

MOULTON ROAD

2

B1063

ASHLEY ROAD

Longholes
Stud

MOULTON ROAD

1

Hascombe
Stud

Mill
House

MILL ROAD

62

Beech
House Stud

B1063

Sandwich
Stud

67 A B 68 C D 69 E F

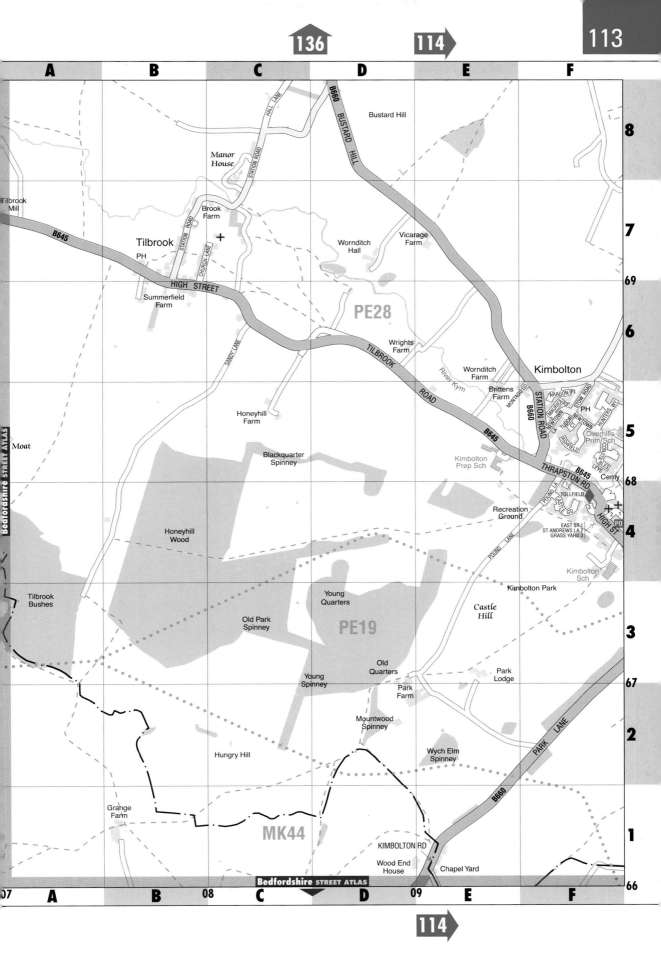

A   B   C   D   E   F

8

Airfield
(disused)

Airstrip

Magpie
Farm

STOCKING LANE

PE28

Mast

GROSVENOR CT

Airfield
(disused)

Bicton
Industrial
Estate

INGRIE RD
KIM RD
RIVER RD
OUSE RD
BROOK RD

EASTON ROAD

High
Park Farm

7

Mast

PE28

69

BIGRAM'S   LANE

6

Bigram's
Farm

Lowen
Wood

EASTON ROAD

Newtown

Warren
Hill

Priory
Farm

Overhills
Prim Sch

5

Warren
Spinney

Dudney
Wood

Three Shires Way

NEWTOWN

68

Cemy

Kimbolton

PE19

Moat

Lady
Grove

EAST ST
LONDON   RD

4

Kimbolton
Sch

B645

EASTON ROAD

Kimbolton
Castle

B660

Kimbolton
Park

Stonely

PARK LANE

3

Stonely
Grange

67

HATCHET LA
HATCHET LA
OLD FORD LANE

Stonely
Hill Farm

Agden Hill
Farm

Claylands
Farm

2

College
Farm

Gimbers End

River Kym

1

Agdengreen
Spinney

B645

66

Lower
Park Farm

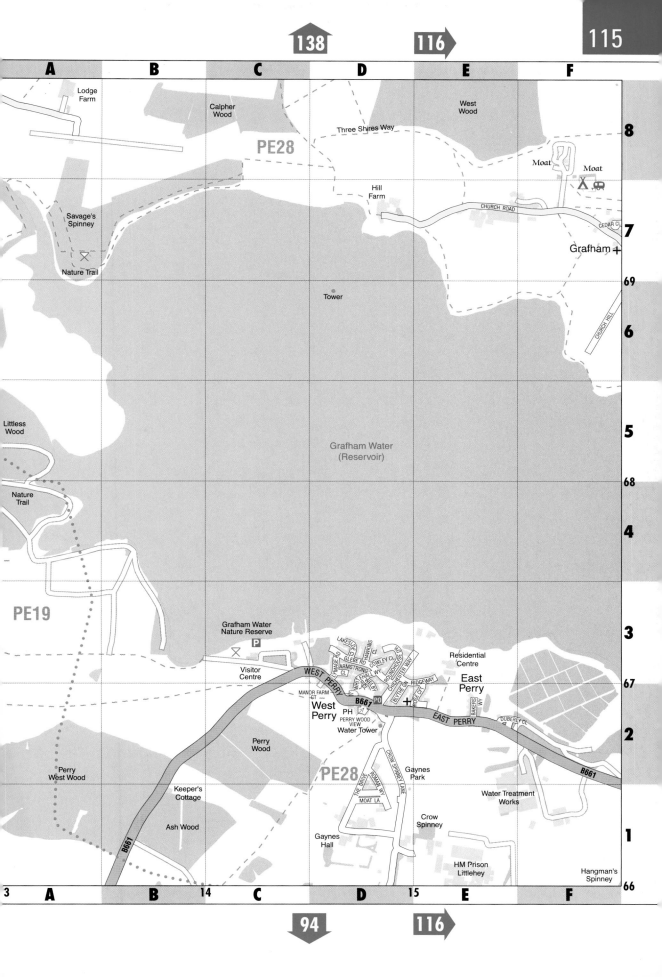

Lodge Farm

Calpher Wood

Three Shires Way

West Wood

PE28

Moat

Moat

Savage's Spinney

CHURCH ROAD

CEDAR CL

Hill Farm

Grafham +

8

7

69

Nature Trail

Tower

CHURCH HILL

6

Littless Wood

Grafham Water (Reservoir)

5

68

Nature Trail

4

PE19

Grafham Water Nature Reserve

P

Residential Centre

3

Visitor Centre

LAKESIDE CL
HAWKINS CL
GLEBE RD
ARMSTRONG CL
WHITEHALL WY
COWLEY CL
LY-MAGE RD
BLYTHE CM
ROUNDHOUSE RD
COLCHESTER WAY
RIDGEWAY
NELBY CL

East Perry

67

MANOR FARM CT

WEST PERRY

West Perry

B667

PO

ROSE CFT

BAKERS WY

PH
PERRY WOOD VIEW
Water Tower

EAST PERRY

DUBERLY CL

B661

2

Perry Wood

Perry West Wood

THE DRIVE
ROMAN WY
CROW SPINNEY LANE
MOAT LA

PE28

Gaynes Park

Water Treatment Works

Keeper's Cottage

Crow Spinney

Ash Wood

Gaynes Hall

HM Prison Littlehey

Hangman's Spinney

1

66

B661

A   B   C   D   E   F

8   Redwood Lodge

Brampton Wood Nature Reserve

7   THE WYVERN
VAN DIEMANS WY
HAYCRAFT CL
BREACH ROAD
MEADOWCROFT
ALSYKE CL
FIELD CL
CEDAR CL
CHURCH HILL
CHESTNUT CL
THE PIGHTLE
INHAMS WY
HARTHAM CL
Playing Fields
Moat
BRAMPTON RD

Thistle Hill

69   CHURCH RD
Grafham
HOME CL
Water Tower
BUCKDEN ROAD

PE28

6   Moat

5   P

68   Grafham Water Exhibition Centre

Hardonian Farm
TAYLORS LANE
Paddock Farm

PE19

Model Farm

4   Buckden Wood
Wood Farm

PERRY ROAD B661

3   Grafham Water (Reservoir)

Tower

Moat

Shooter's Hollow

Westfield Farm

67

2   Three Shires Way

Diddington Wood

Coronation Wood

Jubilee Copse

Diddington Brook

GREAT NORTH ROAD

PE28

1   B661
Highfield Farm
Diddington Wood

Lodge Farm

A1

66

A   B   C   D   E   F

8

7

69

6

5

68

4

3

67

2

1

66

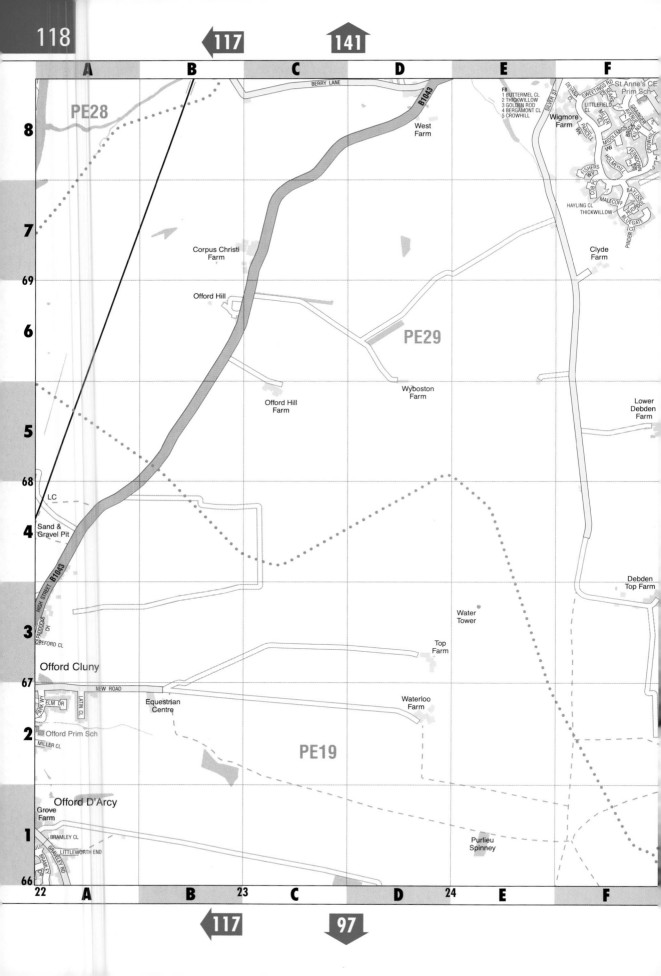

117
141
117
97

PE28

BERRY LANE

B1043

West Farm

St Anne's CE Prim Sch

F8
1 BUTTERMEL CL
2 THICKWILLOW
3 GOLDEN ROD
4 BERGAMONT CL
5 CROWHILL

Wigmore Farm

SILVER ST

DE JADA CL
SWEETINGS RD
BIRCLAS
LITTLEFIELD
GRANGER
AVENUE
MILLER
CROWHILL
PARCEL WK
KESINGHAM
MIDDLEMISS
VW
HOLMEHILL
FISHERS WY
COB PL
MALECOFF
BAYLISS
HUDPOOL
HAYLING CL
THICKWILLOW
BLUEGATE
PINDER CL

Corpus Christi Farm

Clyde Farm

Offord Hill

PE29

Offord Hill Farm

Wyboston Farm

Lower Debden Farm

LC

Sand & Gravel Pit

Debden Top Farm

B1043

HIGH STREET

Water Tower

PADDOCKS

CH

OPEFORD CL

Top Farm

Offord Cluny

NEW ROAD

ELM DR
LATIN CL
KERRY WY

Equestrian Centre

Waterloo Farm

Offord Prim Sch

MILLER CL

PE19

Offord D'Arcy

Grove Farm

BRAMLEY CL

LITTLEWORTH END

Purlieu Spinney

BRAMLEY RD

GRANLEY

A **B** **C** **D** **E** **F**

A14

70

25

8

Bear's
Croft Farm

Emmanuel Knoll
Plantation

New
Farm

CH

Hemingford Abbots
Golf Club

LIONS
CROSS

ROMAN WAY

LONDON RD

MARTIN ST

A1198

Cemy

GODMANCHESTER

DVROVIGVTVM

7

69

Bleakley
Farm

MOATS WAY

6

PE29

Mast

Littlebury
Farm

Rectory
Farm

The Coll of
Animal Welfare

Wood Green
Animal Centre

5

68

Beaconsfield
Equine
Centre

A1198

Top
Farm

PE28

4

Depden
Lodge

3

67

Lattenbury
Farm

2

Brookside
Cottage

Dumptilow
Farm

Top
Plantation

A1198

Graveley
Way Bridge

1

GRAVELEY WAY

66

PE27

PE28

Douglas Farm

Rectory Farm

A14

Gore Tree Farm

Arthur's Meadow Nature Reserve

The Grove

GORE TREE ROAD

GROVE LANE

LONG LA

MARSH LANE

LONDON ROAD

Stepping Stone Bridge

Galley Hill Farm

Galley Hill

26

HUNTINGDON ROAD

A14

Mast

Woolpack Farm

MERE WAY

Topfield Farm

B1040

West Brook

West End Farm

Linton's Farm

POTTON ROAD

Five Arch Bridge

HILTON ROAD

Oxholme Farm

Clayfield Farm

Hilton End Farm

Punch's Grove

NEW ENGLAND

THE PADDOCKS

CHEQUERS CFT

WEST BROOK

WEST BROOK CL

Moat

KIDMANS CL

TRE CL

CROSS FARM CL

FECKS CL

GRAVELEY WAY

B1040

Hilton

SCOTTS CL

HIGH ST

GROVE END

MAZE RD

The Green

Turf Maze

CHAPEL CL

CHURCH LA

SPARROW

CHURCH END

Park Farm

PH

HOME FARM CLOSE

PO

FLACKDALE RD 1
RUTLAND GN 2
MILL HILL END 3

121
208

A B C D E F

Sand & Gravel Works

Church Farm

P

PE27

HOLYWELL FERRY ROAD

HOLYWELL FERRY ROAD

8

Covells Bridge

(dis)   LC   LC

Mare Fen Nature Reserve

STATION ROAD

Brownsfield Farm

High Causeway Bridge

Cloverfield Farm

OVER ROAD

LC

7

Church Bridge

STATION RD

STATION ROAD

Church End

69

Friesland Farm

MILL WAY

Earthworks

TAYLOR'S LA

BLACK HORSE LA

MARKET ST

CHEQUERS CT

MARKET ST

PO

WAL

MAN'S LA

HOBBLEDODDS CL

6

Windmill

WHITEGATE CL

MOAT WY

MOAT WY

B CHANTRY

THISTLE GN

HIGH STREET

GREENSIDE CL

SCHOOL LA

Swavesey

Swavesey Prim Sch

High Causeway Bridge

CB24

CARTER'S WY

PRIORY AVE

GIBRALTER LANE

MIDDLE WATCH

Swavesey Village Coll

Liby

5

CHURCH ST

HORSE AND GATE ST

HONEY HILL

FEN DRAYTON ROAD

Swavesey Sports Centre

WHITTON CL

WHITTON CL

Mill Farm

68

CAMBRIDGE RD

SWAVESEY ROAD

4

St John's College Farm

ROSE AND CROWN ROAD

Dairy Farm

PINE GROVE

Works

BOXWORTH END

3

Boxworth End

67

Boxworth End Farm

2

A14

HUNTINGDON ROAD

TIPPLERS ROAD

Thorpes Farm

CB23

BUCKING WAY ROAD

1

Friesland Farm

A14

ANDERSON RD

66

34   A   B   35   C   D   36   E   F

A   B   C   D   E   F

8 Willingham
Windmill

PH
BERRYCROFT
NEWINGTON
B1050
BALAND FIELD
MILL RD
LONG
MILL RD
30
MILLFIELD
STATION ROAD

Belsars Field

7 West Field

RAMPTON ROAD
Mistletoe Farm
BLACK PIT DROVE
Anstey Farm

Top Field Farm
COW LANE
69 WESTFIELD
New Farm

6
STANTON MERE WAY

RAMPTON ROAD
Ashley Farm

5 New Farm

CB24

HIGH STREET
PH
Manor Farm

68
ORCHARD END
HOME FARM CL
KING STREET
CHURCH END
Rampton
Ivy Farm

4
CUCKOO LANE

New Ground Common

(dis)

REYNOLDS DROVE

3
LC
Brookfield Farm
Brook Field

CUCKOO LANE

The Holme

67
RAMPTON RD

Cuckoo Bridge

2
MAGDALENE CL
MAGDALENE
RAMPTON ROAD
RAMPTON DRIFT

Nether Grove
Oakington Barracks

1
THATCHER'S WOOD
MILLS LANE
LANE
CL
AVE
WOODSIDE
ST MICHAEL'S LA

66
40   A   B   41   C   D   42   E   F

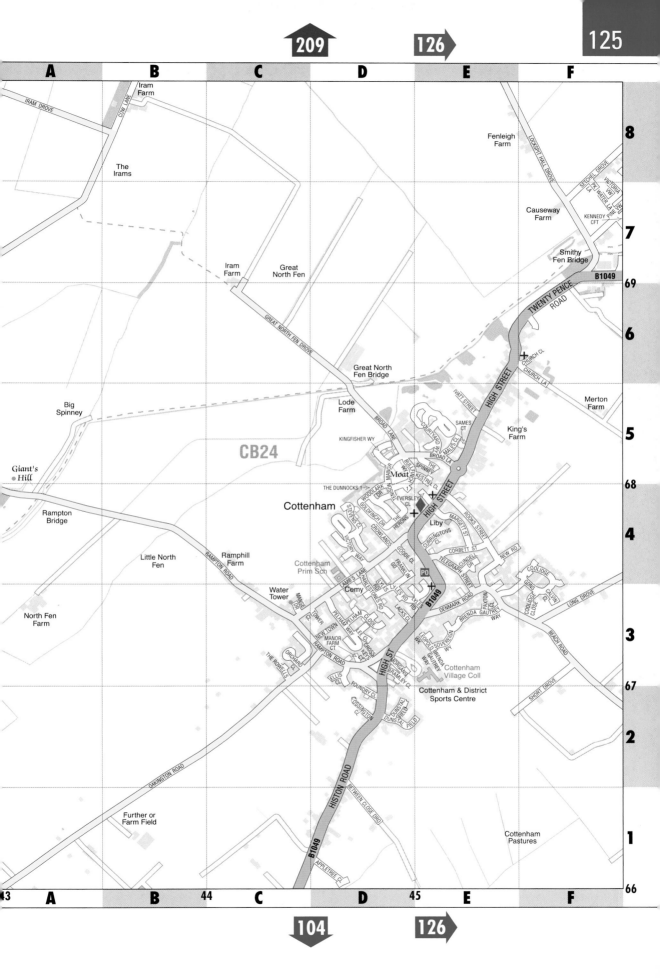

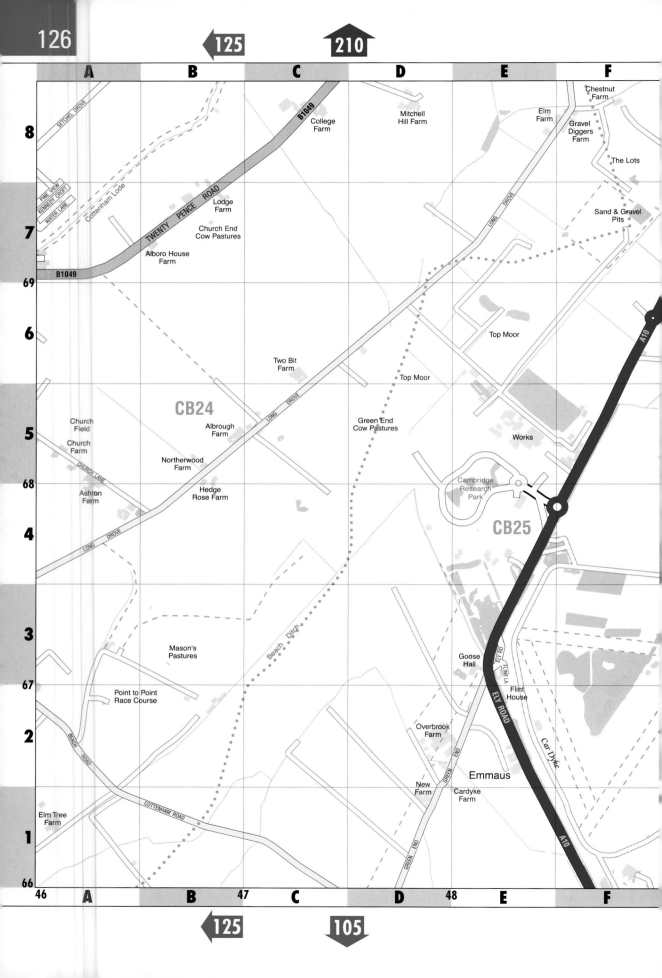

A B C D E F

8

7

69

6

68

5

4

67

3

2

1

66

Vicarage
Farm
Chittering

SCHOOL LANE

CHITTERING DR

SAND DROVE

Varsity
Farm

Denny
Lodge

Causeway
End Farm

A10

ELY ROAD

North Fen

Denny Abbey
(remains of)

Denny Abbey
Farm

Lowlands
Farm

LONG DROVE

Heron
Farm

The Farmland
Museum &
Denny Abbey

CROSS DROVE

Bank
Farm

CB25

Soldiers' Hill

New
Farm

CROSS   DROVE

LC

Waterbeach
Joist Fen

Airfield
(disused)

Hinge
Farm

LONG DROVE

LC

Lower Hinge
Farm

67

Waterbeach
Barracks

MILL DV

ABBEY PL

CODY ROAD

ORCHARD
VW

+

+

Cemetery

CAPPER   ROAD

KIRBY TR

KIRBY   ROAD

FLETCHER AV

River Cam

PROVIDENCE WAY

ORCHARD DR

BANNOLD DROVE

DENNY END ROAD

49

A B 50 C D 51 E F

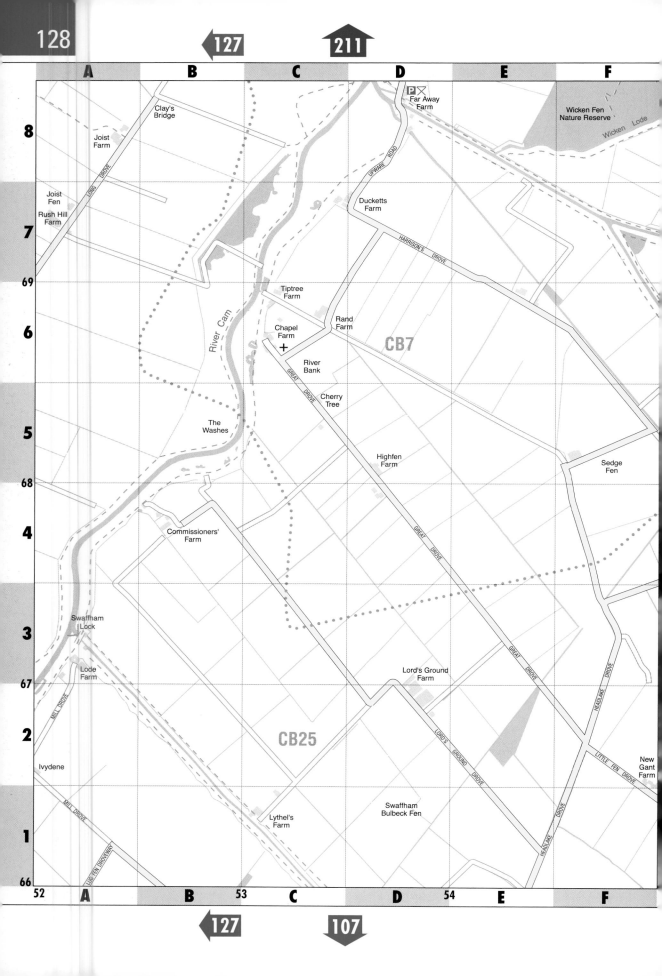

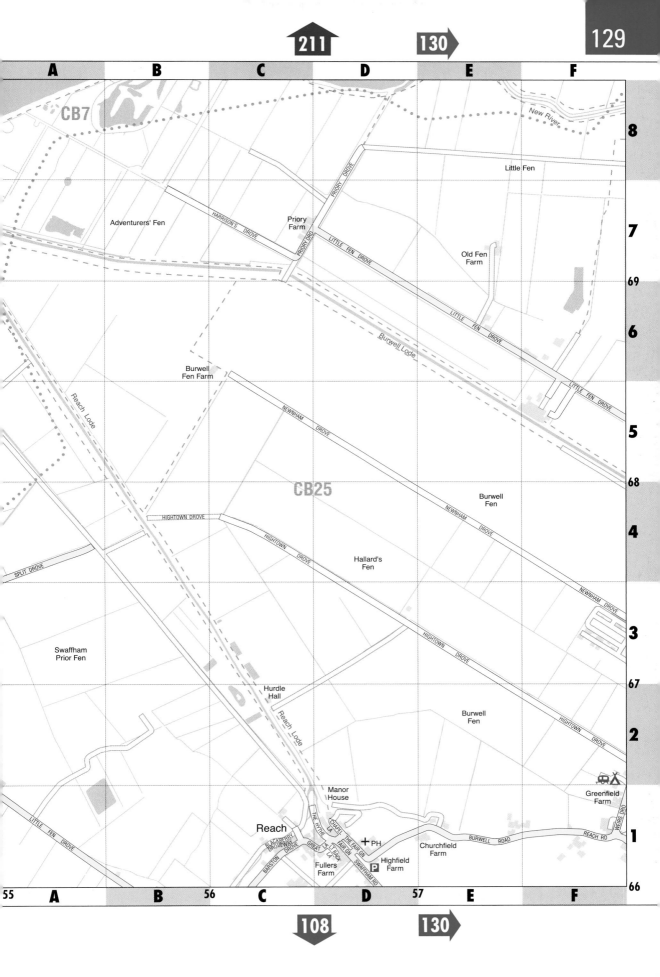

CB7

New River

8

Little Fen

Adventurers' Fen

HARRISON'S DROVE

Priory Farm

PRIORY DRO

PRIORY DROVE

LITTLE FEN DROVE

7

Old Fen Farm

69

Burwell Lode

LITTLE FEN DROVE

6

Reach Lode

Burwell Fen Farm

NEWNHAM DROVE

LITTLE FEN DROVE

5

CB25

68

HIGHTOWN DROVE

Burwell Fen

NEWNHAM DROVE

4

SPLIT DROVE

HIGHTOWN DROVE

Hallard's Fen

NEWNHAM DROVE

3

Swaffham Prior Fen

HIGHTOWN DROVE

67

Hurdle Hall

Reach Lode

Burwell Fen

HIGHTOWN DROVE

2

Manor House

Greenfield Farm

LITTLE FEN DROVE

Reach

THE HYTHE

CHAPEL LA

THE FAIR GN

BACK LA

BLACKBERRY DROVEWAY

BARSTON DROVE

GREAT LA

+PH

SWAFFHAM RD

P

Churchfield Farm

BURWELL ROAD

REACH RD

WEIRS DRO

1

Fullers Farm

Highfield Farm

66

129
212

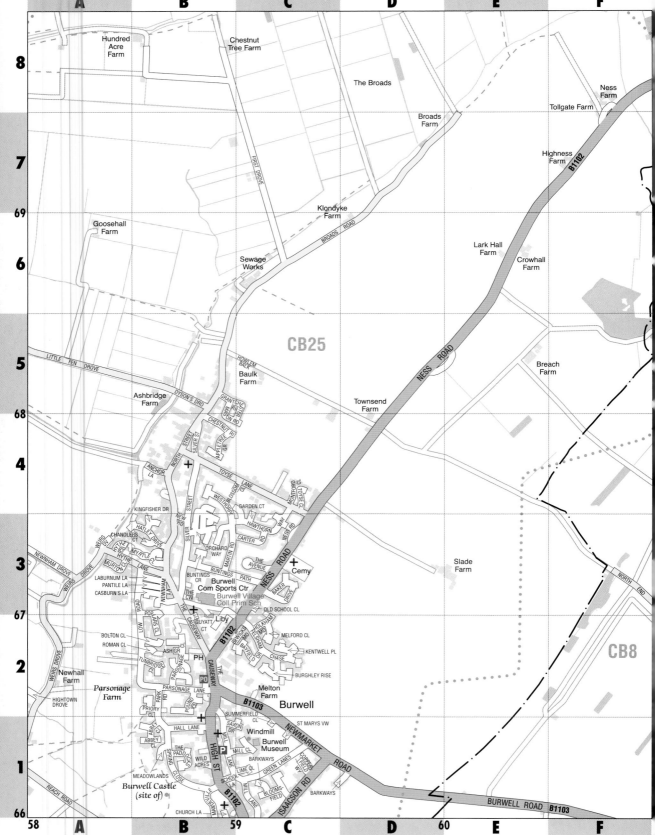

129
109

131
213

Chippenham

PH

NEW STREET

PALACE LANE

HIGH STREET

B1085 PARKSIDE

Chippenham
Lodge

Forty
Acre Wood

Underdown
Plantation

Gifford
Wood

Chippenham
Hall

Chippenham Fen
National
Nature Reserve

Ash
Wood

The
Canal

Chippenham
Park

Jerusalem
Wood

Park
Farm

CB7

High Park
Corner

FORDHAM ROAD

Foxburrow
Plantation

Coachroad
Plantation

Hundred Acre
Plantation

CHIPPENHAM ROAD

PH

Snailwell

Manor
Farm

Four
Ponds

THE STREET

CHURCH LANE

THE GREEN

Church
Farm

Gravelpit
Plantation

CB8

Airstrip

SHORT ROAD

Snailwell
Stud

Sounds
Plantation

Lower
Yard

NEWMARKET ROAD

A14

A14

A1304

131
111

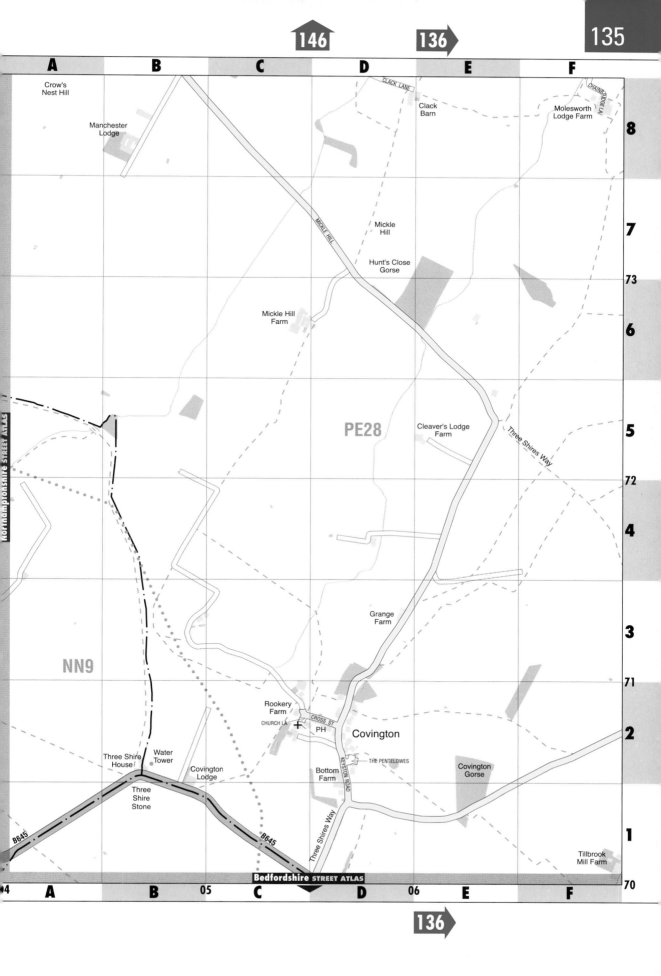

A B C D E F

8
7
73
6
5
72
4
3
71
2
1
70

Crow's Nest Hill

Manchester Lodge

CLACK LANE

Clack Barn

CHAINBRIDGE LA

Molesworth Lodge Farm

MICKLE HILL

Mickle Hill

Hunt's Close Gorse

Mickle Hill Farm

PE28

Cleaver's Lodge Farm

Three Shires Way

Grange Farm

NN9

Rookery Farm

CROSS ST

CHURCH LA

PH

Covington

Three Shire House

Water Tower

Covington Lodge

THE PENTELOWES

Three Shire Stone

Bottom Farm

KEYSTON ROAD

Covington Gorse

B645

B645

Three Shires Way

Tillbrook Mill Farm

Northamptonshire STREET ATLAS

148
138

A B C D E F

8

Catworth
Gorse

Belton's
Hill

A14

17

7

A14

18

Catworth
Farm

West Lodge
Farm

73

THRAPSTON ROAD

LITTLECOTES CL

POUND CL

THRAPSTON RD

CHURCH LA

Spaldwick

PH

HIGH ST

BELTON'S HILL

Little
Catworth

6

MOUNT
PLEASANT

STOW ROAD

FERRIMAN

ROYSTON
RD

FULLER CL

BURTON
WY

Spaldwick
Prim Sch

PE28

5

Lumber
Hill

72

Upthorpe
Lodge

Bunkers
Hill

4

STOW ROAD

3

Home
Farm

Church
Farm

SPALDWICK ROAD

71

CHURCH LA

CHURCH
WK

Manor
Farm

THE
LANE

Stow Longa

2

Rookery
Farm

Sunnyside
Farm

1

Airfield
(dis)

STOCKING LANE

PE19

70

114
138

A B C D E F

8

Moat

Weybridge
Lodge Farm

7

Weybridge
Farm

73

6

PE28

5

20

Grove
Bridge

Sand &
Gravel Pit

72

THRAPSTON ROAD

A14

Moat

4

BLACKSMITHS LA
MALTING LA

HIGH ST

ST PETER'S WAY

Manor Farm

Woodhatch
Farm

Little
Meadow
Farm

Ellington

PARSON'S DR

Low
Harthay

Church
Farm

High
Harthay

3

71

Ellington
Thorpe

2

Moat

Underlands
Wood

Red
Wood

Redwood
Lodge

Brampton Wood
Nature Reserve

Madders
Hill

1

Sparrow's
Spinney

6   A   B   17   C   D   18   E   F   70

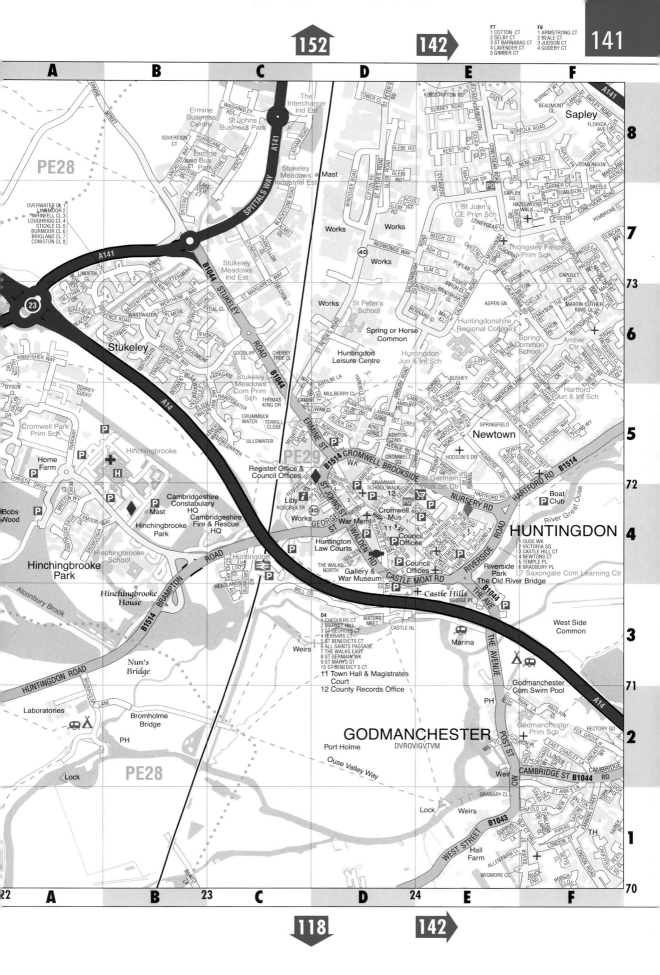

8

7

73

6

5

72

4

3

71

2

1

70

A B C D E F

WALLACE CT
GOSHAWK CL
FLORIDA AV
CONEYGEAR ROAD
KINGS CL
SISLEY RD
PEREGRINE CL
EAGLE WY
HARRIER CL
A141
KITE WY
OSPREY WY
KESTREL
BUZZARD CL

BUZZARD CL

NEWNHAM
VASSE RD
OTHELLO
CLARE RD
VEASEY RD
SAPLEY ROAD
BARR
OWL WAY
MERLIN WY
SPARROWHAWK WAY
SPARROWHAWK WY
SNOWY OWL WY

NF CHARLES DR
ROONEY AV
DESBOROUGH RD
MILL RD
MILL RD
LARK CL
HAWK CL
FALCON DR
TAWNY CL
SNOWY OWL WY
ELIZABETH DR
HOBBY CL
B1514

Hartford

MAYFIELD RD
AIR CIRCLE
LONGSTAFF WY
MAIN STREET
MAIN STREET
THE HOLLOW
THE GROVE
OLD HOUGHTON RD
HOUGHTON ROAD

Hartford Main St
THE SPINNEY
CHURCH LANE
River Great Ouse

HUNTINGDON

PE29

Cook's Stream

Ouse Valley Way

Sand &
Gravel Pit

COW LANE

Sewage
Works

1 ANDERSON CRES
2 MEADOW WAY
3 HARCOURT
4 RECTORY GDNS

Rectory
Farm

Brickyard
Farm

CAMBRIDGE RD
A14
B1044

GODMANCHESTER
DVROVIGVTVM

24

HILSDENS DR
KISBY AVE
WHITE
HART
PETTIT
STUART RD
PETTIT RD
TUDOR ROAD
THE GT
WINDSOR RD
RAVENSHOE
A1198

LEGION
WAY
CARDINAL WAY

Cardinal
Distribution
Park

CHESTER RD
CENTURION WAY
COHORT WAY

1 MOWLANDS
2 ROMAN WY

DOVEHOUSE
CL

A141
New Barn
Farm
Cobwebs

Hartford
Hill

A141

Manor
Farm

RUDDLES LA

Banks End

HUNTINGDON ROAD
A1123

Hertford Marina

PH

Willow
Walk Farm

PE28

Weir

Pathfinder Long Distance Walk

Sewage
Works

Harcourt Farm

70 A14

Emmanuel Knoll
Plantation

SAWTRY WAY

Sewage
Works

SPLASH LANE
Gumsetre
Farm

HUNTINGDON ROAD
WARREN CL

Wyton
PH

Ouse Valley Way

Black
Bridge

ABBOTS CL
WHAEFIELD
COMMON LANE
MEADOW LA
RIVER RD

Hemingford Abbots

Home
Farm

Hemingford
Park

Long
Plantation

RIDGEWAY

Ridgeway
Farm

25 A B 26 C D 27 E F

A B C D E F

ST IVES

Rugby Club

Cottage Farm

Black Bridge

B1040

SANDWICH CL

Westwood Farm

SOMERSHAM ROAD

1 SUFFOLK CL
2 DEVON CL
3 REMBRANDT WY
4 REYNOLDS CL
5 THE WHISTLERS
6 DA VINCI CL
7 GAINSBOROUGH DR
8 RENOIR CL
9 WITHAM CL
10 MANCHESTER WY

Sewage Works

Marley Gap Bridge

Lowndes Drove

8

YORK WY

ARRAN WY

Blackers Hill Farm

Priory Farm

7

EDISON RD
EDISON ROAD

Ind Est

73

Wheatfields Prim Sch

LAVENDER WY
ERICA WY
FORSYTHIA RD

CAXTON ROAD
Works

NUFFIELD ROAD

6

SOMERSHAM ROAD

A1123

Gifford's Farm

PE27

B1040

HOUGHTON RD ST AUDLEYS LANE

Stocks Bridge

5

A1123

Old Railway Industrial Estate

High Street

Priory RL

ST AUDLEY CL

HARRISON WY

Five Acre Farm

Eastfield Cty Inf Sch

72

Recn Gd

Westfield Jun Sch

ELSWORTH CL
ROOKERY CL

BERKELEY GN

A1096

4

HARVEST CT

ORCHARD TER

CROWN CL

PARK SIDE

PARK RD

PARK AVE

GREAT FARTHING CL

LITTLE FARTHING CL

FARTHING LA

HARRISON WAY

Manor Farm

BACK LA

BACK LANE

The Norris Museum

Queen Victoria's Diamond Jubilee Meml

Bridge & Chapel

Statue

War Meml

Liby

1 MEADOW CL
2 NEDDERWORTH RD
3 DARWOOD PL
4 CARLISLE TERR
5 CROMWELL TERR
6 SHEEP MARKET
7 MARKET RD

3

TH
PO

NEW RD

PRIORY MEWS

PRIORY RD

The Wilderness

The Meadow Business Centre

MEADOW LANE

Holy Well

Holywell

71

Works

River Great Ouse

Goodyers Farm

HOLYWELL FRONT

2

HARRISON WAY

A1096

Lock

Marina

1 BIRT LA
2 CHAPEL LA
3 MARKET LA
4 WHITE HART LA
5 OLIVER RD
6 QUAY CT
7 FOUNDRY WK
8 WOOLPACK LA
9 FREE CHURCH PAS
10 MERRYLAND

SECOND DROVE

Works

Mill Farm

LOW ROAD

Sand & Gravel Pit

1

PE28

CB24

Ouse Viaduct (dis)

Sand & Gravel Works

70

31 32 33

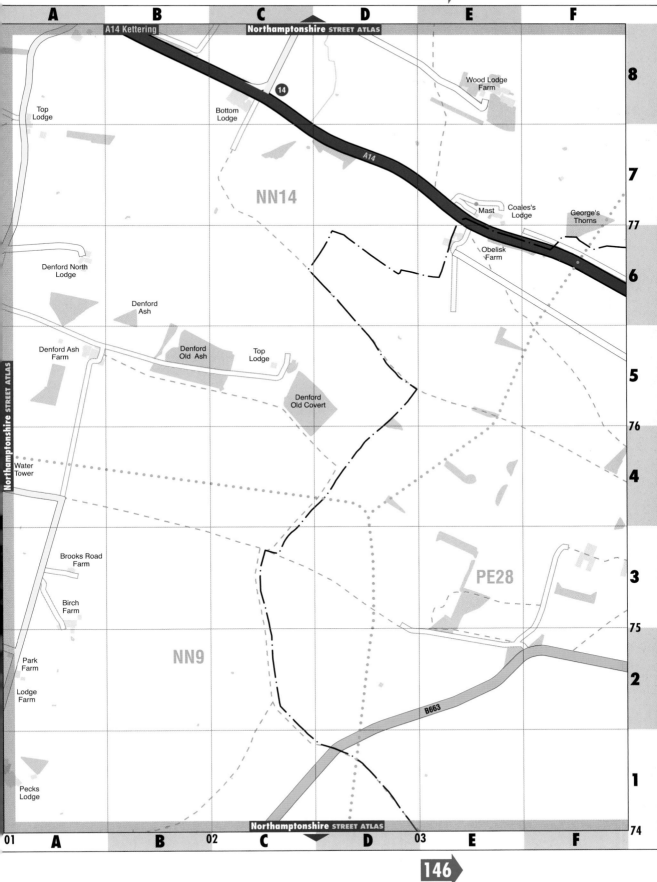

A14 Kettering

Top Lodge

Bottom Lodge

Wood Lodge Farm

NN14

A14

Mast

Coales's Lodge

George's Thorns

Obelisk Farm

Denford North Lodge

Denford Ash

Denford Ash Farm

Denford Old Ash

Top Lodge

Denford Old Covert

Water Tower

Brooks Road Farm

Birch Farm

PE28

Park Farm

Lodge Farm

NN9

B663

Pecks Lodge

Northamptonshire STREET ATLAS

Northamptonshire STREET ATLAS

A B C D E F

8

7

77

6

5

76

4

3

75

2

1

74

COCKBROOK LA

RAF
Molesworth

Old Weston Grove

Glebe
Farm

HILL CL
HILL CL

PE28

Sewage
Works

Manor
Farm

Brington

Yew Tree
Farm

Molesworth

Manor
Farm

PH

Church
Farm

CHURCH LA

Brington CE
Prim Sch

Old Weston

BRINGTON RD
BRINGTON RD
MAIN ST
B660

Manor
Farm

B660

Fox Holes
Farm

Leighton
Gorse

THRAPSTON RD

PH

16

FOX ROAD

B660

New
Bridge

A14

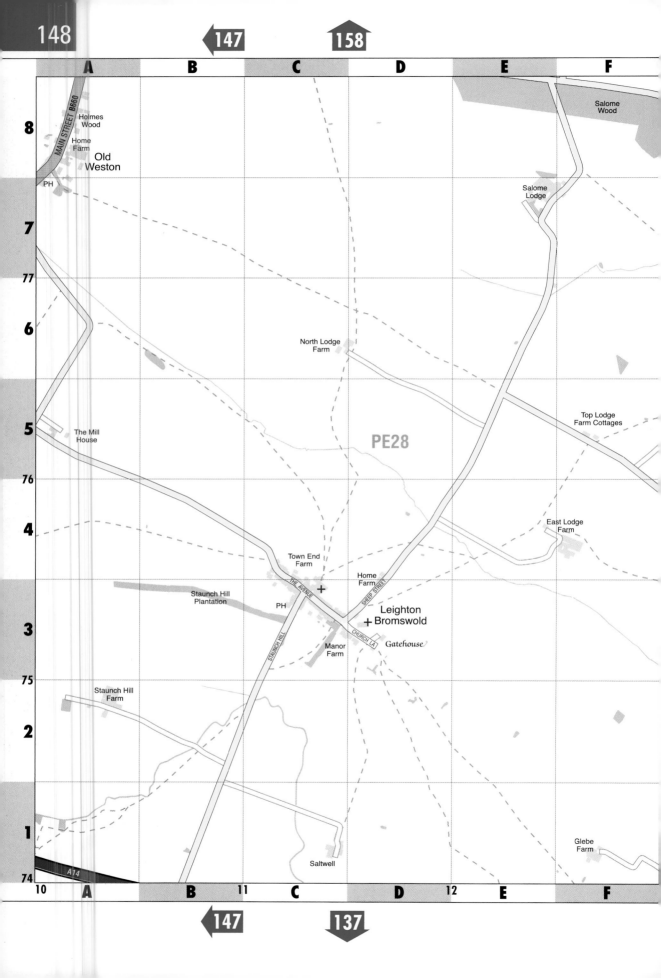

A14

Salome Wood

Holmes Wood

Home Farm

Old Weston

PH

MAIN STREET B660

Salome Lodge

North Lodge Farm

PE28

The Mill House

Top Lodge Farm Cottages

East Lodge Farm

Town End Farm

Home Farm

Staunch Hill Plantation

PH

THE AVENUE

Leighton Bromswold

SHEEP STREET

Manor Farm

CHURCH LA

Gatehouse

STAUNCH HILL

Staunch Hill Farm

Saltwell

Glebe Farm

A   B   C   D   E   F

8

Brook
Lodge

7

Black
Lodge

77

Home
Farm

6

HAMERTON ROAD

BREAM CL

CHURCH RD

Buckworth

Buckworth
Wood

BARHAM RD

Manor
Lodge

PE28

5

76

4

Grange
Farm

3

Barham

WOOLLEY RD

75

2

Trennery
Farm

The Manor
House

New
Manor
Farm

Woolley

ELLINGTON ROAD

1

Hill House
Farm

74

3   A   B   14   C   D   15   E   F

A B C D E F

8

Hermitage
Wood

Little
Less Wood

Long
Coppice

CLAY LANE

7

Top
Farm

77

Alconbury
Airfield
(Dis)

6

A1(M)

A1(M)

13a

B1043

B1043

B1043

5

B1043

P

PE28

Home
Farm

76

Alconbury
House

IOWA

Sewage
Works

KANSAS

MICHIGAN

IOWA

CALIFORNIA

4

Pringle
Farm

TEXAS

GEORGIA

CALIFORNIA

PRINGLE WY

PRINGLE CT

PO

ARIZONA

OKLAHOMA

UTAH

Little Stukeley

MILL RD

CHURCH WY

SANDERS CL

OREGON

COLORADO

COLORADO

MILL CL

LOW RD

ALPHA LA

BIRCH DR

BRAVO LA

CEDAR DRIVE

DELTA LANE

Nook
Farm

ELM DRIVE

ECHO LA

MAPLE DRIVE

3

Brooklands
Farm

A14

FOXTROT LA

OAK DRIVE

GOLF LA

HOTEL LA

SPENCER DRIVE

75

INDIA

ERMINE STREET

PH

Hotel

Tumuli

Hotel

PO

CAMOYS CL

2

Church
End

CHURCH RD

MOOR

WY

CHURCH CL

Great
Stukeley

PARK VW

1

A1

Matcham's
Bridge

74

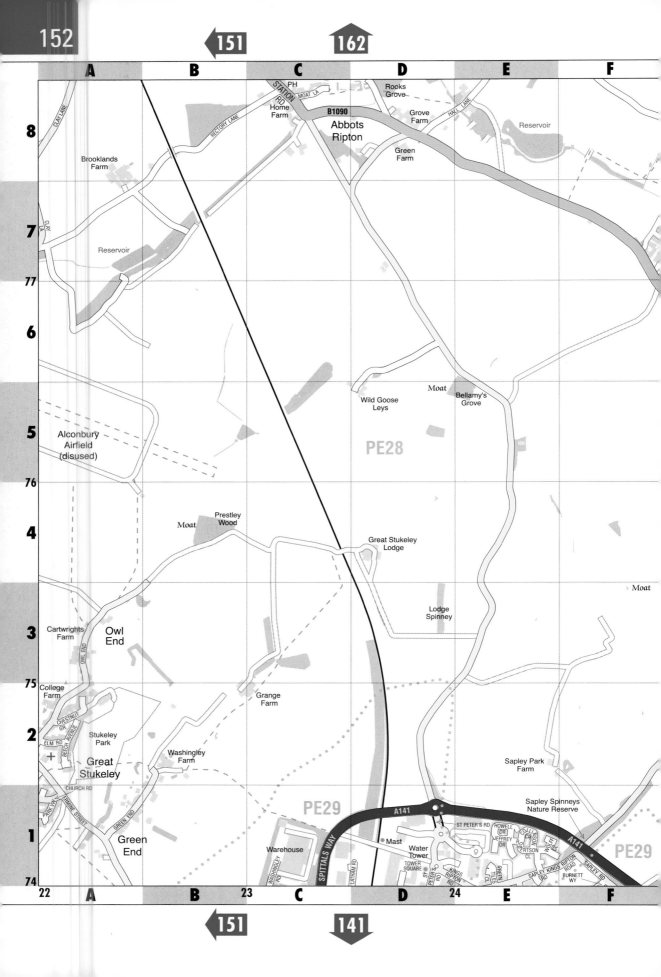

A B C D E F

8

PH
STATION RD
MOAT LA
Rooks Grove
Home Farm
B1090
Grove Farm
HALL LANE
Reservoir
Abbots Ripton
Green Farm

RECTORY LANE
CLAY LANE
Brooklands Farm

7

CLAY LA
Reservoir

77

6

Wild Goose Leys
Moat
Bellamy's Grove

5
Alconbury Airfield (disused)

PE28

76

4
Moat
Prestley Wood
Great Stukeley Lodge
Moat

3
Cartwrights Farm
Owl End
OWL END
Lodge Spinney

75
College Farm
Grange Farm
Sapley Park Farm

2
CHESTNUT GR
ELM RD
BEECH AVENUE
Stukeley Park
Washingley Farm
Great Stukeley

CHURCH RD
PE29
Sapley Spinneys Nature Reserve

1
PARK VW
FERMINE STREET
GREEN END
Green End
WASHINGLEY RD
Warehouse
SPITTALS WAY
LATHAM RD
A141
Mast
Water Tower
TOWER SQUARE
ST PETER'S RD
ST PETER'S RD
KINGS RIPTON RD
HOWELL DR
JEFFREY DR
MASON CL
ROBERTSON CL
GREEN TILES CL
SAPLEY KINGS RIPTON ROAD
BURNETT WY
SAPLEY RD
A141
PE29

74
22 A 23 B C 23 D 24 E F

A   B   C   D   E   F

Cemy

BOUGH LANE

Bridge Farm

Broughton   8

SCHOOL RD

BRIDGE RD

Lodge Farm

7

Grange Farm

Lodge Farm

77

6

B1090

SCHOOL LA

Glebe Farm

Lodge Farm

QUAKER CL

RAMSEY ROAD

Walden Farm

Kings Ripton

Manor Farm

PE28

5

76

4

Hungary Hall

Mayfield Heath Farm

Pathfinder Long Distance Path

Laboratories

SAWTRY WAY

A141

3

75

2

Wyton Airfield

Lodge Farm

St Thomas's Dole Plantation

Hartford Hill Farm

SAWTRY WAY

B1090

YELLOWGATE RD

1

A141

74

A | B | C | D | E | F

8

White Hall Farm

CAUSEWAY ROAD
CAUSEWAY RD
BRIDGE RD
+ PH

BROUGHTON LANE

Sewage Works

A141

Works

WARBOYS ROAD

Old Hurst Grove

7

Mill Barn Farm

RAMSEY RD

60

Church Farm +

Manor Farm

Moat

THE GRANARY

CHURCH STREET

THE LANE

WELLINGTON CL.

Old Hurst

77

PE28

RAMSEY RD

ST IVES RD

LANCASTER CA.

THE LANE

Marsh Farm

6

5

76

4

Mast

A141

3

75

Wyton Airfield

PE27

2

Hiam Farm

OLD RAMSEY RD

Pineview Kennels

1

RAF Wyton

CANBERRA WY.
YELLOWGATE ROAD
KEMBALL WY.
LANCASTER
CANBERRA WAY
HARRIS WY.
PATHFINDER
VICTORY RD.
WELLINGTON WY.
HAWK DRIVE
BLENHEIM WAY
BENNETT ROAD
DRUCE AVENUE
DURHAM WY.
WILTSHIRE RD.
NORFOLK RD.

NIMROD DRIVE
LINDSAY

74

28 | A | B | 29 | C | D | 30 | E | F

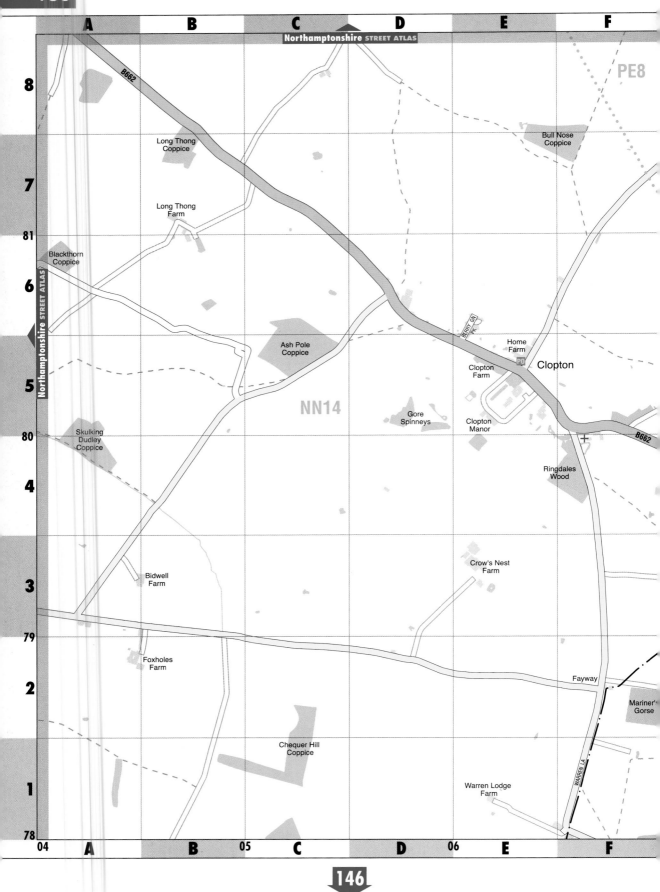

PE8

A B C D E F

8

Long Thong
Coppice

Bull Nose
Coppice

7

Long Thong
Farm

81

Blackthorn
Coppice

6

Ash Pole
Coppice

BERRY GN
PK

Home
Farm

PO

Clopton

Clopton
Farm

5

NN14

Gore
Spinneys

Clopton
Manor

80

Skulking
Dudley
Coppice

B662

Ringdales
Wood

4

Crow's Nest
Farm

3

Bidwell
Farm

79

Foxholes
Farm

Fayway

2

Mariner'
Gorse

WARREN LA

Chequer Hill
Coppice

1

Warren Lodge
Farm

78

04 A B 05 C D 06 E F

B662

Middle
Copse

Common
Wood

Barnwell
Wold

PE8

Gumwells
Wold

THURNING ROAD

81

Winwick
Lodge

Manimeer
Spinney

80

NN14

PE28

Grange
Farm

Fieldbarn
Farm

Cockbrook
Farm

Ash
Copse

South
Farm

COCKBROOK LANE

Sewage
Works

B662

Cockbrook
Lodge

RAF
Molesworth

157

166

A   B   C   D   E   F

8

7

81

6

Pasture
Farm

THURNING ROAD

Moat

Westward
Farm

THE GREEN

Winwick

Bottom
Farm

Mount
Pleasant
Farm

Valley
Farm

HAMERTON ROAD

Hollow
Farm

Manor
Farm

Little
Gidding

Alconbury Brook

B660 WINWICK ROAD

PE28

5

80

OLD WESTON ROAD

B660

Hamerton
Grove

4

3

79

Cottage
Farm

2

Dipslade
Coppice

Grange
Farm

Howson's
Lodge

1

B660

High Street
Farm

78

10   A   B   11   C   D   12   E   F

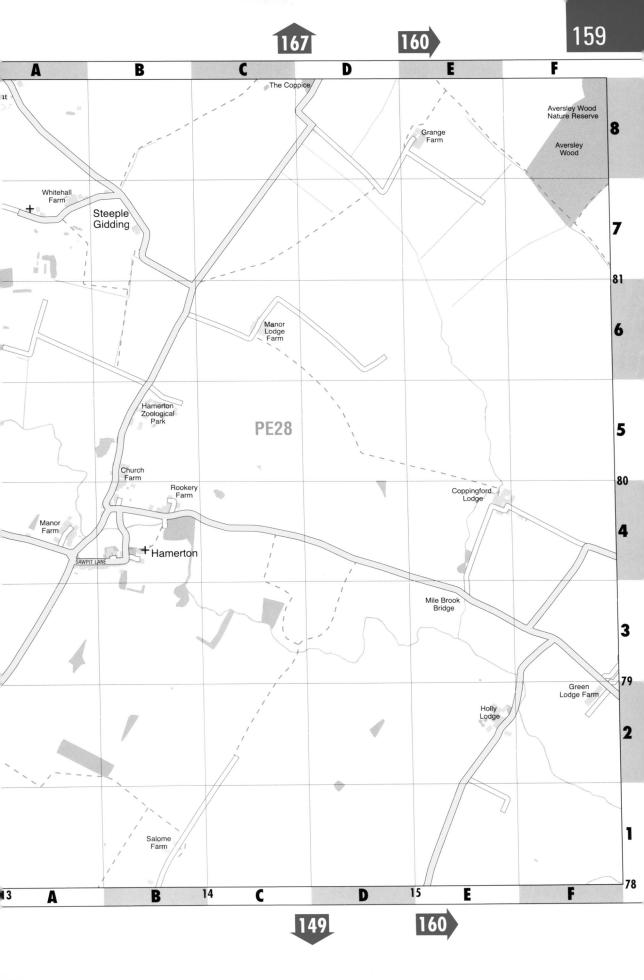

167
160

The Coppice

Aversley Wood
Nature Reserve

Grange
Farm

Aversley
Wood

8

Whitehall
Farm

Steeple
Gidding

7

81

Manor
Lodge
Farm

6

Hamerton
Zoological
Park

PE28

5

80

Church
Farm

Coppingford
Lodge

Rookery
Farm

Manor
Farm

4

SAWPIT LANE

Hamerton

Mile Brook
Bridge

3

79

Green
Lodge Farm

Holly
Lodge

2

Salome
Farm

1

78

A
B
C
D
E
F

149
160

A   B   C   D   E   F

169
162

Riddy
Wood

8

Moat

Grange
Farm

Bottom Lodge
Farm

DOUBLE
BANK
LANE

Woodwalton Marsh
Nature Reserve

NEW ROAD

7

81

Moat
Mill
Mound

THE CROSS
BEVILLE
BEVILLE
RAVELEY ROAD

PH

Red House
Farm

Wood Walton

6

West
Wood

B1090

Abbey
Farm

BRIDGE STREET

WALTON HILL

Monks Wood
Farm

Hill
Farm

5

PE28

Monk's
Wood

80

Monks Wood
National
Nature Reserve

Monks Wood
Experimental
Station

New
England
Bridge

4

STOCKING CLOSE

Bevill's
Wood

B1090

3

79

Heath
Farm

Hill
Wood

2

Boulton's
Hunch Wood

Fellowes
Farm

Round
Wood

Safefield
House

Park Farm
Cottages

Little
Less Wood

1

Alconbury
Hill

Long
Coppice

78

19   A   20   B   C   20   D   21   E   F

A B C D E F

PE26

8

Rose
Wood

Wood
Grounds Farm

7

Chestnut
Farm

High
Holborn Farm

Chestnuts
Farm

Yewe Tree
Farm

St John's Pl

HEATH
LA

Great
Raveley

School
Farm

81

Manor
Farm

Wistow

Grange
Farm

Rookes Grove
Farm

6

Kingsland
Spinney

PE28

5

80

Little
Raveley

Everitts
Farm

4

Greatlands

WOOD LANE

3

Rectory
Farm

79

2

Raveley
Wood

Wood
Farm

1

Raveley Wood
Farm

SCHOOL ROAD

78

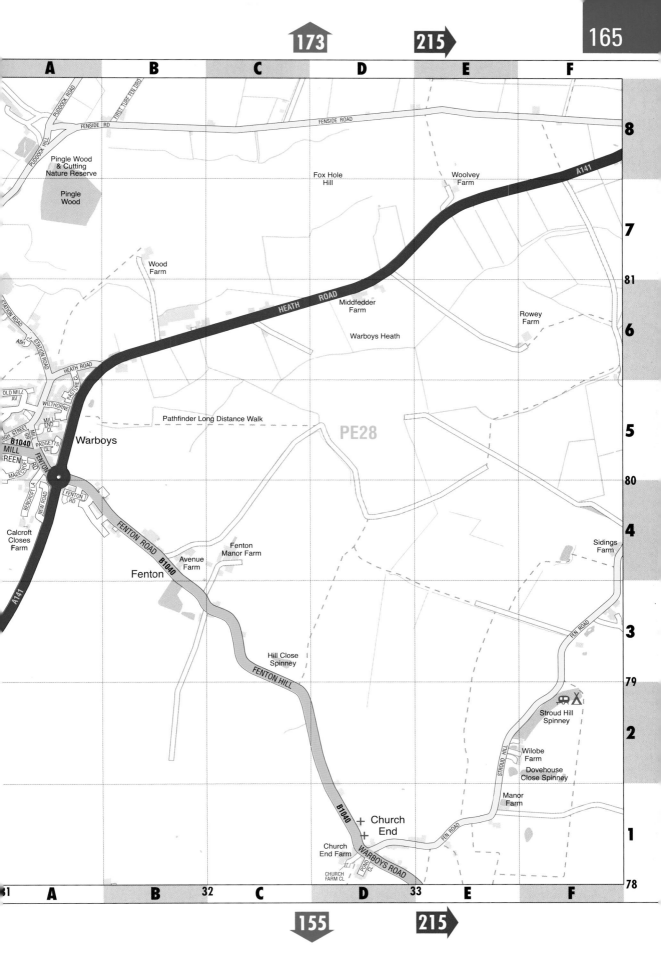

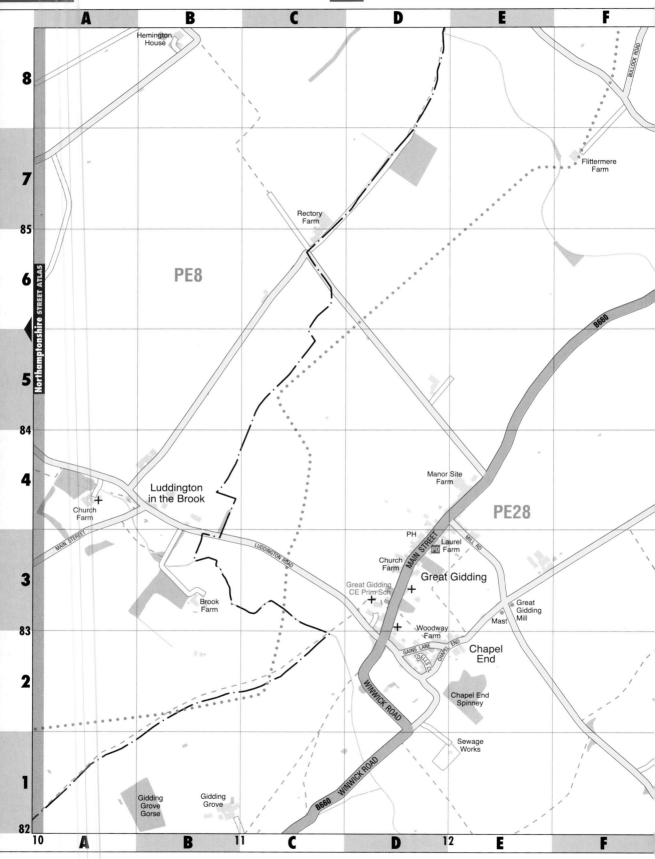

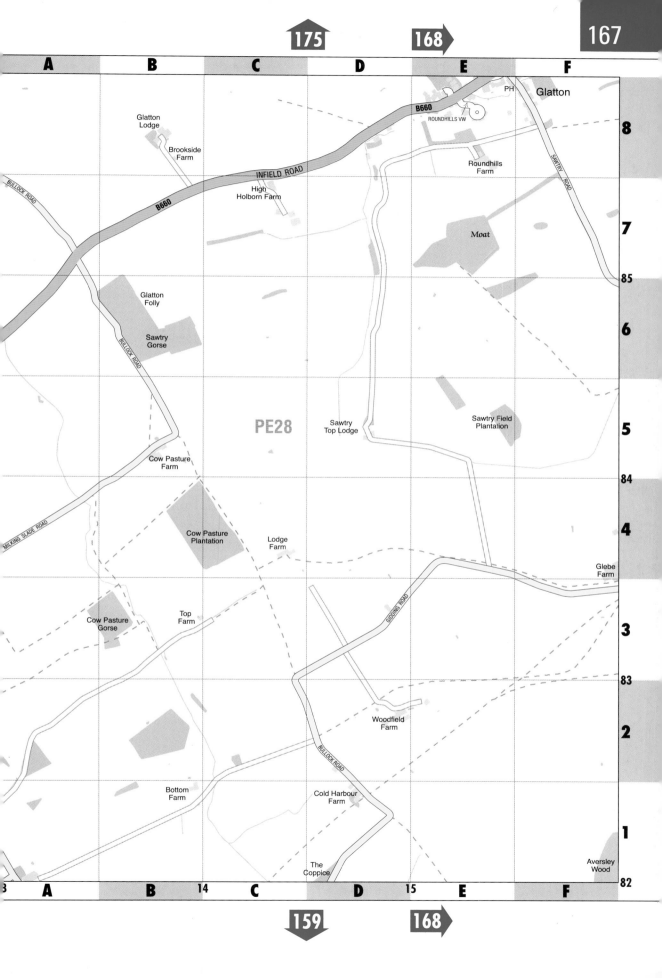

175
168

A   B   C   D   E   F

Glatton
PH
B660
ROUNDHILLS VW
Glatton
Lodge
Brookside
Farm
INFIELD ROAD
Roundhills
Farm
B660
High
Holborn Farm
BULLOCK ROAD
Moat
SAWTRY ROAD

8
7
85

Glatton
Folly
Sawtry
Gorse
BULLOCK ROAD

6

PE28
Sawtry
Top Lodge
Sawtry Field
Plantation

5
84

Cow Pasture
Farm
Cow Pasture
Plantation
Lodge
Farm
Glebe
Farm

4

MILKING SLADE ROAD
Cow Pasture
Gorse
Top
Farm
GIDDING ROAD

3
83

Woodfield
Farm

2

Bottom
Farm
BULLOCK ROAD
Cold Harbour
Farm

1

The
Coppice
Aversley
Wood

82

3   A   B   14   C   D   15   E   F

159
168

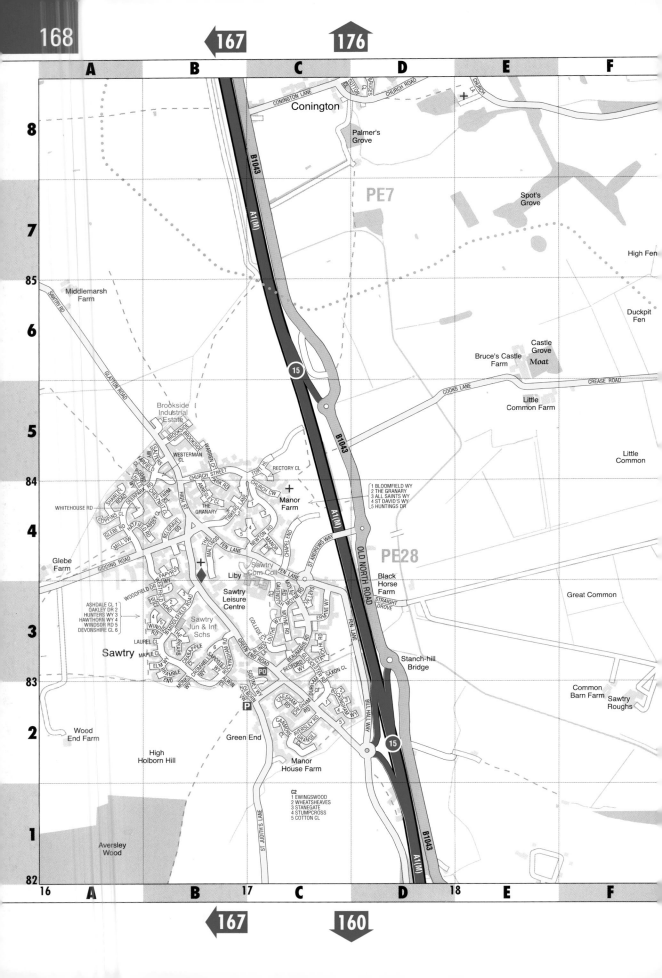

Conington

Palmer's
Grove

PE7

Spot's
Grove

High Fen

Middlemarsh
Farm

Duckpit
Fen

Castle
Grove
Bruce's Castle   Moat
Farm

Cooks Lane   Crease Road

Little
Common Farm

Brookside
Industrial
Estate

Little
Common

1 BLOOMFIELD WY
2 THE GRANARY
3 ALL SAINTS WY
4 ST DAVID'S WY
5 HUNTINGS DR

RECTORY CL

Manor
Farm

WHITEHOUSE RD

THE
GRANARY

PE28

Glebe
Farm

GIDDING ROAD

Sawtry
Com Coll

Liby

Black
Horse
Farm

Great Common

Sawtry
Leisure
Centre

ASHDALE CL 1
OAKLEY DR 2
HUNTERS WY 3
HAWTHORN WY 4
WINDSOR RD 5
DEVONSHIRE CL 6

Sawtry
Jun & Inf
Schs

Stanch-hill
Bridge

LAUREL CL

Sawtry
MAPLE CL

Common
Barn Farm   Sawtry
Roughs

Sawtry

PO

Wood
End Farm

P

Green End

High
Holborn Hill

Manor
House Farm

C2
1 EWINGSWOOD
2 WHEATSHEAVES
3 STANEGATE
4 STUMPCROSS
5 COTTON CL

Aversley
Wood

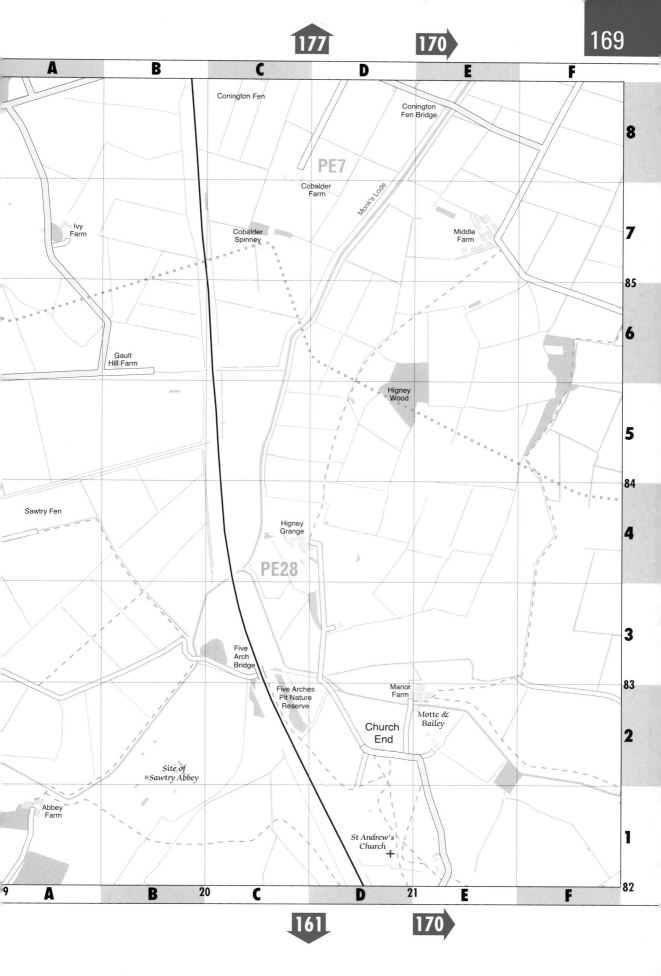

177
170

A B C D E F

8

Conington Fen

Conington
Fen Bridge

PE7

Cobalder
Farm

Monk's Lode

7

Ivy
Farm

Cobalder
Spinney

Middle
Farm

85

6

Gault
Hill Farm

Higney
Wood

5

84

Sawtry Fen

4

Higney
Grange

PE28

3

Five
Arch
Bridge

83

Five Arches
Pit Nature
Reserve

Manor
Farm

Motte &
Bailey

2

Church
End

Site of
Sawtry Abbey

Abbey
Farm

1

St Andrew's
Church

82

9 A 20 B C D 21 E F

161
170

A B C D E F

RAY'S DROVE

MIDDLE DROVE

Lotting
Fen

HARPER'S DROVE

8

7

85

PE7

HEIGHTS DROVE ROAD

Ramsey Heights
Nature Reserve

HEIGHTS DROVE ROAD   CHAPEL ROAD

6

Woodwalton Fen
National
Nature Reserve

Woodwalton Fen

PE26

Common
Farm

5

84

Wheatley's Drain

Great
Raveley Fen

4

Great Raveley Drain

Turf
Fen

TURF FEN ROAD

3

83

2

PE28

Lady's Wood
Nature Reserve

1

Moat
Farm

RAVELEY FEN RD

82

22   A   B   23   C   D   24   E   F

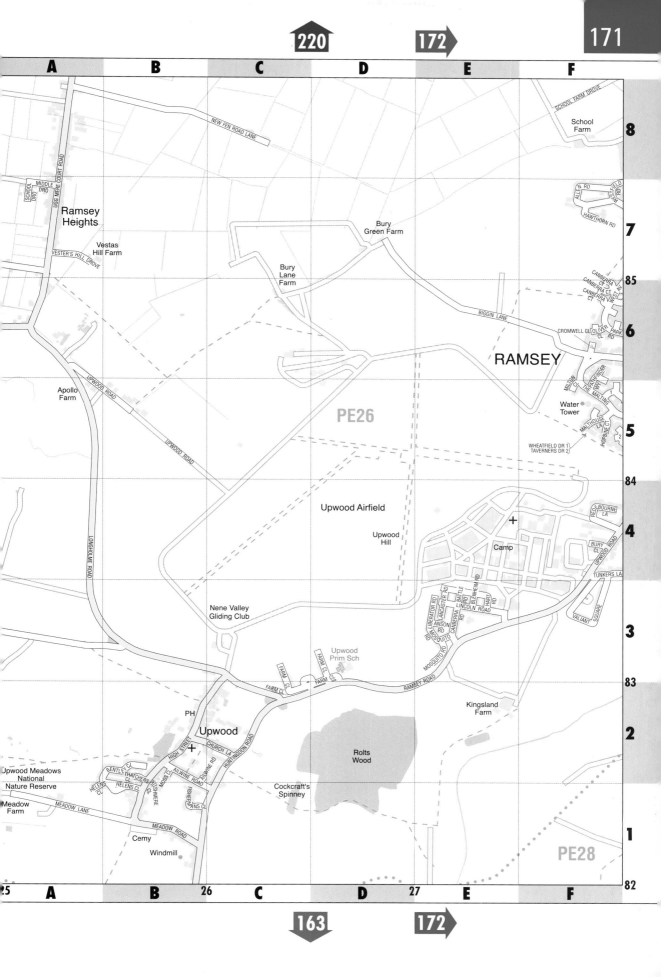

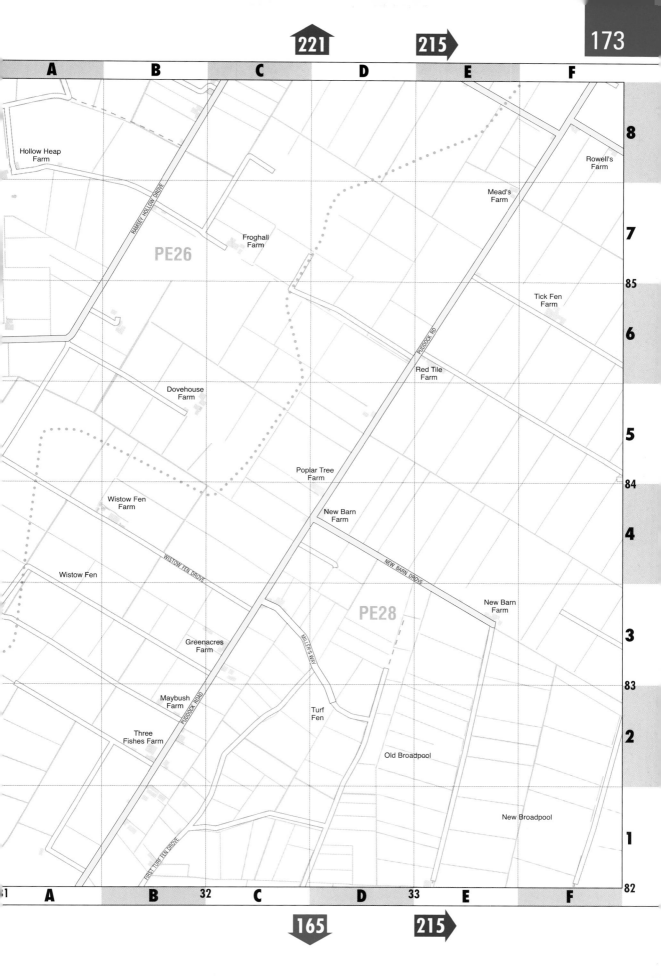

221
215

A B C D E F

8

Hollow Heap
Farm

Rowell's
Farm

Mead's
Farm

PE26

Froghall
Farm

7

85

Tick Fen
Farm

6

Red Tile
Farm

Dovehouse
Farm

5

Poplar Tree
Farm

84

Wistow Fen
Farm

New Barn
Farm

4

Wistow Fen

NEW BARN DROVE

WISTOW FEN DROVE

New Barn
Farm

PE28

3

Greenacres
Farm

MILLER'S WAY

83

Maybush
Farm

PUDDOCK ROAD

Turf
Fen

2

Three
Fishes Farm

Old Broadpool

New Broadpool

1

FIRST TURF FEN DROVE

82

A B C D E F
31 32 33

165
215

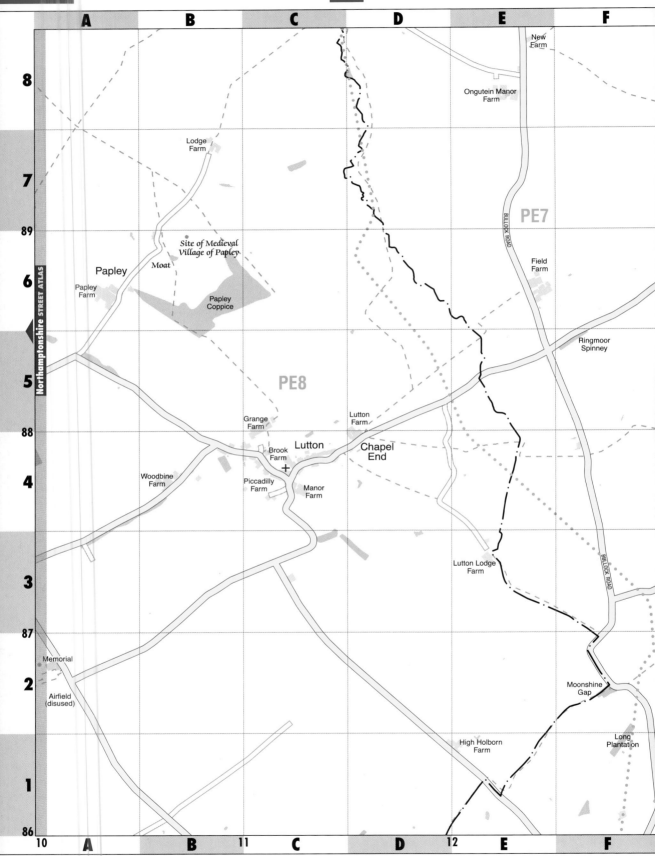

New Farm

Ongutein Manor Farm

PE7

BULLOCK ROAD

Lodge Farm

Site of Medieval Village of Papley

Moat

Papley

Papley Farm

Papley Coppice

Field Farm

Ringmoor Spinney

PE8

Grange Farm

Lutton Farm

Woodbine Farm

Brook Farm

Lutton

Chapel End

Piccadilly Farm

Manor Farm

Lutton Lodge Farm

BULLOCK ROAD

Memorial

Airfield (disused)

Moonshine Gap

High Holborn Farm

Long Plantation

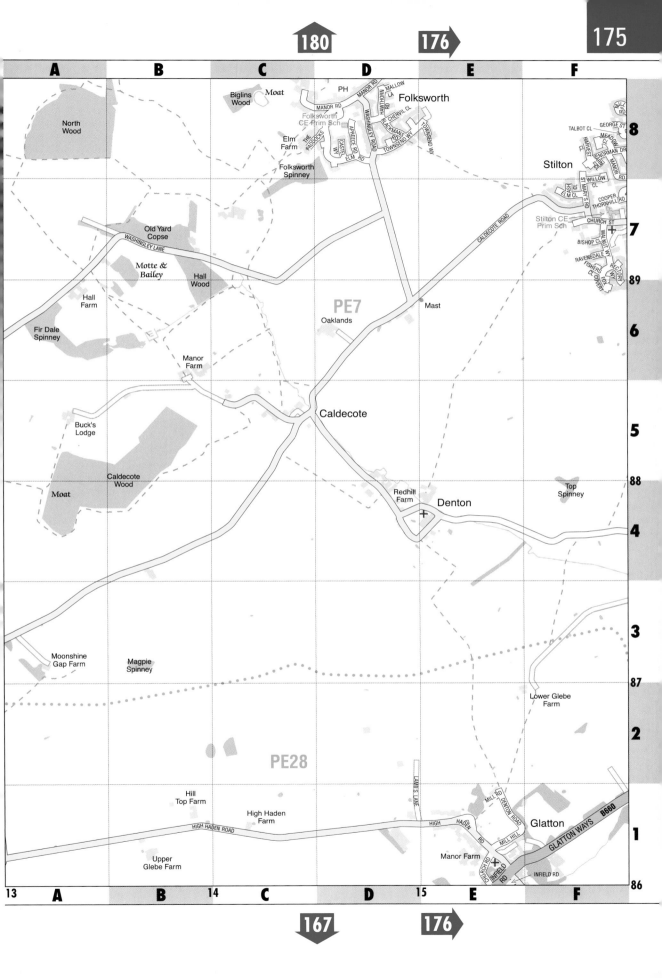

A B C D E F

180
176

North
Wood

Biglins
Wood
Moat

PH
MANOR RD
Folksworth

MANOR RD
Folksworth
CE Prim Sch
Elm
Farm
THE PADDOCKS
CASTEL
APREECE RD
HAWTHORN
WASHINGLEY ROAD
BLACKMANS RD
MALLOW
CHERVIL CL
TOWNSEND WY
TOWNSEND WY

GEORGE ST
TALBOT CL
MEADOW
BENORMAN DR
MANOR RD

Stilton

Folksworth
Spinney

ELM RD
CASTEL

ST MARY'S RD
WILLOW CL
HSP CL
ELM CL
COOPER
THORNHILL RD

CALDECOTE ROAD
Stilton CE
Prim Sch
CHURCH ST

Old Yard
Copse

WASHINGLEY LANE

BISHOP CL
WALNUT WY
RAVENSDALE
FISHERS CL
FOX COVERT
RECTORY
FOX

Motte &
Bailey
Hall
Wood

Hall
Farm

PE7

Mast

Fir Dale
Spinney

Oaklands

Manor
Farm

Buck's
Lodge

Caldecote

Caldecote
Wood

Top
Spinney

Moat

Redhill
Farm
Denton

Moonshine
Gap Farm

Magpie
Spinney

Lower Glebe
Farm

PE28

Hill
Top Farm

High Haden
Farm

LAMB'S LANE

HIGH HADEN ROAD

HIGH
HADEN
RD

MILL RD
DENTON ROAD

MILL HILL

Glatton
GLATTON WAYS
B660

Upper
Glebe Farm

Manor Farm
CHURCH RD
INFIELD RD

INFIELD RD

8
7
89
6
5
88
4
3
87
2
1
86

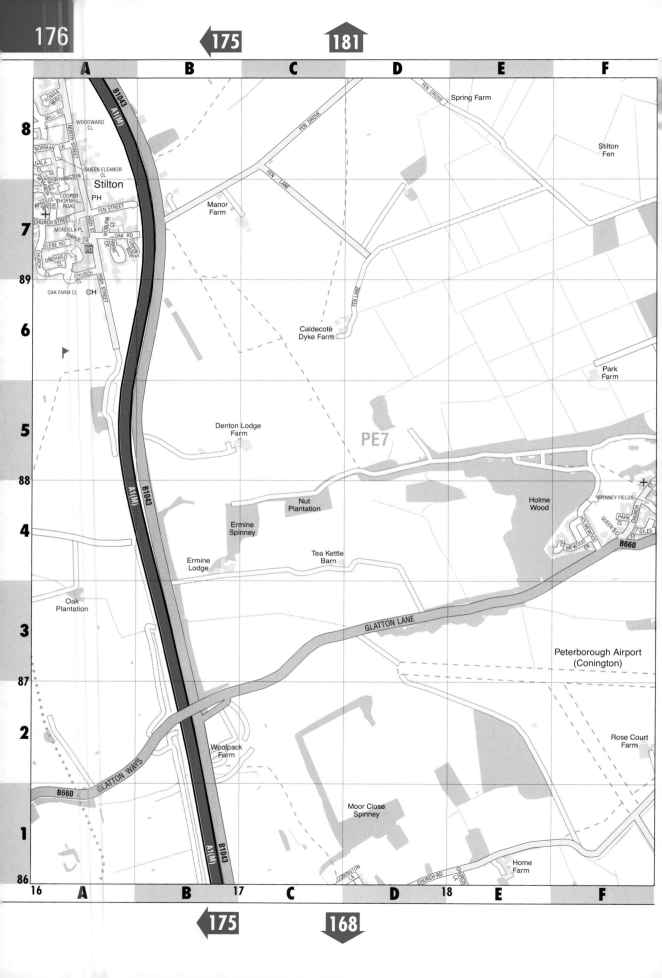

A B C D E F

175
181

ROMAN WAY
MILL RD
WOODWARD CL
NORTH STREET
B1043
A1(M)
NORMAN DR
GALA CL
BELL CL
SAMUEL CL
WORTHINGTON
QUEEN ELEANOR CL
Stilton
PH
COOPER THORNHILL ROAD
APPREECE WY
FEN STREET
CHURCH STREET
HIGH ST
MONDELA PL
MAPLE DR
GLEBE RD
NIMBOW CT
TURPIN'S RIDE
ERMINE
OAK RD
PO
CHURCH CL
ORCHARD CL
CHURCH CL
HIGH STREET
OAK FARM CL
CH

8
7
89
6
5
88
4
3
87
2
1
86

Manor Farm

FEN DROVE
Spring Farm
Stilton Fen

FEN LANE

FEN LANE

Caldecote Dyke Farm

Park Farm

PE7

Denton Lodge Farm

Nut Plantation
Holme Wood
SPINNEY FIELDS
St GILES

Ermine Spinney

HOLMEWOOD CR
QUEEN'S CL
PARK CL
CHURCH CL
B660

Ermine Lodge

Tea Kettle Barn

A1(M) B1043

Oak Plantation

GLATTON LANE

Peterborough Airport (Conington)

Woolpack Farm

Rose Court Farm

GLATTON WAYS

B660

Moor Close Spinney

A1(M) B1043

CONINGTON LA
CHURCH RD
CHURCH LA
Home Farm

16 A B 17 C D 18 E F

175
168

A   B   C   D   E   F

8

Willow Hall

Stilton Roughs

Holme Lode Farm

Caldecote Fen

Denton Fen Covert

Ballard's Covert

Ladyseat Farm

The Roughs

7

HOD FEN DROVE

Holme Fen National Nature Reserve

Denton Covert

Denton Covert

LC

SEYNORY DROVE

89

Fox Covert

Holme Lode Covert

Middle Covert

NEW LONG DROVE

6

North Park

Jackson's Covert

5

Holmewood Hall

WELLS WY

PE7

Holme CE Prim Sch

SHORT DROVE

CHURCH ST

LONG DROVE

88

VICARAGE CL

SHORT DROVE

YAXLEY ROAD

4

PO

PH

Holme

STATION ROAD

LC

B660

Cemy

PINGLE BANK

3

Top Farm

New Dyke

87

Fen Farm

2

Monks Lode

Goose Green Farm

Mill Hill

Windmill

1

LC

Conington Fen

Eternity Hall Farm

86

183

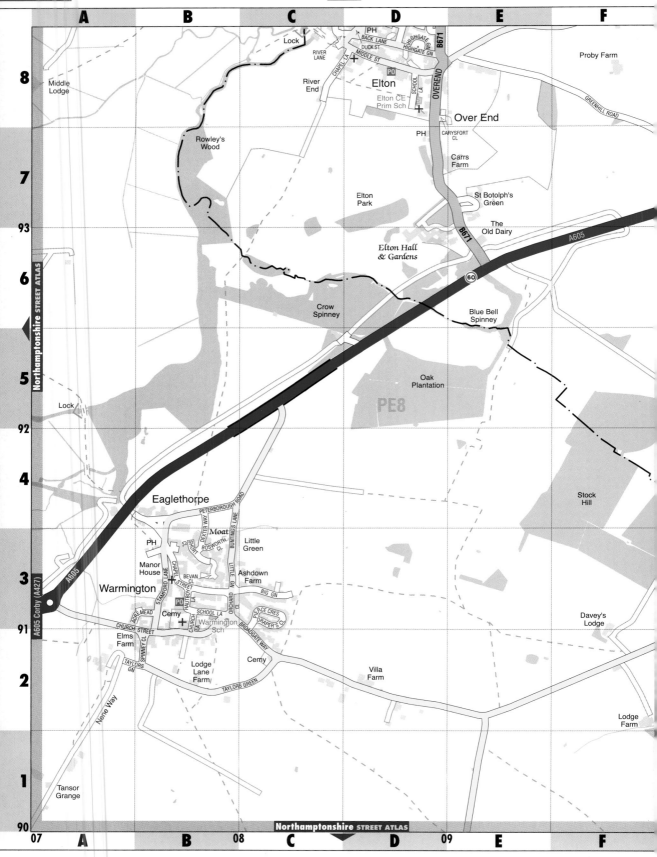

A B C D E F

8

CH

Springlodge
Farm

BULLOCK ROAD

Furze
Farm

Lodge
Farm

Billing Brook

A605

Elton Lodge
Farm

Rectory
Farm

7

60

93

Greenhill
Lodge

Bate's
Lodge

GREENHILL ROAD

6

BULLOCK ROAD

Lawrence's
Lodge

PE7

5

92

Bonser's
Lodge

Stockhill
Lodge

Tookey
Farm

4

PE8

Ashpole
Spinney

Morborne
Hill

Transmitting
Station
Mast

Radio
Station

3

Balaclava
Spinney

91

Long
Spinney

Papley
Gorse

BULLOCK RD

BULLOCK ROAD

2

America
Farm

Morborne
Hill Top

1

90

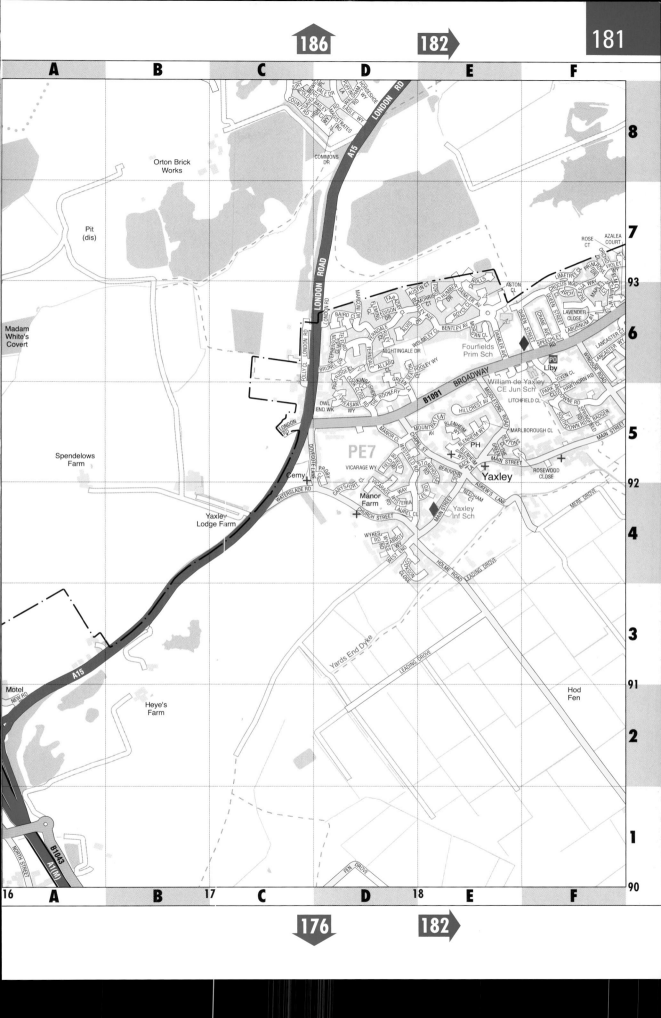

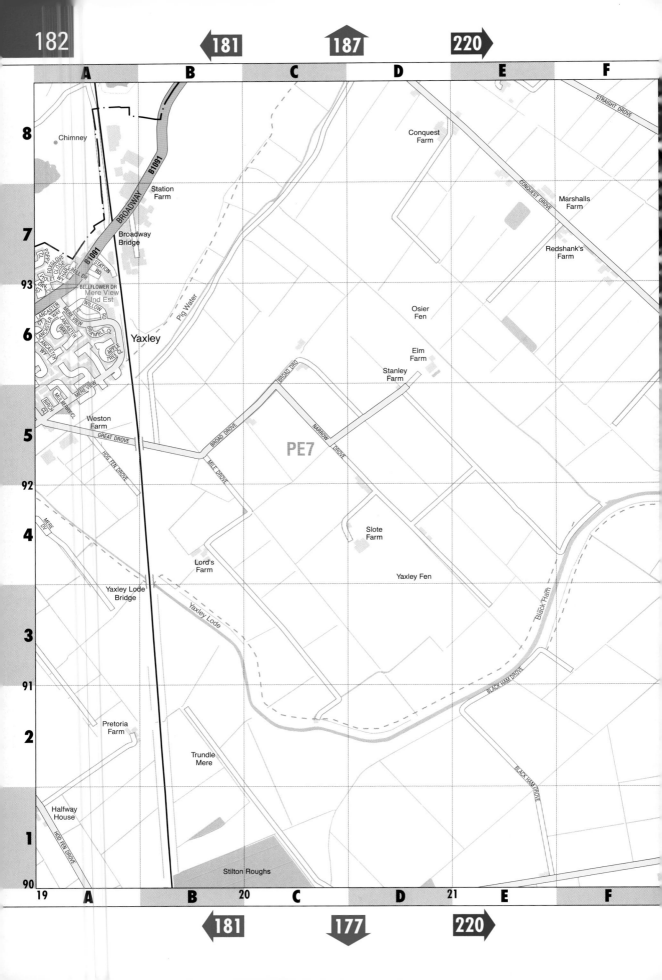

181
187
220

A   B   C   D   E   F

8   Chimney

Conquest
Farm

Station
Farm

STRAIGHT DROVE

CONQUEST DROVE

Marshalls
Farm

7   Broadway
Bridge

B1091

BROADWAY

Redshank's
Farm

93   BELLFLOWER DR
Mere View
Ind Est

Pig Water

STATION RD

Osier
Fen

6   Yaxley

Elm
Farm

BROAD DRO

Stanley
Farm

5   Weston
Farm

GREAT DROVE

MILE DRIVE

BROAD DROVE

PE7

NARROW DRIVE

HOG FEN DRIVE

92

4   MERE DV

Slote
Farm

Lord's
Farm

Yaxley Fen

Black Ham

Yaxley Lode
Bridge

3   Yaxley Lode

BLACK HAM DROVE

91

2   Pretoria
Farm

Trundle
Mere

BLACK HAM DROVE

1   Halfway
House

HOG FEN DRIVE

90   Stilton Roughs

19   A   B   20   C   D   21   E   F

181
177
220

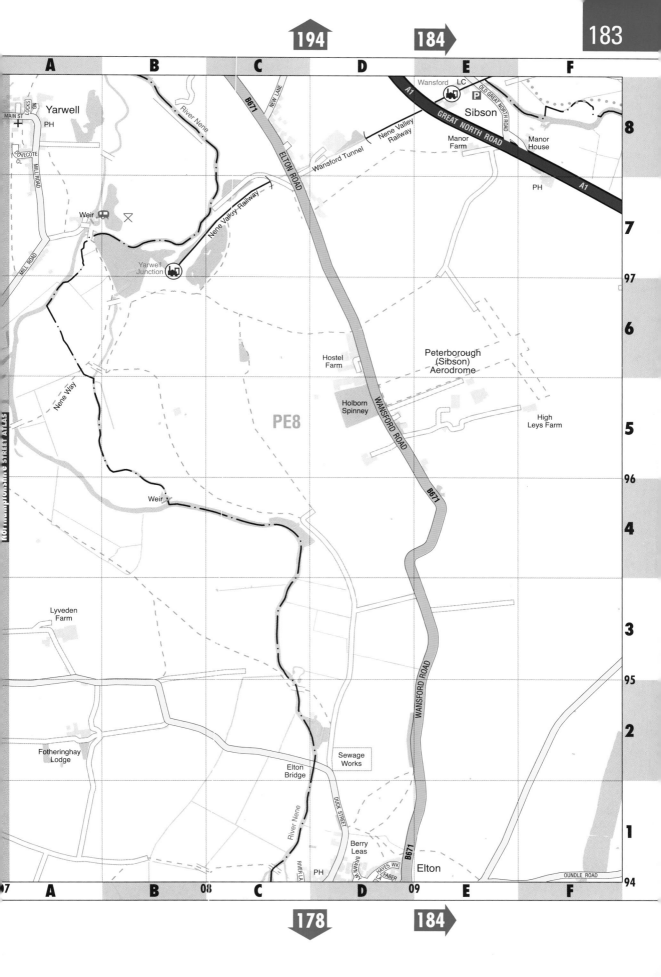

A   B   C   D   E   F

Yarwell
PH
MAIN ST
LOCKS RD
DOVECOTE CL
MILL ROAD
MILL ROAD

River Nene
B671
NEW LANE
ELTON ROAD

Wansford   LC
Sibson
GREAT NORTH ROAD
OLD GREAT NORTH ROAD
A1
A1
Manor Farm
Manor House
PH

8

Nene Valley Railway
Wansford Tunnel

Weir
Nene Valley Railway
Yarwell Junction

7

97

Nene Way

Hostel Farm
Holborn Spinney
Wansford Road
Peterborough (Sibson) Aerodrome
High Leys Farm

6

PE8

5

96

Weir

4

Lyveden Farm

B671

3

95

Fotheringhay Lodge

Sewage Works
Elton Bridge
River Nene
DUCK STREET

2

94

Berry Leas
BRAMBLE
HAYES WK
FABER
PH
RIVER LA
B671
Elton
OUNDLE ROAD

1

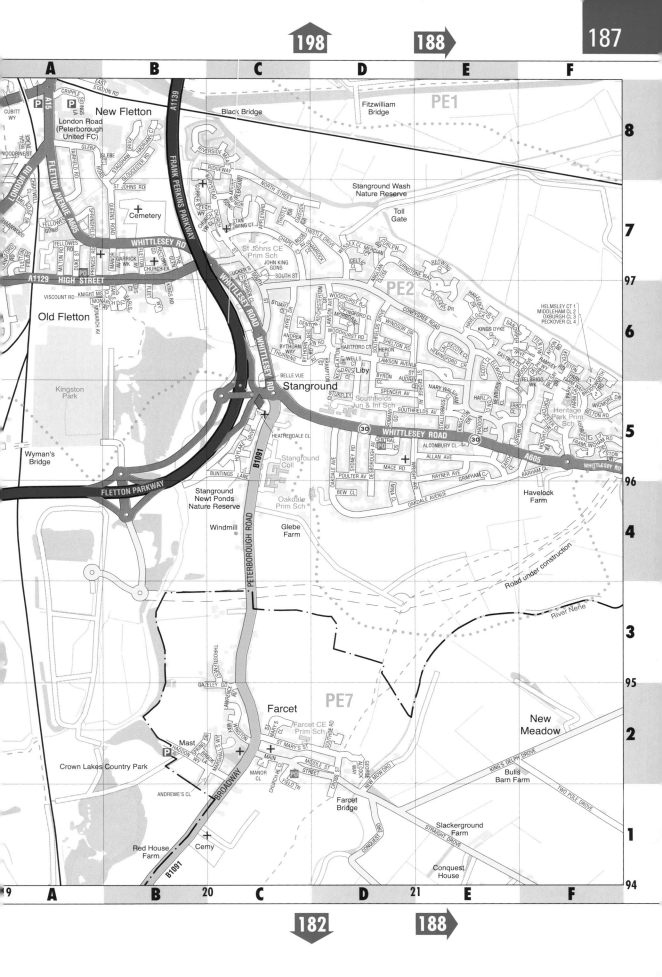

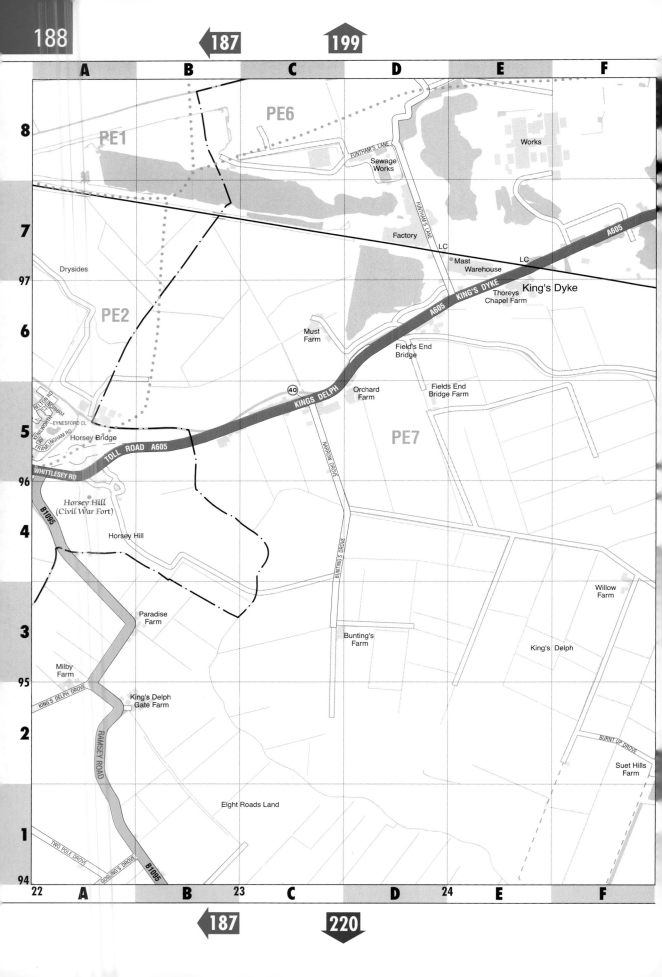

189
201

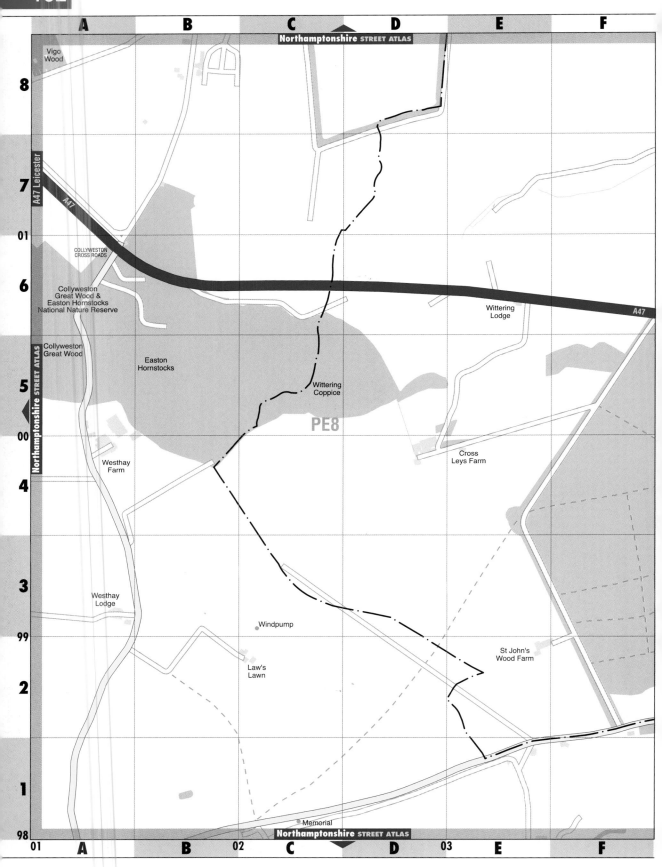

Vigo
Wood

A47 Leicester

A47

COLLYWESTON
CROSS ROADS

Collyweston
Great Wood &
Easton Hornstocks
National Nature Reserve

Wittering
Lodge

A47

Northamptonshire STREET ATLAS

Collyweston
Great Wood

Easton
Hornstocks

Wittering
Coppice

PE8

Cross
Leys Farm

Westhay
Farm

Westhay
Lodge

Windpump

Law's
Lawn

St John's
Wood Farm

Memorial

A   B   C   D   E   F

8

7

01

6

5

00

4

3

99

2

1

98

Wittering

Elms Farm

Church Farm

WOODROFFE RD

TRENT RD

ECCLES RD

EGG ROAD

PARKER ROAD

SUTCLIFFE RD

A1

Sewage Works

Bonemills Farm

Diamond Jubilee Plantation

Abbots Wood

West Wood

Lound Wood

OLD OUNDLE ROAD

Wittering Grange

Thornhaugh Hall

Manor House

Home Farm

Warren Studler Breeding Farm

Thornhaugh

RUSSELL HILL

MEADOW LA

Croft Farm

PE8

Medieval Village of Sibberton (site of)

Sibberton Lodge

Bedford Purlieus National Nature Reserve

Cook's Hole

A47

Bedford Purlieus

Wansford Pasture Nature Reserve

Quarry (dis)

Spoil Heap

Cocker Wood

St John's Wood

WANSFORD ROAD

Cow Wood

Old Sulehay Forest

SULEHAY ROAD

Old Sulehay Lodge

Sand & Gravel Pit

Quarry (dis)

04   A   B   05   C   D   06   E   F

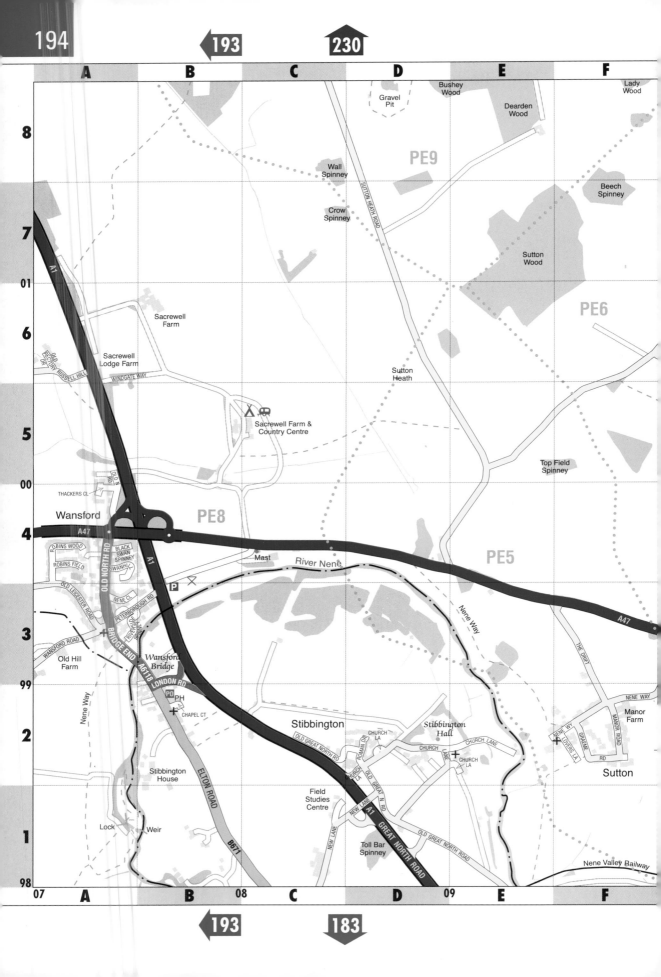

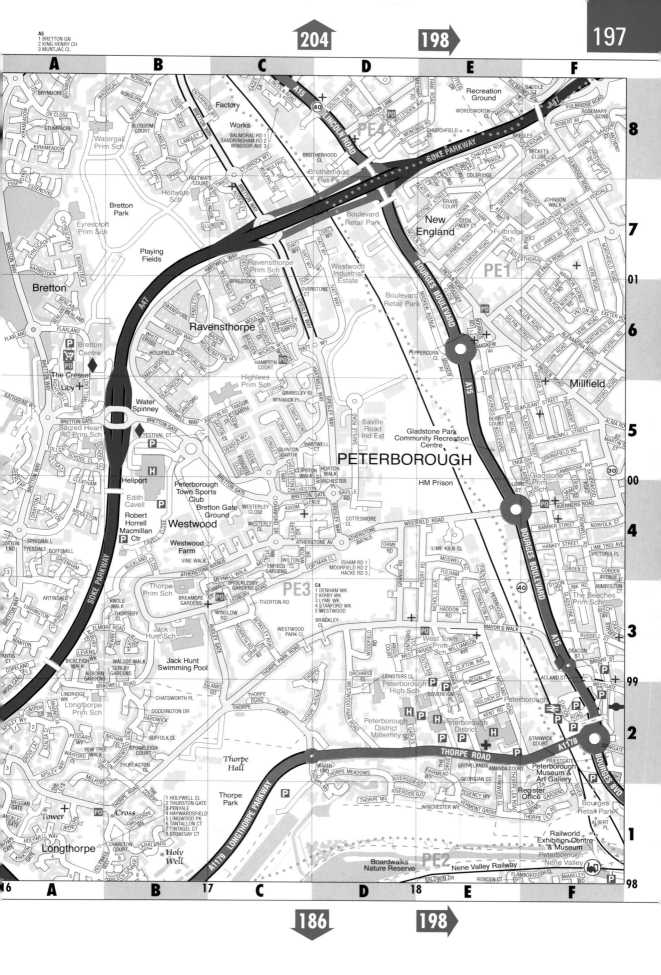

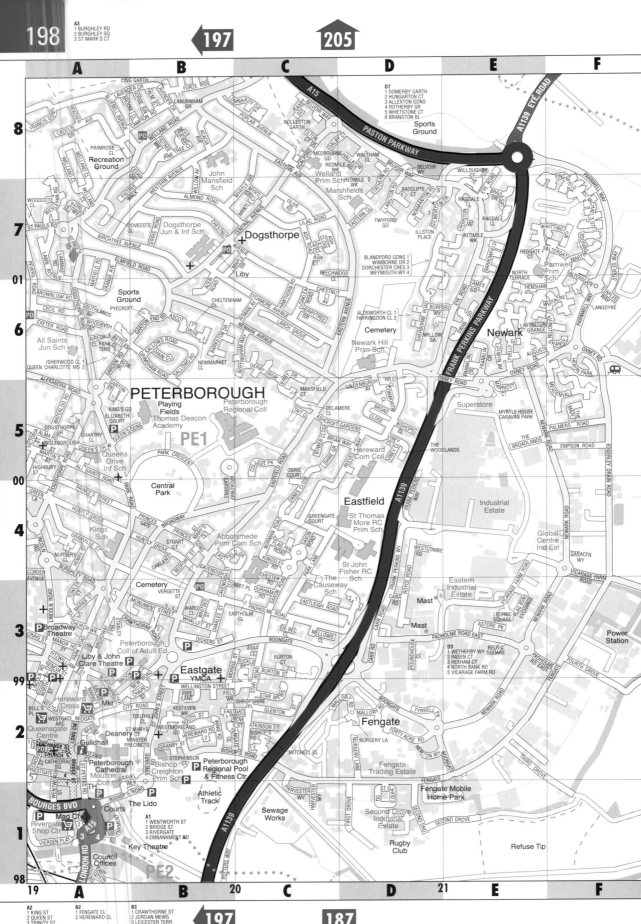

198

A3
1 BURGHLEY RD
2 BURGHLEY SQ
3 ST MARK'S CT

197

205

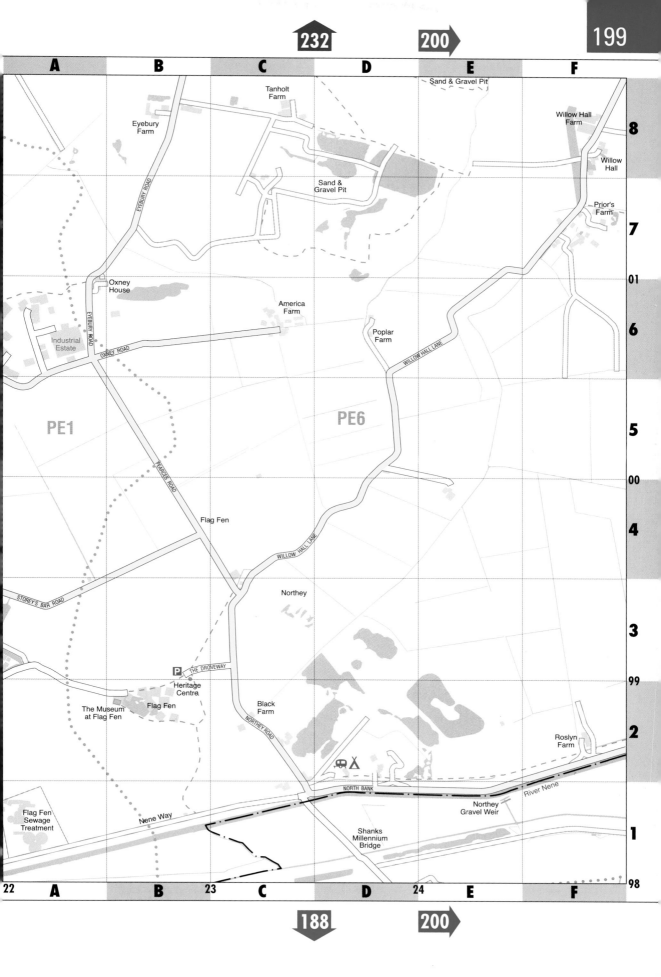

A   B   C   D   E   F

8

7

01

6

PE1   PE6

5

00

4

3

99

2

1

98

Sand & Gravel Pit

Willow Hall Farm

Tanholt Farm

Eyebury Farm

Willow Hall

EYEBURY ROAD

Sand & Gravel Pit

Prior's Farm

Oxney House

America Farm

Poplar Farm

EYEBURY ROAD

OXNEY ROAD

WILLOW HALL LANE

Industrial Estate

PEARCES ROAD

Flag Fen

WILLOW HALL LANE

STOREY'S BAR ROAD

Northey

P

THE DROVEWAY

Heritage Centre

The Museum at Flag Fen

Flag Fen

Black Farm

NORTHEY ROAD

Roslyn Farm

NORTH BANK

River Nene

Northey Gravel Weir

Flag Fen Sewage Treatment

Nene Way

Shanks Millennium Bridge

A B C D E F

8

7

01

6

5

00

4

3

99

2

1

98

The Gores

Gore's Farm

THE CHASE

B1040 WHITTLESEY ROAD

Stone Bridge Corner

Stone Bridge

Prior's Fen

PE6

Teakettle Hall Farm

Teakettle Hall Bridge

NORTH SIDE

GREEN DROVE

Prior's Fen Farm

Bank Farm

Dog-in-a-Doublet Farm

North Side

North Fen

LEVITT'S DROVE

Dog-in-a-Doublet Bridge

PH

Nature Reserve

Lock

LONG DROVE

Nene Way

The Wash

Gull Farm

NORTH BANK

Delph Dike

Plum Tree Farm

River Nene

Little Bridge

B1040

PE7

Morton's Leam

EAST DELPH

YARWELL'S HEADLANDS

25 A B 26 C D 27 E F

A B C D E F

8

7

01

6

Stone Bridge
Farm

Green
Drove Farm

THORNEY DYKE

Walnut
Farm

Crowtree
Farm

Aingers
Farm

Rowletts
Farm

Prospect
House Farm

PE6

Second
Bridge Farm

Bassenhally Moor

5

Popley's Gull

00

4

LONG DROVE

River Nene

3

99

Nene Way

PE7

Bassenhally
Farm

2

Decoy
Farm

Feldale

Feldale
Farm

WHITTLESEY

SHANK
CL

WING

GODNY
CL

SWALLOW

CL

TEAL
RD

DOVE
LA

DRYBREAD ROAD

DRYBREAD ROAD

1

PEAKES
DR

WILLOWBROOK
DR

98

A B 29 C D 30 E F

OLD KNARR FEN DROVE

201
233
227

A B C D E F

8 Harriman's Farm

KNARR FEN ROAD

Knarr Cross Farm

THORNEY DYKE

Poplars' Farm

OLD KNARR FEN DRO

Bassenhally Moor Farm

Bassenhally Moor

7

PE6

01

River Nene

6 Bassnimoor Farm

The Wash

5

00

Moreton's Leam

4 Nene Way Counter Drain St Peter's Farm

PE7

3

99 Elderneil Farm

ELDERNELL LANE

Chapel Farm Man Farm

Engine Farm

2 Flint Farm Kingsland

Eldernell WISBECH ROAD

A605

1 Bishop's Farm

ELDERNELL LANE

Kingsland Farm

98 The Lipneas

31 A B 32 C D 33 E F

201
191
227

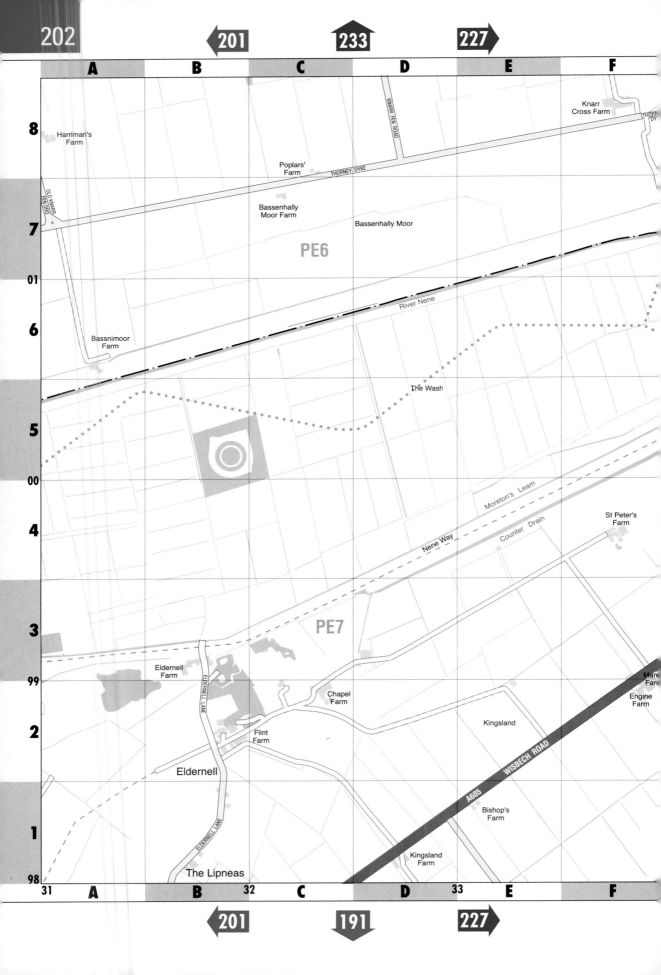

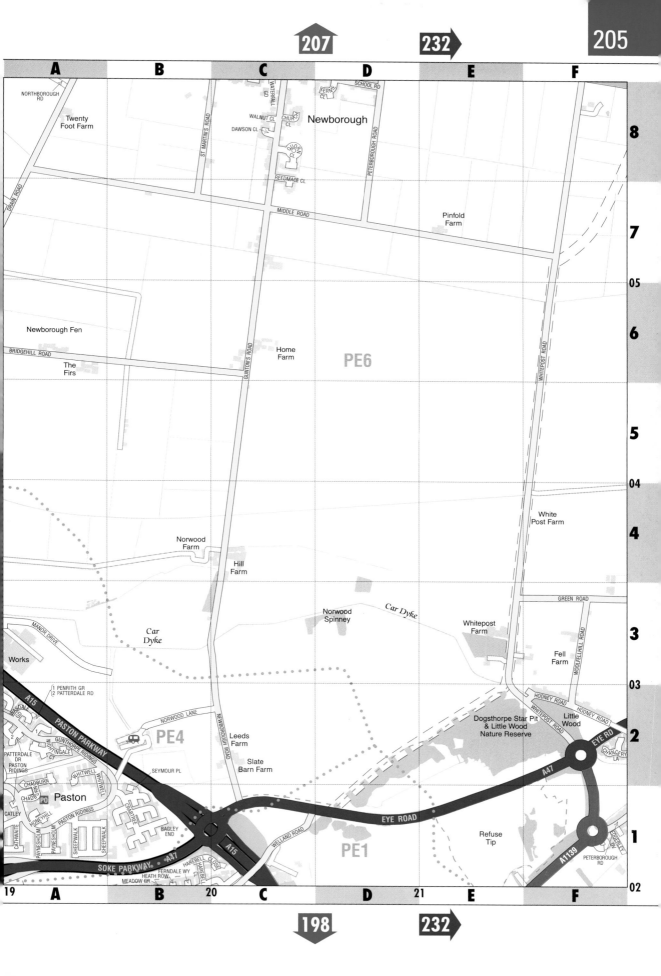

A B C D E F

NORTHBOROUGH RD

Twenty Foot Farm

DRAIN ROAD

ST MARTIN'S ROAD

WATERFALL GD

WALNUT CL

DAWSON CL

CHUR CL

CHOPM CL

REEDMACE CL

FERNE CL

SCHOOL RD

Newborough

PETERBOROUGH ROAD

MIDDLE ROAD

Pinfold Farm

Newborough Fen

BRIDGEHILL ROAD

The Firs

GUNTON'S ROAD

Home Farm

PE6

WHITEPOST ROAD

White Post Farm

Norwood Farm

Hill Farm

Car Dyke

Norwood Spinney

Car Dyke

Whitepost Farm

GREEN ROAD

WOOLFELLHILL ROAD

Fell Farm

MANOR DRIVE

Car Dyke

Works

A15

PASTON PARKWAY

1 PENRITH GR
2 PATTERDALE RD

NORWOOD LANE

PE4

NEWBOROUGH ROAD

Leeds Farm

Slate Barn Farm

HODNEY ROAD

WHITEPOST ROAD

HODNEY ROAD

Dogsthorpe Star Pit & Little Wood Nature Reserve

Little Wood

EYE RD

CHANCERY LA

A47

WISDALE GR

NIGHTINGALE CT

GUNTHORPE RIDINGS

SEYMOUR PL

PATTERDALE DR PASTON RIDINGS

CHADBURN

WHITWELL

WHITWELL

CRABTREE

PASTON RIDINGS

BAGLEY END

WELLAND ROAD

EYE ROAD

A47

EYE ROAD

Refuse Tip

A1139

PETERBOROUGH RD

BUSKLEY RD

CHADS

P.O.

Paston

CATHWAITE

CATLEY

HONEYHILL

PAYNESHOLM

PAYNESHOLM

SHEEPWALK

SHEEPWALK

SOKE PARKWAY

A47

A15

HAREBELL CLOSE

HAREBELL

FERNDALE WY

HEATH ROW

MEADOW GR

PE1

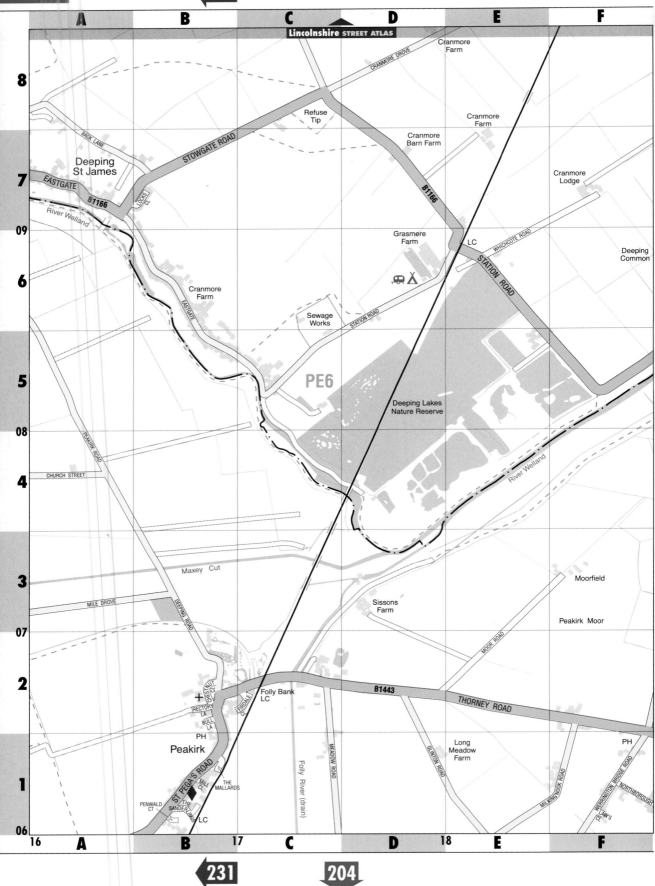

Lincolnshire STREET ATLAS

A B C D E F

Lincolnshire STREET ATLAS

B1166

River Welland

WELLAND BANK

MIDDLE ROAD

MIDDLE ROAD

CORPORATION BANK

LOW ROAD

Wards Farm

8

7

09

6

Eardley Grange

CROWLAND ROAD

Chestnut Farm

B1166

The Wash

Willow Barn Farm

The Willows

DOVE WILLOW

WILLOW DRIVE

SPEECHLEY'S DRO

PE6

5

08

Belmont Farm

DECOY ROAD

Lower Willow Farm

Decoy

Moores Farm

4

The Avenue

Bull Bridge Farm

3

07

DECOY ROAD

WILLOW DRIVE

Pank's Farm

SPEECHLEY'S DRIVE

2

B1443

Slip Bridge

Buildings Farm

DRAIN ROAD

ROWELL CL 1

Bull Bridge

PH

Newborough

GRIFFINS CL

Crowtree Farm

Baxter's Bridge

WHITEPOST RD

1

SEARGEANTS CL

WILLIAMS CL

ST MARTIN'S ROAD

HOLLY CL

HAWTHORN CL

WATERFALL CLOSE

BURTON'S RD

FENSIDE DRIVE

GODFREY CL

P CLOSE

WHITSED RD

EVES CL

EVES CL

THORNEY ROAD

B1443

06

SOKE ROAD

Newborough Prim Sch

SCHOOL BR

155

215

Scale: 1¾ inches to 1 mile

0   ¼   ½ mile
0   250m   500m   750m   1 km

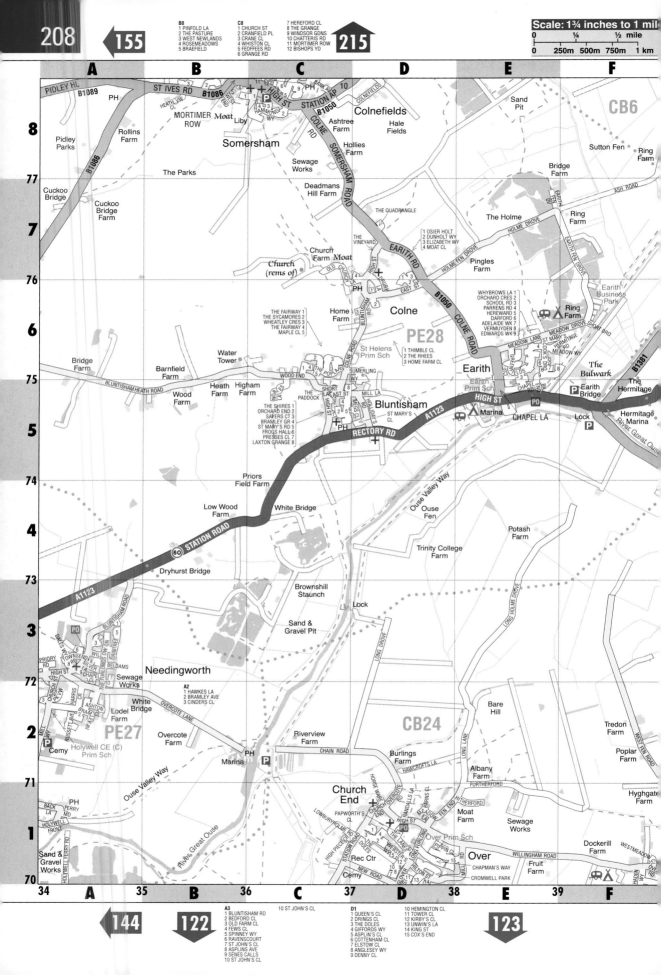

CB6

PIDLEY HL

B1089   PH

Rollins Farm

Pidley Parks

B1086

Cuckoo Bridge

Cuckoo Bridge Farm

St IVES RD   ST IVES RD   B1086

HEATH VW   MORTIMER ROW   Moat   Liby

HAMMONDS   END   WY

HIGH ST   PH

STATION AP

B1050

Somersham

The Parks

Colnefields

COLNE RD

Ashtree Farm

Hale Fields

Sand Pit

Sutton Fen

Ring Farm

Bridge Farm

Sewage Works

Deadmans Hill Farm

Hollies Farm

SOMERSHAM ROAD

THE QUADRANGLE

THE VINEYARD

EARITH RD

1 OSIER HOLT
2 DUNHOLT WY
3 ELIZABETH WY
4 MOAT CL

HOLME DROVE

The Holme

Ring Farm

ASH ROAD

EARITH DRI

EARITH FEN DROVE

Church Farm Moat

OLD CHURCH   DRUBY

Church (rems of)

PH

HIGH ST EAST   EAST ST

Colne

B1050

COLNE ROAD

Pingles Farm

Earith Business Park

Ring Farm

WHYBROWS LA 1
ORCHARD CRES 2
SCHOOL RD 3
PARRENS RD 4
HEREWARD 5
DARFORD 6
ADELAIDE WK 7
VERMUYDEN 8
EDWARDS WK 9

MEADOW LANE

MEADOW DROVE

SHORT BRO

B1381

Bridge Farm

Barnfield Farm

Water Tower

BLUNTISHAM HEATH ROAD

Heath Farm

Higham Farm

Wood Farm

THE FAIRWAY 1
THE SYCAMORES 2
WHEATLEY CRES 3
THE FAIRWAY 4
MAPLE CL 5

Home Farm

PE28

St Helens Prim Sch

WOOD END

THE POPLARS

SUMERLING

MILL LA

1 THIMBLE CL
2 THE RHEES
3 HOME FARM CL

Earith Prim Sch

Earith

CHAPEL LA

HIGH ST

The Bulwark

The Hermitage

THE PADDOCK

THE SHIRES 1
ORCHARD END 2
SAYERS CT 3
BRAMLEY GR 4
ST MARY'S RD 5
FROGS HALL 6
PRESSES CL 7
LAXTON GRANGE 8

SHORT   LAST   EAST ST

HOLIDAYS   WY

HOLIDAYS   MEWS

St MARY'S CL

Bluntisham

A1123

PH

RECTORY RD

PO

Marina

Lock

Hermitage Marina

Rvr Gt Ouse

Priors Field Farm

Low Wood Farm

White Bridge

Ouse Valley Way

Ouse Fen

Potash Farm

STATION ROAD

60

Dryhurst Bridge

A1123

Trinity College Farm

Brownshill Staunch

Lock

LONG HOLME DROVE

LONG DROVE

Sand & Gravel Pit

PO

BLUNTISHAM RD

DALES CL   SILVER   ST   CHAIN TREE   BELDAMS

PRIORY RD   HIGH ST

TOWNSEND LA   THE FURLONGS   LOW GN

Needingworth

A2
1 HAWKES LA
2 BRAMLEY AVE
3 CINDERS CL

Bare Hill

Tredon Farm

CHURCH   CL YW   HARRIS CL   RUSSELL LANE   ASHTON   BRAZE CL   Chapel

CB24

Poplar Farm

Sewage Works

MILL   PO   Cemy   Holywell CE (C) Prim Sch

PE27

Lodel Farm

White Bridge

OVERCOTE LANE

Overcote Farm

Riverview Farm

CHAIN ROAD

Burlings Farm

HAWCROFTS LA

LONG LANE

Albany Farm

FURTHERFORD

WEST FEN ROAD

Hyghgate Farm

PH

Marina

River Great Ouse

PH   FERRY   RD

BACK LA

HOLYWELL FRONT

HOLYWELL FERRY RD

Ouse Valley Way

Church End

PAPWORTH'S CL

HORSE WARE   OVERCOTE LA

CHURCH   WEBSTER'S CL   HIGH ST   PO

HEMING RD   MEADOW   FEN DR

Moat Farm

Sewage Works

Over Prim Sch

Dockerill Farm

WESTMEADOW

Sand & Gravel Works

LOWBURY   HOLME RD

STATION   RD   DOLES   PIPPIN CL   Rec Ctr

HIGH PRIEST FURLONG   THE FURLONG   KINGFISHER   FURLONG   HILTON CL

Over

WILLINGHAM ROAD

Fruit Farm

OVER   RD

HADEN

Cemy   NEW ROAD

Chapman's Way

CROMWELL PARK

144

122

123

Grid references: A B C D E F (columns), 8 77 7 76 6 75 5 74 4 73 3 72 2 71 1 70 (rows); 34 A 35 B 36 C 37 D 38 E 39 F (bottom)

A   B   C   D   E   F

8

77

7

76

South Fen

North Fen

Jolly Bankers
Bridge

CHAIN CAUSEWAY

B1381

New Bedford River or Hundred Foot Drain

Galls
Farm

Hill Row
Doles

Willow
Hall Farm

Third
Bridge

Second
Bridge

New Cut
Bridge

North
Hill

Mast

Haddenham

Eight &
Twenty Farm

Willow Hall
Farm

Willow
Farm

Causeway
Farm

Tree
Farm

Manderly
Farm

HILL ROW

Willow
Farm

HILL ROW CAUSEWAY

A1123

A1123   WEST END

GLEBE
WY

MEADOW LA

NEW TOWN ROAD

Fen
Barn

Gall Fen

6

Hermitage
Farm

UPPER DELPH DROVE

Lower Delphs

Cracknell
Farm

LONG DROVE

CB6

75

B1050

Claytons
Bridge

Adventurers' Fen

Windmill

5

74

Upper
Delphs

Dam Bank
Bridge

DAM BANK DROVE

Parkes
Farm

ALDRETH ROAD

Bridge
Farm

Cut Bridge

Flat Bridge
Farm

Defreville
Farm

HIGH ST

Aldreth

HEREWARD CL

THE BOROUGH

Bedlam
Farm

4

Flat Bridge

SAND LA

THE BOOT

FEN SIDE

MEADOWBROOK

Lakes Drove
Bridge

73

Flat Road
Farm

FLAT ROAD

Ewell Fen

Church
Fen Bridge

CHURCH FEN DRO

CROSS DROVE

LAKES DRO

HOGHILL DROVE

Holme
Fen

3

Middle
Fen Farm

Woodhall
Farm

Queen
Holme

Ford

72

EARITH ROAD

Middle
Fen

MILKING HILLS DRIVE

Milking Hills Corner

QUEENHOLME WY

Smithey Fen
Farm

River Great Ouse

2

B1050

SPRING DROVE

Queenholme
Bloodstock Stables

CB24

Glebe
Farm

SMITHEY FEN ENGINE DROVE

Lingwood
Farm

LITTLE
SETCHEL
DRO

71

Belsar
Farm

MEADOW ROAD

Tibbitts
Farm

Hempsals
Fen

HEMPSALS ROAD OR MEADOW DROVE

Norris
Farm

Fen End
Farm

Smithey
Fen

LOCKSPIT HALL DROVE

LORD-
SHIP
CL

POUND LA

Liby

WILFORD FURLONG

COCKHILL END

CHURCH ST

PRIEST LA

Willingham

Belsar's Hill
(Fort)

Hempsall
Farm

COW LANE

OXHOLME DROVE

Plough
Farm

1

ICU

THODAYS

ELM WY

PYRETHRUM WY

SCHOLE RD

RAMP

SILVER ST

SHORTLS ST

CHURCH GREEN LA

IRAM DROVE

70

40   A   41   B   42   C   43   D   44   E   45   F   70

A1
1 BELSARS CL
2 PYRETHRUM WY
3 OSBORN CL
4 CHURCH LA
5 PEGLER CT
6 BRICKHILLS
7 GEORGE ST
8 HIGH ST
9 STATION RD
10 SAXON WY
11 BOURNEYS MANOR CL
12 COVENT GDN
13 LOVE'S LA
14 ROSE & CROWN YD
15 Willingham
    Prim Sch

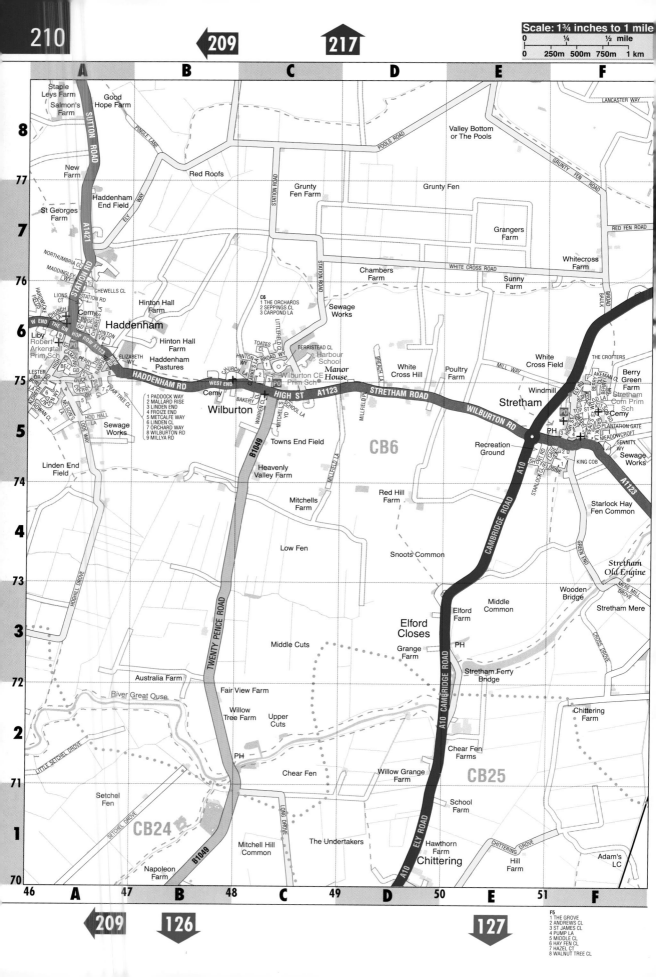

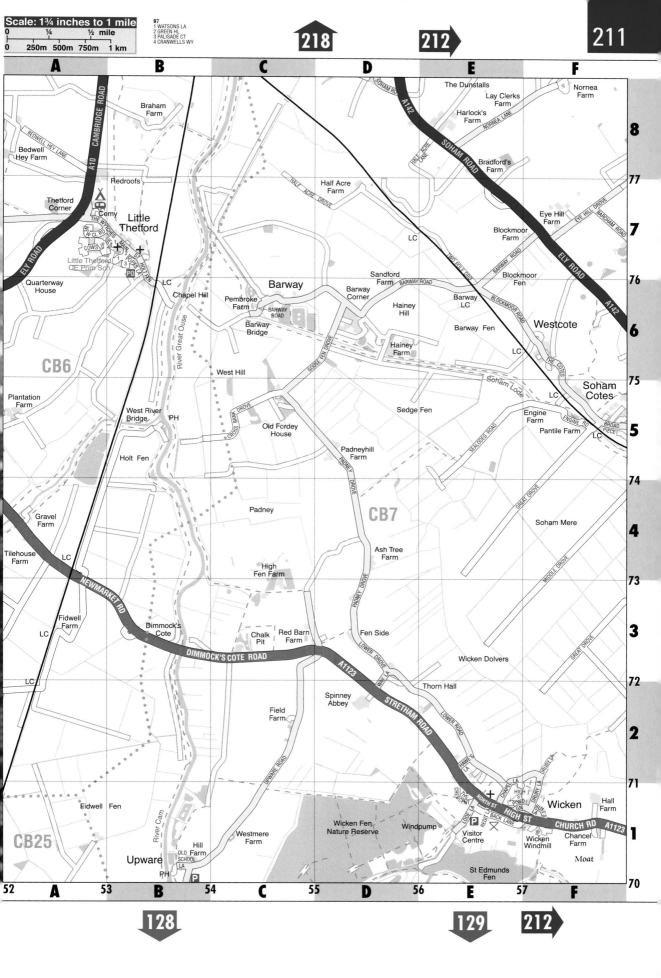

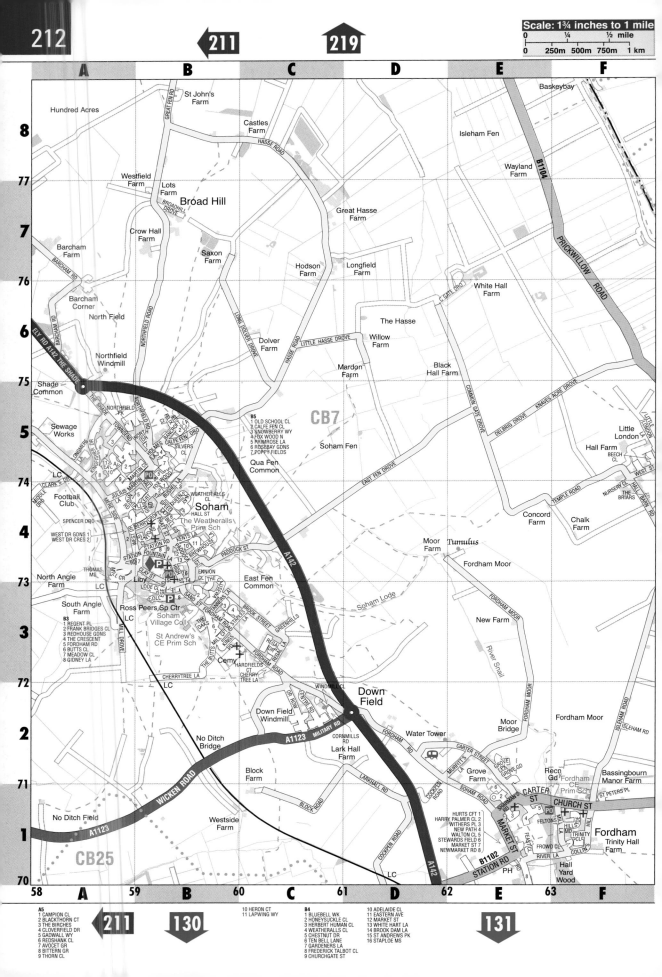

Scale: 1¾ inches to 1 mile
0 ¼ ½ mile
0 250m 500m 750m 1 km

Baskeybay

Hundred Acres

St John's Farm

Castles Farm

Isleham Fen

8

Wayland Farm

Westfield Farm

Lots Farm

Broad Hill

77

BROADHILL DROVE

Great Hasse Farm

7

Crow Hall Farm

Barcham Farm

Saxon Farm

White Hall Farm

76

Hodson Farm

Longfield Farm

Barcham Corner

North Field

The Hasse

6

ELY RD A142 THE SHADE

Northfield Windmill

Dolver Farm

Willow Farm

75

Shade Common

Mardon Farm

Black Hall Farm

CB7

B5
1 OLD SCHOOL CL
2 CALFE FEN CL
3 SNOWBERRY WY
4 FOX WOOD N
5 PRIMROSE LA
6 ROSEBAY GDNS
7 POPPY FIELDS

Soham Fen

Little London

Hall Farm

5

Sewage Works

Qua Fen Common

Football Club

Soham

The Weatheralls Prim Sch

Concord Farm

Chalk Farm

4

WEST DR GDNS 1
WEST DR CRES 2

Moor Farm

Tumulus

Fordham Moor

73

North Angle Farm

Liby

East Fen Common

Soham Lode

Fordham Moor

New Farm

South Angle Farm

Ross Peers Sp Ctr

Soham Village Coll

B3
1 REGENT PL
2 FRANK BRIDGES CL
3 REDHOUSE GDNS
4 THE CRESCENT
5 FORDHAM RD
6 BUTTS CL
7 MEADOW CL
8 GIDNEY LA

St Andrew's CE Prim Sch

Cemy

3

Greenhills

River Snail

Down Field

72

Down Field Windmill

Water Tower

Moor Bridge

Fordham Moor

2

No Ditch Bridge

A1123 MILITARY RD

Lark Hall Farm

Grove Farm

Recn Gd

Bassingbourn Manor Farm

Fordham CE Prim Sch

Block Farm

LARKHALL RD

Fordham

71

WICKEN ROAD

Westside Farm

HURTS CFT 1
HARRY PALMER CL 2
WITHERS PL 3
NEW PATH 4
WALTON CL 5
STEWARDS FIELD 6
MARKET ST 7
NEWMARKET RD 8

CARTER ST

CHURCH ST

1

No Ditch Field

A1123

Trinity Hall Farm

CB25

B1102

STATION RD

PH

Hall Yard Wood

70

A5
1 CAMPION CL
2 BLACKTHORN CT
3 THE BIRCHES
4 CLOVERFIELD DR
5 GADWALL WY
6 REDSHANK CL
7 AVOCET GR
8 BITTERN GR
9 THORN CL

10 HERON CT
11 LAPWING WY

B4
1 BLUEBELL WK
2 HONEYSUCKLE CL
3 HERBERT HUMAN CL
4 WEATHERALLS CL
5 CHESTNUT DR
6 TEN BELL LANE
7 GARDENERS LA
8 FREDERICK TALBOT CL
9 CHURCHGATE ST

10 ADELAIDE CL
11 EASTERN AVE
12 MARKET ST
13 WHITE HART LA
14 BROOK DAM LA
15 ST ANDREWS PK
16 STAPLOE MS

◀ 211
▼ 130
▼ 131

For full street detail of the highlighted area see page 239. ◀ 213

0 ¼ ½ mile
0 250m 500m 750m 1 km

Suffolk STREET ATLAS

A1065 Swaffham

IP27

Tumulus
Foxhole Heath
Rakeheath Farm
Howhill Clump
Chamberlain's Buildings Farm
Codson Plantation
Codson Hill
How Hill (Tumulus)
Dalehole Plantation
Tumulus
Twelve Acre Wood
Highlodge Farm
Holywell Row
Moat
Beck Lodge
Jeagor Farm
Holly Farm
Mildenhall Airfield
Mildenhall Woods
Mildenhall
Snipepit Plantation
Mildenhall Woods
Mildenhall Woods
Avenue Farm
Kingsway
Bury Rd
Cemy
Coll
Barton Mills
Icklingham Plains
Turf Fen
River Lark
Temple Bridge
Nature Reserve
Six Acre Covert
The Grove
IP28
Golf Links Road
Chalk Hill
Mast
Tumulus
Summerhouse Plantation
Bay Farm
Chalkhill Plantation
Weston-Evans Plantation
Clarkstone Plantation
Nethercroft Farm
Thormanby Stud
Tuddenham Heath
Tuddenham
Southgate Farm
Longwood Farm
Tuddenham CE Prim Sch
Sheepskin Plantation
Herringswell Manor Farm
Fen Farm
Park Wood
Park Farm
Waterloo Plantation
Old Hall Farm
Sewage Works
Shortlands Plantation
Hundred Acre Farm
Hall Farm
Berries Wood
Moorhouse Plantation
Mitchel Head
Field Farm

Cavenham Road
Mildenhall Road
Newmarket Road
Worlington Road
Herringswell Road
Cherry Hill
Tuddenham Road
High St
Higham Rd
Icknield Way Path

213 ◀

134

A1
1 CLOVER WY
2 HEATHERSET WY
3 LARKSPUR CL
4 BROOMHILL CL
5 SAINFOIN CL
6 BLACKBERRY WY
7 ROSEMARY CLE
8 GORSE CL
9 LAUREL CL
10 BOUNDARY RD
11 JUNIPER RD
12 HUNDRED ACRE WY
13 BENNETT RD
14 BERGAMOT CL
15 DAMSON CL
16 ELDERBERRY RD
17 HAREBELL RD
18 THYME CL

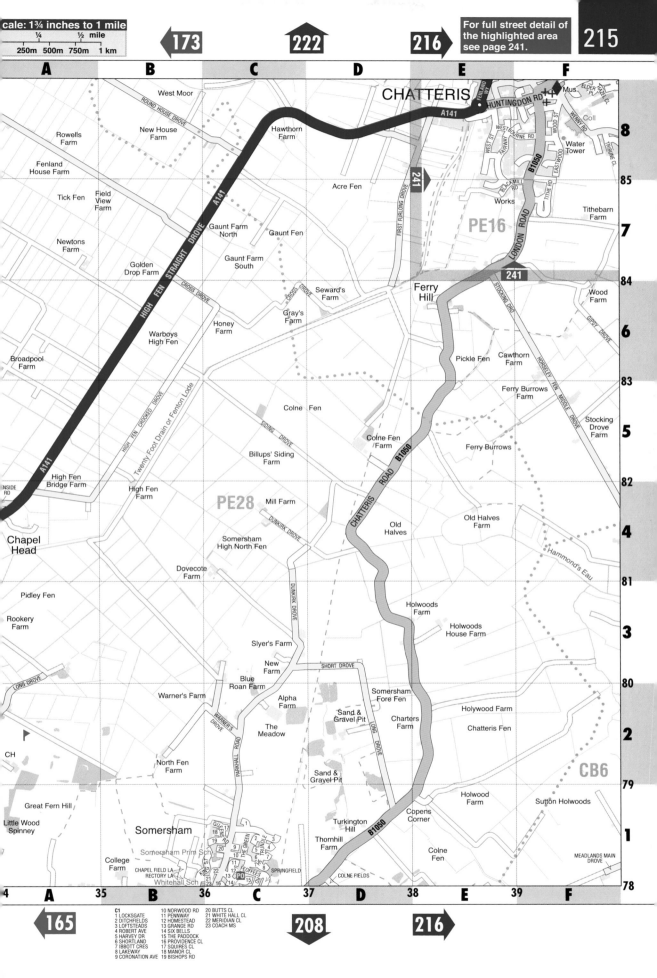

216

For full street detail of the highlighted area see page 241.

215

223

Scale: 1¾ inches to 1 mile

0   ¼   ½ mile

0   250m   500m   750m   1 km

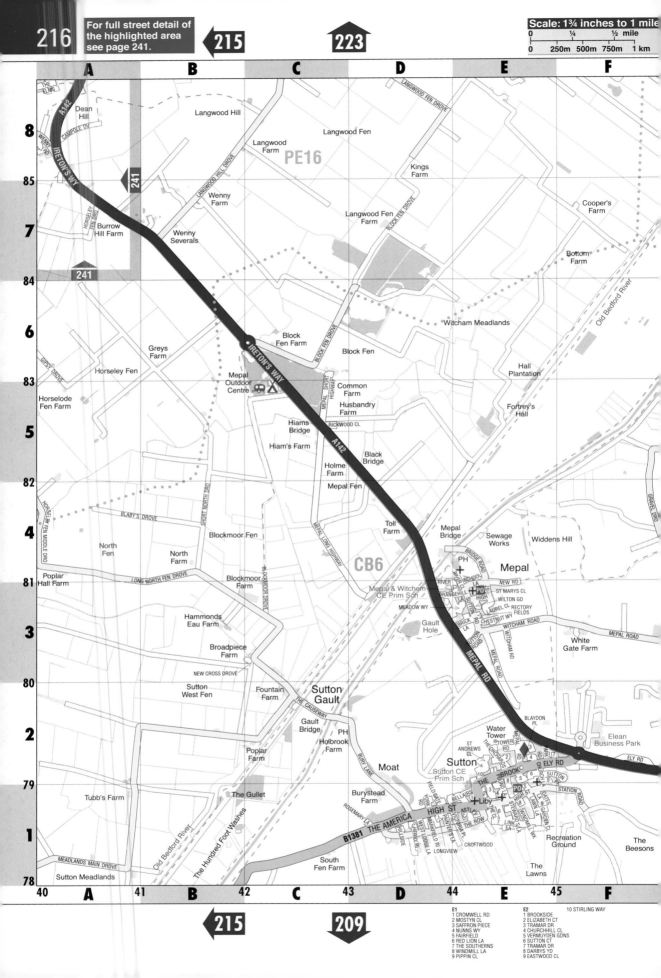

A   B   C   D   E   F

THE ELMS

A142

Dean Hill

IRETON'S WY

CAMPOLE DV

8

Langwood Hill

Langwood Fen

85

Langwood Farm

PE16

Kings Farm

241

WENNY

HORSELEY FEN DRO

Wenny Farm

LANGWOOD HILL DROVE

Cooper's Farm

7

Burrow Hill Farm

Wenny Severals

Langwood Fen Farm

BLOCK FEN DROVE

Bottom Farm

241

84

Witcham Meadlands

Old Bedford River

6

GIPSY DROVE

Greys Farm

IRETON'S WY

Block Fen Farm

Block Fen

Hall Plantation

83

Horseley Fen

Mepal Outdoor Centre

MEPAL SHORT HIGHWAY

Common Farm

RICKWOOD CL

Fortrey's Hall

Horselode Fen Farm

Hiams Bridge

Hiam's Farm

Husbandry Farm

A142

5

HORSELEY FEN MIDDLE DRO

Holme Farm

Black Bridge

82

BLABY'S DROVE

SHORT NORTH DRO

Mepal Fen

4

North Fen

North Farm

Blockmoor Fen

Toll Farm

Mepal Bridge

BRIDGE ROAD

Sewage Works

Widdens Hill

Mepal

GRAVEL DRO

81

Poplar Hall Farm

LONG NORTH FEN DROVE

Blockmoor Farm

BLOCKMOOR DROVE

CB6

MEPAL LONG HIGHWAY

PH

NEW RD

ST MARYS CL

WILTON GD

Mepal & Witcham CE Prim Sch

RECTORY FIELDS

White Gate Farm

MEPAL ROAD

3

Hammonds Eau Farm

MEADOW WY

BRICK LA

CHESTNUT WY

WITCHAM RD

MEPAL ROAD

Broadpiece Farm

Gault Hole

WITCHAM ROAD

80

NEW CROSS DROVE

Sutton West Fen

Fountain Farm

Sutton Gault

THE CAUSEWAY

BLAYDON PL

Elean Business Park

2

Gault Bridge

PH

Holbrook Farm

Water Tower

TOWER RD

ELY RD

Poplar Farm

BURY LANE

Moat

ST ANDREWS CL

Sutton

STATION ROAD

79

Tubb's Farm

The Gullet

Burystead Farm

ROSEMARY LA

Sutton CE Prim Sch

THE BROOK

Liby

PO

Recreation Ground

The Beesons

1

MEADLANDS MAIN DROVE

Old Bedford River

The Hundred Foot Washes

B1381 THE AMERICA

HIGH ST

CROFTWOOD

The Lawns

South Fen Farm

78

Sutton Meadlands

40   A   41   B   42   C   43   D   44   E   45   F

215

209

E1
1 CROMWELL RD
2 MOSTYN CL
3 SAFFRON PIECE
4 NUNNS WY
5 FAIRFIELD
6 RED LION LA
7 THE SOUTHERNS
8 WINDMILL LA
9 PIPPIN CL

E2
1 BROOKSIDE
2 ELIZABETH CT
3 TRAMAR DR
4 CHURCHHILL CL
5 VERMUYDEN GDNS
6 SUTTON CT
7 TRAMAR DR
8 DARBYS YD
9 EASTWOOD CL

10 STIRLING WAY

Scale: 1¾ inches to 1 mile

¼ ½ mile
250m 500m 750m 1 km

224
218

A B C D E F

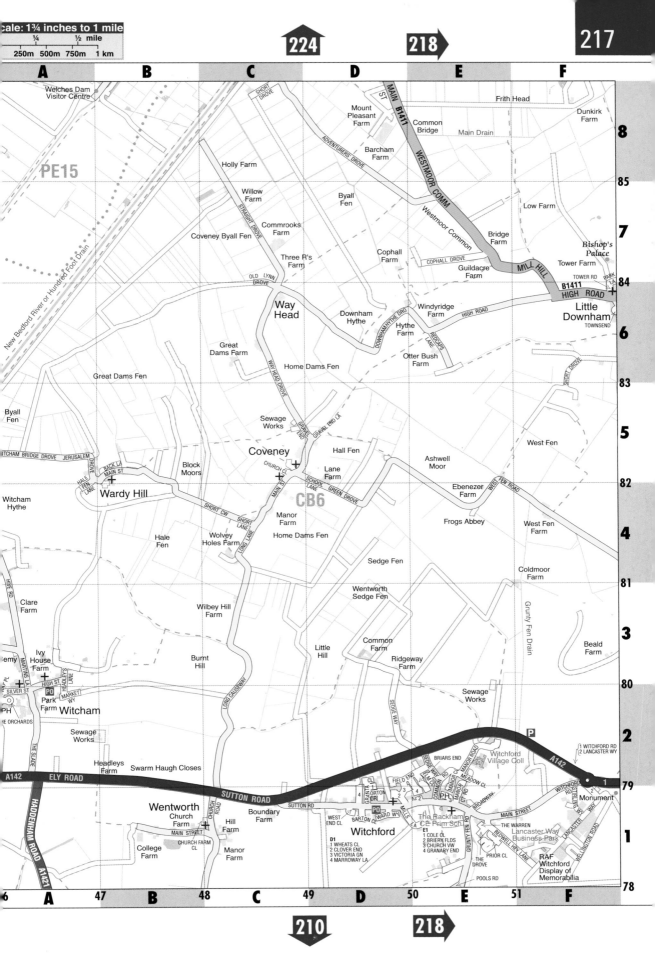

Welches Dam Visitor Centre

Frith Head

Mount Pleasant Farm

Common Bridge

Main Drain

Dunkirk Farm

8

PE15

Holly Farm

Barcham Farm

Low Farm

85

Willow Farm

Byall Fen

Westmoor Common

Bridge Farm

7

Commrooks Farm

Coveney Byall Fen

Cophall Farm

Bishop's Palace

Guildacre Farm

Tower Farm

TOWER RD

PARK LA

Three R's Farm

Cophall Drove

84

Way Head

Downham Hythe

Windyridge Farm

High Road

B1411
HIGH ROAD

Little Downham

TOWNSEND

Great Dams Farm

Hythe Farm

6

Great Dams Fen

Home Dams Fen

Otter Bush Farm

83

Byall Fen

West Fen

5

Witcham Bridge Drove Jerusalem

Coveney

Hall Fen

Ashwell Moor

82

Wardy Hill

Block Moors

Lane Farm

Ebenezer Farm

West Fen Farm

4

Witcham Hythe

Manor Farm

Home Dams Fen

Frogs Abbey

Hale Fen

Wolvey Holes Farm

Sedge Fen

Coldmoor Farm

81

Clare Farm

Wilbey Hill Farm

Wentworth Sedge Fen

Beald Farm

3

Ivy House Farm

Burnt Hill

Little Hill

Common Farm

Ridgeway Farm

80

SILVER ST

PO

Park Farm

Witcham

Sewage Works

2

THE ORCHARDS

Sewage Works

Headleys Farm

Swarm Haugh Closes

A142

Witchford Village Coll

1 Witchford Rd
2 Lancaster Wy

A142
ELY ROAD

SUTTON ROAD

Boundary Farm

PH

Monument

79

HADDENHAM ROAD

Wentworth Church Farm

Hill Farm

SUTTON RD

Witchford

PO

The Rackham's CE Prim Sch

The Warren

Lancaster Way Business Park

1

College Farm

Main Street

Manor Farm

RAF Witchford Display of Memorabilia

78

A1421

210
218

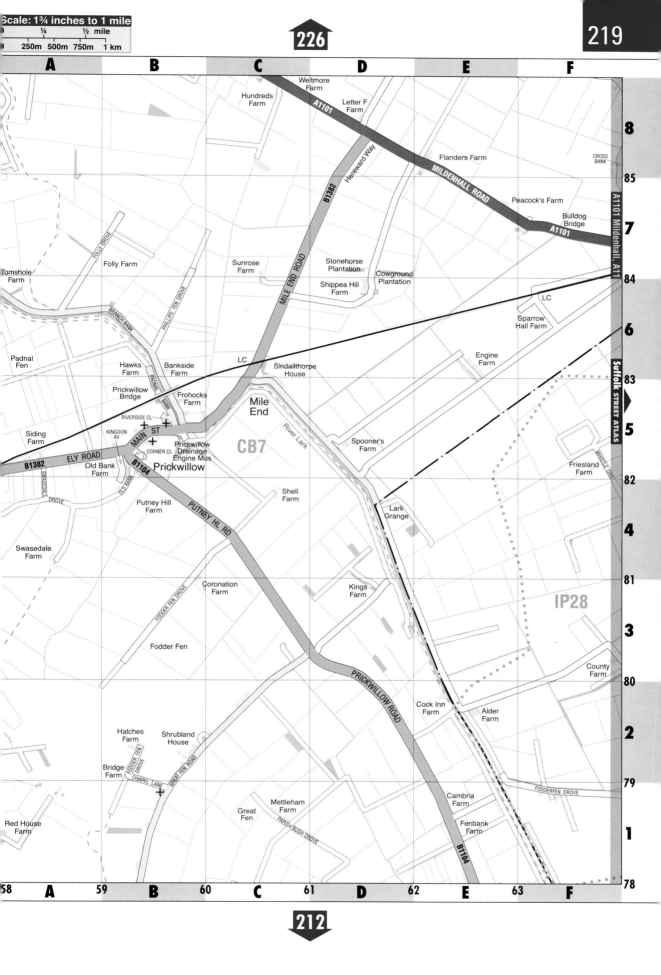

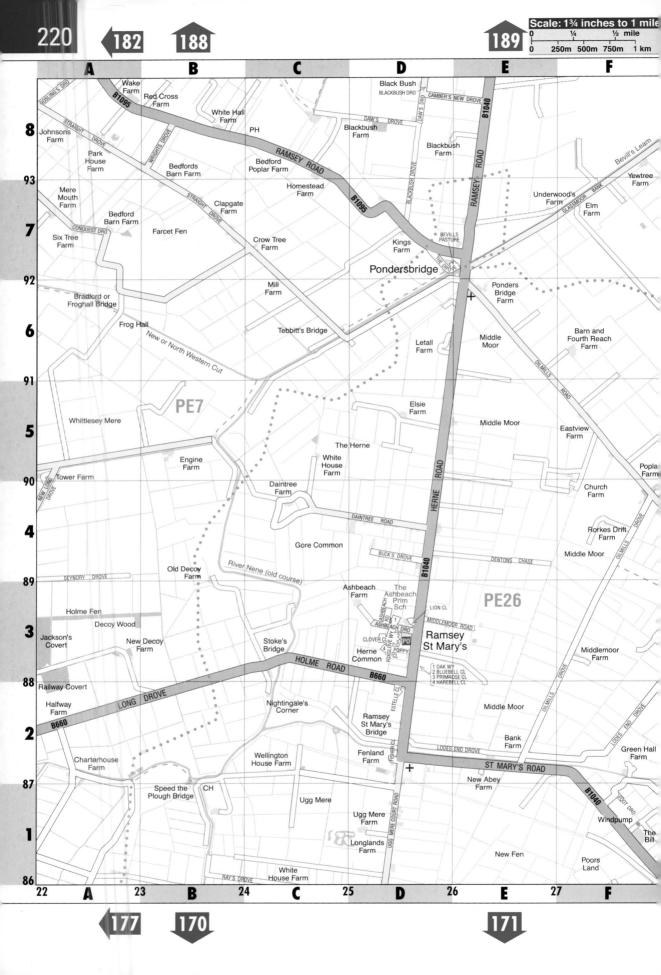

Scale: 1¾ inches to 1 mile

0   ¼   ½ mile
0   250m 500m 750m 1 km

A   B   C   D   E   F

8

Gosling's Dro
B1095
Wake Farm
Red Cross Farm
White Hall Farm
PH
Black Bush
BLACKBUSH DRO
CAMBER'S NEW DROVE
DAW'S DROVE
DAW'S DRO
Johnsons Farm
Straight Drove
Park House Farm
Bedfords Barn Farm
Ramsey Road
Bedford Poplar Farm
Blackbush Farm
Blackbush Farm
B1040
Ramsey Road
Bevill's Leam

93

Mere Mouth Farm
Straight Drove
Clapgate Farm
Homestead Farm
B1095
Underwood's Farm
Glassmoor Bank
Elm Farm
Yewtree Farm

7

Bedford Barn Farm
Conquest Dro
Farcet Fen
Crow Tree Farm
Kings Farm
Bevills Pasture
The Dro
Six Tree Farm

92

Bradford or Froghall Bridge
Frog Hall
Mill Farm
Tebbitt's Bridge
Pondersbridge
Ponders Bridge Farm

6

New or North Western Cut
Letall Farm
Middle Moor
Barn and Fourth Reach Farm

91

PE7
Elsie Farm
Oilmills Road

5

Whittlesey Mere
Engine Farm
The Herne
White House Farm
Middle Moor
Eastview Farm

90

New Long Drove
Tower Farm
Daintree Farm
Herne Road
Church Farm
Popla Farm

4

Old Decoy Farm
Daintree Road
Gore Common
Buck's Drove
Dentons Chase
Rorkes Drift Farm
Middle Moor
Oilmills Drove

89

Seynory Drove
River Nene (old course)
B1040
Ashbeach Farm
The Ashbeach Prim Sch
PE26

3

Holme Fen
Decoy Wood
New Decoy Farm
Stoke's Bridge
Herne Common
Ashbeach Dro
Clover Way
Poppy
Lion Cl
Middlemoor Road
Ramsey St Mary's
Middlemoor Farm
Jackson's Covert

88

Railway Covert
Holme Road
B660
Estelle Cl
1 Oak Wy
2 Bluebell Cl
3 Primrose Cl
4 Harebell Cl
Middle Moor

2

Halfway Farm
Long Drove
B660
Nightingale's Corner
Wellington House Farm
Ramsey St Mary's Bridge
Fenland Farm
Fisher Cl
Bank Farm
Lodes End Drove
Lodes End Drove
Green Hall Farm

87

Charterhouse Farm
Speed the Plough Bridge
CH
Ugg Mere
Ugg Mere Court Road
St Mary's Road
New Abey Farm
B1040
Foot Dro
Windpump

1

Ugg Mere Farm
Longlands Farm
New Fen
Poors Land
The Bill

86

Ray's Drove
White House Farm

22   23   24   25   26   27

A   B   C   D   E   F

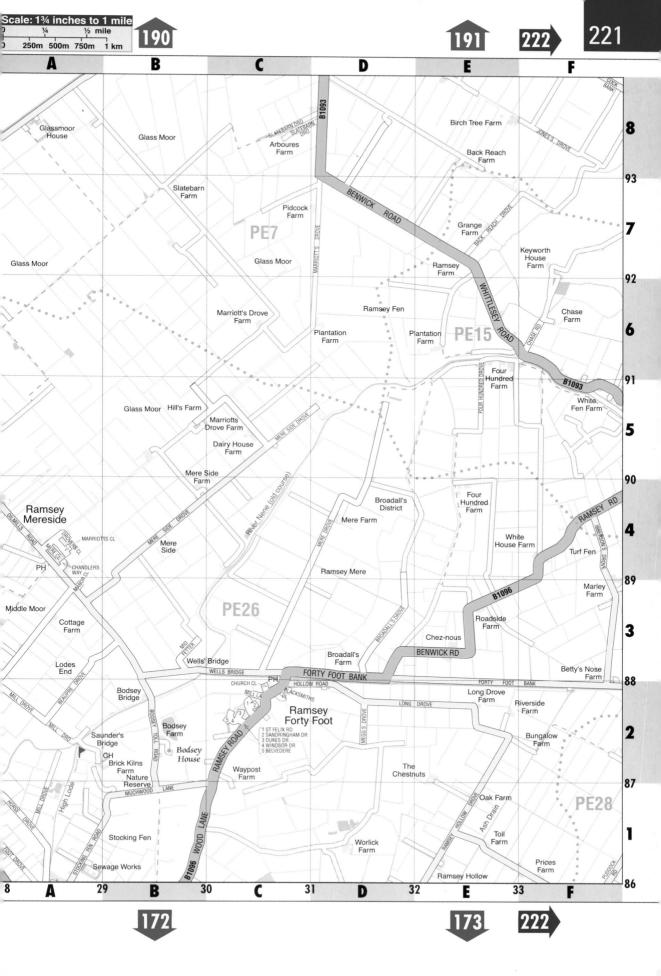

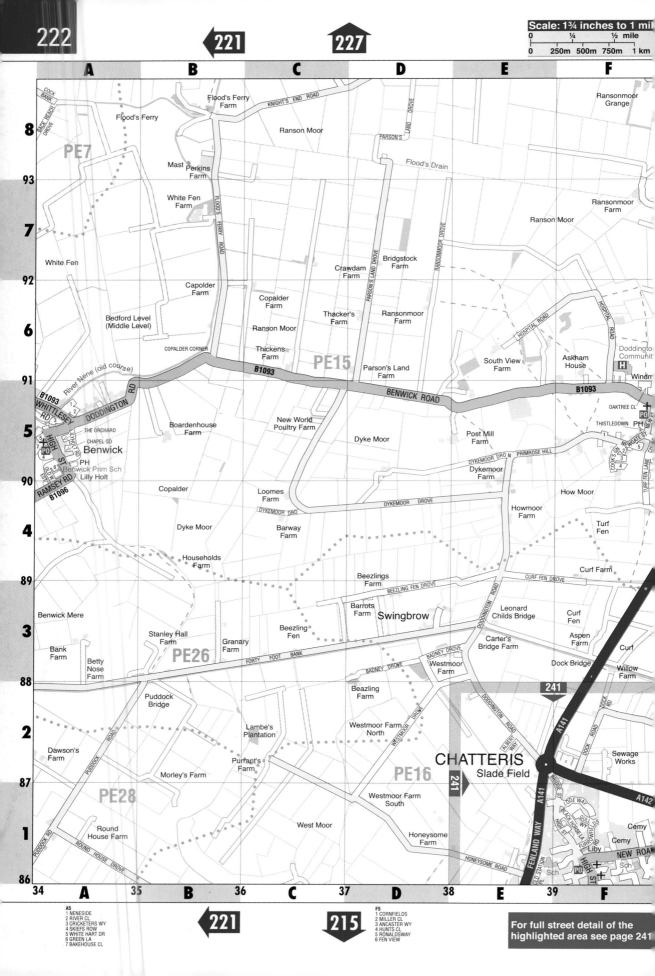

A   B   C   D   E   F

8   PE7
Flood's Ferry Farm
Flood's Ferry
KNIGHT'S END ROAD
Ranson Moor
Ransonmoor Grange
Mast
Perkins Farm
93
White Fen Farm
PARSON'S
Flood's Drain
Ransonmoor Farm
7
White Fen
Capolder Farm
Crawdam Farm
Bridgstock Farm
Ranson Moor
92
Copalder Farm
Thacker's Farm
Ransonmoor Farm
6
Bedford Level (Middle Level)
Ranson Moor
Thickens Farm
PE15
South View Farm
Askham House
Doddington Communi
H
COPALDER CORNER
Parson's Land Farm
91
River Nene (old course)
B1093
BENWICK ROAD
B1093
Windm
B1093
WHITTLESEY RD
DODDINGTON RD
Boardenhouse Farm
New World Poultry Farm
Post Mill Farm
OAKTREE CL
THISTLEDOWN
PH
5
THE ORCHARD
CHAPEL GD
Benwick
Dyke Moor
NEWGATE ST
HIGH ST
PH
Benwick Prim Sch
Lilly Holt
DYKEMOOR DRO N
PRIMROSE HILL
Dykemoor Farm
TURF FEN LANE
90
RAMSEY RD
B1096
Copalder
Loomes Farm
DYKEMOOR DRO
DYKEMOOR DROVE
Howmoor Farm
How Moor
4
Dyke Moor
Barway Farm
Turf Fen
Households Farm
Curf Farm
89
Beezlings Farm
BEEZLING FEN DROVE
CURF FEN DROVE
Benwick Mere
Barrots Farm
Swingbrow
Leonard Childs Bridge
Curf Fen
3
Stanley Hall Farm
Granary Farm
Beezling Fen
Carter's Bridge Farm
Aspen Farm
Curf
Bank Farm
PE26
FORTY FOOT BANK
DODDINGTON DROVE
Dock Bridge
Willow Farm
Betty Nose Farm
BADNEY DROVE
Westmoor Farm
88
Puddock Bridge
BADNEY DROVE
WESTMOOR DROVE
Beazling Farm
241
A141
2
Lambe's Plantation
Westmoor Farm North
DODDINGTON ROAD
ALBERT WAY
CHATTERIS
Slade Field
DOCK RD
Sewage Works
Dawson's Farm
PUDDOCK ROAD
Purfant's Farm
PE16
241
A141
A142
87
PE28
Morley's Farm
Westmoor Farm South
Cemy
1
Round House Farm
ROUND HOUSE DROVE
West Moor
Honeysome Farm
FENLAND WAY
Cemy
Liby
NEW ROA
HONEYSOME ROAD
OLD STATION
Sch
PO
HIGH ST
Sch
86
34   A   35   B   36   C   37   D   38   E   39   F

← 221   ↓ 215

A5
1 NENESIDE
2 RIVER CL
3 CRICKETERS WY
4 SKIEFS ROW
5 WHITE HART DR
6 GREEN LA
7 BAKEHOUSE CL

F5
1 CORNFIELDS
2 MILLER CL
3 ANCASTER WY
4 HUNTS CL
5 RONALDSWAY
6 FEN VIEW

For full street detail of the highlighted area see page 241

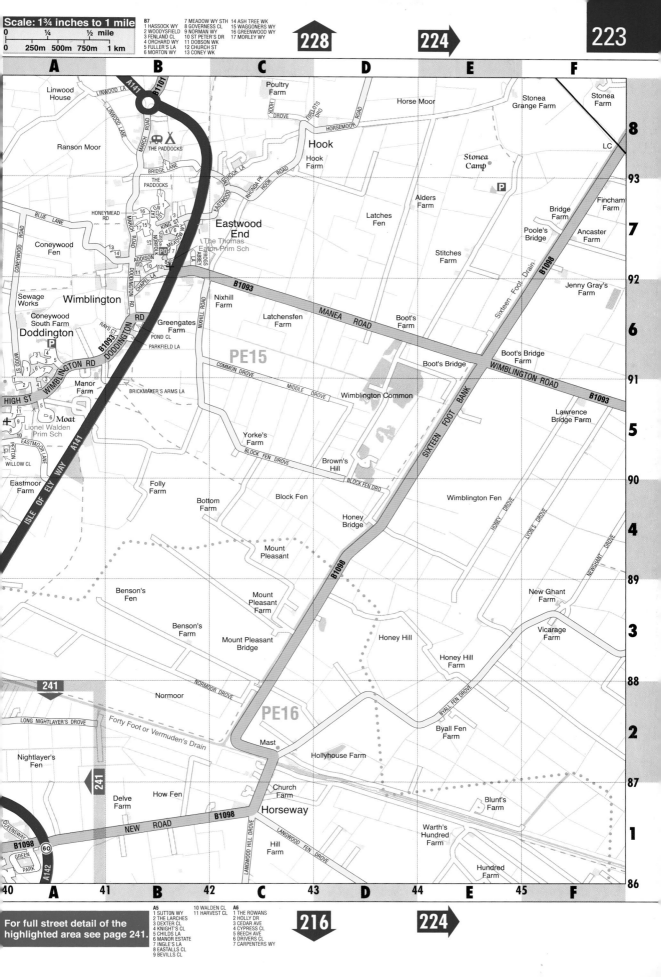

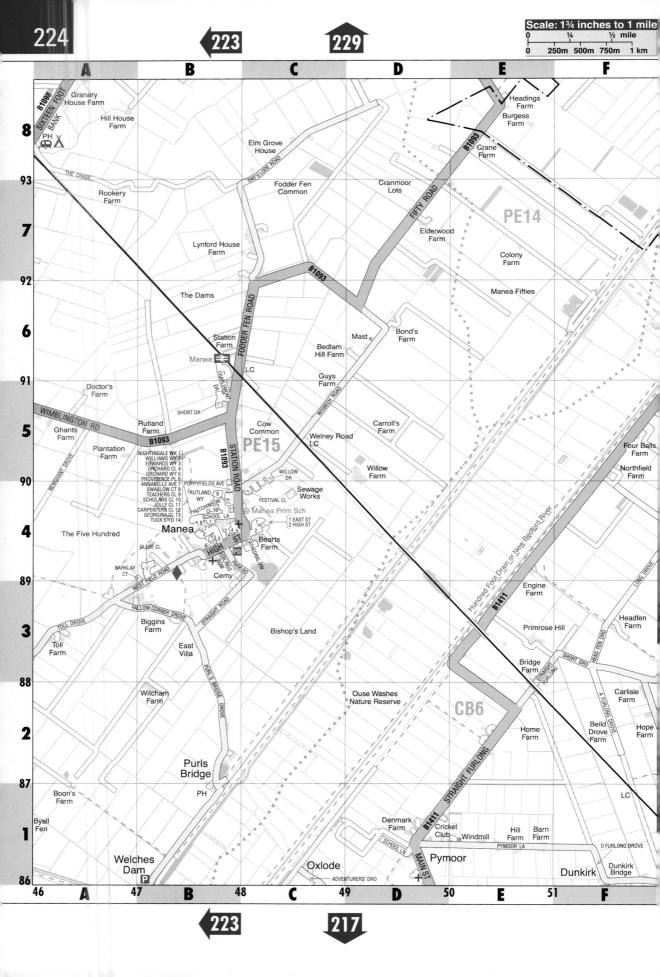

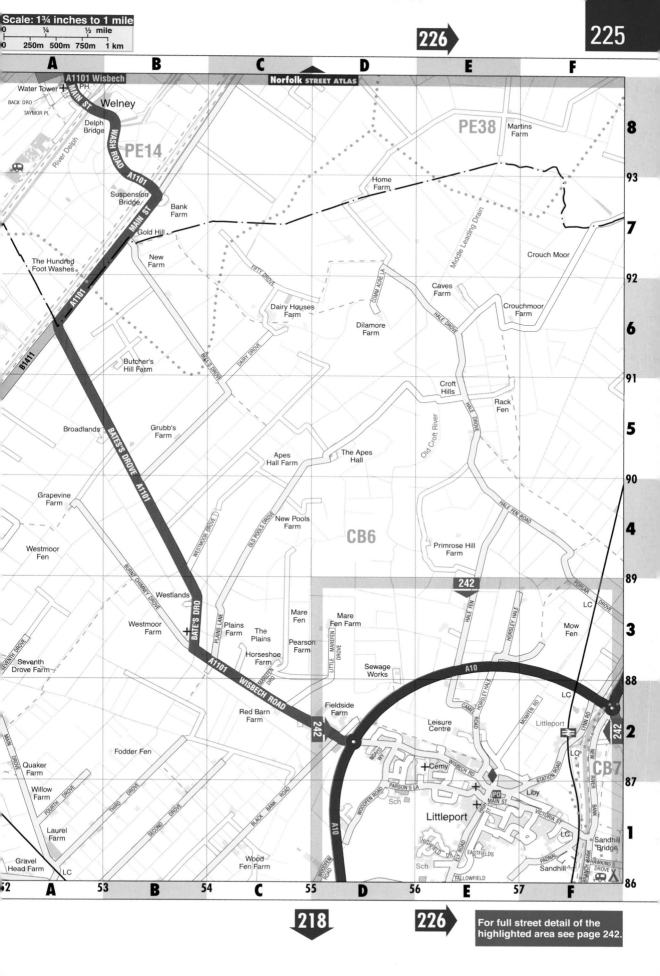

Scale: 1¾ inches to 1 mile

250m 500m 750m 1 km
¼ ½ mile

A B C D E F

Norfolk STREET ATLAS

A1101 Wisbech
Water Tower
BACK DRO
PH
TAYMOR PL
Welney
MAIN ST
Delph Bridge
WASH ROAD
PE14
River Delph
A1101
Suspension Bridge
MAIN ST
Bank Farm
Gold Hill
New Farm
The Hundred Foot Washes
B1411
A1101
FIFTY DROVE
Dairy Houses Farm
Dilamore Farm
COMM ACRE LA
Caves Farm
HALE DROVE
Crouch Moor
Crouchmoor Farm
Butcher's Hill Farm
BELL'S DROVE
DAIRY DROVE
Croft Hills
HALE DROVE
Rack Fen
Broadlands
BATE'S DROVE
A1101
Grubb's Farm
Old Croft River
Grapevine Farm
WESTMOOR DRIVE
Apes Hall Farm
The Apes Hall
HALE FEN ROAD
Westmoor Fen
BURNT CHIMNEY DRIVE
New Pools Farm
OLD POOLS DROVE
CB6
Primrose Hill Farm
PE38
Martins Farm
Home Farm
Middle Leading Drain

Westlands
Westmoor Farm
BATE'S DRO
PLAINS LANE
Plains Farm
The Plains
Horseshoe Farm
Mare Fen
Pearson Farm
Mare Fen Farm
LITTLE MAREFEN DROVE
Sewage Works
242
HALE FEN
HORSLEY HALE
Mow Fen
POPLAR DROVE
LC
A1101
WISBECH ROAD
MAREFEN DRO
242
Red Barn Farm
Fieldside Farm
A10
242
CAMEL ROAD
HORSLEY HALE
Littleport
MOWFEN RD
LC
NEW RIVER BANK
242
CB7
SEVENTH DROVE
Seventh Drove Farm
Fodder Fen
THIRD DROVE
FOURTH DROVE
Quaker Farm
Willow Farm
Laurel Farm
Gravel Head Farm
LC
SECOND DROVE
BLACK BANK ROAD
Wood Fen Farm
WOODFEN ROAD
A10
Leisure Centre
NOATS WY
Cemy
WISBECH RD
PARSON'S LA
Sch
PO
MAIN ST
Littleport
HIGHFIELD DR
ELY ROAD
EASTFIELDS
Sch
FALLOWFIELD
STATION ROAD
Liby
VICTORIA ST
LC
Sandhill Bridge
PADNAL
Sandhill
HAWKINS'S DROVE
BRANCH BANK

8
93
7
92
6
91
5
90
4
89
3
88
2
87
1
86

52 A 53 B 54 C 55 D 56 E 57 F

For full street detail of the highlighted area see page 242.

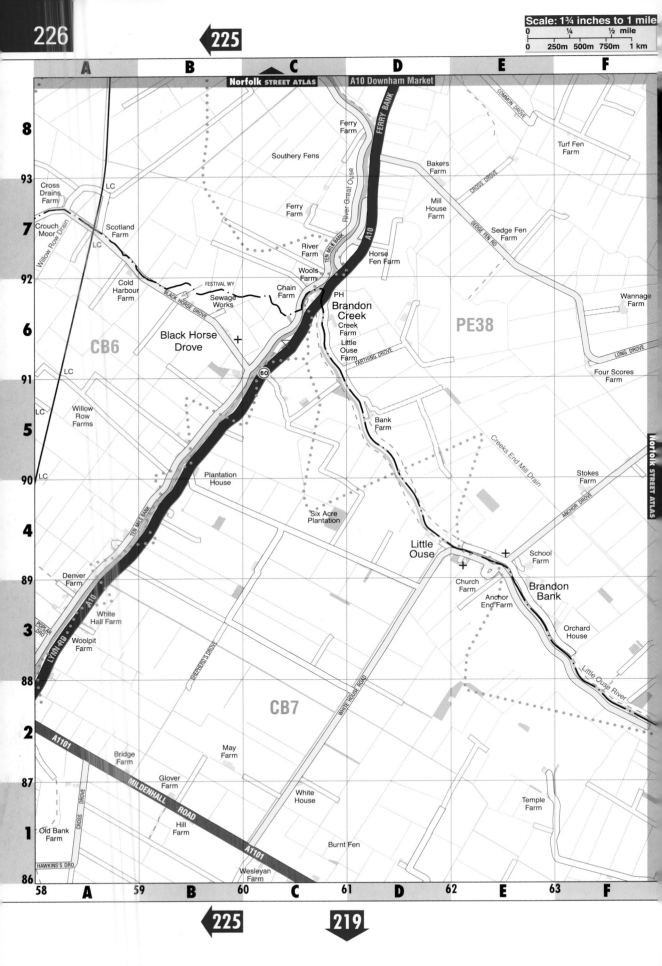

225

Scale: 1¾ inches to 1 mile

0   ¼   ½   mile
0   250m   500m   750m   1 km

Norfolk STREET ATLAS

A10 Downham Market

FERRY BANK

Ferry
Farm

Southery Fens

Bakers
Farm

Turf Fen
Farm

COMMON DROVE

Cross
Drains
Farm

LC

Crouch
Moor Drain

LC

Scotland
Farm

Ferry
Farm

River Great Ouse

Mill House
Farm

CROSS DROVE

SEDGE FEN RD

Sedge Fen
Farm

River
Farm

TEN MILE BANK

Cold
Harbour
Farm

FESTIVAL WY

Sewage
Works

Wools
Farm

Chain
Farm

PH

Brandon
Creek

Horse
Fen Farm

A10

Wannage
Farm

BLACK HORSE DROVE

Creek
Farm

Little
Ouse
Farm

PE38

CB6

Black Horse
Drove

✛

FARTHING DROVE

LONG DROVE

Four Scores
Farm

60

Willow
Row
Farms

LC

LC

Bank
Farm

Creeks End Mill Drain

Stokes
Farm

Plantation
House

TEN MILE BANK

ANCHOR DROVE

Six Acre
Plantation

Little
Ouse

School
Farm

Denver
Farm

A10

White
Hall Farm

SHEPHERD'S DROVE

WHITE HOUSE ROAD

Church
Farm

✛

✛

Anchor
End Farm

Brandon
Bank

POPLAR DRO

LYNN RD

Woolpit
Farm

Orchard
House

Little Ouse River

CB7

A1101

Bridge
Farm

May
Farm

MILDENHALL   ROAD

Glover
Farm

White
House

Temple
Farm

Old Bank
Farm

CROSS DROVE

Hill
Farm

A1101

Burnt Fen

HAWKINS'S DRO

Wesleyan
Farm

Norfolk STREET ATLAS

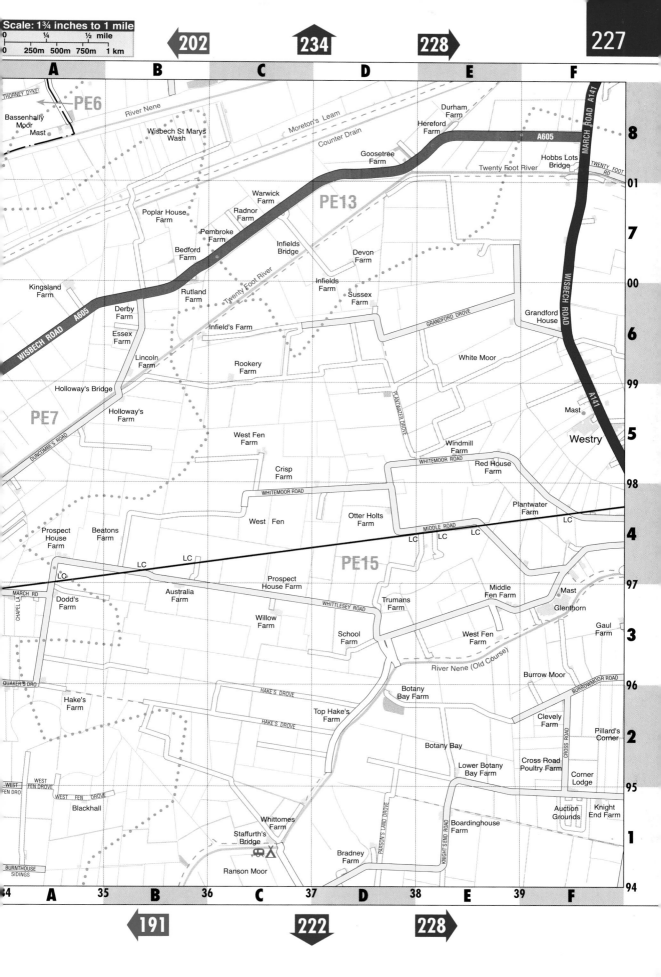

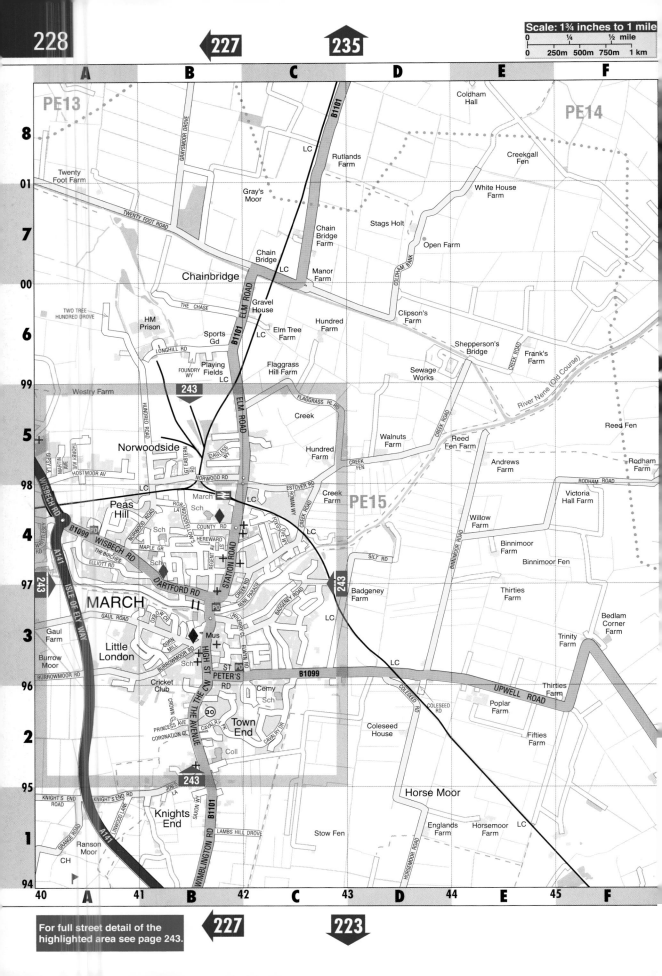

Scale: 1¾ inches to 1 mile
0   ¼   ½   mile
0   250m 500m 750m 1 km

Bottom
Laddus Farm
Laddus Fens
Laddus
Farm
Low Corner
Farm
Riverside
Farm
Low Corner
Farm
Low Nene
Farm
Old Nene
Farm
March Riverside
River Nene (Old Course)
March Riverside
Laddus Drive
Wests
Bridge
Pophams
Eau
Ivy House
Farm
Christchurch
Farm
Euximoor
House Farm
Euximoor Fen
Cherrytree
Farm
Ivy House
Farm
Euximoor Drive
Pear
Tree Farm
Bridge
Farm
PE14
Poulter's Drove
Iron Bridge
Crown
Farm
Ivy
House
Farm
B1098
Upwell Road
Well
Fen Farm
Rodham Road
Exmoor
Grange
Sixteen Foot Bank
Crown Road
Townley Prim Sch
Upwell Rd
PH
Christchurch
Green La
Chapel of Ease
Farm
Padgetts
Farm
Acorn
Farm
B1100
Church Road
PO
PH
The Limes
Scott's Rd
Pear
Tree Farm
Holme
Farm
1 CROWN RD
2 CROWN AV
3 FEN WY
Bedlam
Wheatsheaf Drove
Willow
Farm
Padgett's Road
Bedlam
Farm
Sixteen Foot Drain
Upwell Fen
PE15
B1099
Bedlam
Bridge
B1098
Mortimer
Farm
Stonebridge
Farm
Sparrow Hall
Farm
Darcey Lode
Fifty Road
Hole in the Wall
Farm
Poplar
Farm
Windmill
Farm
B1093
Thurland's Drove
School Rd
Baptist Road
Upwell
Prim Sch
Broad Dro
Green Road
New Road
A1101
Tointons Rd
Low Cottage
Farm
Workhouse La
Priory
Farm
Peartree
Farm
Plaw Field
Townsend Road
Barryke Bank
Dovecote Rd
Back Dro
The Chase
Croft Road
Croft House
Farm
B1098
Main Rd
PH
Three
Holes
Pophams
Eau
Grange
Farm
Fen
Farm
Squire's Drove
Euximoor
House Farm
Black
Sluice
Bridge
Paradise
Farm
Middle Level Main Drain
Cottons
Corner
Rosewood
Farm
Mud S.Armor Dro
Ralingham
Hall
Deptfords
Farm
Mudd's Drove
Mudd
Farm
Poulters
Farm
Lot's Bridge
B1094
Silt Road
Duffins
Farm
Flint Ho Rd
Norfolk Street Atlas
Primrose
Hall Farm
Halfpenny Toll Rd
Lotts
Bridge
Farm
Scotts
Farm
A1101
Small
Acre Farm
Poplar
Farm
Horsehead Drove
B1034
Beechwood
Farm
Old Croft River
Fir Tree
Farm
Grange
Farm
Cock Fen Road
Lakes
End
Wisbech Road
A1101 Littleport, A10
Chestnut
Farm
Pates
Farm
Croft
Farm
Wisbech Road
Tipps
End
Old Croft
Farm
Isle
Farm
Whitehall
Farm
B1100
March Road
Turf Lot Dro
Elder
Farm
Lakes

A B C D E F

8
01
7
00
6
99
5
98
4
97
3
96
2
95
1
94

6 47 48 49 50 51
A B C D E F

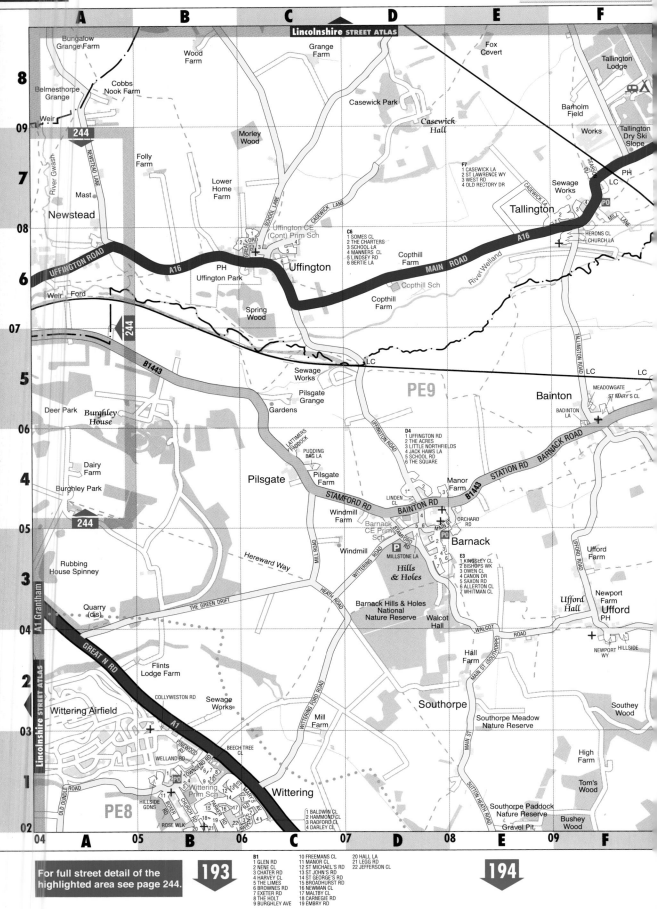

Scale: 1¾ inches to 1 mile

Lincolnshire STREET ATLAS

A B C D E F

8
Bungalow Grange Farm
Belmesthorpe Grange
Cobbs Nook Farm
Wood Farm
Grange Farm
Fox Covert
Tallington Lodge
Casewick Park
Barholm Fjeld
Tallington Dry Ski Slope

09
Weir
244
Morley Wood
Casewick Hall
Works
PH
LC

7
River Gwash
Mast
Folly Farm
Lower Home Farm
F7
1 CASEWICK LA
2 ST LAWRENCE WY
3 WEST RD
4 OLD RECTORY DR
Sewage Works
PO

08
Newstead
School Lane
Uffington CE (Cont) Prim Sch
Casewick Lane
C6
1 SOMES CL
2 THE CHARTERS
3 SCHOOL LA
4 MANNERS CL
5 LINDSEY RD
6 BERTIE LA
Tallington
A16 MAIN ROAD
HERONS CL
CHURCH LA

6
UFFINGTON ROAD
A16
PH
Uffington Park
Uffington
Copthill Farm
Copthill Sch
River Welland

07
Weir Ford
Spring Wood
Copthill Farm
LC
Tallington Road
LC
LC

5
B1443
Sewage Works
Pilsgate Grange Gardens
PE9
Bainton
MEADOWGATE
ST MARY'S CL

06
Deer Park
Burghley House
Lattimers Paddock
D4
1 UFFINGTON RD
2 THE ACRES
3 LITTLE NORTHFIELDS
4 JACK HAWS LA
5 SCHOOL RD
6 THE SQUARE
BADINTON LA

4
Dairy Farm
Burghley Park
Pudding Bag La
Pilsgate Farm
Pilsgate
Windmill Farm
Manor Farm
LINDEN CL
BAINTON RD
STATION RD
BARNACK ROAD
B1443
ORCHARD RD

05
244
Hereward Way
MILL RD
Windmill
Barnack CE Prim Sch
Millstone La
Barnack
E3
1 KINGSLEY CL
2 BISHOPS WK
3 OWEN CL
4 CANON DR
5 SAXON RD
6 ALLERTON CL
7 WHITMAN CL
UFFORD RD
Ufford Farm

3
Rubbing House Spinney
Quarry (dis)
THE GREEN DRIFT
HEATH ROAD
WITTERING ROAD
Hills & Holes
Barnack Hills & Holes National Nature Reserve
Walcot Hall
Ufford Hall
Newport Farm
Ufford
PH

04
A1 Grantham
GREAT N RD
WALCOT ROAD
NEWPORT WY
HILLSIDE

2
Lincolnshire STREET ATLAS
Flints Lodge Farm
COLLYWESTON RD
Sewage Works
A1
Hall Farm
Southorpe
Southorpe Meadow Nature Reserve
Southey Wood

03
Wittering Airfield
PINGWOOD AV
WELLAND RD
BEECH TREE CL
Mill Farm
WITTERING FORD ROAD
MAIN ST (SOUTHORPE)
SUTTON HEATH ROAD
High Farm

1
OLD OUNDLE ROAD
TOWNSEND RD
PO
Wittering Prim Sch
HILLSIDE GDNS
CHURCH RD
MARY'S AV
Wittering
1 BALDWIN CL
2 HAMMOND CL
3 RADFORD CL
4 DARLEY CL
Tom's Wood

02
PE8
ROSE WLK
Southorpe Paddock Nature Reserve
Gravel Pit
Bushey Wood

04 A 05 B 06 C 07 D 08 E 09 F

For full street detail of the highlighted area see page 244.

193 194

B1
1 GLEN RD
2 NENE CL
3 CHATER RD
4 HARVEY CL
5 THE LIMES
6 BROWNES RD
7 EXETER RD
8 THE HOLT
9 BURGHLEY AVE
10 FREEMANS CL
11 MANOR CL
12 ST MICHAEL'S RD
13 ST JOHN'S RD
14 ST GEORGE'S RD
15 BROADHURST RD
16 NEWMAN CL
17 MALTBY CL
18 CARNEGIE RD
19 EMBRY RD
20 HALL LA
21 LEGG RD
22 JEFFERSON CL

B8
1 ABBOTS DR
2 GLEBE GDNS
3 CORONATION AVE
4 CHAPEL ST
5 STRICKLANDS DR
6 ALDERLANDS CL
7 PENWALD CL
8 TATWIN DR
9 BECCELM DR

Scale: 1¾ inches to 1 mile
0   ¼   ½ mile
0   250m   500m   750m   1 km

A1073 Spalding (A16) **Lincolnshire** STREET ATLAS

C8
1 SNOWDON CL
2 CRAWFORD GDNS
3 KENNULPHS CL
4 HARRINGTON SQ

Crowland High Wash
Corporation Bank   Low Rd
Middle Rd
Crowland
Alderlands
Ashley's Barn
Plank Drove
Harvester Way
Crease Drove
Broadway
Low Rd
Monks Rd
Barbers Drove
Peterborough Road
A1073
Harrington Dr
Barbers Drove South
Barbers Drove
B1040
Green Drove
Sheppard's Drive
Empsons Farm
Old South Eau
Falls Bridge
Empsons Farm
Green Drove
South Eau Farm
Blue Bell Farm
Falls Drove
Blue Bell Bridge

Kennulph's Farm
Poplar Farm
Eardley Grange Farm
Wright's Drove
Speechley's Dro
Toll House Farm
Old Farm
Peterborough Road
A1073
Greenbank Farm
Vine House Farm
Hundreds Farm
Hundreds Road
Nene Terrace
St Vincent's Cross Farm
St Vincent's Cross
French Drove
Old Hall Farm
Bell Drove

Pepper Lake Farm
Horseshoe Bridge
Moor's Farm
Gray's Farm
Olympia Farm
Steam House Farm
Hill Farm
A1073
Singlesole Farm
Cross
B1040
Bennett's Pieces
Hangman's Corner

Flood Farm
B1443 Thorney Road
Hill Farm
Fletchers Farm
Mason's Bridge
Hurn Farm
Thorney Road
Crowland Rd
Powder Blue Farm
B1443
Bukehorn Road
Cat's Water Plantation
Little Tower's Fen
Singlecote Farm
Crowland Road
Lodge Farm
B1040
Buke Horn Farm
B1443
Buke Horn Plantation

Turves Farm
Elm Tree Farm
Oakhurst Farm
Northolm Farm
The Reaches
Cat's Water
Bedford Level (North Level)
Middle West Farm
Rose Farm
Great Towers Fen
Hightrees Farm
Windmill
A47
ASH CL 1
LAUREL DR 2
BERBERIS CL 3
ORCHARD CT 4
B1167 THE CSW
Abbe
Hous

Northam Cl
Newstead Cl
Eye Green
Turves Road
Northolme Coppice
Nipcot Road
Cat's Water Plantation
Catwater Farm
Causeway Toll Farm
The Causeway
Pode Hole Farm
Guys Fen
Toneham Farm
Toneham Lane
B1167

Eye Green Nature Reserve
Green Rd
PH
Pershore Wy
Eye Green Ind Est
Crowland Rd
Guilsborough Rd
A1073
Thorney Road
Hayne's Farm
Pasture House Farm
Willow Hall Lane
Chicell's Hurst
Hill Farm

Malmesbury Dr
Eye Road
A47
Liby
PO
PH
High St
Back Lane
Easby Ri
Thorney Road
Fountains Pl
Eye CE Prim Sch
Eye
1 ENFIELD CT
2 BEVERLEY CL
3 PIONEER WY
Bar Pastures
Bar Pasture Farm
Barlees Fen
Thorney River
Whittlesey Rd

Abbey Cl
The Cloisters
Peterborough Rd
Lindisfarne Rd
The Little Cl
Sand & Gravel Pit

PE6

A1
1 BEAULIEU CT
2 HODNEY RD
3 TINTERN RI
4 MOORE'S LA
5 ST BENET'S GDNS
6 CHANCERY LA
7 BEECH LA
8 IXWORTH CL
9 DELAPRE CT
10 WALSINGHAM WY
11 GLASTONBURY CL
12 CARTMEL WY
13 DEERHURST WY
14 BOXGROVE CL
15 NEW RD
16 WESTMINSTER GDNS
17 MONKS DR
18 ST BEE'S DR
19 ST OLAVE'S DR
20 ST ALBAN'S DR
21 WESTMINSTER GDNS

Scale: 1¾ inches to 1 mile

0 ¼ ½ mile
0 250m 500m 750m 1 km

Lincolnshire STREET ATLAS

A B C D E F

North Fen

Avenue Farm

North Fen

OLD S EAU BANK
WEST DROVE
STATION ROAD
B1166

LORDSHIP END
B1166

8

New South Eau

Gothic House Farm

Sycamore Farm

FRENCH DROVE B1167

Lordship End

LITTLEWORTH DRO
Allens Bridge
COMMON ROAD

09

North Fen

Portsand Farm

New Cut Bridge

New Cut

Malice Farm

PE12

7

French Farm

FRENCH DROVE

Grange Farm

Chestnuts Farm

Lodge Farm

08

GREEN DROVE

Gold Dike

6

Green Drove Farm

Wrydelands Farm

ARCHERS DROVE

Gold Dike Farm

07

Morris Fen

Archer's Drove Farm

Wryde Croft

SOULDING DROVE

PE6

5

Lodge Farm

BLACK DROVE

Priests Farm

English Drove Farm

NEW CUT

Nutsgrove Farm

06

Elder House Farm

CH

ENGLISH DROVE

Wryde Plantation

4

Little House Farm

White Hart Farm

Desford Farm

Fish Fen

WALLACE'S DROVE

05

Lime Tree Farm

Sewage Works

A47

Mast

East Wryde Farm

B1167

Little Knarr Fen

Thorney
Thorney Heritage Mus

Duke of Bedford Prim Sch

Duke's Head Farm

Pigeons' Farm

WISBECH ROAD

Knarr Farm

A47

04

KINGSLINE
STATION RD
GAS
30
Liby
PO
WHITTLESEY RD

Park Farm

WISBECH ROAD

B1167

Corner Farm

Rattlerow Farm

2

High Lands

ASHLEY
POOL LA

Cemy
ST BOTOLPH'S WY 1
ST MARY'S CL 2
ST PETER'S WY 3

North Farm

Knarr Corner Farm

DAIRY DROVE

Glass House Farm

KNARR FEN ROAD

03

B1040

South Farm

West Corner Farm

OLD KNARR FEN DROVE

Upper Knarr Fen

Lower Knarr Fen

1

Hill Plantation

02

A3
1 CHESTNUT DR
2 BEECH CL
3 THE MALTINGS
4 ABBEY PL
5 CHURCH ST
6 THE GREEN
7 RUSSEL CL
8 TAVISTOCK CL
9 TOPHAM CRES

10 BEDFORD CT

1 PARK CL
2 SMITHFIELD

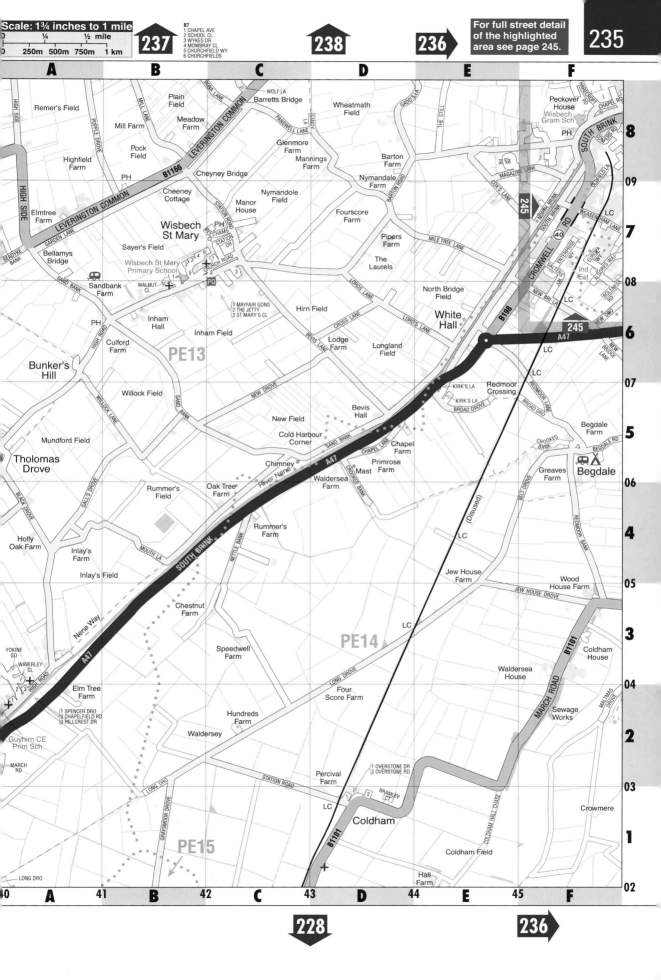

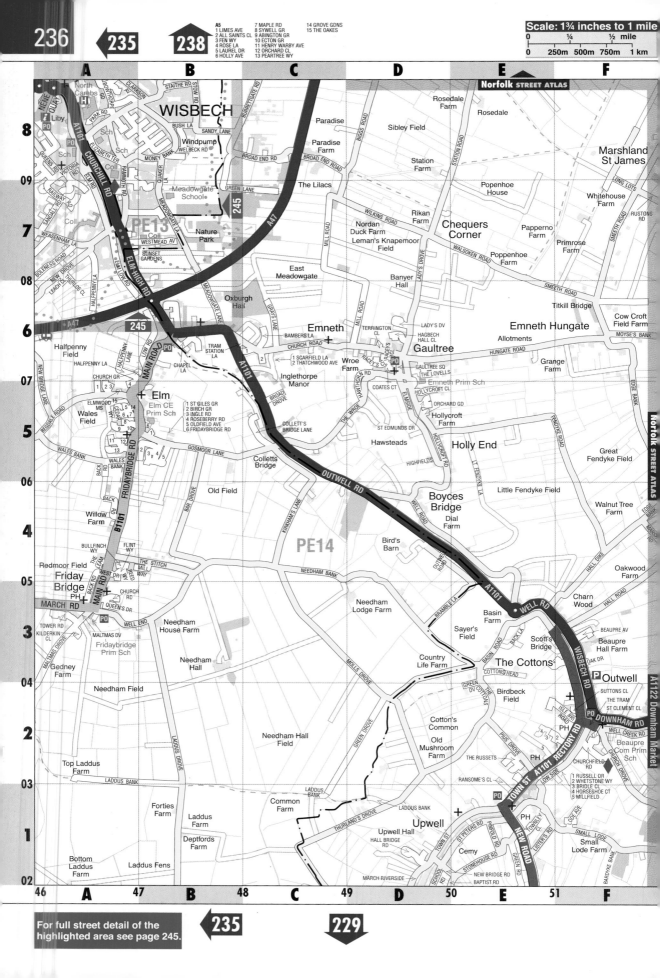

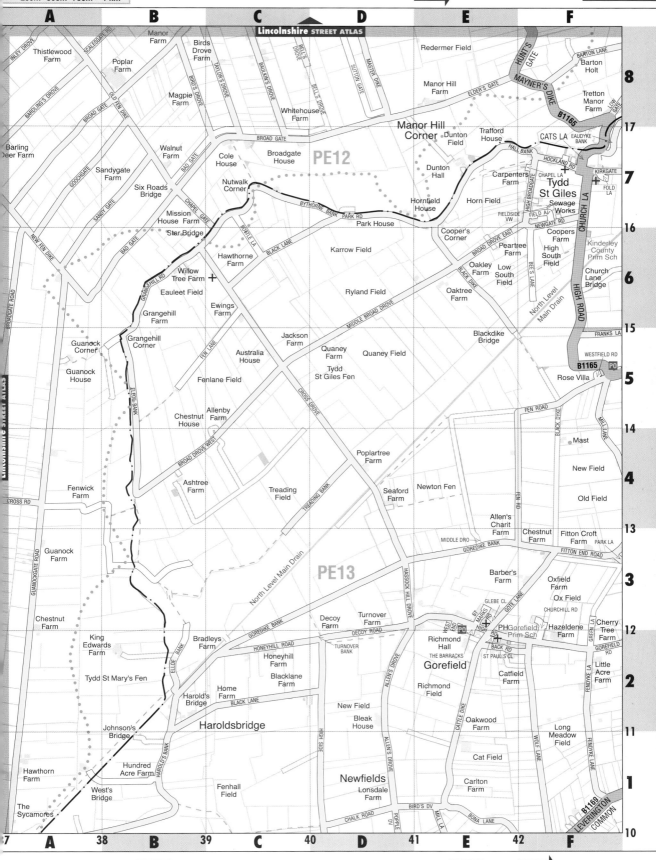

Lincolnshire STREET ATLAS

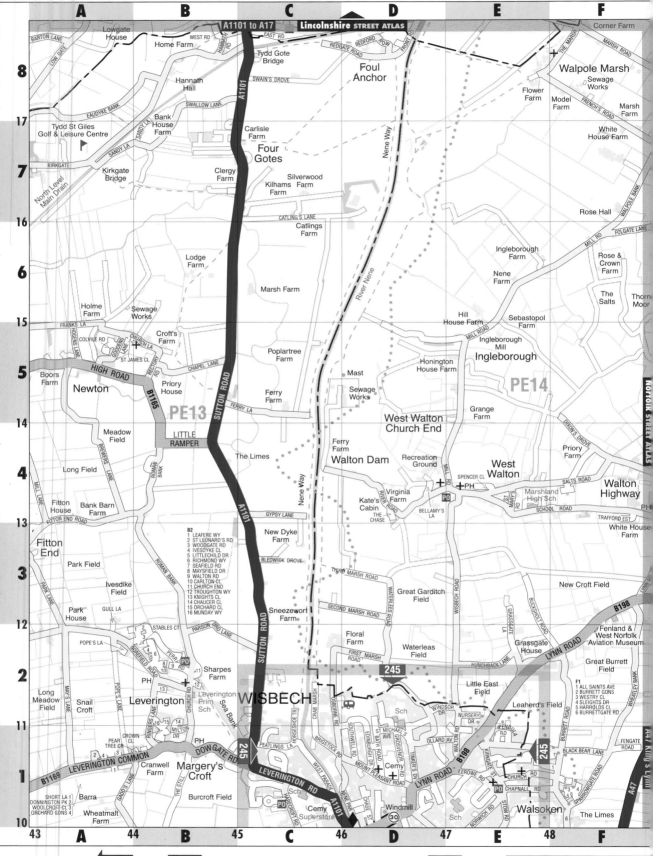

Lincolnshire STREET ATLAS

A1101 to A17

PE13

PE14

Norfolk STREET ATLAS

For full street detail of the highlighted area see page 245

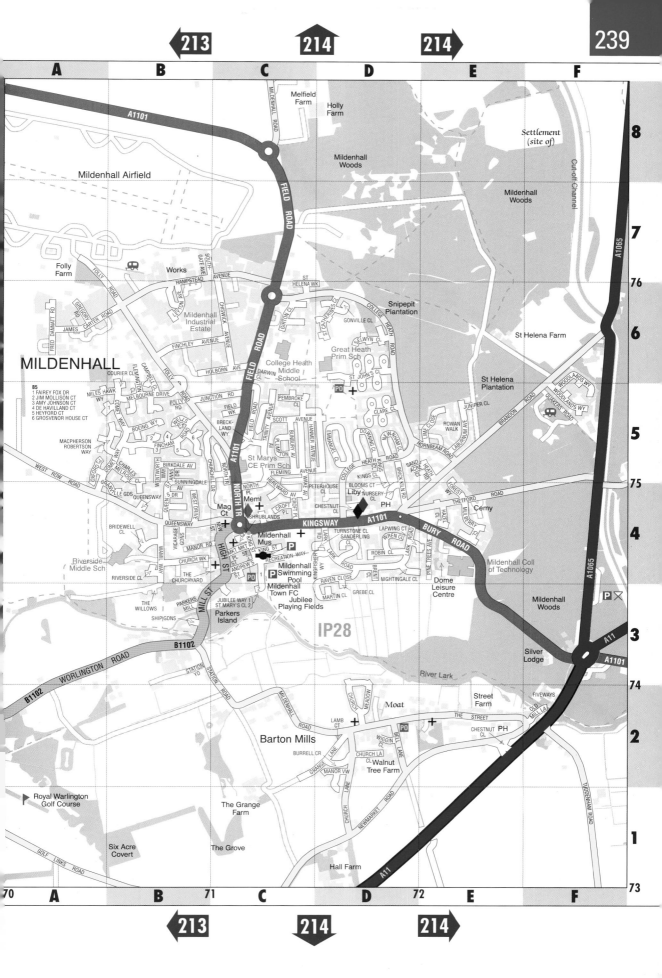

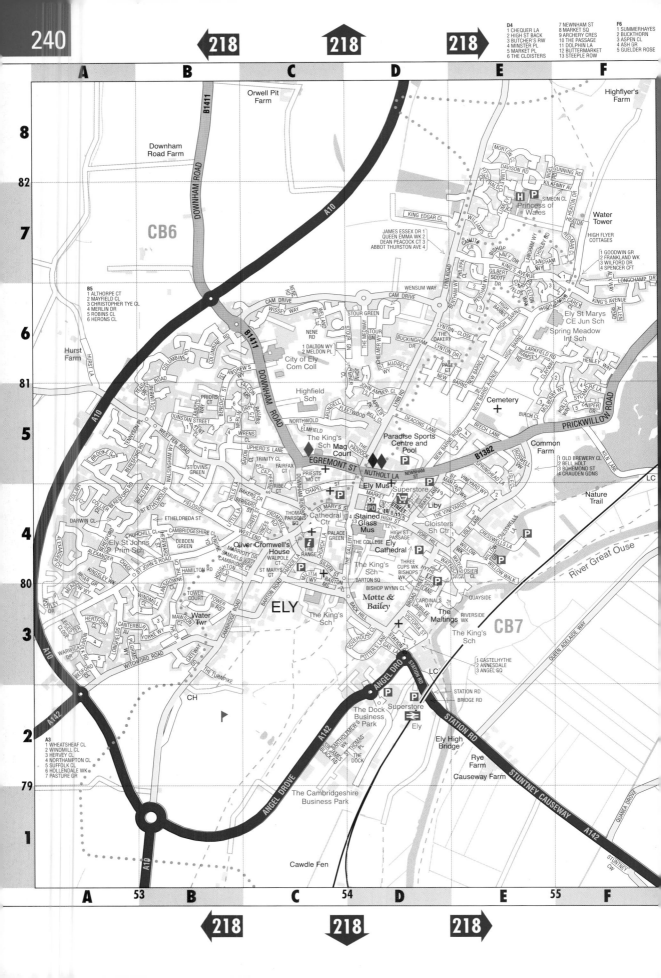

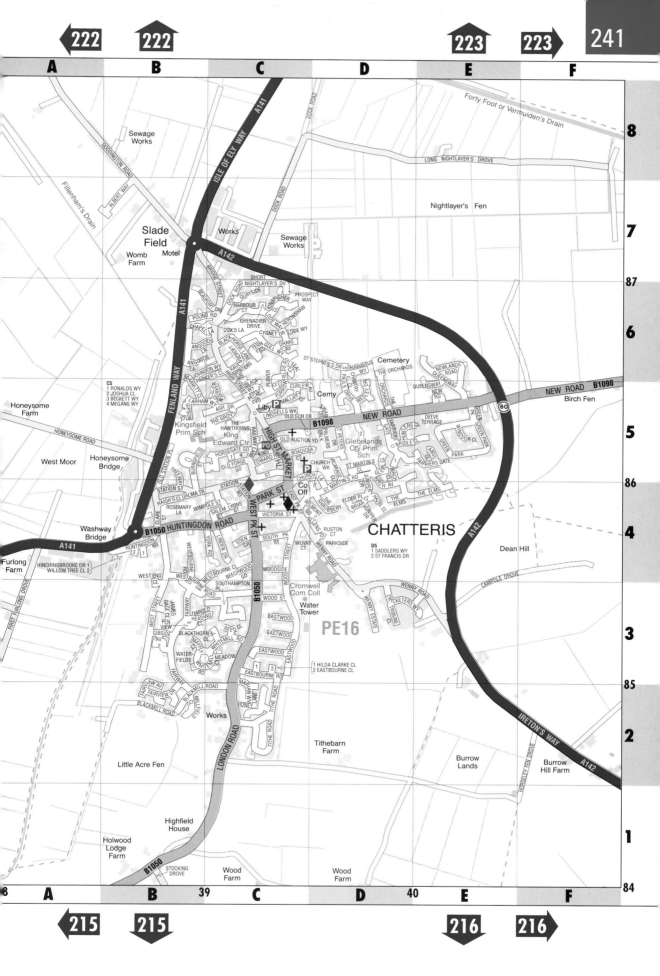

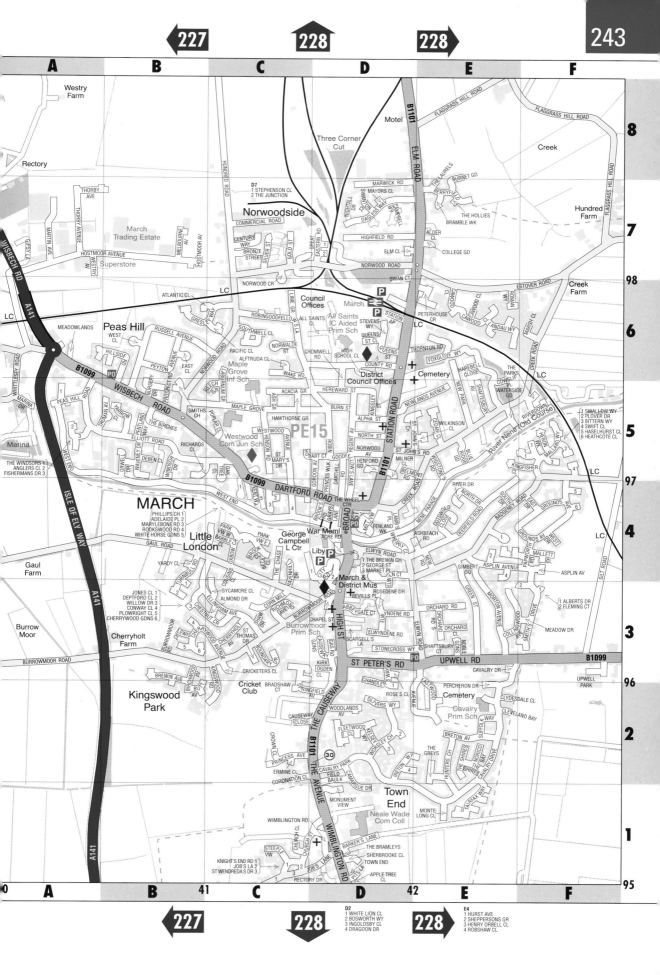

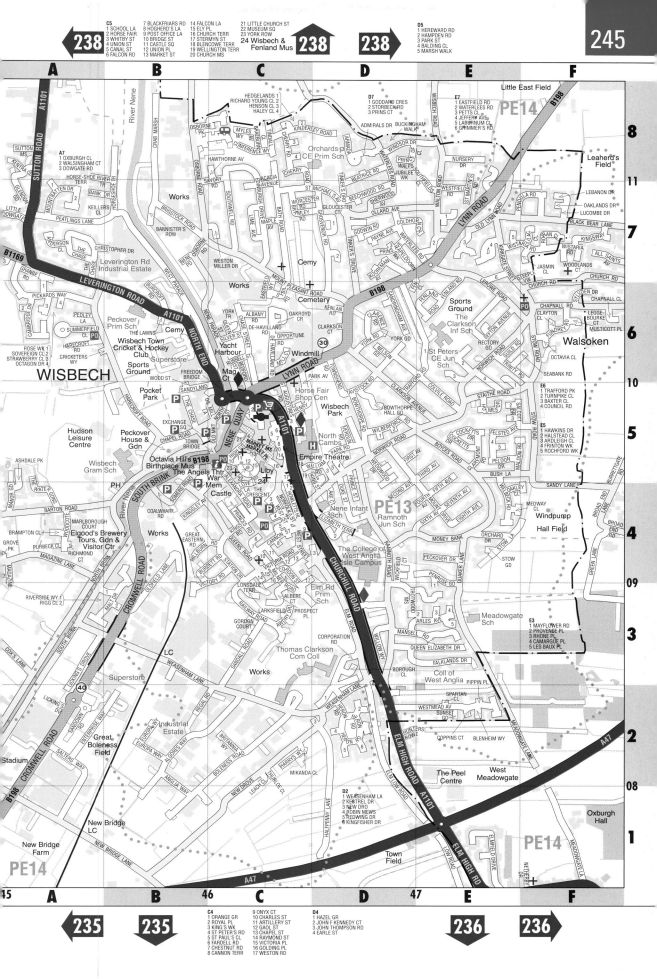

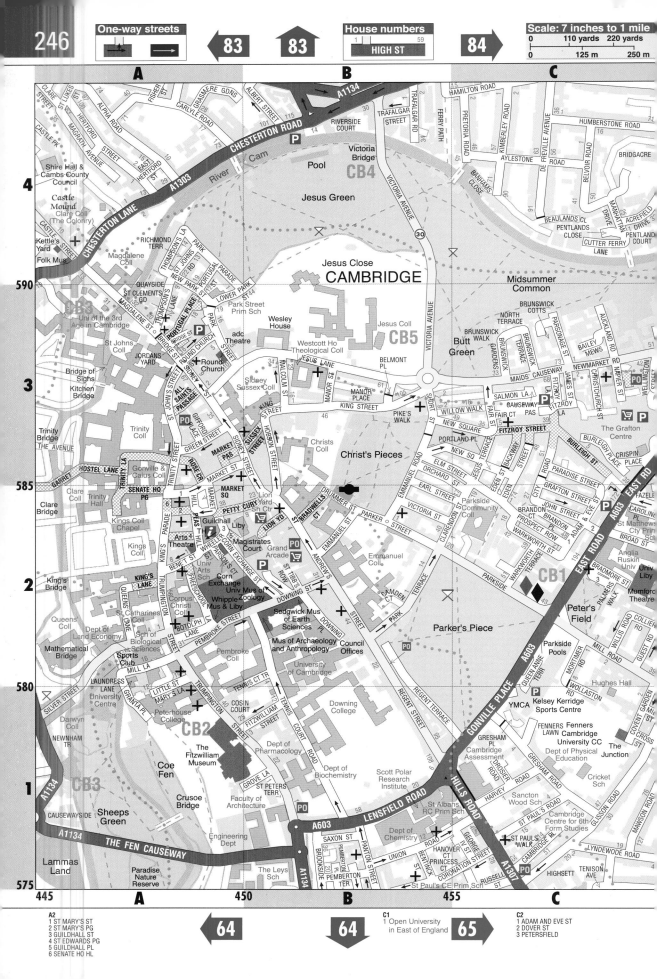

Index

Place name May be abbreviated on the map

Location number Present when a number indicates the place's position in a crowded area of mapping

Locality, town or village Shown when more than one place has the same name

Postcode district District for the indexed place

Page and grid square Page number and grid reference for the standard mapping

Church Rd **6** Beckenham BR2..........**53** C6

Cities, towns and villages are listed in CAPITAL LETTERS

Public and commercial buildings are highlighted in magenta **Places of interest** are highlighted in blue with a star★

Abbreviations used in the index

Acad	**Academy**	Comm	**Common**	Gd	**Ground**	L	**Leisure**	Prom	**Promenade**
App	**Approach**	Cott	**Cottage**	Gdn	**Garden**	La	**Lane**	Rd	**Road**
Arc	**Arcade**	Cres	**Crescent**	Gn	**Green**	Liby	**Library**	Recn	**Recreation**
Ave	**Avenue**	Cswy	**Causeway**	Gr	**Grove**	Mdw	**Meadow**	Ret	**Retail**
Bglw	**Bungalow**	Ct	**Court**	H	**Hall**	Meml	**Memorial**	Sh	**Shopping**
Bldg	**Building**	Ctr	**Centre**	Ho	**House**	Mkt	**Market**	Sq	**Square**
Bsns, Bus	**Business**	Ctry	**Country**	Hospl	**Hospital**	Mus	**Museum**	St	**Street**
Bvd	**Boulevard**	Cty	**County**	HQ	**Headquarters**	Orch	**Orchard**	Sta	**Station**
Cath	**Cathedral**	Dr	**Drive**	Hts	**Heights**	Pal	**Palace**	Terr	**Terrace**
Cir	**Circus**	Dro	**Drove**	Ind	**Industrial**	Par	**Parade**	TH	**Town Hall**
Cl	**Close**	Ed	**Education**	Inst	**Institute**	Pas	**Passage**	Univ	**University**
Cnr	**Corner**	Emb	**Embankment**	Int	**International**	Pk	**Park**	Wk, Wlk	**Walk**
Coll	**College**	Est	**Estate**	Intc	**Interchange**	Pl	**Place**	Wr	**Water**
Com	**Community**	Ex	**Exhibition**	Junc	**Junction**	Prec	**Precinct**	Yd	**Yard**

Index of towns, villages, streets, hospitals, industrial estates, railway stations, schools, shopping centres, universities and places of interest

A

Abbey Cl
Burwell CB25............**130** B1
Eye PE6 ....**232** A1
Sawtry PE28 ....**168** B4
Abbey Coll PE26 ....**172** C7
Abbey Coll Cambridge 3
CB1................**64** F7
Abbey Fields PE26 ....**172** C7
Abbeygate Ct PE15....**243** D3
Abbey La
Lode CB25 ....**107** C2
Swaffham Bulbeck CB25..**108** B3
Abbey Meadows Com Sch
CB5................**84** D2
Abbey Pl
4 Thorney PE6........**233** A3
Waterbeach CB25 ......**127** B1
Abbey Rd
Cambridge CB5 ......**84** A3
Peterborough PE4........**204** C3
Ramsey PE26............**172** C6
Abbey Rooms La PE26..**172** B6
Abbey St
Cambridge CB1 ......**84** A2
Ickleton CB10 ....**17** F3
Abbey Way PE7........**189** C7
Abbey Wlk CB1........**84** A2
Abbotsbury PE2........**186** A3
Abbots Cl
Cambridge CB4 ......**83** E7
Hemingford Abbots PE28 ..**142** F3
Ramsey PE26............**172** C7
Abbot's Cl PE28........**155** A5
Abbots Cres PE27 ......**144** A6
Abbots Dr 1 PE6 ......**232** B8
ABBOTSLEY........**57** C5
Abbotsley Rd PE19 ......**57** E8
Abbotsmede Prim Com Sch
PE1................**198** C4
ABBOTS RIPTON........**162** C1
Abbots Ripton CE Prim Sch
PE28................**162** C1
Abbots Way
Ely CB6 ....**240** B5
Horningsea CB25........**106** A1
Abbott Cl PE28............**146** C4
Abbot Thurston Ave CB6 **240** E6
Abbotts Cl SG8 ....**12** A2
Abbott's Cl PE9............**244** D4
Abbotts Ct 2 CB9........**24** E5

Abbotts Gr PE4 ....**204** B6
Abbott's Grove Cotts CB9. **24** F3
Abbotts Rd CB9.........**39** A1
Abbot Way PE7 ....**181** D4
Abercorn Ct CB9.........**23** F6
Abercorn Pl 6 CB4 ......**83** E8
Abington Gr 6 PE14 ....**236** A5
ABINGTON PIGGOTS...**11** E5
Abington Pl CB9 ....**39** A1
Abington Rd SG8 ....**11** F2
Aboyne Ave PE2 ......**185** F5
Abrahams Cl CB25 ......**105** D6
Abram's La SG8........**8** C4
Acacia Ave
Peterborough PE1.......**198** B8
St Ives PE27 ....**143** E6
Wisbech PE13 ....**245** C8
Acacia Gr
March PE15 ....**243** C5
St Neots PE19 ....**75** A6
Acer Rd PE1............**198** B6
Acheson Rd PE28........**117** B8
Ackerman Gdns 4 PE19..**74** C2
Ackerman St PE19 ......**74** C2
Ackroyd Rd 2 SG8........**5** E8
Acland St PE1............**197** F3
Acorn Ave CB23..........**102** C4
Acorn La CB23 ....**79** C4
Acrefield Dr CB4........**246** C4
Acremead PE8............**178** A3
Acre Rd
Carlton CB8 ....**55** B8
March PE15 ....**243** D4
Acre The 2 PE9 ....**230** D4
Acre The 2............**150** F4
Acton Way CB4 ....**83** D5
Adam & Eve St 1 CB1...**246** C1
Adam's La PE19..........**96** E4
Adams Rd
Cambridge CB3 ....**83** B2
Swaffham Prior CB25 ...**108** D5
Adastral Cl CB8............**110** E4
adc Theatre★ CB1 .....**246** A3
Addenbrookes Hospl CB2 **65** A3
Adderley PE3............**197** C7
Addington Way 1 PE4 . **204** C3
Addington Wlk 6 PE19...**74** C2
Addison Rd PE15........**223** B7
Adelaide Cl 10 CB7......**212** B4
Adelaide Pl PE15........**243** C4
Adelaide St PE9........**244** C5

Adelaide Wlk PE28......**208** E6
Admirals Dr PE13 ......**245** D8
Admirals Way PE19......**74** A2
Adventurers' Dro CB6...**224** C1
A Furlong Dro CB6......**224** F2
AILSWORTH........**195** D3
Ailwine Rd PE26 ......**171** B2
Aingers Rd CB24........**104** B4
Ainsdale CB1 ....**65** F5
Ainsdale Dr PE4 ......**204** B4
Ainsworth Ct 4 CB1....**84** A1
Ainsworth Pl CB1........**84** B1
Ainsworth St CB1 ......**84** A1
Aintree Rd SG8...........**5** F6
Airedale Cl PE1 ......**198** A6
Airedale Rd 1 PE9......**244** A4
Airport Way PE1........**85** B2
Akeman Cl CB6........**210** F6
Akeman St
Cambridge CB4 ....**83** C5
Landbeach CB25 ......**105** C6
Akerly Dr CB23..........**79** A4
Alamein Ct PE19 ......**74** C5
Albany Rd PE13........**245** C6
Albany Wlk PE2........**186** D7
Alba Rd PE7 ....**186** B2
Albemarle Rd PE27.....**143** F7
Albemarle Way CB4.....**83** E7
Alberta Cres PE29.....**141** E6
Albert Ct PE13 ....**245** C3
Albert Pl PE3 ....**197** F1
Albert Rd
Stamford PE9.........**244** C5
Stow cum Quy CB25 ...**86** A5
Albert's Dr PE15 ......**243** F3
Albert St CB4............**246** B4
Albert Way PE16........**241** B7
Albion Row 6 CB3......**83** C3
Albion Yd 5 CB3 ......**83** C3
ALCONBURY........**150** E4
Alconbury CE Prim Sch
PE28................**150** F5
Alconbury Cl PE2 ......**187** C3
ALCONBURY WESTON..**150** D6
Alder Cl
1 Eaton Socon PE19 ...**74** B5
January PE15 ....**243** E7
Alder Rd CB9............**39** A1
Alder Dr
Bourn CB23............**79** C3
Huntingdon PE29........**141** D6
Alderlands PE6 ....**232** B8

Alderlands Cl 6 PE6....**232** B8
Alderman Jacobs Prim Sch
PE7................**189** F8
Alderman's Dr PE3......**197** E3
Alder Rd PE7 ....**186** C3
Alderton Cl CB9........**38** E2
Aldham Ct 12 CB9......**23** E7
Aldous Ct SG8 ....**15** E8
ALDRETH........**209** E4
Aldreth Rd CB6........**209** F5
Aldsworth Cl PE1......**198** D6
Alec Rolph Cl CB21......**66** D5
Alexander Chase CB6...**240** A4
Alexander Rd SG19.....**25** B4
Alexandra Rd
Littleport CB6 ....**242** E4
Peterborough PE1.......**197** F6
Stamford PE9..........**244** B6
Wisbech PE13 ....**245** C5
Alex Wood Rd CB4......**83** E6
Alfric Sq PE2 ....**186** D6
Alftruda Cl PE15........**243** C6
Algar Dr CB8 ....**70** F8
Algores Way PE13.....**245** B2
Alington Rd PE19 ......**74** E1
Aliwal Rd PE7..........**189** E3
Alix Way CB7 ....**240** F7
Allan Ave PE2 ....**187** E5
Allard Cl PE2............**181** D6
Allen Ct CB2 ....**64** D2
Allen Farm Cl PE29.....**141** E1
Allen Rd
Ely CB6 ....**240** F6
Peterborough PE1.......**197** E6
Ramsey PE26 ....**171** F7
Allens Cl CB23 ....**63** B4
Allen's Dro PE13......**237** D1
Allen's Orch PE28......**140** E1
Allens Yd PE16.........**241** D4
Allerton Cl 6 PE9......**230** D3
Allerton Garth PE7.....**185** A4
Allexton Gdns 3 PE1...**198** D7
Alley The CB8............**90** A2
Allington Wlk CB9 ......**23** E8
Allotment La PE5 ......**195** E2
Allotments Dro CB6.....**211** B7
All Saints Ave PE13.....**245** F7
All Saints CE Prim Sch
CB8................**111** B3
All Saints Cl
January PE15 ....**243** D6
St Ives PE27 ....**144** A6
2 Wisbech PE14........**236** A5

All Saints Gn PE27 ......**144** A6
All Saints IC Aided Prim Sch
PE15................**243** D6
All Saints Jun Sch PE1...**198** A6
All Saints Mews 10 PE9..**244** B5
All Saints Pas
Cambridge CB2 ....**246** A3
6 Huntingdon PE28......**141** D4
All Saints' Pl 12 PE9....**244** B5
All Saints Rd
Fulbourn CB21..........**66** F5
Newmarket CB8.........**111** A3
Peterborough PE1.......**198** A5
All Saints' St PE9 ......**244** B5
All Saints Way PE28.....**168** C4
All Saints Wlk IP28 .....**213** F4
All Souls La CB3 ....**83** B4
Alma Rd PE1............**197** F5
Alma Terr PE16..........**241** B4
Almond Cl PE29.........**142** A1
Almond Dr PE15 ......**243** C3
Almond Gr CB23 ......**102** C4
Almond Rd
Peterborough PE1.......**198** B7
St Neots PE19 ....**74** F6
Almoners' Ave CB1......**65** C3
Almoners La PE3........**197** E3
Alms Ct PE29 ....**141** C7
Alms Hill CB23..........**60** D7
Alms La SG7 ....**2** D4
Alnwick Ct 1 PE19......**74** C7
Alpha La PE28 ....**151** E3
Alpha Rd CB4...........**246** A4
Alpha St PE9 ....**244** C5
Alpha Terr CB2 ....**64** D3
Alstead Rd CB24 ......**104** B5
Alsyke Cl PE28..........**116** A7
Althorpe Ct 1 CB6......**240** B5
Alvis Dr PE7............**181** D6
ALWALTON........**185** B4
Alwin Cl PE28..........**168** B3
Alwyn Cl PE27 ....**144** B6
Alwyne Rd CB1..........**65** C2
Amanda Ct PE3 ......**197** E2
Amber Ctr PE29..........**141** F6
Amberley Slope PE4....**204** C3
Ambleside Gdns PE4.....**204** D3
Ambrose Way CB24.....**104** C4
Ambury Hill PE29.......**141** E5
Ambury Rd PE29 ......**141** D5

Ambury Road S PE29 .... 141 D5
Ambuscade Rd PE19 .... 74 C1
Amcotts CB23 .... 60 B8
American Air Mus★ CB22 16 F8
American La PE29 .... 141 E5
America The CB6 .... 216 D1
Amwell Rd CB4 .... 83 F8
Amy Johnson Ct [3] IP28. 239 B5
Ancaster Rd [2] PE9 ...... 244 A7
Ancaster Way
  Cambridge CB1 .... 65 D7
  [3] Doddington/Wimblington
  PE15 .... 222 F5
Anchor Ct
  Littleport CB6 .... 242 E3
  Peterborough PE4 ...... 205 F1
Anchor Dro PE38 .... 226 F4
Anchor La CB25 .... 130 B4
Anderson Cl PE13 .... 245 A7
Anderson Cres PE29 .... 142 A2
Anderson Rd
  Boxworth CB8 .... 101 D8
  Swavesey CB24 .... 122 D1
Andrea Cl PE5 .... 187 C6
Andrew Cl PE5 .... 195 D2
Andrew's Cl PE7 .... 187 B1
Andrew Rd
  Newmarket CB8 .... 110 E5
  [1] Stamford PE9 .... 244 B6
  St Neots PE19 .... 74 F2
Andrews Cl [2] CB6 ...... 210 F5
Andrews Cres PE4 ..... 204 F2
Angel Dro CB7 .... 240 D2
Angell's Mdw SG7 ...... 2 D4
Angel Sq CB7 .... 240 D3
Angle End CB21 .... 67 F8
Angle La SG8 .... 29 E5
Anglers Cl PE15 .... 243 A5
Anglers Way CB4 ...... 84 C5
Anglesey Abbey (& remains
  of Priory)★ CB25 ..... 107 B1
Anglesey Way [8] PE4 .. 208 D1
Angles Theatre The★
  PE13 .... 245 C5
Anglian Bsns Pk SG8 .....5 E3
Anglian [1] PE13 .... 187 D6
Anglia Way PE13 .... 245 B2
Anglia Ruskin Univ CB1. 246 C2
Angoods La PE16 .... 241 B6
Angus Cl [2] CB1 .... 65 A8
Angus Ct PE3 .... 197 D3
Annabelle Ave PE15 .... 224 B4
Anne Rd PE9 .... 244 A6
Anne's Cl CB8 .... 110 B8
Annesdale CB7 .... 240 D3
Annesley CB1 .... 65 E5
Annesley Cl PE28 ...... 168 B4
Annington Cres SG8 .... 13 A8
Ann's Rd CB5 .... 84 E4
Ansley Way PE27 .... 143 E5
Anson Cl PE26 .... 171 E3
Anson Dr PE27 .... 143 F6
Anson Pl PE19 .... 74 A2
Anstey Way CB2 .... 64 D2
Antelope Way CB1 ..... 66 A7
Anthony Cl
  Peterborough PE1 ..... 197 F8
  [1] Whittlesey PE7 ..... 189 C8
Antonia Cl CB9 .... 24 E7
Anvil Ave SG8 .... 12 A2
Anvil Cl
  Chatteris PE16 .... 241 E5
  Great Shelford CB22 .. 49 C4
Apeldoorn Wlk PE13 .... 245 D7
Apley Way CB23 .... 79 A4
Apollo Way CB4 .... 83 E8
Apple Acre Rd CB9 ..... 38 C1
Appleby Pk CB6 .... 240 D5
Apple Cl PE19 .... 96 F8
Apple Orch The PE28 ... 143 D2
Appletree Cl CB24 ..... 125 D1
Apple Tree Cl
  Hardwick CB23 .... 80 F3
  January PE15 .... 243 D1
  Yaxley PE7 .... 182 A6
Appletree Gr CB25 ..... 130 B4
Appletrees CB23 .... 102 C3
Applewood Cl CB1 ..... 65 F5
Applewood Dr PE7 ..... 186 C3
Appleyard PE2 .... 187 C7
Approach Cotts CB9 .... 38 D2
Apreece Rd PE7 .... 175 D8
Apreece Way PE7 ...... 176 A7
Apsley Way PE3 .... 197 A2
Apthorpe St CB21 ..... 66 F6
Apthorpe Way CB4 .... 84 A7
Aragon Cl
  Buckden PE19 .... 117 B4
  Cambridge CB4 ...... 83 E7
Aragon Pl PE28 .... 113 F5
Aragon Rd CB9 .... 23 D6
Arber Cl PE25 .... 86 E6
Arborfield Cl PE6 ..... 231 C4
Arbour La CB23 ...... 79 A4
Arbroath Gdns PE2 ... 185 C4
ARBURY 83 D6
Arbury Banks★ SG7 ... 2 C1
Arbury Cl PE3 .... 197 A3
Arbury Ct CB4 .... 83 E6
Arbury Prim Sch CB4 .. 83 E5
Arbury Rd CB4 .... 83 E6
Arcadia Gdns CB24 ... 103 C5
Archers Cl CB25 ..... 108 B3

Archers Dro PE6 .... 233 D6
Archers Wood PE7 ..... 186 C3
Archers Wood Nature
  Reserve★ PE28 ...... 160 C7
Archery Cres [9] CB7 .... 240 D4
Archway Ct CB3 .... 64 B7
Arden Rd CB4 .... 83 F8
Ardleigh Cl [3] PE13 .... 245 E5
Ardross Ct CB8 .... 68 F6
Argent Pl CB8 .... 111 A6
Argyle St CB1 .... 65 B8
Argyll Ct CB9 .... 23 F6
Arizona PE28 .... 151 F4
Arles Ave PE13 .... 245 E5
Armada Cl PE13 .... 245 D8
Armingford Cres SG8 ... 14 E7
Armitage Way CB4 ..... 83 F8
Armley Gr PE9 .... 244 D7
Armshold Rd CB23 ..... 61 D2
Armstrong Cl
  Newmarket CB8 .... 111 B3
  Perry PE28 .... 115 D3
Armstrong Ct [1] PE29 .. 141 F8
Arnhem Ct PE19 .... 74 C5
Arnold's La PE7 ...... 189 E7
Arran Cl CB1 .... 65 F6
Arran Way PE7 .... 144 A8
Arrendene Rd CB9 ..... 38 F1
ARRINGTON 44 C1
Arrow Ct PE7 .... 186 C3
Art Gall & War Mus★
  PE29 .... 141 D4
Arthur Mellows Village Coll
  PE6 .... 203 D8
Arthur's Meadow Nature
  Reserve★ PE28 ...... 120 C7
Arthur St CB4 .... 83 C4
Artillery St [11] PE13 ... 245 C4
Artindale PE3 .... 197 A3
Artis Ct PE3 .... 197 A3
Arundel Cl CB4 .... 83 C5
Arundel Cres PE19 .... 74 E2
Arundell CB6 .... 240 C5
Arundel Rd
  Huntingdon PE29 ..... 142 A6
  Peterborough PE4 .... 204 C1
Arundel Wlk [1] CB9 .... 23 E8
Ascham Cl CB4 .... 32 B4
Ascham Rd CB4 .... 83 E4
Ascot Dr PE1 .... 198 B6
Ascot Rd SG8 .... 5 F6
Ashbeach Dro PE26 ... 220 D3
Ashbeach Prim Sch The
  PE26 .... 220 D3
Ashbeach Rd
  March PE15 .... 243 D4
  Ramsey PE26 .... 220 D3
Ashburn Cl PE6 .... 203 F7
Ashbury Cl CB1 .... 65 B6
Ash Cl
  Huntingdon PE29 ..... 141 E7
  Peterborough PE1 .... 198 C7
  Stilton PE7 .... 175 F7
  Thorney PE6 .... 232 F3
  Warboys PE28 .... 165 A6
Ashcroft PE19 .... 98 B2
Ashcroft Ct CB4 ..... 83 E7
Ashcroft Gdns PE1 ... 198 C5
Ash Ct
  Brampton PE28 ...... 140 C3
  Peterborough PE1 .... 198 C7
Ashdale Cl PE28 ..... 168 B3
Ashdale Pk PE13 ..... 245 A5
ASHDON 21 B1
Ashdon Pl CB10 ...... 21 C2
Ashdon Prim Sch CB10. 21 B1
Ashen Gn CB22 ...... 49 A5
Ashes The PE2 ...... 186 F5
Ashfield PE28 ...... 113 F5
Ashfield Rd CB4 .... 84 B5
Ashfields [1] PE6 .... 231 F7
Ash Gn CB10 .... 18 D1
Ash Gr
  Burwell CB25 ...... 130 B2
  Chatteris PE16 .... 241 C5
  [4] Ely CB7 .... 240 F5
  Haverhill CB9 ..... 38 E1
  March PE15 .... 243 C5
  Melbourn SG8 ...... 14 C5
Ashlea Cl CB9 ..... 24 B6
Ashlea Rd CB9 ..... 24 B6
Ashleigh PE2 ...... 185 C6
ASHLEY 91 F7
Ashley Ct [9] CB1 ... 84 A1
Ashley Gdns CB6 ... 242 D3
Ashley Pool La PE6 . 233 A2
Ashley Rd
  Cheveley CB8 ...... 112 A1
  Newmarket CB8 ..... 111 C6
Ashley Way CB22 ... 32 F8
Ashline Gr PE7 .... 189 C6
Ashmead Dr CB23 ... 81 A3
Ash Pk PE4 .... 204 B6
Ash Pl CB6 .... 210 F5
Ash Rd
  Earith PE28 ...... 208 F7
  Peterborough PE1 .. 198 C7
ASHTON 231 A4
Ashton Cl PE27 .... 208 A2
Ashton Gdns PE29 .. 141 D5
Ashton Rd PE3 .... 197 B5
Ash Tree Cl [14] PE15. 223 B7
Ashvale CB4 ...... 83 D7
Ash Way SG8 ...... 5 F6
ASHWELL 2 E4
Ashwell Bury SG7 .. 2 C5
ASHWELL END 2 A5
Ashwell & Morden Sta SG7 3 D2

Ashwell Prim Sch SG7 ... 2 D4
Ashwell Rd
  Guilden Morden SG8 ... 10 F2
  Newnham SG7 .... 2 A1
Ashwell St
  Ashwell SG7 .... 2 D3
  Bassingbourn cum Kneesworth
  SG8 .... 13 A3
Ashwell Village Mus★ SG7. 2 D4
Askers Field CB23 .... 78 E2
Askew's La PE7 ...... 181 E4
Aspal Cl [8] IP28 ..... 213 F8
Aspal Hall Rd IP28 ... 213 F8
Aspal La IP28 .... 214 A8
Aspal Pk
  Beck Row, Holywell Row &
  Kenny Hill IP28 ... 214 A8
  Mildenhall IP28 ... 213 F8
Aspal Pl [9] IP28 .... 213 F8
Aspen Cl
  [3] Ely CB7 .... 240 E5
  Haverhill CB9 .... 38 E1
Aspen Gn PE29 .... 141 E6
Asplin Ave PE15 ... 243 E4
Asplins Ave [8] PE27 . 208 A3
Asplin's Cl [5] CB24 . 208 D1
Asplin's La PE19 .. 117 F3
Aster Dr PE4 ..... 204 D3
Astile La CB29 .... 141 D5
Astley Cl CB6 .... 216 E1
Astore Pk PE1 .... 198 E3
Atherstone Ave PE3 . 197 B4
Atherton Cl CB4 .. 83 E5
Athlone [7] CB1 .... 84 A1
Athlone Cl CB23 .. 99 A3
Atkins Cl
  Cambridge CB4 .... 84 A7
  Littleport CB6 ... 242 C5
Atkinson St PE1 ... 198 C2
Atlantic Cl PE15 .. 243 B6
Atterton Rd CB9 ... 38 D1
Auberry Way CB23 .. 78 F3
Auborn Gdns PE3 .. 197 A3
Aubretia Ave PE4 .. 204 D3
Auckland Rd CB5 .. 246 C3
Audley Cl SG19 ... 58 E4
Audley Gate PE3 .. 197 C3
Audley Way PE21 .. 37 A3
Augers Rd [4] CB1 .. 65 F6
Augusta Cl PE1 ... 198 E6
Augustus Cl
  [4] Cambridge CB4 .. 83 E8
  Haverhill CB9 .... 24 D7
Augustus Way PE16 . 241 D6
Aureole Wlk CB8 .. 110 E8
Austin Cl PE7 .... 181 D6
Austin Friars La [3] PE9. 244 B4
Austin St PE9 .... 244 B4
Australia Ct CB3 .. 83 B4
Avenells Way [2] SG19. 41 D5
Avenue Rd
  Huntingdon PE29 .. 141 D5
  St Neots PE19 .... 74 F6
Avenue The
  Borough Fen PE6 .. 207 E3
  Burwell CB25 ..... 130 C3
  Cambridge CB3 .... 246 A3
  Girton CB3 .... 103 B1
  Godmanchester PE29. 141 E3
  Leighton CB23 .... 148 C3
  Madingley CB23 ... 81 F7
  March PE15 .... 243 D2
  Newmarket CB8 .... 111 A3
  Ramsey PE26 ...... 172 A7
Aversley Rd PE28 .. 168 C2
Aversley Wood Nature
  Reserve★ PE28 .... 159 F8
Aves Cl CB7 ...... 213 A5
Avocet Gr [7] CB7 .. 212 A5
Avon Ct
  Eaton Socon PE19 . 74 C3
  Peterborough PE4 .. 204 E2
Avro Ct PE29 ..... 141 B8
Awdry Dr PE13 .... 245 C3
Axiom Ave PE3 .... 197 C4
Axiom Ct PE9 ..... 244 D4
Axis Way [6] PE19 .. 74 B5
Aydon Rd PE7 .... 187 F6
Aylesborough Cl [4] CB4. 83 D7
Aylesford Way CB22 . 49 A4
Aylestone Rd CB4 .. 246 C4
Aylington Cl PE8 .. 184 B1
Ayre Ct [5] PE19 ... 75 A5
Ayres Dr PE2 ..... 187 C6
Azalea Cl PE3 .... 197 A2
Azalea court PE7 .. 181 F6

B

Babble Cl PE15 .... 243 C4
BABRAHAM 50 E1
Babraham CE Prim Sch
  CB22 .... 50 D1
Babraham Rd
  Babraham CB22 ... 50 B1
  Cambridge CB2 ... 65 C2
  Fulbourn CB21 ... 50 E8
  Great Shelford CB22. 49 E8
  Sawston CB22 .... 32 F8
  Stapleford CB22 .. 50 B6
Back Dro
  Upwell PE14 ..... 229 D8
  Welney PE14 ..... 225 A8
Back Hill
  Ely CB7 .... 240 D8
  Hadstock CB21 ... 20 B6

Back La
  Barrington CB22 .... 29 E8
  Bourn CB23 .... 79 B4
  Burrough Green CB8 . 70 F4
  Cambourne CB23 .... 79 C4
  Coveney CB6 .... 217 B5
  [14] Deeping St James PE6. 231 E8
  Elton PE8 .... 178 D8
  Ely CB7 .... 240 D4
  Eye PE6 .... 232 A1
  Haslingfield CB23 . 47 B4
  Holywell-cum-Needingworth
  PE27 .... 144 F2
  Ickleton CB10 ..... 18 A3
  Market Deeping PE6 . 206 A2
  Melbourn SG8 ...... 14 C4
  Outwell PE14 ...... 236 E3
  Stamford PE9 ...... 244 C5
  Wicken CB7 .... 211 E1
  Yaxley PE7 .... 181 E5
Back Rd
  Elm PE14 .... 236 A5
  Gorefield PE13 .... 237 C8
  Linton CB21 .... 35 C3
  Murrow PE13 .... 234 D6
  Wisbech PE14 ...... 236 A3
Back Reach Dro PE15. 221 E7
Back St SG7 .... 2 D3
Bacon's Yd SG7 .... 2 D4
Badcock Rd CB23 ... 47 B5
Bader Cl
  Peterborough PE3 .. 197 B6
  Ramsey PE26 ...... 172 A4
Bad Gate PE12 ..... 237 B7
Badgeney Rd PE15 .. 243 E4
Badger Cl PE7 ..... 181 F5
Badgers Holt CB24 . 103 A8
Badinton La PE9 ... 230 F5
BADLINGHAM 213 C1
Badlingham Rd CB7 . 213 C1
Badminton Cl CB4 .. 83 C6
Badney Dro PE16 ... 222 D3
Bagley End PE4 .... 205 B1
Bagot Pl [5] CB4 .... 83 F8
Bagsham La IP28 ... 213 E6
Bahram Cl CB8 ..... 110 E4
Bailey Cl PE7 ..... 24 D7
Bailey Mews CB5 ... 246 C3
Bailey Way PE2 .... 186 D8
Bain Cl PE9 .... 244 C7
Baines Coney CB9 .. 38 D1
BAINTON 230 F5
Bainton Green Rd PE9. 231 A4
Bainton Rd
  Barnack PE9 ...... 230 D4
  Newborough PE6 ... 204 F8
Baird Cl PE7 ...... 181 D6
Bakehouse Cl [7] PE15. 222 E5
Bakehouse Hill CB8 . 70 E8
Baker Dr CB25 .... 130 C3
Bakers Cl CB23 ... 62 D6
Bakers Field CB23 . 102 C1
Bakers La
  Barley SG8 .... 6 F3
  Linton CB21 ...... 35 D2
  Peterborough PE2 .. 186 E7
Bakers Link PE19 .. 74 E2
Bakers Row CB8 ... 111 A4
Bakers Way
  Perry PE28 .... 115 D3
  Tuddenham IP28 ... 214 D2
Bakery Cl
  Fen Ditton CB5 ... 84 E5
  Wilburton CB6 .... 210 C5
Bakewell Rd PE2 ... 185 C2
Bala Ct PE4 ...... 204 E3
Balaton Pl CB8 ... 111 A6
Balding Cl [4] PE13. 245 D5
Baldock Rd SG8 ... 4 C4
Baldock St SG8 ... 5 D6
Baldock Way CB1 .. 65 B5
Baldwin Cl PE8 ... 230 C1
Baldwins Cl CB23 . 60 C5
Baldwin's Cnr SG7 . 2 E5
Baldwins Manor SG19. 58 F4
Balingdon La CB21 . 35 D3
Balintore Rise PE2 . 185 D4
Balland Field CB24 . 124 A8
Balland Hill PE19 . 75 C5
Ballard Cl CB24 .. 105 D3
Balmoral Dr [5] CB9 . 23 E8
Balmoral Rd PE4 .. 197 C8
Balmoral Way PE19 . 74 E2
BALSHAM 53 A2
Balsham La CB8 ... 70 B7
Balsham Rd
  Fulbourn CB21 .... 67 B2
  Linton CB21 ...... 35 D3
Bambers La PE14 .. 236 C6
Bamber St PE1 .... 197 F4
Bancroft Cl CB1 .. 65 B6
Bancroft La CB7 .. 212 B5
Bandon Rd CB3 ... 82 F6
Banff Cl [2] CB4 .. 83 E7
Banham Mews CB9 . 38 B1
Banhams Cl CB4 .. 246 C4
Bank Ave
  Hampton Hargate PE7. 186 D2
  Somersham PE28 ... 208 C8
Bank Cl PE7 ..... 189 E5
Bank Dr PE13 .... 245 A7
Bank Rd PE27 .... 144 B7
Banks Cnr CB6 ... 240 C4
Banks Ct PE19 ... 74 E2
Bank's End PE28 .. 142 D6
Bank The PE13 ... 234 C7
Bannister Gdns SG8. 5 E8

Bannister's Row PE13 ... 245 A4
Bannold Ct CB25 ...... 106 B8
Bannold Dro CB25 ..... 106 C8
Bannold Rd CB25 ...... 106 B8
Banworth La CB25 ..... 105 D6
Baptist Rd PE14 ...... 229 D8
Barbara Stradbroke Ave
  CB8 .... 89 B7
Barber Cl PE2 .... 187 C7
Barbers Dro PE6 ...... 232 C8
Barbers Drove S PE6 .. 232 C8
Barbers Hill PE4 ..... 204 B7
Barcham Rd CB7 .... 211 F7
Bar Cl CB22 .... 49 C5
Bardling's Dro PE12 .. 237 A8
Bardney PE2 .... 186 A4
Bar Dro PE14 .... 236 B4
Bardyke Bank PE14 .... 229 C7
Baretts Cl PE7 .... 189 C8
Barford Ct PE2 .... 186 C7
Barford Rd PE19 ...... 74 E2
Bargate La IP28 ...... 213 D5
Bargate Rd IP28 ...... 213 D6
BARHAM 149 B3
Barham Cl PE2 .... 187 F5
Barham Ct SG8 .... 14 D6
Barham Rd PE28 ...... 149 C6
BAR HILL 102 C3
Bar Hill Prim Sch CB23. 102 B3
Barker Cl
  Hail Weston PE19 .. 95 A1
  Waterbeach CB25 ... 106 B8
Barker's La PE15 .... 243 D1
Barkham's La CB6 .... 242 B4
Barklay Ct PE15 .... 224 A4
Barkston Dr PE1 .... 198 B6
Barkway Rd SG8 .... 5 C5
Barkways CB25 ..... 130 C1
Barkway St SG8 .... 5 D5
Bar La
  Hatley SG19 ...... 42 E8
  Stapleford SG22 .. 49 C4
  Tadlow SG19 ...... 25 E8
BARLEY 6 F2
Barley Cl [2] CB8 .... 111 B3
Barleyfields CB21 .. 67 A5
Barley Mews PE2 ... 186 D7
Barley Rd
  Eaton Socon PE19 . 74 C3
  Great & Little Chishill SG8. 7 A3
Barley VP Fst Sch SG8. 7 A2
Barley Way CB21 ... 35 D2
Barlings Ct CB24 .. 111 A4
Barnabas Ct CB24 .. 105 D1
Barnabas Oley CE Prim Sch
  SG19 .... 58 E4
BARNACK 230 E4
Barnack CE Prim Sch
  PE9 .... 230 D4
Barnack Gr SG8 .... 5 C7
Barnack Hills & Holes
  National Nature Reserve★
  PE9 .... 230 D3
Barnack Rd
  Bainton PE9 ...... 230 E4
  St Martin's Without PE9. 244 C4
Barnard Cl [1] PE7 .. 74 F1
Barnard Way
  [1] Cambridge CB4 .. 83 D5
  Peterborough PE3 .. 196 F3
Barn Cl
  Huntingdon PE29 .. 142 A7
  [6] Maxey PE6 ..... 231 C7
  Peterborough PE4 .. 204 B3
  Ramsey PE26 ...... 172 A4
  Stilton PE7 ...... 175 F8
Barnes Cl
  Cambridge CB5 .... 84 D2
  St Neots PE19 .... 74 F4
Barnes Way
  Peterborough PE4 .. 204 B3
  Whittlesey PE7 ... 189 B8
Barnfield Gdns PE7 . 190 F8
Barnfield La PE28 .. 98 C7
Barn Hill PE9 ..... 244 B5
Barns Cl CB24 .... 208 A1
Barns The
  Buckden PE19 ..... 117 B4
  Littleport CB6 ... 242 C3
Barnstock PE3 .... 197 A4
Barnwell Dr [8] CB9 . 84 E2
Barnwell Rd CB1 ... 84 D1
Baron Ct
  Eaton Socon PE19 . 74 B4
  [2] Paston PE4 .... 204 F1
  Peterborough PE4 .. 204 D4
Barons La CB22 .... 30 C5
Baron's Way
  Papworth Everard CB23. 99 B3
  Stamford PE9 ..... 244 C4
Baros Cl CB1 ..... 22 A7
Barra PE13 .... 238 A1
Barracks The PE13 . 237 E2
Barringer Way PE19 . 74 F1
BARRINGTON 29 E8
Barrington CE Prim Sch
  CB22 .... 29 E8
Barrington Nature Reserve★
  CB22 .... 29 F7
Barrington Rd
  Orwell SG8 ...... 45 F1
  Shepreth SG8 .... 29 E8
Barron's Gn SG8 .. 29 F4
Barrons Way [1] CB23. 62 C5
Barrow Cl CB2 .... 64 E5
Barrowcrofts CB24 . 104 B5
Barrowfield PE1 .. 198 E2
Barrow La CB23 ... 79 A4

Barrow Rd CB2 . . . . 64 E5
Barr's St PE7 . . . . 189 D7
Barry Lynham Dr CB8 . . 111 C2
Barry Wlk **3** PE2 . . . . . . 186 F7
Barsey Cl CB9 . . . . 38 C1
Barston Dro CB25 . . . . 108 C7
Bartholemew's Wlk CB7. 240 C2
Bartholomew Cl CB10 . . . . 18 E2
BARTLOW 21 A7
Bartlow Hills (Tumuli)★
  CB21 . . . . 21 B6
Bartlow Pl CB9 . . . . 39 B1
Bartlow Rd
  Castle Camps CB21 . . . . . 22 D4
  Hadstock CB21 . . . . 20 D7
  Linton CB21 . . . . 35 E2
BARTON 63 B3
Barton CE Prim Sch CB23 63 B4
Barton Cl
  Cambridge CB3 . . . . 64 B8
  Peterborough PE4 . . . . . 204 F1
  Witchford CB6 . . . . 217 D1
Barton Holt PE13 . . . . 237 F8
Barton La PE13 . . . . 237 F8
Barton Mews CB7 . . . . 240 C4
BARTON MILLS 239 C2
Barton Rd
  Cambridge CB3 . . . . 64 B8
  Comberton CB23 . . . . 62 D5
  Ely CB7 . . . . 240 C3
  Haslingfield CB23 . . . . . . 47 A7
  Wisbech PE13 . . . . 245 A4
Bartons Cl CB21 . . . . 53 B2
Bartons Pl CB8 . . . . 110 E5
Barton Sq CB7 . . . . 240 C3
Bartram Gate PE4 . . . . . . 204 E1
BARWAY 211 C6
Barway Cnr CB7 . . . . 211 D6
Barway Rd CB7 . . . . 211 E7
Bascraft Way PE29 . . . . . . 142 A1
Basil Gn PE2 . . . . 186 D6
Basin Rd PE14 . . . . 236 E3
Bassenhally Ct PE7 . . . . . . 189 E7
Bassenhally Rd PE7 . . . . . 189 E8
Bassenthwaite PE29 . . . . . 141 B6
Basset Cl **3** CB4 . . . . 83 B8
Bassett Cl CB4 . . . . 83 B8
Bassingboum Barracks
  SG8 . . . . 12 F4
BASSINGBOURN 12 F4
Bassingbourn Prim Sch
  SG8 . . . . 12 D4
Bassingbourn Rd SG8 . . . 12 B3
Bassingbourn Village Coll
  SG8 . . . . 12 E4
Bateman Mews CB2 . . . . . 64 E7
Bateman St CB2 . . . . 64 E7
Bate's Dro CB6 . . . . 225 B3
Bateson Cl CB4 . . . . 83 D4
Bates's Dro CB6 . . . . 225 B5
Bath Rd PE13 . . . . 245 C7
Bath Row PE9 . . . . 244 B4
Bathurst PE2 . . . . 186 A4
Battle Gate CB23 . . . . 80 A8
Battle Gate Rd CB23 . . . . 80 A8
Battle Rd PE26 . . . . 171 E4
Baulkin's Dro PE12 . . . . . . 237 C8
Baulk La SG19 . . . . 43 A3
Baulks The CB22 . . . . 32 E7
Baulk The
  Thriplow SG8 . . . . 31 B2
  Whittlesey PE7 . . . . 189 E8
Bawtree Cres CB21 . . . . . . 35 E3
Baxter Cl **3** PE13 . . . . . . 245 E6
Baxter Dr **4** PE19 . . . . . . 74 E2
Baycliffe Cl **1** CB1 . . . . . 65 D5
Bayfield Dr CB25 . . . . 130 C2
Bayford Pl **1** CB4 . . . . . . 83 F8
Bayliss PE29 . . . . 118 F7
Bayston Ct PE2 . . . . 186 E8
Beachampstead Rd **1**
  PE19 . . . . 93 F6
Beach Rd CB24 . . . . 125 F3
Beacon Cl PE29 . . . . 141 A6
Beaconsfield Ct **4** CB9. . 23 F7
Beaconsfield Terr CB4 . . . 83 D4
Beald Way CB6 . . . . 240 B4
Beale Ct **2** PE29 . . . . 141 F8
Beales Way CB4 . . . . 84 A7
Bean Ct **2** PE19 . . . . 75 A6
Bear La SG7 . . . . 2 D4
Beatrice Rd PE13 . . . . 245 D7
Beatty Rd PE19 . . . . 74 B2
Beauchamp Cl PE19 . . . . . 74 B3
Beaufort Ct **3** CB9 . . . . . 23 F7
Beaufort Dr
  Chatteris PE16 . . . . 241 B6
  Hardwick PE19 . . . . 117 A5
Beaufort Gdns PE19 . . . . . 75 C6
Beaulands CB4 . . . . 246 C4
Beaulieu Cl **1** PE6 . . . . . 232 A1
Beaumaris Rd PE28 . . . . . 168 C3
Beaumont Cl PE29 . . . . . . 141 F8
Beaumont Cres CB1 . . . . . 65 D3
Beaumont Ct CB9 . . . . 24 B6
Beaumont Rd CB1 . . . . 65 D3
Beaumont Vale CB9 . . . . . 24 B6
Beaumont Way PE7 . . . . . 186 C2
Beaupre Ave PE14 . . . . . . 236 F3
Beaupre Com Prim Sch
  PE14 . . . . 236 F2
Beaupre Dro PE26 . . . . . . 221 A2
Beauvale Gdns PE4 . . . . . . 204 E3
Beauvoir Pl PE7 . . . . 181 E5
Beaver Cl **8** PE19 . . . . . . 74 B5
Beccelm Dr **9** PE6 . . . . . 232 B8
Beche Rd CB5 . . . . 84 A2

Beche Way CB25 . . . . 105 C7
Beck Cl PE15 . . . . 243 C4
Beckets Cl PE1 . . . . 197 F8
Becket's Cl PE26 . . . . 172 B8
Beckett Way **3** PE16 . . . 241 C5
Beck Rd CB7 . . . . 213 B4
BECK ROW 213 F8
Beck Row Prim Sch
  IP28 . . . . 213 F8
Bec Rd PE19 . . . . 74 E5
Bede Pl PE1 . . . . 198 A6
Bedford Ave PE28 . . . . . . 143 B8
Bedford Cl
  Ely CB6 . . . . 240 A3
  2 Needingworth PE27 . 208 A3
  St Ives PE27 . . . . 143 F7
Bedford Ct
  5 Haverhill CB9 . . . . . . 23 F7
  10 Thorney PE6 . . . . . . 233 A3
Bedford Purlieus National
  Nature Reserve★ PE8 . . 193 A4
Bedford Row PE13 . . . . . . 238 D8
Bedford St
  Peterborough PE1 . . . . . 198 B4
  St Neots PE19 . . . . 74 E6
  Wisbech PE13 . . . . 245 C6
Bedford Way PE28 . . . . . . 168 C3
Bedwell Hey La
  Little Thetford CB6 . . . . . 211 A8
  Witchford CB6 . . . . 217 E1
Beechams Cl PE13 . . . . . . 235 C7
Beech Ave
  7 Doddington/Wimblington
  PE15 . . . . 223 A6
  Little Stukeley PE28 . . . . 152 A2
  Peterborough PE1 . . . . . 197 F3
Beech Cl
  Great Shelford CB22 . . . . 48 E3
  Huntingdon PE29 . . . . . . 141 E7
  Isleham CB7 . . . . 212 F5
  2 Thorney PE6 . . . . . . 233 A3
  Warboys PE28 . . . . 164 E4
Beech Croft CB8 . . . . 70 D2
Beech Dr PE27 . . . . 143 F5
Beech End PE28 . . . . 150 E4
Beeches Cl **1** PE28 . . . . 213 D7
Beeches Prim Sch The
  PE1 . . . . 197 F3
Beeches Rd IP28 . . . . 213 D7
Beeches The
  Cambridge CB4 . . . . 85 B1
  Royston SG8 . . . . 5 D6
Beech Gr
  Haverhill CB9 . . . . 23 E8
  March PE15 . . . . 243 C5
  St Neots PE19 . . . . 74 E6
Beech La
  Ely CB7 . . . . 240 E5
  7 Eye PE6 . . . . 232 A1
  Pampisford CB22 . . . . 33 B3
Beech Rd PE6 . . . . 203 D8
Beechside SG19 . . . . 41 C6
Beech Tree Cl PE8 . . . . . . 230 B1
Beech Way CB21 . . . . 35 C2
Beechwood Ave
  Bottisham PE25 . . . . 86 F6
  Melbourn SG8 . . . . 14 C5
Beechwood Cl
  Exning CB8 . . . . 110 C8
  Peterborough PE1 . . . . . 198 C7
Beechwood Gdns PE16 . . 241 C4
Beechwood Nature Reserve★
  CB1 . . . . 65 F2
Beechwood Rd PE13 . . . . 245 D7
Beehive Centre Ret Pk
  CB1 . . . . 84 B2
Bee's La PE13 . . . . 237 F6
Beeson Pl **5** PE19 . . . . . 95 F2
Beeston Dr PE7 . . . . 187 F5
Beeton Cl SG8 . . . . 14 C6
Beetons Cl PE7 . . . . 181 E5
Beevor Ct PE29 . . . . 152 E1
Beezling Cl **9** PE19 . . . . 74 C6
Beezling Fen Dro PE26 . . 222 D3
BEGDALE 235 F5
Begdale Rd PE14 . . . . 235 F5
Begwary Cl **7** PE19 . . . . 74 B5
Beild Dro CB6 . . . . 218 B7
Belbin Way CB22 . . . . 32 B8
Beldam Ave SG8 . . . . 5 E5
Beldams Ct PE7 . . . . 207 A3
Beldam's Cl CB23 . . . . 61 D4
Belgic Sq PE2 . . . . 198 E3
Belgrave Rd CB1 . . . . 65 C8
Belgrave Sq PE28 . . . . 168 B4
Belham Rd PE1 . . . . 197 E7
Bellairs CB6 . . . . 216 E1
Bellamy Cl PE19 . . . . 74 E2
Bellamy's La PE14 . . . . . . 238 D4
Bell Cl
  Ely CB6 . . . . 240 D5
  Meldreth SG8 . . . . 14 A8
  Stilton PE7 . . . . 176 A7
Bell Dro PE26 . . . . 232 F6
Belle Isle PE28 . . . . 140 B3
Belle Isle Cres PE28 . . . . . 140 B3
Belle Vue PE7 . . . . 187 C6
Bellfield PE28 . . . . 140 F3
Bellflower Dr PE7 . . . . 182 A6
Bell Gdns
  Haddenham CB6 . . . . 210 A6
  Soham CB7 . . . . 212 B4
Bell Hill CB24 . . . . 104 B4
Bell Holt CB7 . . . . 240 E4
Bellings Rd CB9 . . . . 38 E2

Bell La
  Alconbury PE28 . . . . 150 F4
  Barton Mills IP28 . . . . . . 239 D2
  Fenstanton PE28 . . . . . . 121 B5
  4 Market Deeping PE6 . 231 F8
  Nuthampstead SG8 . . . . . 1 A1
  Southoe & Midloe PE19 . . 95 E6
Bellman's Ct PE7 . . . . 189 F7
Bellmans Gr PE7 . . . . 190 A7
Bellman's Rd PE7 . . . . 189 F6
Bellows Cl CB25 . . . . 86 E5
Bell's Dro
  Littleport CB6 . . . . 225 B6
  Sutton St James PE12 . . 237 C8
Bells Mdw SG8 . . . . 11 A5
Bell's Pl PE1 . . . . 198 A2
Belmont Ct **8** CB9 . . . . . 23 F7
Belmont Gdns PE16 . . . . . 241 C4
Belmont Pl CB5 . . . . 246 B3
Belmont Rd PE15 . . . . 243 D5
Belmore Cl **1** CB4 . . . . . 83 C5
Belsar's Cl **1** CB24 . . . . 209 A1
Belsar's Hill (Fort)★
  CB24 . . . . 209 C1
Belsay Ct CB9 . . . . 23 D8
Belsay Dr PE2 . . . . 187 E5
Belsize Ave PE2 . . . . 186 E6
Belt Dro PE14 . . . . 235 F4
Belton Gdns **10** PE9 . . . 244 C5
Belton Rd PE7 . . . . 187 F5
Belton's Hill PE28 . . . . . . 137 F7
Belton St PE9 . . . . 244 C5
Belt The CB7 . . . . 73 D8
Belvedere PE26 . . . . 221 C2
Belvoir Ct **4** CB9 . . . . . . 23 E8
Belvoir Rd CB4 . . . . 246 C4
Belvoir Terr CB2 . . . . 64 E7
Belvoir Way PE1 . . . . 198 C8
Benacre CB9 . . . . 38 B1
Benams PE5 . . . . 195 E2
Bencroft La PE28 . . . . 165 A4
Bendyshe Way
  Barrington CB22 . . . . 30 A8
  Harston CB22 . . . . 47 A1
Benedict Sq PE4 . . . . 204 A2
Benedict St CB6 . . . . 240 B5
Benefield Rd CB8 . . . . 112 F6
Benet Cl CB24 . . . . 105 C1
Bene't St CB2 . . . . 246 A2
Benians Ct CB3 . . . . 83 B3
Benland PE3 . . . . 197 A6
Bennett Rd
  13 Red Lodge IP28 . . . . 214 A1
  Wyton PE28 . . . . 154 A1
Benny's Way CB3 . . . . 82 B2
Benson Pl **5** CB4 . . . . . . 83 C4
Benson St CB4 . . . . 83 C4
Benstead PE2 . . . . 185 E3
Bentham Way CB6 . . . . . . 240 E6
Bentinck St CB2 . . . . 246 B1
Bentley Ave PE7 . . . . 181 E6
Bentley Cl PE26 . . . . 171 B2
Bentley Rd 64 E5
Bentley St PE9 . . . . 244 C5
BENWICK 222 A5
Benwick Prim Sch PE15 . 222 A5
Benwick Rd
  Doddington PE15 . . . . . . 222 D5
  Ramsey PE26 . . . . 221 E3
  Whittlesey PE7 . . . . 221 D7
Benyon Gr PE2 . . . . 186 B4
Berberis Cl PE6 . . . . 232 F3
Beresford Rd CB4 . . . . 240 A5
Bergamont Cl **5** PE29 . . 118 F8
Bergamot Rd PE29 . . . . . . 23 C8
Bergholt Cl **4** CB5 . . . . . 84 E4
Berkeley Gn PE27 . . . . . . 144 C4
Berkeley Rd PE3 . . . . 197 C3
Berkley Cl **1** PE19 . . . . . 74 E4
Berkley St PE19 . . . . 74 E4
Bermuda Rd CB4 . . . . 83 C4
Bernard Cl PE29 . . . . 141 D6
Bernard Rd PE28 . . . . 140 D3
Bernard St CB6 . . . . 240 B4
Berristead Cl CB6 . . . . 210 C6
Berrybut Way PE9 . . . . . . 244 D7
Berry Cl CB6 . . . . 210 F5
Berrycroft
  Soham CB7 . . . . 212 B4
  Willingham CB24 . . . . . . 124 A8
Berryfield PE15 . . . . 243 E7
Berry Gn CB6 . . . . 210 F5
Berry Green Pk NN14 . . . 156 C5
Berry La PE29 . . . . 118 C8
Berry Leas PE8 . . . . 183 D1
Bertie La **6** PE9 . . . . 230 C6
Betjamin Rd SG8 . . . . 5 B8
Betony Vale SG8 . . . . 5 E5
Betony Wlk CB9 . . . . 23 D8
Bettles Cl PE1 . . . . 198 A6
Betts Cl PE29 . . . . 141 F1
Between Close Dro
  CB24 . . . . 125 D2
Bevan Cl
  Huntingdon PE29 . . . . . . 141 E6
  Warmington PE8 . . . . 178 B3
Beverley Cl SG8 . . . . 5 B8
Beverley Ct PE6 . . . . 232 B1
Beverley Gdns PE9 . . . . . . 244 A6
Beverley Way **4** CB2 . . . 64 D3
Beverstone PE2 . . . . 185 D5
Beville CB28 . . . . 161 F6
Bevills Cl **16** PE15 . . . . . 223 A5
Bevills Pasture PE26 . . . . 220 D7
Bevills Pl PE15 . . . . 243 D3

Bevington Way PE19 . . . . 74 E2
Bevishall PE4 . . . . 204 F1
Bevis La PE13 . . . . 235 C6
Bew Cl PE2 . . . . 187 D4
Bewick Pl PE7 . . . . 181 D8
Bewicks Mead CB25 . . . . . 130 C2
Bickerley Ct CB23 . . . . 79 A3
Bickleigh Wlk PE3 . . . . . . 197 A3
Bicton Ind Est PE28 . . . . . 114 B7
Bifield PE2 . . . . 185 D3
Biggen The CB22 . . . . 17 E8
Biggin Abbey★ CB5 . . . . . 84 F8
Biggin La
  Fen Ditton CB5 . . . . 84 F8
  Ramsey PE26 . . . . 171 E6
Big Gn PE8 . . . . 178 C3
Biggs Rd PE14 . . . . 236 B3
Bigram's La PE19 . . . . 114 C7
Bilberry Cl **1** PE19 . . . . . 74 C5
Bilberry End CB21 . . . . . . 20 C7
Bill Hall Way PE28 . . . . . . 168 D2
Billings Cl CB9 . . . . 38 F2
Bill Rickaby Dr CB8 . . . . . 111 A3
Binnimoor Rd PE15 . . . . . 228 E4
Birch Ave PE16 . . . . 241 D5
Birch Cl
  Cambridge CB4 . . . . 83 F5
  Chatteris PE16 . . . . 241 C5
  Ely CB7 . . . . 240 E5
  Yaxley PE7 . . . . 182 A5
Birch Dr PE28 . . . . 151 E3
Birchen Cl PE7 . . . . 186 C3
Birchin Cl PE7 . . . . 186 C3
Birchtree Ave PE1 . . . . . . 198 A7
Birch Trees Rd CB22 . . . . 49 A6
Birchwood PE2 . . . . 186 A3
Birchwood Ave PE15 . . . . 243 B6
Bird Farm Rd CB21 . . . . . 66 E5
Bird La PE19 . . . . 95 A1
Birds Cl CB10 . . . . 18 A3
Bird's Dro
  Gorefield PE13 . . . . 237 D1
  Sutton St James PE12 . . 237 B8
BIRD'S HUNDRED 189 C5
Birdwood Rd CB1 . . . . 65 D6
Birkdale Ave
  Mildenhall IP28 . . . . 239 B5
  Peterborough PE4 . . . . . 204 B3
Birt La PE27 . . . . 144 A3
Biscay Cl CB9 . . . . 24 C7
Bishop Cl PE7 . . . . 175 F7
Bishop Creighton Prim Sch
  PE1 . . . . 198 B2
Bishops Cl
  Haverhill CB9 . . . . 23 E8
  Little Downham CB6 . . . . 218 A7
  Peterborough PE1 . . . . . 198 D5
Bishops Ct **8** CB9 . . . . . 23 E8
Bishop's Ct CB2 . . . . 64 C1
Bishopsfield PE4 . . . . 204 D1
Bishops Rd
  19 Somersham PE28 . . 215 C1
  St Neots PE19 . . . . 74 F2
Bishop's Rd
  Cambridge CB2 . . . . 64 D1
  Peterborough PE1 . . . . . 198 A1
Bishops Way
  Buckden PE19 . . . . 117 B4
  Great Paxton PE19 . . . . . 96 E4
Bishops Wlk
  2 Barnack PE9 . . . . . . 230 D3
  Ely CB7 . . . . 240 D4
Bishops Yd **12** PE28 . . . 208 C8
Bishop Way CB24 . . . . . . 104 C3
Bishop Wynn Cl CB7 . . . . 240 D3
Bittern Cl PE27 . . . . 143 F7
Bittern Gr **8** CB7 . . . . . . 212 A5
Bittern Way PE15 . . . . 243 F5
Blaby's Dro CB6 . . . . 216 A4
Black Bank CB6 . . . . 218 B8
Black Bank Rd CB6 . . . . . . 218 B8
Black Bear La
  Leverington PE13 . . . . . . 245 F7
  Newmarket CB8 . . . . 110 F3
  Walsoken PE14 . . . . 238 F1
Blackberry Droveway
  CB25 . . . . 129 C1
Blackberry Way **6** IP28 . 214 A1
Blackbird Way PE4 . . . . . . 150 E4
Blackbush Dro PE7 . . . . . . 220 D8
Blackdown Garth PE4 . . . 204 D3
Black Dro
  March PE15 . . . . 223 E8
  Thorney PE6 . . . . 233 A5
  Wisbech St Mary PE13 . . 234 B3
Black Dyke PE13 . . . . 237 F4
Black Ham Dro PE15 . . . . 182 E2
Black Hill Rd PE27 . . . . . . 143 E6
Black Horse Dro CB6 . . . . 226 B6
BLACK HORSE DROVE . . 226 B6
Black Horse La
  Chatteris PE16 . . . . 241 C6
  Swavesey CB24 . . . . 122 E6
Black La
  Gorefield PE13 . . . . 237 C2
  Tydd St Giles PE13 . . . . . 237 C6

Blackmans Rd PE7 . . . . . . 175 D8
Blackmead PE2 . . . . 186 B4
Blackmill Rd PE16 . . . . . . 241 E6
Blackmore Cl **4** CB9 . . . . 38 F1
Blacksmith Cl SG19 . . . . . 40 C3
Blacksmiths Cl
  Abbotsley PE7 . . . . 57 B5
  Ramsey Forty Foot PE26 . 221 C2
Blacksmiths La
  Abbotsley PE19 . . . . 57 B5
  Ellington PE28 . . . . 139 A4
  Shudy Camps CB21 . . . . . 22 C5
Blackstone Rd PE29 . . . . . 141 C4
Black Swan Cres PE7 . . . . 186 B2
Black Swan Spinney
  PE8 . . . . 194 A4
Blackthorn Cl
  Cambridge CB4 . . . . 83 F6
  Chatteris PE16 . . . . 241 C3
Blackthorn Ct
  Coates/Eastrea PE7 . . . . 190 F8
  2 Soham CB7 . . . . 212 A5
Blackwell Rd PE7 . . . . 186 C2
Blackwood Rd PE19 . . . . . 74 B3
Bladon Way CB9 . . . . 39 B1
Blair Par CB9 . . . . 23 E8
Blair Way PE19 . . . . 74 E2
Blake Cl SG8 . . . . 13 D1
Blakeland Hill CB22 . . . . . 17 D8
Blakes Way PE15 . . . . 74 B2
Blandford Gdns PE1 . . . . 198 E7
Blandford Wlk **1** CB4 . . . 83 C6
Blanford Wlk CB4 . . . . 83 C7
Blashfield Cl **2** PE9 . . . . 244 A6
Blaxhall Cl **13** CB9 . . . . . 23 E7
Blaydon Pl CB6 . . . . 216 E2
Blea Wr PE29 . . . . 141 B6
Bledwick Dro PE13 . . . . . . 238 C3
Blench La CB21 . . . . 34 F6
Blencowe Terr **18** PE13 . 245 C5
Blenheim Cl
  2 Cambridge CB1 . . . . 65 E5
  3 Eaton Socon PE19 . . 74 C4
  Haverhill CB9 . . . . 39 B1
  Shepreth SG8 . . . . 29 E4
  Thistley Green IP28 . . . . 213 D7
Blenheim Dr PE27 . . . . . . 143 F7
Blenheim Gr PE19 . . . . . . 96 F8
Blenheim Rd
  Ramsey PE26 . . . . 172 A7
  Upwood PE26 . . . . 171 E3
Blenheim Way
  Emneth PE14 . . . . 245 E2
  1 Hardwick CB23 . . . . . 81 A4
  Wyton PE28 . . . . 154 A1
  Yaxley PE7 . . . . 181 E5
Blethan Dr PE29 . . . . 141 A6
Blinco Gr CB1 . . . . 65 B5
Blind La
  3 Maxey PE6 . . . . 231 C7
  Sawtry PE28 . . . . 168 C3
Bliss Way CB1 . . . . 66 A6
Block Fen Dro
  Chatteris PE16 . . . . 216 C6
  Wimblington PE15 . . . . . 223 C5
Blockmoor Dro CB6 . . . . . 216 C4
Blockmoor Rd CB7 . . . . . . 211 E6
Block Rd CB7 . . . . 212 C1
Blois Rd CB9 . . . . 24 F1
Bloomfield Cl PE19 . . . . . . 95 F2
Bloomfield Way PE28 . . . . 168 C4
Blooms Ct IP28 . . . . 239 D4
Bloomsfield CB25 . . . . 130 B4
Blossom Cl CB25 . . . . 130 B4
Blossom Ct PE3 . . . . 197 B8
Blossom St CB1 . . . . 84 A1
Bluebell Ave PE1 . . . . 198 A8
Bluebell Cl PE26 . . . . 220 D3
Bluebell Dr CB23 . . . . 79 C5
Bluebell Wlk **1** CB7 . . . . 212 B4
Blue Boar Dro CB6 . . . . . . 218 B7
Bluecoat Prim Sch PE9 . . 244 B6
Bluegate PE29 . . . . 118 F7
Blue La PE15 . . . . 223 A7
Blue Ridge Gdns PE15 . . 243 E5
Blue Water Rise PE7 . . . . 186 C1
BLUNTISHAM 208 D5
Bluntisham Heath Rd
  PE28 . . . . 155 F3
Bluntisham Rd
  Bluntisham/Colne PE28 . 208 D6
  1 Needingworth PE27 . 208 A3
Blunt's La PE7 . . . . 189 E7
Blythe Gn PE28 . . . . 115 D2
Blythe Way
  Caldecote CB23 . . . . 80 C1
  Gamlingay SG19 . . . . 41 D5
Blyton Rd CB23 . . . . 99 A3
Boadicea Ct PE16 . . . . 241 C5
Boardman Cl PE19 . . . . . . 95 F2
Boardwalks Nature Reserve★
  PE3 . . . . 197 D3
Bodiam Way PE19 . . . . . . 74 F2
Bodian Wlk **3** CB9 . . . . . 23 E8
Bodsey Toll Rd PE26 . . . . 221 B2
Boeing Way IP28 . . . . 239 B5
Bogmoor Rd SG8 . . . . 7 C1
Bogs Gap La SG8 . . . . 11 B3
Bohemond St CB7 . . . . . . 240 E5
Boleness Rd PE13 . . . . . . 245 C2
Boleyn Ave PE2 . . . . 186 C8
Boleyn Way CB9 . . . . 23 D7
Boleyn Wlk CB8 . . . . 111 C3
Bolton Cl CB25 . . . . 130 A2

Bona La PE13 . . . . **235** B8
Boongate PE1 . . . . **198** C3
Booth Way PE19 . . . . **95** F1
Boot La CB22 . . . . **29** E8
Boot's Rd PE15 . . . . **223** F6
Boot The CB6 . . . . **209** D4
BORDEVILLE **244** D8
Boretree Way PE29 . . . . . **141** A7
Borley Way CB1 . . . . **85** B1
Borough Cl PE13 . . . . **245** D3
Borough The CB6 . . . . . . **209** E4
Borrowdale CB4 . . . . **83** C6
Borrowdale Cl PE4 . . . . . **204** E3
Borthwick Pk PE2 . . . . . . **185** D6
Bossers's Way CB23 . . . . **80** C2
Boswell Cl PE1 . . . . **197** E8
Bosworth Cl PE8 . . . . **178** B3
Bosworth Rd CB1 . . . . **65** D5
Bosworth Way **2** PE15 . **243** D2
Botolph Gn PE2 . . . . **186** C7
Botolph La CB2 . . . . **246** A2
Bottels Rd PE28 . . . . **164** E5
BOTTISHAM **86** F6
Bottisham Prim Sch CB25 **86** E5
Bottisham Swimming Pool &
Sports Ctr CB25 . . . . . . **86** E6
Bottisham Village Coll
CB25 . . . . **86** E6
Bottle La PE13 . . . . **237** C7
Bough La PE28 . . . . **162** F1
Boulevard Ret Pk PE1 . . . **197** D7
Boundary Dr PE15 . . . . . **243** C3
Boundary Rd
Haverhill CB9 . . . . **24** D5
10 Red Lodge IP28 . . . . **214** A1
Boundary Road Ind Est
CB9 . . . . **24** C5
Bourdillon Cl **1** PE28 . . **121** B6
Bourges Bvd PE1 . . . . . . **197** D7
Bourges Ret Pk PE3 . . . . **197** F1
BOURN **60** C6
Bourn Bridge Rd CB21 . . . **34** A8
Bourn CE Prim Sch CB23 . **60** C6
Bourne Rd
Cambridge CB4 . . . . **84** C5
Haverhill CB9 . . . . **24** B8
Bourneys Manor Cl **11**
CB24 . . . . **209** A1
Bourn Rd CB23 . . . . **59** F8
Bourns The CB21 . . . . **67** A4
Bourn Windmill★ CB23 . . **79** A1
Bower Cl PE1 . . . . **198** C5
Bowers Croft CB1 . . . . . . **65** C3
Bower's La **4** CB7 . . . . **213** A5
Bowker Way PE7 . . . . **189** C8
Bowlings Ct PE27 . . . . . . **144** A3
Bowness Way **2** PE4 . . **204** F2
Bowsers CB10 . . . . **20** D3
Bowsers La CB10 . . . . . . **20** B2
Bowthorpe Hall Gdns
PE13 . . . . **245** D5
Bowthorpe Rd PE13 . . . . **245** D5
Boxer Rd PE8 . . . . **230** B1
Boxford Cl **20** CB9 . . . . . **23** E7
Boxgrove Cl **14** PE6 . . . **232** A4
BOXWORTH **101** B5
Boxworth End **123** E3
Boxworth Rd CB24 . . . . . **122** E3
Boxworth Rd CB23 . . . . . **100** C4
Boyce Cl PE7 . . . . **189** D7
BOYCES BRIDGE **236** B4
Boyces Rd PE13 . . . . **245** E5
Boyton Cl CB7 . . . . **39** A2
Bozeat Way PE3 . . . . **197** C6
Brackenbury Cl CB24 . . . **104** C3
Brackenwood PE2 . . . . . . **185** D6
Brackhill Fen Dro PE28 . . **208** E8
Brackley Cl
3 Cambridge CB4 . . . . **83** D6
Peterborough PE3 . . . . . **197** C6
Brackwood PE2 . . . . **185** D6
Brackyn Rd CB1 . . . . **65** B7
Bradbury Pl PE29 . . . . . . **141** E4
Bradden St PE3 . . . . **197** C6
Bradegate Dr PE1 . . . . . . **198** C2
Bradford's Cl CB25 . . . . . . **86** E6
Bradley Rd CB8 . . . . **72** F1
Bradmore St CB1 . . . . . . **246** C2
Bradrushe Fields CB3 . . . **82** F3
Bradshaw Cl PE29 . . . . . **141** E6
Bradshaw Ct PE15 . . . . . **243** C2
Bradwell Rd PE3 . . . . **197** A2
Bradwells Ct CB1 . . . . . . **246** B2
Braeburn Ave PE13 . . . . . **245** C8
Braeburn Wlk SG8 . . . . . . **5** C7
Braefield
Hemingford Abbots PE28 . **142** F3
5 Somersham PE28 . . . **208** B8
Braemar Gdns PE7 . . . . . **189** D6
Braggs La
Hemingford Grey PE28 . . **143** C1
Wrestlingworth SG19 . . . . **25** B4
Brailsford Cl PE3 . . . . **197** A4
Bramall Ct PE3 . . . . **197** C3
Bramble Cl
Haverhill CB9 . . . . **38** D1
Whittlesey PE7 . . . . **189** D6
Yaxley PE7 . . . . **182** A6
Bramble Ct
2 Brampton PE28 . . . **140** C3
6 Great Cambourne CB23 **79** C3
Bramble End
Alconbury PE28 . . . . **150** F5
Sawtry PE28 . . . . **168** B3
Bramble La PE14 . . . . **236** D3

Brambles The
Balsham CB21 . . . . **53** C1
Bar Hill CB23 . . . . **102** D3
Girton CB3 . . . . **83** A6
Hemingford Grey PE27 . . **143** F1
Littleport CB6 . . . . **242** D3
3 Royston SG8 . . . . **5** E5
Bramble Wlk PE15 . . . . . **243** E7
Bramley Ave
Melbourn SG8 . . . . **14** D6
Needingworth PE27 . . . . **208** A2
Bramley Cl
Cottenham CB24 . . . . . . **125** D3
Offord Cluny PE19 . . . . . **118** A1
Bramley Ct
Cambridge CB4 . . . . **84** B6
Coldham PE14 . . . . **235** D1
Bramley Dr PE19 . . . . . . **118** A1
Bramley Gr PE28 . . . . . . **208** C5
Bramley Rd
Haverhill CB9 . . . . **23** C7
St Ives PE27 . . . . **144** B5
Wisbech PE13 . . . . **245** C7
Bramleys The
March PE15 . . . . **243** D1
Shepreth SG8 . . . . **29** E4
Bramley Way CB23 . . . . . . **81** A4
BRAMPTON **140** C2
Brampton Cl PE13 . . . . . **245** A4
Brampton Ct PE7 . . . . . . **187** D6
Brampton Gdns PE19 . . . . **75** A4
BRAMPTON LODGE **140** A1
BRAMPTON PARK **140** C1
Brampton Rd
Buckden PE19 . . . . **117** C6
Cambridge CB1 . . . . **84** B1
Grafham PE28 . . . . **116** B7
Huntingdon PE29 . . . . . . **141** B3
Royston SG8 . . . . **5** C8
Brampton Village Prim Sch
PE28 . . . . **140** C2
Brampton Wood Nature
Reserve★ PE19 . . . . . . **139** D1
Brancepeth Pl PE2 . . . . . **186** E7
Branch Bank
Ely CB7 . . . . **218** F6
Littleport CB7 . . . . **242** F2
Branch Rd CB23 . . . . **62** C7
Brandon Bank **226** E3
BRANDON CREEK **226** D6
Brandon Ct CB1 . . . . **246** C2
Brandon Pl CB1 . . . . **246** C2
Brandon Rd IP28 . . . . . . **239** E5
Brands Cl PE26 . . . . **172** A5
Brangehill La CB6 . . . . . **216** D3
Branston Rise **6** PE1 . . **198** D7
Brassey Cl PE1 . . . . **197** E6
Bravo La PE28 . . . . **151** B2
Brawn Way PE8 . . . . **183** D1
Bray **6** CB1 . . . . **84** A1
Braybrook Pl CB1 . . . . **65** F8
Braybrooke Pl CB1 . . . . . . **65** F8
Braymere Rd PE7 . . . . . . **186** D2
Brays La CB7 . . . . **240** C4
Brazilian Terr CB8 . . . . . . **110** F3
Breach La CB6 . . . . **210** D6
Breach Rd PE28 . . . . **116** A7
Bream Cl PE28 . . . . **149** D6
Breamore Gdns PE3 . . . . **197** B3
Breckenwood Rd CB21 . . . **66** C6
Breckland Way IP28 . . . . **239** C5
Brecon Way PE29 . . . . . . **141** A4
Brenda Gautrey Way
CB24 . . . . **125** E3
Brendon Garth PE4 . . . . **204** E1
Brent Cl IP28 . . . . **239** D4
Brentwood Cl **6** CB5 . . . **84** E4
Brentwood Ct CB5 . . . . . . **84** E4
Breton Ave PE15 . . . . **243** E2
BRETTON **197** A6
Bretton Ctr PE3 . . . . **197** A6
Bretton Gate PE3 . . . . . . **197** A5
Bretton Gn **1** PE3 . . . . **197** A5
Bretton Way
Bretton PE3 . . . . **197** A7
Peterborough PE3 . . . . . **196** F2
Brewerne PE2 . . . . **186** C4
Brewers Cl CB24 . . . . . . **123** F3
Brewers La PE13 . . . . . . **238** A4
Brewery Cl PE13 . . . . . . **234** D7
Brewery La SG8 . . . . **29** B2
Brewery Rd CB22 . . . . **33** A5
Brewhouse La CB7 . . . . . **212** B4
Brewin Ave PE15 . . . . . . **243** B3
Brewin Chase The PE15 . **243** D4
Brewster Ave PE2 . . . . . . **186** F8
Brewster Avenue Inf Sch
PE2 . . . . **186** E8
Briar Cl PE16 . . . . **241** D4
Briar Gr CB6 . . . . **240** A4
Briars End CB6 . . . . **217** E2
Briars The
Isleham CB7 . . . . **212** F4
Sawtry PE28 . . . . **168** B3
Briar Way PE1 . . . . **198** C5
Briary La SG8 . . . . **5** C5
Brickberry Cl PE7 . . . . . . **186** C2
Brickfields Ave CB8 . . . . **110** D7
Brickfields Dr CB9 . . . . . . **38** E2
Brickhills CB24 . . . . **209** A1
Brickkiln La CB6 . . . . . . **218** B7
Brick Kiln Rd IP28 . . . . . **239** D5
Brick Kilns PE29 . . . . . . **118** F8
Brick La CB6 . . . . **216** E2
Brickmaker's Arms La
PE15 . . . . **223** B5

Brickmakers Way CB6 . . . **242** B1
Brick Row SG8 . . . . **8** D3
Brickstead Rd PE7 . . . . . **186** D2
Bridewell Cl IP28 . . . . . . **239** B4
Bridewell Rd CB1 . . . . **66** A5
Bridgacre CB1 . . . . **246** C4
Bridge Cl CB22 . . . . **48** F6
Bridge Dro PE13 . . . . . . **234** B7
Bridge End
Earith PE28 . . . . **208** E5
Wansford PE8 . . . . **194** A3
Bridge End Rd IP28 . . . . **213** C1
Bridgefoot
Great & Little Chishill SG8 . . **15** B2
St Ives PE27 . . . . **144** A3
Bridgehill Rd PE6 . . . . . . **205** A6
Bridge La
Great Shelford CB22 . . . . **48** E4
Wimblington PE15 . . . . . **223** D1
Bridge of Sighs★ CB3 . . **246** A3
Bridge Pl CB1 . . . . **141** E3
Bridge Rd
Broughton PE28 . . . . . . **153** F8
Ely CB7 . . . . **240** E2
Histon CB24 . . . . **104** C2
Impington CB24 . . . . **83** C8
Mepal CB6 . . . . **216** E4
Bridge St
Cambridge CB2 . . . . **246** A3
Chatteris PE16 . . . . **241** B7
Market Deeping PE6 . . . . **231** E8
Moulton CB8 . . . . **112** F5
2 Peterborough PE1 . . . **198** A1
St Ives PE27 . . . . **144** A3
Whaddon SG8 . . . . **13** B8
10 Wisbech PE13 . . . . . **245** C5
Wistow PE28 . . . . **163** F7
Wood Walton PE28 . . . . **161** E6
Bridle Cl
Chatteris PE16 . . . . **241** D5
The Cottons PE14 . . . . . **236** E2
Bridle End PE19 . . . . **98** B2
Bridle Way PE28 . . . . **63** F4
Brierley Wlk CB4 . . . . **83** C7
Briery Fields **2** CB6 . . . **217** E1
BRIGGATE **189** E6
Briggate Cres PE7 . . . . . **189** C6
Briggate E PE7 . . . . **189** D6
Briggate W PE7 . . . . **189** C6
Bright St PE1 . . . . **197** F3
Brigland Cl PE29 . . . . . . **141** B6
Brigstock Ct PE3 . . . . . . **197** C6
Brigstock Rd PE13 . . . . . **245** B7
Brimbles Way PE2 . . . . . **185** E5
Brimley Rd CB4 . . . . **83** D6
Bringhurst PE2 . . . . **186** A4
BRINGTON **147** D4
Brington CE Prim Sch
PE28 . . . . **147** C4
Brington Rd PE28 . . . . . . **147** F7
BRINKLEY **70** E2
Brinkley Rd
Brinkley CB8 . . . . **69** A6
Carlton CB8 . . . . **54** F8
Westley Waterless CB8 . . . **70** D3
Weston Colville CB21 . . . . **54** C8
Brinkman Rd CB21 . . . . . . **35** D3
Bristol Ave PE4 . . . . **204** B3
Britannia Way PE13 . . . . **245** C2
Britannic Way CB1 . . . . . . **65** F7
British Racing Sch CB8 . . **111** B8
Brittain Cl **5** PE19 . . . . **74** E2
Britten Pl CB1 . . . . **65** D7
Broadall's Dro PE26 . . . . **221** D3
Broad Baulk CB6 . . . . . . **210** F6
Broad Cl PE1 . . . . **198** D5
Broadcroft Cres CB9 . . . . **23** E8
Broad Dro
Emneth PE14 . . . . **236** C5
Upwell PE14 . . . . **229** D8
Wisbech PE14 . . . . **235** F5
Yaxley PE7 . . . . **182** B5
Broad Drove E PE13 . . . . **237** C6
Broad Drove W PE13 . . . **237** B4
Broad End CB23 . . . . **100** A4
Broad End La PE13 . . . . . **245** F4
Broad End Rd PE14 . . . . **245** F4
Broad Gate PE12 . . . . . . **237** A8
Broadgate La PE6 . . . . . . **231** F8
Broadgate Rd PE12 . . . . **234** C8
Broadgate Way PE8 . . . . **178** B3
BROAD GREEN
Newmarket **91** D4
Royston **8** C3
Broad Hill CB7 . . . . **212** B7
Broadhill Dro CB7 . . . . . **212** B7
Broadhurst Rd **15** PE8 . **230** B1
Broad La
Cottenham CB24 . . . . . . **125** E5
Haslingfield CB23 . . . . . . **47** A5
Broadlands CB6 . . . . **225** A5
Broadlands The PE1 . . . . **198** E5
Broad Leas PE27 . . . . . . **144** A4
Broadmeadow CB22 . . . . **49** F1
Broad Piece CB7 . . . . **211** F5
Broads Rd CB25 . . . . **130** C6
Broad St
Bourn CB23 . . . . **79** B4
Cambridge CB1 . . . . **246** C2
Ely CB7 . . . . **240** D3
Haverhill CB9 . . . . **23** F8
March PE15 . . . . **243** D4
Stamford PE9 . . . . **244** B5
Whittlesey PE7 . . . . **189** D7
Broadway
Bourn CB23 . . . . **60** D8
Cambourne CB23 . . . . . . **79** C3
Crowland PE6 . . . . **232** B8

Broadway continued
Farcet PE7 . . . . **187** C1
Grantchester CB3 . . . . . . **64** A4
Witchford CB6 . . . . **217** E1
Yaxley PE7 . . . . **181** E5
Broad Way CB6 . . . . **210** C6
Broadway Gdns PE1 . . . . **198** B5
Broadway The
Oakington/Longstanton
CB24 . . . . **103** B5
Romsey Town CB1 . . . . . . **76** A3
St Ives PE27 . . . . **144** A3
Broadway Theatre★ PE1 **198** A3
Broadweir PE28 . . . . **138** C4
Broad Wheel Rd PE6 . . . **231** B6
Broad Wlk The PE13 . . . . **74** E3
Brockholme Mews CB23 . . **79** C5
Brockholt Rd CB2 . . . . . . **78** E2
Brocklesby Gdns PE3 . . . **197** C3
Brockley Rd CB23 . . . . . **100** B4
Brockwood Cl **2** SG19 . . **41** D6
Brocks Bsns Ctr CB9 . . . . **23** F5
Brodsworth Rd PE7 . . . . **187** D5
Bromholme La PE28 . . . . **141** A3
Bronze St PE15 . . . . **243** C7
Brook Cl
Alconbury PE28 . . . . **150** F4
Histon CB24 . . . . **104** A4
March PE15 . . . . **243** C4
Brookdale CB23 . . . . **102** C3
Brook Dam La **14** CB7 . . **212** B4
Brooke Gr CB6 . . . . **240** A5
BROOK END **136** B6
Brooke Rd SG8 . . . . **5** D8
Brook End SG8 . . . . **11** C3
Brookfield Cl CB22 . . . . . . **32** F5
Brookfield Dr CB24 . . . . **123** F3
Brookfield Home Pk PE4 **204** B2
Brookfield Rd
Coton CB3 . . . . **82** B2
Papworth Everard CB23 . . **99** A4
Sawston CB22 . . . . **32** F5
Brookfields CB1 . . . . **65** D7
Brookfields Cl CB8 . . . . . **111** B5
Brookfields Ind Pk PE4 . . **204** B4
Brookfield Way
Cambourne CB23 . . . . . . **79** A3
Ramsey PE26 . . . . **172** A4
Brookfurlong PE3 . . . . . . **197** B6
Brookhampton St CB10 . . **18** A5
Brook La
Coton CB23 . . . . **82** C2
Farcet PE7 . . . . **187** B2
Stretham CB6 . . . . **210** F5
Brooklands PE28 . . . . . . **150** F2
Brooklands Ave CB2 . . . . **64** E5
Brook Rd
Bassingbourn cum Kneesworth
SG8 . . . . **12** C4
Eaton Socon PE19 . . . . . **74** C4
Kimbolton PE28 . . . . **114** B7
Newton CB22 . . . . **31** B6
Brook Service Rd CB9 . . . **24** A8
Brookside
Alconbury PE28 . . . . **150** F4
Cambridge CB2 . . . . **246** B1
Dalham CB8 . . . . **92** E4
Exning CB8 . . . . **110** C8
Great Paxton PE19 . . . . . **96** A3
Huntingdon PE29 . . . . . . **141** D5
Moulton CB8 . . . . **112** F5
Oakington/Longstanton
CB24 . . . . **123** F2
Orwell SG8 . . . . **45** D1
Peterborough PE4 . . . . . **204** D2
Sawtry PE28 . . . . **168** B5
St Ives PE28 . . . . **143** B5
1 Sutton CB6 . . . . **216** E2
Toft CB23 . . . . **61** D4
Brookside Gr CB6 . . . . . **242** C5
Brookside Ind Est PE28 . . **168** B5
Brookside La **1** CB2 . . . . **64** E7
Brooks Rd CB1 . . . . **65** D8
Brook's Rd PE15 . . . . . . **243** D4
Brook St
Elsworth CB23 . . . . **100** B3
Peterborough PE1 . . . . . **198** A4
Soham CB7 . . . . **212** C3
St Neots PE19 . . . . **74** C5
Brook The CB6 . . . . **216** E1
Brookway PE27 . . . . **144** C4
Broom Cl
7 Littleport CB7 . . . . . **242** D4
Peterborough PE1 . . . . . **198** A8
Broomhill Cl **4** IP28 . . . **214** A1
Broom Way PE27 . . . . . . **144** B5
Broom Wlk **5** IP28 . . . . **213** F8
Brotherhood Cl PE4 . . . . **197** D8
Brotherhood Ret Pk PE4 **197** D8
Brothers Pl CB1 . . . . **65** D6
BROUGHTON **153** F8
Broughton La CB3 . . . . . **154** B8
Brownes Rd **6** PE8 . . . . **230** B1
Browning Dr PE19 . . . . . . **74** C6
Brownlow Dr **8** PE6 . . . **231** F8
Brownlow Quay PE9 . . . . **244** C5
Brownlow Rd
Cambridge CB4 . . . . **83** C6
Peterborough PE1 . . . . . **198** A6
Brownlow St **6** PE9 . . . **244** C5
Brownlow Terr PE27 . . . . **144** C5
Brownshill Staunch
PE27 . . . . **208** C3
Brown's Sq **6** PE19 . . . . **74** F5
Broxbourne Cl CB1 . . . . . . **66** A7
Bruces PE7 . . . . **168** D3
Brudenell PE2 . . . . **185** E2

Brunel Ct PE27 . . . . **144** B6
Brunel Dr PE7 . . . . **181** D6
Brunswick Cotts CB1 . . . **246** C3
Brunswick Ct CB21 . . . . . . **66** E5
Brunswick Gdns CB5 . . . **246** C3
Brunswick Terr CB5 . . . . **246** C3
Brunswick Wlk CB1 . . . . **246** C3
Bryan Cl PE26 . . . . **172** B6
Brybank Rd CB9 . . . . **38** C1
Brynmore PE3 . . . . **204** A1
Bryony Cl
Coates/Eastrea PE7 . . . . **190** C7
Haverhill CB9 . . . . **38** E1
Buchan St CB4 . . . . **83** C7
BUCKDEN **118** B3
Buckden CE Prim Sch
PE19 . . . . **117** B4
Buckden Marina PE19 . . **117** E3
Buckden Rd
Brampton PE28 . . . . **117** D7
Grafham PE28 . . . . **116** A6
Buckingham Dr CB6 . . . . **240** D6
Buckingham Rd
Cambridge CB3 . . . . **83** C3
Haverhill CB9 . . . . **23** E7
Buckingham Way PE28 . . **168** C2
Buckingham Wlk PE13 . . **245** D8
Buckingway Bsns Pk
CB24 . . . . **101** E8
Bucking Way Rd CB3 . . . **101** D8
Buckland Cl PE3 . . . . **197** B4
Buckles Gdns PE7 . . . . . **189** F7
Buckle St PE1 . . . . **198** C3
Buckley Rd PE19 . . . . **74** E4
Bucksherd Cl CB23 . . . . . **79** B2
Bucksholt Rd PE14 . . . . . **238** E3
Buck's La CB23 . . . . **45** F7
Buckthorn **2** CB7 . . . . . **240** F6
Buckthorne Rd **4** PE7 . . **186** D3
Buckthorn Rd PE7 . . . . . **186** D3
BUCKWORTH **149** E6
Buckworth Rd PE28 . . . . **150** C5
Budge Cl PE28 . . . . **140** E2
Budleigh Cl CB1 . . . . **65** D7
Buffalo Way CB1 . . . . **66** A7
Buff La SG19 . . . . **43** A1
Building End SG8 . . . . **1** F8
Building End Rd SG8 . . . . **1** F7
Bukehorn Rd PE6 . . . . . . **232** D4
Bulbeck Mill CB2 . . . . **29** F7
Bullard Laboratories CB3 **83** A4
Bullen Cl
Cambridge CB1 . . . . **65** D5
Longstanton CB24 . . . . . **123** E2
Bullfinch Way
Cottenham CB24 . . . . . . **125** D5
Friday Bridge PE14 . . . . **236** A4
Bull La
Broughton PE28 . . . . . . **164** A1
Langley CB11 . . . . **1** F2
Peakirk PE6 . . . . **206** B2
West Wratting CB21 . . . . . **53** F6
Bullock Rd
Elton PE8 . . . . **184** B1
Folksworth & Washingley
PE7 . . . . **174** C7
Great Gidding PE28 . . . . **167** B6
Little Gidding PE28 . . . . **167** D2
Bullrush La CB23 . . . . **79** C3
Bulstrode Gdns CB3 . . . . **83** A2
Bulteel Cl CB24 . . . . **105** C3
Bumpstead Rd CB9 . . . . . **24** B5
Bunbury Ave IP28 . . . . . **239** C5
BUNKER'S HILL **235** A6
Buntings Cres CB23 . . . . **130** B3
Bunting's Dro PE7 . . . . . **188** C4
Buntings La PE7 . . . . **187** B5
Bunting's La CB23 . . . . . . **78** B3
Buntings Path CB23 . . . . **130** B3
Bunyan Cl **4** SG19 . . . . . **41** D5
Burberry Rd PE19 . . . . . . **117** B3
Burcroft Rd PE13 . . . . . . **245** B6
Burdett Gr PE7 . . . . **189** F6
Burdett Rd PE13 . . . . . . **245** B4
Bure Cl PE27 . . . . **144** B6
Bures Ct **14** CB9 . . . . **23** E7
Burford Way PE1 . . . . . . **198** D6
Burgess Rd CB25 . . . . . . **106** B7
Burgess's Dro CB25 . . . . **106** C7
Burghley Ave **9** PE8 . . . **230** B1
Burghley Cl **9** PE6 . . . . **231** F8
Burghley Ct PE9 . . . . . . **244** C5
Burghley House★ PE9 . . **244** F3
Burghley La PE9 . . . . . . **244** C5
Burghley Rd
1 Peterborough PE1 . . **198** A3
4 Stamford PE9 . . . . . **244** A7
Burghley Rise CB25 . . . . **130** C2
Burghley Sq **2** PE1 . . . **198** A3
Burghley Rd
Burleigh Ave **9** PE8 . . . **230** B1
Burleigh Cl **9** PE6 . . . . **231** F8
Burleigh Pl CB1 . . . . **246** C3
Burleigh Rd PE27 . . . . . . **143** F8
Burleigh St CB1 . . . . **246** C3
Burleigh Terr PE27 . . . . . **144** A3
Burling Ct CB1 . . . . **65** C6
Burling Wlk CB24 . . . . . . **105** D3
Burma Rd CB22 . . . . **32** A1
Burmer Rd PE1 . . . . **197** E2
Burmoor Cl PE29 . . . . . . **141** B6
Burnaby Cl PE28 . . . . . . **140** C3
Burnet Gdns PE15 . . . . . **243** C2
Burnett Way PE29 . . . . . **141** B4

Burnham Cl CB1 . . . . 66 A6
Burns Cl PE1 . . . . 197 F7
Burns Ct **3** PE19 . . . . . . 74 D5
Burnsfield St PE16 . . . . 241 B5
Burnside CB1 . . . . 65 D7
Burns Rd SG8 . . . . 5 C8
Burn St PE15 . . . . 243 D5
Burns Way PE27 . . . . . . 143 F5
Burnt Chimney Dro CB6 . 225 B4
Burnt Cl
  Grantchester CB3 . . . . 64 A4
  St Neots PE19 . . . . 74 E3
Burnt House Cl CB9 . . . . . 38 C1
Burnthouse Rd PE7 . . . . 191 E4
Burnthouse Sidings PE7. 191 F1
Burnt Up Dro CB7 . . . . . 188 F2
Burntwood End CB10 . . . . 19 C6
Burrell Cres IP28 . . . . . 239 C2
Burrell Way CB21 . . . . . . 53 B2
Burrel Rd PE27 . . . . 144 B6
Burrettgate Rd
  6 Leverington PE14 . . . 238 F1
  Walsoken PE13 . . . . 245 F6
Burrett Gdns **2** PE14 . . 238 F1
Burrett Rd PE14 . . . . . . 238 F1
BURROUGH END 70 E4
Burrough Field CB24 . . . 104 C1
BURROUGH GREEN 70 F3
Burrough Green CE Prim Sch
  CB8 . . . . 70 F3
Burrowmoor Prim Sch
  PE15 . . . . 243 C3
Burrowmoor Rd PE15 . . . 243 C3
Burrows Dr PE29 . . . . . . 141 C3
Burstellars PE27 . . . . . . 144 A6
Burswood PE2 . . . . 185 F2
Burton Cl CB9 . . . . 23 E7
Burton Ct PE1 . . . . 198 C3
BURTON END 37 C8
Burton End
  Haverhill CB9 . . . . 23 E7
  West Wickham CB1 . . . . . . 37 C8
Burton End CP Sch CB9 . . 23 D7
Burton Hill CB9 . . . . 38 D5
Burtons SG8 . . . . 28 F1
Burton St PE1 . . . . 198 C1
Burton Way PE28 . . . . . 137 F6
BURWELL 130 C2
Burwell Castle (site of)★
  CB25 . . . . 130 B1
Burwell Mus★ CB25 . . . . 130 C1
Burwell Rd
  Eaton Socon PE19 . . . . . . 74 C6
  Exning CB8 . . . . 110 A8
  Reach CB25 . . . . 129 E1
  Swaffham Prior CB25 . . . 108 E5
Burwell Reach PE2 . . . . . 186 C7
Burwell Village Prim Sch
  CB25 . . . . 130 B3
BURY 172 B4
Bury CE Prim Sch PE26 . 172 B4
Bury Cl
  Ramsey PE26 . . . . 171 F4
  St Ives PE27 . . . . 143 F5
Buryfield PE26 . . . . 172 A4
Bury Gn CB6 . . . . 218 A7
Bury La
  Chrishall SG8 . . . . 8 D1
  Haddenham CB6 . . . . . . 210 A3
  Lidgate CB8 . . . . 73 F8
  Meldreth SG8 . . . . 14 A5
  Moulton CB8 . . . . 112 F6
  Sutton CB6 . . . . 216 D2
Bury Plantation SG8 . . . . . 5 F6
Bury Rd
  Great Shelford CB22 . . . . . 49 C4
  Kentford CB8 . . . . 134 B2
  Mildenhall IP28 . . . . . . 239 E4
  Newmarket CB8 . . . . 111 C5
  Ramsey PE26 . . . . 172 A5
  Snailwell CB8 . . . . 111 E8
Burystead PE2 . . . . 187 B8
Bury The CB25 . . . . 86 C5
Bury Way PE27 . . . . 143 F5
Bush Cl CB23 . . . . 62 D5
Bushel La CB7 . . . . 212 B4
Bushey Cl PE29 . . . . 141 E5
Bushfield PE2 . . . . 185 E3
Bushfield Com Coll PE2 . 185 E3
Bushfield Sports Ctr
  PE2 . . . . 185 E4
Bush La PE13 . . . . 245 D5
Bushmead Gdns PE19 . . . 74 B3
Bushmead Prim Sch PE19 74 A3
Bushmead Rd PE19 . . . . . 74 A3
Bushy Cl PE7 . . . . 186 D3
Bustard Hill PE28 . . . . . 113 D8
Bustler's Rise CB22 . . . . . 17 D8
Butcher Cl CB24 . . . . . . 105 C3
Butchers Cl PE28 . . . . . . 150 D6
Butcher's Hill CB10 . . . . . 18 A4
Butcher's La SG19 . . . . . . 25 B4
Butcher's Row **3** CB7 . . 240 D4
Bute Ct CB9 . . . . 23 F6
Butlers Way CB22 . . . . . . 32 F7
Butler Way
  Cambridge CB4 . . . . 83 D6
  Haslingfield CB23 . . . . . . 47 A3
Butley Ct **2** CB9 . . . . . . 23 E6
Butt Ave PE15 . . . . 243 D2
Buttercup Rd CB4 . . . . . . 83 D7
Buttermarket CB6 . . . . . 240 D4
Buttermel Cl **1** PE29 . . 118 F8
Buttermere CB1 . . . . 141 B6
Buttermere Pl **4** PE4 . . 204 C4
Butt La
  Great Wilbraham CB21 . . . 68 A7
  Milton CB24 . . . . 105 B3

Button End CB22 . . . . 47 D4
Butts Cl
  6 Soham CB7 . . . . . . 212 B3
  20 Somersham PE28 . . 215 C1
Butts Gn CB22 . . . . 32 D5
Buttsgrove Way PE29 . . 141 F7
Butt's La CB7 . . . . 211 F1
Butts The
  Fowlmere SG8 . . . . 15 D8
  Soham CB7 . . . . 212 B3
Buxtons La SG8 . . . . 10 F3
Buzzard Cl PE28 . . . . . . 142 B8
Byall Fen Dro PE15 . . . . 223 E2
Bydand La PE19 . . . . 95 F2
Byng Cl PE19 . . . . 74 B2
Byres The PE7 . . . . 189 F7
Byron Cl
  Huntingdon PE29 . . . . . . 141 F6
  Peterborough PE2 . . . . . 187 D6
Byron Pl **10** PE19 . . . . . 74 C5
Byron Rd **4** SG8 . . . . 5 E8
Byron Sq PE2 . . . . 64 D2
BYTHORN 146 D4
Bythorne Bank PE13 . . . 237 C7
Bythorn Rd PE2 . . . . 187 C6
Bythorn Way PE2 . . . . . . 187 C6

C

Cabbage Moor CB22 . . . . 48 E8
Cadenham Rd CB25 . . . . 108 E3
Cadwin Field CB4 . . . . . . 83 F7
Caernarvon Rd PE19 . . . . 74 F2
Caernarvon Wlk CB9 . . . . 23 E8
Cage Hill CB25 . . . . 108 D5
Cage La
  Great Staughton PE19 . . . 94 B6
  Stretham CB6 . . . . 210 F5
Cairns CB8 . . . . 131 A3
Caithness Ct CB4 . . . . . . 83 E8
Calcot St PE7 . . . . 186 D2
Caldbeck Cl PE4 . . . . . . 204 F2
CALDECOTE
  Highfields 61 B7
  Highfields 80 B1
  Stilton 175 D5
  St Neots 76 B1
Caldecote Cl PE2 . . . . . . 187 E6
Caldecote Prim Sch CB23 80 C2
Caldecote Rd
  Stilton PE7 . . . . 175 E7
  St Neots PE19 . . . . 74 E3
Caldervale PE2 . . . . 186 C6
Caledon Way **3** CB4 . . . 83 E8
Calfe Fen Cl **2** CB7 . . . 212 B5
Calfe Fen Dro CB7 . . . . . 212 B5
Calford Dr CB9 . . . . 23 C8
CALFORD GREEN 24 F7
California CB4 . . . . 125 F3
California Rd
  Huntingdon PE29 . . . . . . 141 E6
  St Ives PE27 . . . . 143 E6
Callander Cl CB4 . . . . 83 D7
Calvin Cl CB24 . . . . 125 F3
Camargue Dr PE15 . . . . . 243 D2
Camargue Pl **4** PE13 . . 245 E3
Cambanks CB4 . . . . 84 A4
Camber's New Dro PE7 . 220 D8
CAMBOURNE 79 D4
Cambourne Bsns Pk CB23 79 B3
Cambourne Rd CB23 . . . . 79 B5
Cambrian Way PE4 . . . . . 204 E1
CAMBRIDGE 246 A2
Cambridge Airport CB1 . . 84 F2
Cambridge Assessment
  CB1 . . . . 246 C1
Cambridge Ave PE1 . . . . 197 F5
Cambridge Bsns Pk CB4 . 84 C7
Cambridge Cl
  Haverhill CB9 . . . . 38 E1
  St Ives PE27 . . . . 143 F6
Cambridge Cres SG8 . . . . 13 A8
Cambridge Ct **10** PE19 . . 74 F5
Cambridge Ctr for Sixth
  Form Studies CB1 . . . . 246 C1
Cambridge & Cty Folk Mus★
  CB3 . . . . 246 A4
Cambridge Dr
  St Ives PE27 . . . . 143 F6
  Wisbech PE13 . . . . 245 A6
Cambridge Gdns PE19 . . . 74 F5
Cambridge Leisure CB1 . . 65 A6
Cambridge Pl CB1 . . . . . 246 C1
Cambridge Rd
  Babraham CB22 . . . . 50 D4
  Balsham CB21 . . . . 52 F2
  Barley SG8 . . . . 7 A3
  Barton CB23 . . . . 62 E1
  Ely CB7 . . . . 65 B8
  Eynesbury Hardwicke PE19. 76 B4
  Fenstanton PE28 . . . . . . 121 A6
  Foxton CB22 . . . . 30 C7
  Fulbourn CB1 . . . . 66 A5
  Girton CB3 . . . . 82 E8
  Godmanchester PE29 . . . 141 F2
  Great Shelford CB22 . . . . . 48 F7
  Hardwick CB23 . . . . 81 B3
  Hauxton CB22 . . . . 48 A5
  Histon CB24 . . . . 83 C8
  Madingley CB23 . . . . 81 F5
  Melbourn SG8 . . . . 14 E7
  Milton CB24 . . . . 105 C1
  Newton CB22 . . . . 31 B8
  Oakington/Longstanton
  CB24 . . . . 103 C4
  Orwell SG8 . . . . 45 C1

Cambridge Rd continued
  Sawston CB22 . . . . 32 E8
  Stamford PE9 . . . . 244 A6
  St Neots Rural PE19 . . . . . 75 C5
  Stretham CB6 . . . . 210 E3
  Thetford CB6 . . . . 211 A8
  Thriplow SG8 . . . . 30 F3
  Waterbeach CB25 . . . . . 105 F7
  Wimpole SG8 . . . . 27 F6
Cambridge Regional Coll
  (City Centre Campus)
  CB5 . . . . 84 A2
Cambridge Regional Coll
  (Science Park Campus)
  CB4 . . . . 83 F8
Cambridge Ret Pk CB5 . . 84 B3
Cambridge Science Pk
  CB4 . . . . 84 B8
Cambridgeshire Arts
  Theatre★ CB1 . . . . 246 A2
Cambridgeshire Cl CB6 . 240 D4
Cambridge Sq PE28 . . . . 143 B7
Cambridge St
  Godmanchester PE29 . . . 141 F2
  St Neots PE19 . . . . 75 A5
Cambridge Sta CB1 . . . . . 65 A7
Cambridge Steiner Sch
  CB21 . . . . 66 D5
Cambridge Univ Botanic
  Gdn★ CB2 . . . . 64 F7
Cambridge Univ Ctr CB2 246 A1
Cambridge Univ Press
  CB2 . . . . 64 F5
Cambridge Way CB1 . . . . 38 C1
Cambridge Womens
  Resources Ctr CB1 . . . . . 84 A1
Cam Cl PE27 . . . . 144 A7
Cam Cswy CB6 . . . . 84 B6
Camden Ct CB1 . . . . 246 C2
Camel Rd CB6 . . . . 240 C6
Camelia Cl PE4 . . . . 204 D3
Camel Rd CB6 . . . . 242 C6
Cameron Rd CB4 . . . . 83 E7
Camoys Cl PE28 . . . . 151 F2
Campaign Ave PE28 . . . . 186 D8
Campbell Cl IP28 . . . . . . 239 B6
Campbell Dr PE4 . . . . . . 204 E4
Campbell La CB2 . . . . 64 C2
Campbell St **1** CB1 . . . . 65 B8
Campbell Way PE15 . . . . 243 D7
Camping Cl CB6 . . . . 210 A6
Campion Cl **1** CB7 . . . . 212 A5
Campion Rd PE1 . . . . . . 198 B8
Campion Way SG8 . . . . . . 5 E5
Campkin Ct CB4 . . . . 83 F7
Campkin Rd CB4 . . . . 83 F7
Campole Dro PE16 . . . . . 241 E3
Camps Cl CB25 . . . . 106 B7
CAMPS END 22 A1
Camps Rd
  Bartlow CB21 . . . . 21 B7
  Haverhill CB9 . . . . 23 F7
  Helions Bumpstead CB9 . . 23 B1
Camside CB4 . . . . 84 A4
Canal St **5** PE13 . . . . . 245 C5
Canberra Cl
  Bassingbourn SG8 . . . . . . 13 B5
  Mildenhall IP28 . . . . 213 E8
Canberra Ct PE5 . . . . 171 F7
Canberra Dr PE27 . . . . . 143 F7
Canberra Rd PE26 . . . . . 171 E3
Canberra Way PE4 . . . . . 154 A1
Candidus Ct PE4 . . . . . . 204 B5
Candy St PE2 . . . . 186 E8
Cane Ave PE2 . . . . 186 D7
Cangle Junc CB9 . . . . 24 A8
Canmore Cl PE29 . . . . . . 168 C2
Canners Ct CB21 . . . . 61 E5
Cannon's Cl SG8 . . . . 10 F5
Cannon St
  Little Downham CB6 . . . . 218 A6
  Wisbech PE13 . . . . 245 C4
Cannon Terr **8** PE13 . . 245 C4
Canon Cl CB9 . . . . 39 A1
Canon Dr **4** PE9 . . . . . 230 D3
Canonsfield PE4 . . . . . . 204 A4
Cantelupe Rd CB23 . . . . . 47 C7
Canterbury Ave CB6 . . . . 240 C5
Canterbury Cl CB4 . . . . . 83 C4
Canterbury Rd PE4 . . . . 204 B3
Canterbury St CB4 . . . . . 83 C4
Cant's Dro PE13 . . . . . . 234 C4
Canute Cres CB6 . . . . . . 240 E7
Canwell PE4 . . . . 204 C4
Capio Fitzwilliam Hospl
  PE6 . . . . 196 C2
Capital Pk CB21 . . . . 66 C5
Capper Rd CB25 . . . . . . 127 C1
Capstan Cl CB4 . . . . 84 A3
Capthorne Cl PE7 . . . . . 186 C2
Capuchin Cl CB1 . . . . 66 A7
Capulet Cl PE19 . . . . 74 C5
Capulet St PE29 . . . . . . 141 F7
Caravere Cl **2** CB4 . . . . 83 F8
Caraway Rd CB21 . . . . . . 66 E5
Cardiff Pl SG8 . . . . 13 A8
Cardigan St CB8 . . . . . . 111 A3
Cardinal Distribution Pk
  PE29 . . . . 142 B1
Cardinals Gate PE4 . . . . 204 A5
CARDINAL'S GREEN 37 B1
Cardinals Way CB7 . . . . 240 D4
Cardinal Way
  Godmanchester PE29 . . . 142 B1
  5 Haverhill CB9 . . . . . 38 F1
Car Dyke Rd
  Landbeach CB25 . . . . . . 105 F6
  Waterbeach CB25 . . . . . 106 A6

Carey Cl CB7 . . . . 240 F6
Caribou Way CB1 . . . . 66 A7
Carisbrook Ct PE3 . . . . . 186 B8
Carisbrooke Rd CB4. . . . . 83 C5
Carisbrooke Way **8** PE19 74 F2
Carleton Crest PE4. . . . . 204 D1
Carleton Terr PE7 . . . . . 144 B3
Carlisle Terr PE27 . . . . . 144 B3
Carlow **9** CB1 . . . . 84 A2
CARLTON. 55 A7
Carlton Cl
  Haverhill CB9 . . . . 38 F2
  10 Leverington PE13 . . 238 F2
Carlton Ct PE5 . . . . 195 D2
CARLTON GREEN 55 A4
Carlton Green Rd CB8 . . . 55 A6
CARLTON HILL 55 A8
Carlton Rd CB8 . . . . 70 E1
Carlton Rise SG8 . . . . 14 D5
Carlton Way CB4 . . . . 83 D5
Carlyle Rd CB4 . . . . 246 A4
Carmel Ave PE2 . . . . 186 E8
Carmel St CB10 . . . . 18 D2
Carmen St CB10 . . . . 18 D3
Carnaby Cl PE29 . . . . . . 142 A1
Carnation Way PE28 . . . 133 F8
Carnegie Rd **18** PE8 . . . 230 B1
Caroline Pl CB1 . . . . 246 C2
Carpenters Cl PE15 . . . . 224 B4
Carpenters Way **9** PE15. 224 A4
Carpond La **3** CB6 . . . . 210 C6
Carradale PE2 . . . . 185 D5
Carrick Cl CB1 . . . . 65 E5
Carrier Cl PE2 . . . . 186 D8
Carrington Pl PE28 . . . . 140 C3
Carrington's Dro PE6 . . . 232 B8
Carron Dr PE4 . . . . 204 A3
Carrops The CB8 . . . . . . 134 A6
Carr Rd PE1 . . . . 198 D3
Carr's Lodge PE9 . . . . . . 244 F8
Carsey Hill CB21 . . . . 22 B6
Carson Wlk CB8 . . . . 110 F6
Carter Cl
  Brampton PE28 . . . . 140 C3
  Duxford CB22 . . . . 17 E8
Carter Rd CB25 . . . . 130 C3
Carters Cl PE3 . . . . 196 F3
Carters Croft CB10 . . . . . 21 B1
Carter St CB7 . . . . 212 E1
Carter's Way CB24 . . . . . 122 E5
Cartmel Way **12** PE6. . . 232 A1
Cartwright Rd **5** SG8 . . . 5 D5
Caryer Cl PE2 . . . . 186 D6
Carysfort Cl
  Over End PE8 . . . . 178 D8
  Yaxley PE7 . . . . 181 D4
Casburn's La CB25 . . . . . 130 A3
Casewick La **1** PE9 . . . . 230 F7
Casewick Rd PE9 . . . . . . 230 E7
Cassander Cl SG8 . . . . . . 15 E8
Castelhythe CB7 . . . . . . 240 D3
Castel Way PE7 . . . . 175 D8
Casterton Rd PE9 . . . . . 244 A6
Castle Ave CB9 . . . . 23 E7
CASTLE CAMPS 22 E3
Castle Camps CB21 . . . . . 22 D1
Castle Camps CE Prim Sch
  CB21 . . . . 22 E3
Castle Dr **7** PE6 . . . . . 231 F7
Castle Dyke PE9 . . . . . . 244 B5
CASTLE END 231 C7
Castle End Rd PE6 . . . . . 231 C7
Castle Gdns CB28 . . . . . 113 F4
Castle Hill PE29 . . . . . . 141 D3
Castle Hill Cl PE19 . . . . . 74 C2
Castle Hill Ct PE29 . . . . 141 E4
Castle Hill Mid Sch CB9 . . 23 D7
Castle La CB9 . . . . 23 E8
Castle Manor Bus & Enter
  Coll CB9. . . . . 23 E8
Castle Moat Rd PE29 . . . 141 D4
Castle Pk CB1 . . . . 246 A4
Castle Row **8** CB3 . . . . . 83 C3
Castle Specl Sch CB4 . . . 83 E5
Castle Sq **11** PE13 . . . . 245 C5
Castle St
  Cambridge CB3 . . . . 246 A4
  7 Stamford PE9 . . . . . 244 B5
Castle Wlk CB9 . . . . 23 E8
CASTOR. 195 D1
Castor CE Prim Sch PE5 . 195 E2
Castor Hanglands National
  Nature Reserve★ PE6 . . 195 E7
Castor Mills PE8 . . . . . . 184 F6
Castor Rd
  Castor PE6. . . . . 196 C6
  Marholm PE6 . . . . 203 D1
Casworth Way PE5. . . . . 195 D2
Cat Field PE13 . . . . 237 E1
Catharine St CB1 . . . . . . 65 B8
Cathedral Sq PE3 . . . . . 198 A2
Cathedral View PE15 . . . 224 C4
Catherine Cl PE2 . . . . . . 186 B7
Cathwaite PE4 . . . . 204 F1
Catkin Cl CB9 . . . . 38 E1
Catley PE4 . . . . 205 A1
Catling's La PE13 . . . . . . 238 C2
Catley Pk CB1 . . . . 19 D6
Cats La PE13 . . . . 237 F7
Cattle Dike PE13 . . . . . . 237 E2
Cattle Market Rd PE1 . . . 198 A2
Cattle Market Way **6**
  PE4 . . . . 198 A2
CATWORTH. 136 D2
Causeway
  Godmanchester PE29 . . . 141 E1
  Great Staughton PE19. . . . 93 F6
  Pampisford CB22 . . . . 33 C5

Causeway Cl
  Great Staughton PE19. . . . 93 F6
  March PE15 . . . . 243 C2
Causeway Gdns PE15. . . . 243 D3
Causeway Pas CB1. . . . . 246 C3
Causeway Rd PE28 . . . . . 154 A8
Causeway Sch The PE1. . 198 C3
Causeway Sh Ctr PE7 . . . 189 F7
Causewayside CB1. . . . . 246 A1
Causeway The
  Bassingbourn SG8 . . . . . . 13 A5
  Burwell CB25. . . . . 130 B2
  Elsworth CB23 . . . . 100 B4
  Haverhill CB9. . . . . 23 E8
  Isleham CB7 . . . . 213 A5
  March PE15 . . . . 243 D2
  Soham CB7 . . . . 212 B4
  Sutton CB6. . . . . 216 C2
  Thorney PE6. . . . . 232 E2
  West Wratting CB21 . . . . . 53 E5
Cavalry Dr PE15 . . . . 243 D2
Cavalry Pk PE15 . . . . . . 243 E2
Cavalry Prim Sch PE15 . 243 D2
Cavell Cl PE3 . . . . 197 B4
Cavendish Ave CB1 . . . . . 65 B5
Cavendish Cl PE28 . . . . . 168 C3
Cavendish Ct **5** CB9 . . . 23 E6
Cavendish Rd CB1 . . . . . . 84 B1
Cavendish St PE1 . . . . . . 198 B4
Cavendish Way CB23 . . . . 80 C1
Cavenham Rd PE28 . . . . 214 E2
Caverstede Rd PE4. . . . . 204 D1
Cavesson Ct CB4 . . . . 83 C6
Cawdor Pl **6** PE19 . . . . . 74 F2
Cawood Cl PE15 . . . . . . 243 E6
CAXTON. 78 E3
Caxton Drift PE19 . . . . . . 77 F3
Caxton End
  Bourn CB23 . . . . 60 B7
  Eltisley PE19 . . . . 77 F3
Caxton La CB22 . . . . 30 B5
Caxton Rd
  Bourn CB23 . . . . 60 C7
  Great Gransden SG19 . . . . 58 E5
  St Ives PE27 . . . . 144 B6
Cecil Lodge Cl CB8. . . . . 110 F3
Cecil Pacey Ct PE1. . . . . 197 E7
Cecil Rd PE1. . . . . 198 A6
Cedar Ave **5** PE15 . . . . 223 A6
Cedar Cl
  Grafham PE28 . . . . 115 F7
  March PE15 . . . . 243 E5
  Melbourn SG8 . . . . 14 C5
Cedar Cres SG8. . . . . 5 B6
Cedar Ct CB7 . . . . 242 D4
Cedar Dr PE28 . . . . 151 E3
Cedar Gr PE1 . . . . 198 B8
Cedar Rd PE27 . . . . 143 F6
Cedar Wlk CB25 . . . . 86 F6
Celta Rd PE2 . . . . 186 F6
Celtic Cl PE2 . . . . 187 D7
Cemetery Hill CB8 . . . . . 110 D7
Cemetery Rd
  St Neots PE19 . . . . 74 F5
  1 Whittlesey PE7 . . . . 189 E7
Cenacle The **1** CB3. . . . . 64 C7
Centenary Way PE28 . . . 140 C2
Central Ave
  Brampton PE28 . . . . 140 D1
  Peterborough PE1 . . . . . 198 C7
Central Sq PE2 . . . . 187 D2
Central Ave CB8 . . . . 111 D2
Centre Dr CB8 . . . . 111 D2
Centre for Mathematical
  Sciences CB3. . . . . 83 B2
Centre Rd CB7 . . . . 212 C2
Centurion Way PE29 . . . 142 B1
Century Way PE15 . . . . . 243 C2
Cerris Rd PE2 . . . . 198 B7
Chadburn PE4 . . . . 205 A1
Chadley La PE29 . . . . . . 141 F2
Chadwick Ct **9** CB4. . . . 83 E8
Chaffinch Way CB23 . . . . 79 C4
CHAINBRIDGE. 228 D2
Chainbridge La PE28 . . . 135 F8
Chain Cl PE1. . . . . 198 B6
Chain Cswy CB6 . . . . . . 209 B8
Chain Rd CB24 . . . . 208 C2
Chalfont Cl **2** CB1 . . . . . 65 F6
Chalk Gr CB1 . . . . 65 D4
Chalkhill Barrow SG8 . . . . 14 C4
Chalklands CB21 . . . . 35 C3
Chalk Rd PE13 . . . . 237 D1
Chalkstone Mid Sch CB9 . 24 A8
Chalkstone Way CB9 . . . . 39 A1
Chalky La SG8 . . . . 8 D2
Chalky Rd CB1 . . . . 34 C3
Challis Cl CB22 . . . . 29 F8
Challis Gn CB22 . . . . 29 F8
Chalmers Rd CB1 . . . . . . 65 C6
Chamberlain Way PE19 . . 74 F7
Chambers Dr **10** CB4 . . . 83 E8
Chamois Cl PE2. . . . . 32 F6
Champions Cl SG8 . . . . . . 15 E8
Champneys Wlk CB3. . . . . 64 C8
Chancellor Cl PE29. . . . . 141 C7
Chancellors Wlk **2** CB4 . . 83 C6
Chancery La **6** PE6 . . . . 232 A1
Chandlers PE2 . . . . 185 E5
Chandlers Ct CB25 . . . . . 130 B3
Chandlers Way PE26 . . . . 221 A4
Chandler's Way PE15 . . . 243 D2
Chandlers Wharf **8** PE19. 74 E5
Chantry Cl
  Cambridge CB4 . . . . 83 F4
  Chatteris PE16. . . . . 241 D6

Chantry Cl continued
Peterborough PE1......**198** A5
Swavesey CB24.......**122** E6
Chantry The CB21......**67** A5
Chapel Ave 1 PE13.....**235** B7
Chapel Cl
Hilton PE28..........**120** B1
Litlington SG8.........**12** A2
Needingworth PE27....**208** A3
Waterbeach CB25.....**106** B7
Wrestlingworth SG19....**25** B4
Chapel Ct PE8.........**194** B2
CHAPEL END.........**174** D4
Chapel End
Great Gidding PE28....**166** D2
Sawtry PE28.........**168** C4
Chapel Field SG19......**41** D4
Chapel Field La PE28...**215** B1
Chapelfield Rd PE13....**235** A2
Chapelfield Way CB22....**32** F8
Chapel Gate PE12......**237** B7
Chapel Gdns
Benwick PE15........**222** A5
Coates/Eastrea PE7....**190** C7
Chapel Hill CB23.......**47** A3
Chapel La
Alwalton PE2.........**185** F5
Chatteris PE16........**241** B6
Downham CB6........**218** A6
Easton PE28.........**138** B4
Elm PE14............**236** B6
Elton PE8...........**178** C8
Fowlmere SG8.........**15** E8
Harston CB22.........**47** F3
Houghton PE28.......**143** A5
Kirtling CB8...........**72** C5
Melbourn SG8.........**14** C6
Newton PE13.........**238** B5
4 Peterborough PE4...**204** C3
Reach CB25..........**129** D1
Soham CB7...........**219** B2
St Ives PE27.........**144** A3
Tydd St Giles PE13....**237** F7
Whittlesey PE7.......**227** A3
Wicken CB7..........**211** E1
Willingham CB4.......**208** E5
Wimblington PE15.....**223** B6
Wisbech PE14........**235** D5
Chapel Rd
Beck Row, Holywell Row & Kenny Hill IP28...**213** D6
Earith PE28..........**208** E5
Great Eversden CB23....**45** F8
Ramsey Heights PE26...**170** F6
Weston Colville CB21....**54** B5
Wisbech PE13........**245** B5
Chapel Row CB8........**91** F8
Chapel St
Alconbury PE28.......**150** F4
Cambridge CB4........**84** A4
4 Crowland PE6......**232** B8
Duxford CB22.........**32** D1
Ely CB6.............**240** C4
Exning CB8..........**110** B8
March PE15..........**243** D3
Peterborough PE1.....**198** B2
Stanground PE2.......**187** C7
Stretham CB6........**210** F5
Warmington PE8......**178** B3
Waterbeach CB25.....**106** B7
13 Wisbech PE13.....**245** C4
Yaxley PE7..........**181** D5
Chapelwent Rd CB9.....**38** E2
Chapel Yd
Kimbolton MK44......**113** B1
Stamford PE9.........**244** C5
Chaplains Cl 6 CB9.....**38** F1
Chaplins PE7.........**190** F8
Chaplin's Cl CB21......**66** F5
Chapman Ct CB4.......**83** E7
Chapmans Cl CB25....**105** C7
Chapman's Cl SG8.....**14** C6
Chapmans Dr 5 CB23...**79** C3
Chapman's Way CB24..**208** E1
Chapman Way PE19....**74** E1
Chapnall Cl PE13......**245** F6
Chapnall Rd PE13.....**245** F6
Chapple Dr CB9........**38** F1
Charcoal La PE28......**140** C3
Charding Cres SG8......**5** C7
Chariot Way CB4.......**83** D8
Charlemont Dr PE15...**224** B5
Charles Babbage Rd CB3..**82** F2
Charles Cl
Newmarket CB8......**110** E3
Ramsey PE26........**172** A7
Charles Cope Rd PE2...**185** F5
Charles Dr PE29.......**142** A6
Charles Melrose Cl IP28.**239** B5
Charles Rd
Stamford PE9........**244** A7
Whittlesey PE7.......**189** F6
Charles St
Cambridge CB1........**65** B7
Peterborough PE1.....**198** B3
10 Wisbech PE13.....**245** C4
Charles' St PE19.......**74** F5
Charlton Ct PE3.......**197** B1
Charnocks Cl 3 SG19...**41** D5
Charnwood Cl PE27....**187** A7
Charrington Cl CB9.....**24** C6
Charters The 2 PE9...**230** C6
Chartfield Rd CB1......**65** F6
Chartwell Cl PE2......**187** A7
Chase Cl CB9.........**39** A1

Chase Rd PE15.......**221** F6
Chase St PE13.......**245** C6
Chase The
Ely CB6.............**240** B4
March PE15.........**243** C4
Thorney PE6.........**200** E7
Upwell PE14.........**229** D7
Walton Dam PE14....**238** D4
Whittlesey PE7.......**220** E7
Wimblington PE15....**224** B8
Wisbech PE13.......**245** A4
Chaston Rd CB22......**49** A5
Chater Rd 3 PE8......**230** B1
Chatsfield PE4.......**204** A6
Chatsworth Ave CB4....**83** C5
Chatsworth Pl PE3....**197** B2
CHATTERIS.........**241** D4
Chatteris Mus ★ PE16..**241** D4
Chatteris Rd
Chatteris PE28.......**215** D4
10 Somersham PE28..**208** C8
Chaucer Cl
Cambridge CB2.......**64** E6
12 Wisbech PE13....**238** B2
Chaucer Pl PE19......**74** D6
Chaucer Rd
Cambridge CB2.......**64** D7
Peterborough PE1....**197** D8
Royston SG8...........**5** C8
Chaucer Way PE27....**143** F6
Chauntry Rd CB9.......**23** F7
Chawston Cl 9 PE19...**74** C5
Chedburgh Pl CB9......**39** B1
Cheddars La CB5.......**84** B3
Chedworth St CB3......**64** C7
Cheere Way CB23......**99** B3
Chelmer Cl PE27......**144** E7
Chelmer Garth PE4....**204** F1
Chelmer Rd CB9........**24** B8
Chelmer Way CB6.....**240** D6
Cheltenham Cl PE1....**198** B6
Chelveston Way PE3...**197** C5
Chelwood Rd CB1......**65** F6
Cheney Ct PE2........**186** C4
Cheney Way CB4.......**84** C5
Chequer La 1 CB7....**240** D4
Chequers Cl
Alconbury Weston PE28..**150** C6
Cambridge CB1.......**65** F5
Fenstanton PE28.....**121** B6
Orwell SG8...........**45** E1
Chequers Cnr PE14....**236** E7
Chequers Croft PE28...**120** B2
Chequers Ct
Church End CB24.....**122** E7
1 Huntingdon PE29..**141** D4
Chequers La CB23......**99** B3
Chequers Rd CB24....**104** C2
Chequer St PE28.....**121** B6
Chequers Way PE29...**141** D4
Cherry Bounds Rd CB3..**82** E8
Cherry Cl
Cambridge CB1.......**65** E5
Linton CB21..........**35** B3
Milton CB24.........**105** D3
Cherry Ct CB23........**79** A4
Cherry Dr SG8..........**5** E7
Cherryfields PE2......**185** E6
Cherry Hill IP28......**214** C3
CHERRY HINTON.......**65** F5
Cherry Hinton CE Inf Sch
CB1................**65** E6
Cherry Hinton Close Limekiln Close Nature Reserve ★
CB1................**65** E4
Cherry Hinton Com Jun Sch
CB1................**66** A6
Cherry Hinton Rd
Cambridge CB1.......**65** B6
Great Shelford CB22...**65** D1
Teversham CB1.......**66** A8
Cherry Hinton West Pit Nature Reserve ★ CB1..**65** E4
Cherryholt Ave PE15...**243** C3
Cherry Holt La PE9....**244** D5
Cherryholt Rd PE9....**244** D5
Cherry Orch
Fulbourn CB21.......**66** D5
Haddenham CB6.....**210** A5
Oakington/Longstanton CB24...**103** C5
Cherry Orton Rd PE2..**185** F5
Cherry Rd PE13.......**245** C4
Cherry Rise CB6......**216** D1
Cherry Tree CB7......**128** C5
Cherry Tree Ave CB22..**49** C4
Cherry Tree Cl
Huntingdon PE29....**141** C6
Litlington SG8........**12** A1
Cherry Tree Gr PE1...**198** C6
Cherry Tree Gr PE7...**189** F6
Cherrytree La CB7....**212** B3
Cherry Tree La CB7....**212** C3
Cherry Trees CB22.....**48** E7
Cherry Tree Way PE28.**121** B6
Cherrywood Ave PE15.**243** B3
Cherrywood Gn PE15.**243** B3
Chervil Cl PE7.......**175** D8
Chervil Way 1 CB23...**79** C3
Cherwell Ct CB3.......**64** C7
Chesham Rd PE28....**168** C2
Chesnut Gr CB4.......**83** F4
Chester Cl PE28......**143** B7
Chester Ct 8 CB9.....**23** E6
Chesterfield Rd CB4....**84** A6
Chesterfield Way 8 PE19 **74** E2
CHESTERFORD PARK....**19** D1

Chesterford Research Pk
CB10................**19** D1
Chester Rd
Peterborough PE1....**198** C3
St Neots PE19........**74** C1
Wyton Airfield PE28..**143** B7
CHESTERTON
Cambridge...........**84** A5
Peterborough........**184** B3
Chesterton Com Coll CB4 **83** E4
Chesterton Gr PE2....**187** D6
Chesterton Hall Cres CB4..**83** F4
Chesterton La CB4....**246** A4
Chesterton Rd CB4....**246** A4
Chester Way PE29....**142** B1
Chestnut Ave PE1....**198** C6
Chestnut Cl
Brampton PE28......**140** D2
Glinton PE6.........**203** D8
Grafham PE28.......**116** A7
Haslingfield CB23.....**47** B4
Haverhill CB9.........**23** F8
Huntingdon PE29....**141** E7
Mildenhall IP28......**239** E2
Peakirk PE6.........**206** B2
Sawston CB22.........**32** E7
Sawtry PE28........**168** B4
Chestnut Cres
March PE15.........**243** B3
Whittlesey PE7......**189** E6
Chestnut Dr
5 Soham CB7.......**212** B4
1 Thorney PE6......**233** A3
Chestnut Gr
Cambridge CB4.......**83** F4
Little Stukeley PE28..**152** A2
St Neots PE19........**74** A4
Chestnut La SG8.......**13** B6
Chestnut Rd
St Ives PE27........**143** F6
7 Wisbech PE13....**245** C4
Chestnut Rise
Bar Hill CB23........**102** D3
Burwell CB25.......**130** B4
Chestnuts The
Elton PE8...........**178** C8
Harston CB22.........**48** A4
Chestnut Way CB6....**216** E3
Chestnut Wlk 6 SG8....**5** E5
Chettisham PE28......**218** C5
CHEVELEY............**91** C6
Cheveley CE Prim Sch
CB8................**91** C7
Cheveley Rd
Newmarket CB8......**111** C3
Woodditton CB8.......**91** C3
Cheviot Ave PE4.....**204** D2
Chewells Cl CB6......**210** A6
Chewells La CB6.....**210** A6
Cheyney Cl SG8........**11** B1
Cheyney St SG8........**11** B1
Chichester Way PE28..**115** D2
Chiefs St CB6........**240** C4
Chieftan Way CB4.....**83** D8
Chigwell Ct 7 CB5.....**84** E4
Chilcourt SG8..........**5** C6
CHILDERLEY..........**80** C8
CHILDERLEY GATE.....**80** C4
Childerley Hall ★ CB23...**80** D8
Childers St PE7......**189** C8
Childs La 12 PE15....**223** A5
Child's Pond Rd PE19...**75** A6
Chilford Hall Vineyard ★
CB21................**35** D6
Chiltern Rise PE4....**204** D2
Chimswell Way CB9....**23** C8
CHIPPENHAM.........**133** D8
Chippenham Fen National Nature Reserve ★ CB7..**132** C7
Chippenham Mews PE2.**186** C7
Chippenham Rd
Chippenham CB8....**133** C2
Fordham CB7........**213** A1
Moulton CB8........**133** D3
Chisenhale PE2......**185** E6
Chishill Rd
Barley SG8...........**7** A2
Great & Little Chishill SG8..**7** F3
Heydon SG8..........**8** A4
Chishill St SG8.........**7** F3
Chiswick Ave IP28....**239** C6
Chiswick End SG8......**14** A7
CHITTERING.........**127** B8
Chittering Dro CB25...**127** C8
Chivers Rd CB9........**23** D7
Chivers Way CB24....**104** B2
CHRISHALL............**8** D4
Chrishall Holy Trinity CE Prim Sch SG8....**8** C3
Chrishall Rd SG8......**15** F6
CHRISTCHURCH.......**229** D3
Christ Church Cl PE9..**244** B6
Christchurch St CB1...**246** C3
Christie Dr PE29......**141** A5
Christopher Cl PE1....**197** F8
Christopher Dr PE13..**245** A7
Christopher Tye Cl 3
CB6................**240** B5
Christs Coll CB1......**246** B3
Church Cl
Bassingbourn SG8....**12** E5
Cottenham CB24....**125** F6
Coveney CB6.......**217** C5
Dullingham CB8.......**70** E8
Exning CB8..........**110** C8
Great & Little Abington CB21...**34** C7
Great Wilbraham CB21..**67** F7

Church Cl continued
Newborough PE6....**205** C8
Ramsey PE26........**221** C2
Stilton PE7.........**176** A7
The Stukeleys PE28..**151** F2
Whittlesford CB22.....**32** C5
Church Cswy PE28....**168** C4
Church Dr PE2.......**185** F5
Church Dro PE14.....**236** F2
CHURCH END.........**136** E1
CHURCH END CB3......**82** B2
CHURCH END..........**77** D4
Church End
Everton SG19.........**40** C3
Gamlingay SG19......**41** E5
CHURCH END.........**151** F2
Church End
Hilton PE28..........**99** B8
Horningsea CB25....**106** A2
11 Leverington PE13.**238** B2
CHURCH END.........**208** C1
Church End
Over CB24..........**208** D1
Parson Drove PE13..**234** B8
CHURCH END CB24....**124** F4
CHURCH END.........**122** E7
Church End
Weston Colville CB21..**54** A7
Whaddon SG8........**28** B2
CHURCH END.........**169** D2
Church Farm Cl
Church End PE28....**165** D1
Wentworth PE28.....**217** B1
Church Farm La SG8....**11** B1
Church Fen Dro CB6..**209** E3
Churchfield SG8........**7** A1
CHURCH FIELD.......**189** B7
Churchfield Ave CB22...**32** F8
Churchfield Ct
Girton CB3..........**103** E3
Peterborough PE4...**197** E8
Churchfield Rd
Peterborough PE4...**197** D8
Upwell PE14.........**236** F2
Churchfields PE13....**235** B7
Churchfield Way
Whittlesey PE7......**189** C7
5 Wisbech St Mary PE13.**235** B7
Church Gate 13 PE6...**231** F8
Churchgate St 9 CB7..**212** B4
Church Gdns
Beck Row, Holywell Row & Kenny Hill IP28...**213** D6
North Green PE7.....**190** B8
Church Gn CB10.......**18** B7
Church Gr PE14.......**236** A6
Church Hill
Castor PE5..........**195** E2
Grafham PE28.......**115** F6
Churchhill Cl 4 CB6...**216** E2
Church Hill Cl PE7....**187** C1
Churchill Ave
Haverhill CB9.........**39** B1
Houghton & Wyton PE28..**143** B7
Newmarket CB8......**110** D5
Churchill Cl CB6.....**240** A4
Churchill Coll CB3.....**83** B3
Churchill Ct
Little Downham CB6..**218** A6
Newmarket CB8......**110** F3
Churchill Dr IP28.....**239** B5
Churchill Rd
Cambridge CB3.......**83** B3
Gorefield PE13......**237** F3
Stamford PE9.......**244** B7
Wisbech PE13.......**245** D4
Church La
Abington Pigotts SG8..**11** F1
Alwalton PE2.......**185** F5
Arrington SG8........**44** D1
Ashwell SG7...........**2** D4
Balsham CB1..........**53** B2
Barton CB23..........**63** B4
Barton Mills IP28....**239** D1
Beck Row, Holywell Row & Kenny Hill IP28...**213** D6
Brington & Molesworth PE28...**147** C4
Burwell CB25.......**130** B1
Cambridge CB2.......**64** C2
Castle Camps CB21....**22** E3
Chatteris PE16......**241** C4
Cheveley CB8.........**91** C6
Comberton CB23......**62** C3
Conington PE7......**168** E8
Cottenham CB24....**125** F6
Covington PE28......**135** C2
Croydon SG8.........**27** A8
Doddington/Wimblington PE15...**222** F5
Ellington PE28......**138** F4
Elsworth CB23.......**100** B4
Ely CB7............**240** C4
Exning CB8..........**110** C8
Fenstanton PE28....**121** B6
Fulbourn CB21.......**67** A5
Gamlingay SG19......**41** D5
Girton CB3...........**82** E8
Graveley PE19........**97** F5
Great & Little Abington CB21...**34** B7
Great Paxton PE19...**96** D5
Guilden Morden SG8...**10** F5

Church La continued
Haddenham CB6.....**210** A6
Helpston PE6........**231** B4
Hemingford Abbots PE28.**143** A3
Hemingford Grey PE28..**143** C2
Hilton PE28.........**120** B1
Huntingdon PE29....**142** A5
Isleham CB7.........**213** A5
Kennett CB8.........**133** F5
Kingston CB23........**61** B3
Leighton PE28.......**148** B3
Linton CB21..........**35** C2
Little Eversden CB23...**46** A7
1 Littleport CB6.....**242** D4
Little Staughton MK44..**93** B2
Madingley CB23......**81** E4
Milton CB24.........**105** D2
Newmarket CB8......**111** A3
Newton PE13........**238** A5
Pampisford CB22......**33** B3
Papworth Everard CB23..**99** A2
Peterborough PE2....**187** B7
Ramsey PE26........**171** B2
Royston SG8...........**5** D6
Sawston CB22........**32** F7
Sibson cum Stibbington PE8...**194** E2
Snailwell CB8........**132** A3
Spaldwick PE28......**137** F6
Stamford PE9.......**244** C4
Stetchworth CB8......**90** A2
Stow Longa PE28....**137** B3
Sutton CB6..........**216** E2
Tallington PE9.......**230** F6
Tilbrook PE28.......**113** B7
Tydd St Giles PE13...**237** F6
Warmington PE8.....**178** B2
Westley Waterless CB8..**70** B5
Whittlesford CB22....**32** C5
Wilburton CB6......**210** B6
4 Willingham CB24..**209** A1
Worlington IP28.....**213** F4
Wrestlingworth SG19...**25** B3
Church Lane Cl IP28..**239** D2
Church Leys PE28.....**121** C6
Church Mdw IP28....**239** D2
Church Mdws PE19....**74** F5
Church Mews 20 PE13.**245** C4
Church Path CB21.....**20** B6
Church Pl PE29......**141** E2
Church Rate Wlk CB3..**64** C8
Church Rd
Brampton PE28......**140** E2
Buckworth PE28......**149** D6
Carlton CB8..........**55** A6
Catworth PE28......**136** D7
Chrishall SG8..........**8** D3
Christchurch PE14...**229** D3
Conington PE7......**168** D8
Easton PE28.........**138** B4
Everton SG19.........**40** C3
Friday Bridge PE14..**236** A3
Glatton PE28........**175** E4
Grafham PE28.......**115** E7
Great Wilbraham CB21..**67** F8
Hauxton CB22.........**48** A5
Leverington PE13....**245** F7
Little Stukeley PE28..**151** F2
Little Wilbraham CB1...**86** F2
Moulton CB8.........**112** F5
Shepreth SG8.........**29** E4
Shudy Camps CB21....**22** C5
Stow cum Quy CB25...**85** F4
Teversham CB1.......**85** B2
Thistley Green IP28..**213** D6
Toft CB23............**61** E4
Warboys PE28.......**164** E4
Wentworth CB6......**217** C1
Wicken CB7.........**211** F1
Wisbech PE13.......**238** B1
Wisbech St Mary PE13.**235** B7
Wittering PE8.......**230** B1
Church St
Alwalton PE7........**185** A4
Ashley CB8...........**91** F8
Bourn CB23...........**60** C5
Buckden PE19........**117** A4
Cambridge CB4........**84** A4
12 Doddington/Wimblington PE15...**223** B7
Exning CB8..........**110** C8
Fen Ditton CB5........**84** E6
Fen Drayton CB24...**121** F5
Fenstanton PE28....**121** B6
Fordham CB7........**212** F1
Gamlingay SG19......**41** D5
Great Chesterford CB10..**18** D2
Great Eversden CB23...**45** E7
Great Gransden SG19...**58** E4
Great Shelford CB22...**48** E4
Great Wilbraham CB21..**67** F8
Guilden Morden SG8...**10** F4
Harston CB22.........**47** D2
Haslingfield CB23.....**47** A5
Hemingford Grey PE28..**143** C2
Histon CB24.........**104** B5
Holme PE7...........**176** F4
Ickleton CB10........**18** A4
6 Isleham CB7.......**213** A5
Litlington SG8........**12** A2
Little Gransden SG19...**58** E3
March PE15..........**243** C1
Market Deeping PE6..**231** F8
Needingworth PE27...**208** A2
Northborough PE6...**231** F6
Old Hurst PE28......**154** D7
Peterborough PE1....**198** A2
Sawtry PE28........**168** B4

Church St *continued*
1 Somersham PE28...... 208 C8
Stamford PE9........... 244 B4
Stanground PE2........ 187 C7
Stapleford CB22....... 49 C4
Steeple Morden SG8.... 11 B1
Stilton PE7............ 175 F7
St Ives PE27........... 143 F4
St Neots PE19.......... 74 F5
5 Thorney PE6......... 233 A3
Thriplow SG8.......... 31 C1
Warmington PE8....... 178 A3
Werrington PE4........ 204 C3
Whaddon SG8........... 28 B2
Whittlesey PE7........ 189 D6
Willingham CB24....... 209 A1
Wistow PE28........... 163 F7
Withersfield CB9....... 38 C4
Woodhurst PE28....... 155 B6
Yaxley PE7............ 181 D4
Church Terr 16 PE13... 245 C5
Church View
Keyston PE28.......... 146 A3
9 Northborough PE6.... 231 F7
Oakington/Longstanton
CB24............... 103 C6
4 St Neots PE19........ 74 F5
3 Witchford CB6...... 217 E1
Church View Cl PE2... 187 B7
Church Way
Alconbury PE28......... 150 E5
Downham CB6.......... 218 A7
Haslingfield CB23...... 47 A5
Little Stukeley PE28.... 151 D4
Church Wlk
Chatteris PE16......... 241 D5
Little Gransden SG19... 58 F3
Mildenhall IP28....... 239 B4
Peterborough PE1...... 198 A3
6 St Neots PE19........ 74 F5
Stow Longa PE28....... 137 B3
Sturmer CB9........... 24 E4
Upton PE6............. 195 B5
Churchyard The IP28.. 239 B4
Cinders Cl 3 PE27.... 208 A2
Cinques Rd SG19....... 41 C6
Cinques The SG19...... 41 B6
Cirrus Ct PE29........ 141 D7
Cissbury Ring PE4.... 204 C2
City of Ely Com Coll CB6 240 C6
City Rd
Cambridge CB1......... 246 C2
Littleport CB6......... 242 E4
March PE15............ 243 D4
Peterborough PE1...... 198 A2
Civic Ind Est CB9....... 23 F5
Clack La PE28......... 135 D8
Clare Cl
Mildenhall IP28....... 239 D5
Stamford PE9.......... 244 A5
Waterbeach CB25...... 106 A8
Clare Coll CB2........ 246 A2
Clare Coll Pavilion CB2.. 64 F5
Clare Coll (The Colony)
CB4................. 246 A4
Clare Ct PE27......... 144 A4
Clare Dr CB23.......... 80 C2
Claremont 1 CB1....... 64 F7
Claremont Rd PE13..... 245 E5
Clarence Rd
Peterborough PE1...... 197 F5
Wisbech PE13.......... 245 D6
Clarendale Est CB8..... 55 F6
Clarendon Rd
Cambridge CB2......... 64 F6
Haverhill CB9.......... 23 F7
Clarendon St CB1...... 246 B2
Clarendon Way PE6.... 203 F8
Clare Pl CB8.......... 111 B2
Clare Rd
Cambridge CB3......... 64 C8
Huntingdon PE29....... 142 A7
5 Northborough PE6... 231 F7
Peterborough PE1...... 197 F6
Clare St
Cambridge CB4......... 246 A4
Chatteris PE16......... 241 B4
Clarke's La CB6....... 210 C5
Clarkes Way SG8....... 12 F5
Clark Rd SG8........... 5 D7
Clarkson Ave PE13..... 245 D5
Clarkson Cl CB3....... 83 B2
Clarkson Ct PE13...... 245 D6
Clarkson Inf Sch The
PE13................ 245 E6
Clarkson Rd CB3....... 83 B2
Claudian Cl CB9........ 24 D7
Clayburn Rd PE7...... 186 C1
Claybush Rd SG7......... 2 D3
Clay Cl La CB24....... 104 D3
Claydon Cl CB21........ 22 E4
Claygate PE7.......... 189 D7
Claygate Rd CB1........ 65 F6
CLAYHITHE............ 106 D5
Clayhithe Rd CB25..... 106 C6
Clayhive Dr 6 CB9..... 23 F7
Clay La
Abbots Ripton PE28.... 162 A1
Castor PE5............ 195 E2
Little Stukeley PE28... 151 D4
CLAYPIT HILL.......... 61 D2
Claypole Dr 3 PE6.... 231 F7
Clay St
Histon CB24........... 104 B5
Soham CB7............ 212 D4
Clayton PE2........... 186 A4
Clayton Cl PE13....... 245 E4

Claytons Way PE29..... 141 F5
Clayway CB7.......... 240 E6
Clear Cres SG8......... 14 D5
Cleatham PE3.......... 197 A4
Clematis Cl IP28...... 213 F1
Clement Dr PE2....... 186 D8
Clements Cl CB9........ 23 F7
Clements Dr CB9........ 23 F7
Clement's La CB9....... 23 F7
Clements Prim Sch CB9.. 23 F7
Clement's Way 1 IP28.. 213 F8
Clerk Maxwell Rd CB3.. 83 A2
Cleveland Bay PE15.... 243 E2
Cleveland Ct PE4...... 204 E2
Cleve Pl PE6.......... 232 A1
Cleves Rd CB9......... 23 D6
Cley Cl CB9........... 38 C1
Clifden Cl SG8......... 44 D1
Cliff Cres PE9......... 244 B5
Cliff Rd PE9.......... 244 B5
Clifton Ave PE3....... 197 E3
Clifton Ct CB1......... 65 A6
Clifton Rd
Cambridge CB1......... 65 A6
Huntingdon PE29...... 141 D7
Clifton Way CB1........ 65 A7
Clipston Wlk PE3...... 197 C5
Cliveden Cl CB4........ 83 C5
Clive Hall Dr CB24.... 124 A1
Cloisters Sh Ctr CB7.. 240 D4
Cloisters The
6 Ely CB7............ 240 D4
Eye PE6.............. 232 A1
CLOPTON.............. 156 E5
Close The
Babraham CB22......... 50 E2
Godmanchester PE29... 142 A1
Kennett CB8........... 133 F5
Papworth Everard CB23.. 99 B3
Royston SG8............ 5 F7
St Neots PE19......... 74 E6
Sutton CB6............ 216 E1
Close Victoria SG19.... 25 B4
Cloughs Cross PE13... 234 D8
Clover Cl PE26........ 220 D3
Clover Ct
Cambridge CB1......... 66 A5
Linton CB21........... 35 C2
Clover Field 2 CB6.... 217 D1
Clover Field CB9....... 23 D8
Cloverfield Dr 4 CB7.. 212 A5
Clover Rd PE19......... 74 C3
Clover Way 1 IP28.... 214 A1
Club Way PE7.......... 186 E4
Clydesdale Cl PE15.... 243 E2
Clydesdale Rd 6 SG8..... 5 E6
Coach Dr CB23......... 46 D5
Coach House La CB22.... 31 B7
Coach La CB8.......... 91 D5
Coach Mews 23 PE28... 215 C1
Coalwharf Rd PE13.... 245 B4
COATES............... 190 F8
Coates Ct PE14........ 236 D6
Coates Dro PE28...... 213 A5
Coates Prim Sch PE7... 190 F8
Coates Rd PE7......... 190 D7
Cobbet Pl PE1......... 198 B3
Cobble Yd CB1......... 246 C3
Cobden Ave PE1....... 197 F4
Cobden St PE1......... 197 F4
Cobholm Pl 4 CB4..... 83 F8
Cob Pl PE29.......... 118 F7
Cobwebs PE28......... 142 D8
COCKAYNE HATLEY..... 25 C8
Cock Bank PE7........ 191 C2
Cockbrook La
Brington & Molesworth
PE28.............. 147 C8
Old Weston PE28...... 157 C2
Cockburn St CB1........ 65 B5
Cockcroft Pl CB3....... 83 B2
Cockerell Rd CB4....... 83 D5
Cockerton Rd CB3..... 103 E1
Cocketts Dr PE13..... 245 E5
Cockfen La CB25....... 105 C7
Cock Fen Rd PE14..... 229 F3
Cockhall Cl SG8........ 12 A1
Cockhall La SG8........ 12 A1
Cockle Cl CB22........ 31 C7
Cockpen Rd CB7....... 131 A8
Cockrells PE19......... 75 C7
Codling Wlk CB23...... 78 F4
Codrington Ct 2 PE19... 74 B3
Cody Rd CB25......... 127 B1
Coggeshall Cl 5 CB5.... 84 E4
Cohort Way PE29...... 142 B1
Colbeck Rd CB9........ 38 E2
Colbron Cl SG7.......... 2 C4
Colbrook CB21......... 66 D6
Cold Arbour SG19...... 56 A1
COLDHAM.............. 235 D1
Coldham Bank PE15.... 228 D6
COLDHAM HALL........ 228 E8
Coldham Hall Chase
PE14................ 235 E1
Coldham La Bus Pk CB1.. 65 E8
COLDHAM'S COMMON.... 84 D2
Coldhams Cres PE29.... 141 F6
Coldham's Gr CB1....... 84 C1
Coldham's La CB1....... 84 C2
Coldhams N PE29...... 141 F6
Coldham's Rd CB1....... 84 B2
Coldhams S PE29...... 141 F5
Cold Harbour SG7........ 2 E7
Cold Harbour Cnr PE13.. 235 C7
Coldhorn Cres PE13.... 245 D7
Cole Cl 1 CB4........ 217 D1
Coleridge Com Coll CB1.. 65 C7

Coleridge Ct 1 PE19... 74 C6
Coleridge Pl PE1...... 197 E8
Coleridge Rd CB1....... 65 B6
COLESEED HOUSE...... 228 D2
Coleseed Rd PE15..... 228 D2
Colesfield CB24....... 123 E2
Coles La
Brinkley CB8........... 70 D2
Linton CB21........... 35 C2
Oakington/Longstanton
CB24.............. 103 C6
Coles St CB24........ 105 D2
College Bus Pk CB1..... 65 F7
College Cl CB25........ 86 E6
College Cres CB23...... 47 B5
College Ct PE28...... 168 C3
College Fields CB4..... 83 F6
College Gdns PE15..... 243 E7
College Heath Mid Sch
IP28............... 239 C6
College Heath Rd IP28.. 239 D6
College Pk PE1....... 198 C5
College Rd
Histon CB24........... 104 B1
Soham CB7............ 212 B3
College The CB7....... 240 D4
Collett's Bridge La PE14. 236 C5
Collier Rd CB1........ 246 C2
Colliers La CB25........ 86 A6
Collier Way CB22....... 49 C4
Collingham PE2........ 185 F3
Collings PE15......... 110 E5
Collingwood Ave PE15.. 243 E3
Collingwood Dr CB24... 123 E2
Collingwood Rd PE19.... 74 B2
Collin's Hill CB22...... 49 A3
Collin's Hill PE7...... 212 F1
Collinson Cres PE28.... 152 E1
Coll of Animal Welfare The
PE29............... 119 C3
Coll of West Anglia - Isle
Coll The PE16........ 241 C5
Coll of West Anglia - Milton
Coll The CB24........ 105 A8
Collyweston Great Wood &
Easton Hornstocks National
Nature Reserve★ PE8. 192 A6
Collyweston Rd PE9.... 230 B2
Colmworth Bsns Pk PE19. 74 C2
Colmworth Rd MK44..... 93 B1
COLNE................ 208 D6
COLNEFIELDS.......... 208 D8
Colne Fields
Colne PE28........... 215 D1
Somersham PE28....... 208 D8
Colne Rd
Bluntisham PE28...... 208 C6
Colne PE28........... 208 C8
Earith PE28........... 208 D6
Colne Valley Rd CB9.... 24 A7
Colorado PE28........ 151 F3
Colts Croft SG8......... 7 C2
Coltsfoot Cl CB1........ 66 A5
Coltsfoot Dr
Peterborough PE2...... 186 E7
Royston SG8............ 5 E6
Columbine Rd CB6..... 240 B6
Colvile Rd
Newton PE13.......... 238 A5
Wisbech PE13......... 245 E5
Colville Cty Prim Sch CB1 65 F5
Colville Rd CB1......... 65 F6
Colwyn Ave PE1....... 198 E6
Colwyn Cl CB4......... 83 D5
COMBERTON........... 62 C5
Comberton Rd
Barton CB23........... 62 F5
Little Eversden CB23.... 46 C8
Toft CB23............. 61 E5
Comberton Village Coll
CB23................ 62 A4
Comet Rd PE29........ 143 A8
Comet Way
Mildenhall IP28....... 239 B5
St Ives PE27.......... 144 A7
Comfrey Ct CB1........ 66 A5
Commerce Rd PE2...... 185 C5
COMMERCIAL END CB25. 108 C3
Commercial End CB25... 108 C3
Commercial Rd PE15.... 243 C7
Common Acre La CB6... 225 D6
Common Dro
Southery PE38......... 226 E8
2 Whittlesey PE7...... 189 C8
Wimblington PE15...... 223 C6
Common Gate Dro CB7.. 212 E5
Common La
Ashwell SG7............ 2 B6
Chrishall SG8........... 1 F7
Hemingford Abbots PE28. 142 F3
Sawston CB22.......... 32 D7
Common Rd
Parson Drove PE12..... 233 F7
Weston Colville CB21.... 54 E4
West Wratting CB21.... 54 E2
Whittlesey PE7....... 189 C8
Witchford CB6........ 217 E1
Commons Dr PE7....... 181 D8
Commons Rd PE7....... 189 C8
Common The CB21....... 53 F4
Compton Fields CB7.... 240 E7
Conder Cl CB24....... 105 C3
Conduit Head Rd CB3.... 82 F3
Conduit Rd PE15...... 243 C6
Coneygear Ct PE29.... 141 E7
Coneygear Rd PE29.... 141 E8
Coneygree Rd PE7..... 187 D6
Coneywood Rd PE15... 223 A7

Conference Way PE13... 245 C8
Conifers The PE2...... 185 F6
Coningsby Rd PE3..... 204 A2
CONINGTON
Fenstanton........... 121 C1
Sawtry.............. 168 C3
Conington La PE28.... 168 C8
Conington Rd CB3..... 121 B3
Coniston Cl PE29..... 141 B6
Coniston Rd
Cambridge CB1......... 65 B6
Peterborough PE4..... 204 E3
Conley Cl PE26........ 172 B7
Connaught Rd CB9...... 23 E7
Connor's Cl SG8........ 10 F4
Conquest Dro PE7..... 187 D1
Constable Ave 4 PE19... 74 D6
Constable Cl PE7..... 190 A8
Constable Cres PE7... 190 A8
Constable Rd
1 Haverhill CB9....... 38 D1
St Ives PE27......... 144 A7
Constables Leys PE28... 113 F5
Consul Ct 8 CB4....... 83 E7
Control Tower Mus★ CB8. 12 F8
Convent Ct CB25...... 105 D4
Conway Ave PE4....... 204 C2
Conway Cl
3 Cambridge CB1....... 65 F6
Haverhill CB9......... 23 D8
March PE15........... 243 B3
Conway Pl 4 PE19..... 74 F2
Conworth Cl PE1...... 198 C5
Cook Cl CB4........... 84 B6
Cook Close Rd PE7.... 181 D6
Cook Dr PE19.......... 74 E2
Cook's Dro
Beck Row, Holywell Row &
Kenny Hill IP28....... 213 B8
Earith PE28........... 208 E6
Cook's Hole PE8...... 193 C4
Cooks La PE28........ 168 D5
Cookson Cl PE7....... 181 D4
Coolidge Gdns CB24.... 125 F4
Coombelands SG8....... 13 L1
Coombelands Rd 3 SG8... 5 E8
Coombe Rd SG8.......... 4 A1
Cooper Cl CB23......... 79 B2
Cooper's Cl CB22....... 90 A1
Cooper Thornhill Rd 1
PE7................. 175 F7
Cootes La CB24........ 121 E5
Cootes Mdw PE21...... 144 B3
Copalder Cnr PE15.... 222 B6
Copeland
Longthorpe PE3........ 196 F2
Peterborough PE3..... 197 A3
Copel Cl CB23.......... 80 B1
Copellis Cl CB9........ 39 A2
Copes Cl PE19........ 117 B4
Cophall Dro CB6...... 217 E7
Coploe Rd CB10......... 17 F3
Coploe Rise CB10........ 18 A3
Copperbeech Cl PE7.... 144 A5
Copper Beech Way PE2.. 187 B2
Copperfields SG8......... 5 E6
Copperfield Way CB25... 130 C1
Coppice Ave CB22....... 49 B6
Coppice Dr CB23........ 79 A4
Coppice The
Histon CB24........... 104 C1
Littleport CB6........ 242 C1
Coppingford Cl PE2.... 187 D6
Coppins Cl PE28...... 168 A4
Coppins Ct PE14...... 245 E2
Copse The PE29........ 140 F5
Copsewood PE4....... 204 C4
Copy Hill CB9.......... 23 E3
Coral Park Trading Est
CB1................. 84 E2
Corbett St CB24....... 125 E4
Cordell Ct PE27...... 143 E6
Cordon St PE13....... 245 C4
Coree Cl CB2.......... 65 A5
Corfe Ave PE4........ 204 D3
Corfe Pl 3 PE19....... 74 F2
Cormas Cl 5 SG8........ 5 E8
Corner Cl CB7........ 219 B5
CORNER LODGE........ 227 F2
Corn Exchange St CB2... 246 A2
Cornfield La CB6...... 242 C4
Cornfields 1 PE15.... 222 F5
Cornish Cl CB21........ 37 A3
Corn Mill PE15....... 243 C3
Cornmills Rd CB7...... 212 D2
Cornstall Bldgs 3 PE9.. 244 C5
Cornwall Ct PE19....... 74 B4
Cornwallis Dr PE19..... 74 A3
Cornwallis Rd CB9...... 23 F6
Cornwall Rd
6 Stamford PE9........ 244 B6
Wyton Airfield PE28.... 143 A8
Corona Rd CB4......... 83 E4
Coronation Ave
3 Crowland PE6....... 232 B8
Huntingdon PE29...... 141 E5
Parson Drove PE12..... 234 A7
Royston SG8............ 5 C5
9 Somersham PE28.... 215 C1
Warboys PE28......... 164 F6
Whittlesey PE7....... 189 F7
Coronation Cl
March PE15........... 243 C2
Waterbeach CB25...... 106 A7
Coronation Mews 2 CB2. 64 E7
Coronation Pl CB2....... 64 E7
Coronation St CB2..... 246 B1

Corporation Bank PE6... 207 F7
Corporation Rd PE13... 245 D3
Corpus Christi Coll CB2. 246 A2
Corpus Christi La PE29. 141 L1
Corrie Rd CB1.......... 65 B7
Corsican Pine Cl CB8... 110 F5
Corunna Cl 7 PE19..... 74 C5
Corvus Cl SG8........... 5 E8
Cosgrove Cl PE3....... 197 C6
Cosin Ct CB1.......... 246 A1
Cossington Cl CB24.... 125 D2
Cotes The CB7........ 211 F6
COTON................ 82 B2
Coton CE Prim Sch CB23. 82 B2
Coton Rd CB3.......... 63 E5
Cotswold Cl
March PE15........... 243 E4
Peterborough PE4..... 204 E1
COTTENHAM........... 125 C4
Cottenham Cl 6 PE28... 208 D1
Cottenham Prim Sch
CB24............... 125 D4
Cottenham Rd
Histon CB24........... 104 B5
Landbeach CB24....... 126 A3
Cottenham Village Coll
CB24............... 125 L1
Cottesmore Cl PE3..... 197 D4
Cotton Cl
Conington PE7......... 168 C3
5 Sawtry PE28........ 168 C2
Cotton Ct 1 PE29..... 141 F7
Cotton End Rd PE7.... 197 A4
Cotton End Rd CB8.... 110 C4
Cottons Cnr PE14..... 229 D6
Cotton's Field CB23... 102 B1
Cottons Head PE14.... 236 E3
COTTONS THE......... 236 E3
Cottons The PE14..... 236 E2
Cottrell's La CB23.... 100 B4
Coulson Cl CB24...... 105 C2
Coulson Way PE28.... 150 F4
Council Rd 4 PE13.... 245 E6
Council St PE4....... 197 D8
Countess Cl PE19...... 74 B3
County Rd
Hampton Vale PE7..... 181 C8
March PE15........... 243 D6
Coupals Cl CB9......... 24 D6
Coupals Prim Sch CB9... 24 D7
Coupals Rd CB9......... 24 E6
Courier Cl IP28....... 239 B6
Courtland Ave CB1...... 65 C3
Courtney Way CB4....... 83 E4
Courtyards CB22........ 48 F3
Courtyard Way CB24... 125 E5
Cousins Cl PE15...... 243 C4
Covehite Ct 6 CB9..... 23 E6
COVENEY............. 217 C5
Covent Gdn
Cambridge CB1......... 246 C1
12 Willingham CB24.... 209 A1
Covent Gdns CB24..... 209 A1
Coventry Cl PE4...... 204 B3
Covert Cl CB9......... 39 A1
Covert The
1 Comberton CB23..... 62 D6
Peterborough PE3..... 197 B1
COVINGTON........... 135 D2
Cowbridge Hall Dro CB6 218 B6
Cow Brook La CB23..... 99 A3
Cow Brook Pl 2 CB23... 99 A3
Cowdell End CB23..... 100 B4
Cowgate PE1.......... 197 F2
Cow & Hare Pas PE27... 144 A3
Cow La
Fulbourn CB21......... 66 E5
Godmanchester PE29... 142 C2
Great Chesterford CB10.. 19 A4
Rampton CB24......... 124 F6
Cowley Cl PE28....... 115 D3
Cowley Pk CB4......... 84 B7
Cowley Rd CB4......... 84 C7
COWLINGE............. 73 D1
Cowlinge Cnr CB8....... 73 D8
Cowper Rd
Cambridge CB1......... 65 B6
Huntingdon PE29...... 141 D5
Peterborough PE1...... 197 F7
Cowpers Ct 4 PE19..... 74 D6
Cow & Sheep Dro IP28.. 213 C7
Cowslip Cl SG8........... 5 F5
Cowslip Dr CB6....... 211 L4
Cowslip Pl PE15...... 243 E5
Cow Way PE7.......... 190 D8
Coxons Cl PE29....... 141 E5
Coxs Cl CB22.......... 49 C4
Cox's Dro CB21........ 66 F6
Cox's End 15 CB24.... 208 D1
Cox's La
Chatteris PE16........ 241 C6
Wisbech PE13......... 245 A3
Crabapple Cl PE28.... 168 B3
Crabapple Gdns PE2... 185 D6
Crab Apple Way SG19... 41 C5
Crab Marsh PE13...... 245 B8
Crabtree PE4......... 205 B1
Crabtree Croft CB21.... 35 B3
Crafts Way CB23...... 102 C3
Craft Way SG8......... 11 B2
Craig St PE1......... 197 F3
Craister Ct CB4....... 83 E7
Cramswell Cl CB21..... 23 E6

Crandal Way CB22 . . . . . . **49** A4
Crane Ave PE7 . . . . **181** F6
Crane Cl **3** PE28 . . . . . **208** C8
Cranemore PE4 . . . . **204** A4
Crane's La CB23 . . . . **61** A2
Crane St PE28 . . . . **140** C3
Cranfield Pl **2** PE28 . . . **208** C8
Cranfield Way
  Brampton PE28 . . . . **140** D2
  Buckden PE19 . . . . **117** A3
Cranford Dr PE3 . . . . . . **197** C4
Cranleigh Cl CB2 . . . . **64** D1
Cranmer Rd CB3 . . . . **83** B1
Cranmore Dro PE6 . . . . . **206** D8
Cranny The PE19 . . . . . . **117** F2
Cranwells Way **4** CB6 . . **211** B8
Cratherne Way CB4 . . . . . **83** F7
Crathern Way CB4 . . . . . . **83** F7
Crauden Gdns CB7 . . . . . **240** E5
Craven Cl CB2 . . . . **64** D2
Craven Ct CB8 . . . . **110** F7
Craven Way CB8 . . . . . . **110** E6
Crawford Cl **11** CB4 . . . . **83** E8
Crawford Gdns **2** PE6 . . **232** C8
CRAWLEY END **8** D5
Crawley End SG8 . . . . **8** D4
Crawthorne Rd PE1 . . . . **198** A3
Crawthorne St **1** PE1 . . **198** B3
Crease Dro PE6 . . . . **232** B8
Crease Rd
  Conington PE28 . . . . . . **168** F5
  Sawtry PE28 . . . . **169** B6
Crecy Ct PE19 . . . . **74** C5
Creek Fen PE15 . . . . **228** D5
Creek Rd PE15 . . . . **243** D4
Crescent Cl PE7 . . . . **190** A7
Crescent Rd
  Histon CB24 . . . . **104** C1
  Whittlesey PE7 . . . . **189** F6
Crescent The
  Cambridge CB3 . . . . **83** B3
  Dullingham CB8 . . . . **89** C1
  Eaton Socon PE19 . . . . . . **74** C3
  Eye PE6 . . . . **232** A1
  Impington CB24 . . . . . . **104** C1
  Littleport CB6 . . . . **242** C3
  Peterborough PE2 . . . . . **186** E7
  4 Soham CB7 . . . . **212** B3
  St Ives PE27 . . . . **144** A5
  St Neots PE19 . . . . **74** F6
  Wicken CB7 . . . . **211** E1
  Wisbech PE13 . . . . **245** C4
Cressbrook Dr CB23 . . . . . **79** C3
Cressener Terr **3** PE19 . . **74** F5
Cresset The **3** PE3 . . . . **197** A4
Cresswells La CB7 . . . . . **240** E4
Crester Dr **3** PE4 . . . . . **204** C3
Criccieth Way PE2 . . . . . . **74** F1
Cricketers Cl PE15 . . . . . **243** C3
Cricketers Way
  3 Benwick PE15 . . . . . **222** A5
  Chatteris PE16 . . . . **241** D3
  Wisbech PE13 . . . . **245** A6
Cricketfield La PE26 . . . . **172** A6
Cricket Field Rd CB8 . . . . **111** B2
Cricket Sch CB1 . . . . **246** C1
Crick's Rd IP28 . . . . **213** D6
Cripple Sidings La PE2 . . **187** A8
Crispin Cl
  Haverhill CB9 . . . . **23** D7
  1 Impington CB4 . . . . . **83** D7
Crispin Pl CB1 . . . . **246** C3
Crockfords Rd CB8 . . . . . **111** A2
Crocus Gr PE1 . . . . **198** A8
Crocus Way PE7 . . . . **181** F6
Croft Cl
  Brampton PE28 . . . . **140** D2
  Histon CB24 . . . . **104** B5
Crofters The CB6 . . . . . . **210** F6
Croftfield Rd PE29 . . . . . **141** F1
Croftgate CB3 . . . . **64** A7
Croft Gdns CB3 . . . . **64** C7
Croft La
  Haverhill CB9 . . . . **24** B6
  Oakington/Longstanton
  CB24 . . . . **103** B6
Croft Park Rd CB6 . . . . . **242** D3
Croft Pl IP28 . . . . **239** C4
Croft Rd
  Isleham CB7 . . . . **213** A5
  Newmarket CB8 . . . . . . **110** E5
  Outwell PE14 . . . . **229** D7
Crofts The PE19 . . . . **95** F1
Croft The
  Christchurch PE14 . . . . . **229** D3
  Fulbourn CB21 . . . . **66** E5
  Stamford PE9 . . . . **244** D5
Croft Way PE7 . . . . **186** C2
Croftwood CB6 . . . . **216** D1
Crome Ditch Cl CB3 . . . . . **64** A4
Cromwell Cl
  2 Northborough PE6 . . **231** F7
  Ramsey PE26 . . . . **171** F6
Cromwell Com Coll
  PE16 . . . . **241** C4
Cromwell Ct **4** PE19 . . . . **74** F3
Cromwell House* PE19 . . **141** D5
Cromwell Mews PE6 . . . . **231** C4
Cromwell Mus* PE29 . . . **141** D4
Cromwell Park Prim Sch
  PE29 . . . . **141** A4
Cromwell Pk CB24 . . . . . **208** E1
Cromwell Pl PE27 . . . . . . **144** B3
Cromwell Rd
  Cambridge CB1 . . . . **84** B1

Cromwell Rd continued
  Ely CB6 . . . . **240** C4
  March PE15 . . . . **243** D6
  Peterborough PE1 . . . . . **197** F4
  St Neots PE19 . . . . **74** F3
  1 Sutton CB6 . . . . **216** E1
  Wisbech PE13 . . . . **245** B3
Cromwell Sq PE29 . . . . . **141** D5
Cromwell Terr PE27 . . . . **144** B3
Cromwell Way PE28 . . . . **168** B3
Cromwell Wlk PE29 . . . . **141** D5
Crooked Bank
  Begdale PE14 . . . . **235** F5
  Wisbech PE14 . . . . **235** D5
Croot Cl PE28 . . . . **140** B2
Cropley Grove **92** D3
Cropston Rd PE1 . . . . . . **198** E7
Crosfield Cl CB4 . . . . **83** E7
Cross Bank CB7 . . . . . . **219** F8
Cross Bank Dro CB7 . . . . **211** C5
Crossberry Way PE6 . . . . **231** B4
Cross Cl CB9 . . . . **39** A1
Cross Dro
  Haddenham CB6 . . . . . . **209** E3
  Littleport CB7 . . . . **226** A1
  Southery PE38 . . . . **226** C3
  Stretham CB6 . . . . **210** F3
  Tydd St Giles PE13 . . . . . **237** D5
  Warboys PE28 . . . . **215** C6
  Waterbeach CB25 . . . . . **127** A4
  Whittlesey PE7 . . . . **190** F6
  Wilburton CB6 . . . . **210** C3
  Wistow PE28 . . . . **172** E1
Cross Farm Ct PE28 . . . . **120** C2
Cross Gn CB8 . . . . **70** F8
Crosshall Inf Sch PE19 . . . **74** C6
Crosshall Jun Sch PE19 . . **74** C6
Crosshall Rd PE19 . . . . . . **74** D6
Cross Hall Rd PE19 . . . . . **74** D6
Cross Keys Ct CB24 . . . . **125** D3
Cross La
  Little Downham CB6 . . . . **218** A6
  Melbourn SG8 . . . . **14** C6
  Wisbech PE13 . . . . **235** B5
Cross Lane Cl SG8 . . . . . . **45** E1
Cross Rd
  March PE15 . . . . **227** F2
  Sutton St Edmund PE12 . . **237** A4
  Whittlesey PE7 . . . . **189** C7
Crossroad Cotts CB10 . . . **17** E2
Cross St
  Cambridge CB1 . . . . **246** C1
  Covington PE28 . . . . **135** D2
  Farcet PE7 . . . . **187** D1
  Huntingdon PE29 . . . . . **141** E5
  Peterborough PE1 . . . . . **198** A2
Cross The PE28 . . . . **161** B6
Crossway Hand PE7 . . . . **189** B8
Crossways
  Barley SG8 . . . . **6** F1
  Linton CB21 . . . . **35** C7
Crossways Gdns CB2 . . . . **64** D2
Crow Dean CB23 . . . . **79** A3
CROW END **60** D7
Crowhill **6** PE29 . . . . . **118** F8
Crow Hill La CB23 . . . . . . **79** B3
Crowhurst PE4 . . . . **204** C5
Crowland **232** B8
Crowland Rd
  Deeping St James PE6 . . **207** A3
  Eye PE6 . . . . **232** A3
  Haverhill CB9 . . . . **23** F8
  Newborough PE6 . . . . . . **232** A2
  Thorney PE6 . . . . **232** E5
Crowlands CB24 . . . . **125** C5
Crowland Way CB4 . . . . . . **83** F7
Crown Ave PE14 . . . . . . **229** D3
Crown Cl
  Hail Weston PE19 . . . . . . **95** A1
  March PE15 . . . . **243** C2
  Margery's Croft PE13 . . . **238** B1
  St Ives PE27 . . . . **144** A4
  Warboys PE28 . . . . **164** F6
Crown Gdns
  Alconbury PE28 . . . . **150** E4
  Little Downham CB6 . . . . **218** A6
Crown La **6** CB24 . . . . . **242** D4
Crown Lakes Ctry Pk*
  PE7 . . . . **187** B2
Crown Mews PE26 . . . . . **172** B7
Crown Pl PE27 . . . . **144** A3
Crown Rd PE14 . . . . **229** D3
Crown St
  Peterborough PE1 . . . . . **197** C7
  Stamford PE9 . . . . **244** B5
  St Ives PE27 . . . . **144** A3
Crown Wlk
  Newmarket CB8 . . . . . . **111** A4
  St Ives PE27 . . . . **144** A3
Crowson Cres **6** PE6 . . . **231** F7
Crow Slang La PE28 . . . . **115** D2
Crowthorne Cl CB1 . . . . . . **65** F6
Crow Tree St SG19 . . . . . . **58** D4
Croxton **76** B2
Croxton Gdns PE28 . . . . **136** D6
Croydon **27** A7
Croydon Hill SG8 . . . . **26** E8
Croydon Rd
  Arrington SG8 . . . . **44** C1
  Croydon SG8 . . . . **27** B8
Croyland Rd PE4 . . . . . . **204** D1
Crummock Wr PE29 . . . . . **141** C5
Crunch Croft CB9 . . . . **24** E5
Crystal Dr PE2 . . . . **186** D8
Cubitt Way PE2 . . . . **187** A8
Cuckoo La
  Lolworth CB23 . . . . **101** F5
  Rampton CB24 . . . . **124** E3

Culley Ct PE2 . . . . **185** B2
Culloden Cl PE19 . . . . **74** C5
Cumberland Cl PE28 . . . . **143** A4
Cumberland Way **3** PE19 **74** F1
Cundell Dr CB4 . . . . **123** E4
Cunningham Cl CB4 . . . . . **83** E6
Cunningham Rd PE2 . . . . **186** E8
Cunningham Way PE19 . . . **74** A2
Curf PE16 . . . . **222** F3
Curf Fen Dro PE16 . . . . . **222** E4
Curlew Ave PE16 . . . . . . **241** C5
Curlew Cl PE7 . . . . **189** F8
Curlew Cres **6** SG8 . . . . . . **5** E8
Curlew Gr PE2 . . . . **187** D2
Curlew Pl **2** PE19 . . . . . **75** B6
Curringtons Cl CB24 . . . . **125** E4
Cutter Ferry Cl CB4 . . . . . **84** A3
Cutter Ferry La CB4 . . . . **246** C4
Cygnet Dr PE16 . . . . **241** C6
Cygnet Pk PE7 . . . . **186** E3
Cygnet Rd PE7 . . . . **186** E3
Cypress Cl
  6 Doddington PE15 . . **223** A6
  Peterborough PE3 . . . . . **197** A2
Cyprus Rd CB1 . . . . **65** C7

D

Dacre Gn SG8 . . . . **5** F6
Daffodil Gr PE2 . . . . **187** C7
Dagless Way PE15 . . . . . **243** D7
Daimler Ave PE7 . . . . . . **181** E6
Daintree PE27 . . . . **208** A3
Daintree Rd PE26 . . . . . . **220** D4
Daintrees Rd CB24 . . . . . **121** F6
Daintree Way PE28 . . . . **143** D1
Dairy Dro
  Littleport CB6 . . . . **225** C6
  Thorney PE6 . . . . **233** E2
Daisy Cl CB4 . . . . **83** D7
Dakota Rd IP28 . . . . **213** E8
Dalby Ct PE1 . . . . **198** C8
Dale Cl PE2 . . . . **185** F5
Dalegarth CB24 . . . . **83** F4
Dales Way CB24 . . . . **208** A3
Dale The CB24 . . . . **123** F1
Dale Way CB22 . . . . **32** F8
Dalham **92** E8
Dalham Pl CB9 . . . . **24** B8
Dalham Rd
  Ashley CB8 . . . . **92** B7
  Moulton CB8 . . . . **112** F4
Dalton Sq CB4 . . . . **84** B5
Dalton Way CB6 . . . . **240** D6
Dam Bank Dro CB6 . . . . . **209** C4
Damms Pastures CB23 . . . **80** D2
Damson Way CB23 . . . . . . **79** A3
Damson Wlk SG7 . . . . **3** A3
Dane Dr CB3 . . . . **83** A1
Dane Hill CB8 . . . . **133** E5
Dane Hill Rd CB8 . . . . . . **133** D5
Danesbury Ct CB1 . . . . . . **84** C1
Danes Cl PE1 . . . . **198** C4
Daniel Ct PE9 . . . . **244** C4
Danish Ct PE4 . . . . **204** A4
Daphmoir Cl CB2 . . . . **29** F8
Dapple Gdns PE7 . . . . . . **189** D3
Darford PE28 . . . . **208** E6
Darley Cl PE8 . . . . **230** C1
Darrington Cl **1** PE19 . . . **74** B3
Dart Cl PE27 . . . . **144** B6
Dartford Rd PE15 . . . . . . **243** C4
Darthill Rd PE15 . . . . . . **243** D5
Dartmoor Dr PE29 . . . . . **141** A4
Darwin Cl
  Ely CB6 . . . . **240** A4
  Mildenhall IP28 . . . . . . **239** C6
  3 Stamford PE9 . . . . . **244** A1
Darwin Coll CB3 . . . . . . **246** A1
Darwin Dr CB4 . . . . **83** D5
Darwin Pl CB8 . . . . **111** B1
Darwood Ct PE27 . . . . . . **144** B3
Daules Rd PE28 . . . . **140** E1
Davey Cl CB24 . . . . **104** C3
Davey Cres CB22 . . . . **49** A6
David Bull Way CB24 . . . . **105** D3
David Chalmers Cl PE2 . . **186** F8
David's Cl PE14 . . . . **203** F4
David's La PE4 . . . . **204** B6
David St **5** CB1 . . . . **65** A8
Davie La PE7 . . . . **201** A1
Da Vinci Pl PE27 . . . . . . **144** A7
Davis Cl PE19 . . . . **96** A2
Davison Rd CB6 . . . . **240** E8
Davy Rd CB1 . . . . **65** B7
Daws Cl **5** CB1 . . . . **65** F6
Daw's Dro PE7 . . . . **220** D8
Daymond St PE2 . . . . . . **186** D7
Days Cl SG8 . . . . **5** C5
Day's Lode Rd PE15 . . . . **224** C7
Days Mdw CB24 . . . . **103** C6
Deaconscroft PE3 . . . . . . **197** B5
Deacons La CB7 . . . . **240** D5
Deacon St PE1 . . . . **197** F3
Deal Gr PE29 . . . . **141** E8
Deal Gr CB22 . . . . **32** F8
Dean Dr CB1 . . . . **65** B4
Dean Dro PE15 . . . . **215** F6
Dean Peacock Ct CB6 . . . **240** E6
Dean Rd CB21 . . . . **21** B8
Deans Cl CB9 . . . . **39** A1
Dean's Ct PE15 . . . . **198** A2
Debdale Cl PE2 . . . . **185** E4
Debdale Ct PE7 . . . . **189** F5
Debden Gn CB6 . . . . **240** B4
De Bec Cl PE1 . . . . **198** C3

De Beche Cl CB23 . . . . . . **99** B3
Deben Ave PE27 . . . . . . **144** A7
Deben Cl PE15 . . . . **243** B5
Deben Rd CB9 . . . . **24** B8
Decoy Rd
  Borough Fen PE6 . . . . . **207** A3
  Gorefield PE13 . . . . **237** D2
DEEPING GATE **231** E8
Deeping Lakes Nature
  Reserve* PE6 . . . . **206** D5
Deeping Rd PE6 . . . . **206** B3
DEEPING ST JAMES **206** A7
Deeping St James Com Prim
  Sch **18** PE6 . . . . **231** F8
Deeping St James Rd
  PE6 . . . . **231** E7
Deepings Sch The **17**
  PE6 . . . . **231** F8
Deerfield Rd PE15 . . . . . **243** E4
Deerhurst Way **13** PE6 . . **232** A1
Deerleap PE3 . . . . **197** A5
Deerpark Rd PE28 . . . . . **168** A4
Deer Valley Rd **1** PE2 . . **186** E8
De Freville Ave CB4 . . . . **246** C4
De Freville Rd CB22 . . . . . **49** A6
Degas Dr PE15 . . . . **243** D4
De Havilland Ct **4** IP28 . **239** B5
De Havilland Rd PE13 . . . **245** C4
De-Havilland Rd PE13 . . . **245** C4
Deighton Cl PE27 . . . . . . **144** B5
De La Haye Cl CB23 . . . . . **99** B3
Delamere Cl
  Little Wilbraham CB8 . . . . **68** F6
  Peterborough PE1 . . . . . **198** C5
Delapre St **9** PE6 . . . . . **232** A1
De La Warre Way CB23 . . . **79** B4
Delbrig Dro CB7 . . . . **212** E5
De Lisle Cl CB23 . . . . **99** B3
Dells Cl PE28 . . . . **166** D2
Dell The
  Peterborough PE2 . . . . . **186** E7
  Royston SG8 . . . . **5** C5
Delph PE7 . . . . **189** D7
Delph Ct PE2 . . . . **187** F6
Delph Dro IP28 . . . . **212** F8
Delph St PE7 . . . . **189** D7
Delta La PE28 . . . . **151** E3
Delves Way PE7 . . . . **186** D2
Delve Terr PE16 . . . . **241** E5
Dendys PE28 . . . . **143** D1
Dengaine Cl CB23 . . . . . . **99** B2
Denham Rd CB8 . . . . **92** E8
Denham Wlk **1** PE3 . . . . **197** C4
Denis Dr PE2 . . . . **186** A4
Denmark Dr PE2 . . . . . . **186** A4
Denmark Rd CB24 . . . . . **125** E3
Dennis Gn SG19 . . . . **41** C4
Dennis Rd CB5 . . . . **84** F4
Dennis Green **41** C4
Dennis Wilson Ct CB2 . . . **64** D4
Denny Cl **9** CB24 . . . . . **208** D1
DENNY END **105** F8
Denny End Rd CB25 . . . . **105** F8
Denson Cl CB25 . . . . **106** A8
DENTON **175** E4
Denton Rd
  Glatton PE28 . . . . **175** E1
  Peterborough PE7 . . . . . **187** C6
Dentons Chase PE26 . . . . **220** E4
Depot Rd CB8 . . . . **110** E6
Deptford PE15 . . . . **243** B3
Derby Dr PE1 . . . . **198** C6
Derby Rd CB1 . . . . **65** B6
Derby St CB3 . . . . **64** C7
Derby Way CB1 . . . . **110** D5
Derwent Cl
  Cambridge CB1 . . . . **65** D5
  Huntingdon PE29 . . . . . **141** B5
  St Ives PE27 . . . . **144** B6
Derwent Dr PE4 . . . . **204** E2
Derwood Gr PE4 . . . . . . **204** B5
Desborough Ave PE2 . . . . **187** D5
Desborough Rd PE29 . . . **142** A6
Desmond Ave CB1 . . . . . . **65** F6
Devana Cl PE29 . . . . **118** F8
De Vere Cl PE28 . . . . **143** B1
Devills Pl PE16 . . . . **243** D4
Devil's Dyke Nature
  Reserve* CB25 . . . . **109** B5
Devoke Cl PE29 . . . . **141** B6
Devon Cl PE27 . . . . **144** A8
Devonshire Cl PE28 . . . . **168** B3
Devonshire Mews CB23 . . **80** C1
Devonshire Rd CB1 . . . . . **65** A8
Dewpond Cl **4** PE19 . . . . **75** A6
Dexter Cl **10** PE15 . . . . . **223** A5
Dexter La CB6 . . . . **242** C3
Dexter Way PE8 . . . . **178** B3
Dial Cl PE19 . . . . **95** F2
Diamond Cl CB2 . . . . **64** E5
Diana Cl PE7 . . . . **190** A6
Dickasons CB8 . . . . **14** D7
Dickens St PE1 . . . . **198** B3
Dickerson Cl **1** SG19 . . . . **96** A8
DIDDINGTON **96** A8
Digby Ct **3** PE19 . . . . . . **74** B3
Dillestone Ct CB9 . . . . . . **24** E5
DILLINGTON **94** C7
Dimmock's Cote CB6 . . . . **211** B3
Dimmock's Cote Rd CB7 . . **211** B3
Dingley Ct PE3 . . . . **197** C5
Dip The CB8 . . . . **111** D2
Discovery Way CB4 . . . . . . **84** C6
Ditchburn Pl
  6 Cambridge CB1 . . . . **65** A8
  Cambridge CB1 . . . . **84** A1
Ditchfield CB25 . . . . **108** D8

Ditchfields **2** PE28 . . . . **215** C1
Ditton Cl CB8 . . . . **111** A1
Ditton Fields CB5 . . . . **84** C3
Ditton Gn CB8 . . . . **90** D1
DITTON GREEN **90** E1
Ditton La CB5 . . . . **84** E4
Ditton Lodge Fst Sch
  CB8 . . . . **111** B2
Ditton Wlk **11** CB5 . . . . . **84** C4
Dixies Cl SG7 . . . . **2** D3
Dixon's Dro PE14 . . . . . . **238** F5
Dixons Rd **1** PE6 . . . . . . **231** E8
Dobson Wlk **11** PE15 . . . **223** B7
Dock Bsns Pk The CB7 . . . **240** D2
Dockings La **10** CB7 . . . . **213** A5
Dock La CB25 . . . . **106** A2
Dock Rd PE16 . . . . **241** C6
Dock The PE7 . . . . **240** D2
Doctor's Cl CB24 . . . . . . **104** D3
Docwra Rd CB23 . . . . **99** A3
Docwra's Cl SG8 . . . . **29** D5
DODDINGTON **223** A6
Doddington Com Hospl
  PE15 . . . . **222** F6
Doddington Dr PE3 . . . . . **197** B2
Doddington Rd
  Benwick PE15 . . . . **222** A5
  Chatteris PE16 . . . . **241** A8
  Doddington/Wimblington
  PE15 . . . . **223** B6
Dodds Mead CB23 . . . . . . **47** A5
Dodford La CB3 . . . . **103** E2
Dogget La CB21 . . . . **66** F4
Doggett Rd CB1 . . . . **65** E6
Dog Kennel La SG8 . . . . . . **5** D6
Dogsthorpe Gr PE1 . . . . . **198** A5
DOGSTHORPE **198** C7
Dogsthorpe Jun & Inf Sch
  PE1 . . . . **198** B7
Dogsthorpe Rd PE1 . . . . . **198** A5
Dogsthorpe Star Pit & Little
  Wood Nature Reserve*
  PE6 . . . . **205** E2
Doles The **3** CB24 . . . . . **208** D1
Dole The CB24 . . . . **104** C3
Dolls Cl CB21 . . . . **53** C1
Dolphin Cl
  Cambridge CB1 . . . . **66** A7
  Linton CB21 . . . . **35** C7
Dolphin La
  11 Ely CB7 . . . . **240** D4
  Melbourn SG8 . . . . **14** B6
Dolphins Way SG19 . . . . . **41** D6
Dolphin Way CB22 . . . . . . **49** A6
Dome Leisure Ctr IP28 . . **239** E4
Donaldson Dr PE4 . . . . . **204** F2
Donegal 7 CB1 . . . . **84** A2
Donegal Cl PE4 . . . . **204** D2
Donne Cl SG8 . . . . **5** C8
Donnington Pk PE13 . . . . **238** A1
Dorchester Cres **3** PE1 . **198** D7
Dorchester Way PE28 . . . **143** B7
Doris St CB3 . . . . **110** F3
Dorling Way PE28 . . . . . . **140** B3
Dorral Dean CB23 . . . . . . **80** B1
Dorvis La CB10 . . . . **21** B1
Double Bank La PE28 . . . **161** B7
Doughty St PE9 . . . . **244** D7
Douglas House Hospl CB2 **64** E5
Douglas Rd **8** PE6 . . . . . **231** E8
Douglas Way CB23 . . . . . . **79** B3
Doug Smith Cl CB8 . . . . . **110** F6
Dove Cl PE28 . . . . **121** C5
Dovecote
  Peterborough PE1 . . . . . **198** A7
  Yarwell PE8 . . . . **183** A8
Dove Cote Cl CB24 . . . . . **121** F5
Dovecote La PE7 . . . . . . **181** C5
Dovecote Rd
  Great Paxton PE19 . . . . . **96** D3
  Upwell PE14 . . . . **229** D7
Dovehouse Cl
  Ely CB7 . . . . **240** D3
  Fowlmere SG8 . . . . **15** E8
  Godmanchester PE29 . . . **142** A1
  St Neots PE19 . . . . **74** F6
Dove House Rd CB9 . . . . . **24** A8
Dovehouse Wood PE28 . . **162** B1
Dover Cl PE29 . . . . **141** E8
Dover Rd PE4 . . . . **204** C2
Dover St **2** CB1 . . . . **246** C2
Dove Willow PE6 . . . . . . **207** D6
Dovey Cl PE27 . . . . **144** B6
Dowding Way CB4 . . . . . . **83** D6
Dowgate Rd **3** PE13 . . . . **245** A7
Downe Cl CB23 . . . . **99** A2
DOWN FIELD **212** D2
Down Gate PE3 . . . . **197** A4
Downham Feoffees Prim Sch
  CB6 . . . . **218** A6
DOWNHAM HYTHE **217** D6
Downham Hythe Dro
  CB6 . . . . **217** D6
Downham Rd
  Ely CB6 . . . . **240** B7
  Outwell PE14 . . . . **236** D2
Downham's La CB4 . . . . . . **84** A6
Downing Cl
  Bottisham CB25 . . . . **86** E6
  Mildenhall IP28 . . . . . . **239** D5
  Newmarket CB8 . . . . . . **111** A2
Downing Coll CB2 . . . . . . **246** B1
Downing Cres PE9 . . . . . **244** B7
Downing Ct CB25 . . . . . . **108** A1
Downing Pl CB2 . . . . **246** B2
Downing St CB2 . . . . **246** B2
Downlands SG8 . . . . **5** C6
Downs Cres CB9 . . . . **23** F8

Downs Pl CB9 ... 23 F8
Downton Dr CB9 ... 23 E8
Dowsdale Bank PE6 ... 233 A8
Dragon Fly Cl PE7 ... 186 C2
Dragoon Dr 4 PE15 ... 243 D2
Drain Rd PE6 ... 205 A7
Drake Ave PE6 ... 241 C6
Drake Cl PE29 ... 141 F6
Drake Rd PE19 ... 74 B2
Drake Way CB24 ... 104 C5
Draper's Cl PE8 ... 178 C3
DRAPERS GREEN ... 23 A2
Drapers La CB9 ... 23 B2
Drapery Row 1 CB8 ... 111 A3
Drayhorse Rd PE26 ... 172 A5
Drayton PE3 ... 197 A4
Drayton Cl CB1 ... 66 A5
Drayton Rd CB1 ... 66 A5
Drewels La PE19 ... 56 D4
Driffield Way PE2 ... 186 D8
Drift Ave PE9 ... 244 D7
Drift Gdns PE9 ... 244 D7
Drift PE9 ... 244 C6
Drift The
  Elsworth CB23 ... 100 B4
  Exning CB8 ... 110 A8
  Newmarket CB8 ... 111 B2
  Oakington/Longstanton CB24 ... 103 B5
  Sutton PE5 ... 194 F3
Drings Cl 2 CB24 ... 208 D1
Drinkwater Cl CB8 ... 110 E4
Drivers Ave PE15 ... 141 E5
Drivers Cl 8 PE15 ... 223 A6
Drive The
  Perry PE28 ... 115 D1
  Peterborough PE3 ... 197 E2
  St Ives PE27 ... 143 F4
Drosier Rd CB1 ... 246 C1
Drove Gdns CB23 ... 79 C3
Drove Rd SG19 ... 41 A4
Drovers Cl PE26 ... 221 C4
Drove The
  Farcet PE26 ... 220 D7
  Witchford CB6 ... 217 E1
Droveway The PE6 ... 199 B3
Druce Ave PE28 ... 154 A1
Drummer St CB1 ... 246 B2
Drury La
  Bluntisham/Colne PE28 ... 208 D7
  Melbourn SG8 ... 14 D6
  Wicken CB7 ... 211 F4
Drybread Rd PE7 ... 189 F8
Dryden Cl PE27 ... 143 E6
Dryden Ct 7 PE19 ... 75 A5
Dryden Rd PE1 ... 197 E7
DRY DRAYTON ... 102 C1
Dry Drayton CE Prim Sch CB23 ... 102 C1
Dry Drayton Rd
  Madingley CB23 ... 81 D7
  Oakington & Westwick CB24 ... 103 A4
Dry Leys PE2 ... 186 C6
Dubbs Knoll Rd SG8 ... 10 F5
Duberly Cl PE28 ... 115 E2
Duchess Cl PE19 ... 74 A3
Duchess Dr
  Newmarket CB8 ... 111 D2
  Wooddition CB8 ... 90 E8
Duck Dro CB7 ... 219 D5
DUCK END ... 97 C5
Duck End
  Girton CB3 ... 82 D8
  Godmanchester PE29 ... 141 F1
Duck La
  Haddenham CB6 ... 210 A6
  St Neots PE19 ... 74 F4
DUCKPUDDLE BUSH ... 4 F2
Ducks La CB8 ... 110 C7
Duck St PE8 ... 178 D8
Duckworth Cl 2 PE7 ... 189 E7
Duddery Hill CB9 ... 23 F6
Duddery Rd CB9 ... 24 A7
Duddington Gdns PE7 ... 189 D7
Duddle Dr CB24 ... 123 F5
Dudley Ave PE4 ... 204 C2
Dudley Rd CB5 ... 84 C4
Duke of Bedford Prim Sch PE6 ... 233 B3
Dukes Dr PE2 ... 221 C2
Dukes Mdw CB22 ... 49 C5
Dukesmead PE4 ... 204 B2
Dukesmead Mobile Home Pk PE4 ... 204 B2
Dukes Rd PE19 ... 74 B4
Duke St
  Peterborough PE2 ... 187 A7
  Wisbech PE13 ... 245 D4
DULLINGHAM ... 70 D8
DULLINGHAM LEY ... 71 A5
Dullingham Rd
  Newmarket CB8 ... 110 F1
  Stetchworth CB8 ... 89 D3
  Wooddition CB8 ... 89 F7
Dullingham Sta CB8 ... 89 B2
DULOE ... 74 A6
Duloe Rd PE19 ... 74 B5
Dunblane Dr PE2 ... 185 D4
Duncan Way PE29 ... 141 F7
Duncock La CB23 ... 100 B4
Duncombe's Rd PE7 ... 191 F8
Dundee Cl CB4 ... 84 A5
Dundee Ct PE2 ... 185 C5
Dungate La CB21 ... 52 B6
Dunholt Way PE28 ... 208 D6
DUNKIRK ... 224 F1
Dunkirk Dro PE28 ... 215 C4

Dunmowe Way CB21 ... 66 E5
Dunnocks The CB24 ... 125 D4
Dunsberry
  Marholm PE3 ... 203 F1
  Peterborough PE3 ... 196 F8
Dunsbridge Turnpike SG8 ... 29 F2
Dunsey Wood CB9 ... 38 E1
Dunsmore Cl CB5 ... 84 E4
Dunstal Field CB24 ... 125 D2
Dunstall's Dro CB7 ... 218 E1
Dunstan St CB6 ... 240 B5
Dunster Dr CB9 ... 23 E8
Durham Cl PE28 ... 168 C2
Durham Rd PE1 ... 198 C3
Durham Way
  Newmarket CB8 ... 110 E5
  Wyton Airfield PE28 ... 143 B8
Durnford Way CB4 ... 83 E5
DUXFORD ... 17 D8
Duxford Aircraft Mus (Imperial War Mus at Duxford)* CB22 ... 31 F1
Duxford Airfield CB22 ... 17 A8
Duxford Camp CB22 ... 31 F1
Duxford CE Com Prim Sch CB22 ... 32 D1
Duxford Rd
  Hinxton CB10 ... 18 A7
  Ickleton CB10 ... 17 F5
  Whittlesford CB22 ... 32 D4
Dwyer-Joyce Cl CB24 ... 104 B4
DYER'S GREEN ... 13 C8
Dykemoor Dro PE15 ... 222 C4
Dykemoor Drove N PE15 ... 222 E5
Dyson Cl
  Peterborough PE1 ... 197 F3
  The Stukeleys PE29 ... 141 A5
Dyson's Dro CB25 ... 130 B5

E

Eachard Rd CB3 ... 83 B5
Eagle Cl PE19 ... 75 B7
Eagle La CB8 ... 89 D1
Eagle's La CB6 ... 218 A7
Eaglesthorpe PE1 ... 197 E7
EAGLETHORPE ... 178 A4
Eagle Way PE29 ... 142 A8
Eames Gdns PE1 ... 198 E6
Eardley Grange PE6 ... 207 F6
EARITH ... 208 E6
Earith Bsns Pk PE28 ... 208 F6
Earith Fen Dro PE28 ... 208 F7
Earith Prim Sch PE28 ... 208 E5
Earith Rd
  Bluntisham/Colne PE28 ... 208 D7
  Willingham CB24 ... 209 A2
Earl Cl 1 PE19 ... 74 B4
Earle St 4 PE13 ... 245 D4
Earls Cl PE2 ... 187 B6
Earls Hill Gdns SG8 ... 5 C6
Earl Spencer Ct PE2 ... 186 E8
Earl St CB1 ... 246 B2
Earlswood PE2 ... 185 E5
Earning St PE29 ... 141 F1
Earth Cl PE2 ... 187 E5
Easby Rise PE6 ... 232 B2
Eastalls Cl 15 PE15 ... 223 A5
Eastbourne Cl 2 PE16 ... 241 C3
Eastbourne Rd PE16 ... 241 C3
East Chadley La PE29 ... 141 F2
East Cl PE15 ... 243 B6
East Delph PE7 ... 189 D4
East Dr
  Caldecote CB23 ... 80 C1
  March PE15 ... 243 F4
Eastern Ave
  Haverhill CB9 ... 23 E8
  Peterborough PE1 ... 198 C8
  11 Soham CB7 ... 212 B4
Eastern Cl PE1 ... 198 D7
Eastern Ind Est PE1 ... 198 E3
East Fen Comm CB7 ... 212 C4
East Fen Dro CB7 ... 212 D4
East Fen Rd CB7 ... 213 B5
EASTFIELD ... 198 D4
Eastfield CB4 ... 84 A5
Eastfield Cty Inf Sch PE27 ... 144 A4
Eastfield Dr PE7 ... 189 F6
Eastfield Gr PE1 ... 198 B4
Eastfield Rd
  Peterborough PE1 ... 198 C4
  Royston SG8 ... 5 E6
  1 Wisbech PE13 ... 245 E4
Eastfields CB6 ... 242 C3
Eastfield Way PE13 ... 245 C6
EASTGATE ... 198 B2
Eastgate
  Great Chesterford CB10 ... 18 D2
  15 Market Deeping PE6 ... 231 F8
  Peterborough PE1 ... 198 B2
  Whittlesey PE7 ... 189 E7
Eastgate Mews PE7 ... 189 E7
East Hatley SG19 ... 43 A1
East Hertford St CB4 ... 246 A4
Eastholm PE1 ... 198 C3
East La SG19 ... 41 C6
Eastleigh Rd PE1 ... 198 C4
East Meadowgate PE14 ... 236 C7
Eastmoor La PE15 ... 223 C4

Easton Rd PE19 ... 114 C3
East Park St PE16 ... 241 C4
EAST PERRY ... 116 E3
East Perry PE28 ... 115 E2
East Rd
  Cambridge CB1 ... 246 C2
  Isleham CB7 ... 213 A5
  8 Northborough PE6 ... 231 F7
  Tydd St Mary PE13 ... 238 C8
EASTREA ... 190 D7
Eastrea Ct PE2 ... 187 E6
Eastrea Rd PE7 ... 189 F7
East St
  Bluntisham/Colne PE28 ... 208 C5
  Great Gransden SG19 ... 58 E4
  Huntingdon PE29 ... 141 F5
  1 Kimbolton PE28 ... 113 F4
  Manea CB6 ... 224 C4
  Stamford PE9 ... 244 C5
  St Neots PE19 ... 74 F5
East Sta Rd PE2 ... 187 A8
East View IP28 ... 213 C3
East Villa PE15 ... 224 B3
East Water Cres PE7 ... 186 C1
East Way CB22 ... 50 A1
Eastwood PE16 ... 241 C3
Eastwood Ave PE15 ... 243 E3
Eastwood Cl CB6 ... 216 E2
Eastwood End PE15 ... 223 C7
Eaton Cl
  Cambridge CB4 ... 84 A6
  Huntingdon PE29 ... 142 A7
Eaton Ct PE19 ... 74 C1
Eaton Est PE15 ... 223 B7
EATON FORD ... 74 C5
EATON SOCON ... 74 A5
Eaudyke Bank PE13 ... 237 F7
Eayre Ct PE19 ... 75 A5
Eccles Cl CB22 ... 32 F8
Eccles Rd PE8 ... 193 D8
Echo Hill SG8 ... 5 C5
Echo La PE28 ... 151 E3
Ecton Gr 7 PE14 ... 236 A5
Eden Cres PE16 ... 241 C4
Edendale Cl CB1 ... 65 C5
Edenfield PE2 ... 186 C6
Eden Rd CB9 ... 24 A7
Eden St Backway CB1 ... 246 C2
Eden St CB1 ... 246 C3
Edgcote Cl PE15 ... 223 C5
Edge Bank PE14 ... 236 F6
Edgeborough Cl CB8 ... 134 A1
Edgecombe CB4 ... 83 F7
Edgerley Drain Rd PE1 ... 198 F5
Edgerley Dro PE7 ... 205 F8
Edinburgh Ave
  Peterborough PE4 ... 204 B3
  Sawston CB22 ... 32 F8
Edinburgh Dr
  Eaton Socon PE19 ... 74 B4
  St Ives PE27 ... 143 F7
  Wisbech PE13 ... 245 C8
Edinburgh Rd
  Cambridge CB4 ... 84 A5
  Newmarket CB8 ... 110 E4
  Stamford PE9 ... 244 B7
Edis Ct PE2 ... 187 B6
Edison Dr PE7 ... 181 D6
Edison Rd PE27 ... 144 C6
Edis Way CB22 ... 30 C5
Edith Cavell Hospl PE3 ... 197 B4
Edmonds Cl PE9 ... 244 D6
Edmund Cl
  Haverhill CB9 ... 23 F7
  Milton CB24 ... 105 C2
Edwalton Ave PE3 ... 197 E3
Edward Rd
  Stamford PE9 ... 244 B7
  St Neots PE19 ... 74 F2
Edward St CB1 ... 84 A1
Edwards Way PE15 ... 224 B4
Edwards Wlk PE28 ... 208 E6
Edwinstowe Cl CB2 ... 64 E6
Egar Way PE1 ... 196 F2
Egerton Cl CB5 ... 84 D4
Egerton Rd CB5 ... 84 E4
Egremont Rd CB23 ... 81 A3
Egremont St CB6 ... 240 C5
Ehringshausen Way CB9 ... 24 B6
Eight Acres PE9 ... 244 A5
Eighth Ave PE13 ... 245 E4
Ekin Rd CB5 ... 84 D4
Eland Way CB1 ... 66 A7
Elbourn Way SG8 ... 12 F5
Elbow La PE13 ... 234 F8
Elder Cl
  Cambridge CB4 ... 83 F6
  Sawston CB22 ... 32 D8
Eldern PE2 ... 186 C4
ELDERNELL ... 202 B2
Eldernell La PE7 ... 191 B8
Elder Pl PE16 ... 241 D4
Elder's Way PE12 ... 237 E8
Eldith Ave CB7 ... 213 A1
Eldo Gdns PE19 ... 213 D6
Eldo La IP28 ... 214 B8
Eldo Rd PE28 ... 213 D6
Elean Bsns Pk CB6 ... 216 E2
Eleanor Cl PE9 ... 244 A6
Elecks La SG8 ... 11 D8
Elfleda Rd CB5 ... 84 C3
Elford Closes PE15 ... 210 E3
Elgar Way 5 PE9 ... 244 A6
Elgood's Brewery Tours, Gdn & Visitors Ctr* PE13 ... 245 A4
Elin Way SG8 ... 14 B8

Eliot Rd SG8 ... 5 D8
Elizabethan Way PE28 ... 140 B2
Elizabeth Ave CB8 ... 110 E5
Elizabeth Ct
  5 Eaton Socon PE19 ... 74 C4
  Hemingford Grey PE27 ... 143 F1
  Peterborough PE1 ... 198 A5
  2 Sutton CB6 ... 216 E2
Elizabeth Dr PE29 ... 142 B6
Elizabeth Par CB8 ... 110 E5
Elizabeth Rd PE9 ... 244 A6
Elizabeth Terr PE13 ... 245 D4
Elizabeth Way
  Bluntisham/Colne PE28 ... 208 D7
  Burrough Green CB8 ... 70 F4
  Cambridge CB4 ... 83 F4
  Gamlingay SG19 ... 41 C6
  Haddenham CB6 ... 210 A6
  Manea CB6 ... 224 C4
Ellesmere Rd CB4 ... 83 D6
Ellindon PE3 ... 197 B7
Ellingham Ave PE15 ... 243 C3
ELLINGTON ... 139 A4
Ellington Rd PE28 ... 149 E1
ELLINGTON THORPE ... 139 A2
Elliot Ave PE3 ... 196 F2
Elliott Cl CB8 ... 111 A6
Elliott Rd PE15 ... 243 B5
Ellis Cl CB24 ... 125 D3
Ellison Cl CB4 ... 83 D7
Ellison La CB23 ... 81 A4
Elloe Bank
  Newton PE13 ... 237 B2
  Tydd St Giles PE13 ... 237 B5
Ellwood Ave PE2 ... 187 B5
Ellwoods Cl CB7 ... 213 A5
ELM ... 236 B5
Elm CE Prim Sch PE14 ... 236 B5
Elm Cl
  Dullingham CB8 ... 70 D8
  Haverhill CB9 ... 23 F8
  Huntingdon PE29 ... 141 E7
  March PE15 ... 243 D7
  5 Market Deeping PE6 ... 231 F8
  Stilton PE7 ... 175 F2
  Witchford CB6 ... 217 E2
  Yaxley PE7 ... 181 F7
Elm Cres PE16 ... 241 C4
Elm Croft PE19 ... 95 F3
Elmcroft Cl 6 IP28 ... 213 F8
Elm Ct
  Elmdon CB11 ... 9 B4
  5 Sturmer CB9 ... 24 E5
ELMDON ... 9 A4
Elmdon Lee CB11 ... 9 E1
Elmdon Pl CB9 ... 24 B8
Elm Dr
  Little Stukeley PE28 ... 151 E3
  Offord Cluny PE19 ... 118 A2
  St Ives PE27 ... 143 F6
Elm End PE28 ... 150 F4
Elmfield CB6 ... 240 C5
Elmfield Dr PE14 ... 245 E1
Elmfield Rd
  Cambridge CB4 ... 84 A5
  Peterborough PE1 ... 198 A7
Elm High Rd PE14 ... 245 E1
Elmhurst Cl CB9 ... 24 B7
Elm Low Rd PE14 ... 245 D2
Elmondbury CB11 ... 9 A4
Elmore Rd PE3 ... 197 A3
Elm Pk PE7 ... 189 E7
Elm Rd
  Folksworth PE7 ... 175 D8
  Little Stukeley PE28 ... 152 A1
  March PE15 ... 243 D8
  Wisbech PE13 ... 245 D3
Elm Rd Prim Sch PE13 ... 245 D4
Elm's Ave CB22 ... 49 A5
Elms Cl CB22 ... 32 D1
Elmside CB14 ... 236 D5
Elm Side CB6 ... 242 B5
Elms Rd
  Freckenham IP28 ... 213 E2
  Red Lodge IP28 ... 213 F1
Elm St
  Cambridge CB1 ... 246 B3
  Peterborough PE2 ... 186 F7
  Stamford PE9 ... 244 C5
Elms The
  Chatteris PE16 ... 241 E4
  Great Chesterford CB10 ... 18 E3
  Haslingfield CB23 ... 47 C5
  Milton CB24 ... 105 C2
Elm Tree Cl CB23 ... 79 C3
Elm Tree Dr SG8 ... 12 F4
Elm Way
  Melbourn SG8 ... 14 C5
  Papworth Everard CB23 ... 99 A3
  Sawtry PE28 ... 168 B3
  Willingham CB24 ... 209 A1
Elm Wlk SG8 ... 5 F7
Elsie's Way PE29 ... 141 F6
Elstone PE2 ... 186 A4
Elstow Cl 7 CB24 ... 208 D1
ELSWORTH ... 100 C4
Elsworth CE Prim Sch CB23 ... 100 A4
Elsworth Cl PE27 ... 144 C5
Elsworth Pl CB1 ... 65 A6
Elsworth Rd
  Boxworth CB23 ... 101 A5
  Conington CB23 ... 100 C8
Elter Wlk PE4 ... 204 E3
Elter Wr PE29 ... 141 B5
ELTISLEY ... 77 C4
Eltisley Ave CB3 ... 64 C7
Eltisley Rd SG19 ... 58 E6
ELTON ... 178 D8

Elton CE Prim Sch PE8 ... 178 D8
Elton Hall & Gdns* PE8 ... 178 D6
Elton Rd
  Sibson cum Stibbington PE8 ... 183 C8
  Water Newton PE8 ... 184 B7
Elvedon Way
  Haverhill CB9 ... 38 E1
  Newmarket CB8 ... 110 E5
Elwyn Ct PE15 ... 243 D3
Elwyndene Rd PE15 ... 243 D3
Elwyn Rd PE15 ... 243 D4
ELY ... 240 C3
Ely Cath CB7 ... 240 C4
Ely Cl PE4 ... 204 B3
Ely Mus* CB7 ... 240 C4
Ely Pl 15 PE13 ... 245 C5
Ely Rd
  Downham CB6 ... 218 B6
  Ely CB7 ... 218 D4
  Landbeach CB25 ... 105 F8
  Littleport CB6 ... 242 C2
  Milton CB24 ... 105 E3
  Soham CB7 ... 211 F7
  Stretham CB6 ... 210 F5
  Sutton CB6 ... 216 F2
  Waterbeach CB25 ... 126 E3
  Wentworth CB6 ... 217 A2
Ely St John's Prim Sch CB6 ... 240 A4
Ely St Marys CE Jun Sch CB7 ... 240 F6
Ely Way CB6 ... 210 A7
Embankment Rd 4 PE1 ... 198 A1
Embry Rd 19 PE8 ... 230 B1
Emery Pl PE28 ... 140 C2
Emery Rd CB1 ... 84 A1
Emery St CB1 ... 84 A1
Emlyns Gdns PE9 ... 244 C6
Emlyns St PE9 ... 244 C6
Emmanuel Cl IP28 ... 239 D5
Emmanuel Coll CB1 ... 246 B2
Emmanuel Rd
  Cambridge CB1 ... 246 B2
  Stamford PE9 ... 244 B7
Emmanuel St CB1 ... 246 B2
EMMAUS ... 127 E2
EMNETH ... 236 C6
EMNETH HUNGATE ... 236 E6
Emneth Prim Sch PE14 ... 236 D6
Emperor Ct 8 CB4 ... 83 E8
Empingham Rd PE9 ... 244 A5
Empire Theatre* PE13 ... 245 C5
Empson Rd PE1 ... 198 F5
Emson's Cl CB21 ... 35 D2
Enderbys Wharf PE27 ... 144 A3
Enfield 8 CB1 ... 84 A2
Enfield Ct PE6 ... 232 B1
Enfield Gdns PE3 ... 197 C4
Engaine Rd CB7 ... 186 B5
Engine Rd CB7 ... 211 F5
Engine Yd CB6 ... 240 B4
Engleric SG8 ... 8 D4
English Rd PE6 ... 233 B4
English St PE1 ... 197 E5
Ennerdale Cl PE29 ... 141 B6
Ennerdale Rise PE4 ... 204 D2
Ennion Cl CB7 ... 212 B3
Ennisdale Cl 9 CB4 ... 83 E7
Enniskillen Rd CB4 ... 84 B5
Enterprise Way
  Bretton PE3 ... 197 B8
  Wisbech PE13 ... 245 A2
Erasmus Cl CB4 ... 83 D5
Erica Rd PE27 ... 144 A3
Eriswell Rd
  Beck Row, Holywell Row & Kenny Hill IP28 ... 214 B8
  Haverhill CB9 ... 24 B8
Ermine Bsns Ctr PE29 ... 141 B8
Ermine Bsns Pk PE29 ... 141 B8
Ermine Cl
  March PE15 ... 243 C2
  Royston SG8 ... 5 D8
Ermine Cres PE7 ... 176 A7
Ermine Ct PE29 ... 141 C5
Ermine St
  Caxton CB23 ... 78 E2
  Huntingdon PE29 ... 141 C5
  Little Stukeley PE28 ... 151 F2
  The Stukeleys PE28 ... 141 A8
Ermine Street N CB23 ... 99 A4
Ermine Street S CB23 ... 78 C8
Ermine Way
  Arrington SG8 ... 44 C4
  Sawtry PE28 ... 168 C3
Erratts Hill CB8 ... 73 D1
Eskdale Cl 1 PE4 ... 204 E3
Essendyke PE3 ... 197 A7
Essex Cl CB4 ... 83 E5
Essex Hill CB11 ... 9 B2
Essex Rd
  Huntingdon PE29 ... 141 E8
  5 Stamford PE9 ... 244 B6
Estelle Ct PE26 ... 220 D2
Estover Rd PE15 ... 243 E6
Etheldreda St CB6 ... 240 B4
Ethelred Cl PE26 ... 172 B8
ETTON ... 231 D5
Eurocentre Sch CB2 ... 64 F7
Europa Way PE13 ... 245 B2
Euston St PE29 ... 141 E4
Euximoor Dro PE14 ... 229 B5

Evans Cl
Brampton PE28 . . . .**140** D3
Royston SG8 . . . .**5** D7
Evans Gr CB22 . . . .**32** E8
Everdon Way PE3 . . . .**197** C5
Ever Gn CB8 . . . .**55** F6
Evergreen Dr PE7 . . . . . .**186** B2
Evergreen La CB8 . . . .**55** F7
Evergreens CB4 . . . .**84** B5
Everingham PE2 . . . .**185** D5
Eversden Cl CB23 . . . .**61** D5
Eversden Rd CB23 . . . .**46** C5
Eversley Cl CB24 . . . . . .**125** D4
EVERTON **40** C3
Everton Hill SG19 . . . .**40** B3
Everton Lower Sch SG19 .**40** D3
Everton Rd
Gamlingay Great Heath
SG19 . . . .**40** E3
Sandy SG19 . . . .**40** B3
Eves Cl PE6 . . . .**207** D1
Ewingswood 1 PE28 . . . .**168** C2
Exchange Sq PE13 . . . . . .**245** B5
Exchange St PE1 . . . .**198** A2
Exeter Cl
Cambridge CB2 . . . .**64** D1
2 Market Deeping PE6 .**231** F8
Exeter Ct 10 CB9 . . . .**23** E6
Exeter Rd
Newmarket CB8 . . . .**111** A4
Peterborough PE1 . . . . .**197** F6
7 Wittering PE8 . . . . . .**230** B1
Exmoor Cl PE29 . . . .**141** A4
EXMOOR GRANGE **229** B4
EXNING **110** A8
Exning Prim Sch CB8 . . . .**110** B8
Exning Rd CB8 . . . .**110** D6
EYE **232** B1
Eyebury Rd PE6 . . . .**199** A6
Eye CE Prim Sch PE6 . . . .**232** B1
EYE GREEN **232** B2
Eye Green Ind Est PE6 . .**232** A2
Eye Green Nature Reserve★
PE6 . . . .**232** B2
Eye Hill Dro CB7 . . . .**211** F7
Eye Rd PE1 . . . .**198** E2
Eyeworth Rd SG19 . . . .**25** B2
EYNESBURY **74** F3
Eynesbury CE Prim Sch
PE19 . . . .**74** E4
Eynesbury Gn PE19 . . . . . .**74** F4
Eynesford Cl PE7 . . . .**188** A5
Eyrescroft PE3 . . . .**197** A2
Eyrescroft Prim Sch PE3 .**197** A2
Eyresford Cl PE7 . . . .**188** A5

F

Faber La PE8 . . . .**183** D1
Fairacre CB10 . . . .**18** C3
Fairbairn Rd CB4 . . . .**84** C5
Fairchild Way PE1 . . . . . .**198** A7
Fair Ct CB1 . . . .**246** C3
Fairey Ave PE29 . . . .**141** F1
Fairey Fox Dr 1 IP28 . . . .**239** B5
Fairfax Ct
Ely CB6 . . . .**240** C4
St Neots PE19 . . . .**74** F3
Fairfax Rd CB1 . . . .**84** B1
Fairfax Way
March PE15 . . . .**243** E1
10 Market Deeping PE6 .**231** F8
Fairfield
Gamlingay SG19 . . . .**41** C5
5 Sutton CB6 . . . .**216** E1
Fairfield Dr PE26 . . . .**172** A6
Fairfield Rd PE2 . . . .**187** A8
Fairfields
Sawston CB22 . . . .**50** A1
St Ives PE27 . . . .**144** A4
Fairfields Cres PE27 . . . . .**144** B4
Fairfield Way CB21 . . . .**35** D3
Fair Green The CB25 . . . .**129** D1
Fairhaven Cl
Duxford CB22 . . . .**32** D1
Lode CB25 . . . .**107** C2
Fairhaven Way CB8 . . . . .**110** E5
Fairlawns CB8 . . . .**110** F2
Fairlawns Rd CB8 . . . .**110** F2
Fairmead Way PE3 . . . . . .**197** E2
Fairsford Pl CB1 . . . .**84** A2
Fair St CB1 . . . .**246** C3
Fairstead House Sch
CB8 . . . .**111** B4
Fairview Ave PE16 . . . . . .**241** B5
Fairview Dr PE16 . . . .**241** B2
Fairview Gr CB25 . . . .**108** E5
Fairway
Chatteris PE16 . . . .**241** B3
Girton CB3 . . . .**103** E2
Fairway The
Bar Hill CB23 . . . .**102** D3
Bluntisham/Colne PE28 .**208** C6
Falcon Cl
Haverhill CB9 . . . .**24** C8
5 St Neots PE19 . . . .**75** B7
Falconer Rd CB23 . . . .**24** C5
Falcon La
4 Whittlesey PE7 . . . . .**189** D6
14 Wisbech PE13 . . . . .**245** C5
Falcon Mews CB6 . . . . . .**240** B5
Falcon Rd
Stukeley PE29 . . . .**141** A6

Falcon Rd continued
6 Wisbech PE13 . . . . . .**245** C5
Falcon Way
Buckden PE19 . . . .**117** B3
Peterborough PE7 . . . . .**186** C1
Falklands Dr PE13 . . . . . .**245** E3
Falklands Rd CB9 . . . .**39** A1
Falkner Rd CB22 . . . .**33** A8
Fallodan Rd PE2 . . . .**185** C3
Fallow Corner Dro PE15 .**224** A3
Fallow Dr PE19 . . . .**74** B5
Fallowfield
Cambridge CB4 . . . .**84** B5
Littleport CB6 . . . .**242** C3
Peterborough PE2 . . . . .**185** D5
Fallowfield Ct 8 CB9 . . . . .**23** E7
Fall's Dro PE13 . . . .**232** F7
Falmouth Ave CB8 . . . . . .**110** F3
Falmouth Gdns CB8 . . . . .**111** A6
Falmouth St 1 CB8 . . . . .**110** F3
Falstaff Rd PE19 . . . .**74** C3
Fane Cl PE9 . . . .**244** B7
Fane Rd PE4 . . . .**197** E8
Fanshawe Rd CB1 . . . .**65** A6
Faraday Cl PE7 . . . .**181** D6
FARCET **187** C2
Farcet CE Prim Sch PE7 .**187** C2
Farcet Cl 5 PE19 . . . .**74** C6
Fardell Rd 6 PE13 . . . . . .**245** C4
Fardell's La CB23 . . . .**100** A4
Farendon Rd PE28 . . . . . .**140** E1
Farfield Cl PE28 . . . .**168** A5
Farleigh Fields PE2 . . . . .**185** D7
Farm Cl
Ramsey PE26 . . . .**171** C3
Sawtry PE28 . . . .**168** B4
Farmer's End CB23 . . . .**61** E5
Farmer's Row CB21 . . . . . .**66** E4
Farm La
Papworth Everard CB23 . .**99** C2
Thriplow SG8 . . . .**31** B1
Farmland Mus & Denny
Abbey The★ CB25 . . . .**127** A5
Farm Rise CB22 . . . .**32** C5
Farmstead Cl CB24 . . . . . .**104** B5
Farm View PE5 . . . .**195** E2
Far Pasture PE4 . . . .**204** B5
Farrier Ct SG8 . . . .**5** C7
Farriers Ct PE2 . . . .**186** D7
Farriers Gate PE16 . . . . . .**241** D5
Farriers Way PE26 . . . . . .**164** F5
Farringdon Cl PE1 . . . . . .**198** D6
Farringford Cl 4 CB4 . . . . .**83** C6
Farthing Dro PE38 . . . . . .**226** D6
Farthing La PE27 . . . .**144** B4
Fassage Cl CB25 . . . .**107** C2
Fastnet Cl CB9 . . . .**24** D8
Faulkner Cl CB24 . . . .**125** D3
Fawcett Prim Sch CB2 . . . .**64** D3
Fawsley Garth PE3 . . . . . .**197** C6
Fayway NN14 . . . .**156** F2
Fazeley CB1 . . . .**246** C2
Feast Cl CB7 . . . .**212** E1
Feilden Way CB8 . . . .**110** E5
Felbrigg Wlk PE2 . . . .**187** F6
Feldale Pl PE7 . . . .**189** F8
Fellowes Dr PE15 . . . .**172** A6
Fellowes Gdns PE2 . . . . . .**187** A7
Fellowes Rd PE2 . . . .**187** A7
Felsham Chase PE25 . . . . .**130** C2
Felsted Ave PE13 . . . .**245** E5
Feltons CB7 . . . .**212** E1
Felton St CB1 . . . .**65** A8
Felton Way CB7 . . . .**240** E6
Fen Bank Rd CB7 . . . .**213** A6
Fenbridge Rd PE4 . . . .**204** C4
Fen Cl PE13 . . . .**245** E6
Fen Cswy★ PE7 . . . .**189** A8
Fen Cswy The CB3 . . . . . .**246** A1
FEN DITTON **84** F5
Fen Ditton Prim Sch CB5 .**84** F5
Fendon Cl CB1 . . . .**65** B3
Fendon Rd CB1 . . . .**65** B3
FEN DRAYTON **122** F6
Fen Drayton Nature
Reserve★ CB24 . . . . . .**121** F7
Fen Drayton Prim Sch
CB24 . . . .**121** F6
Fen Drayton Rd CB24 . . . .**122** C5
Fen Dro PE7 . . . .**176** C8
Fendyke La PE13 . . . .**237** F1
Fendyke Rd PE14 . . . .**236** E5
FEN END **57** D6
Fen End
Over CB24 . . . .**208** D1
Willingham CB24 . . . . . .**209** A1
FENGATE **198** D2
Fengate PE1 . . . .**198** D1
Fengate Cl 1 PE1 . . . .**198** B2
Fengate Mobile Home Pk
PE1 . . . .**198** D1
Fengate Rd PE14 . . . .**238** F1
Fengate Trad Est PE1 . . . .**198** D2
Fenhall Field PE13 . . . . . .**237** C1
Fen La
Sawtry PE28 . . . .**168** C3
Stilton PE7 . . . .**176** C8
Swaffham Bulbeck CB25 .**108** A4
Tydd St Giles PE13 . . . . .**237** B5
Fenland Cl 3 PE15 . . . . . .**223** B7
Fenland & District Ind Est
PE7 . . . .**189** F5
Fenland Rd PE13 . . . .**245** E6
Fenland Way PE16 . . . . . .**241** B5
Fenland & West Norfolk
Aviation Mus★ PE14 . .**238** F3
Fenland Wlk PE15 . . . . . .**243** D4

Fenleigh Cl CB25 . . . .**106** B8
Fennec Cl CB1 . . . .**66** B6
Fennels Cl CB9 . . . .**24** A7
Fenners Lawn CB1 . . . . . .**246** C1
Fenny La SG8 . . . .**29** A1
Fen Rd
Bassingbourn cum Kneesworth
SG8 . . . .**12** B7
Little Wilbraham CB1 . . . .**86** D2
Lode CB25 . . . .**107** B4
Milton CB4 . . . .**84** D6
Newton PE13 . . . .**237** E4
Parson Drove PE12 . . . .**234** C7
Pidley cum Fenton PE28 .**165** E1
Shingay cum Wendy SG8 . .**26** F1
Wisbech St Mary PE13 . .**234** E2
Fen Side
Haddenham CB6 . . . . . .**209** A4
Wicken CB7 . . . .**211** D3
Fenside Dr PE26 . . . .**207** C1
Fenside Rd PE26 . . . .**165** D8
Fen St PE7 . . . .**176** A7
FENSTANTON **122** C5
Fenstanton & Hilton Prim
Sch PE28 . . . .**121** C6
FENTON **165** B4
Fenton Hill PE28 . . . .**165** C3
Fenton Rd
Haverhill CB9 . . . .**24** B8
Warboys PE28 . . . .**165** A4
Fen View
Chatteris PE16 . . . .**241** B3
Christchurch PE14 . . . . .**229** D3
6 Doddington/Wimblington
PE15 . . . .**222** F5
Peterborough PE7 . . . . .**187** F6
Fen View Ct CB4 . . . .**84** D5
Fen Way 3 PE14 . . . .**236** A5
Feoffees Rd 5 PE28 . . . . .**208** C8
Ferndale
Teversham CB1 . . . .**66** C8
Yaxley PE7 . . . .**181** D6
Ferndale Cl CB8 . . . .**111** B5
Ferndale Rise CB8 . . . .**84** C4
Ferndale Way PE1 . . . .**205** B1
Ferndown Dr PE29 . . . . . .**118** F8
Ferneley Cres 8 CB8 . . . . .**111** A4
Fern Gr CB9 . . . .**23** E8
Fernie Cl PE6 . . . .**205** D8
Fernlea Cl CB1 . . . .**65** F7
Ferrars Ave PE19 . . . .**74** E4
Ferrars Ct 4 PE29 . . . .**141** D4
Ferrars Rd PE29 . . . .**141** D5
Ferrars Way CB4 . . . .**83** D6
Ferriman Rd PE28 . . . .**137** F6
Ferry Bank PE38 . . . .**226** D8
Ferry Cutter La CB4 . . . . .**246** C4
Ferry Dr PE6 . . . .**196** D3
Ferry Hill
Castor PE5 . . . .**196** B1
Chatteris PE16 . . . .**215** E6
Ferry La
Beck Row, Holywell Row &
Kenny Hill IP28 . . . .**213** D5
Cambridge CB4 . . . .**84** B4
Newton PE13 . . . .**238** B5
Ferry Mdw PE27 . . . .**208** A1
Ferry Meadows Ctry Pk★
PE2 . . . .**185** D4
Ferry Path PE1 . . . .**246** B4
Ferryview PE2 . . . .**185** E6
Ferry Way CB6 . . . .**242** D4
Festival Cl PE15 . . . .**224** C4
Festival Ct PE3 . . . .**197** B5
Festival Rd CB7 . . . .**213** A5
Festival Way PE26 . . . . . .**226** B6
Fews Cl 4 PE27 . . . .**208** A3
Field Ave PE13 . . . .**237** F7
Field Baulk PE15 . . . .**243** D2
Field Cl
Abbotsley PE19 . . . .**57** A6
Alconbury PE28 . . . .**150** F4
Buckden PE19 . . . .**117** B4
Grafham PE28 . . . .**116** A7
Linton CB21 . . . .**35** B2
Little Paxton PE19 . . . . . .**95** F2
Warboys PE28 . . . .**164** F5
Field Cottage Rd PE19 . . . .**74** C3
Field Cres SG8 . . . .**5** F7
Field End
Balsham CB21 . . . .**53** B2
Witchford CB6 . . . .**217** D2
Fielden Way CB8 . . . .**110** E5
Fieldfare Dr PE2 . . . .**187** E6
Fieldfare Way 10 SG8 . . . . .**11** D8
Field Farm Cotts CB10 . . . .**18** F7
Field Gate PE6 . . . .**216** D2
Fielding Ct 2 PE19 . . . .**74** C6
Fielding Pl PE19 . . . .**97** F4
Field La CB5 . . . .**84** E6
Field Rd
Kingston SG23 . . . .**61** B3
Mildenhall IP28 . . . .**239** C5
Ramsey PE26 . . . .**172** A7
Field Rise PE7 . . . .**181** D5
Field Row SG23 . . . .**61** B3
Fields End Cl PE7 . . . .**186** D3
Fieldside
Ely CB6 . . . .**240** B4
Stretham CB6 . . . .**210** E5
Whittlesey PE7 . . . .**190** F8
Fieldside View PE13 . . . . .**237** F7
Field Terr PE7 . . . .**187** C2
Field Terr Rd CB8 . . . .**110** F5
Field View
Bar Hill CB23 . . . .**102** B2
Harston CB22 . . . .**48** A4

Field View continued
Haverhill CB9 . . . .**38** C1
Field Way CB1 . . . .**65** C3
Field Wlk
Mildenhall IP28 . . . .**239** C5
Peterborough PE1 . . . . .**198** B2
Fifth Ave PE13 . . . .**245** E4
Fifty Dro CB6 . . . .**225** C7
Fifty Rd
Christchurch PE14 . . . . .**229** D1
Manea PE14 . . . .**224** D7
Figtree Wlk PE1 . . . .**198** B8
Fillance The SG8 . . . .**12** D5
Fincham Rd IP28 . . . .**239** B5
Fincham's Cl CB21 . . . .**35** D2
Finchfield PE1 . . . .**198** F7
Finchley Ave IP28 . . . .**239** B6
Finchley Gn PE3 . . . .**197** A4
Finch Rd CB4 . . . .**83** D5
Finch's Cl CB22 . . . .**49** C5
Finch's Rd CB23 . . . .**46** A7
Finch's Field CB23 . . . .**46** A7
Firdale Cl PE6 . . . .**206** C2
Firelots Dro PE15 . . . .**223** C8
First Ave
Warboys PE28 . . . .**164** E6
Wisbech PE13 . . . .**245** D5
First Broadpool Dro
PE28 . . . .**165** E8
First Drift PE9 . . . .**244** B2
First Dro
Burwell CB25 . . . .**130** C7
Peterborough PE1 . . . . .**198** D1
First Furlong Dro PE16 . . .**241** A3
Firs The CB22 . . . .**32** D2
First Marsh Rd PE14 . . . . .**238** D2
First Turf Fen Dro PE15 . .**165** B8
Fisher Cl
Duxford CB22 . . . .**17** E8
Haverhill CB9 . . . .**24** D7
Ramsey St Mary's PE26 . .**220** D7
Fishermans Cl PE26 . . . . .**171** B1
Fishermans Dr PE15 . . . . .**243** A5
Fishers Bank CB6 . . . .**242** E3
Fishers Cl PE7 . . . .**175** F7
Fisher's La
Cambridge CB1 . . . .**65** F6
Orwell SG8 . . . .**45** D2
Fisher St CB4 . . . .**246** A4
Fishers Way PE29 . . . .**118** F8
Fishers Yd 4 PE19 . . . .**74** E5
Fish Hill SG8 . . . .**5** D6
Fison Rd CB5 . . . .**84** E4
FITTON END **238** A3
Fitton End Rd PE13 . . . . . .**237** F3
Fitzgerald Cl CB6 . . . .**240** E8
Fitzroy Cl CB1 . . . .**246** C3
Fitzroy Cl CB5 . . . .**246** C3
Fitzroy St
Cambridge CB1 . . . .**246** C3
Newmarket CB8 . . . .**111** A3
Fitzwilliam Coll CB3 ★ **83** B4
Fitzwilliam Mus The★
CB2 . . . .**246** A1
Fitzwilliam Rd
Cambridge CB2 . . . .**64** F6
Stamford PE9 . . . .**244** A7
Fitzwilliam St
Cambridge CB2 . . . .**246** B1
Peterborough PE1 . . . . .**198** A3
Five Acres PE28 . . . .**28** F1
Five Arches PE2 . . . .**185** C6
Five Arches Pit Nature
Reserve★ PE28 . . . . . .**169** C2
Five Hundred Dro PE15 . . .**224** A4
Fiveways IP28 . . . .**239** F2
Flackdale Rd PE28 . . . .**120** B1
Flag Bsns Exchange PE1 .**198** E3
Flag Fen★ PE6 . . . .**199** D3
Flag Fen Rd PE1 . . . .**198** C4
Flaggrass Hill Rd PE15 . . .**243** E8
Flambards Cl SG8 . . . .**14** B8
Flamborough Cl PE2 . . . . .**197** C1
Flamsteed Dr PE29 . . . . . .**140** F5
Flamsteed Rd CB1 . . . .**65** A6
Flatford Rd CB9 . . . .**23** C8
Flat Rd CB24 . . . .**209** B3
Flat The CB8 . . . .**111** F7
Flavian Cl PE3 . . . .**24** D7
Flawn Way PE19 . . . .**74** D7
Flaxfields CB21 . . . .**35** C3
Flaxland PE3 . . . .**197** A6
Fleam Dyke Cotts CB21 . . .**67** C2
Flecks La
Shingay cum Wendy SG8 . .**26** D1
Steeple Morden SG8 . . . . .**11** D8
Fleet Cl CB6 . . . .**242** D4
Fleet The SG8 . . . .**5** C6
Fleet Way PE7 . . . .**187** B6
Fleetwood CB6 . . . .**240** C5
Fleetwood PE15 . . . .**243** D2
Flegcroft PE7 . . . .**189** F1
Fleming Ave IP28 . . . .**239** C5
Fleming Cl PE7 . . . .**181** D6
Fleming Ct
March PE15 . . . .**243** F3
Woodston PE2 . . . .**186** D8
Flemington Cl IP28 . . . . . .**239** B6
Fletcher Ave CB25 . . . . . .**127** C1
Fletchers Cl PE26 . . . .**172** A7
Fletcher's Terr 3 CB1 . . . . .**65** A8
Fletton Ave PE2 . . . .**187** A8
Fletton Fields PE2 . . . .**187** A7
Fletton Parkway PE2 . . . .**185** F2
Flint Cl PE28 . . . .**140** C2
FLINT CROSS **15** B2
Flint Ct CB21 . . . .**35** B2
Flint House Rd PE14 . . . . .**229** F5

Flint La CB25 . . . .**126** E3
Flint Way
Elm PE14 . . . .**236** A4
St Neots PE19 . . . .**74** E2
Flood's Ferry PE15 . . . . . .**222** A8
Flood's Ferry Rd PE15 . . . .**222** B7
Flore Cl PE3 . . . .**197** C5
Florence Cl PE7 . . . .**189** F6
Florida Ave PE29 . . . .**141** F8
Flowers Cl PE26 . . . .**172** A7
Flower St 2 CB1 . . . .**84** A1
Flowmere Rd SG8 . . . .**8** A5
Fodderfen Dro
Beck Row, Holywell Row &
Kenny Hill IP28 . . . .**219** F1
Wicken CB7 . . . .**211** C3
Fodder Fen Dro CB7 . . . . .**219** B3
Fodder Fen Rd PE15 . . . . .**224** C6
Foder Way PE7 . . . .**186** E3
Fold La PE13 . . . .**237** F7
Fold The PE7 . . . .**190** F8
Folgate La PE14 . . . .**238** F6
FOLKSWORTH
175 D8
Yaxley **180** D1
Folksworth CE Prim Sch
PE7 . . . .**175** D8
Folksworth Rd PE7 . . . . . .**180** E1
Folly Cl PE7 . . . .**181** C5
Folly Dro CB7 . . . .**219** A7
Folly Rd IP28 . . . .**239** B6
Folly's Dro PE13 . . . .**234** F3
Fontwell Ave CB4 . . . .**83** C5
Fontwell Gdns 2 PE9 . . . .**244** B5
Foot Dro PE26 . . . .**172** A8
Footpath The CB23 . . . .**82** C2
Ford Cl
Beck Row, Holywell Row &
Kenny Hill IP28 . . . .**213** D7
Eaton Socon PE19 . . . . . .**74** D5
Yaxley PE7 . . . .**181** C6
Ford End
Alconbury PE28 . . . .**150** F4
Hail Weston PE19 . . . . . .**95** B1
FORDHAM **212** F1
Fordham Abbey★ CB7 . . . .**131** E8
Fordham CE Prim Sch
CB7 . . . .**212** F1
Fordham Cl SG7 . . . .**2** D5
Fordham Moor CB7 . . . . . .**212** E3
Fordham Rd
Exning CB8 . . . .**131** E3
Freckenham IP28 . . . . . .**213** B2
Isleham CB7 . . . .**213** A4
Newmarket CB8 . . . .**110** F8
5 Royston SG8 . . . .**5** E5
Snailwell CB8 . . . .**132** A5
5 Soham CB7 . . . .**212** B3
Fordham Way SG8 . . . .**14** D5
Fordwich Cl 1 CB4 . . . .**83** D6
Fore Hill CB7 . . . .**240** D4
Foreman's Rd SG8 . . . .**31** B2
Forest End CB8 . . . .**134** A6
Forest Glade CB9 . . . .**38** F2
Forest Rd CB1 . . . .**65** E5
Forest Way IP28 . . . .**239** E4
Forge Cl PE19 . . . .**74** B2
Forge End
Great Shelford CB22 . . . . .**49** C4
Peterborough PE7 . . . . .**185** A4
Forge Way PE28 . . . .**164** F5
Forster Rd PE28 . . . .**140** E1
Forsythia Rd PE27 . . . . . .**144** A6
Fortescue Rd CB4 . . . .**83** E6
Forties Cl CB9 . . . .**24** D8
Fortune Way SG8 . . . .**12** E5
Forty Acre Rd PE1 . . . . . .**198** D2
Forty Foot Bank
Doddington PE26 . . . . . .**222** C3
Ramsey Forty Foot PE26 .**221** C3
Ramsey PE26 . . . .**221** C2
Forum Ct 7 CB4 . . . .**83** E7
Foster Ct PE29 . . . .**141** F7
Foster Rd
Cambridge CB2 . . . .**64** D2
Peterborough PE2 . . . . .**186** D8
Foster Way CB23 . . . .**79** B3
Foul Anchor PE13 . . . .**238** D8
Foundry Cl CB24 . . . .**125** D3
Foundry Rd PE9 . . . .**244** A5
Foundry Way
Eaton Socon PE19 . . . . . .**74** B1
March PE15 . . . .**228** B6
Ramsey PE26 . . . .**172** A5
Foundry Wlk PE27 . . . . . .**144** A3
Fountain La
Haslingfield CB23 . . . .**47** B5
Soham CB7 . . . .**212** B4
Fountains Pl PE6 . . . .**232** B1
Four Acres
Fenstanton PE28 . . . . . .**121** C6
Great Chesterford CB10 . . .**18** D3
Four Chimneys Cres
PE7 . . . .**186** C2
Fourfields Prim Sch PE7 .**181** E6
Four Gotes PE13 . . . .**238** C7
Four Hundred Dro PE15 . . .**221** E5
Fourth Ave PE13 . . . .**245** E4
Fourth Dro
Downham CB6 . . . .**225** A1
Peterborough PE1 . . . . .**198** F3
Four Went Ways CB21 . . . . .**51** A1
FOWLMERE **15** D8
Fowlmere Nature Reserve★
SG8 . . . .**15** B8
Fowlmere Prim Sch SG8 . .**15** D8
Fowlmere Rd
Foxton SG8 . . . .**30** D3

Fowlmere Rd *continued*
Heydon SG8 . . . . 7 F8
Newton CB22 . . . . 31 B6
Shepreth SG8 . . . . 29 F4
Thriplow SG8 . . . . 31 A2
Fox Brook PE19 . . . . 75 C5
Foxburrow Cl CB9 . . . . . . 38 F1
Fox Cl PE19 . . . . 75 A5
Fox Cnr SG8 . . . . 10 F5
Fox Covert
Stilton PE7 . . . . 175 F7
St Neots PE19 . . . . 75 C5
Foxcovert Rd
Peakirk PE6 . . . . 204 A8
Werrington PE4 . . . . . . 204 B4
Foxdale PE1 . . . . 197 F7
Fox Dale PE9 . . . . 244 A4
Foxenfields PE28 . . . . . . 162 C1
Foxglove Cl
3 Eaton Socon PE19 . . . 74 C5
Yaxley PE7 . . . . 182 A7
Foxglove Way
January PE15 . . . . 243 E6
Ramsey St Mary's PE26. . 220 D3
Fox Gn CB8 . . . . 55 F7
Fox Gr PE29 . . . . 141 F2
Fox Hill SG8 . . . . 11 A5
Fox Hill Rd SG8 . . . . 10 F5
Foxhollow CB23 . . . . 79 B2
Fox Hollow CB23 . . . . . . 102 C4
Foxley Cl PE4 . . . . 204 C4
Fox Rd
Balsham CB21 . . . . 52 F3
Bourn CB23 . . . . 60 D5
Catworth PE28 . . . . . . 136 D8
Fox's Cl CB24 . . . . 105 D2
Fox St SG19 . . . . 58 E5
Fox's Way CB23 . . . . 62 D6
FOXTON. 30 D5
Foxton Prim Sch CB22 . . 30 C5
Foxton Rd
Barrington CB22 . . . . . . 29 F8
Foxton CB22. . . . . 30 A7
Foxton Sta CB22. . . . . . 30 C6
Foxtrot La PE28. . . . . . . 151 F3
Fox Wood N **4** CB7 . . . . 212 B5
Fox Wood S CB7. . . . . . 212 B4
Framlingham Rd PE7. . . . 187 F5
Francis Cl CB9 . . . . 23 F8
Francis Darwin Ct CB4 . . 83 C5
Francis Gdns PE1 . . . . . . 197 F6
Francis Pas **3** CB2 . . . . . 64 E7
Frank Bridges Ct **2** CB7. 212 B4
Frankland Wlk CB7 . . . . 240 F6
Franklin Cres PE1. . . . . . 198 E6
Franklin Gdns CB24 . . . . 125 D4
Frank Perkins Parkway
PE2 . . . . 187 B8
Frank Perkins Way PE1. . 198 D4
Franks La PE13 . . . . 237 F5
Frank's La CB4. . . . . 84 B5
Fraserburgh Way **2** PE2 185 C4
Fraser Dr PE27. . . . . 144 A7
Fraser Rd CB4 . . . . 84 A6
FRECKENHAM 213 C3
Freckenham Rd IP28. . . . 213 E3
Fred Archer Way CB8 . . . 111 A3
Fred Dannatt Rd IP28. . . 239 A6
Frederick Talbot Cl **8**
CB7 . . . . 212 B4
Free Church Pas PE27. . . 144 A4
Freedom Bridge PE13 . . . 245 B6
Freeman Cl **10** PE8. . . . . 230 B1
Freemantle Ct **5** PE19 . . 74 B3
Free Sch La CB2 . . . . . . 246 C2
Freesia Way PE7. . . . . . . 181 F6
Freewood La CB11. . . . . . 9 B3
French Dro PE6. . . . . . . 232 E7
French's Rd
Cambridge CB4 . . . . . . 83 D4
Walpole PE14 . . . . 238 F8
Freshfields CB8. . . . . . . 110 F4
Freston PE4 . . . . 204 F2
Friar Cl CB9 . . . . 38 F1
Friar's Cl CB1. . . . . 65 F5
Friars Nine CB8. . . . . . . 242 C4
Friar's Pl CB6. . . . . 242 C5
Friar's Way CB6. . . . . . . 242 C5
Friar Way CB23 . . . . 79 B2
FRIDAY BRIDGE 236 A4
Fridaybridge Prim Sch
PE14 . . . . 236 A3
Fridaybridge Rd PE14 . . . 236 A4
Friday St IP28 . . . . 213 D6
Friends Cl PE19. . . . . 98 C2
Frinton Way **4** PE13 . . . . 245 E5
Fritton Ct **7** CB9 . . . . . . 23 E6
Frobisher Cl PE29. . . . . . 141 F6
Frog End
Great Wilbraham CB21 . . 67 F7
Haslingfield CB23 . . . . . 47 A6
Little Wilbraham CB1. . . . 86 C2
Shepreth SG8. . . . . 29 F2
Frogge St CB10 . . . . 18 B3
Frogmore CB8. . . . . 110 B4
Frogs Abbey CB6 . . . . . . 217 E4
Frogs Abbey La PE15. . . 223 B7
Frogs Hall PE28. . . . . . . 208 C5
Froize End CB6. . . . . . . 210 A5
Froment Way CB24. . . . . 105 C3
Fromont Cl CB21. . . . . . . 66 E4
Front Rd
Murrow PE13. . . . . 234 D6
Tydd St Giles PE13. . . . 238 D8
Front St CB8. . . . . 92 F4
Frowd Cl CB7. . . . . 212 E1
Frumetty La PE28. . . . . . 150 F4

Fryers Callis PE9. . . . . . 244 C3
Fryth Cl CB9 . . . . 39 A1
FULBOURN 66 F4
Fulbourn Hospl CB1. . . . 66 B5
Fulbourn Nature Reserve★
CB21 . . . . 67 B4
Fulbourn Old Drift CB1. . 66 A4
Fulbourn Prim Sch CB21. 66 F5
Fulbourn Rd
Cambridge CB1 . . . . . . 65 F5
Fulbourn CB1. . . . . 66 D7
Fulbridge Rd PE1 . . . . . . 197 F8
Fulbridge Rd PE1 . . . . . . 197 F7
Fulbrooke Rd CB3 . . . . . 64 A7
Fulham Rd PE3 . . . . 197 E4
Fullards Cl PE29 . . . . . . 155 B4
Fuller Cl PE28 . . . . 137 F6
Fuller's Hill SG19 . . . . . . 42 D7
Fuller's La **5** PE15 . . . . . 223 B7
Fuller Way CB3 . . . . 83 B3
Fundrey Rd PE13. . . . . . 245 F6
Funtham's La PE7. . . . . . 188 D7
Furlongs The PE27 . . . . . 208 A2
Furlong Way CB23 . . . . . 80 B1
Furrells The CB21. . . . . . 35 C3
Furrowfields Rd PE16 . . . 241 C5
Furrows The PE27 . . . . . 144 A4
Furrow The CB6 . . . . . . 242 C3
Furtherford CB24 . . . . . 208 E1
Furze Gr SG8 . . . . 5 E5
Furze Ride PE7 . . . . 198 B8
Fydell Cl PE19 . . . . 75 B7

G

Gables Cl SG8 . . . . 29 A1
Gables Dr PE3 . . . . 197 D2
Gables The PE28 . . . . . . 121 A5
Gadd's La PE13 . . . . 235 D8
Gadwall Way **5** CB7 . . . 212 B5
Gage Cl SG8 . . . . 5 D8
Gainsborough Ave **6**
PE19. . . . . 74 C5
Gainsborough Cl CB4 . . . 84 B6
Gainsborough Dr PE27 . . 144 A7
Gainsborough Rd CB9. . . 38 D1
Gains La PE28 . . . . 166 D2
Gala Cl PE7. . . . . 176 A8
Galfrid Rd CB5. . . . . 84 D2
Gallery The CB7 . . . . . . 240 D4
Gallions Cl PE4 . . . . 204 D1
Gallows Hill (Tumulus)★
SG7. . . . . 3 E1
Gall's Dro PE13 . . . . 235 A4
GAMLINGAY 41 D5
GAMLINGAY CINQUES. . . 41 B6
Gamlingay Cinques Nature
Rerserve★ SG19 . . . . . 41 A7
Gamlingay Fst Sch SG19 . 41 D5
GAMLINGAY GREAT
HEATH 40 E3
Gamlingay Meadows Nature
Reserve★ SG19 . . . . . . 41 A4
Gamlingay Rd
Gamlingay SG19 . . . . . . 41 D8
Potton SG19. . . . . 41 C1
Waresley SG19 . . . . . . 57 E1
Gamlingay Village Coll
SG19. . . . . 41 E5
Gamlingay Wood Nature
Reserve★ SG19 . . . . . . 41 E8
Gamsey Wood Nature
Reserve★ PE28 . . . . . . 162 A8
Gannet Cl PE28 . . . . 24 C8
Gannocks Cl PE2. . . . . . 185 F5
Gannocks The PE2 . . . . . 185 F5
Ganwick Cl CB5 . . . . 38 F2
Gaol St **12** PE13. . . . . . . 245 C4
Garden Cl
Royston SG8 . . . . 5 E7
St Ives PE27 . . . . 144 A4
Sutton CB6 . . . . 216 E1
GARDEN COTTAGE. 93 D5
Garden Ct
Burwell CB25. . . . . 130 C4
Ramsey PE26. . . . . . . 172 A4
Garden End SG8 . . . . . . 14 D5
Garden End Rd PE1 . . . . 198 B6
Gardeners La **7** CB7. . . . 212 B4
Garden Fields CB22 . . . . 48 E3
Garden Gr PE7. . . . . 189 D6
Garden La
Royston SG8 . . . . 5 D5
Wisbech St Mary PE13. . 235 A7
Garden Rd PE1 . . . . 198 A6
Gardens The PE15 . . . . . 243 A6
Garden Wlk
Cambridge CB4 . . . . . . 83 D4
Histon CB24. . . . . 104 C5
Royston SG8 . . . . 5 E7
Gardiners La SG7 . . . . . . 2 D4
Garlic Row CB5. . . . . . . 84 B3
Garner Ave PE28. . . . . . 164 E5
Garner Cl CB24 . . . . 105 C3
Garner Ct PE29 . . . . 141 F7
Garratt Rd **4** PE9 . . . . . 244 B4
Garret Hostel La CB2. . . 246 A3
Garrick Wlk PE2 . . . . . . 187 B7
Garry Dr CB4 . . . . 84 A7
Garton St PE1 . . . . 198 A5
Gascoigne PE6 . . . . 203 F5
Gas La
Ely CB7 . . . . 240 C4
Stamford PE9. . . . . . . 244 C5
Thorney PE6. . . . . 233 A3
Gas Rd PE15 . . . . 243 D3
Gas St PE9 . . . . 244 C5

Gatenby PE4 . . . . 204 C4
Gateway Gdns CB6. . . . . 240 B3
Gateways CB8 . . . . 90 F6
GATLEY END. 3 C7
Gaul Rd PE15 . . . . 243 B4
Gault Bank PE15 . . . . . . 227 D1
GAULTREE. 236 D6
Gaultree Sq PE14 . . . . . 236 D6
Gavel St PE7. . . . . 181 C8
Gayton Cl **3** CB2 . . . . . . 64 D3
Gayton Ct PE3 . . . . 197 C5
Gazeley Gdns PE7. . . . . 187 B2
Gazeley Rd
Ashley CB8. . . . . 92 A8
Cambridge CB2 . . . . . . 64 D4
Kentford CB8 . . . . 134 C1
Moulton CB8 . . . . 112 F6
Gazelle Cl **4** PE19 . . . . . 74 B5
Gazelle Way CB1. . . . . . . 66 B7
Geddington Rd PE2 . . . . 186 E8
Geneva St PE1 . . . . 198 A3
Geoffrey Bishop Ave
CB21 . . . . 67 A4
George Alcock Way PE7. 189 D7
George Campbell Leisure Ctr
PE15 . . . . 243 C4
George Gdns PE7 . . . . . . 189 D8
George Gibson Cl CB8. . . 110 C8
George IV St CB2 . . . . . 246 C1
George La
Buckden PE19 . . . . 117 A3
Royston SG8 . . . . 5 D5
Warboys PE28 . . . . . . 164 E5
George Lambton Ave
CB8 . . . . 110 F6
George Nuttall Cl CB4. . . 84 A6
George Pateman Ct **2**
CB1 . . . . 64 F7
George Pl **7** PE19 . . . . . 74 F2
George St
Cambridge CB4 . . . . . . 83 F4
Huntingdon PE29. . . . . 141 D4
March PE15 . . . . 243 D4
Peterborough PE2. . . . . 186 F8
Stilton PE7. . . . . 175 F8
7 Willingham CB24 . . . 209 A1
Georgia PE28 . . . . 151 E4
Georgian Ct PE3 . . . . . . 197 E2
Georgina Cl PE15 . . . . . 224 B4
Gerard Cl CB5 . . . . 84 C2
Gerard Rd CB5. . . . . 84 D3
Gery Ct PE19 . . . . 74 C5
Giant's Hill **3** CB24 . . . . 125 A5
Gibralter La CB24 . . . . . 122 E5
Gibside Ave PE16 . . . . . 241 B3
Gibson Cl CB25 . . . . 106 A7
Gidding Gr PE28 . . . . . . 166 B1
Gidding Rd PE28 . . . . . . 167 D3
Giddings Cl PE2. . . . . . . 185 F4
Gidney La **8** CB7 . . . . . . 212 B3
Gifford Pl CB2 . . . . 246 A3
Gifford's Cl CB3 . . . . 82 E8
Giffords Way **4** CB24 . . . 208 D1
Gilbert Cl CB4 . . . . 83 C5
Gilbert Rd
Cambridge CB4 . . . . . . 83 D5
Littleport CB6 . . . . 242 B5
Gilbert Scott Dr CB6 . . . 240 E7
Gildale PE4. . . . . 204 D4
Gildenburgh Ave PE1 . . . 198 D5
Gill's Hill CB23 . . . . 60 D5
Gilmerton Ct CB2 . . . . . 64 D4
Gilmorton Dr PE1 . . . . . 198 D7
Gilmour Rd CB2. . . . . . . 64 D4
Gilpin Pl CB2. . . . . 64 F6
Gilpin Rd CB2. . . . . 64 F6
Gilpin St PE1 . . . . 197 E6
Gimber Ct **5** PE29 . . . . . 141 F7
GIMBERS END 115 B2
Gimbert Rd CB7 . . . . . . 212 B4
Gimbert Sq PE15. . . . . . 243 E4
Gipping Cl **4** CB9. . . . . . 23 E6
Gipsey Cnr PE19 . . . . . . 56 C5
Gipson Cl PE16. . . . . . . 241 B5
Gipsy Dro PE16 . . . . 215 F6
Gipsy La PE15. . . . . 243 A7
GIRTON. 82 F8
Girton Cl
Mildenhall IP28 . . . . . . 239 C6
Woodditton CB8. . . . . . 111 B1
Girton Coll
Cambridge CB3 . . . . . . 83 B2
Girton CB3. . . . . 82 F6
Girton Cres PE29. . . . . . 142 A7
Girton Glebe Prim Sch
CB3. . . . . 103 E1
Girton Rd
Girton CB3 . . . . 82 F7
Haverhill CB9. . . . . 24 B7
Girton Way PE1 . . . . 244 A7
Gisborne Rd CB1. . . . . . . 65 C6
Gladeside CB23 . . . . . . 102 C4
Gladstone Park Com Recn
Ctr PE1 . . . . 197 E5
Gladstone Prim Sch PE1 197 F5
Gladstone St PE1 . . . . . . 197 F3
Gladstone Way CB1. . . . . 65 F5
Glamis Cl PE19 . . . . 23 D8
Glamis Gdns PE3. . . . . . 197 B2
Glanely Gdns CB8. . . . . 110 C8
Glassmoor Bank PE7. . . 220 F7
GLATTON. 175 D7
Glatton Dr PE2. . . . . . . 187 D6
Glatton La PE7. . . . . 176 D3
Glatton Rd PE28 . . . . . . 168 A6
Glatton Ways PE28 . . . . 175 F1
Glebe Ave PE2 . . . . 185 E4

Glebe Cl
Chatteris PE16. . . . . . . 241 D5
Gorefield PE13. . . . . . . 237 E3
Great Paxton PE19 . . . . 96 E4
Toft CB23. . . . . 61 E5
Wimblington PE15 . . . . 224 B4
Glebe Cres CB22 . . . . . . 33 B4
Glebe Ct PE2 . . . . 187 A8
Glebe Gdns **2** PE6 . . . . . 232 B8
Glebe La
Buckden PE19 . . . . 117 A3
Cambourne CB23 . . . . . 79 C4
Great Shelford CB22 . . . 49 B5
Glebelands Cty Prim Sch
PE16 . . . . 241 D5
Glebe Rd
Barrington CB22 . . . . . . 29 F8
Brampton PE28 . . . . . . 140 E2
Cambridge CB1 . . . . . . 65 B3
Hemingford Grey PE28 . . 143 D1
Huntingdon PE29. . . . . 141 D7
Perry PE28. . . . . 115 D3
Peterborough PE2. . . . . 187 A8
Sawtry PE28 . . . . 168 A4
Stilton PE7. . . . . 176 A7
Waterbeach CB25 . . . . 106 A7
Glebe The
Haverhill CB9. . . . . 39 A1
Ramsey PE26. . . . . . . 172 B4
Glebe Way
Haddenham CB6 . . . . . 209 F6
Histon CB24. . . . . 104 C4
Glemsford Pl **2** CB9 . . . . 24 B8
Glemsford Rise PE2 . . . . 186 C7
Glenacre Cl **3** CB1. . . . . 65 E5
Glenariff Cl **7** CB1. . . . . 74 E4
Glencoe Way PE2 . . . . . 185 D3
Glen Cres PE9 . . . . 244 C7
Glendale PE2 . . . . 185 D6
Glendon Gdns PE13 . . . . 245 A7
Gleneagles PE2 . . . . 185 F6
Glenfields PE7 . . . . 189 C8
Glenmere Cl CB1 . . . . . . 65 D5
Glen Rd **1** PE8 . . . . 230 B1
Glen The PE2 . . . . 187 B7
GLENTHORN 227 F3
Glenton St PE1 . . . . 198 C2
Glenville Cl CB1. . . . . . . 85 B1
GLINTON 203 E8
Glinton Rd
Helpston PE6. . . . . 203 A8
Newborough PE6 . . . . . 204 E8
Glisson Rd CB1 . . . . 246 C1
Globe La
Alconbury PE28 . . . . . . 150 E3
3 Littleport CB6. . . . . . 242 D4
Gloucester Ct PE13 . . . . 245 D7
Gloucester Pl **4** PE1. . . . 198 B3
Gloucester Rd
Brampton PE28 . . . . . . 140 D1
Haverhill CB9. . . . . 23 F7
Peterborough PE2. . . . . 187 B7
Sawtry PE28 . . . . 168 A4
7 Stamford PE9 . . . . . 244 B6
Wyton Airfield PE28. . . . 143 B8
Glover Cl CB22. . . . . 32 F6
Glover Cl PE7 . . . . 208 D1
Goddard Cres **1** PE13. . . 245 D7
Godeby Cl **4** PE29. . . . . 141 F8
Godesdone Rd CB5 . . . . 84 A3
Godfrey Cl PE6 . . . . 207 D1
Goding Way CB24 . . . . . 105 D2
GODMANCHESTER. 141 E2
Godmanchester Com
Swimming Pool PE29 . . 141 F2
Godmanchester Prim Sch
PE29. . . . . 141 F2
Godric Sq PE2 . . . . 186 D6
Godsey La **2** PE6 . . . . . . 231 E8
Godwin Cl CB1. . . . . 65 C4
Godwin Rd PE13 . . . . . . 245 D7
Godwin Way CB1 . . . . . . 65 C4
Godwit Cl PE7 . . . . 201 A1
Goffers Knoll (Tumulus)★
SG8. . . . . 14 E1
Goffsmill PE3. . . . . 197 A4
Gog Magog Way CB22. . . 49 C5
Goldcrest Ct **8** CB23. . . . 79 C3
Golden Drop PE6 . . . . . . 231 C4
Golden Miller Cl CB8. . . . 110 D7
Golden Rod **8** PE29. . . . . 118 F8
Goldhay Way PE2 . . . . . 185 F2
Goldie La PE2 . . . . 185 F6
Golding Pl **15** PE13 . . . . 245 C4
Golding Rd CB1. . . . . 65 B6
Goldings Cl CB9 . . . . 39 A2
Goldpits PE28. . . . . 164 F5
Gold St PE15. . . . . 243 C4
Golf La PE28 . . . . 151 F3
Golf Links Rd
Barton Mills IP28 . . . . . 214 A3
Worlington IP28 . . . . . . 239 A1
Gonville & Caius Coll
CB2. . . . . 246 B1
Gonville Cl IP28 . . . . 239 D6
Gonville Pl CB1 . . . . 246 C1
Goochgate PE12 . . . . . . 237 A7
Goodacre PE2. . . . . 186 A4
Goodchilds Gdns **5** CB7 213 A5
Goode Cl CB24. . . . . . . 125 D4
Goodens La PE13 . . . . . 238 A5
Goodliff Cl PE29 . . . . . . 141 C6
Goodliffe Ave CB21 . . . . 53 C2
Goodwin Gr CB7 . . . . . . 240 F7
Goodwin Wlk PE4 . . . . . 204 C4

Goodwood Rd
Peterborough PE3 . . . . . 196 F3
Royston SG8 . . . . 5 F6
Goose Cross. 80 B1
Goose Fen Dro CB7 . . . . 211 C6
Gordon Ave
March PE15 . . . . 243 D4
Peterborough PE2. . . . . 186 E7
Gordon Cl PE19 . . . . 95 F1
Gordon Ct PE13. . . . . . . 245 C3
Gordon Rd PE19 . . . . . . 95 F1
Gordon Richards Cl CB8. 110 F6
Gordon Way PE13. . . . . 186 C7
Goredike Bank PE13 . . . 237 E3
GOREFIELD 237 E2
Gorefield Prim Sch PE13 237 E2
Gorefield Rd PE13 . . . . . 237 F2
Gore Tree Rd PE28. . . . . 120 C7
Gorse Cl **8** IP28 . . . . 214 A1
Gorse Gn PE1. . . . . 198 B8
Gorse Way PE27 . . . . . . 144 B5
Goshawk Cl PE29 . . . . . 142 A5
Gosling's Dro PE7. . . . . 220 A8
Gosling Way CB22. . . . . . 33 A8
Gosmoor La PE14. . . . . 236 B5
Gosslan Cl CB27 . . . . . . 144 A6
Gostwick PE2. . . . . 185 D5
Gote La PE13 . . . . 237 E3
Gough Way CB3 . . . . 64 A8
Governess Cl **8** PE15 . . . 223 B7
Gower Rd SG8 . . . . 5 C7
Gowers The CB3 . . . . . . 103 E1
Grace Sch of Medicine
CB1. . . . . 65 A8
Gracious St PE7 . . . . . . 189 D7
Graeme Rd PE5 . . . . 194 F7
GRAFHAM 116 A7
Grafham Cl PE2. . . . . . . 187 E4
Grafham Rd PE28 . . . . . 138 F4
Grafham Water Ex Ctr★
PE28 . . . . 116 B5
Grafham Water Nature
Reserve★ PE28 . . . . . . 115 C3
Grafton Ave PE3 . . . . . . 197 C3
Grafton Cl PE27. . . . . . . 143 F3
Grafton Ctr The CB1. . . . 246 C3
Grafton Dr CB23 . . . . . . 80 D3
Grafton St CB1. . . . . 246 C2
Graham Rd CB4. . . . . . . 83 E8
Grain Cl CB22 . . . . 49 A5
Grainger Ave PE29 . . . . 118 F8
Grammar Sch Wlk PE29. 141 D4
Granary Ct CB23 . . . . . . 81 F5
Granary End **4** CB6 . . . . 217 E1
Granary La **5** CB6 . . . . . 242 D4
Granary Rd CB8. . . . . . . 111 B2
Granary The
Old Hurst PE28 . . . . . . 154 D7
Sawtry PE28 . . . . 168 B4
Granary Way CB23 . . . . . 79 B3
Granby St
Littleport CB6 . . . . 242 D4
Newmarket CB8. . . . . . 111 B3
Peterborough PE1 . . . . 198 B2
Grand Arc CB2. . . . . 246 B2
Grandford Dro PE15. . . . 227 E6
GRANDFORD HOUSE. . . 227 F6
Grandridge Cl CB21 . . . . 66 F4
Grange Ave PE1 . . . . . . 198 A6
Grange Bottom SG8. . . . . 5 E5
Grange Cl PE28 . . . . 168 C2
Grange Cres PE2. . . . . . 186 A5
Grange Ct CB3 . . . . 64 B8
Grange Dr CB3. . . . . 82 E7
Grange Farm Cl PE19 . . . 57 F5
Grange Farm The IP28 . . 239 C1
Grangehill Rd PE13 . . . . 237 B6
Grange La
Barton Mills IP28 . . . . . 239 C2
Littleport CB6 . . . . 242 B2
Grange Rd
Cambridge CB3 . . . . . . 64 B8
Duxford CB22 . . . . 17 A6
Ickleton CB10 . . . . 9 A8
March PE15 . . . . 228 A1
Peterborough PE3. . . . . 197 D4
6 Somersham PE28 . . . 208 C8
Wisbech PE13 . . . . 245 A7
Grange The
Meldreth SG8. . . . . 14 B8
8 Somersham PE28 . . . 208 C8
Granhams Cl CB22 . . . . . 49 A6
Granham's Rd
Cambridge CB2 . . . . . . 65 C1
Great Shelford CB22 . . . 49 A7
Gransden Rd
Abbotsley PE19 . . . . . . 57 E6
Caxton CB23 . . . . 59 D8
Gransley Rise PE2 . . . . . 197 C5
Granta Cl
Great Chesterford CB10 . 18 F1
St Ives PE27 . . . . 144 B7
Witchford CB6 . . . . . . 217 D1
Granta Cotts CB10 . . . . . 18 C2
Granta Leys CB21 . . . . . 35 B3
Granta Pk CB21. . . . . . . 34 A6
Granta Pl CB2 . . . . 246 A1
Granta Sch CB21. . . . . . 35 B3
Granta Terr CB22 . . . . . . 49 B4
Granta Vale CB21. . . . . . 35 D2
GRANTCHESTER. 64 A4
Grantchester Mdws CB3. 64 C7

Grantchester Rd
Barton CB23 . . . . **63** D7
Cambridge CB2 . . . . **64** B2
Coton CB23 . . . . **82** C1
Grantchester CB3 . . . . **64** B6
Grantchester Rise CB25 . **130** B5
Grantchester St 3 CB3. . . **64** C7
Grantham Cl SG8 . . . . **5** B8
Granville Ave PE6 . . . . **231** F7
Granville Gdns IP28 . . . . . . **239** A4
Granville St PE1 . . . . **198** A4
Grasmere PE29 . . . . **141** B6
Grasmere Gdns
Cambridge CB1 . . . . **246** A4
Peterborough PE4 . . . . **204** D3
Grassgate La PE14 . . . . . . **238** E3
Grass Plant Cotts CB8 . . . **131** B4
Grass Yd 3 PE28 . . . . **113** F4
Gravel Bridge Rd CB24 . . **123** C6
Gravel Dro
Beck Row, Holywell Row &
Kenny Hill IP28. . . . . . . **213** C6
Witcham CB6. . . . . **216** F4
Gravel End CB6 . . . . **217** C5
Gravel End La
Coveney CB6 . . . . **217** D5
Witchford CB6. . . . . **217** E1
GRAVELEY. **97** F4
Graveley Rd PE19 . . . . **97** A8
Graveley Way PE28. . . . . . . **98** E8
GRAVEL HOUSE **228** C4
Gravel Pit Hill SG8 . . . . . . **16** C8
Gravel Wlk PE1 . . . . **198** A2
Gray Ct PE1 . . . . **197** B8
Grayling Cl CB4. . . . . **84** A4
Gray Rd CB1. . . . . **65** D6
Grays Cl SG8 . . . . **5** C8
Grays Gr MK44 . . . . **93** B2
Grays La
Emneth PE14. . . . . **236** C6
March PE15 . . . . **243** D4
Graysmoor Dro PE14 . . . . **228** B8
Gray's Rd SG19 . . . . **41** D6
GREAT ABINGTON **34** C5
Great Abington Prim Sch
CB21 . . . . **34** C5
GREAT BRADLEY **55** F7
GREAT CAMBOURNE **79** B2
Great Chesterfield Prim Sch
CB10. . . . . **18** D2
GREAT CHESTERFORD . . . **18** D2
Great Chesterford Sta
CB10. . . . . **18** C1
GREAT CHISHILL **7** F2
Great Cl CB23. . . . . **63** B4
Great Dro
Soham CB7 . . . . **211** F3
Swaffham Prior CB7 . . . . . **128** C6
Yaxley PE7 . . . . **182** A5
Great Eastern Rd
March PE15 . . . . **243** D7
Wisbech PE13 . . . . **245** B4
Great Eastern St CB1 . . . . . **65** B8
Greater Foxes CB21 . . . . . . **66** F5
GREAT EVERSDEN **45** E8
Great Farthing Cl PE27 . . **144** B4
Great Fen Rd CB7 . . . . **212** B8
Greatford Rd PE9 . . . . **230** C6
GREAT GIDDING **166** E3
Great Gidding CE Prim Sch
PE28 . . . . **166** D3
Great Gn SG8 . . . . **11** A5
GREAT GRANSDEN **58** D5
Great Heath Prim Sch
IP28 . . . . **239** C6
Great How PE27 . . . . **143** F7
Great La CB25 . . . . **129** C1
Greatlands PE28 . . . . **163** B4
Great & Little Shelford CE
Prim Sch CB22. . . . . **48** F4
Great Northern St PE29 . **141** D5
Great North Fen Dro
CB24 . . . . **125** C6
Great North Rd
Alconbury PE28. . . . . **150** E4
Buckden PE19 . . . . **117** A5
Eaton Socon PE19 . . . . **74** B2
Peterborough PE2 . . . . **185** A4
Sibson cum Stibbington
PE8 . . . . **183** E8
Southoe & Midloe PE19. . . **95** F4
St Neots PE19 . . . . **74** C7
Wothorpe PE9 . . . . **244** A2
Great Parlow Cl PE19 . . . . . **97** E7
GREAT PAXTON **96** E4
Great Paxton CE Prim Sch
PE19 . . . . **96** F5
GREAT RAVELEY **163** B7
GREAT SHELFORD **48** F5
GREAT STAUGHTON **94** B6
Great Staughton Prim Sch
PE19 . . . . **93** F6
GREAT STUKELEY **152** A2
Great Whyte PE26 . . . . **172** A8
GREAT WILBRAHAM **68** A7
Great Wilbraham CE Prim
Sch CB21 . . . . **67** F8
Great Wilbraham Rd CB1. **86** F1
GREAT WRATTING **39** D5
Grebe Cl
Mildenhall IP28 . . . . **239** A1
Whittlesey PE7 . . . . **190** A8
Grebe Ct PE7 . . . . **190** A8
Grebe Way 3 PE19 . . . . . . **75** B7

Greenacres
Duxford CB22 . . . . **32** D1
Peterborough PE4 . . . . **204** A4
Green Acres SG19 . . . . **41** C5
Green Bank Rd CB25 . . . . **108** B2
Greenbanks SG8 . . . . **14** C5
Greenbury Cl SG8. . . . . **6** F1
Green Cl PE19 . . . . **94** A6
Greendale PE29. . . . . **141** A6
Green Drift SG8. . . . . **5** B6
Green Drift The PE9. . . . . **230** B3
Green Dro
Coveney CB6 . . . . **217** D4
Crowland PE6 . . . . **232** D8
Elm PE14 . . . . **236** D2
Northside PE6 . . . . **200** F4
Thorney PE6. . . . . **233** A6
GREEN END. **62** B6
Green End
Comberton CB23 . . . . **62** C6
Fen Ditton CB5. . . . . **84** E6
Gamlingay SG19 . . . . **41** C5
GREEN END. **152** A1
Green End CB25 . . . . **105** D8
GREEN END. **93** A3
Green End
Little Staughton MK44. . . . . **93** A3
Little Stukeley PE28. . . . . . **152** A1
Sawtry PE28 . . . . **168** B2
Stretham CB6 . . . . **210** F4
Green End Ind Est SG19 . . . **41** C5
Green End Rd
Cambridge CB4 . . . . **84** B6
Sawtry PE28 . . . . **168** B3
St Neots PE19 . . . . **75** A5
Green Farm Ct PE5. . . . . . **195** E2
Greenfield SG8 . . . . **5** B7
Greenfield Cl CB22. . . . . . . **49** D4
Greenfields
Earith PE28 . . . . **208** E6
Eltisley PE19 . . . . **77** E4
Hemingford Grey PE27 . . . **143** F1
Newmarket CB8. . . . . **111** C3
1 St Neots PE19 . . . . **75** A4
Greenfields Way CB9. . . . . . **23** F6
Greenford Cl SG8 . . . . **28** D8
Greengage Cl SG8 . . . . **14** C5
Greengage Rise SG8 . . . . . **14** C5
Greengarth PE27. . . . . **144** A5
Greengate Ct PE1. . . . . **198** C4
Greenham PE3. . . . . **197** A4
Greenhaze La CB23 . . . . . . **79** B3
Green Head Rd CB25 . . . . **108** D4
Green Hill 2 CB6 . . . . **211** B7
Greenhill Rd PE8. . . . . **178** F8
Greenhills CB7 . . . . **212** C3
Green How PE27 . . . . **143** E6
Green La
Ashwell SG7. . . . . **2** E5
6 Benwick PE15. . . . . **222** A5
Brampton PE28 . . . . **140** D2
Christchurch PE14. . . . . . . **229** D3
Ellington PE28 . . . . **138** F4
Everton SG19. . . . . **40** C3
Great Staughton PE19 . . . . **93** F6
Hail Weston PE19 . . . . **95** A1
Leverington PE13. . . . . **237** F2
Linton CB21 . . . . **35** C2
Peterborough PE1. . . . . . . **198** A4
Red Lodge IP28 . . . . **133** F8
Stamford PE9 . . . . **244** B7
St Ives PE28 . . . . **143** A5
Upton & Coppingford PE28 **160** C2
Walsoken PE14 . . . . **245** C4
Yaxley PE7 . . . . **181** D6
Greenlands CB23 . . . . **65** B3
Green Lanes CB25 . . . . . . **130** C1
Greenleas CB24. . . . . **104** B5
Green Leys PE27 . . . . **143** F5
Greenlow SG8. . . . . **14** A4
Green Man La CB22 . . . . . . **47** E3
Green Pk
Brinkley CB8 . . . . **70** D2
Cambridge CB4 . . . . **84** B6
Chatteris PE16. . . . . **241** E5
Green Rd
Newborough PE6. . . . . **205** F3
Newmarket CB8. . . . . **111** B2
Upwell PE14. . . . . **229** E8
Green Rd The CB22 . . . . . . **33** A8
Green Side CB25 . . . . **106** B7
Greenside Cl CB24 . . . . . . **122** E6
Green's Rd CB4 . . . . **83** E4
Green St
Cambridge CB2 . . . . **246** A3
Duxford CB22 . . . . **32** D1
Haverhill CB9. . . . . **24** C8
March PE15 . . . . **243** E3
Royston SG8 . . . . **5** D8
Willingham CB24 . . . . **209** A1
Greenstock La PE13 . . . . . **238** A6
Green The
Ashley CB8. . . . . **91** F8
Beck Row, Holywell Row & Kenny
Hill IP28 . . . . **213** C7
Brampton PE28 . . . . **140** D2
Cambridge CB4 . . . . **84** B5
Castor PE5. . . . . **195** E2
Foxton CB22. . . . . **30** B5
Glinton PE6 . . . . **203** E8
Great Staughton PE19 . . . . **93** F7
Haddenham CB6. . . . . **210** A6
Histon CB24. . . . . **104** B4
Kingston CB23 . . . . **61** B3
Kirtling CB8 . . . . **72** C5
Lolworth CB23. . . . . **101** F5
Peterborough PE4 . . . . **204** D5
Royston SG8 . . . . **5** D6

Green The continued
Snailwell CB8. . . . . **132** A3
Somersham PE28. . . . . **215** C1
Steeple Morden SG8 . . . . . **11** C1
6 Thorney PE6 . . . . **233** A3
Winwick PE28 . . . . **158** A6
Yaxley PE7 . . . . **181** E5
Green Tiles Cl PE29 . . . . . **152** E1
Greenway PE19 . . . . **117** B4
Greenwood Cl
1 Haverhill CB9 . . . . **23** E7
Ramsey PE26. . . . . **172** A5
Greenwood Way 16
PE15. . . . . **223** B7
Gregory Rd IP28 . . . . **239** A6
Grenadier Dr PE16 . . . . . . **241** C6
Grenadier Rd CB9. . . . . **23** C8
Greneway Mid Sch SG8 . . . **5** E7
Grenfell Cl PE16 . . . . **172** A5
Grenville Way PE19 . . . . . . **74** B2
Gresham Pl CB1 . . . . **246** C1
Gresham Rd CB1 . . . . **246** C1
Gresley Dr PE9 . . . . **244** B4
Gresley Way
March PE15 . . . . **243** B6
Peterborough PE3 . . . . **197** C6
Gretton Cl PE2 . . . . **186** C7
Greville Rd CB1. . . . . **65** B7
Greville Starkey Ave CB8 **110** F5
Greys SG8 . . . . **5** A4
Greys The PE15 . . . . **243** E2
Greystoke Ct 1 CB1 . . . . . **65** E5
Greystoke Rd CB1. . . . . **65** E5
Grieve Ct CB4. . . . . **84** C5
Griffins Cl PE6 . . . . **207** D1
Griffiths Ct PE2 . . . . **185** E5
Grimeshaw Wood Nature
Reserve★ PE3 . . . . **196** F6
Grimmer's Rd 6 PE13. . . **245** E7
Grimshaw Rd PE1. . . . . . . **198** B6
Grip The CB21 . . . . **35** B1
Groat La SG19 . . . . **41** D8
Grosvenor Gdns PE19 . . . . **74** E6
Grosvenor House Ct 6
IP28. . . . . **239** B5
Grosvenor Rd PE13. . . . . . **245** D7
Grosvenor Yd CB8 . . . . **111** A3
Grounds Ave PE15 . . . . . . **243** F4
Grounds Way PE7. . . . . . . **191** A8
Grove Cl CB23 . . . . **80** B1
Grove Ct
Little Paxton PE19 . . . . **95** F2
St Ives PE28 . . . . **144** A4
Grove End PE28. . . . . **120** C1
Grove Gdns
14 Elm PE14 . . . . **236** A5
Fordham CB7. . . . . **212** E2
Grove La
Brampton PE28 . . . . **140** D3
Cambridge CB1 . . . . **246** B1
Hilton PE28 . . . . **120** C7
Peterborough PE3 . . . . **197** A2
Grovelands PE3. . . . . **197** E2
Grovemere Ct PE28 . . . . . **114** B7
Grove Pk
Fordham CB7. . . . . **212** E2
Wisbech PE13 . . . . **245** C8
Grove Prim Sch The CB4 . **83** F6
Grove Rd
Little Paxton PE19 . . . . **95** F2
Sawston PE22. . . . . **33** A8
Grove St PE2 . . . . **186** F8
Grove The
Cambourne CB23 . . . . **79** C5
Cambridge CB4 . . . . **84** B6
Chatteris PE16. . . . . **241** C5
Huntingdon PE29 . . . . **142** B6
Linton CB21 . . . . **35** B3
Mildenhall IP28 . . . . **213** D8
Orwell SG8. . . . . **28** D8
St Neots PE19 . . . . **74** E6
1 Stretham CB6. . . . . **210** F5
Whittlesey PE7 . . . . **189** F6
Wistow PE28. . . . . **163** F6
Grove Way PE26 . . . . **172** A4
Grunty Fen Rd CB6. . . . . . **210** F8
Guanockgate Rd PE12. . . . **234** C8
Guash Way PE9 . . . . **244** D7
Guelder Rd 2 PE7 . . . . . . **186** D3
Guelder Rose 5 CB7. . . . . **240** F5
Guernsey Way CB6. . . . . . **242** C3
Guest Rd CB1. . . . . **246** C2
Guildenburgh Cres PE7 . . **190** A7
GUILDEN MORDEN. **10** F4
Guilden Morden CE Prim Sch
SG8. . . . . **10** F5
Guildhall Pl 5 CB1 . . . . . . **246** A2
Guildhall St 3 CB1 . . . . . . **246** A2
Guild Rd PE13 . . . . **245** E6
Guilsborough Rd PE6 . . . . **232** B2
Guineas Cl CB8 . . . . **110** E6
Guineas The CB8. . . . . **110** A4
Guise La SG8 . . . . **12** D6
Gull Bank PE13 . . . . **234** E3
Gull Dro PE13. . . . . **234** D3
Gull La PE13 . . . . **238** A3
Gull Rd PE13 . . . . **234** F3
Gull Way
Chatteris PE16. . . . . **241** C6
Whittlesey PE7 . . . . **190** A8
Gullymore PE3. . . . . **196** F8
Gunhild Cl CB1 . . . . **65** D5
Gunhild Cl CB1 . . . . **65** C5
Gunhild Way CB1 . . . . **65** C5
Gunnell Ct CB24 . . . . **105** D2
Gunning Rd CB6 . . . . **240** E8
Gunnings Way PE28. . . . . **143** C1
Gunning Way CB4. . . . . **83** C6

GUNTHORPE. **204** D2
Gunthorpe Prim Sch
PE4 . . . . **204** E2
Gunthorpe Rd
Newborough PE6. . . . . **204** F4
Peterborough PE4 . . . . **204** E2
Gunthorpe Ridings PE4 . **205** A2
Guntons Cl CB7. . . . . **212** B4
Gunton's Rd PE6. . . . . **205** C6
Gurlings Cl CB9. . . . . **39** A2
Gurnard Leys PE3. . . . . . . **204** A1
Gurney Way CB4. . . . . **83** E4
Guthlac Ave PE4 . . . . **204** D1
Guyatt Cl CB25. . . . . **130** B2
GUYHIRN. **234** F2
Guyhirn CE Prim Sch
PE13 . . . . **235** A2
Guyhirn Gull PE13. . . . . . . **234** E3
Gwydir St CB1 . . . . **65** A8
Gypsy Cnr PE28 . . . . **150** B6
Gypsy La PE13 . . . . **238** C4
Gypsy's Wlk CB8 . . . . **91** A8

H

Hacke Rd PE3 . . . . **197** D3
HADDENHAM **210** B6
Haddenham End Field
CB6 . . . . **210** A7
Haddenham Rd CB6. . . . . . **217** A1
HADDON. **180** B6
Haddon Cl PE2. . . . . **187** C5
Haddon Rd
Haddon PE7. . . . . **180** C6
Peterborough PE3 . . . . **197** C3
Haddon Way PE7 . . . . **187** B2
Haddow's Cl CB24 . . . . . . **123** F2
Haden Way
Over CB24 . . . . **208** F1
Willingham CB24 . . . . **123** F8
Hadleigh Ct CB5 . . . . **84** E4
Hadley Rd PE4. . . . . **204** D1
Hadrian Cl CB9 . . . . **24** D7
Hadrians Ct PE2 . . . . **187** B8
HADSTOCK **20** C6
Hadstock Rd CB21 . . . . **35** B1
Hagbech Hall Cl PE14 . . . . **236** D6
Haggers CB10 . . . . **18** D2
Hagger's Cl SG8 . . . . **14** D6
Haggis Gap CB21 . . . . **66** F5
Haig Ct CB4. . . . . **84** A4
Haigh's Cl PE16 . . . . **241** B4
HAIL WESTON **95** B1
Hake's Dro PE15 . . . . **227** C2
Halcyon Cl PE29 . . . . **141** C6
Hale Ave CB4 . . . . **83** D4
Hale Cl SG8. . . . . **14** D6
Hale Dro CB6 . . . . **225** E6
Hale Fen CB6. . . . . **242** C8
Hale Fen La CB6 . . . . **217** A4
Hale Fen Rd CB6. . . . . **225** E4
Hales Barn Rd CB9. . . . . . . **38** E2
Haley Cl
Hemingford Grey PE28 . . . **143** B1
Wisbech PE13 . . . . **245** C8
Half Acre Dro CB7 . . . . . . **211** C2
Half Acre La CB7. . . . . **211** D8
Halfpenny La PE14 . . . . . . **245** D1
Halfpenny Toll Rd PE14 . . **229** E4
Halifax Rd
Cambridge CB4 . . . . **83** B4
Mildenhall IP28 . . . . **213** E8
Halifax Way CB8 . . . . **110** E5
Hallards The 6 PE19. . . . . **74** C6
Hallaton Rd PE1 . . . . **198** B8
Hall Bank PE13 . . . . **237** E7
Hall Barn Rd CB7 . . . . **212** F4
Hall Bridge Rd PE14. . . . . **236** D1
Hall Cl
Bourn CB23. . . . . **60** C5
Foxton CB22. . . . . **30** B6
Huntingdon PE29 . . . . **142** A6
Little Paxton PE19 . . . . **95** F2
Hall Cres CB22 . . . . **33** A7
Hallcroft Rd PE7. . . . . **189** C8
Hall Dike PE14 . . . . **236** F4
Hall Dr
Hardwick CB23 . . . . **80** F3
Highfields CB23 . . . . **80** C3
Hall End CB24 . . . . **105** D2
Halley Cl PE29 . . . . **141** A5
Hall Farm La SG19 . . . . **58** D4
Hall Farm Rd 2 CB4 . . . . . **83** D5
Hallfields La PE4 . . . . **204** E1
Hall Gate Rd PE12. . . . . . . **234** B8
Hall Green La PE28. . . . . . **121** B6
Hall La
Abbots Ripton PE28. . . . . . **152** D8
Brinkley CB8 . . . . **70** E2
Burwell CB25 . . . . **130** B1
Great & Little Chishill SG8. . **7** F2
Peterborough PE4 . . . . **204** C4
Tilbrook PE28 . . . . **113** C8
20 Wittering PE8 . . . . **230** B1
Hall Rd
Outwell PE14 . . . . **236** F3
St Neots PE19 . . . . **74** E3
Hall St CB7 . . . . **212** B5
Hallwyck Gdns CB8 . . . . . **110** F2
Hamden Way CB23. . . . . . . **99** B3
HAMERTON. **159** B4
Hamerton Rd
Alconbury Weston PE28. . . **150** C7
Buckworth PE28 . . . . **149** D6
Winwick PE28 . . . . **158** C5

Hamerton Zoological Pk★
PE28 . . . . **159** B5
Hamilton Ct CB8. . . . . **110** E2
Hamilton Rd
Cambridge CB4 . . . . **246** B4
Ely CB6 . . . . **240** B4
Newmarket CB8. . . . . **110** E3
Hamiltons The CB8 . . . . . **110** E2
Ham La PE2 . . . . **185** E7
Hamlet Cl PE29 . . . . **141** F6
Hamlet Rd CB9 . . . . **24** B7
Hamlet The CB6 . . . . **218** C6
Hammond Cl
Cowlinge CB8. . . . . **73** D1
Newmarket CB8. . . . . **110** E6
Pampisford CB22. . . . . **33** B5
Wittering PE8. . . . . **230** C1
Hammond Way PE28 . . . . **208** C8
Hampden Gdns CB1. . . . . . **84** B1
Hampden Rd 2 PE13. . . . . **245** D5
Hampden Rise SG8 . . . . **5** D4
Hampden Way PE19 . . . . . . **75** A3
Hampshire Rd PE28 . . . . . **143** B8
Hampstead Ave IP28 . . . . **239** B6
Hampton Cl PE28 . . . . **121** C6
Hampton Coll PE7 . . . . **186** D1
Hampton Ct PE3 . . . . **197** C6
HAMPTON HARGATE **186** D2
Hampton Hargate Prim Sch
PE7. . . . . **186** C2
Hampton Vale Prim Sch
PE7. . . . . **186** C1
Hanaper Dr SG8 . . . . **6** F1
Hanbury PE2 . . . . **185** F3
HANCHET END **38** C1
Hanchet End CB9 . . . . **38** B1
HANCHETT VILLAGE **23** B8
Hankey St PE1 . . . . **197** F4
Hanmer Ave IP28 . . . . **239** C5
Hannath Rd PE13 . . . . **238** B8
Hannington Cl PE7 . . . . . . **190** A7
Hanover Cl
Bar Hill CB23. . . . . **102** B3
Eaton Socon PE19 . . . . **74** D5
Hanover Ct
Brampton PE28 . . . . **140** D3
Cambridge CB1 . . . . **246** B1
Peterborough PE3 . . . . **197** A8
Hansel Cl PE2 . . . . **186** E8
Hansell Rd PE28 . . . . **140** B3
Hanson Ct CB4. . . . . **83** E7
Harbins La PE19 . . . . **57** C6
Harbour Ave CB23 . . . . **62** D6
Harbour Ct PE16 . . . . **241** C6
Harbour Sch CB6 . . . . **210** C6
Harcombe Rd CB1 . . . . **65** E6
Harcourt PE29 . . . . **142** A2
Hardfields Cl CB7. . . . . . . **212** C3
Harding Cl 1 CB25 . . . . . **106** A7
Harding Way
Cambridge CB4 . . . . **83** C5
Histon CB24. . . . . **104** B4
St Ives PE27 . . . . **144** B5
Hardman Rd CB22. . . . . **30** C5
HARDWICK
Buckden. **117** A5
Cambridge. **81** B3
Hardwick Com Prim Sch
CB23 . . . . **81** A3
Hardwick Ct PE3. . . . . **197** B2
Hardwicke Cl CB6. . . . . . . **242** C5
Hardwicke La PE19. . . . . . . **57** B6
Hardwicke Rd SG19 . . . . . . **58** F6
Hardwicke Fields CB6. . . . **210** A6
Hardwicke Road Ind Est
SG19 . . . . **58** F6
Hardwick La PE19. . . . . . . **117** C5
Hardwick Rd
Haverhill CB9. . . . . **24** B8
St Neots PE19 . . . . **74** E3
Toft CB23. . . . . **61** E6
Hardwick St CB3. . . . . **64** C7
Hardy Cl
Huntingdon PE29 . . . . **141** F6
Longstanton CB24 . . . . . . **123** E2
Hardy Dr SG8. . . . . **5** D8
Hardy Pl 1 PE19. . . . . **74** D6
Hardy's La PE7 . . . . **189** E6
Harebell Cl
Cambridge CB1 . . . . **66** A5
Huntingdon PE29 . . . . **141** D6
January PE15 . . . . **243** E4
Peterborough PE1. . . . . . . **205** A4
Ramsey St Mary's PE26. . . **220** D3
Harebell Dr PE7 . . . . **182** A7
Harefield Rise CB21. . . . . . **35** E2
HARE PARK. **88** A3
Harewood Gdns PE3 . . . . **197** B2
Hargate Way
Hampton Hargate PE7. . . . **186** B2
Peterborough PE7. . . . . . . **186** D3
Hargood Ct 4 PE19. . . . . . **74** B3
Hargreaves Rd 6 SG8. . . . . **5** D5
Harland Rd PE19. . . . . **74** E6
Harlech Ct 5 PE19. . . . . . . **74** F2
Harlech Grange PE3 . . . . . **197** B1
Harlestones Rd CB24 . . . . **125** D4
Harley Ind Pk PE3 . . . . **96** D2
HARLTON. **46** C5
Harlton Cl PE2 . . . . **187** E5
Harlton Rd
Great Eversden CB23 . . . . . **45** F7
Haslingfield CB23 . . . . **46** F5
Harn Rd PE7. . . . . **186** D3
Harold Heading Cl PE16 . **241** B3
Harold's Bank PE13 . . . . . **237** B1
HAROLDSBRIDGE **237** C2
Harper's Dro PE26 . . . . . . **170** F7

Harradine Cl PE29 . . . . 155 B5
Harrier Cl PE29 . . . . . . 142 A8
Harrington Dr PE6 . . . . 232 C8
Harrington Sq 10 PE6 . . 232 B8
Harris Cres PE27 . . . . . 208 A2
Harris La PE28 . . . . . . 163 E6
Harrison Cl PE3 . . . . . . 196 F3
Harrison Pl PE1 . . . . . . 144 A5
Harrison's Dro
  Burwell CB25. . . . . . . 129 A8
  Swaffham Prior CB7 . . 128 D7
Harrison Way PE27. . . . 144 B3
Harris Rd CB4 . . . . 83 D6
Harris's La PE28 . . . . . 163 E7
Harris St PE1 . . . . 197 F6
Harris Way PE28 . . . . . 154 A1
Harrold Dro PE12 . . . . 234 C8
Harrolds Cl 5 PE14 . . . 238 F1
Harrow Rd CB9 . . . . 23 E7
Harry Palmer Cl PE27 . . 212 E1
Harry Scott Ct CB4 . . . . 83 E7
Harrys Way PE13 . . . . . 245 C2
HARSTON 48 A3
Harston Mill CB22. . . . . 47 D2
Harston & Newton Sch
  CB22. . . . . 47 F2
Harston Rd CB22 . . . . . 31 B8
Hart Cl CB9. . . . . 38 F1
Hartfield Rd CB8. . . . . . 70 E4
HARTFORD 142 A6
Hartford Ct PE2. . . . . . 187 D6
Hartford Jun & Inf Sch
  PE29 . . . . 141 F5
Hartford Rd PE29 . . . . . 141 E4
Hartington Gr CB1 . . . . 65 A5
Hartlands PE7 . . . . 190 E8
Hartley Cl CB25 . . . . . . 106 B8
Hart Rd PE26 . . . . 171 E3
Hartwell Ct PE3. . . . . . 197 C5
Hartwell Way
  Peterborough PE3. . . . 197 B5
  Ravensthorpe PE3. . . . 197 C6
Harvest Cl
  11 Doddington PE15 . . 223 A5
  Stilton PE7 . . . . 175 F8
Harvest Ct PE27. . . . . . 144 A4
Harvester Way
  Crowland PE6 . . . . . . 232 B8
  Peterborough PE1. . . . 198 C1
Harvest Way CB1 . . . . . 84 A2
Harvey Cl 4 PE8. . . . . . 230 B1
Harvey Dr 5 PE28 . . . . 215 C1
Harvey Goodwin Ave CB4. 83 D4
Harvey Goodwin Gdns
  CB4 . . . . 83 D4
Harvey Rd CB1 . . . . . . 246 C1
Harvey St 3 PE19. . . . . 74 C8
Haselhurst Cl PE15. . . . 243 F4
HASLINGFIELD 47 B6
Haslingfield Endowed Prim
  Sch CB23. . . . . 47 A5
Haslingfield Rd
  Barrington CB22 . . . . . 29 F8
  Barton CB23 . . . . 63 B2
  Harlton CB23. . . . . . . 46 E6
  Haslingfield CB23 . . . . 47 C3
Hasse Rd CB7. . . . . . . 212 C8
Hassock Hill Dro PE13. . 237 D3
Hassock Way 1 PE15 . . 223 B7
Hastings Rd PE4 . . . . . 204 C2
Hatchet La PE19 . . . . . 114 B2
Hatfield Rd PE28. . . . . 168 A4
Hathaway Cl PE19. . . . . 74 C3
Hatherdene Cl CB1. . . . 65 E8
Hatley Cl PE19 . . . . . . 75 A7
Hatley Dr CB25 . . . . . . 130 B3
HATLEY END. 25 B5
Hatley Rd
  Gamlingay SG19 . . . . . 41 F4
  Wrestlingworth & Cockayne
   Hatley SG19 . . . . 25 B7
HATLEY ST GEORGE . . . 43 A3
Hatton Park Prim Sch
  CB24. . . . . 123 F2
Hatton's Pk CB24 . . . . 123 F2
Hatton's Rd CB23 . . . . 102 C7
Hautboy La PE8. . . . . . 178 B3
HAUXTON 48 B4
Hauxton Prim Sch CB22. 48 C4
Hauxton Rd
  Cambridge CB2 . . . . . 48 C8
  Great Shelford CB22 . . 48 D4
Havelock Cl SG19 . . . . . 41 C5
Havelock Dr PE7 . . . . . 187 E6
Haven The CB21 . . . . . 66 F5
HAVERHILL 24 C8
Haverhill Bsns Pk CB9 . . 24 A5
Haverhill Leisure Ctr CB9 24 B7
Haverhill Rd
  Castle Camps CB21 . . . 22 E4
  Horseheath CB21 . . . . 37 A3
  Little Wratting CB9 . . . 39 F3
  Stapleford CB22 . . . . . 49 E5
  Steeple Bumpstead CB9 . 24 B1
Haveswater Cl 1 PE4 . . 204 E2
Haviland Way CB4 . . . . 83 F6
Hawcrofts La CB24. . . . 208 D2
Hawe's La CB7. . . . . . . 211 E2
Haweswater PE29. . . . . 141 C5
Hawk Dr
  Huntingdon PE29. . . . 142 B7
  Wyton PE28 . . . . 154 A1
Hawkesden Rd PE19 . . . 75 B6
Hawkes End PE28 . . . . 140 E2
Hawkesford Way PE19 . . 74 F7
Hawkes La PE27 . . . . . 208 A2
Hawkins Dr 1 PE13. . . . 245 E5

Hawkins Rd CB4 . . . . . . 83 F7
Hawkins's Dro CB7. . . . 242 F3
Hawkshead Way 2 PE4 . 204 E3
Hawthorn Ave
  Hauxton CB22 . . . . . . 48 B4
  Sawston CB22 . . . . . . 32 F6
Hawthorn Cl
  Little Paxton PE19 . . . . 95 F2
  Littleport CB6 . . . . . . 242 E3
  Newborough PE6. . . . . 207 C1
  Royston SG8 . . . . 5 F7
Hawthorn Dr PE29 . . . . 141 D5
Hawthorne Ave PE13. . . 245 C8
Hawthorne Dr PE7 . . . . 189 F6
Hawthorne Gr PE15 . . . 243 C5
Hawthorn End 1 PE28 . . 150 F5
Hawthorne Rd CB22. . . . 49 B4
HAWTHORN LODGE . . . 93 D5
Hawthorn Rd
  Emneth PE14 . . . . . . 236 D5
  Folksworth PE7 . . . . . 175 D8
  Haverhill CB9. . . . . . . 38 D1
  Peterborough PE1. . . . 198 C6
  Ramsey PE26. . . . . . . 171 F3
  St Neots PE19 . . . . . . 74 E6
  Yaxley PE7 . . . . 181 F5
Hawthorns The PE16. . . 241 C5
Hawthorn Way
  Burwell CB25. . . . . . . 130 C3
  Cambridge CB4 . . . . . 83 F4
  Royston SG8 . . . . 5 F7
  Sawtry PE28 . . . . 168 B3
  St Ives PE27 . . . . 144 A3
Hawthorn Wlk 4 IP28 . . 213 F8
Hawtreys The CB23 . . . . 62 D5
Hay Cl CB21 . . . . 53 B1
Haycocks Rd CB9 . . . . . 23 C8
Haycraft Cl PE28 . . . . . 116 A7
Haycroft The PE19 . . . . 117 F2
Haydock Rd SG8. . . . . . . 5 F6
Hayes Wlk PE8. . . . . . . 178 D8
Hay Fen Cl 6 CB6 . . . . 210 F5
Hayfield Ave CB22 . . . . 32 F7
Hayland Dro IP28. . . . . 213 B7
Hayley Cl PE19. . . . . . . 95 A1
Hayley Wood Nature
  Reserve ★ CB23 . . . . . 43 C6
Hayling Ave PE19 . . . . . 96 A2
Hayling Cl 4 PE29 . . . . 118 F7
Hayman's Way CB23 . . . 99 A2
Haymarket Rd 7 CB3 . . 83 C3
Hay St SG8 . . . . 11 B2
Hayster Dr CB1 . . . . . . 65 E6
Hayter Cl PE21. . . . . . . 53 F4
Haywardsfield PE3. . . . 197 A1
Haywoods La SG8. . . . . . 5 F7
Hayzen Cl CB22 . . . . . . 29 F8
Hazel Cl
  Chatteris PE16. . . . . . 241 D4
  Haverhill CB9. . . . . . . 23 E7
  Mildenhall IP28 . . . . . 239 E4
Hazel Croft PE4 . . . . . . 204 A4
Hazel Ct 7 CB6 . . . . . . 210 F5
Hazel Gdns 1 PE13 . . . 245 C8
Hazel La CB23 . . . . 79 C5
HAZEL STUB 23 C7
Hazel Way PE27 . . . . . . 144 B4
Hazelwood Cl CB4 . . . . 83 D6
Hazelwood Wlk PE29. . . 141 F7
Head Fen Dro CB6 . . . . 224 F3
Headford Cl CB5. . . . . . 84 D4
Headington Cl CB1. . . . 65 F5
Headington Dr CB1 . . . . 65 F5
Headlake Dro CB25 . . . 128 E1
Headland Ave CB9 . . . . 23 E7
Headlands
  Fenstanton PE28 . . . . 121 C5
  Huntingdon PE29 . . . . 141 C3
Headlands Way PE7. . . . 189 D8
Headley Gdns CB22 . . . . 49 B4
Headley's La CB6 . . . . . 217 A2
Heasman Cl CB24 . . . . 208 C1
Heath Ave SG8 . . . . 5 C6
Heathbell Rd CB8 . . . . 111 C3
Heathcote Cl PE15 . . . . 243 F4
Heather Ave PE1. . . . . . 198 A8
Heatherdale Cl PE7 . . . 187 C5
Heathersett Cl CB8. . . . 110 E7
Heatherset Way 1 IP28 . 213 F1
Heath Farm Rd IP28 . . . 213 F1
Heathfield
  Royston SG8 . . . . 5 B6
  Thriplow CB22. . . . . . 31 E1
Heath House CB4 . . . . . 84 A5
Heath La PE28 . . . . . . 163 A7
Heath Rd
  Barnack PE9 . . . . 230 C3
  Bottisham CB25. . . . . 87 B4
  Burwell CB25. . . . . . . 109 D5
  Exning CB8. . . . . 110 B4
  Gamlingay SG19 . . . . . 41 A4
  Helpston PE6. . . . . . . 231 C4
  Mildenhall IP28 . . . . . 239 E5
  Newmarket CB8. . . . . 111 C3
  Swaffham Bulbeck CB25 108 B2
  Swaffham Prior CB25 . . 109 A3
  Warboys PE28 . . . . . . 165 C6
Heath Row PE1. . . . . . 205 B1
Heath View Cl PE28 . . . 208 B8
Heaton Cl
  Ely CB6. . . . . 240 F7
  Peterborough PE3. . . . 197 B3
Heaton Dr CB6. . . . . . . 240 F7
Hectare The CB22. . . . . 48 F7
Hedda Dr PE7 . . . . 186 D3
Heddon Way PE27 . . . . 144 B6
Hedgelands
  Peterborough PE4. . . . 204 C5

Hedgelands continued
  Wisbech PE13 . . . . . . 245 C8
Hedgerley Cl CB3 . . . . . 83 A2
Heffer Cl CB22. . . . . . . 49 C4
Heights Dro Rd PE26 . . . 170 D6
Helen Cl 3 CB5. . . . . . . 84 E4
Helens Cl PE26 . . . . . . 171 B1
Helions Bumpstead Rd
  CB9 . . . . 23 F5
Helions Park Ave CB9 . . 24 A7
Helions Park Gdns CB9. . 24 A7
Helions Park Gr CB9 . . . 24 A7
Helions Service Rd CB9 . 24 A7
Helions Wlk CB9. . . . . . 24 A7
Helmsdale Gdns PE4 . . . 204 B2
Helmsley Ct PE7 . . . . . 187 F5
HELPSTON 231 C4
Helpston Rd
  Castor PE5. . . . . 195 D2
  Etton PE6 . . . . 203 C8
Heltwate PE3 . . . . 197 C7
Heltwate Ct PE3 . . . . . 197 C7
Heltwate Sch PE3 . . . . 197 B7
HEMINGFORD ABBOTS . 142 E3
Hemingford Cres PE2 . . 187 E6
HEMINGFORD GREY . . . 143 E1
Hemingford Grey Prim Sch
  PE28 . . . . 143 D2
Hemingford Rd
  Cambridge CB1 . . . . . 65 B8
  Hemingford Grey PE27 . 143 F3
Hemington Cl 10 CB24. . 208 D1
Hemlocks The CB23 . . . 47 B5
Hemmerley Dro PE7. . . 189 E8
Hempfield Pl CB6 . . . . . 242 D4
Hempfield Rd CB6 . . . . 242 D4
Hempsals 12 PE19. . . . . 74 C6
Hempsals Rd or Meadow Dro
  CB24 . . . . 209 F1
Hempstead Rd
  2 Haverhill CB9. . . . . 38 C1
  Peterborough PE7. . . . 186 C1
Hen Brook PE19 . . . . . 74 F4
Henderson Cl CB9. . . . . 38 C1
Henford Gdns PE15 . . . 243 D5
Henley Rd CB1. . . . . . . 84 B2
Henley Way CB7 . . . . . 240 F6
Henry Cl CB9 . . . . 23 D9
Henry Crabb Rd CB6 . . . 242 A6
Henry Morris Rd
  Histon CB24. . . . . . . 104 C3
  Sawston CB22 . . . . . . 33 A8
Henry Orbell Cl 3 PE15 . 243 E4
Henry St
  Peterborough PE1. . . . 198 A4
  Wisbech PE13 . . . . . . 245 C5
Henry Warby Ave 8
  PE14. . . . . 236 A5
Henshaw PE1. . . . . 198 E6
Henson Cl PE13. . . . . . 245 C8
Henson Rd PE15 . . . . . 243 D5
Herbert Human Cl 3
  CB7. . . . . 212 B4
Herbert St CB4 . . . . . . 83 E4
Herbert Twinn Ct CB5. . 84 D4
Hercules Cl 5 CB4. . . . . 83 E8
Hereford Cl 7 PE28. . . . 208 C8
Hereward Ave IP28 . . . . 239 C5
Hereward Cl
  Haddenham CB6 . . . . 209 E4
  Histon CB24. . . . . . . 104 C3
  2 Peterborough PE1 . . 198 B2
Hereward Com Coll PE1 . 198 D5
Hereward Rd
  Peterborough PE1. . . . 198 B2
  1 Wisbech PE13. . . . . 245 C5
Hereward St
  Ely CB6 . . . . 240 B4
  March PE15. . . . . 243 D5
Hereward Way PE6 . . . . 231 F8
Herewood Cross Sh Ctr
  PE1. . . . . 198 A2
Heritage Park Prim Sch
  PE7. . . . . 187 F5
Hermitage Rd PE28 . . . 208 E6
Herne Rd PE26. . . . . . . 220 D4
Heron Cl PE7 . . . . 189 F8
Heron Ct
  Peterborough PE2. . . . 187 D6
  10 Soham CB7. . . . . . 212 A5
  1 St Neots PE19 . . . . 75 B6
Heron Pk PE1. . . . . 198 F6
Heronry Dr PE6 . . . . . . 196 E2
Herons Cl
  6 Ely CB6. . . . . 240 B5
  Tallington PE9 . . . . . . 230 F6
Heron's Cl CB1 . . . . . . 65 D4
Heronshaw PE16. . . . . . 241 D6
Herons The CB24 . . . . . 125 D4
Heron Way PE27 . . . . . 143 F7
Heron Wlk PE15 . . . . . 243 F5
Herrick Cl PE1. . . . . . . 197 E8
Herring's Cl CB25 . . . . . 85 F5
HERRINGSWELL 113 E4
Herringswell Rd
  Herringswell IP28 . . . . 214 B2
  Kentford CB8. . . . . . . 134 B4
Herschel Rd CB3. . . . . . 83 B1
Hertford Cl CB6. . . . . . 240 A3
Hertford La SG8 . . . . . . 8 E5
Hertford St CB4. . . . . . 246 A4
Hervey Cl 3 CB6. . . . . . 240 B3
Hethersett Cl CB8. . . . . 110 E8
Hetley Pl PE2 . . . . 186 A4
Hexham Ct 3 PE1 . . . . 198 D3
HEYDON 8 A5

Heydon La
  Elmdon CB11 . . . . 8 F4
  Heydon SG8. . . . . 8 B5
Heydon Rd SG8 . . . . 7 F2
Heyford Cl PE4 . . . . . . 204 F2
Heyford Ct 5 IP28 . . . . 239 B5
Hiblings Row PE15 . . . . 224 B4
Hickling Wlk PE4 . . . . . 204 E3
Hicks La
  Girton CB3 . . . . 82 E8
  Peterborough PE7 . . . . 186 F5
Hicks Way 4 CB9 . . . . . 24 E5
Hide Cl CB22 . . . . 32 F6
Higham Rd IP28 . . . . . . 214 E1
Highbridge PE13 . . . . . 237 F7
Highbury St PE1 . . . . . 198 A5
High Cl SG8 . . . . 8 A5
Highclere Cl CB8 . . . . . 110 D8
Highclere Rd 1 PE7 . . . 186 D3
High Court Way PE7 . . . 181 D8
HIGH CROSS 82 E2
High Cswy PE7 . . . . . . 189 E7
Highdene Rd CB1 . . . . . 66 A6
High Ditch Rd CB5 . . . . 85 A4
High Fen Crooked Dro
  PE28. . . . . 215 B5
High Fen Straight Dro
  PE28. . . . . 215 B6
Highfield Ave
  Alconbury Weston PE28. 150 D6
  Cambridge CB4 . . . . . 83 E5
Highfield Cl CB22 . . . . . 17 D8
Highfield Cotts SG8 . . . . 4 B7
Highfield Dr CB6. . . . . . 242 C5
Highfield Gate CB21. . . . 66 F6
Highfield Rd
  Helpston PE6. . . . . . . 231 A3
  Histon CB24. . . . . . . 104 C1
  March PE15 . . . . 243 D7
HIGHFIELDS 80 D2
Highfields PE14. . . . . . 236 D5
Highfields Sch CB6 . . . . 240 C5
Highfields Rd CB23 . . . . 80 C2
High Flyer Cotts CB7 . . . 240 F7
Highgate Gn PE8. . . . . . 178 D8
High Gn
  Abbotsley PE19 . . . . . 57 B6
  Great Shelford CB22 . . 49 A6
High Haden Rd PE28 . . . 175 B1
HIGH HARTHAY 139 E3
Highlands SG8. . . . . 5 E6
Highlands The CB8. . . . . 110 D8
Highlees Prim Sch PE3 . 197 C6
High Leys PE27 . . . . . . 143 F5
High Mdw
  Harston CB22 . . . . . . 47 F3
  Ramsey PE26. . . . . . . 172 A3
High Park Cnr CB7. . . . . 132 D5
High Piece Cres CB24 . . 208 C1
High Rd
  Downham CB6 . . . . . . 217 F6
  Gorefield PE13. . . . . . 237 E3
  Newton PE13. . . . . . . 238 A5
  Tydd St Giles PE13. . . 237 F7
  Wisbech St Mary PE13 . 235 A6
High Sch Cl PE15 . . . . 243 D6
Highsett CB1 . . . . 246 C1
High Side PE13 . . . . . . 235 A8
High St
  Abbotsley PE19 . . . . . 57 B6
  Abington Pigotts SG8. . 11 F5
  Alconbury PE28 . . . . . 150 A4
  Alconbury Weston PE28. 150 D6
  Ashley CB8. . . . . 91 F8
  Ashwell SG7. . . . . 2 D4
  Babraham CB22. . . . . 33 D8
  Balsham CB21 . . . . . . 53 A2
  Barley SG8. . . . . 6 F2
  Barrington CB22 . . . . . 29 E8
  Barton CB23 . . . . 63 B4
  Bassingbourn SG8. . . . 12 F4
  Benwick PE15 . . . . . . 222 A5
  Bluntisham/Colne PE28. 208 C5
  Bottisham CB25. . . . . 86 F5
  Bourn CB23 . . . . 60 C6
  Boxworth CB23 . . . . . 101 B5
  Brampton PE28 . . . . . 140 E2
  Brinkley CB8 . . . . 70 D2
  Buckden PE19 . . . . . . 117 A4
  Burwell CB25. . . . . . . 109 B8
  Cambourne CB23. . . . 79 B3
  Castle Camps CB21 . . . 22 E3
  Castor PE5. . . . . 195 F2
  Catworth PE28. . . . . . 136 D7
  Chatteris PE16. . . . . . 241 C5
  Cherry Hinton CB1. . . . 66 A7
  Cheveley CB8. . . . . . . 91 C7
  Chippenham CB7 . . . . 132 E8
  Chrishall SG8. . . . . 8 D3
  Conington CB23. . . . . 121 C1
  Coton CB23 . . . . 82 B2
  Cottenham CB24 . . . . 125 E4
  Croxton PE19. . . . . . . 76 F4
  Croydon SG8 . . . . 27 A7
  Doddington/Wimblington
   PE15. . . . . 223 A5
  Dry Drayton CB23 . . . . 102 B1
  Earith PE28 . . . . 208 E5
  Ellington PE28 . . . . . . 139 A4
  Ely CB7 . . . . 240 D4
  Eye PE6 . . . . 232 A1
  Eyeworth SG19 . . . . . 10 A8
  Fen Ditton CB5. . . . . . 84 E5
  Fen Drayton CB24 . . . 121 F5
  Fenstanton PE28 . . . . 121 A6
  Fowlmere SG8. . . . . . 15 E8
  Foxton CB22. . . . . . . 30 B5

High St continued
  Fulbourn CB21 . . . . . . 66 F5
  Girton CB3 . . . . 103 E1
  Glinton PE6 . . . . 203 E8
  Grantchester CB3 . . . . 64 A4
  Graveley PE19 . . . . . . 97 F5
  Great Chesterford CB10. 18 E2
  Great Eversden CB23 . . 45 E8
  Great & Little Abington
   CB21. . . . . 34 C6
  Great Paxton PE19 . . . 96 D4
  Great Shelford CB22 . . 48 E3
  Great Wilbraham CB21 . 67 F7
  Guilden Morden SG8 . . 10 F4
  Haddenham CB6 . . . . 209 E4
  Hail Weston PE19 . . . . 74 B8
  Harlton CB23. . . . . . . 46 D5
  Harston CB22 . . . . . . 47 F3
  Haslingfield CB23 . . . . 47 B5
  Hauxton CB22 . . . . . . 48 C5
  Haverhill CB9. . . . . . . 24 A7
  Hemingford Abbots PE28 143 A3
  Hemingford Grey PE28 . 143 C2
  Hildersham CB21. . . . . 34 E5
  Hilton PE28 . . . . 120 B1
  Hinxton CB10. . . . . . . 18 B7
  Histon CB24. . . . . . . 104 B4
  Holywell-cum-Needingworth
   PE27. . . . . 144 F5
  Hornsea CB25. . . . . . 106 A1
  Huntingdon PE29 . . . . 141 D4
  Kimbolton PE28 . . . . . 113 F4
  Knapwell CB23. . . . . . 100 E3
  Landbeach CB25 . . . . 105 D6
  Linton CB21 . . . . 35 C2
  Little Paxton PE19 . . . . 95 F2
  Littleport CB6 . . . . . . 242 D4
  Little Staughton MK44. . 93 B1
  Little Wilbraham CB1. . . 86 F1
  Lode CB25 . . . . 107 C2
  Longstanton CB24 . . . 123 F3
  Longstowe CB23 . . . . 59 F2
  Madingley CB23. . . . . 81 F5
  Manea PE15. . . . . . . 224 C4
  March PE15. . . . . 243 D3
  Market Deeping PE6 . . 231 D8
  Maxey PE6. . . . . 231 C7
  Melbourn SG8 . . . . . . 14 C5
  Meldreth SG8. . . . . . . 14 B8
  Mepal CB6 . . . . 216 E3
  Mildenhall IP28 . . . . . 239 C4
  Milton CB24. . . . . 105 D2
  Needingworth PE27. . . 208 A3
  Newmarket CB8. . . . . 110 F3
  Oakington CB24. . . . . 103 C6
  Offord Cluny PE19 . . . . 96 F3
  Orwell SG8. . . . . 45 E1
  Over CB24 . . . . 208 D1
  Pampisford CB22. . . . . 33 B5
  Peterborough PE2. . . . 187 A6
  Pidley cum Fenton PE28. 155 E8
  Rampton CB24 . . . . . 124 E5
  Ramsey PE26. . . . . . . 172 A6
  Royston SG8 . . . . 5 D6
  Sawston CB22 . . . . . . 32 F6
  Sawtry PE28 . . . . 168 B4
  Shepreth SG8. . . . . . . 29 E4
  Soham CB7. . . . . 212 B4
  Somersham PE28. . . . 208 C8
  Spaldwick PE28 . . . . . 137 F6
  Stamford PE9. . . . . . . 244 B5
  Stetchworth CB8 . . . . 90 A2
  Stilton PE7 . . . . 176 A7
  St Neots PE19 . . . . . . 74 E5
  Stourbridge Common CB4. 84 A4
  Stretham CB6 . . . . . . 210 F5
  Sutton CB6. . . . . 216 D1
  Swaffham Bulbeck CB25 108 B8
  Swaffham Prior CB25 . . 108 D5
  Swavesey CB24 . . . . . 122 E6
  Tadlow SG8. . . . . 26 A3
  Teversham CB1. . . . . . 66 C8
  Tilbrook PE28 . . . . . . 113 B6
  Toft CB23. . . . . 61 D4
  Tuddenham IP28 . . . . 214 D2
  Upwood PE26 . . . . . . 171 B2
  Warboys PE28 . . . . . . 164 F5
  Waterbeach CB25 . . . . 106 B8
  West Wickham CB21. . . 37 A7
  West Wratting CB21 . . . 53 F5
  Whittlesford CB22 . . . . 32 C5
  Wicken CB7. . . . . 211 E1
  Wilburton CB6 . . . . . . 210 C5
  8 Willingham CB24 . . . 209 A1
  Wisbech PE13 . . . . . . 245 C5
  Witcham CB6. . . . . . . 217 A3
  Wrestlingworth SG19 . . 25 B4
  Yelling PE19. . . . . 98 C1
High Street Back 2 CB7 . 240 D4
High Street Pas CB7 . . . 240 D4
High Street St Martin's
  PE9 . . . . 244 C4
Hightown Dro CB25 . . . 129 C4
Highway The PE19 . . . . 94 A6
Highworth Ave CB4 . . . . 83 F5
Higney Rd PE7. . . . . . . 186 C1
Hilda Clarke Cl 1 PE16 . 241 C3
Hilda St CB4. . . . . 83 D4
HILDERSHAM 34 F5
Hildersham Mill CB21. . . 34 F5
Hildersham Rd CB21 . . . 34 D7
Hillary Cl PE9 . . . . 244 D6
Hillburn Rd PE13. . . . . 245 B4

Hill Cl
Brington & Molesworth
PE28 ....147 C5
Little Stukeley PE28....151 F1
Newmarket CB8.........110 E3
Peterborough PE1......198 D5
Sawtry PE28...........168 B3
Hill Cres CB9 ....39 A1
Hillcrest CB23 ....102 C3
Hillcrest Ave PE7 .....181 E5
Hillcrest Dr PE13.....235 A2
Hill Est
Ramsey PE26..........172 B4
St Ives PE28..........143 B5
Hill Farm Rd CB22 ....32 B3
Hill Farms CB1........66 C2
Hillfield
Alconbury PE28 ....150 F5
Foxton CB22...........30 C5
Hillfield Rd CB23.....62 D6
Hill La CB9 ....24 F3
Hill Rd
Over CB24............208 E1
Wistow PE26..........164 A8
Hill Rise
St Ives PE27..........143 E7
St Neots PE19.........75 A5
Hill Row CB6 ....209 E6
Hill Row Cswy CB6....209 A6
Hills Ave CB1 ....65 B5
Hillside
Orwell SG8............45 E2
Royston SG8...........5 D5
Sawston CB22.........32 F8
Sutton CB6............216 D1
Hillside Cl
Ellington PE28........138 F4
Ufford PE9............230 F2
Hillside Cotts PE28...146 A4
Hillside Gdns PE9.....230 B1
Hillside La SG8 ......44 C4
Hillside Mdw CB7......212 F1
Hillside Rd PE15......243 B5
Hills La CB6 ....240 B4
Hills Rd CB2 ....246 C1
Hills Rd Sixth Form Coll
CB1....................65 A6
Hillstead CB22........49 D7
Hills View CB22.......49 B6
Hill View
Dry Drayton CB23 .....102 D1
Lidgate CB8...........73 F8
Hillward Cl PE2.......186 C6
Hillway CB21 ....35 C2
Hilsdens Dr PE29.....142 A1
HILTON 121 B1
Hilton Rd PE28........120 E3
Hilton St CB24........208 D1
Hinchcliffe PE2.......185 E2
Hinchinbrooke Rd PE28.117 D8
Hinchingbrooke Ctry Pk★
PE29 ....140 F4
Hinchingbrooke Dr PE16 241 B4
Hinchingbrooke Hospl
PE29 ....141 B5
Hinchingbrooke House★
PE29 ....141 B3
**HINCHINGBROOKE
PARK.** 206 D5
Hinchingbrooke Sch
PE29 ....141 A4
Hines Cl CB23 ....63 A4
Hines La CB23 ....62 C5
Hinkins Cl SG8........14 D6
Hinton Ave CB1........65 C5
Hinton Cl PE7.........189 C4
Hinton Rd CB21.......66 D5
Hinton View CB6.......210 A6
Hinton Way
Great Shelford CB22 ..49 C6
Wilburton CB6........210 A4
HINXTON 18 A7
Hinxton Rd CB22......17 E8
Hinxworth Rd SG7 ....2 B4
HISTON 104 C4
Histon & Impington Inf Sch
CB24.................104 B3
Histon & Impington Jun Sch
CB24.................104 C4
Histon Rd
Cambridge CB4 ....83 C4
Cottenham CB24......104 C8
Hitches St CB4.......242 D4
Hitherford CB24......208 E1
Hive Rd CB6...........217 A4
Hives The PE19........74 D4
Hoadly Rd CB3........83 B5
Hobart Ct PE15.......243 C5
Hobart Rd CB1........65 C7
Hobbledodds Cl CB24..122 E6
Hobby Cl PE29........142 B6
Hobsons Acre CB22....48 F6
Hobson St CB1........246 B3
Hockland Rd PE13.....237 F7
Hockley Cl CB21......22 B5
Hod Fen Dro
Denton & Caldecote PE7.177 A7
Yaxley PE7...........181 B4
Hodgson Ave PE4......204 B6
Hod Hall La CB6......210 A5
Hodley PE23...........99 B1
Hodney Rd PE6........232 A1
Hodson's Dr PE29.....141 E5
Hodwell SG7...........2 D4
Hogarth Cl PE27......144 A7

Hogarth Pl [2] PE19 ....74 D5
Hogens La PE13........238 A5
Hog Fen Dro PE7......182 A5
Hogherd's La [8] PE13.245 C5
Hoghill Dro CB6......209 F3
Hogsden Leys PE19....75 C7
Hog's La SG8 ....8 D3
Holbein Rd PE27......144 A7
Holben Cl CB23.......63 B3
Holborn Ave IP28.....239 B6
Holbrook Rd
Cambridge CB1 ....65 B4
Haverhill CB9.........23 E6
Holburn View PE28....168 B2
Holcroft PE2..........186 B3
Holden End CB10......21 B2
Holdfield PE3.........197 B6
Holdich St PE1.......197 C4
Holdsworth Valley Prim Sch
CB8...................110 F3
Holgate La PE4.......204 B7
Holkham Mead CB25...130 C2
Holkham Rd PE2......185 D3
Holland Ave PE4......204 D1
Holland Pk CB8.......91 C7
Holland Rd PE9.......244 D6
Hollands Bsns Ctr CB9..24 B6
Hollands St CB9......24 A6
Hollands Road Ind Est
.......................24 A6
Hollans Ctr The CB9..24 A6
Hollendale Wlk [6] CB6.240 A3
Hollesley Ave CB3....23 C8
Holliday's Rd PE28...208 D5
Hollies Cl SG8........5 E6
Hollies The PE15.....243 E7
Hollmans Cl CB21.....66 F4
Hollow Hill CB9......38 A4
Hollow La PE26.......172 E6
Hollow Rd
Chrishall SG8.........8 D1
Elmdon CB11..........9 C4
Ramsey Forty Foot PE26..221 C2
Holly Dr [4] PE15....223 A6
Hollymount [6] CB1...84 A2
Hollytrees CB23......102 C3
Holly Way [7] PE6....231 E8
Holly Wlk
Ely CB7...............240 F5
[3] Mildenhall IP28...213 F8
Peterborough PE7....186 D3
HOLME.................177 A4
Holme Cl
Castor PE5............195 D2
Oakington/Longstanton
CB22.................103 C5
Holme Dro CB6........208 E7
Holme Fen Dro PE28...208 D7
**Holme Fen National Nature
Reserve**★ PE7........177 C7
Holmehill PE29.......118 F8
Holme La CB6.........218 A6
Holme Rd
Ramsey PE26.........220 C3
Yaxley PE7...........181 E4
Holmes Dr PE13......245 E5
Holmes La CB7........212 B5
Holmes Rd PE6.......203 F7
Holmes The CB6......242 E4
Holmes Way PE4......204 E2
Holme Way CB22......32 F8
Holmewood PE7.......176 F4
Holmewood Cres PE7..176 F4
Holmsey Gn IP28.....213 F8
Holmsey Green Gdns [2]
IP28..................213 F8
Holt Cl [8] PE8......230 B1
Holt Fen CB6.........211 B7
Holyrood Cl CB4......83 C6
HOLYWELL.............144 F2
Holywell CE (C) Prim Sch
PE27..................208 A2
Holywell Cl PE3......197 A1
Holywell Ferry Rd CB24.121 F6
Holywell Front PE27..144 F2
HOLYWELL ROW........214 A8
Home Cl
Burton End CB21......37 B8
Grafham PE28.........116 A6
Histon CB24..........104 B4
Home End CB10........67 A4
Home Farm Cl
Abbotsley PE19.......57 B6
Colne PE28...........208 D6
Hilton PE28..........120 B1
Rampton CB24.........124 F4
Home Farm Rd PE28...143 B5
Homefield Cl CB24....104 C3
Homefield Rd CB9.....23 F5
Homefield Rd Units CB9..23 F5
Home Pasture PE4.....204 B5
Homerton Coll CB2....65 A5
Homerton St CB2.....65 A6
Homestall Cres CB9...38 B4
Homestead [12] PE28..215 C1
Homing The CB5.......84 E3
Honeydon Ave PE19....74 B5
Honey Dro PE15.......223 E4

Honeyhill PE4 ....205 A1
Honey Hill
[9] Cambridge CB3 ...83 C3
Fen Drayton CB24.....122 A4
Fenstanton PE28......121 B6
Gamlingay SG19.......41 D4
West Wratting CB21...53 E5
Honey Hill Mews CB3...83 C3
Honeyhill Rd PE13....237 C2
Honey La PE16........241 C2
Honeymead Rd PE15...223 B7
Honeysome Rd PE16...241 A5
Honeysuckle Cl
Haverhill CB9.........38 E1
Red Lodge IP28.......134 A8
[2] Soham CB7........212 B4
Honeysuckle Ct PE2...186 D7
Honeyway SG8.........5 E6
Hoo Cl PE19...........117 B4
Hoof Cl CB6...........242 D3
HOOK..................223 D8
Hook Dro PE15........228 B1
Hook La PE15.........223 C7
Hook Rd PE15.........223 C7
Hook's Dro PE13......234 C4
Hook's Mill SG8......10 E7
Hooper St CB1........84 A1
Hopbine Ct PE26......171 F5
Hope St CB1..........65 B8
Hop Gdns CB23........78 F3
Hopkins Cl CB4.......84 A6
Hop Row CB6..........210 A6
Hopton Rise CB9......38 B1
Hornbeam Rd
Hampton Hargate PE7..186 B2
Mildenhall IP28......239 D5
HORNINGSEA...........106 A1
Horningsea Rd
Fen Ditton CB5.......84 F6
Horningsea CB5.......85 A8
Horn La
Kirtling CB8..........72 B5
Linton CB21..........35 B2
Horse Comm Cl PE29...141 E5
Horse Comm La PE29...141 E5
Horse Dro PE26.......221 A1
Horse Fair Sh Ctr PE13.245 C5
Horsegate
Market Deeping PE6...231 E8
Whittlesey PE7.......189 D7
Horsegate Gdns PE16..241 C5
Horsegate La PE7.....189 C7
Horse & Gate St PE7..121 F5
Horsehead Dro PE14...229 F4
HORSEHEATH...........37 A3
Horseheath Gn CB21...37 C1
Horseheath Pk CB21...37 D3
Horseheath Rd
Linton CB21..........35 D2
Withersfield CB9.....38 A4
Horseley Fen Dro PE16..37 A1
HORSE MOOR...........228 D1
Horsemoor Rd PE15....223 D8
Horseshoe Cl
Balsham CB21.........53 C2
Barley SG8............6 F1
Elmdon CB11..........9 B4
Horseshoe Ct CB14....236 E2
Horseshoe La
[4] Haverhill CB9.....23 E7
[4] Stamford PE9.....244 B5
Horseshoes La CB21...54 D5
Horseshoes Way PE28..140 D2
Horseshoe Terr PE13..245 B7
Horseshoe Way PE7...186 D2
Horse Ware CB24......208 D2
Horseway PE16........54 D5
Horsey Hill (Civil War Fort)★
PE7...................188 A4
Horsham Cl [3] CB23..38 C1
Horsley Hale CB6.....242 D6
Horton Wlk PE3.......197 D5
Hospital Rd PE15.....222 E6
Hostmoor Ave PE15...243 A7
Hotel La PE28.........151 F3
HOUGHTON..............143 A5
Houghton Ave PE2.....187 F5
Houghton Gdns CB6....240 B4
Houghton Grange PE28.143 C5
Houghton Hill Rd PE28..143 B5
**Houghton Meadows Nature
Reserve**★ PE28........143 C4
Houghton Mill★ PE28..143 A4
Houghton Prim Sch
PE28..................143 A5
Houghton Rd
Huntingdon PE29......142 C6
St Ives PE27..........143 E5
Houghtons La CB7.....213 B5
Houldsworth Terr CB8.110 F3
Housman Ave SG8......5 C8
Howard Cl CB5........84 D4
Howard Ct CB5........84 E4
Howard De Walden Way
CB8...................111 A4
Howard Rd
Cambridge CB5 ....84 E4
Eaton Socon PE19.....74 C1
Meldreth SG8.........14 A8
Howard Road Ind Est
PE19..................74 C1
Howard's La CB21.....37 A2
Howell Dr PE28.......152 E1
Howe Rd CB6..........38 F1
Howes Pl CB3.........83 A5
Howgate Rd CB4.......83 D7

How Hill (Tumulus)★
IP27..................214 F7
Howitt's Gdns PE19...75 A2
Howitts La PE19......74 F4
Howitt's La [5] PE19..74 F3
Howland PE2..........186 A3
Howletts Hill PE13...245 C4
Howlett Way PE25....86 E6
Hoylake Dr PE7.......187 C5
Huddleston Way CB22..33 A7
Hudpool PE29.........118 F7
Hudson Cl PE19.......24 C6
Hudson Leisure Ctr
PE13..................245 A5
Hughes Hall CB1......246 C1
Hulatt Rd CB1........65 C4
Humberdale Way PE28..164 F5
Humber Dr PE7........181 E6
Humberley Cl [1] PE19..74 F3
Humber Rd PE29.......141 F7
Humberstone Rd CB4..246 C4
Humphreys Rd CB4....83 E6
Humphries Way SG24...105 D3
Humphrys St PE2.....186 D8
Hunchback La PE14....238 E2
Hundon Pl CB9........24 B8
Hundred Acre Way [12]
IP28..................214 A1
Hundred Rd PE15.....243 C8
Hundreds Rd PE6.....232 C6
Hungarton Ct [2] PE1.198 D7
Hungate Rd PE14.....236 E6
Hunsbury Cl PE7......189 F6
Hunters Chase PE15...243 E2
Hunters Cl PE16......241 D5
Hunters Rowe PE14...245 D2
Hunters Way
Kimbolton PE28.......113 F5
Royston SG8..........5 E6
Sawtry PE28..........168 B3
Hunting Ave PE2......186 F7
HUNTINGDON...........141 F4
Huntingdon Jun & Inf Sch
PE29..................141 E6
Huntingdon Leisure Ctr
PE29..................141 D6
Huntingdon Racecourse
PE28..................140 C5
Huntingdon Rd
Boxworth PE28........101 E7
Brampton PE28........141 A2
Cambridge CB3 ....83 A5
Chatteris PE16.......241 B4
Fen Drayton CB24.....121 D4
Houghton & Wyton PE28.142 F5
Lolworth CB23........102 B5
Ramsey PE26.........171 C2
Sawston CB22.........33 A8
St Neots PE19.........75 A8
**Huntingdonshire Regional
Coll**
Huntingdon PE29......141 E6
St Neots PE19.........74 F6
Huntingdon St PE19...74 F6
Huntingdon Sta PE29.141 C4
Hunting Gr CB23......101 B5
Huntings Dr PE28.....168 B4
Huntley Cl CB5.......84 E4
Huntly Gr PE1........198 B4
Huntly Rd PE2........186 E7
Hunts Cl [4] PE15....222 F5
Hunts End PE19.......117 B4
Hunts End Ct PE19...117 B4
Hunt's Gate PE12....237 F8
Hunts La CB10........18 B7
Huntsmans Gate PE3..196 F3
Huntsmill CB21.......66 E4
Hunts Rd CB22........17 D8
Hurdleditch Rd SG8...28 D8
Hurdle Dro IP28......213 D8
Hurdles The PE28.....140 E2
Hurdles Way CB22.....31 E1
Hurn Rd PE6..........203 E3
Hurrell Rd CB4.......83 C6
Hurrell's Row CB22...47 E2
Hurricane Cl PE29....141 B8
Hurrys Cl CB22.......32 E7
Hurst Ave [1] PE15...243 E4
Hurstingstone PE27...144 A5
Hurst La CB6.........240 A6
Hurst Park Ave CB4...83 E5
Hurts Croft CB7......212 E1
Hutchinson Cl PE15...224 A4
Hut Field La CB23....99 A3
Huttles Gn SG8.......29 E4
Hyholmes PE3.........196 F7
Hyll Cl CB10.........18 D3
Hyperion Way CB8.....110 D8
Hythe Cl CB23........130 A3
Hythegate PE4........204 D4
Hythe La
Burwell CB25.........130 A3
Ely CB7...............240 F4
Hythe The
Littleport CB6.......242 D5
Reach CB25...........129 D1

I

Ibberson's Dro PE15...221 F4
Ibbot Cl PE2.........187 E5
Ibbott Cres [7] PE28..215 C1
Iceni Way
Exning CB8...........110 B8
Kings Hedges CB4.....83 D7
Icewell Hill CB8.....111 A4
ICKLETON.............18 A4

Ickleton Grange CB10....17 A1
Ickleton Pl CB9......24 E8
Ickleton Rd
Duxford CB22.........17 C2
Elmdon CB11.........9 A4
Great Chesterford CB10.18 C2
Hinxton CB10.........18 B6
Icknield Cl
Cheveley CB8.........91 C5
Ickleton CB10........18 A3
Icknield Fst Sch SG8...5 F1
Icknield Prim Sch The
CB22.................33 A8
Icknield Wlk SG8.....5 F6
Ida Darwin Hospl CB21.66 D5
Ihlee Cl PE4.........204 E1
Ilex Cl PE7..........186 C3
Ilex Rd PE7..........144 B6
Illing's La PE28......164 A1
Illingworth Way CB22..30 C5
Illston Pl PE1.......198 D4
Impala Dr CB1........66 A7
Impett's La CB21.....67 A4
IMPINGTON............104 C2
Impington La PE24....104 C3
Impington Village Coll
CB24.................104 D3
India La PE28.........151 F2
Infield Rd PE7.......167 C7
Ingham Hall Gdns PE13.234 D7
Ingham Rd CB9........24 A8
INGLEBOROUGH.........238 E5
Ingleborough PE1.....198 A5
Ingleborough Mill PE14.238 E5
Ingle Rd PE14........236 E5
Ingle's La [14] PE15..223 A5
Ingoldsby Cl [3] PE15.243 D2
Ingram St PE29.......141 E4
Inhams Cl PE13.......234 D5
Inhams Ct PE7........189 E6
INHAM'S END..........189 E6
Inham's Rd PE7.......189 E6
Inhams Way PE14......116 A7
Inkerman Rise PE19...74 C5
Inley Dro PE12.......237 A8
Innovation Way PE2...185 E2
Interchange Ind Est The
PE29..................141 C8
Inverness Cl CB4.....84 A5
Iowa PE28.............151 E4
Iram Dro CB24........209 B1
Irchester Pl PE3.....197 D4
Ireton Cl PE19.......74 F3
Ireton's Way
Chatteris PE16.......241 F2
Mepal PE16...........216 C6
Ireton Way PE15......243 D2
Iris Dr PE2...........186 E8
Irnham Rd PE9........244 C7
Ironmonger St [2] PE9.244 C5
Irving Burgess Cl PE7.189 C8
Isaacson Rd CB25.....109 C8
Isham Rd PE3.........197 C4
Isherwood Cl
Dogsthorpe PE1.......198 A6
Royston SG8..........5 C8
Isinglass Cl CB8.....111 E2
Isis Way PE2.........185 E3
ISLANDS COMMON......74 E7
Isle Bridge Rd PE14..236 F2
ISLEHAM..............213 A5
Isleham CE Prim Sch
CB7...................213 A5
Isleham Marina IP28..213 B6
Isleham Rd CB7.......212 F2
Isle of Ely Way
Chatteris PE16.......241 C7
March PE15...........243 A4
Isons Cl SG8.........15 E8
Itter Cres PE4.......197 E8
Ivan Clark's Cnr CB21.34 C7
Ivatt St CB24........125 E5
Ivatt Way PE3........197 C2
Ivelbury Cl PE19.....117 A3
Ivel Cl CB1...........65 F7
Ives Dro PE7.........189 A2
Ivesdyke Cl [4] PE13.238 B2
Ivett's Cl CB23......45 E7
Ivydene CB25.........128 A2
Ivy Field CB23.......63 B4
Ivy Gr PE4...........204 D2
Ivy Way PE28.........138 A6
Ixworth Cl PE6.......232 A1
Ixworth Rd [3] CB9...23 E6
Izaak Walton Way CB4.84 C5
Izzard Rise PE19.....96 E4

J

Jack Haws La [4] PE9...230 D4
Jack Hunt Sch PE3....197 B3
Jack Hunt Swimming Pool
PE3...................197 B3
Jack Jarvis Cl [5] CB8.111 A3
Jack's Corner Dro PE26.172 E3
Jackson Cl CB22......48 C5
Jackson's La CB10....18 D3
Jackson's Sq CB10....18 D3
Jackson's Way SG8....15 E8
Jack Warren Gn CB5...84 F3
James Carter Rd IP28.239 A6
James Ct PE19........74 F2
James Essex Dr CB6...240 E2
James Gage Cl PE16...241 B3
James Gdns PE7.......189 E2
James Nurse Cl CB1...66 A6

James St CB5 246 C3
Janus Cl CB9 24 D6
Jarman's La IP28 213 D7
Jarman Way SG8 5 B7
Jarvis Way CB8 110 E5
Jasmin Cl PE13 245 F7
Jasmine Ct
Cambridge CB1 65 C5
Peterborough PE2 185 E2
Jasmine Way PE7 181 F6
Jay Cl CB9 24 C7
Jaywick Rd CB9 24 A8
Jeavons La 6 CB23 79 C3
Jedburgh Cl 3 CB4 83 E7
Jefferson Cl 22 PE8 230 B1
Jeffery Ave 4 PE13 245 E7
Jeffrey Cl SG8 5 C8
Jeffrey Dr PE28 152 E1
Jellicoe Pl PE19 74 A2
Jenkins Cl PE19 74 B2
Jennings Ave PE19 74 E2
Jenyns Cl CB25 86 E7
Jepps La SG8 5 D6
Jermyn Cl CB4 83 D6
Jersey Way CB6 242 C3
Jerusalem Dro CB6 217 A5
Jesus Coll CB5 246 B3
Jesus La CB1 246 B3
Jesus Terr CB1 246 C3
Jetty The PE13 235 C7
Jew House Dro PE14 235 E3
Jim Mollison Ct 2 IP28 239 B5
JJ Thompson Ave CB3 82 F2
Job's La PE15 243 C1
John Amner Cl CB6 240 D6
John Bends Way PE13 234 D7
John Breay Cl SG8 29 D4
John Clare Prim Sch
PE6 231 B4
John Clare Theatre★
PE1 198 A2
John Clarke Ct CB4 84 A6
John Conder Ct CB1 65 C7
John Falkner Inf Sch
CB22 32 E7
John F Kennedy Ct 2
PE13 245 D4
John Impey Way SG8 14 D6
John King Gdns PE2 187 C7
John Mansfield Sch PE1 198 B8
John Paxton Jun Sch
CB22 32 F8
John's Acre CB22 32 F6
John Sale Cl SG7 2 C4
John's Cl SG8 15 E8
Johnson's Dro PE13 234 B7
Johnson Way PE16 241 C6
Johnson Wlk PE1 197 F7
John St
Cambridge CB1 246 C2
Royston SG8 5 D6
John Thompson Rd 3
PE13 245 D4
John Wesley Rd PE4 204 A2
Joiner's Ct CB21 35 B2
Joiner's Rd CB21 35 B2
Jolley Cl PE15 224 B4
Jolley Way CB4 83 F6
Jones Cl PE15 243 B3
Jones Ct PE26 172 B7
Jones Dr CB23 99 A3
Jones La PE7 190 C7
Jone's Dro PE7 221 F8
Jopling Way CB22 48 C4
Jordan Mews 2 PE1 198 B3
Jordans Yd CB1 246 A3
Jorose St PE3 197 A3
Jorose Way PE3 197 F3
Joscelynes CB22 49 C4
Joshua Cl 2 PE16 241 C5
Josiah Ct CB25 106 C8
Joyce's Cl CB22 32 F6
Jubilee Ave PE28 164 D6
Jubilee Cl
Brampton PE28 140 B3
Isleham CB7 213 A5
Little Paxton PE19 95 F2
Waterbeach CB25 106 A8
Jubilee Ct CB8 90 A1
Jubilee End SG8 11 B2
Jubilee St PE2 186 F8
Jubilee Terr CB7 240 D3
Jubilee Way
Mildenhall IP28 239 C4
Steeple Morden SG8 11 B2
Jubilee Wlk
Haverhill CB9 24 A7
Wisbech PE13 245 D8
Judson Ct 3 PE29 141 F8
Julian Cl CB9 24 D7
Julius Martin La CB7 212 A4
Junction Rd IP28 239 B5
Junction The★ CB1 246 C1
Junction The 2 PE15 243 D7
Juniper Cl IP28 239 E5
Juniper Cres PE3 197 A2
Juniper Dr
Chatteris PE16 241 D5
Ely CB7 240 F5
Juniper Rd 11 IP28 214 A1
Jupiter Cl 2 CB9 24 C6
Jury Rd PE7 181 C8
Justinian Cl CB9 24 D6
Jutland Rise PE19 74 C5

K

Kaldor Ct CB4 83 E7
Kansas PE28 151 E4
Katharine Way PE3 197 A5
Kathleen Elliot Way CB1 65 F7
Kay Hitch Way CB24 104 B2
Keates Rd CB1 66 A5
Keats Cl SG8 5 C8
Keats Ct PE19 74 C6
Keats Way PE1 197 D7
Keble Cl PE9 244 A7
Keble Ct PE9 244 A7
Kedleston Rd PE7 187 F6
Keep The CB9 23 E7
Keeton Rd PE1 197 E7
Kefford Cl SG8 12 F5
Keillers Cl PE13 245 A7
Keith Day Rd CB2 65 A3
Kelful Cl PE7 190 D7
Kelsey Cres CB1 66 A7
Kelsey Kerridge Sports Ctr
CB1 246 C1
Kelsey Way PE15 243 D2
Kelso Ct PE4 204 C1
Kelvin Cl CB1 65 D5
Kemmann La CB23 79 B3
Kendal Cl PE4 204 F2
Kendall Croft PE7 189 E6
Kendall Way PE28 154 A1
Kendal Way CB4 84 A6
Kendrick Cl PE2 187 D6
Kenilworth Ave PE7 188 A5
Kenilworth Cl 3 PE19 74 C3
Kenlan Rd PE13 245 D6
Kennedy Croft CB24 126 A7
Kennedy Rd CB7 213 A5
Kennels Rd PE6 196 D4
Kennet Gdns PE4 204 E1
Kennetside CB8 73 D1
KENNETT 134 F5
KENNETT END 113 A2
Kennett Prim Sch CB8 133 F5
Kennett Rd or Moulton Rd
CB8 112 F7
Kennett Sta CB8 133 F3
Kennulphs Cl 3 PE6 232 C8
Ken Stimpson Com Sch
PE4 204 B4
Ken's Way CB24 105 D2
Kent Cl
Ely CB6 240 B5
St Ives PE27 143 F7
KENTFORD 113 B2
Kentings CB23 62 B5
Kentmere Pl 1 PE4 204 F2
Kentra Cl PE13 245 A8
Kent Rd
Huntingdon PE29 141 E8
Peterborough PE3 197 E2
Kents La CB7 212 B4
Kent Way
Cambridge CB4 83 F7
January PE15 243 C4
Kentwell Pl CB25 130 C2
Kenwood Gdns CB21 35 E2
Kerridge Cl CB1 84 A1
Kespar CB8 73 D6
Kesters Cl CB23 81 B2
Kesteven Cl 6 PE6 231 E8
Kesteven Rd PE9 244 B7
Kesteven Wlk PE1 198 B2
Kestrel Cl
Cottenham CB24 125 E5
Huntingdon PE29 142 A7
Kestrel Ct PE3 197 F2
Kestrel Dr 2 PE14 245 D2
Kestrel Pl 4 PE19 75 B7
Kestrel Rd CB9 24 C7
Kestrel Way 7 SG8 5 E8
Keswick Cl PE4 204 F3
Kettering Rd PE9 244 B2
Kettlefields CB8 89 F1
Kettlefields CP Sch CB8 89 F1
Kettles Cl CB24 103 C5
Kettle's Yd★ CB1 246 A4
Keynes Rd CB5 84 D4
KEYSTON 146 B3
Keyston Rd PE28 135 D2
Key Theatre★ PE1 198 A1
Kidmans Cl
Hilton PE28 120 B1
Newton CB22 31 B7
Kildare Dr PE3 197 C4
Kilderkin Cl PE14 236 A3
Kilham PE2 185 E2
Kilkenny Ave CB6 240 E7
Killem's Gn CB11 1 E4
Kilmaine Cl CB4 83 F8
Kiln Cl
2 Little Downham CB6 218 B7
St Ives PE27 143 E6
Kiln House Yd SG8 5 C6
Kiln La CB7 240 F5
Kilverstone PE4 204 B6
Kimberley Rd CB4 246 C4
KIMBOLTON 113 F6
Kimbolton Ct PE1 197 F3
Kimbolton Prep Sch
PE28 113 E5
Kimbolton Rd
Hail Weston PE19 74 A8
Pertenhall MK44 113 D1
Kimbolton Sch PE28 113 F4
Kim Rd PE28 114 A7
Kinderley Cty Prim Sch
PE13 237 F6
Kinderley Rd PE13 245 C8
King Cob CB6 210 F5
Kingdon Ave CB7 219 B5
King Edgar Cl CB6 240 D7
King Edward Ctr (Cromwell
Com Coll) PE16 241 C5
King Edward Rd PE16 241 C5
King Edward VII Rd CB8 110 E5
Kingfisher Cl
Bourn CB23 60 C6
Chatteris PE16 241 C6
Haverhill CB9 24 C8
Little Paxton PE19 96 A2
March PE15 243 E5
Sawston CB22 32 E6
Yaxley PE7 181 D5
Kingfisher Dr
Burwell CB25 130 B4
Soham CB7 212 A5
6 Wisbech PE14 245 D2
Kingfisher Gn PE27 143 F7
Kingfisher Rd PE7 189 F8
Kingfishers PE2 185 D6
Kingfisher Way
Cambridge CB2 64 F6
Cottenham CB24 125 D5
Mildenhall IP28 239 D4
The Stukeleys PE29 141 A6
King George Ave CB8 110 B8
King Henry Chase 2
PE3 197 A5
King James Way SG8 5 D6
King's Ave CB7 240 E7
Kingsbridge Ct PE4 204 A5
Kingsbrook PE27 144 A5
Kings Cl
Huntingdon PE29 142 A7
Mildenhall IP28 239 D5
North Green PE7 190 F8
Kings Coll CB2 246 A2
Kings Coll Sch CB3 83 C1
Kings Ct
Exning CB8 110 B8
Newmarket CB8 110 F7
Kings Delph PE7 188 C5
King's Delph Dro PE7 187 E2
Kings Dr CB8 111 B1
KING'S DYKE 188 E6
King's Dyke PE7 188 E6
Kings Dyke Cl PE2 187 E6
Kingsfield Prim Sch
PE16 241 B5
King's Gate CB23 78 E1
King's Gdns
Huntingdon PE29 141 D5
Peterborough PE1 198 A5
Kings Gr CB23 63 B4
KINGS HEDGES 83 E7
Kings Hedges PE27 144 A6
Kings Hedges Prim Sch
CB4 83 F7
King's Hedges Rd CB4 83 D7
Kings Jun Sch The CB7 240 C4
King's Jun Sch The CB6 240 C5
King's La
Cambridge CB1 246 A2
Elmdon CB11 9 A3
St Neots PE19 75 A5
Kingsland Way SG7 2 D4
Kingsley Ave PE13 245 B4
Kingsley Cl 1 PE9 230 D3
Kingsley Rd PE1 198 C4
Kingsley St PE15 243 D5
Kingsley Wlk CB6 240 A4
Kingsline Cl PE6 233 A3
Kings Mead CB8 91 C7
Kingsmead Ct CB6 242 E4
Kings Mill La
Great Shelford CB22 48 F4
2 Stamford PE9 244 B4
Kings Par CB7 212 B3
King's Par CB2 246 A2
Kings Rd
Eaton Socon PE19 74 B3
Hardwick CB23 81 A2
Peterborough PE2 187 B6
Stamford PE9 244 B6
St Ives PE27 144 A4
St Neots PE19 74 F6
Wisbech PE13 245 C4
King's Rd CB3 64 B7
Kings Ride SG8 4 C3
KINGS RIPTON 153 C5
Kings Ripton Rd PE29 152 D1
King's Sch PE1 198 A4
King St
Cambridge CB1 246 B3
Doddington/Wimblington
PE15 223 B7
Mildenhall IP28 239 C4
14 Over CB24 208 D1
1 Peterborough PE1 198 A2
Rampton CB24 124 E4
Royston SG8 5 D6
Somersham PE28 215 B1
West Deeping PE6 231 A8
Wisbech PE13 245 C5
Kings Theatre★ 3 CB8 110 F3
KINGSTON 61 A3
Kingston Cl PE29 141 E8
Kingston Dr PE2 187 E5
Kingston Pas 2 CB8 111 A3
Kingston Rd CB23 61 D1
Kingston St CB1 65 A8
Kingston Vale SG8 5 E5
Kingston Way PE28 163 F6
Kingsway
Arbury CB4 83 D6
Kingsway *continued*
Duxford Airfield CB22 31 F1
Leverington PE13 245 F7
Mildenhall IP28 239 C4
Newmarket CB8 110 F4
Royston SG8 5 D8
King's Wk 3 PE13 245 C4
KINGSWOOD PARK 243 B2
Kingswood Rd PE15 243 C3
Kinnaird Way CB1 65 C4
Kinnears Wlk PE2 185 F2
Kinross Rd CB4 84 A5
Kintbury CB22 17 D8
Kipling Ct PE1 197 E8
Kipling Pl 1 PE19 74 D5
Kipling Rd 1 SG8 5 E8
Kirby Cl CB4 83 F5
Kirby Cross Ave CB6 242 B5
Kirby Rd CB25 127 C1
Kirby's Cl 12 CB24 208 D1
Kirby Terr CB25 127 B1
Kirby Wlk PE3 197 C5
Kirkgate PE13 237 F7
Kirkgate St PE13 245 E7
Kirkham's La PE14 236 C4
Kirkmeadow PE3 197 A8
Kirk Ogden Cl PE15 243 D3
Kirk's La PE14 235 E5
Kirkstall PE2 186 B3
Kirkton Gate PE3 197 A1
Kirkwood Cl PE3 197 E2
Kirkwood Rd CB4 83 F7
KIRTLING 72 D6
KIRTLING GREEN 72 C4
Kirtling Pl 5 CB9 24 B8
Kirtling Rd
Kirtling CB8 72 D7
Woodditton CB8 90 E1
KIRTLING TOWERS 72 D7
Kisby Ave PE29 142 A1
Kite Cl PE29 142 A7
Kitson Gdns CB6 210 F5
Knapp Rise CB23 47 A5
Knapp The CB23 47 A5
KNAPWELL 100 E2
Knaresborough Ct 10
PE19 74 F1
Knarr Fen Rd PE6 202 D8
Knaves Acre Dro CB7 212 E5
KNEESWORTH 13 A6
Kneesworth House (Hospital)
SG8 13 C5
Kneesworth Rd SG8 13 F8
Kneesworth St SG8 5 C7
Knight Mews PE2 187 A6
Knighton Cl PE7 186 D1
Knights Cl
Eaton Socon PE19 74 B4
13 Leverington PE13 238 B2
Knight's Cl 11 PE15 223 A5
Knights Ct CB9 23 E7
KNIGHTS END 228 A1
Knight's End Rd PE15 243 C1
Knights Way CB24 105 D3
Knipe Cl PE29 141 B7
Knole Wlk PE3 197 B3
Knowle Ct CB6 242 B5
Knowles Ave PE28 164 E5
Knowles Cl PE28 140 E2
Knox End CB10 21 A2
Knutsford Rd SG8 12 E4
Kooreman Ave PE13 245 D7
Kyle Cres PE28 140 D2
Kym Rd PE19 74 C4

L

Laburnhum Gr PE1 198 B8
Laburnum Ave
Mildenhall IP28 239 E5
Yaxley PE7 181 F6
Laburnum Cl
Cambridge CB4 83 F4
Red Lodge IP28 213 F1
5 Wisbech PE13 245 E7
Laburnum Gr PE15 243 C6
Laburnum La CB25 130 A3
Laburnum Way PE27 144 A5
Lacey's La CB8 110 B7
Lacey's Way CB22 32 D1
Lacks Cl CB24 125 D3
Laddus Bank PE14 236 C1
Laddus Dro PE14 229 B8
LADDUS FENS 236 B1
Ladies Hill SG19 58 D4
Ladybower Way PE4 204 E3
Lady Charlotte Rd PE7 186 C3
Ladygate 1 CB9 23 E6
Lady Jermy Way CB1 85 B1
Lady Lodge Dr PE2 186 A5
Lady Margaret Rd 1 CB3 83 C3
Lady Romayne Cl PE9 244 C4
Lady's Dro PE14 236 D6
Lady Smith Ave PE7 189 F8
Lady's Wood Nature
Reserve★ PE26 170 E2
Ladywalk CB24 123 F3
Lady Way PE19 74 B4
Laith Rd CB23 79 B2
Lake Ave PE14 229 F3
Lake Ct PE13 245 D4
Lake Dro PE7 190 E6
Lakefield Ave PE19 96 A2
Lakes Dro CB6 209 F3
LAKES END 229 F3
Lakeside
Hamrton Hargate PE7 186 C2
Lakeside *continued*
Peterborough PE4 204 D4
Lakeside Cl
Little Paxton PE19 96 A2
Perry PE28 115 D3
Lakeview Ct PE29 141 B7
Lakeview Way PE7 186 D2
Lakeway 8 PE28 215 C1
Lake Way PE29 141 C5
Lamb Dro CB23 79 C3
Lambert Mews PE9 244 C4
Lambes Ct PE4 204 A4
Lambeth Wlk PE9 244 A6
Lamb Fair Ct CB21 35 D2
Lamble Cl IP28 213 F8
Lambourn Cl 1 CB2 64 D3
Lambourne Rd CB23 81 A3
Lambs' Cross CB24 103 F8
Lambs Hill Dro PE15 228 B1
Lamb's La
Cottenham CB24 125 D3
Glatton PE28 175 D2
Lamb's Pl PE15 243 D4
Lammas Field 4 CB3 64 C7
Lammas Gdns PE29 141 D5
Lammas Rd PE1 198 A7
Lammas Way
St Ives PE27 143 F4
St Neots PE19 74 E6
Lamport Dr PE29 141 F8
Lancaster Cl
Old Hurst PE28 154 D6
Warboys PE28 164 F4
Lancaster Ct PE7 181 F6
Lancaster Dr PE27 144 A6
Lancaster Rd
Mildenhall IP28 213 E8
Ramsey PE26 171 E3
10 Stamford PE9 244 B6
Lancaster Way
Ely CB6 217 F1
Godmanchester PE29 141 F2
Huntingdon PE29 141 B8
Wyton PE28 154 A1
Yaxley PE7 181 F6
Lancaster Way Bsns Pk
CB6 217 F1
Lancelot Way PE28 121 C5
Lancing Cl PE4 204 C3
Landau Way PE15 243 E6
LANDBEACH 105 D7
Landbeach Rd CB24 105 D3
Landcliffe Cl PE27 144 B5
Lander Cl CB24 105 C3
Landseer Ct CB9 23 F6
LANDWADE 132 C4
Landwade Rd
Exning CB8 131 B4
Fordham CB8 131 D5
Lane End CB9 38 B1
Lanes The
Great Wilbraham CB21 67 F8
Over CB24 208 D1
St Ives PE28 143 A5
Lane The
Easton PE28 138 B4
Hauxton CB22 48 B4
Old Hurst PE28 154 E6
St Neots PE19 75 A5
Stow Longa PE28 137 B2
West Deeping PE6 231 B7
Langdale Cl CB1 66 A7
Langdyke PE1 198 F6
Langford Rd PE2 187 A7
Langham Rd CB1 65 C6
Langham Way
Ely CB7 240 E7
Haverhill CB9 38 B1
Langley PE3 197 B8
Langley Cl PE27 144 A4
Langley Ct PE27 144 A4
Langley Lawn CB11 1 D2
Langley Way PE28 143 B1
Langton Rd PE1 198 D7
Langwood Cl 7 PE19 74 C6
Langwood Fen Dro PE16 216 D8
Langwood Hill Dro PE16 216 B7
Lankester Rd SG8 5 C5
Lannesbury Cres PE19 75 C7
Lansbury Cl 4 PE19 74 E4
Lansdowne Cl CB6 240 B3
Lansdowne Rd
Cambridge CB3 82 F3
Yaxley PE7 181 F6
Lansdowne Way PE2 186 D7
Lansdowne Wlk PE2 186 D7
Lanthorn Stile CB21 67 A5
Lantree Cres CB2 64 D1
Lanwades Pk CB8 133 F1
Lapwing Ct IP28 239 D4
Lapwing Dr PE7 190 A8
Lapwings Cl CB1 85 B1
Lapwing Way 11 CB7 212 A5
Larch Cl PE7 181 F6
Larches The 2 PE15 223 A5
Larch Gr PE1 198 C6
Larham Way PE16 241 B5
Lark Cl IP28 213 F4
Lark Cres PE29 142 A6
Lark End PE19 117 B3
Larkfield Rd CB7 240 E6
Lark Grange CB7 219 D4
LARK HALL CORNER 69 B1
Larkhall Rd CB7 212 D1
Lark Hill CB8 112 E5

Larkin Cl CB4 . . . . 84 A6
Larkin Pl SG8 . . . . 13 D1
Larkins Rd SG8 . . . . 26 F6
Larklands PE3 . . . . 197 B1
Lark Rd IP28 . . . . 239 D4
Lark Rise CB23 . . . . 80 F3
Larks Cl CB9 . . . . 24 C7
Larkspur Cl 4 IP28 . . . . . 213 F1
Larkspur Wlk PE4 . . . . . 204 D3
Lark Way PE28 . . . . 150 E4
Larmor Dr CB3 . . . . 83 B3
Laroc Cl PE29 . . . . 141 F1
Latham Ave PE2 . . . . 186 C6
Latham Cl CB2 . . . . 64 D6
Latham Rd
    Cambridge CB2 . . . . . . 64 D6
    Huntingdon PE29 . . . . 141 C8
Latimer Cl CB5 . . . . 84 E3
Latin Cl PE19 . . . . 118 A2
LATTERSEA FIELD 190 B6
Lattersey Cl PE7 . . . . 189 F7
Lattersey Nature Reserve★
    PE7 . . . . 190 A5
Lattimers Paddock PE9 . 230 C4
Laughton's La PE28 . . . . 143 A5
Laundress La CB3 . . . . . . 246 A2
Laundry La CB1 . . . . 65 D5
Laureate CP Sch CB8 . . . 110 E6
Laureate Gdns CB8 . . . . . 110 E6
Laureate Paddocks CB8 . 110 E6
Laureate Sch Rd CB8 . . . 110 E6
Laurel Cl
    Haverhill CB9 . . . . 38 D2
    Mepal CB6 . . . . 216 E3
    9 Red Lodge IP28 . . . 214 A1
    Sawtry PE28 . . . . 168 A3
    Yaxley PE7 . . . . 181 D4
Laurel Dr
    Elm PE14 . . . . 236 A5
    Thorney PE6 . . . . 232 F3
Laurels Cl PE19 . . . . 74 F4
Laurels The PE15 . . . . . . 243 E7
Lauriston Pl 1 CB4 . . . . . 83 E8
Lavender Cl
    3 Red Lodge IP28 . . . 213 F1
    Yaxley PE7 . . . . 181 F6
Lavender Cres PE1 . . . . . 198 B8
Lavender Ct 4 PE29 . . . . 141 F7
Lavender Field CB9 . . . . . 23 D8
Lavender Rd CB4 . . . . 84 A7
Lavender Way PE27 . . . . 144 A6
Lavenham Ct PE2 . . . . . . 186 C7
Lavington Grange PE1 . . 198 E6
Law Cl CB6 . . . . 242 D3
Lawn Ave PE1 . . . . 198 A7
Lawn La
    Little Downham CB6 . . 218 A7
    Sutton CB6 . . . . 216 E1
Lawns Cres CB6 . . . . 218 A7
Lawns Ct SG8 . . . . 5 D6
Lawns The
    Cambridge CB3 . . . . . . 83 A2
    Everton SG19 . . . . 40 C3
    Melbourn SG8 . . . . 14 C5
    Walton PE4 . . . . 204 E1
    Wisbech PE13 . . . . . . 245 B6
Lawn The CB2 . . . . 32 C5
Lawrence Lea CB22 . . . . . 47 F2
Lawrence Ave PE7 . . . . . 187 C2
Lawrence Cl CB3 . . . . 82 D8
Lawrence Rd
    Eaton Socon PE19 . . . . 74 C5
    Ramsey PE26 . . . . . . 172 C7
    Wittering PE8 . . . . . . 230 B1
Lawrence Way CB4 . . . . . 83 F7
Law's Cl PE6 . . . . 206 F1
Laws Cres PE28 . . . . 140 C4
Law's Lawn PE8 . . . . 192 C2
Lawson Ave PE2 . . . . 187 D6
Lawson Cl CB24 . . . . 104 B4
Laxton Ave CB23 . . . . 81 A3
Laxton Cl PE19 . . . . 74 C4
Laxton Grange PE28 . . . . 208 C5
Laxton Way CB4 . . . . 84 C6
Layer Rd CB9 . . . . 23 E7
Layston Pk SG8 . . . . 5 D5
Layton Cres PE28 . . . . . . 140 D2
Lea Brooks Cl PE28 . . . . 164 F4
Leach Cl PE13 . . . . 245 C2
Leaden Hill SG8 . . . . 28 D8
Leaden's La PE19 . . . . . . 117 C3
Leader's Way CB8 . . . . . 110 E4
Leading Dro PE7 . . . . 181 E4
Leaf Ave PE7 . . . . 186 D3
Leafere Way 1 PE13 . . . 238 B2
Leaford Dr CB6 . . . . 218 B6
Lea Gdns PE3 . . . . 197 F1
Leam The PE14 . . . . 236 A4
Lea Rd PE28 . . . . 143 C1
Leas Cl PE27 . . . . 144 A4
Leather La CB8 . . . . 23 E7
Lebanon Dr PE13 . . . . . . 245 F7
Ledbury Rd PE3 . . . . 197 C3
Ledham PE2 . . . . 185 D4
Ledo Rd CB22 . . . . 31 F2
Leechcroft PE28 . . . . 121 C6
Lee Cl
    Cottenham CB24 . . . . 125 D3
    Hanchet End CB9 . . . . 38 F2
Lee Rd PE7 . . . . 181 E4
Lees La PE19 . . . . 95 E5
Lees Way CB3 . . . . 103 E1
Leete Pl SG8 . . . . 5 C7
Leete Rd CB1 . . . . 65 F5

Leete's La CB23 . . . . 46 A8
Leeway Ave CB22 . . . . . . 49 B5
Legge-Bourke Ct PE13 . . 245 F6
Leger Cl PE27 . . . . 144 A6
Legg Rd 21 PE8 . . . . 230 B1
Legion Cl CB4 . . . . 83 E7
Legion Way PE29 . . . . . . 142 B1
Leicester Cl CB6 . . . . 240 A3
Leicester Terr 3 PE1 . . . 198 B3
Leighton PE2 . . . . 186 C4
LEIGHTON
    BROMSWOLD 148 D3
Leighton Prim Sch PE2 . 186 C4
Leinsters Ct PE3 . . . . 197 D3
Leiston Cl PE6 . . . . 232 A1
Leiston Rd CB9 . . . . 23 E7
Lemur Dr CB1 . . . . 66 B7
Lensfield Rd CB2 . . . . . . 246 B1
Lenton Cl PE28 . . . . 140 D2
Lents Way CB4 . . . . 84 C5
Leofric Sq PE1 . . . . 198 E3
Leonard Cl 2 CB5 . . . . . . 84 E4
Leopold Wlk CB24 . . . . . 125 E3
Lerowe Rd PE13 . . . . 245 E7
Les Baux Pl 5 PE13 . . . . 245 E3
Leslie Green Rd PE28 . . . 143 B5
Lessingham PE2 . . . . 185 D4
Lester Dr CB6 . . . . 210 A6
Lester Piggott Way CB8 . 110 F6
Lethbridge Rd PE4 . . . . . 204 E2
Levellers La PE19 . . . . . . 74 F3
Leveret Way PE19 . . . . . 75 C5
LEVERINGTON 238 B2
Leverington Comm PE13 235 B8
Leverington Prim Sch
    PE13 . . . . 238 B2
Leverington Rd PE13 . . . 245 A6
Leverington Road Ind Est
    PE13 . . . . 245 B7
Levers Wr PE29 . . . . 141 C5
Levitt's Dro PE6 . . . . 200 C4
Lewes Gdns PE4 . . . . . . 204 C3
Lewis Cl
    Great & Little Abington
        CB21 . . . . 34 C5
    March PE15 . . . . 243 B3
Lewis Cres CB21 . . . . 34 C5
Lexington Cl 3 CB4 . . . . 83 C5
Leyburn Cl CB4 . . . . 66 A7
Ley Rd CB8 . . . . 90 A1
Leys Ave CB4 . . . . 83 F5
Leys Rd
    Cambridge CB4 . . . . . . 83 F5
    St Neots PE19 . . . . . . 74 E4
Leys Sch The CB2 . . . . . 246 B1
Leys The
    Alconbury PE28 . . . . . 150 F4
    Little Gransden SG19 . 58 B3
    Peterborough PE3 . . . 197 A1
    Sawtry PE28 . . . . 168 C3
Leys Wlk CB22 . . . . 48 C4
Leyton Ave IP28 . . . . . . 239 B6
Liberator Rd PE26 . . . . . 171 C3
Lichfield Ave PE4 . . . . . . 204 B3
Lichfield Cl CB1 . . . . 65 B6
Licking's Dro PE13 . . . . . 245 A2
LIDGATE 73 E8
Lidgate Cl PE2 . . . . 186 C7
Lidgate Rd CB8 . . . . 92 E7
Lifelong Learning Office
    CB1 . . . . 65 C7
Lilac Cl
    Haslingfield CB23 . . . . 47 B5
    Wisbech PE13 . . . . . . 245 F7
Lilac Ct CB1 . . . . 65 C5
Lilac End CB23 . . . . 47 B4
Lilac Rd PE1 . . . . 198 C7
Lilac Way PE27 . . . . 144 B6
Lilley Cl CB4 . . . . 84 B5
Lilyholt Rd PE15 . . . . . . 222 A5
Lime Ave PE13 . . . . 245 C7
Lime Cl
    Burwell CB25 . . . . . . 130 C1
    Mildenhall IP28 . . . . . 239 E5
Lime Gr
    March PE15 . . . . 243 C6
    Royston SG8 . . . . 5 E8
    St Neots PE19 . . . . . . 74 F6
Limekiln Cl SG8 . . . . 5 E5
Lime Kiln Cl PE3 . . . . . . 197 E4
Limekiln Rd CB1 . . . . 65 E3
Lime Rd PE26 . . . . 172 A8
Limes Ave 1 PE14 . . . . 236 A5
Limes Cl
    Bassingbourn SG8 . . . 12 E5
    Littleport CB6 . . . . . . 242 C4
Limes Ct PE27 . . . . 143 F1
Limes Park Rd PE27 . . . 143 F1
Limes Rd CB23 . . . . 81 A3
LIMES THE 229 C3
Limes The
    Bassingbourn SG8 . . . 12 E5
    Castor PE5 . . . . 195 F1
    Harston CB22 . . . . . . 47 F2
    Sawston CB22 . . . . . . 32 F8
    5 Wittering PE8 . . . 230 B1
Limestone Cl 7 CB7 . . . 213 A5
Lime Tree Ave PE1 . . . . 197 F4
Limetree Cl
    3 Cambridge CB1 . . . 65 D5
    Yaxley PE7 . . . . 181 F7
Limlow SG8 . . . . 4 B8
Linclare Pl 7 PE19 . . . . . 74 C4
Lincoln Ave PE27 . . . . . 143 F7
Lincoln Cl PE19 . . . . 117 A5
Lincoln Rd
    Deeping Gate PE6 . . . 231 E7

Lincoln Rd continued
    Mildenhall IP28 . . . . . 213 E8
    Peterborough PE4 . . . 197 C8
    Ramsey PE26 . . . . . . 171 E3
    Stamford PE9 . . . . . . 244 D7
    Wyton Airfield PE28 . . 143 A8
Linden Cl
    Barnack PE9 . . . . 230 D4
    Cambridge CB4 . . . . . 83 C4
    Haddenham CB6 . . . . 210 A5
Linden Dr PE16 . . . . 241 C4
Linden End CB6 . . . . 210 A5
Linden Gdns PE2 . . . . . . 185 C5
Linden Gr PE29 . . . . 141 F2
Lindens Cl PE13 . . . . 234 A2
Linden Way CB6 . . . . . . 210 A5
Lindeth Cl PE29 . . . . 141 A7
Lindisfarne Cl 9 PE19 . . 74 F1
Lindisfarne Rd PE6 . . . . 232 A1
Lindridge Wlk PE3 . . . . 197 A2
Lindsay Cl
    Royston SG8 . . . . 13 C1
    Wyton PE28 . . . . 143 A4
Lindsells Wlk PE16 . . . . 241 C5
Lindsey Cl PE4 . . . . 204 D1
Lindsey Rd
    Stamford PE9 . . . . . . 244 C6
    5 Uffington PE9 . . . . 230 D6
Lingfield Rd 1 SG8 . . . . . 5 E6
Ling Garth PE1 . . . . 198 B8
Lingholme Cl 2 CB4 . . . . 83 C5
Lingmoor PE29 . . . . 141 A6
Lingrey Ct CB2 . . . . 64 D2
Lingwood Pk PE3 . . . . . 197 A1
Link Dr PE28 . . . . 140 C3
Link La CB6 . . . . 216 E1
Link Rd
    Peterborough PE1 . . . 197 F3
    Sawston CB22 . . . . . . 32 F8
Links Cl IP28 . . . . 213 F4
Linkside PE3 . . . . 204 B1
Links The CB8 . . . . 89 D8
Links Way PE27 . . . . . . 143 F4
Linley Rd
    St Neots PE19 . . . . . . 74 E3
    Whittlesey PE7 . . . . . 189 E6
Linlithgow Cl CB23 . . . . . 99 A3
Linnet PE2 . . . . 185 D6
LINTON 35 E3
Linton CE Inf Sch CB21 . 35 C2
Linton Cl CB8 . . . . 110 F5
Linton Hts Jun Sch CB21 . 35 D2
Linton Pl CB9 . . . . 24 B3
Linton Rd
    Balsham CB21 . . . . . . 52 F2
    Great Abington CB21 . 34 D6
    Hadstock CB21 . . . . . 20 B8
    Horseheath CB21 . . . . 36 F3
Linton Village Coll CB21 . 35 B2
Linton Zoological Gdns★
    CB21 . . . . 35 B1
Linwood La PE15 . . . . . . 223 A8
Lion Cl PE26 . . . . 220 D3
Lionel Walden Prim Sch
    PE15 . . . . 223 A5
Lion Farm Ct PE19 . . . . . 57 C6
Lions Cross PE29 . . . . . . 119 A8
Lions Ct CB6 . . . . 210 A6
Lion Wlk PE26 . . . . 172 A5
Lion Yard Sh Ctr CB1 . . 246 B2
Lion Yd
    Cambridge CB1 . . . . . 246 B2
    Ramsey PE26 . . . . . . 172 B6
LIPNEAS THE 202 B1
Lisburn Rd CB8 . . . . 111 B3
Lisle Cl CB7 . . . . 240 E5
Lisle La CB7 . . . . 240 E4
Lisle Wlk CB1 . . . . 66 A6
Lister Rd PE1 . . . . 197 F1
Lister's Rd PE14 . . . . . . 236 E1
Litchfield Cl PE7 . . . . . . 181 F5
LITLINGTON 12 B2
Litlington Rd SG8 . . . . . . 11 E1
LITTLE ABINGTON 34 B7
Little Back La CB25 . . . . 129 D1
Little Bowsers CB10 . . . . 20 D3
LITTLEBURY GREEN 9 F2
Little Casterton Rd PE9 . 244 A4
LITTLE CATWORTH . . . 137 A6
Littlechild Dr 6 PE13 . . 238 B2
Little Chilfords CB21 . . . 35 B4
LITTLE CHISHILL 1 C7
Little Chishill Rd SG8 . . . . 1 C6
Little Church St 21 PE13 . 245 C5
Little Cl PE28 . . . . 232 A1
Littlecotes Cl PE28 . . . . 137 F7
LITTLE DITTON 90 F2
Little Ditton CB8 . . . . 90 F2
Little Dowgate PE13 . . . 245 A4
LITTLE DOWNHAM 218 B6
LITTLE END 74 C1
Little End Rd PE19 . . . . . 74 B1
Little End Road Ind Est
    PE19 . . . . 74 B2
LITTLE EVERSDEN 46 A7
Little Farthing Cl PE27 . 144 A4
Little Fen Dro
    Burwell CB25 . . . . . . 129 E6
    Swaffham Prior CB25 . 129 A1
Little Fendyke La PE14 . 236 E5
Littlefield Cl
    Godmanchester PE29 . 118 F8
    Wilburton CB6 . . . . . 210 C6
LITTLE GIDDING 158 F8
Little Gn
    Cheveley CB8 . . . . 91 C5
    Guilden Morden SG8 . . 11 A7
    Warmington PE8 . . . . 178 B3

LITTLE GRANSDEN 58 D3
Little Gransden La SG19 . 58 D4
LITTLE GREEN 178 C3
LITTLE HASSE DRO CB7 . 212 C6
LITTLE HEATH 41 C4
Little Heath SG19 . . . . . . 41 C4
Little How PE27 . . . . 143 C6
Little Johns Cl PE3 . . . . 196 F3
Little La
    Ely CB6 . . . . 240 B4
    Great Gransden SG19 . 58 E4
    Melbourn SG8 . . . . . . 14 C6
LITTLE LINTON 35 B3
LITTLE LONDON 243 C4
Little London CB7 . . . . . 212 F5
Little London CB7 . . . . . 212 F5
Little London La CB7 . . . 212 F5
Little Marefen Dro CB6 . 242 A7
Little Mdw CB23 . . . . . . 102 B2
Littlemeer PE2 . . . . 185 F4
Little Moor PE28 . . . . . . 121 C5
Little Northfields 3 PE9 230 D4
LITTLE OUSE 226 D4
Little Paddocks CB10 . . . 19 A4
LITTLE PAXTON 95 E2
Little Paxton La PE19 . . . 95 F2
Little Paxton Prim Sch
    PE19 . . . . 95 F1
LITTLEPORT 242 C4
Littleport Com Prim Sch
    CB6 . . . . 242 B4
Littleport Sta CB6 . . . . . 242 E6
Little Ramper PE13 . . . . 238 B4
LITTLE RAVELEY 163 B4
Little St Mary's La 2 . . . 246 A1
Little Setchel Dro CB24 . 209 F2
LITTLE SHELFORD 48 E3
Little St CB6 . . . . 218 B6
LITTLE STAUGHTON 93 B2
LITTLE STUKELEY 151 C4
LITTLE THETFORD 211 B7
Little Thetford CE Prim Sch
    CB6 . . . . 211 B7
Little Whyte PE26 . . . . . 172 B7
LITTLE WILBRAHAM 86 E1
Little Wilbraham Rd CB1 . 86 D4
Littleworth Dro PE13 . . 233 F8
Littleworth End PE19 . . 118 A1
LITTLE WRATTING 39 D3
Livermore Gn PE4 . . . . . 204 A6
Loch Fyne Cl PE2 . . . . . 185 C4
Loch Lomond Way PE2 . 185 C4
Locks Cl PE6 . . . . 206 B7
Locksgate 1 PE28 . . . . . 215 C1
Locks Gn PE8 . . . . 183 A8
Lockspit Hall Dro
    Cottenham CB24 . . . . 125 F8
    Ottenham CB24 . . . . . 209 F1
LODE 107 C2
Lode Ave
    Outwell PE14 . . . . . . 236 F1
    Waterbeach CB25 . . . 106 B7
Lode Cl CB7 . . . . 212 B3
Lode La CB7 . . . . 211 L1
Loder Ave PE3 . . . . 196 F2
Lode Rd
    Bottisham CB25 . . . . . 86 D7
    Lode CB25 . . . . 107 D1
Lodes End Dro PE26 . . . 220 F2
Lode Way
    Chatteris PE16 . . . . . 241 C6
    Haddenham CB6 . . . . 210 A5
Lodge Cl PE29 . . . . 141 C4
Lodge Gdns CB6 . . . . . . 210 A6
Lodge Rd SG8 . . . . 31 A1
Loftsteads 3 PE28 . . . . 215 C1
Logan's Way CB4 . . . . . . 84 A3
Loire Ct PE1 . . . . 197 E4
LOLWORTH 101 F5
Lomax Dr CB2 . . . . 140 C3
Lombardy Dr PE1 . . . . . 198 B8
London La PE19 . . . . 96 E4
London Rd
    Barley SG8 . . . . 6 F1
    Chatteris PE16 . . . . . 241 C2
    Fenstanton PE28 . . . . 120 E7
    Fowlmere SG8 . . . . . . 15 D5
    Godmanchester PE29 . 141 F1
    Great Chesterford CB10 . 18 C2
    Great Shelford CB22 . . 49 B4
    Harston CB22 . . . . . . 48 B3
    Hemingford Grey PE27 . 143 F1
    Kimbolton PE28 . . . . 114 A4
    Peterborough PE7 . . . 186 F3
    Royston SG8 . . . . 5 D4
    Sawston CB22 . . . . . . 32 F5
    Stamford PE9 . . . . . . 244 C2
    Wansford PE8 . . . . . . 194 B2
    Yaxley PE7 . . . . 181 C5
London St
    Godmanchester PE29 . 141 F1
    Whittlesey PE7 . . . . . 189 D6
Lone Tree Ave CB24 . . . . 83 C8
Lone Tree Gr CB24 . . . . . 83 C8
Longchamp Dr CB7 . . . . 240 F6
Long Cswy
    Peterborough PE1 . . . 198 A2
    Witcham CB6 . . . . . . 217 C2
Long Dolver Dro CB7 . . . 212 B6
Long Dro
    Bury PE26 . . . . 172 F5
    Cottenham CB24 . . . . 125 F3
    Downham CB6 . . . . . . 224 F3
    Elm PE14 . . . . 235 B1
    Feltwell PE38 . . . . . . 226 F4
    Haddenham CB6 . . . . 209 C5
    Holme PE7 . . . . 177 D5
    Over CB24 . . . . 208 D3

Long Dro continued
    Parson Drove PE13 . . . 234 B5
    Ramsey PE26 . . . . . . 221 D2
    Somersham PE28 . . . . 215 D2
    Waterbeach CB25 . . . 106 D8
    Whittlesey PE7 . . . . . 200 F3
Longfellow Pl 5 PE19 . . . 74 D5
Longfield Gate PE2 . . . . 186 A6
Longfield Rd CB6 . . . . . . 242 B5
Longfields CB6 . . . . 240 A3
Long Furlong CB24 . . . . 208 D1
Longhead La PE14 . . . . . 238 D1
Longhill Rd PE15 . . . . . . 228 B6
Long Holme Dro CB24 . . 208 E3
Longholme Rd PE26 . . . 171 A4
Long La
    Coveney CB6 . . . . 217 C4
    Fowlmere SG8 . . . . . . 15 D8
    Gamlingay SG19 . . . . 41 F6
    Hemingford Grey PE28 . 120 C8
    Linton CB21 . . . . 35 C1
    Over CB24 . . . . 208 E2
    Spaldwick PE28 . . . . 137 F5
    Willingham CB24 . . . . 124 A8
Long Lots PE14 . . . . 236 F8
LONG MEADOW 107 F2
Long Meadow Field
    PE13 . . . . 237 F2
Long Meadow Rd CB25 . 107 F2
Longmere La CB7 . . . . . 212 A5
Long Nightlayer's Dro
    PE16 . . . . 241 E6
Long North Fen Dro CB6 216 A4
Long Pasture PE4 . . . . . 204 B5
Long Rd
    Cambridge CB2 . . . . . 64 F4
    Comberton CB23 . . . . 81 D2
Long Reach Rd CB7 . . . . 211 F6
Long Road Sixth Form Coll
    CB2 . . . . 64 F3
Longsands Coll PE19 . . . 75 A6
Longsands Par 3 PE19 . . 75 A6
Longsands Rd PE19 . . . . 75 A5
Longstaff Way PE29 . . . 142 A6
LONGSTANTON 124 E2
Longstanton Rd
    Oakington/Longstanton
        CB24 . . . . 103 B6
    Over CB24 . . . . 123 B7
LONGSTOWE 59 F3
LONGTHORPE 197 A1
Longthorpe Cl PE3 . . . . 197 A2
Longthorpe Gn PE3 . . . . 197 B1
Longthorpe House Mews
    PE3 . . . . 196 F2
Longthorpe Parkway
    PE3 . . . . 186 A8
Longthorpe Prim Sch
    PE3 . . . . 197 A2
Longueville Ct PE2 . . . . 186 B5
Longview PE3 . . . . 216 D1
Longwater PE2 . . . . 186 B6
Longwood CB23 . . . . 81 B8
Longworth Ave CB4 . . . . 84 A3
Lonsdale CB21 . . . . 35 E2
Lonsdale Terr PE13 . . . . 245 C2
Loop Rd PE28 . . . . 146 A4
Lophams Cl CB9 . . . . 38 F2
Lord's Croft La CB9 . . . . 24 A7
Lordship Cl
    Orwell SG8 . . . . 45 E1
    Willingham CB24 . . . . 209 A1
Lordship Dr SG8 . . . . . . 14 C7
Lordship End PE12 . . . . 233 E8
Lords La PE13 . . . . 235 D7
Lord's La PE13 . . . . 235 D6
Loris Ct CB1 . . . . 66 A7
Lorna Ct PE27 . . . . 143 F6
Lornas Field PE7 . . . . . . 186 D2
Losecoat Cl PE9 . . . . . . 244 D7
Lotfield St SG8 . . . . 45 E1
Lottings Way PE7 . . . . . . 74 C6
Loughborough Univ of
    Peterborough PE1 . . . 198 A3
Loughrigg Cl PE29 . . . . 141 B7
Loughton Ct CB5 . . . . . . 84 E4
Louthe Way PE28 . . . . . 168 C3
Loveday Cl SG8 . . . . 8 D3
Love La
    Ashwell SG7 . . . . 2 A5
    Houghton & Wyton PE28 . 143 A5
    Whittlesey PE7 . . . . . 189 D6
    Wisbech PE13 . . . . . . 245 C4
Lovell Rd CB4 . . . . 84 A7
Lovells The PE14 . . . . . . 236 D6
Lovers La PE5 . . . . 194 F2
Love's Cl CB24 . . . . 104 C2
Love's Hill PE5 . . . . 195 F1
Love's La 13 CB24 . . . . . 209 A1
Lowbury Cres CB24 . . . . 103 B6
Lowburyholme Rd CB24 . 208 C4
Low Cross PE7 . . . . 189 D8
LOWER CAMBOURNE . . . 78 F4
Lower Downs Slade CB9 . 24 A6
Lower Dro CB7 . . . . 211 D3
Lower End CB25 . . . . . . 108 E5
Lowerfield SG8 . . . . 6 D5
Lower Gn CB11 . . . . 1 F1
Lower Gower Rd SG8 . . . . 5 D8
Lower King St SG8 . . . . . 5 D6
Lower Park St CB5 . . . . 246 A1
Lower Rd
    Croydon SG8 . . . . 26 D5
    Ely CB7 . . . . 218 D3
    Wicken CB7 . . . . 211 E2
Lower St SG8 . . . . 31 B3

Lower Wood Nature
Reserve★ CB8 . . . . .54 C6
Lower Yd CB8 . . . . .132 A2
Loweswater PE29 . . . . .141 C5
Low Fen Dro Way CB5. . . .85 B4
Lowfields CB23 . . . . .46 B8
Low Gate PE13. . . . . .237 F8
Low Harthay PE28. . . . . . .139 D3
Lowick Gdns PE3 . . . . . . .197 C5
Lowndes Dro PE27 . . . . . .144 F7
Low Park Cnr CB7. . . . . . .133 A6
Low Rd
  Burwell CB25. . . . . .130 B2
  Crowland PE6 . . . . .207 F7
  Fenstanton PE28 . . . . . . .121 A7
  Hemingford Grey PE27 . . .144 A1
  Little Stukeley PE28. . . . .151 D3
  Queen Adelaide CB7 . . . .218 F4
  The Stukeleys PE28 . . . . .140 C7
  Wisbech PE14 . . . . .245 E1
Lowry Cl
  Haverhill CB9. . . . . .38 D1
  St Ives PE27 . . . . .144 A7
Lowry Rd PE19. . . . . .74 C6
Low Side PE14. . . . . .236 E2
Lowther Gdns PE4 . . . . . .204 D2
Lowther St CB8 . . . . .110 F3
Loxley CI PE4 . . . . .204 A4
Loxley Rd PE28 . . . . .142 F5
Luard Cl CB2 . . . . .65 A5
Luard Rd CB2 . . . . .65 A5
Lucas Ct PE29 . . . . .141 F7
Lucas La SG7 . . . . .2 E4
Lucerne Cl
  Cambridge CB1 . . . . .66 A6
  Red Lodge IP28 . . . . . . .213 F1
Lucketts Cl CB24 . . . . . . .104 B5
Luck's La PE19. . . . . .117 A4
Lucombe Dr PE13 . . . . . .245 F7
Lucy Cavendish Coll CB3 . .83 C3
Luddington Cl PE19 . . . . . .96 E4
LUDDINGTON IN THE
  BROOK 166 B4
Luddington Rd
  Great Gidding PE28 . . . . .166 C3
  Peterborough PE4 . . . . . .204 D1
Ludlow La CB21. . . . . .67 A5
Lug Fen Droveway CB25. .107 A5
Luke St PE19 . . . . .74 E4
Lulworth Dr CB9 . . . . .23 E8
Lumen Rd SG8. . . . . .5 D7
Lumley Cl CB6 . . . . .240 E8
Lundy Cl CB9 . . . . .24 D7
LUTTON 174 C4
Lutton Gate Rd PE12 . . . .234 A8
Lutton Gr PE3 . . . . .197 C6
Lye Cl PE14 . . . . .94 A6
Lyles Rd CB24 . . . . .125 D4
Lymage Rd PE28 . . . . . . .115 D3
Lyme Wlk PE3 . . . . .197 C6
Lynch La SG8 . . . . .15 E8
Lynchwood PE2. . . . . . . .185 C5
Lyndale Pk PE2 . . . . .185 C6
Lyndewode Rd CB1 . . . . .246 C1
Lyndhurst Cl CB24 . . . . . .105 C2
Lynfield La CB4 . . . . .84 A4
Lynn Rd
  Ely CB6 . . . . .240 D6
  Littleport CB6 . . . . .242 F6
  Wisbech PE13 . . . . .245 D6
Lynton Cl CB6 . . . . .240 D6
Lynton Dr CB6 . . . . .240 D6
Lynton Rd PE1 . . . . .197 F6
Lynton Way CB22 . . . . . . .33 D8
Lynx The CB1 . . . . .66 A7
Lyons Ct PE16 . . . . .241 C4
Lyon's Dro PE15 . . . . . . .223 F4
Lysander Cl PE27 . . . . . . .143 F7
Lythemere PE2 . . . . .186 C4
Lyvelly Gdns PE1. . . . . . .198 E6

M

Maarnford Cl CB22. . . . . . .17 D8
MacAulay Ave CB22 . . . . . .49 B6
Macbeth Cl PE29. . . . . . . .141 F6
McCalmont Way CB8. . . . .111 E2
Mace Rd PE2 . . . . .187 D5
Macfarlane Cl CB24 . . . . .104 C2
Mackenzie Rd ⑤ CB1 . . . .84 A1
MacKerel Hall SG8. . . . . . . .5 B6
Macpherson Robertson Way
  IP28. . . . . .239 A5
Maddingley Way CB6. . . . .210 A7
Madecroft PE28. . . . . .165 A5
Madeley Ct PE28 . . . . . . .143 C2
MADINGLEY 81 E5
Madingley Rd
  Cambridge CB3 . . . . .83 B3
  Dry Drayton CB3 . . . . . .102 B1
Madingley Sch CB23 . . . . . .81 F5
Madingley Wood CB23 . . . .82 A4
Madras Rd CB1 . . . . .65 C7
Maffit Rd PE5. . . . . .195 D3
Magazine Cl PE13 . . . . . .245 A4
Magazine La PE13. . . . . . .245 A4
Magdalene Cl CB24 . . . . .123 F2
Magdalene Coll CB4 . . . . .246 A4
Magdalene St CB2 . . . . . .246 A3
Magee Rd PE4 . . . . .204 D1
Magistrates Rd PE7. . . . . .181 D8
Magna Cl CB21 . . . . .34 D7
Magnolia Ave PE3. . . . . . .197 A2
Magnolia Cl
  Cambridge CB1 . . . . .65 B5
  ② Red Lodge IP28 . . . . .213 F1

Magrath Ave CB4 . . . . . . .246 A4
Maiden La PE9. . . . . .244 C5
Maids' Cswy CB5. . . . . . . .246 C3
Mailes Cl CB23. . . . . .63 B4
Main Dro CB6. . . . . .225 A2
Main Rd
  Etton PE6 . . . . .203 B8
  Little Gransden SG19. . . . .58 D3
  Parson Drove PE13 . . . . .234 E7
  Uffington PE9. . . . . .230 D6
  Upwell PE14. . . . . .229 E7
  Wisbech PE14 . . . . .236 A3
Main St
  Ailsworth PE5. . . . . .195 D2
  Barnack PE9 . . . . .230 D3
  Bythorn & Keyston PE28 . .146 D4
  Caldecote CB23 . . . . .61 B6
  Castor PE5. . . . . .195 D3
  Coveney CB6 . . . . .217 B5
  Downham CB6 . . . . .217 D8
  Ely CB7 . . . . .219 B5
  Farcet PE7 . . . . .187 C2
  Great Gidding PE28 . . . . .166 D3
  Hardwick CB23 . . . . .81 A1
  Hatley SG19. . . . . .43 A3
  Huntingdon PE29. . . . . . .142 A6
  Little Downham CB6 . . . . .218 A6
  Littleport CB6 . . . . .242 D4
  Old Weston PE28 . . . . . .147 F7
  Shudy Camps CB21 . . . . . .21 F6
  Southorpe PE9 . . . . .230 E1
  Stow cum Quy CB25 . . . . .85 F5
  Thetford PE28 . . . . .211 B7
  Ufford PE9. . . . . .230 F3
  Upton PE28 . . . . .160 D1
  Welney PE14. . . . . .225 A8
  Wentworth CB6 . . . . . . .217 B1
  Witchford CB6 . . . . .217 E1
  Yarwell PE8 . . . . .183 A6
  Yaxley PE7 . . . . .181 D5
Main Streeet PE28 . . . . . .166 A3
Maio Rd CB4. . . . . .83 F5
Maitland Ave CB4 . . . . . . .84 B6
Major Haddock Cl SG8 . . . . .5 C7
Malborne Way PE2. . . . . .186 B4
Malcolm St CB1. . . . . .246 B3
Malcolm Way CB8 . . . . . .111 B5
Malden CI CB5. . . . . .84 D3
Malden Way PE19. . . . . . . .74 D2
Malecoff PE29 . . . . .118 F7
Males Cl CB24 . . . . .125 E5
Malin Cl CB9. . . . . .24 D7
Mallard Cl
  Chatteris PE16. . . . . . . .241 C5
  Whittlesey PE7 . . . . .189 F8
Mallard Ct PE9. . . . . .244 B4
Mallard La PE19 . . . . .75 A4
Mallard Rd
  Peterborough PE3 . . . . . .204 A1
  Royston SG8 . . . . .5 C6
Mallard Rise CB6 . . . . . . .210 A6
Mallards The
  Peakirk PE6. . . . . .206 B1
  St Ives PE27 . . . . .143 F7
Mallard Way PE15. . . . . . .243 F5
Mallett Cl PE15 . . . . .243 F4
Mallory La ⑪ PE9 . . . . . . .244 B5
Mallory Rd CB1 . . . . .66 A5
Mallow La PE7 . . . . .175 D8
Mallows Cl ② CB23 . . . . . .62 D6
Mallow Wlk
  Haverhill CB9. . . . . .23 C8
  ① Royston SG8. . . . . .5 E5
Malmesbury Dr PE6 . . . . .232 A1
Malory Pl CB23 . . . . .99 A3
Malta Rd CB1 . . . . .65 B7
Maltby CI ⑰ PE8. . . . . . . .230 B1
Malt Cl ⑨ CB8 . . . . .111 B3
Malt Dr PE13 . . . . .245 B3
Malthouse Cl PE29 . . . . . .141 D4
Malthouse La PE26. . . . . .171 F5
Malthouse Way CB22 . . . . .29 F8
Malting End CB8 . . . . .72 D4
Malting La
  Cambridge CB3 . . . . .64 C3
  Ellington PE28 . . . . .139 A4
  Foxton CB22. . . . . .30 C5
  Isleham CB7 . . . . .213 A5
  Litlington SG8 . . . . .12 A2
Maltings Cl
  Moulton CB8 . . . . .112 E5
  Royston SG8 . . . . .5 C7
Maltings La SG8 . . . . .7 E2
Maltings Pl SG19. . . . . . . .41 D5
Maltings The
  Alconbury PE28 . . . . . . .150 E5
  Cambourne CB23. . . . . . .80 B2
  Eaton Socon PE19 . . . . . .74 C5
  Gamlingay SG19 . . . . . . .41 D6
  Sawtry PE28 . . . . .168 B4
  St Martin's Without PE9 . .244 C2
  ③ Thorney PE6 . . . . . . .233 A3
Malting The PE26 . . . . . . .171 F5
Maltmas Dro PE14 . . . . . .235 F2
Malton La SG8 . . . . .29 B4
Malton Rd
  Meldreth SG8. . . . . .29 C3
  Orwell SG8. . . . . .45 F1
Malsters Way CB4. . . . . . . .84 A4
Malus Cl PE7 . . . . .186 C3
Malvern Cl CB8 . . . . .111 B2
Malvern Rd
  Cambridge CB1 . . . . .65 E6
  Peterborough PE4 . . . . . .204 C2
Manasty Rd PE2 . . . . .185 D2
Mancetter Sq PE4. . . . . . .204 B1

Manchester Rd PE28 . . . .117 D8
Manchester Way PE27. . . .144 A8
Mandene Gdns SG19 . . . . .58 E4
Manderston Rd CB8. . . . . .110 E4
Mander Way CB1 . . . . .65 C5
Mandeville
  Burwell CB25. . . . . .109 B8
  Peterborough PE2 . . . . . .185 F4
Mandeville Rd PE28 . . . . .140 C3
Mandrill Cl CB1. . . . . .66 A7
MANEA 224 B4
Manea Prim Sch PE15. . . .224 C4
Manea Rd PE15 . . . . .223 D6
Manea Sta PE15 . . . . .224 B6
Maners Way CB1. . . . . .65 C4
Mangers La CB22 . . . . .32 D1
Manhattan Dr CB4 . . . . . .246 C4
Manners Cl ④ PE29 . . . . .230 C6
Manor at Hemingford Grey
  The★ 143 B2
Manor Ave PE2 . . . . .187 B7
Manor Cl
  Brampton PE28 . . . . .140 E2
  Buckden PE19 . . . . .117 A3
  Farcet PE7 . . . . .187 C2
  Graveley PE19 . . . . .98 A5
  ② Great Staughton PE19 . . .93 F6
  Harston CB22 . . . . .47 F3
  Little Paxton PE19 . . . . . .95 F2
  Little Wilbraham CB1. . . . .86 D1
  Ramsey Forty Foot PE26 . .221 A3
  ⑱ Somersham PE28 . . . .215 C1
  St Ives PE27 . . . . .142 F5
  Witchford CB6 . . . . .217 E1
  ⑪ Wittering PE8 . . . . . . .230 B1
  Yaxley PE7 . . . . .181 D5
Manor Com Coll CB4. . . . . .83 F6
Manor Cres CB23 . . . . .81 A1
Manor Ct CB3. . . . . .64 B8
Manor Ct Rd CB6 . . . . . . .217 E1
Manor Dr
  Fenstanton PE28 . . . . . . .121 B6
  Peterborough PE6 . . . . . .205 A4
  Sawtry PE28 . . . . .168 C4
Manor Est ⑬ PE15 . . . . . .223 A5
Manor Farm Cl
  Haverhill CB9. . . . . .24 B7
  Oakington & Westwick
  CB24. . . . . .103 C6
Manor Farm Ct
  Cottenham CB24 . . . . . . .125 D3
  Perry PE28. . . . . .115 D2
Manor Farm La PE5 . . . . .195 E2
Manor Farm Rd
  Beck Row, Holywell Row &
  Kenny Hill IP28. . . . . . . .213 D7
  Girton CB3. . . . . .103 D2
  St Neots PE19 . . . . .75 A5
  Waresley SG19 . . . . .57 C2
Manor Gdns
  Buckden PE19 . . . . .117 A4
  Peterborough PE2 . . . . . .187 C7
  Wisbech PE13 . . . . .245 A4
Manor Gr PE19 . . . . .75 A5
Manor House Cl ① PE19 . .74 C2
Manor House St PE1 . . . . .198 A3
Manor La
  Alconbury PE28 . . . . .150 F5
  Boxworth CB23 . . . . .101 C6
  Great Chesterford CB10 . . .18 D2
  Great Gransden SG19 . . . .58 D4
Manor Leisure Ctr PE7 . . .189 E6
Manor Pk CB24 . . . . .104 A4
Manor Pl CB1. . . . . .246 B3
Manor Rd
  Folksworth PE7 . . . . .180 D1
  Gamlingay SG19 . . . . . . .41 D6
  Haverhill CB9. . . . . .24 B7
  Hemingford Grey PE28 . . .143 B1
  Little Shelford CB22. . . . . .48 E4
  Meldreth SG8. . . . . .29 A1
  Mildenhall IP28 . . . . . . .239 B4
  Sutton PE5. . . . . .194 F2
  Witchford CB6 . . . . .217 E2
Manor St
  Cambridge CB1 . . . . .246 B3
  Wistow PE28 . . . . .164 A7
Manor View
  Barton Mills IP28 . . . . . . .239 D2
  Whittlesey PE7 . . . . .189 D6
Manor Way
  Hail Weston PE19 . . . . . . .95 A1
  Market Deeping PE6 . . . . .231 F8
Manor Wlk CB21 . . . . .67 A5
Manse Dr CB24 . . . . .125 C3
Mansel Ct CB4 . . . . .83 E6
Mansel Way CB4 . . . . .83 E6
Mansfield Cl CB24 . . . . . .105 C2
Mansfield Ct PE1 . . . . . . .198 C5
Manton PE3 . . . . .197 A3
Maple Ave
  Sawston CB22 . . . . .32 F5
  Wisbech PE13 . . . . .245 C7
Maple Cl
  Bluntisham/Colne PE28. . .208 C6
  Bottisham CB25. . . . . . . .86 F5
  ④ Bourn CB23 . . . . .79 C3
  Cambridge CB4 . . . . .83 F5
  Linton CB21 . . . . .35 B3
  Sawtry PE28 . . . . .168 A3
Maple Dr
  Gamlingay SG19 . . . . . . .41 C5
  Yaxley PE7 . . . . .181 F6

Maple End PE28 . . . . .150 F4
Maple Gr
  March PE15 . . . . .243 C5
  Peterborough PE1 . . . . . .198 C7
Maple Grove Inf Sch
  PE15. . . . . .243 C5
Maple Rd PE14. . . . . .236 A5
Maples The
  Fulbourn CB21. . . . . .66 E5
  Peterborough PE1 . . . . . .198 C5
Maple Way
  Melbourn SG8 . . . . .14 C5
  Royston SG8 . . . . .5 E8
Maple Wlk PE7 . . . . .186 C2
MARCH 243 B4
March & District Mus★
  PE15. . . . . .243 D4
Marchioness Way ⑧
  PE19. . . . . .74 B4
March La CB1. . . . . .65 F8
March Rd
  Coates/Eastrea PE7 . . . .191 A8
  Coldham PE14 . . . . .235 F2
  Elm PE13 . . . . .227 F8
  Guyhirn PE13 . . . . .235 A2
  Welney PE14 . . . . .229 F1
  Whittlesey PE7 . . . . .191 D7
  Wimblington PE15 . . . . . .223 B7
March Riverside PE14 . . . .229 C8
March's Cl CB21 . . . . .66 E5
March Sta PE15 . . . . .243 D6
March Trad Est PE15 . . . .243 E7
Marconi Dr PE7. . . . . .181 D6
Marcus Cl CB9. . . . . .24 D7
Mardale Gdns PE4 . . . . . .204 F2
Marefen Dro CB6 . . . . .5 E6
Mare Fen Nature Reserve★
  CB24. . . . . .122 F8
Marfleet Cl CB22. . . . . .48 F7
MARGERY'S CROFT 238 B1
Margetts PE28 . . . . .143 D1
Margett St CB24 . . . . .125 E4
MARHOLM. 203 E1
Marholm Rd
  Castor PE6. . . . . .196 B3
  Peterborough PE3 . . . . . .204 B1
  Ufford PE9. . . . . .231 A2
Marian Way PE16 . . . . . . .241 C2
Marigold Dr IP28 . . . . . . .133 F8
Marina Dr PE15 . . . . .243 A5
Mariner's Way CB4. . . . . . .84 A3
Marino Cl CB8 . . . . .110 F3
Marion Cl CB3 . . . . .83 B4
Maris Gn CB22 . . . . .49 A6
Maris La CB2 . . . . .64 C2
Marius Cres PE7 . . . . .186 C3
Markby Cl CB22. . . . . .17 D8
MARKET DEEPING 231 D8
Market Hill
  Cambridge CB2 . . . . .246 A2
  Chatteris PE16. . . . . . . .241 C5
  ② Huntingdon PE29 . . . . .141 D4
  Royston SG8 . . . . .5 D6
  St Ives PE27 . . . . .144 A3
Market La
  Linton CB21 . . . . .35 B2
  St Ives PE27 . . . . .144 A3
Market Mews PE13. . . . . .245 C5
Market Pas CB1. . . . . .246 A3
Market Pl
  ⑤ Ely CB7 . . . . .240 D4
  Little London PE15. . . . . .243 D4
  Mildenhall IP28 . . . . . . .239 C4
  St Neots PE19 . . . . .74 E5
  Whittlesey PE7 . . . . .189 E7
  Wisbech PE13 . . . . .245 C5
Market Rd PE27 . . . . .144 B3
Market Sq
  Cambridge CB2 . . . . .246 A2
  ⑧ Ely CB7 . . . . .240 D4
  Royston SG8 . . . . .5 D5
  St Neots PE19 . . . . .74 E5
Market St
  Cambridge CB2 . . . . .246 A3
  Ely CB7 . . . . .240 D4
  Fordham CB7. . . . . .212 E1
  Mildenhall IP28 . . . . . . .239 C4
  ③ Newmarket CB8 . . . . .111 A3
  ⑫ Soham CB7 . . . . .212 B4
  Swavesey SG24 . . . . . . .122 E6
  Whittlesey PE7 . . . . .189 D7
  ⑬ Wisbech PE13. . . . . . .245 C5
Marketstede PE7 . . . . . . .186 B2
Market Way CB4. . . . . .83 A2
Markfield Rise CB6 . . . . . .216 D1
Markham Cl CB4 . . . . .84 A7
Markham Ret Pk PE9. . . . .244 D7
Markhams Cl ③ CB9 . . . . .38 F1
Mark's Way CB3 . . . . .103 E1
Marlborough Cl
  St Ives PE27 . . . . .143 F7
  Yaxley PE7 . . . . .181 E5
Marlborough Ct
  ⑲ Haverhill CB9. . . . . . . .23 E7
  Newnham CB3 . . . . .64 B8
  Wisbech PE13 . . . . .245 A4
Marley Rd PE27 . . . . .143 F8
Marlowe Ct ② PE19 . . . . . .74 D6
Marlowe Gr PE4 . . . . .197 E8
Marlowe Rd CB3 . . . . .64 C7
Marmora Rd CB1 . . . . .65 B7
Marne Ave PE4 . . . . .204 C1
Marne Rd PE7 . . . . .189 F5
Marquis Cl ④ PE19 . . . . . .74 B4
Marriott Ct PE1 . . . . .198 C5
Marriott Dr PE26 . . . . . . .221 A4
Marriotts Cl PE26 . . . . . . .221 A4
Marriott's Dro PE26 . . . . .221 A4

Marritt Cl PE16 . . . . .241 B6
Marroway La ④ CB6 . . . . .217 D1
Marshall Rd CB1 . . . . .65 A5
Marshall's Bank PE13 . . . .234 D8
Marshall's Cl CB1. . . . . . . .85 A1
Marshall's La CB6 . . . . . . .218 B6
Marshall's Way PE7 . . . . . .187 C2
Marsham PE2. . . . . .185 F3
Marsh Cl PE15 . . . . .243 F6
Marsh La PE14 . . . . .143 D1
Marshfields Sch PE1 . . . . .198 D7
Marshland High Sch
  PE14 . . . . .238 E4
MARSHLAND ST JAMES . .236 F8
Marsh Rd
  Outwell PE14. . . . . .236 F4
  Walpole PE14 . . . . .238 F8
Marsh The PE14 . . . . .238 F8
Marsh Wlk ⑤ PE13 . . . . . .245 D5
Marston Rd PE19 . . . . .75 A3
Martin Ave PE15 . . . . .243 A7
Martin Cl
  Godmanchester PE29 . . . .119 A8
  Mildenhall IP28 . . . . . . .239 D3
  Soham CB7 . . . . .212 A5
Martin Ct
  Peterborough PE4 . . . . . .204 C4
  Whittlesey PE7 . . . . .189 C7
Martindale Way CB22 . . . . .32 E8
Martingale Cl ③ CB4. . . . . .83 C6
Martingale Rd ④ SG8. . . . . .5 E6
Martin Luther King Cl
  PE29. . . . . .141 F6
Martin Rd CB25 . . . . .130 B3
Martinsbridge PE1 . . . . . .198 F7
Martins La
  Linton CB21 . . . . .35 E2
  Witcham CB6 . . . . .217 A3
Martin's La CB6 . . . . .218 A6
Martins Mews CB9 . . . . . . .38 C1
Martins Way PE2. . . . . . . .185 F5
Marwick Rd PE15 . . . . . . .243 D7
Mary Armyne Rd PE2. . . . .186 B5
Maryland Ave
  Huntingdon PE29 . . . . . . .141 F8
  Swaffham Bulbeck CB25 . .108 B2
Marylebone Rd PE15 . . . . .243 C4
Mary Walsham Cl PE2. . . .187 E5
Masefield Rd PE19 . . . . . . .74 C6
Masefield Way SG8 . . . . . .13 D1
Maskew Ave PE1. . . . . . . .197 E6
Mason Cl CB9. . . . . .38 F2
Mason Gdns IP28 . . . . . . .213 D6
Mason Rd CB25 . . . . .130 B5
Master Dike PE12 . . . . . . .237 D8
Masterton Cl PE29 . . . . . .244 D7
Masterton Rd PE29. . . . . .244 C7
Matley PE2 . . . . .185 E5
Matley Prim Sch PE2. . . . .185 E5
Matt Dawson Cl CB8 . . . . .110 F6
Matthew Parker Cl CB25 . .105 D7
Matthews La CB8 . . . . .55 F6
Matthew Wren Cl CB6. . . .218 A6
Maule Cl
  Huntingdon PE29 . . . . . . .141 E6
  St Neots PE19 . . . . .74 E1
Maurice Cl PE28 . . . . .113 F5
Mawson Cl CB8 . . . . .240 B3
Mawson Rd CB1 . . . . .246 C1
MAXEY 231 C7
Maxey Rd
  Helpston PE6 . . . . .231 C5
  Northborough PE6 . . . . . .231 D7
Maxey View ⑩ PE6 . . . . . .231 E8
Maxham's Green Rd PE6 . .203 B6
Maxwell Rd PE2 . . . . .186 D6
Mayes Mdw CB8 . . . . .112 E5
Mayfair Gdns PE13 . . . . . .235 C7
Mayfield PE19 . . . . .117 A3
Mayfield Cl ② CB6 . . . . . .240 B5
Mayfield Cres PE29 . . . . . .141 F6
Mayfield Prim Sch CB4. . . . .83 C5
Mayfield Rd
  Coates/Eastrea PE7 . . . .190 D7
  Girton CB3. . . . . .82 D7
  Huntingdon PE29 . . . . . . .141 F6
  Peterborough PE1 . . . . . .198 A6
Mayfield Way CB23. . . . . . .79 C2
Mayflower Rd ① PE13. . . . .245 E3
Mayfly Cl PE16. . . . . .241 B3
Maynards CB22 . . . . .32 C5
Mayner's Dike PE12 . . . . .237 E8
Mayors Cl PE15 . . . . .243 D7
Mayor's Wlk PE3. . . . . . . .197 E3
Maypole Croft CB21. . . . . .37 C8
Maypole La CB8 . . . . .90 E3
May's Ave CB21 . . . . .53 A2
Maysfield Dr ⑧ PE13. . . . .238 B2
May's La PE13 . . . . .238 A2
May St SG8 . . . . .7 E2
Mays Way CB4. . . . . .84 C5
Maytrees PE27 . . . . .143 F1
Maze Rd PE28 . . . . .120 C1
Mead Cl PE3. . . . . .204 B1
Meadenvale PE1. . . . . . . .198 F5
Meadlands Main Dro
  CB6 . . . . .215 F1
Meadowbrook CB6. . . . . . .209 E4
Meadow Bsns Ctr The
  PE27. . . . . .144 B2
Meadow Cl
  Chatteris PE16. . . . . . . .241 C3
  Little Paxton PE19 . . . . . .95 F2
  ⑦ Soham CB7 . . . . .212 B3
  Stilton PE7. . . . . .175 F8

Meadow Cl continued
St Ives PE27 . . . . **144** B3
Witcham CB6 . . . . **217** E2
Meadowcroft CB6 . . . . . . **210** F5
Meadowcroft Way SG8 . . . **28** E8
Meadow Ct CB6 . . . . **242** B5
Meadow Dr PE15 . . . . **243** F3
Meadow Drift CB23 . . . . . **100** B5
Meadow Dro PE28 . . . . . . **208** E6
Meadow Farm Cl CB24 . . . **103** D6
Meadowfield Rd CB22 . . . . **32** E6
Meadowgate PE9 . . . . **230** F5
Meadowgate La PE14 . . . . **245** E2
Meadowgate Sch PE13 . . . **245** E3
Meadow Gr PE1 . . . . **205** B1
Meadow How PE27 . . . . . **143** F6
Meadow La
Earith PE28 . . . . **208** E6
Haddenham CB6 . . . . . . **209** F6
Hemingford Abbots PE28 . **142** F3
Hemingford Grey PE28 . . . **143** D3
Houghton & Wyton PE28 . . **143** D4
Linton CB21 . . . . **35** B2
Little Heath SG19 . . . . . . **41** D3
Newmarket CB8 . . . . **111** D4
Offord Darcy PE19 . . . . . **117** F2
Over CB24 . . . . **208** D1
Ramsey PE26 . . . . **172** B4
St Ives PE27 . . . . **144** C3
Thornhaugh PE8 . . . . . . **193** F5
Meadowlands
Burwell CB25 . . . . **130** B1
March PE15 . . . . **243** A6
Meadowlands Sch CB8 . . . **84** E3
Meadow Prim Sch The
CB21 . . . . **53** B2
Meadow Rd
Great Chesterford CB10 . . **18** D3
Great Gransden SG19 . . . **58** B5
Newborough PE6 . . . . . . **204** D8
Peakirk PE6 . . . . **206** C1
Ramsey PE26 . . . . **171** B4
Willingham CB24 . . . . . . **209** B1
Meadow Rise
Bourn CB23 . . . . **60** C6
Stukeley PE29 . . . . **140** F5
Meadows Cl 5 PE19 . . . . **74** F5
Meadows The
Haslingfield CB23 . . . . . . **47** B5
Worlington IP28 . . . . **213** F4
Meadowsweet PE19 . . . . . **74** B6
Meadowsweet Cl
2 Cambourne CB23 . . . . **79** A4
Haverhill CB9 . . . . **38** E1
MEADOW THE **215** C2
Meadow View PE19 . . . . . **77** E4
Meadow Way
Doddington/Wimblington
PE15 . . . . **223** B7
Earith PE28 . . . . **208** E6
Ely CB6 . . . . **240** A3
Godmanchester PE29 . . . **142** A2
Great Paxton PE19 . . . . . **96** E4
Harston CB22 . . . . **48** A3
Melbourn SG8 . . . . **14** C6
Mepal CB6 . . . . **216** E3
Warboys PE28 . . . . **164** F5
Meadow Way S 7 PE15 . . **223** B7
Meadow Wlk CB21 . . . . . . **34** C6
Mead The PE4 . . . . **204** B1
Mead View CB24 . . . . **103** B5
Mealsgate PE4 . . . . **204** F2
Medallion Ct 1 PE19 . . . . **74** F5
Medbourne Gdns PE1 . . . . **198** C8
Medcalfe Way SG8 . . . . . . **14** D6
Medeswell PE2 . . . . **186** C4
**Medieval Village of Clopton
(site of)** ★ SG8 . . . . **26** E6
**Medieval Village of Croydon
(site of)** ★ SG8 . . . . **27** B8
**Medieval Village of Great
Childerley (site of)** ★
CB23 . . . . **80** D8
**Medieval Village of
Landbeach (site of)** ★
CB25 . . . . **105** C7
**Medieval Village of Papley
(site of)** ★ PE8 . . . . **174** B7
**Medieval Village of
Sibberton (site of)** ★
PE8 . . . . **193** E5
**Medieval Village of
Wintringham (site of)** ★
PE19 . . . . **75** F4
Medland Gr 6 PE19 . . . . . **75** A5
Medlar Way CB23 . . . . **79** A4
Medway Cl PE13 . . . . **245** E4
Medway Rd PE29 . . . . **141** E7
Medway The CB8 . . . . **240** D6
Medworth PE2 . . . . **185** F3
Meeting La
Litlington SG8 . . . . **12** A2
Melbourn SG8 . . . . **14** C6
Meeting Wlk CB9 . . . . **24** B8
Megans Way 4 PE16 . . . . **241** C5
Meggan Gate PE3 . . . . . . **197** A1
Megg's Dro PE26 . . . . . . **221** D2
Megs Cl PE28 . . . . **208** D5
MELBOURN **14** D5
Melbourn Bury SG8 . . . . . **14** B5
Melbourne Ave PE15 . . . . **243** B7
Melbourne Dr IP28 . . . . . **239** B5
Melbourne Rd PE9 . . . . . . **244** D6
Melbourn Prim Sch SG8 . . **14** C6

Melbourn Rd SG8 . . . . **5** D7
Melbourn Science Pk
SG8 . . . . **14** D7
Melbourn St SG8 . . . . **5** D6
Melbourn Village Coll
SG8 . . . . **14** C7
Meldon Pl CB6 . . . . **240** D5
MELDRETH **29** A2
Meldreth Manor Sch SG8 . **29** A1
Meldreth Rd
Shepreth SG8 . . . . **29** D4
Whaddon SG8 . . . . **28** C1
Meldreth Sta SG8 . . . . **14** B7
Meldreth Prim Sch SG8 . . . **14** B8
Melford Cl
Burwell CB25 . . . . **130** C2
Peterborough PE3 . . . . . **197** A2
Mellis Cl PE9 . . . . **38** B1
Mellows Cl PE1 . . . . **198** C3
Melrose Dr PE2 . . . . **187** A7
Melrose Gdns CB8 . . . . . . **110** E4
Melton Cl 1 CB8 . . . . **111** B2
Melvin Way CB24 . . . . **104** A4
Memorial Ct CB3 . . . . **83** C1
Mendip Gr PE4 . . . . **204** E2
MEPAL **216** E4
Mepal Long Highway
CB6 . . . . **216** C4
Mepal Outdoor Ctr PE16 . **216** C6
Mepal Rd CB6 . . . . **216** E2
Mepal Short Highway
CB6 . . . . **216** C5
**Mepal & Witcham CE Prim
Sch** CB6 . . . . **216** D3
Mercers Row CB5 . . . . **84** B4
Mercian Ct PE2 . . . . **187** D7
Mere Cl PE26 . . . . **221** A4
Mere Dro
Ramsey PE26 . . . . **221** D4
Yaxley PE7 . . . . **181** F4
Merelade Gr PE4 . . . . **204** B5
Mere Mill Dro CB6 . . . . . . **210** F4
Mere Side CB7 . . . . **212** A4
Mere Side Dro PE26 . . . . . **221** B4
Mere View PE7 . . . . **182** A5
Mere View Ind Est PE7 . . . **182** A6
Mere Way
Cambridge CB4 . . . . **83** E6
Hemingford Grey PE28 . . **120** B5
Houghton & Wyton PE28 . . **143** A6
Meridian Ct 22 PE28 . . . . **215** C1
Meridian Dr CB23 . . . . . . **101** F4
Meridian Prim Sch CB23 . . **62** C5
Meridian Sch The SG8 . . . . . **5** E7
Meriton PE2 . . . . **185** F2
Merivale Way CB23 . . . . . . **79** A4
Merlin Cl
Huntingdon PE29 . . . . . . **142** B7
St Neots PE19 . . . . **75** B7
Merlin Dr 4 CB6 . . . . **240** B5
Merritt St PE29 . . . . **141** C5
Merryland PE27 . . . . **144** A3
Merryvale CB22 . . . . **64** D1
Merton Grange SG19 . . . . **41** F5
Merton Rd CB24 . . . . **104** B3
Merton St CB3 . . . . **64** C7
Mertoun Paddocks CB8 . . . **90** A8
Metcalfe Rd CB4 . . . . **83** D5
Metcalfe Way CB6 . . . . . . **210** A5
Metro Ctr The PE2 . . . . . . **186** D6
Mewburn PE3 . . . . **204** A1
Mews Cl PE26 . . . . **172** B7
Meynell Gdns CB8 . . . . . . **111** A5
Meynell Wlk PE3 . . . . **197** B3
Michael's Cl CB3 . . . . **103** E1
Michigan PE28 . . . . **151** E4
Michigan Rd PE27 . . . . . . **143** E6
Mickle Gate PE3 . . . . **197** A1
Mickle Hill PE28 . . . . **135** D7
Mid Career Coll CB1 . . . . . **67** B4
Middle Broad Dro PE13 . . **237** D5
Middle Cl 5 CB6 . . . . **210** F5
Middledrift SG8 . . . . **5** C6
Middle Dro
Newton PE13 . . . . **237** E3
Ramsey PE26 . . . . **171** A7
Soham CB7 . . . . **211** F3
Wimblington PE15 . . . . . **223** C5
Middlefield PE7 . . . . **186** D3
Middlefield Prim Sch
PE19 . . . . **74** F2
Middlefield Rd PE28 . . . . . **168** B3
Middleham Cl PE7 . . . . . . **187** F5
Middlemiss View PE29 . . . **118** F8
Middlemoor Rd
Ramsey PE26 . . . . **220** D3
Whittlesford CB22 . . . . . **32** A5
Middle Pasture PE4 . . . . . **204** B5
Middle Rd
Crowland PE6 . . . . **207** E2
March PE15 . . . . **243** A6
Newborough PE6 . . . . . . **205** C7
Middle St
Elton PE8 . . . . **178** D8
Farcet PE7 . . . . **187** C2
Great Gransden SG19 . . . **58** E4
Litlington SG8 . . . . **12** A2
Thriplow SG8 . . . . **31** B1
Middleton PE3 . . . . **197** A4
Middleton Prim Sch PE3 . . **197** A4
Middletons Rd PE7 . . . . . . **181** E5
Middleton Way CB24 . . . . **121** E4
Middle Watch CB24 . . . . . **122** C5
Middle Way CB20 . . . . **50** A1
Mid Fetter PE26 . . . . **221** B3
Midfield CB24 . . . . **103** D4
Midgate PE1 . . . . **198** A2
Midhurst Cl CB4 . . . . **84** A5

Midland Rd PE3 . . . . **197** E3
Midloe Grange PE19 . . . . . **95** A6
Mikanda Cl PE14 . . . . **245** C2
Milburn Dro CB8 . . . . **112** E5
MILDENHALL **239** A6
Mildenhall Airfield IP28 . . **239** B8
Mildenhall Coll of Tecnology
IP28 . . . . **239** E4
Mildenhall Ind Est IP28 . . **239** D6
Mildenhall Mus ★ IP28 . . . **239** C4
Mildenhall Pl CB9 . . . . **24** B8
Mildenhall Rd
Barton Mills IP28 . . . . . **239** C2
Beck Row, Holywell Row & Kenny
Hill IP28 . . . . **239** C8
Ely CB7 . . . . **219** E8
Fordham IP28 . . . . **213** A2
Freckenham IP28 . . . . . **213** D3
Icklingham IP28 . . . . . . **214** E4
Littleport CB7 . . . . **242** F6
Mildenhall Swimming Pool
IP28 . . . . **239** C4
Mildmay Rd PE14 . . . . . . **197** D8
Mile Dro
Glinton PE6 . . . . **231** F5
Yaxley PE7 . . . . **182** B5
MILE END **219** C5
Mile End Rd CB7 . . . . **219** C6
Mile Rd CB22 . . . . **50** C4
Miles Hawk Way IP28 . . . **239** A5
Mile Tree La PE13 . . . . . . **235** E7
Milford St CB1 . . . . **84** A1
Military Rd CB7 . . . . **212** C2
Militia Way CB7 . . . . **240** C4
Milking Nook Rd PE6 . . . . **206** E1
Milking Slade Rd PE28 . . . **167** A4
Milk & Water Dro PE7 . . . **188** A4
Millards La CB25 . . . . **107** D2
Millbank CB8 . . . . **110** F4
Mill Cl
Burwell CB25 . . . . **130** B1
Exning CB8 . . . . **110** B8
Hemingford Grey PE28 . . **143** D3
Huntingdon PE29 . . . . . . **142** A6
Murrow PE13 . . . . **234** D5
Peakirk PE6 . . . . **206** B1
The Stukeleys PE28 . . . . **151** D3
Wisbech PE13 . . . . **245** C4
Mill Cnr CB7 . . . . **212** A4
Mill Comm PE29 . . . . **141** C3
Mill Cres PE2 . . . . **185** E4
Mill Croft CB7 . . . . **212** B3
Mill Cswy SG8 . . . . **8** C5
Mill Ct CB22 . . . . **49** A5
Mill Dro
Crowland PE6 . . . . **207** F7
Lode CB25 . . . . **128** A1
Ramsey PE26 . . . . **221** A2
Soham CB7 . . . . **212** A3
Southery PE38 . . . . **226** E8
MILL END **72** E5
Mill End SG19 . . . . **25** A4
Mill End Cl
Cambridge CB1 . . . . **65** F5
Warboys PE28 . . . . **165** A5
Mill End Rd CB1 . . . . **65** E6
Miller Cl
2 Doddington/Wimblington
PE15 . . . . **222** F5
Godmanchester PE29 . . . **118** F8
Offord Cluny PE19 . . . . . **118** A2
Millers Cl CB21 . . . . **35** D3
Miller's Rd CB23 . . . . **61** D5
Miller's Way PE13 . . . . . . **173** C3
Miller Way
Brampton PE28 . . . . **140** C3
Cambourne CB23 . . . . . . **79** B3
Mill Farm La CB22 . . . . . . **32** F4
MILLFIELD **197** F5
Millfield
Littleport CB6 . . . . **242** C3
Upwell PE14 . . . . **236** E2
Willingham CB24 . . . . . . **124** A8
Mill Field 3 CB6 . . . . **216** E2
Millfield Cl IP16 . . . . **241** B2
Mill Field Cl PE6 . . . . **231** C4
Millfield La CB6 . . . . **210** C5
Millfield Pl CB6 . . . . **210** D5
Millfield Prim Sch CB6 . . . **242** C3
Millfield Rd
Market Deeping PE6 . . . . **231** F8
Maxey PE6 . . . . **231** D8
Millfields
Ramsey PE26 . . . . **172** B8
Stetchworth CB8 . . . . . . **89** F1
Millfields Way CB9 . . . . . . **24** B8
Millfields Way PE7 . . . . . . **189** F6
Mill Gn PE28 . . . . **165** A5
MILL GREEN **22** D7
Mill Hill
Conington PE7 . . . . **177** C1
Downham CB6 . . . . **217** F7
Glatton PE28 . . . . **175** E1
Haverhill CB9 . . . . **23** F7
Newmarket CB8 . . . . . . **111** A4
Royston SG8 . . . . **5** E4
Swaffham Prior CB5 . . . . **108** E5
Weston Colville CB21 . . . **54** C6
Mill Hill End PE28 . . . . . . **120** B1
Mill Hill Rd 7 PE19 . . . . . **74** D5
Mill Hole **33** E8
Millington Rd CB3 . . . . . . **64** C7
Mill La
Arrington SG8 . . . . **44** C3
Barrington CB22 . . . . . . **29** E4
Bassingbourn SG8 . . . . . **12** D5
Bluntisham/Colne PE28 . . **208** D5
Burwell CB25 . . . . **130** B1

Mill La continued
Cambridge CB2 . . . . **246** A2
Castor PE5 . . . . **184** F7
Duxford CB22 . . . . **32** E1
Exning CB8 . . . . **110** B8
Fordham CB7 . . . . **212** F1
Gorefield PE13 . . . . **235** B8
Hauxton CB22 . . . . **48** A6
Hemingford Grey PE28 . . **143** D3
Hinxton CB10 . . . . **18** A7
Histon CB24 . . . . **104** D6
Ickleton CB10 . . . . **18** B4
Impington CB24 . . . . . . **104** D5
Linton CB21 . . . . **35** C2
Newton PE13 . . . . **237** F5
Peterborough PE7 . . . . . **185** A5
Potton SG19 . . . . **40** D1
Ramsey PE26 . . . . **172** B8
Sawston CB22 . . . . **32** E7
Shingay cum Wendy SG8 . **27** B4
Stetchworth CB8 . . . . . . **89** F1
St Neots PE19 . . . . **74** F8
Swaffham Bulbeck CB25 . **108** B3
Tallington PE9 . . . . **230** F7
Toft CB23 . . . . **61** D5
Water Newton PE8 . . . . . **184** C7
West Walton PE14 . . . . . **238** F4
Whittlesford CB22 . . . . . **32** D5
Mill Pit Furlong CB6 . . . . **242** D3
Mill Quern CB23 . . . . **80** C2
Mill Rd
Alconbury PE28 . . . . **150** E4
Ashley CB8 . . . . **91** F8
Barnack PE9 . . . . **230** C3
Buckden PE19 . . . . **117** C3
Cambridge CB1 . . . . **246** C2
Emneth PE14 . . . . **236** D6
Fen Drayton CB24 . . . . . **121** D5
Glatton PE28 . . . . **175** E1
Great Gidding PE28 . . . . **166** E3
Great Wilbraham CB21 . . **67** F7
Harston CB22 . . . . **47** D2
Haverhill CB9 . . . . **24** A7
Histon CB24 . . . . **104** B1
Huntingdon PE29 . . . . . . **142** A6
Kirtling CB8 . . . . **72** E5
Little Gransden SG19 . . . **58** E4
Little Stukeley PE28 . . . . **151** D4
Little Wilbraham CB1 . . . . **86** D1
Lode CB25 . . . . **107** C2
Maxey PE6 . . . . **231** C7
Nassington PE8 . . . . **183** A7
Oakington/Longstanton
CB24 . . . . **103** D6
Royston SG8 . . . . **5** D7
Stilton PE7 . . . . **175** F8
Walpole PE14 . . . . **238** F6
Waterbeach CB25 . . . . . **106** A7
West Walton PE14 . . . . . **238** D4
West Wickham CB21 . . . . **36** E8
West Wratting CB21 . . . . **53** F2
Whittlesey PE7 . . . . **189** E6
Willingham CB24 . . . . . . **124** A8
Wisbech St Mary PE13 . . **234** C5
Wistow PE28 . . . . **163** F6
Mill Reef Cl CB8 . . . . **110** D7
Mills La
Longstanton CB24 . . . . . **124** A1
Witchford CB6 . . . . **217** D1
Mill St
Ashwell SG7 . . . . **2** D4
Cambridge CB1 . . . . **246** C1
Gamlingay SG19 . . . . . . **41** D5
Isleham CB7 . . . . **213** A5
Mildenhall IP28 . . . . **239** B3
St Ives PE27 . . . . **143** C6
Millstone La PE9 . . . . **230** D3
Mill View
March PE15 . . . . **243** D4
Peterborough PE7 . . . . . **185** A5
Sawtry PE28 . . . . **168** A4
Mill View Ct PE19 . . . . . . **74** C2
Mill Way
Grantchester CB3 . . . . . . **64** A3
Holywell-cum-Needingworth
PE27 . . . . **144** F3
Stretham CB6 . . . . **210** E6
Swavesey CB24 . . . . **122** C6
Wisbech PE14 . . . . **236** A4
Millyard CB6 . . . . **210** A6
Mill Yd PE29 . . . . **141** C2
Milner Cl
March PE15 . . . . **243** D5
Sawston CB22 . . . . **32** E7
Milner Rd
Comberton CB23 . . . . . . **62** D6
Wisbech PE13 . . . . **245** C4
Milners Row 13 PE9 . . . . **244** C5
Milnyard Sq PE2 . . . . **185** C2
MILTON **105** E2
Milton Ave PE19 . . . . **74** C6
Milton CE Prim Sch
CB24 . . . . **105** C2
Milton Cl
Huntingdon PE29 . . . . . . **141** E6
Ramsey PE26 . . . . **171** F5
Royston SG8 . . . . **13** C1
St Ives PE27 . . . . **143** F6
Milton Ctry Pk ★ CB24 . . **105** D1
Milton Dr CB23 . . . . **238** D1
Milton Rd
Cambridge CB4 . . . . **246** B4
Impington CB24 . . . . . . **104** F4
Peterborough PE2 . . . . . **187** A7
Milton Rd Prim Sch CB4 . . **83** E5
Milton Way PE3 . . . . **196** F3
Mina Cl PE2 . . . . **187** D4

Minden Ct 8 PE19 . . . . . . **74** C5
Minerva Cl CB9 . . . . **24** D6
Minerva Way CB4 . . . . **83** E8
Mingle La CB22 . . . . **49** B5
Minster Pl 4 CB7 . . . . . . **240** D4
Minster Precincts PE1 . . . **198** B2
Minster Rd
Haverhill CB9 . . . . **39** A1
Royston SG8 . . . . **5** C8
Minter Cl CB25 . . . . **86** A5
Mint La PE19 . . . . **96** E4
Minton Ent Pk CB8 . . . . . **110** F2
Missleton Ct CB1 . . . . **65** C5
Misterton PE2 . . . . **185** E3
Misty Mdws CB5 . . . . **84** D4
Mitchell Cl PE1 . . . . **198** C2
Mitchells CB10 . . . . **20** B1
Mitchells Cotts CB10 . . . . **20** B1
Mitchell's Yd CB6 . . . . . . **210** C5
Moat Cl PE27 . . . . **208** D7
Moat La
Abbots Ripton PE28 . . . . **152** C8
Melbourn SG8 . . . . **14** D7
Perry PE28 . . . . **115** D1
Moats' Way PE28 . . . . **119** E7
Moat Way CB24 . . . . **122** E6
Moat Wlk CB9 . . . . **23** E8
Mobb's Hole SG7 . . . . **10** C4
Moggswell La PE2 . . . . . . **186** B4
Mole Dro PE12 . . . . **233** F8
MOLESWORTH **147** A5
Molewood Cl CB4 . . . . **83** C6
Molls Dro PE14 . . . . **236** C3
Monarch Ave PE2 . . . . . . **187** A6
Monarch Rd PE19 . . . . . . **74** B4
Moncrieff Cl 1 CB4 . . . . . **83** E7
Mondela Pl PE7 . . . . **176** A7
Monet Cl PE27 . . . . **144** A7
Money Bank PE13 . . . . . . **245** E4
Money Hill (Tumulus) ★
CB23 . . . . **47** B3
Moneypiece Cl 1 CB9 . . . . **38** F1
Monk Dr CB23 . . . . **79** C4
Monkfield La CB23 . . . . . . **79** C3
Monkfield Park Prim Sch
CB23 . . . . **79** B4
Monks Cl PE7 . . . . **189** D8
Monks Dr 17 PE6 . . . . . . **232** A1
Monks Gr PE4 . . . . **204** A5
Monks Hardwick PE19 . . . **75** E8
Monks Mdw PE6 . . . . **232** B8
Monks Way PE28 . . . . . . **168** B2
Monkswell CB2 . . . . **64** D3
Monkswood CB6 . . . . **242** C5
**Monks Wood National
Nature Reserve** ★ PE28 . **161** B4
Montagu Ct 2 PE19 . . . . . **74** E4
Montague Rd
Brampton PE28 . . . . **117** D3
Cambridge CB4 . . . . **84** A3
Montagu Gdns PE28 . . . . **113** E5
Montagu Rd
Huntingdon PE29 . . . . . . **141** D4
Little Stukeley PE28 . . . . **151** F2
Peterborough PE4 . . . . . **197** D8
Montagu Sq PE19 . . . . . . **74** E4
Montagu St PE19 . . . . . . **74** E4
Monte Long Cl PE15 . . . . **243** E1
Montford Cl CB25 . . . . . . **130** C4
Montfort Way CB4 . . . . . . **83** E6
Montgomery Rd CB4 . . . . **83** E6
Montreal Rd CB1 . . . . **65** C7
Montrose Cl CB4 . . . . **83** E7
Monument St PE1 . . . . . . **198** A3
Monument View PE15 . . . **243** A5
Moonhall Bsns Pk CB9 . . . **24** A5
Moon Hall La CB9 . . . . . . **24** A6
Moore Cl CB4 . . . . **84** A6
Moor End SG8 . . . . **29** D3
Moore's La 4 PE6 . . . . . . **232** A1
Moores Wlk PE19 . . . . . . **74** F5
Moorfield PE6 . . . . **206** B3
Moorfield Rd
Duxford CB22 . . . . **32** E3
Peterborough PE3 . . . . . **197** D3
Moorfield Way PE28 . . . . **151** F2
Moorhen Rd PE7 . . . . **201** A1
Moorhouse Dr PE29 . . . . **141** E7
Moor Pasture Way CB9 . . . **39** B4
Moor Rd
Great Staughton MK44 . . . **93** B4
Newborough PE6 . . . . . . **206** E2
Moor The SG8 . . . . **14** C7
Moory Croft Cl PE19 . . . . **94** A6
Moot Way PE28 . . . . **155** A5
MORBORNE **180** B3
Morborne Cl PE2 . . . . **187** D6
Morborne La PE7 . . . . . . **180** D4
Morborne Rd PE7 . . . . . . **180** C2
MORDEN GREEN **11** C1
Morden Rd CB23 . . . . **99** B3
More's Mdw CB22 . . . . . . **48** F6
Moreton Cl PE7 . . . . **189** F8
Moretons Cl PE7 . . . . **190** A8
Morgan Cl PE7 . . . . **181** E6
Morgans CB24 . . . . **125** D4
Morland Way PE27 . . . . . **144** A7
Morley Cl 7 IP28 . . . . . . **213** F8
Morley Dr CB6 . . . . **240** A3
Morley Meml Prim Sch
CB1 . . . . **65** B5
Morley Way
17 Eastwood End PE15 . . **223** B7
Peterborough PE2 . . . . . **186** D3
Morpeth Cl PE2 . . . . **186** C6
Morpeth Rd PE3 . . . . **197** C3
Morrice Gn SG8 . . . . **1** A3

Morris Cl PE19 . . . . 117 A3
Morris Ct PE7 . . . . 181 E6
Morris St PE1 . . . . 198 B3
Mortimer La IP28 . . . . 213 C3
Mortimer Rd
  Cambridge CB1 . . . . 246 C2
  Royston SG8 . . . . 5 E6
Mortimer Row 11 PE28 . . 208 C8
Mortimers La CB22 . . . . . . 30 C5
Mortlock Ave CB4 . . . . 84 B6
Mortlock Cl SG8 . . . . 14 C6
Mortlock Gdns CB21 . . . . . 34 C5
Mortlock St PE15 . . . . 14 C6
Morton Ave PE15 . . . . . . 243 E4
Morton Cl CB6 . . . . 240 E8
Morton's Leam ★ PE7 . . . 200 C1
Morton St SG8 . . . . 5 D7
Morton Way 6 PE15 . . . . 223 B7
Mosquito Rd PE26 . . . . . . 171 E3
Moss Bank CB4 . . . . 84 C5
Moss Cl PE26 . . . . 171 B1
Moss Dr CB23 . . . . 47 C5
Moss-Nook CB23 . . . . 79 B3
Mostyn Cl 2 CB6 . . . . . . 216 E1
Moules La CB21 . . . . 20 C6
Moules Yd SG7 . . . . 2 D3
MOULTON 112 E6
Moulton Ave CB8 . . . . . . 134 A2
Moulton CE Prim Sch
  CB8 . . . . 112 E6
Moulton Coll PE1 . . . . . . 198 A1
Moulton Gr PE3 . . . . 197 C6
Moulton Paddocks CB8 . 111 F6
Moulton Rd .
  Ashley CB8 . . . . 112 D1
  Cheveley CB8 . . . . 91 D8
  Newmarket CB8 . . . . 111 D4
Moulton Rd or Kennett Rd
  CB8 . . . . 112 C1
Mountbatten Ave
  Stamford PE9 . . . . 244 A6
  Yaxley PE7 . . . . 181 D5
Mountbatten Ct 6 PE19 . 74 F3
Mountbatten Dr PE13 . . . 245 A7
Mountbatten Way
  Peterborough PE3 . . . . . 197 B6
  Whittlesey PE7 . . . . 190 A6
Mount Dr PE13 . . . . 245 E4
Mounteagle 2 SG8 . . . . . . 5 D5
Mountford Cl CB22 . . . . . . 48 C4
Mountfort Cl 3 PE19 . . . . 74 F3
Mount Pleasant
  3 Cambridge CB3 . . . . . 83 C3
  Great Paxton PE19 . . . . . 96 F4
  Peterborough PE7 . . . . . 187 C2
  Spaldwick PE28 . . . . 137 E6
Mount Pleasant Rd PE13 245 C7
Mount Pleasant Wlk 2
  CB3 . . . . 83 C3
Mount Rd CB9 . . . . 24 A7
Mountsteven Ave
  Gunthorpe PE4 . . . . 204 D2
  Peterborough PE4 . . . . . 204 C1
Mount The
  Barley SG8 . . . . 6 E1
  Toft CB23 . . . . 61 D5
Mouth La PE13 . . . . 235 B4
Mowbray Cl 4 PE13 . . . . 235 B7
Mowbray Rd
  Bretton PE3 . . . . 203 F1
  Cambridge CB1 . . . . 65 C4
Mowfen Rd CB6 . . . . 242 D5
Mowlam Cl CB24 . . . . 104 C2
Mowlands PE29 . . . . 142 A1
Moyne Cl CB4 . . . . 83 D7
Moyne Rd PE28 . . . . 168 C3
Moyse's Bank PE14 . . . . . 236 F6
Muchwood La PE26 . . . . . 221 B1
Mudd's Dro PE14 . . . . . . 229 E6
Mugglestons La PE26 . . . 172 B6
Mulberry Cl
  Bottisham CB25 . . . . 86 F6
  Cambridge CB4 . . . . 83 F5
  Mildenhall IP28 . . . . . . 239 E4
  Whittlesey PE7 . . . . 189 F5
  Yaxley PE7 . . . . 182 B5
Mulberry Way CB7 . . . . . 240 E5
Mullard Radio Astronomy
  Obsy ★ CB23 . . . . 46 E7
Mullein Cl 4 PE19 . . . . . . 74 C5
Mumby's Dro PE14 . . . . . 229 E6
Mumford Theatre ★ CB1 . 246 C2
Muncey Wlk CB24 . . . . . . 104 C5
Munday Way 16 PE13 . . . 238 B2
Munnings Cl
  Haverhill CB9 . . . . 38 D1
  Newmarket CB8 . . . . 111 A4
Muntjac Cl
  3 Bretton PE3 . . . . 197 A5
  5 Eaton Socon PE19 . . . 74 B5
Murfitt's La CB7 . . . . 212 E2
Murfitt Way SG19 . . . . 41 D6
Muriel Cl CB23 . . . . 99 B2
Murrell Cl PE19 . . . . 74 F7
Murrell Ct PE19 . . . . 74 F7
MURROW 234 D5
Murrow Bank PE13 . . . . . 234 D6
Murrow La PE13 . . . . 234 D5
Murrow Prim Sch PE13 . . 234 D5
Murton Cl CB25 . . . . 130 A3
Murton Slade 5 CB9 . . . . 24 A7
Museum of Archaeology &
  Anthropology ★ CB2 . . 246 B2
Museum of Classical
  Archaeology ★ CB3 . . . . 64 C8
Museum of Flag Fen The ★
  PE6 . . . . 199 B2
Museum of Tech ★ CB5 . . 84 B3

Museum Sq 22 PE13 . . . . 245 C5
Musgrave Way
  Fen Ditton CB5 . . . . 84 F6
  7 St Neots PE19 . . . . . . 74 F5
Musker Pl CB23 . . . . 99 B1
Muskham PE3 . . . . 196 F4
Mustards Gapp 5 CB9 . . . 24 C7
Musticott Pl PE13 . . . . . . 245 F6
Mustill's La CB24 . . . . . . 123 B8
Muswell Rd PE3 . . . . 197 C4
Mutlow Hill (Tumulus) ★
  CB21 . . . . 67 F1
Myles Way PE13 . . . . 245 C8
Myrtle Ave PE1 . . . . 198 C7
Myrtle Cl CB25 . . . . 130 B3
Myrtle Ct PE1 . . . . 198 C7
Myrtle Gn PE27 . . . . 144 A5
Myrtle Gr PE1 . . . . 198 C7
Myrtle House Cvn Pk
  PE1 . . . . 198 E5
Myrtle Way PE27 . . . . 144 A5

N

Nansicles Rd PE2 . . . . . . 186 D6
Napier Pl PE2 . . . . 185 C6
Napier St CB1 . . . . 246 C3
Narrow Dro
  Whittlesey PE7 . . . . 188 C5
  Yaxley PE7 . . . . 182 C5
Narrow La CB24 . . . . 104 B4
Naseby Cl PE3 . . . . 197 C5
Naseby Gdns PE19 . . . . . . 75 A4
Nash Rd 7 SG8 . . . . 5 D5
Natal Rd CB1 . . . . 65 C7
Nat Flatman St CB8 . . . . . 111 B3
Nathan Cl PE3 . . . . 197 B2
National Extension Coll
  CB2 . . . . 64 F5
National Horseracing Mus ★
  CB8 . . . . 111 A3
Natures Way PE7 . . . . . . 186 B2
Navigation Wharf 6 PE19 74 E5
Nayland Rd CB9 . . . . 23 E6
Neal Dr CB4 . . . . 83 E8
Neale Cl CB1 . . . . 65 F7
Neale Wade Com Coll
  PE15 . . . . 243 D1
Neaverson Rd PE6 . . . . . 203 F7
Nedderworth Rd PE27 . . . 144 B3
Needham Bank PE14 . . . . 236 C4
Needham Ct PE7 . . . . 181 E4
NEEDINGWORTH 208 B3
Needingworth Rd PE27 . . 144 B4
Nelson Gdns CB24 . . . . . . 245 D6
Nelson Rd
  Eaton Socon PE19 . . . . . 74 B3
  Huntingdon PE29 . . . . . . 142 A4
Nelson's La CB6 . . . . 210 A5
Nene Cl
  Wansford PE8 . . . . 194 A3
  Whittlesey PE7 . . . . 189 D6
  2 Wittering PE8 . . . . . . 230 B1
Nene Inf Sch PE13 . . . . . . 245 D4
Nene Par
  March PE15 . . . . 243 E4
  Wisbech PE13 . . . . 245 B7
Nene Parkway PE3 . . . . . . 196 F1
Nene Quay PE13 . . . . 245 C5
Nene Rd
  Eaton Socon PE19 . . . . . 74 C4
  Ely CB6 . . . . 240 C6
  Huntingdon PE29 . . . . . . 141 E6
  Kimbolton PE28 . . . . 114 A7
  Whittlesey PE7 . . . . 189 E6
Nene Way
  St Ives PE27 . . . . 144 A7
  Sutton PE5 . . . . 194 F2
  Warmington PE8 . . . . . . 178 A2
Neptune Cl CB4 . . . . 83 E7
Ness Rd CB25 . . . . 130 C3
Netherby Dr PE14 . . . . . . 245 E1
Nether Gr CB24 . . . . 123 F2
Netherhall Sch The CB1 . . 65 E4
Netherhall Way CB1 . . . . . 65 D4
Nettle Bank PE14 . . . . . . 235 C4
Neve Gdns IP28 . . . . 213 E6
Neville Rd CB1 . . . . 65 C6
NEWARK 198 E6
Newark Ave PE1 . . . . 198 C6
Newark Cl SG8 . . . . 5 C8
Newark Hill Prim Sch
  PE1 . . . . 198 D6
Newark Rd PE1 . . . . 198 F4
New Barn Dro PE28 . . . . . 173 C4
New Barns Ave CB8 . . . . . 240 D6
New Barns Rd CB7 . . . . . 240 D5
Newbey Cl PE3 . . . . 197 B3
Newbolt Sch SG8 . . . . 5 D8
Newborn Cl PE2 . . . . 187 E5
NEWBOROUGH 207 D1
Newborough Prim Sch
  PE6 . . . . 207 C1
Newborough Rd PE4 . . . . 205 C2
Newboults La PE9 . . . . . . 244 A5
New Bridge La
  Elm PE14 . . . . 235 F6
  Wisbech PE13 . . . . 245 A1
New Bridge Rd PE14 . . . . 236 E1
New Broadpool PE28 . . . . 173 F1
New Cangle Com Prim Sch
  CB9 . . . . 38 F1
Newcastle Dr PE2 . . . . . . 186 D6
New Cheveley Rd CB8 . . . 111 C2

New Cl SG8 . . . . 12 B2
New Close Rd CB6 . . . . . 211 A7
Newcomb Ct PE9 . . . . . . 244 B5
Newcombe Way PE2 . . . . 185 D2
New Cross Dro CB6 . . . . . 216 B3
New Cross Rd PE9 . . . . . . 244 B5
New Cut
  Newmarket CB8 . . . . 111 A3
  Thorney PE6 . . . . 233 D5
New Dro
  Soham PE7 . . . . 211 E4
  3 Wisbech PE13 . . . . . . 245 D2
  Wisbech St Mary PE13 . . 235 C5
Newell Cl SG8 . . . . 44 D1
Newell Wlk CB1 . . . . 65 F7
NEW ENGLAND 197 E7
New England PE28 . . . . . 120 B2
New Farm Cl SG8 . . . . 15 E8
New Farm Cotts CB1 . . . . 20 E7
New Fen Dike PE12 . . . . . 237 A6
New Fen Rd La PE26 . . . . 171 C8
New Field
  Gorefield PE13 . . . . 237 D2
  Newton PE13 . . . . 237 F4
NEWFIELDS 237 D1
New Fields Cvn Pk CB4 . . 84 D6
NEW FLETTON 187 B8
Newgate Rd PE13 . . . . . . 237 F6
Newgates 11 PE9 . . . . . . 244 C5
Newgate St PE15 . . . . . . 222 F5
Newgate Wharf PE15 . . . 223 F4
Newham Rd PE9 . . . . 244 A7
Newington CB24 . . . . 124 B8
New La PE8 . . . . 183 C8
New Lakeside PE7 . . . . . . 186 B1
Newlands Ave PE15 . . . . 243 D5
Newlands Bldgs SG19 . . . 42 A4
Newlands Rd
  Chatteris PE16 . . . . 241 E6
  Parson Drove PE13 . . . . 234 D7
  Whittlesey PE7 . . . . 190 A8
New London Rd
  (Peterborough United FC)
  PE2 . . . . 187 A8
New Long Dro PE7 . . . . . 177 F6
Newman Ave SG8 . . . . 5 F6
Newman 16 PE8 . . . . 230 B1
NEWMARKET 111 B5
Newmarket Bus Pk CB8 . 110 F7
Newmarket Cl PE1 . . . . . 198 B6
Newmarket Coll CB8 . . . . 110 F4
Newmarket Hospl CB8 . . 111 A3
Newmarket Leisure Ctr
  CB8 . . . . 110 F4
Newmarket Rd
  Ashley CB8 . . . . 91 E8
  Barton Mills IP28 . . . . . 239 D1
  Burwell CB25 . . . . 130 C1
  Cambridge CB5 . . . . 246 C3
  Cheveley CB8 . . . . 91 C8
  Cowlinge CB8 . . . . 73 D3
  Fen Ditton CB5 . . . . 85 D3
  Fordham CB7 . . . . 131 D7
  Great Chesterford CB10 . 18 C3
  Lidgate CB8 . . . . 73 C6
  Moulton CB8 . . . . 112 E5
  Royston SG8 . . . . 5 F6
  Snailwell CB8 . . . . 132 B2
  Stow cum Quy CB25 . . . . 85 F4
  Stretham CB6 . . . . 211 A3
Newmarket Sta CB8 . . . . 111 A2
Newmarket Swimming Pool
  CB8 . . . . 110 F3
NEW MEADOW 187 F2
New Meadow Dro PE7 . . . 187 D1
NEWNHAM 64 C8
Newnham Cl
  Huntingdon PE29 . . . . . . 142 A7
  Mildenhall IP28 . . . . . . 239 D5
Newnham Coll CB3 . . . . . 64 C8
NEWNHAM CROFT 64 D7
Newnham Croft Prim Sch
  CB3 . . . . 64 C7
Newnham Croft St 2
  CB3 . . . . 64 C7
Newnham Dro CB25 . . . . 129 C5
Newnham La CB25 . . . . . 130 B3
Newnham Rd CB3 . . . . 64 C7
Newnham St 7 CB7 . . . . 240 D4
Newnham Terr
  Cambridge CB1 . . . . 246 A1
  Newnham CB3 . . . . 64 C8
Newnham Way SG7 . . . . . . 2 B2
Newnham Wlk CB3 . . . . . . 64 C8
New Orchard Pk CB6 . . . 242 E4
New Park St CB5 . . . . 246 A4
New Path CB7 . . . . 212 E1
New Pk PE15 . . . . 243 E5
Newport Ave CB7 . . . . . . 213 A1
Newport Way PE9 . . . . . . 230 F2
New Rd
  Barton CB23 . . . . 63 B4
  Burwell CB25 . . . . 130 B3
  Chatteris PE16 . . . . 241 E5
  Cottenham CB24 . . . . . . 125 E4
  Exning CB8 . . . . 110 B8
  15 Eye PE6 . . . . 232 A1
  Girton CB3 . . . . 103 E4
  Great & Little Chishill SG8 . 15 B1
  Guilden Morden SG8 . . . . 11 A5
  Haddenham CB6 . . . . . . 210 A6
  Harston CB22 . . . . 47 E3
  Haslingfield CB23 . . . . . . 47 B5
  Hemingford Abbots PE28 . 144 E8
  Hinxton CB10 . . . . 18 B6
  Histon CB24 . . . . 104 C3

New Rd continued
  Littleport CB6 . . . . 242 D5
  March PE15 . . . . 243 E4
  Melbourn SG8 . . . . 14 E4
  Mepal SG8 . . . . 216 E3
  Offord Cluny PE19 . . . . 118 A2
  Outwell PE14 . . . . 236 E1
  Over CB24 . . . . 208 D1
  Peterborough PE2 . . . . . 185 E4
  Ramsey PE26 . . . . 172 B7
  Sawston CB22 . . . . 32 E8
  Shudy Camps CB21 . . . . 22 C7
  St Ives PE27 . . . . 144 B3
  Upwell PE14 . . . . 229 E8
  Warboys PE28 . . . . 165 A4
  Whittlesey PE7 . . . . 189 F6
  Woodston PE2 . . . . 186 F7
  Wood Walton PE28 . . . . 161 E7
New River Bank CB7 . . . . 242 F5
New River Gn CB8 . . . . . . 110 B8
New Road Prim Sch PE7 . 189 F6
New Row 8 PE6 . . . . 231 E8
New School Rd CB24 . . . . 104 B3
New Sq CB1 . . . . 246 B3
New St
  Cambridge CB1 . . . . 84 A2
  Chippenham CB7 . . . . . . 132 E8
  Doddington/Wimblington
    PE15 . . . . 222 F5
  Godmanchester PE29 . . 141 F1
  Mildenhall IP28 . . . . . . 239 C4
  Stamford PE9 . . . . 244 C6
  St Neots PE19 . . . . 74 E5
NEWSTEAD 244 E6
Newstead Cl PE6 . . . . . . 232 A2
Newstead La PE14 . . . . . 244 F8
Newstead Rd PE9 . . . . . . 230 A8
NEWTON
  Harston 31 C7
  Wisbech 238 A5
Newton Fen PE13 . . . . . . 237 E4
Newton Pl 9 PE9 . . . . 24 B8
Newton Prim Sch PE19 . . 77 E3
Newton Rd
  Cambridge CB2 . . . . 64 E5
  Great Shelford CB22 . . . 48 D3
  Harston CB22 . . . . 47 F1
  Newton CB22 . . . . 31 A8
  Sawtry PE28 . . . . 168 C4
Newtons Ct PE29 . . . . . . 141 E4
Newton Way PE1 . . . . . . 198 D2
NEWTOWN 64 E7
Newtown PE19 . . . . 74 B8
NEWTOWN
  Huntingdon 141 E5
  Kimbolton 114 A5
Newtown
  Kimbolton PE28 . . . . . . 113 F5
  Stamford PE9 . . . . 244 C4
New Town CB8 . . . . 125 D3
Newtown La PE28 . . . . . . 113 F5
Newtown Rd PE26 . . . . . 172 B7
New Town Rd CB6 . . . . . 209 F6
Next Odsey SG7 . . . . 3 C3
Nicholas Taylor Gdns
  PE3 . . . . 196 F3
Nicholls Ave PE3 . . . . . . 197 E3
Nicholson Way CB4 . . . . . 83 E6
Nigel Rd CB6 . . . . 240 E8
Nightall Dr PE15 . . . . 243 D7
Nightall Rd CB7 . . . . 212 A4
Nightingale Ave
  Bassingbourn SG8 . . . . . 13 A5
  Cambridge CB1 . . . . 65 C3
Nightingale Cl IP28 . . . . 239 D4
Nightingale Ct PE4 . . . . . 205 A2
Nightingale Dr PE7 . . . . . 181 D6
Nightingale Way
  Royston SG8 . . . . 5 E8
  1 St Neots PE19 . . . . . . 75 B7
Nightingale Wlk PE15 . . . 224 B4
Nimbus Way CB8 . . . . . . 110 E8
Nimrod Dr PE28 . . . . 143 A8
Nine Chimneys La CB21 . . 53 B2
Nipcut Rd PE6 . . . . 232 C2
Nixhill Rd PE15 . . . . 223 B6
Noahs Ark CB6 . . . . 242 B5
Noble Gdns PE15 . . . . . . 243 E3
Nobles Cl PE7 . . . . 190 F8
Nobles La PE28 . . . . 208 C5
Noel Murless Dr CB8 . . . . 110 F5
Nook The PE6 . . . . 231 C4
Norburn PE3 . . . . 197 B8
Norfolk Ave CB8 . . . . 110 C5
Norfolk Rd
  Ely CB6 . . . . 240 A3
  Huntingdon PE29 . . . . . . 141 E8
  St Ives PE27 . . . . 144 A8
  Wyton Airfield PE28 . . . 143 B8
Norfolk Sq 3 PE9 . . . . . . 244 B6
Norfolk St
  Cambridge CB1 . . . . 84 A1
  Doddington/Wimblington
    PE15 . . . . 223 B7
  Peterborough PE1 . . . . . 197 F4
  Wisbech PE13 . . . . 245 C4
Norfolk Terr CB1 . . . . 84 A1
Norgett's La SG8 . . . . 14 D6
Norham Ct PE7 . . . . 188 A5
Norico Bay PE15 . . . . 243 E2
Norman Cl PE7 . . . . 189 E8
NORMAN CROSS 180 F2
Norman Dr PE7 . . . . 175 F8
Norman Pk CB25 . . . . . . 102 C4
Norman Rd PE1 . . . . 198 C4
Norman's La 8 SG8 . . . . . 5 D5
Normanton Rd PE1 . . . . . 198 C4
Normanton Way CB24 . . . 104 B5

Mor—Nuf **265**

Norman Way
  Cherry Hinton CB1 . . . . . 65 E7
  9 Doddington/Wimblington
    PE15 . . . . 223 B7
  Over CB24 . . . . 123 B7
Normoor Dro PE16 . . . . . 223 B2
Nornea La CB7 . . . . 211 F8
Norris Mus The ★ PE27 . 144 A3
Norris Rd PE27 . . . . 144 A4
Northam Cl PE6 . . . . 232 A2
Northampton Cl 4 CB6 . . 240 A3
Northampton St CB3 . . . . 83 C2
North Ave CB9 . . . . 23 E8
North Bank PE6 . . . . 199 D1
North Bank Rd 4 PE1 . . . 198 D3
NORTHBOROUGH 231 F7
Northborough Prim Sch
  PE6 . . . . 231 F6
Northborough Rd PE6 . . . 206 F1
North Brink PE13 . . . . . . 245 A4
North Cambridgeshire Hospl
  PE13 . . . . 245 D5
North Cl SG8 . . . . 5 C8
North Cotts CB2 . . . . 64 D4
North Dr
  March PE15 . . . . 243 E4
  Newmarket CB8 . . . . 110 F5
  Soham CB7 . . . . 212 B5
North End
  Bassingbourn cum Kneesworth
    SG8 . . . . 12 D6
  Exning CB8 . . . . 130 F3
  Meldreth SG8 . . . . 29 B2
  Wisbech PE13 . . . . 245 B6
North End Rd CB10 . . . . . 18 A8
Northey Rd PE6 . . . . 199 C2
North Fen Dro CB6 . . . . . 218 B8
North Fen Rd PE6 . . . . . 231 F5
Northfield
  Fulbourn CB21 . . . . 67 A5
  Girton CB3 . . . . 103 E2
Northfield Cl SG19 . . . . . . 41 C6
Northfield Pk CB7 . . . . . . 212 A5
Northfield Rd
  Ashwell SG7 . . . . 2 C7
  Peterborough PE1 . . . . . 197 C7
  Soham CB7 . . . . 212 A5
  Wyboston PE19 . . . . 74 A1
NORTHFIELDS 244 C6
Northfields Ave CB8 . . . . 83 E7
Northfields Ct PE9 . . . . . 244 C6
Northfields Rd CB25 . . . . 107 D2
Northgate PE7 . . . . 189 D8
Northgate Cl PE7 . . . . . . 189 D8
NORTH GREEN 190 E8
North La SG19 . . . . 41 B7
North Lodge Dr CB23 . . . . 99 B2
Northminster PE1 . . . . . . 198 A3
North Pl IP28 . . . . 239 C4
North Rd
  Alconbury Weston PE28 . 150 E5
  Brampton PE28 . . . . 140 D1
  Great Abington CB21 . . . 33 F5
  St Ives PE27 . . . . 144 A4
  Whittlesford CB22 . . . . . 32 B6
NORTH SIDE 200 F4
North Side PE6 . . . . 200 F5
North St
  Burwell CB25 . . . . 130 B4
  Cambridge CB4 . . . . 83 C4
  Folksworth & Washingley
    PE7 . . . . 181 A1
  Freckenham IP28 . . . . . 213 C3
  Huntingdon PE29 . . . . . . 141 E5
  March PE15 . . . . 243 D5
  Peterborough PE1 . . . . . 198 A2
  Stamford PE9 . . . . 244 B5
  Stilton PE7 . . . . 176 A8
  Wicken CB7 . . . . 211 E1
  Wisbech PE13 . . . . 245 C5
North Terr
  Cambridge CB1 . . . . 246 C3
  Mildenhall IP28 . . . . . . 239 C4
  Peterborough PE1 . . . . . 198 E7
  Sawston CB22 . . . . 32 F5
Northumberland Ave 4
  PE9 . . . . 244 A6
Northumberland Cl 2
  CB4 . . . . 83 D6
Northumbria Cl CB6 . . . . 210 A7
Northwold CB6 . . . . 240 C5
Norton Cl
  Cambridge CB5 . . . . 84 D3
  Papworth Everard CB23 . 99 A2
Norton Rd
  Haverhill CB9 . . . . 23 E6
  Peterborough PE1 . . . . . 197 F6
Norwalde St PE15 . . . . . . 243 C6
Norwich Rd PE13 . . . . . . 245 D5
Norwich St CB2 . . . . 64 E7
Norwood Ave PE15 . . . . . 243 D5
Norwood Cres PE15 . . . . 243 C6
Norwood La PE4 . . . . 205 B2
Norwood Prim Sch PE4 . . 204 F3
Norwood Rd
  March PE15 . . . . 243 D7
  10 Somersham PE28 . . . 215 C1
NORWOODSIDE 243 C7
Notley Dr CB9 . . . . 38 C1
Nottingham Way PE1 . . . 198 C6
Nuffield Cl CB4 . . . . 84 B7
Nuffield Hospl CB2 . . . . . 64 E6

Nuffield Rd
Cambridge CB4 . . . . **84** B6
St Ives PE27 . . . . **144** C6
Nunns Way 4 CB6 . . . . . . **216** E1
Nun's Orch CB24 . . . . **104** B4
Nuns Way CB4 . . . . **83** F7
Nursery Cl
Isleham CB7 . . . . **212** F4
Mildenhall IP28 . . . . **239** D4
Peterborough PE1 . . . . . . **198** A4
Nursery Dr
March PE15 . . . . **243** B5
Wisbech PE13 . . . . **245** E8
Nursery Gdns
Little Paxton PE19 . . . . . **96** A2
St Ives PE27 . . . . **144** B5
Whittlesey PE7 . . . . **189** F6
Nursery La PE13 . . . . **198** D2
Nursery Rd
Huntingdon PE29 . . . . . . **141** E4
St Neots PE19 . . . . **74** F4
Nursery Way 2 CB23 . . . . **62** C5
Nursery Wlk
Brampton PE28 . . . . **140** C3
Cambridge CB4 . . . . **83** C5
Nutholt La CB6 . . . . **240** D5
Nutters Cl CB3 . . . . **64** A4
Nuttings Rd CB1 . . . . **84** D1

O

Oak Ave PE7 . . . . **186** B2
Oak Cl PE19 . . . . **75** A5
Oak Ct PE7 . . . . **182** A6
Oakdale Ave PE2 . . . . **187** D4
Oakdale Prim Sch PE7 . . **187** C4
Oak Dr
Brampton PE28 . . . . **140** C4
Huntingdon PE29 . . . . . . **141** E8
Little Stukeley PE28 . . . . **151** F3
Mildenhall IP28 . . . . **213** F8
Outwell PE14 . . . . **236** A5
Oak End PE28 . . . . **150** F4
Oakery The CB7 . . . . **240** D6
Oak Farm Cl PE7 . . . . **176** A7
OAKINGTON **103** B5
Oakington Barracks
CB24 . . . . **124** B1
Oakington CE Prim Sch
CB24 . . . . **103** C5
Oakington Rd
Cottenham CB24 . . . . **125** B1
Dry Drayton CB23 . . . . . . **102** D2
Girton CB3 . . . . **103** E3
Oakington & Westwick
CB24 . . . . **103** E7
Oak La
Cheveley CB8 . . . . **91** C4
Littleport CB6 . . . . **242** A2
Oaklands
Fenstanton PE28 . . . . . . **121** B5
Peterborough PE1 . . . . . . **198** B4
Oaklands Ave PE28 . . . . . **163** F7
Oaklands Dr PE13 . . . . . . **245** F7
Oakleaf Rd PE1 . . . . **198** C6
Oakleigh Cres PE29 . . . . . **141** F1
Oakleigh Dr PE2 . . . . **186** C6
Oakley Cl PE13 . . . . **245** E4
Oakley Dr PE28 . . . . **168** B3
Oak Rd
Glinton PE6 . . . . **231** E5
Stilton PE7 . . . . **176** A4
Oakrits SG8 . . . . **14** B8
Oakroyd Cres PE13 . . . . . . **245** C6
Oaks Bsns Pk The CB8 . . . **110** F7
Oaks Dr CB8 . . . . **110** F7
Oaks The
15 Elm PE14 . . . . **236** A5
Milton CB24 . . . . **105** C2
Soham CB7 . . . . **212** B3
Oak Tree Ave CB4 . . . . **83** F5
Oaktree Cl PE15 . . . . **222** F5
Oak Tree Cl
March PE15 . . . . **243** C5
St Ives PE27 . . . . **143** F5
Oaktree Rd CB24 . . . . **121** D6
Oak Tree Way CB24 . . . . . **104** B3
Oak View PE5 . . . . **196** F2
Oak Way PE26 . . . . **220** D3
Oakwood Dr CB23 . . . . **79** B2
Oasthouse Way PE26 . . . . **172** A5
Oates' La CB6 . . . . **216** L1
Oates Way PE26 . . . . **172** C1
Oatlands Ave CB23 . . . . . . **102** B4
Occupation Rd
Cambridge CB1 . . . . **84** A2
Peterborough PE1 . . . . . . **197** E6
Ockendon Cl PE19 . . . . **74** B3
Octagon Dr PE13 . . . . **245** A6
Octavia Cl PE13 . . . . **245** F6
Octavia Hill Birthplace
House★ PE13 . . . . **245** B5
Odecroft PE3 . . . . **197** C7
Odin Cl PE7 . . . . **189** E8
ODSEY **3** C1
Offa Lea CB22 . . . . **31** B7
OFFORD CLUNY **118** F3
OFFORD D'ARCY **118** F1
Offord Prim Sch PE19 . . . **118** A2
Offord Rd PE19 . . . . **97** F6
O Furlong Dro CB6 . . . . . . **224** F1
Ogden Cl SG8 . . . . **14** D6
Oil Mill La PE13 . . . . **245** B5
Oilmills Dro PE26 . . . . **220** F4

Oilmills Rd PE26 . . . . **220** E6
Oklahoma PE28 . . . . **151** F4
Old Allots The MK44 . . . . . **93** A1
Old Auction Yd PE16 . . . . **241** C5
Old Bailey Rd PE7 . . . . . . **181** C8
Old Bank CB7 . . . . **219** B4
Old Brewery Cl CB7 . . . . . **240** E4
Old Broadpool PE28 . . . . . **173** D2
Oldbrook PE3 . . . . **204** A1
Old Bull Yd PE19 . . . . **74** E5
Old Church La PE28 . . . . . **208** C7
Old Clements La 7 CB9 . . . **23** F7
Old Court Hall PE29 . . . . . **141** E1
Oldeamere Way PE7 . . . . . **190** A7
Old Farm Cl
Histon CB24 . . . . **104** B5
8 Needingworth PE27 . . **208** A3
Old Fen Dike PE12 . . . . . . **237** B8
Old Field PE13 . . . . **237** F4
Oldfield Ave PE14 . . . . **236** B5
Oldfield Gdns PE17 . . . . . **189** D7
Oldfield La PE13 . . . . **245** B4
OLD FLETTON **187** A6
Old Fletton Prim Sch
PE2 . . . . **186** F6
Old Ford La PE19 . . . . **114** B2
Oldforge Gdns PE16 . . . . . **241** C5
Old Forge Way PE2 . . . . . . **32** E8
Old Glebe PE28 . . . . **150** E5
Old Great North Rd PE8 . . **194** C2
Old Haverhill Rd CB9 . . . . . **39** E4
Old Houghton Rd PE29 . . **142** B6
Old House Rd CB21 . . . . . . **53** C2
OLD HURST **154** E7
Oldhurst Rd PE28 . . . . . . **155** E8
Old Knarr Fen Dro PE6 . . . **233** C2
Old Leicester Rd PE8 . . . . **194** A3
Old Lynn Dro CB6 . . . . **217** C2
Old Lynn Rd PE13 . . . . . . **245** E4
Old Mill Ave PE28 . . . . **165** A5
Old Mill Cl CB22 . . . . **29** D7
Old Mill La IP28 . . . . **239** F2
Old Mkt PE13 . . . . **245** C5
Old North Rd
Bassingbourn cum Kneesworth
SG8 . . . . **13** B4
Longstowe CB23 . . . . **60** A3
Royston SG8 . . . . **5** C7
Sawtry PE28 . . . . **168** D4
Wansford PE8 . . . . **194** A3
Old Orch The PE15 . . . . . . **222** A5
Old Oundle Rd PE8 . . . . . . **193** A6
Old Pinewood Way CB23 . . **99** B4
Old Pond La PE5 . . . . **195** E2
Old Pools Dro CB6 . . . . . . **225** C4
Old Pound Ct PE28 . . . . . . **143** D2
Old Priory Farm PE6 . . . . **231** F8
Old Railway Ind Est
PE27 . . . . **144** D4
Old Ramsey Rd
St Ives PE28 . . . . **143** E8
Woodhurst PE28 . . . . **154** E2
Old Rectory Dr
Dry Drayton CB23 . . . . . . **102** B1
4 Tallington PE9 . . . . . . **230** F7
Thornhaugh PE8 . . . . **194** A6
Old Rope Wlk CB9 . . . . **23** E7
Old Rorge Gdns PE16 . . . . **241** C5
Old School Cl
Burwell CB25 . . . . **130** C3
Littleport CB6 . . . . **242** D5
1 Soham CB7 . . . . **212** B3
Old School Dr PE16 . . . . . **241** C5
Old School Gdns 3 PE19 . **74** C2
Old School La
Brinkley CB8 . . . . **70** E1
Milton CB24 . . . . **105** D2
Whittlesford CB22 . . . . . . **32** C5
Wicken CB7 . . . . **211** B1
Old South Eau Bank PE6 . **233** E8
Old Stable Wlk PE26 . . . . **172** A4
Old Station Pl PE16 . . . . . **241** B5
Old Station Rd
Newmarket CB8 . . . . **111** B4
Ramsey PE26 . . . . **172** A6
Old West Est PE15 . . . . . . **222** A5
OLD WESTON **148** A8
Old Weston Rd PE28 . . . . . **158** A5
OLD WIMPOLE **44** F3
Oliver Cl PE26 . . . . **171** F6
Oliver Cromwell's House★
CB7 . . . . **240** C4
Olive Rd PE1 . . . . **198** C7
Oliver Rd PE27 . . . . **144** B3
Olivers Way PE15 . . . . **243** D2
Olivia Rd PE28 . . . . **140** C3
Ollard Ave PE13 . . . . **245** D7
Ongar Cl PE15 . . . . **84** F4
Onyx Ct 9 PE13 . . . . **245** C4
Opeford Cl PE19 . . . . **118** A3
Open Univ in East of England
1 CB2 . . . . **246** C1
Opportune Rd PE13 . . . . . **245** C6
Orange Gr 1 PE13 . . . . . . **245** C4
Orchard Ave CB4 . . . . **83** E5
Orchard Cl
Balsham CB21 . . . . **52** F3
Bassingbourn SG8 . . . . . . **13** A5
Cottenham CB24 . . . . **125** C3
Eaton Socon PE19 . . . . . . **74** C4
Elsworth CB23 . . . . **100** B4
Girton CB3 . . . . **103** E1
Hail Weston PE19 . . . . . . **95** A1
Haverhill CB9 . . . . **23** F7
Lidgate CB8 . . . . **73** E8
Littleport CB6 . . . . **242** D4
Little Wilbraham CB1 . . . **86** E2
Manea PE15 . . . . **224** B4

Orchard Cl continued
March PE15 . . . . **243** E3
9 Market Deeping PE6 . . **231** E8
Peterborough PE3 . . . . . . **197** D3
Stamford PE9 . . . . **244** B5
Stilton PE7 . . . . **176** A7
Warboys PE28 . . . . **164** F6
Warmington PE8 . . . . . . **178** B3
15 Wisbech PE13 . . . . . . **238** B2
9 Wisbech PE14 . . . . . . **236** A5
Orchard Cres PE28 . . . . . . **208** E6
Orchard Ct PE6 . . . . **232** F3
Orchard Dr
Girton CB3 . . . . **82** E7
Waterbeach CB25 . . . . . . **127** B1
3 Wisbech PE13 . . . . . . **245** E4
Orchard End
Bluntisham/Colne CB28 . . **208** C5
Rampton CB24 . . . . **124** E4
Orchard Est
Cambridge CB1 . . . . **65** F7
1 Little Downham CB6 . . **218** B7
Orchard Gate SG8 . . . . **14** C6
Orchard Gdns
Fenstanton PE28 . . . . . . **121** B5
Gaultree PE14 . . . . **236** D5
Leverington PE13 . . . . . . **238** A1
Orchard Gr PE6 . . . . **231** C7
Orchard La
Brampton PE28 . . . . **140** E3
Huntingdon PE29 . . . . . . **141** E4
Orchard Mews PE2 . . . . . . **186** F8
Orchard Park Prim Sch
CB4 . . . . **83** D8
Orchard Pightle CB21 . . . . **20** B6
Orchard Rd
Barnack PE9 . . . . **230** E4
Eaton Socon PE19 . . . . . . **74** C4
Great Shelford CB22 . . . . **49** B6
Haslingfield CB23 . . . . . . **47** B5
Histon CB24 . . . . **104** C5
March PE15 . . . . **243** E3
Melbourn SG8 . . . . **14** C5
Royston SG8 . . . . **5** B7
Sawston CB22 . . . . **32** F7
Stamford PE9 . . . . **244** B5
Orchard Road S PE15 . . . . **243** E3
Orchard Row CB7 . . . . **212** C2
Orchards CE Prim Sch
PE13 . . . . **245** D8
Orchard St
Cambridge CB1 . . . . **246** B3
Peterborough PE2 . . . . . . **186** F7
Stow cum Quy CB25 . . . . **85** F5
Whittlesey PE7 . . . . **189** D7
Orchards The
Cambridge CB1 . . . . **65** F5
Chatteris PE16 . . . . **241** D5
Great Shelford CB22 . . . . **49** B6
Peterborough PE2 . . . . . . **185** F4
Sutton CB6 . . . . **216** E2
1 Wilburton CB6 . . . . . . **210** C6
Witcham CB6 . . . . **217** A2
Orchard Terr
St Ives PE27 . . . . **144** A4
Whittlesford CB22 . . . . . . **32** C4
Orchard The
Ashley CB8 . . . . **91** F7
Fen Drayton CB24 . . . . . **121** F5
Little Paxton PE19 . . . . . **95** F2
Peterborough PE4 . . . . . . **204** C3
Orchard View
Ashwell SG7 . . . . **3** A3
Waterbeach CB25 . . . . . . **127** B1
Orchard Way
Burwell CB25 . . . . **130** B3
Cambourne CB23 . . . . **79** A3
4 Doddington/Wimblington
PE15 . . . . **223** B7
Godmanchester PE29 . . . **141** F2
Haddenham CB6 . . . . **210** A5
Manea PE15 . . . . **224** B4
Melbourn SG8 . . . . **14** D6
Oakington/Longstanton
CB24 . . . . **103** C5
Offord Cluny PE19 . . . . . . **97** A8
Ramsey PE26 . . . . **172** A4
Royston SG8 . . . . **5** C8
Orchid Cl
13 Eaton Socon PE19 . . . **74** C6
Yaxley PE7 . . . . **181** F7
Orchid Fare CB23 . . . . **80** C2
Oregon PE28 . . . . **151** E4
Orford Rd CB9 . . . . **23** F6
Orkney Cl CB9 . . . . **24** D7
Orme Rd PE3 . . . . **197** D4
Orthwaite PE29 . . . . **141** B6
Orton Ave PE2 . . . . **186** E7
ORTON BRIMBLES **185** D5
Orton Dr CB6 . . . . **217** D1
Ortongate Sh Ctr PE2 . . . **185** E3
ORTON GOLDHAY **185** F3
ORTON LONGUEVILLE . . . **186** B5
Orton Longueville Sch
PE2 . . . . **186** A5
ORTON MALBOURNE **186** B4
Orton Mere Rd PE2 . . . . . . **186** B7
Orton Parkway PE2 . . . . . **185** D4
ORTON SOUTHGATE **185** C2
ORTON WATERVILLE **185** E4
ORTON WISTOW **185** C6
Orton Wistow Prim Sch
PE2 . . . . **185** C6
ORWELL **45** E1
Orwell Cl PE27 . . . . **144** A6
Orwell Dr PE15 . . . . **243** B5
Orwell Furlong CB4 . . . . . . **84** C7
Orwell Gr PE4 . . . . **204** F1

Orwell Rd CB22 . . . . **29** C8
Orwell Terr CB22 . . . . **29** D8
Osborn Cl 3 CB24 . . . . . . **209** A1
Osborne Pk PE13 . . . . **245** C8
Osborne Rd PE13 . . . . **245** B7
Osbourne Cl 3 PE4 . . . . . **204** F1
Osier Ave PE7 . . . . **186** D2
Osier Cl CB7 . . . . **240** E4
Osier Ct 4 PE19 . . . . **74** C6
Osier Holt PE28 . . . . **208** D6
Osiers The PE19 . . . . **117** A3
Osier Way CB23 . . . . **79** C5
Oslar's Way CB21 . . . . **66** E5
Osprey PE2 . . . . **185** F2
Osprey Cl PE29 . . . . **142** A7
Osprey Ct PE29 . . . . **141** A5
Osprey Rd CB9 . . . . **24** C7
Osric Ct PE1 . . . . **198** C5
Oswald Rd PE2 . . . . **186** D7
Otago Cl PE7 . . . . **189** F8
Otago Rd PE7 . . . . **189** E8
Othello Cl PE29 . . . . **142** A7
Otterbrook PE2 . . . . **185** D5
Otter Cl CB23 . . . . **102** B4
Otter Way 9 PE19 . . . . **74** B5
Oundle Rd
Elton PE8 . . . . **183** F1
Peterborough PE2 . . . . . . **185** E6
Ouse Fen Rd Or Bank
CB24 . . . . **208** D3
Ouse Rd
Eaton Socon PE19 . . . . . . **74** C4
Kimbolton PE28 . . . . **144** B7
St Ives PE28 . . . . **144** A7
Ouse Valley Way PE19 . . . **117** E4
Ouse Washes Nature
Reserve★ CB6 . . . . **224** D2
Ouse Wlk PE29 . . . . **141** E4
Outfield PE3 . . . . **204** A1
OUTWELL **236** F3
Outwell Rd
Boyces Bridge PE14 . . . . **236** D4
Elm PE14 . . . . **236** C5
Outwell PE14 . . . . **236** E3
OVER **208** L1
Overchurch Cl CB9 . . . . **23** F7
Overcote La PE27 . . . . **208** B2
Overcote Rd CB24 . . . . . . **208** D1
Overend PE8 . . . . **178** D8
OVER END **178** D7
Overhall Grove Nature
Reserve★ CB23 . . . . . . **100** F3
Over Hall La CB10 . . . . **21** D2
Overhills Prim Sch PE28 . **113** F5
Over Prim Sch CB24 . . . . . **208** D1
Over Rd
Swavesey CB24 . . . . **122** F8
Willingham CB24 . . . . . . **208** F1
Overstone Ct PE3 . . . . **197** D4
Overstone Dr 1 PE14 . . . . **235** D1
Overstone Rd 2 PE14 . . . **235** D1
Overton Way PE2 . . . . **185** F4
Overwater Cl PE29 . . . . . . **141** A6
Ovington Pl 3 CB9 . . . . . . **24** B8
Owall Wlk 3 SG8 . . . . **5** E8
Owen Cl 3 PE9 . . . . **230** D3
Owen Dr SG8 . . . . **13** D1
Owens Gdns PE7 . . . . **189** C8
OWL END **152** A3
Owl End PE28 . . . . **151** D7
Owl End Wlk PE7 . . . . **181** D5
Owls End PE26 . . . . **172** A4
Owlstone Rd CB3 . . . . **64** C7
Owl Way PE29 . . . . **142** B7
Oxbow Cres PE15 . . . . **243** C4
Oxburgh Cl
Peterborough PE7 . . . . . . **187** F5
Wisbech PE13 . . . . **245** A4
Ox Cl PE3 . . . . **197** A8
Oxclose PE3 . . . . **197** A8
Ox Field PE13 . . . . **237** F3
Oxford Cl
Bassingbourn SG8 . . . . . . **12** F7
Mildenhall IP28 . . . . **239** A5
Wyton PE29 . . . . **143** B8
Oxford Gdns PE7 . . . . **189** C7
Oxford Rd
Cambridge CB4 . . . . **83** B4
Peterborough PE1 . . . . . . **197** F5
Stamford PE9 . . . . **244** A4
St Ives PE27 . . . . **144** A4
Oxford St CB8 . . . . **110** B8
Oxholme Dro CB24 . . . . . . **209** F1
OXLODE **224** C1
Oxney Rd PE1 . . . . **198** C5
Oyster Row CB5 . . . . **84** B3

P

Pacific Cl PE15 . . . . **243** C6
Paddock Cl CB24 . . . . **104** C4
Paddock Row CB23 . . . . . . **100** B4
Paddocks Chase PE19 . . . **118** A3
Paddocks Dr CB23 . . . . . . **111** A1
Paddocks Prim Sch CB8 . **110** E4
Paddock St CB7 . . . . **212** B4
Paddocks The
Alconbury PE28 . . . . **150** F5
Burwell CB25 . . . . **130** B1
Cambridge CB1 . . . . **84** C1
Eastwood End PE15 . . . . **223** B7
Folksworth PE7 . . . . **175** D8
Hilton PE28 . . . . **120** B2
Little Wilbraham CB8 . . . . **68** F6
Peterborough PE4 . . . . . . **204** A5
Whittlesey PE7 . . . . **189** E7
Woodhurst PE29 . . . . . . **155** B4

Paddocks The continued
Worlington IP28 . . . . **213** F4
Paddock The
Bluntisham PE28 . . . . . . **208** C5
Eaton Socon PE19 . . . . . . **74** D4
Ely CB6 . . . . **240** D5
Harston CB22 . . . . **47** F2
Huntingdon PE29 . . . . . . **141** E5
15 Somersham PE28 . . . **215** C1
Stamford PE9 . . . . **244** A5
Paddock Way
Haddenham CB6 . . . . **210** A6
Sawston CB22 . . . . **32** F7
Padgetts Cl PE28 . . . . **165** A5
Padgett's Rd PE14 . . . . . . **229** C3
Padholme Rd PE1 . . . . **198** E3
Padholme Road E PE1 . . . **198** E3
Padlock Rd CB21 . . . . **53** F4
Padnal Bank CB7 . . . . **219** B6
Padnal Dro CB6 . . . . **242** E3
Padney Dro CB7 . . . . **211** D5
Page Ct CB7 . . . . **240** D6
Pages Way 3 PE28 . . . . . . **140** C3
Paget Cl CB2 . . . . **64** E3
Paget Pl CB8 . . . . **111** A6
Paget Rd CB2 . . . . **64** D2
Painter's La CB6 . . . . **216** D1
Pakenham Cl CB4 . . . . **84** A5
Pakenham Pl CB9 . . . . **24** B7
Palace Gdns SG8 . . . . **5** C6
Palace Gn CB7 . . . . **240** C4
Palace La CB7 . . . . **132** D8
Palace St CB8 . . . . **111** A3
PALE GREEN **23** D1
Palisade Ct 3 CB6 . . . . . . **211** B7
Palm Ct PE1 . . . . **198** B8
Palmer Ct PE7 . . . . **189** F6
Palmers Cl CB21 . . . . **35** B3
Palmers La
Alconbury PE28 . . . . **150** F4
Chrishall SG8 . . . . **8** C4
Palmers Rd PE1 . . . . **198** F5
Palmerston Rd PE2 . . . . . . **186** F7
Palmers Way SG8 . . . . **14** C2
Palmers Wlk
Cambridge CB1 . . . . **246** C5
Chatteris PE16 . . . . **241** D5
Pamment's La IP28 . . . . . . **213** D2
PAMPISFORD **33** B5
Pampisford Rd CB21 . . . . . **34** C5
Pamplin Ct 1 CB1 . . . . **65** F6
Panswell La PE14 . . . . **235** C8
Panther Way CB1 . . . . **66** A7
Pantile La CB25 . . . . **130** A3
Pantiles CB21 . . . . **20** B7
Pantiles The PE7 . . . . **189** D8
Panton St CB2 . . . . **246** B1
PAPLEY **174** A6
Papley Grove Farm Cotts
PE19 . . . . **77** C7
Papley Hollow PE19 . . . . . . **77** F8
PAPWORTH EVERARD **99** B3
Papworth Hospl CB23 . . . . **99** F3
Papworth Rd
Graveley PE19 . . . . **98** A5
March PE15 . . . . **243** F4
PAPWORTH ST AGNES . . . **98** A8
Papworth's Cl CB24 . . . . . **208** D1
PAPWORTH VILLAGE
SETTLEMENT **99** A2
Papyrus Rd PE4 . . . . **203** F3
Papyrus Way PE28 . . . . . . **168** B4
Parade La CB7 . . . . **240** C4
Paradise La
Northborough PE6 . . . . . **231** F6
3 Whittlesey PE7 . . . . . **189** D6
Paradise Nature Reserve★
CB1 . . . . **246** C1
Paradise Sports Ctr & Pool
CB7 . . . . **240** D5
Paradise St CB1 . . . . **246** C2
Paragon Rd PE27 . . . . **144** A3
Parcell Wlk PE29 . . . . **118** F3
Parish Bush Dro CB7 . . . . **219** C3
Park Ave
Histon CB24 . . . . **104** A4
Little Paxton PE19 . . . . . **95** F1
Newmarket CB8 . . . . **111** B3
St Ives PE27 . . . . **144** B4
Wisbech PE13 . . . . **245** C6
Park Cl
Bassingbourn SG8 . . . . . . **12** E7
Holme PE7 . . . . **176** F7
Little Paxton PE19 . . . . . **95** E1
Moulton CB8 . . . . **112** F7
Thorney PE6 . . . . **233** B8
Yaxley PE7 . . . . **181** F7
Park Cotts 1 CB8 . . . . **111** B8
Park Cres
Little Paxton PE19 . . . . . **95** F1
Peterborough PE1 . . . . . . **198** B6
Thorney PE6 . . . . **233** B8
Waterbeach CB25 . . . . . . **106** C2
Park Dr
Histon CB24 . . . . **104** C4
Little Paxton PE19 . . . . . **95** F1
Park End CB25 . . . . **87** B4
Parker Rd PE8 . . . . **230** B8
Parker Cl PE19 . . . . **74** E1
Parker's Cl PE16 . . . . **241** B8
Parker's Dro IP28 . . . . **213** D2
Parkers Mill PE28 . . . . **239** C2
Park St CB1 . . . . **246** B1
Parker's Terr 2 CB1 . . . . . **84** A4
Park Est 1 PE6 . . . . **231** F6
Park Farm Cotts CB10 . . . . **18** F6
Park Farm Cres PE7 . . . . . **187** F1
Park Farm Dr IP28 . . . . . . **214** A4

Park Farm La SG8 . . . . 1 A2
Park Farm Rd PE6 . . . . . . 196 E5
Park Farm Way PE7 . . . . 187 F6
Parkfield La PE15 . . . . . . 223 B6
Parkgate PE29 . . . . 141 C6
Parkhall Rd PE28 . . . . . . 215 C2
Park Hill PE21 . . . . 37 C2
Park Home Rd PE7 . . . . . 186 D1
Parkinson's La 1 PE7 . . 189 D6
Park La
  Brampton PE28 . . . . 117 C8
  Castle Camps CB21 . . . . . . 22 F3
  Cottenham CB24 . . . . 125 D4
  Dry Drayton CB23 . . . . 81 C8
  Fen Drayton CB24 . . . . . . 121 F6
  Gamlingay SG19 . . . . 41 C5
  Godmanchester PE29 . . . 141 F2
  Histon CB24 . . . . 104 D4
  Kimbolton PE19 . . . . 113 F2
  Langley CB11 . . . . 1 F2
  Leverington PE13 . . . . . . 238 A3
  Little Downham CB6 . . . . 217 F6
  Longstowe CB23 . . . . 59 F3
  Madingley CB23 . . . . 81 F6
  Newmarket CB8 . . . . 111 B3
  Newton PE13 . . . . 237 F3
  Peterborough PE1 . . . . . . 198 C4
  Stamford PE9 . . . . 244 C4
  Whittlesey PE7 . . . . 189 C7
Parklands SG8 . . . . 5 E6
Park Lane Prim Sch PE7 189 C6
Park Par CB5 . . . . 246 A4
Park Rd
  Brampton PE28 . . . . 140 F2
  Buckden PE19 . . . . 117 B4
  Burwell CB25 . . . . 130 B2
  Cheveley CB8 . . . . 91 C6
  Great Chesterford CB10 . . 18 E5
  Haverhill CB9 . . . . 23 F6
  Manea PE15 . . . . 224 B4
  Market Deeping PE6 . . . . 231 F6
  Peterborough PE1 . . . . . . 198 A3
  Ramsey PE26 . . . . 171 F6
  Sawston CB22 . . . . 32 F5
  Sawtry PE28 . . . . 168 B5
  St Ives PE27 . . . . 144 B4
  St Neots PE19 . . . . 74 F6
  Sutton CB6 . . . . 216 E4
  Tydd St Giles PE13 . . . . . 237 D7
  Wisbech PE13 . . . . 245 D5
Parkside
  Cambridge CB1 . . . . 246 C2
  Chatteris PE16 . . . . 241 C4
  Chippenham CB7 . . . . . . 132 E8
  Haverhill CB9 . . . . 23 F6
  Mildenhall IP28 . . . . 214 A8
  Peterborough PE2 . . . . . . 186 B6
Park Side
  Little Paxton PE19 . . . . . . 95 E1
  St Ives PE27 . . . . 144 B4
Parkside Coll CB1 . . . . . . 246 C2
Parkside Pools CB1 . . . . 246 C2
Park St
  Cambridge CB5 . . . . 246 A4
  Chatteris PE16 . . . . 241 C4
  Dry Drayton CB23 . . . . . . 102 C1
  Peterborough PE2 . . . . . . 186 F7
  2 Wisbech PE13 . . . . 245 D5
Parks The PE15 . . . . 243 F5
Park Street Prim Sch
  CB5 . . . . 246 A3
Park Terr
  Cambridge CB1 . . . . 246 B2
  Peterborough PE1 . . . . . . 198 A6
Park The PE28 . . . . 146 E4
Park View
  Bassingbourn SG8 . . . . . . 12 E5
  Little Stukeley PE28 . . . . 151 F1
  Needingworth PE27 . . . . 208 A4
Park View E PE15 . . . . . . 243 C4
Park View W PE15 . . . . . 243 C4
Parkway
  Shudy Camps CB21 . . . . . . 22 C6
  St Ives PE27 . . . . 144 B4
  The Stukeleys PE29 . . . . 141 A5
Park Way
  Little Paxton PE19 . . . . . . 95 F1
  Offord Cluny PE19 . . . . . 118 A2
  St Neots PE19 . . . . 74 F7
Parkway Mid Sch CB9 . . . 23 D8
Parliament St PE1 . . . . . 197 F5
Parlour Cl CB24 . . . . 104 B5
Parnwell Prim Sch PE1 . 198 E4
Parnwell Way PE1 . . . . . . 198 F6
Parr CB24 . . . . 104 C2
Parrens Rd PE28 . . . . 208 E6
Parr Rd CB9 . . . . 23 D6
Parsonage Barns CB25 . . 86 F5
Parsonage Cl
  Burwell CB25 . . . . 130 B2
  Duxford CB22 . . . . 17 E8
Parsonage Farm La CB8 . 90 D7
Parsonage Gdns CB9 . . . . 23 F7
Parsonage La CB25 . . . . . 130 B2
Parsonage St
  Cambridge CB5 . . . . 246 C3
  Wistow PE28 . . . . 163 F6
Parsonage Way CB21 . . . . 35 D2
Parson Dro La PE13 . . . . 238 B2
PARSON DROVE 234 D7
Parson's Ct CB2 . . . . 246 A4
Parson's Dr PE28 . . . . . . 139 A4
Parsons Gn PE27 . . . . . . 144 C4
Parson's La CB6 . . . . 242 C4
Parson's Land Dro PE15 222 D4
Parthia Cl SG8 . . . . 5 E6
Partridge Cl PE7 . . . . 181 C5
Partridge Dr CB23 . . . . . 102 B3

Partridge Gr PE4 . . . . 204 A5
Partridge Hill SG7 . . . . 2 C3
Paske Ave CB9 . . . . 23 F7
Passage The 10 CB7 . . . . 240 D4
PASTON 204 B4
Paston La PE4 . . . . 197 D8
Paston Parkway PE4 . . . 204 E4
Paston Ridings PE4 . . . . 204 F1
Paston Ridings Prim Sch
  PE4 . . . . 204 F1
Pasture Cl PE28 . . . . 165 A5
Pasture Gr 7 CB6 . . . . . . 240 A3
Pasture La PE6 . . . . 231 F6
Pastures The CB23 . . . . . . 81 A1
Pasture The 2 PE28 . . . . 208 B8
Pates Cl CB23 . . . . 47 A6
Pathfinder Way
  Ramsey PE26 . . . . 171 F5
  Warboys PE28 . . . . 164 F4
  Wyton PE28 . . . . 143 A8
Patterdale Dr PE4 . . . . . . 205 A2
Patterdale Rd PE4 . . . . . 205 A2
Paulsgrove PE2 . . . . 185 D5
Pavement The PE27 . . . . 144 A3
Pavilion Cl PE29 . . . . 141 F2
Pavilion Ct
  Haverhill CB9 . . . . 24 B7
  7 Kings Hedges CB4 . . . 83 E8
Paxton Cl CB24 . . . . 125 E3
Paxton Hill PE19 . . . . 96 D2
Paxton Pitts Nature
  Reserve ★ PE19 . . . . 96 A3
Paxton St
  Offord Darcy PE19 . . . . . . 96 F7
  Peterborough PE2 . . . . . 185 D4
Payne Ave PE13 . . . . 245 D7
Paynells PE2 . . . . 186 A3
Payne Prim Sch PE13 . . . 234 D7
Paynesholm PE4 . . . . 205 A1
Paynes Mdw CB21 . . . . . . 35 C3
Payton Way CB25 . . . . . . 106 B7
Peacock Dr CB25 . . . . 86 F7
Peacocks CB22 . . . . 49 A4
Peacock Way
  Littleport CB6 . . . . 242 E4
  Peterborough PE3 . . . . . . 196 F2
Peake Cl PE2 . . . . 186 F6
Peakes Dr PE7 . . . . 201 F1
PEAKIRK 206 B1
Peakirk cum Glinton Prim
  Sch PE6 . . . . 203 E8
Peakirk Rd
  Deeping Gate PE6 . . . . . 231 F8
  Glinton PE6 . . . . 203 F8
  Northborough PE6 . . . . . 206 A4
Pearks Ct PE29 . . . . 141 A5
Pearce Cl CB3 . . . . 64 B8
Pearces Rd PE6 . . . . 199 B5
Pearl Cl CB4 . . . . 84 A4
Pearmain Ct CB4 . . . . 84 C5
Pearmains Cl SG8 . . . . 45 E1
Pearson Cl
  Milton CB24 . . . . 105 D1
  St Neots PE19 . . . . 74 E2
Pear Tree La CB24 . . . . . 234 C2
Pear Tree Cl
  Fenstanton PE28 . . . . . . 121 A5
  Haddenham CB6 . . . . . . 210 A5
Pear Tree Cres PE13 . . . 238 A2
Peartree Way 10 PE14 . . 236 A5
Pease Way CB24 . . . . 103 F4
PEAS HILL 243 B6
Peas Hill CB2 . . . . 246 A2
Peas Hill PE15 . . . . 243 A5
Peas Mkt Hill CB9 . . . . . . 24 A8
Peate Cl PE29 . . . . 141 F1
Peatlings La PE13 . . . . . . 245 A6
Peckover Dr PE7 . . . . 187 F5
Peckover Dr PE13 . . . . . . 245 E4
Peckover House & Gdn ★
  PE13 . . . . 245 B5
Peckover Prim Sch PE13 245 B6
Pecks Cl PE28 . . . . 120 C1
Pecks Yd PE16 . . . . 241 C5
Peddars Way PE3 . . . . . . 197 A2
Pedley La PE13 . . . . 245 A6
Peer Rd PE19 . . . . 74 B4
Pegler Ct 5 CB24 . . . . . . 209 A1
Pegton Dr PE13 . . . . 245 E5
Pelham Cl
  Cottenham CB24 . . . . . . 125 D3
  Peterborough PE2 . . . . . 196 F2
Pelham Ct CB4 . . . . 83 C6
Pelham Way CB24 . . . . . . 125 D3
Pelican Pre-Prep Sch The
  CB1 . . . . 65 B4
Pemberton Pl CB2 . . . . . 246 B1
Pemberton Terr CB2 . . . 246 B1
Pembroke Ave
  Peterborough PE2 . . . . . 185 F5
  9 St Neots PE19 . . . . 74 F2
  Waterbeach CB25 . . . . . 105 F8
Pembroke Cl
  Huntingdon PE29 . . . . . . 141 F7
  Mildenhall IP28 . . . . 239 C5
  2 Newmarket CB8 . . . . . 111 B3
Pembroke Coll CB2 . . . . 246 A2
Pembroke Gr PE6 . . . . . . 203 F8
Pembroke La CB21 . . . . . . 35 E2
Pembroke Rd PE9 . . . . . . 244 A7
Pembroke St CB2 . . . . . . 246 A2
Pembroke Way CB1 . . . . . 85 B1
Penarth Pl CB3 . . . . 64 A8
Pen Cl CB1 . . . . 66 A6
Pendleton PE3 . . . . 197 B6
Pendragon Cty Prim Sch
  CB23 . . . . 99 A3
Pendragon Hill CB23 . . . . 99 A4

Pendula Rd PE13 . . . . 245 E7
Pen Hills Nature Reserve ★
  . . . . 4 E3
Pennine Way PE4 . . . . . . 204 D2
Pennington PE2 . . . . 185 E3
Pennington Rd PE29 . . . 142 A7
Pennway 11 PE28 . . . . . . 215 C1
Penrith Gr PE4 . . . . 205 A2
Penrose Cl PE2 . . . . 245 E4
Penrwyn Ct 5 PE19 . . . . . 74 F1
Pentelowes The PE28 . . 135 D2
Pentlands Cl CB4 . . . . . . 246 C4
Pentlands Cl CB1 . . . . . . 246 C4
Pentlands The PE4 . . . . . 204 E2
Pentlow Hawke Cl CB9 . . 24 B7
Penwald Cl 7 PE6 . . . . . 232 B8
Penwald Ct PE6 . . . . 206 B1
Penyale PE3 . . . . 197 A1
Pepper CL CB25 . . . . 12 F4
Peppercorn Cl PE1 . . . . . 197 E6
Peppercorns La 2 PE19 . 74 C2
Pepperslade PE21 . . . . . . 31 F1
Pepys House ★ PE28 . . . 140 F2
Pepys Rd
  Brampton PE28 . . . . 140 F2
  St Neots PE19 . . . . 75 A4
Pepys Terr CB24 . . . . 104 C1
Pepys Way CB3 . . . . 82 E8
Percheron CB24 . . . . 104 D3
Percheron Dr PE15 . . . . . 243 E2
Percival St PE3 . . . . 197 E2
Peregrine Cl PE29 . . . . . 142 A7
Peregrine St 1 PE7 . . . . 186 D1
Perkins La 7 PE6 . . . . . . 231 C7
Perne Cl CB1 . . . . 65 C6
Perne Rd CB1 . . . . 65 C6
Pernys Cl PE7 . . . . 186 D3
Perowne St CB1 . . . . 84 A1
Perry Cl CB6 . . . . 210 A6
Perry Ct CB3 . . . . 83 A2
Perry Dr SG8 . . . . 5 E7
Perry Rd
  Buckden PE19 . . . . 116 F3
  Leverington PE13 . . . . . . 238 B2
Perry Wood View PE28 . 115 D2
Perse Prep Sch CB2 . . . . . 64 E4
Perse Sch The CB2 . . . . . . 65 A4
Perse Way CB4 . . . . 83 D5
Pershore Rd CB23 . . . . . . 81 A3
Pershore Way PE6 . . . . . 232 B2
Persimmon Wlk PE28 . . 110 E8
PETERBOROUGH 197 D5
Peterborough Airport
  (Conington) PE7 . . . . . . 176 F3
Peterborough Bsns Pk
  PE2 . . . . 185 C5
Peterborough Cath ★
  PE1 . . . . 198 A2
Peterborough Coll of Adult
  Ed PE1 . . . . 198 B3
Peterborough District Hospl
  PE3 . . . . 197 E2
Peterborough Dr
  Bretton PE6 . . . . 196 E2
  Castor PE6 . . . . 196 D3
Peterborough High Sch
  PE3 . . . . 197 D2
Peterborough Mus & Art
  Gall ★ PE3 . . . . 197 F2
Peterborough Nere Valley
  Sta PE3 . . . . 197 F2
Peterborough Rd
  Castor PE5 . . . . 195 E1
  Crowland PE6 . . . . 232 B8
  Eye PE6 . . . . 205 F1
  Newborough PE6 . . . . . . 205 D8
  Peterborough PE7 . . . . . 187 C3
  Wansford PE8 . . . . 194 A3
  Warmington PE8 . . . . . . 178 B4
  Whittlesey PE7 . . . . 189 B7
Peterborough Regional Coll
  PE1 . . . . 198 B5
Peterborough Regional Pool
  & Fitness Ctr PE1 . . . . . 198 B1
Petergate 1 PE9 . . . . 244 B4
Peter Goodin Cl CB24 . . 105 C2
Peterhouse Cl
  Mildenhall IP28 . . . . 239 D4
  Peterborough PE3 . . . . . 197 C3
  Stamford PE9 . . . . 244 B7
Peterhouse Coll CB2 . . . 246 A1
Peterhouse Cres PE15 . . 243 E6
Peterhouse Dr CB8 . . . . . 111 A2
Peterhouse Tech Pk CB1 . 66 A4
Petersfield 3 CB1 . . . . . 246 C2
Petersfield CE Prim Sch
  SG8 . . . . 28 D8
Petersfield Rd CB22 . . . . . 17 D3
Petingo Cl CB8 . . . . 110 D7
Pettis Rd PE13 . . . . 143 E6
Pettis Wlk PE27 . . . . 143 F7
Pettit Rd PE29 . . . . 142 A1
Pettits Cl CB21 . . . . 66 F4
Pettitt's Cl CB23 . . . . 102 C2
Pettitt's La CB23 . . . . 102 C1
Petts Cl 3 PE13 . . . . 245 E7
Petts La CB10 . . . . 19 E1
Petty Cury CB2 . . . . 246 A2
Petworth St CB1 . . . . 84 A2
Peverel Cl CB5 . . . . 84 D3
Peverel Rd CB5 . . . . 84 D3
Peveril Rd PE1 . . . . 197 F6
Peyton Ave PE15 . . . . 243 B6
Peyton Cl PE15 . . . . 223 A5
Pheasant Gr PE4 . . . . . . 204 A5
Pheasant Rise CB23 . . . . 102 A3
Pheasant Way PE7 . . . . . 181 D5

Philip Gdns PE19 . . . . 74 F2
Philippa Cl CB6 . . . . 240 E7
Philipps Cl
  Exning CB8 . . . . 110 B8
  Newmarket CB8 . . . . 110 D4
Phillips Ave SG8 . . . . 5 C8
Phillips Chase PE15 . . . . 243 C4
Phillips Ct PE9 . . . . 244 C5
Phillips' Fen Dro CB7 . . . 219 B6
Phoenix Rd CB9 . . . . 24 A5
Phoenix Sch PE2 . . . . 186 B4
Phoenix Sq PE19 . . . . 74 E6
Phorpres Cl PE7 . . . . 186 D3
Phorpres Houses PE2 . . 186 F4
Phorpres Way PE7 . . . . . 186 F4
Pickards Way PE13 . . . . . 245 A6
Pickle Fen Dro PE16 . . . 215 E6
Picknage Rd SG8 . . . . 7 A2
PIDLEY 155 E8
Pidley Hill PE28 . . . . 208 A8
Pidley Sheep La PE28 . . 155 F7
Pieces La CB25 . . . . 106 B8
Pieces Terr CB25 . . . . . . 106 B7
Pierce Cres PE8 . . . . 178 C3
Pierce La CB21 . . . . 66 F5
Pigeons Cl SG8 . . . . 31 C2
Pightle Cl
  Harston CB22 . . . . 47 D2
  Royston SG8 . . . . 5 C7
Pightle The
  Bottisham CB25 . . . . 86 E6
  Grafham PE28 . . . . 116 A7
  Haverhill CB9 . . . . 24 A8
Pig La CB7 . . . . 144 B5
Pike's Wlk CB1 . . . . 246 B3
Piketts Cl PE7 . . . . 189 D7
Pilgrims Cl CB10 . . . . 18 D2
Pilgrims Way CB6 . . . . . . 240 A3
PILSGATE 230 C4
Pilton Cl 4 PE4 . . . . 204 F2
Pinder Cl PE29 . . . . 118 F7
Pine Gr CB24 . . . . 122 E3
Pines Ind Est The CB8 . . 131 F4
Pines The CB21 . . . . 66 E6
Pine Tree Cl PE15 . . . . . . 198 B8
Pine Trees Ave IP28 . . . . 239 E4
Pine View CB24 . . . . 126 A7
Pinewood Ave
  Whittlesey PE7 . . . . 189 E7
  Wittering PE8 . . . . 230 B1
Pinfold La
  Godmanchester PE29 . . 141 F1
  1 Somersham PE28 . . . 208 B8
  Stamford PE9 . . . . 244 D5
Pinfold Rd PE14 . . . . 236 E1
Pingle Bank PE7 . . . . 177 A4
Pingle Cl PE7 . . . . 189 C7
Pingle Dro CB6 . . . . 216 E6
Pingle La
  Haddenham CB6 . . . . . . 210 B8
  Northborough PE6 . . . . . 231 F6
Pingle The PE7 . . . . 231 F6
Pingle Wood & Cutting
  Nature Reserve ★ PE28 . 165 A8
Pinhoe Dr PE29 . . . . 23 C8
Pinkeneys SG8 . . . . 8 D5
Pioneer Cl CB24 . . . . 104 B2
Pioneer Way PE6 . . . . . . 232 B1
Pipe La PE1 . . . . 198 B2
Piperell Way CB9 . . . . 24 A5
Pipers Cl PE3 . . . . 24 C7
Pipers La PE29 . . . . 141 F1
Pipistrelle Cl PE19 . . . . . 96 A2
Pipistrelle Ct 6 PE4 . . . 204 C3
Pipit Cl SG8 . . . . 5 E8
Pippin Cl
  Offord Darcy PE19 . . . . . 117 F1
  Over CB24 . . . . 208 D1
  9 Sutton CB6 . . . . 216 E1
Pippin Dr CB4 . . . . 84 C6
Pippin Gr SG8 . . . . 5 C7
Pippin Pk CB8 . . . . 73 E8
Pippin Pl PE13 . . . . 245 E2
Pippin Wlk CB23 . . . . 81 A3
Pitfield Cl PE28 . . . . 121 C5
Pitsdean Rd PE19 . . . . 57 A4
Pits La PE15 . . . . 243 D1
Pits The CB7 . . . . 213 A4
Pittneys PE4 . . . . 204 F1
Pius Dro PE14 . . . . 236 E2
Place Farm Com Prim Sch
  CB9 . . . . 23 F8
PLACE HOUSE 93 E6
Plains La CB6 . . . . 225 C3
Plaistow Way SG8 . . . . 7 E2
Plane Tree La SG19 . . . . . 41 C6
Plank Dro PE6 . . . . 232 B8
Plantation Gate CB6 . . . 210 F5
Plantation Rd CB22 . . . . . 33 A7
Plantwater Dro PE15 . . . 227 D5
Plash Dro PE13 . . . . 234 F4
Playles Yd SG8 . . . . 12 E5
Playsteds La CB23 . . . . . . 79 C4
Plough Cl SG8 . . . . 3 B8
Plough Cres 1 PE7 . . . . 189 C8
Plough La PE6 . . . . 207 D1
Plough Rd PE7 . . . . 189 D8
Plover Cl PE16 . . . . 241 C5
Plover Dr PE15 . . . . 243 F5
Ploverly PE4 . . . . 204 C4
Plover Rd PE7 . . . . 189 F8
Plowright Cl PE15 . . . . . . 243 B3
Plumian Way CB21 . . . . . . 53 C2
Plumpton Ave PE19 . . . . 239 C5
Plum Tree Cl 3 CB4 . . . . 83 D7
Polecat La PE28 . . . . 150 E5
Poles Ct PE7 . . . . 189 C7
Pollards La IP28 . . . . 213 D7

Pond Cl
  Eastwood End PE15 . . . 223 B6
  Pidley cum Fenton PE28 . 165 D1
  The Stukeleys PE29 . . . . 140 F5
PONDERSBRIDGE 220 D7
Pond Gn CB7 . . . . 211 E1
Pond La CB6 . . . . 218 A6
Pond The CB6 . . . . 210 A7
Ponsonby Dr PE2 . . . . . . 186 D8
Pont's Hill CB6 . . . . 242 D5
Pooley Way PE7 . . . . 181 D6
Pools Rd CB6 . . . . 210 D8
Pool Way PE5 . . . . 84 C2
Poorsfield Rd 2 CB25 . . 106 A7
Poor's Land SG8 . . . . 6 D4
Pope Rd PE19 . . . . 74 F3
Popes Ct 3 CB9 . . . . 24 E5
Popes La
  Thetford CB6 . . . . 211 B7
  Warboys PE28 . . . . 164 E4
Pope's La PE13 . . . . 238 A2
Pope Way PE1 . . . . 197 E8
Popham Cl PE19 . . . . 74 A3
Pophams Eau ★ PE14 . . 229 C7
Poplar Ave PE1 . . . . 198 C8
Poplar Cl
  Great Gransden SG19 . . . 58 D4
  Great Shelford CB22 . . . . 49 A5
  Haverhill CB9 . . . . 38 D1
  Huntingdon PE29 . . . . . . 141 E7
  March PE15 . . . . 243 C5
  Royston SG8 . . . . 5 E7
Poplar Dr SG8 . . . . 5 E7
Poplar Dro CB6 . . . . 242 F8
Poplar Farm La SG8 . . . . 12 D4
Poplar Rd CB24 . . . . 104 B3
Poplars Cl CB25 . . . . 130 B2
Poplars The
  Bluntisham/Colne PE28 . . 208 C6
  Stukeley PE29 . . . . 140 F5
Poplar Way CB22 . . . . 49 C4
Popple Dro PE13 . . . . 235 A8
Poppy Cl
  Ramsey St Mary's PE26 . 220 D3
  Yaxley PE7 . . . . 182 A7
Poppy Fields 7 PE7 . . . . 212 B5
Poppyfields Ave PE15 . . 224 B4
Porch Cl PE29 . . . . 141 F1
Porson Ct CB2 . . . . 64 E4
Porson Rd CB2 . . . . 64 D5
Portchester Cl PE2 . . . . . 187 F5
Porters Yd PE16 . . . . 241 C6
Port La PE5 . . . . 195 E1
Portland Ave PE1 . . . . . . 197 F7
Portland Gn CB8 . . . . 110 E3
Portland Pl
  Cambridge CB1 . . . . 246 C3
  Whittlesey PE7 . . . . 189 E6
Portland Rd CB8 . . . . 110 E3
Portman PE3 . . . . 197 C4
Portobello La CB22 . . . . . 32 E7
Portugal PE2 . . . . 246 A3
Portugal St CB5 . . . . 246 A3
Portway SG8 . . . . 14 E7
Portway Rd CB23 . . . . 81 A1
Post Office La 9 PE13 . . 245 C5
Post St PE29 . . . . 141 E2
Potter's La CB7 . . . . 240 D3
Potters Way PE1 . . . . 198 B1
Pott Hall Rd IP28 . . . . . . 213 E6
Potton End PE19 . . . . 77 E3
Potton Rd
  Everton SG19 . . . . 40 C3
  Fenstanton PE28 . . . . . . 120 C3
  Gamlingay Great Heath
    SG19 . . . . 40 F3
  Gamlingay SG19 . . . . 41 D3
  Guilden Morden SG8 . . . . 10 F6
  Hilton PE28 . . . . 99 B8
  St Neots PE19 . . . . 74 F2
  Wrestlingworth SG19 . . . 25 B4
Potton Wood ★ SG19 . . . 25 A8
Poulter Ave PE2 . . . . 187 D5
Poulter's Dro PE14 . . . . . 229 D5
Pound Cl
  Bottisham CB25 . . . . 86 E7
  Burwell CB25 . . . . 130 B2
  Hail Weston PE19 . . . . . . 95 B1
  Spaldwick PE28 . . . . 137 F6
Pound Gn SG8 . . . . 10 F5
Pound Hill CB3 . . . . 83 C3
Pound Hill Cl PE27 . . . . . 144 F5
Pound La
  Isleham CB7 . . . . 213 A5
  Kimbolton PE28 . . . . 113 F4
  Sutton CB6 . . . . 216 E2
  14 Willingham CB24 . . . 209 A1
Pound Rd
  Chatteris PE16 . . . . 241 B6
  Hemingford Grey PE28 . . 143 D1
  Ramsey PE26 . . . . 172 A4
Pound The PE27 . . . . 144 A5
Pound Way CB25 . . . . 108 B2
Powell Cl CB23 . . . . 61 D5
Powis Pl 2 PE19 . . . . 74 F1
Pratt Ave PE4 . . . . 204 F2
Pratt St PE27 . . . . 212 B4
Prentice Cl CB24 . . . . . . 123 F2
Presses Cl PE28 . . . . 208 C5
Preston Cl CB23 . . . . 61 D5
Pretoria Rd CB4 . . . . 246 C4
Priam's Way CB22 . . . . . . 49 B4
PRICKWILLOW 219 B5
Prickwillow Drainage Engine
  Mus ★ CB7 . . . . 219 B5

Prickwillow Rd
Ely CB7 . . . . **240** F5
Isleham CB7 . . . . **212** F7
Soham CB7 . . . . **219** D3
Priestgate 4 PE1 . . . . **198** A2
Priest La CB24 . . . . **209** A1
Priests Meadow Ct CB6 . **240** C5
Primary Ct CB4 . . . . **84** B5
Prime Cl SG8 . . . . **14** C6
Primes Cl CB22 . . . . **29** D7
Primrose Cl
Cambridge CB1 . . . . **66** A5
Peterborough PE2 . . . . **187** A6
Ramsey St Mary's PE26 . . **220** D3
Primrose Dr PE7 . . . . **181** F7
Primrose Farm Rd CB1 . . **86** E2
Primrose Hill
Doddington PE15 . . . . **222** E5
Haverhill CB9 . . . . **23** F7
Little Gransden SG19 . . . . . **58** E3
Primrose La
Huntingdon PE29 . . . . **141** E5
5 Soham CB7 . . . . **212** F5
Waterbeach CB25 . . . . **106** A8
Primrose St CB4 . . . . **83** D4
Primrose View SG8 . . . . **5** F5
Prince Andrew's Cl 1 SG8 . . **5** D5
Prince Cl PE19 . . . . **74** B5
Prince of Wales Cl PE13 . **245** D8
Princes Cl CB21 . . . . **53** C1
Princes Dr PE19 . . . . **75** A6
Princes Gate PE1 . . . . **198** A4
Princes Gdns PE1 . . . . **198** A4
Princes Mews SG8 . . . . **5** C6
Prince South Rd PE13 . . . **245** C4
Princes Rd
Peterborough PE2 . . . . **187** A7
Stamford PE9 . . . . **244** B6
Princess Ave PE15 . . . . **243** C2
Princess Ct CB1 . . . . **246** B1
Princess Dr CB22 . . . . **49** F1
Princess of Wales Hospl
CB6 . . . . **240** E7
Prince's St
Huntingdon PE29 . . . . **141** D4
Peterborough PE1 . . . . **198** A4
Ramsey PE26 . . . . **172** A8
Princess Way
Haverhill CB9 . . . . **23** E8
Newmarket CB8 . . . . **110** E4
Prince St PE15 . . . . **245** D5
Princes Wlk PE15 . . . . **243** D3
Prince William Ct 6 CB8 . **83** C4
Prince William Way CB22 . **32** C1
Pringle Ct PE28 . . . . **151** D4
Pringle Way PE28 . . . . **151** D4
Prins Ave PE13 . . . . **245** D7
Prins Ct 3 PE13 . . . . **245** D7
Prior's Cl CB24 . . . . **104** B4
Priors Ct CB6 . . . . **240** B5
Prior's Ct 8 CB6 . . . . **216** E2
Priors Gate PE4 . . . . **204** A4
Priors Rd
Hemingford Grey PE28 . . **143** C1
Whittlesey PE7 . . . . **189** C7
Priory Ave
Haverhill CB9 . . . . **23** F7
Swavesey CB24 . . . . **122** E5
Priory Cl
Burwell CB25 . . . . **130** B2
Ickleton CB10 . . . . **18** A3
7 Market Deeping PE6 . **231** F8
Royston SG8 . . . . **5** E6
Priory Dro CB25 . . . . **129** C2
Priory Gdns
Peterborough PE7 . . . . **184** F3
Stamford PE9 . . . . **244** D5
Waterside CB7 . . . . **213** A3
Priory Gr PE29 . . . . **141** E5
Priory Hill PE19 . . . . **75** B7
Priory Hill Rd PE19 . . . . **75** A7
Priory Jun Sch PE19 . . . . . **75** A6
Priory La
Huntingdon PE29 . . . . **141** E5
Royston SG8 . . . . **5** D5
St Neots PE19 . . . . **74** E5
Priory Mews
St Ives PE27 . . . . **144** A3
St Neots PE19 . . . . **74** E6
Priory Park Inf Sch PE19 . **74** E6
Priory Rd
Cambridge CB5 . . . . **84** A3
Holywell-cum-Needingworth
PE27 . . . . **208** A3
Horningsea CB25 . . . . **106** A1
Huntingdon PE29 . . . . **141** E5
Needingworth PE27 . . . . . **144** F5
Peterborough PE3 . . . . **197** E3
Stamford PE9 . . . . **244** D5
St Ives PE27 . . . . **144** A2
St Neots PE19 . . . . **74** E6
Priory St 3 CB4 . . . . **83** C4
Priory The PE19 . . . . **74** E5
Priory Wlk CB23 . . . . **79** C3
Proby Cl PE7 . . . . **181** D5
Prospect Pl PE13 . . . . **245** C3
Prospect Rd PE15 . . . . **243** B5
Prospect Row
Cambridge CB1 . . . . **246** C2
9 St Neots PE19 . . . . **74** F5
Prospect Way PE16 . . . . . **241** C6
Prospero Cl PE2 . . . . **186** F6
Prospero Way PE29 . . . . . **141** F7
Provence Pl 7 PE13 . . . . . **245** C3
Provence Rd 2 PE29 . . . . **141** A6

Providence Cl 16 PE28 . **215** C1
Providence Pl PE15 . . . . **224** B4
Providence Way CB25 . . . **127** A1
Pryor Cl CB24 . . . . **105** D2
Puddington Dro PE7 . . . . . **190** D6
Pudding Bag La PE9 . . . **230** C4
Pudding La SG8 . . . . **7** A1
Puddock Rd
Ramsey PE28 . . . . **221** F1
Warboys PE28 . . . . **165** A8
Pudgell The SG8 . . . . **7** E2
Puffin La PE7 . . . . **181** D8
Pump La
2 Hardwick CB23 . . . . **81** A3
4 Stretham CB6 . . . . **210** F5
Purbeck Cl PE13 . . . . **245** A4
Purbeck Rd CB2 . . . . **65** A5
Purley Rd 1 CB23 . . . . **79** A4
Purls Bridge PE15 . . . . . . **224** B2
Purl's Bridge Dro PE15 . . **224** B3
Putney Hill Rd CB7 . . . . . **219** B4
Pyecroft PE1 . . . . **198** B6
Pye Terr CB4 . . . . **84** A4
Pyhill PE3 . . . . **197** B8
PYMOOR **224** E1
Pymore (Pymoor) La
CB6 . . . . **224** E1
Pyrecroft CB23 . . . . **79** A3
Pyrethrum Way 2 CB24 . **209** A1

Q

Quadrangle The PE28 . . . **208** D7
Quadrant The
Royston SG8 . . . . **5** C8
St Ives PE27 . . . . **144** B3
Quail Wlk 3 SG8 . . . . **5** E8
Quainton Cl CB5 . . . . **84** D3
Quaker Cl PE28 . . . . **153** C6
Quaker La PE13 . . . . **245** E3
Quaker's Dro PE7 . . . . **191** F5
Quaker's La CB9 . . . . **24** A7
Quaker Way PE16 . . . . **241** C5
Quanea Dro CB7 . . . . **240** F1
Quarry La
Haslingfield CB23 . . . . **47** B4
Maxey PE6 . . . . **231** C6
Swaffham Bulbeck CB25 . . **108** B1
Quay Ct PE27 . . . . **144** A3
Quay Hill CB8 . . . . **242** E4
Quayside
Cambridge CB1 . . . . **246** A4
Chatteris PE16 . . . . **241** C6
Ely CB7 . . . . **240** D3
Quay The PE27 . . . . **144** A3
QUEEN ADELAIDE **218** D4
Queen Adelaide Way
CB7 . . . . **240** E3
Queen Ann Terr CB1 . . . . **246** C2
Queen Charlotte Mews
PE1 . . . . **198** A6
Queen Edith Prim Sch
CB1 . . . . **65** C4
Queen Edith's Way CB1 . . **65** D4
Queen Eleanor Cl PE7 . . **176** A8
Queen Eleanor Tech Coll
PE9 . . . . **244** B6
Queen Elizabeth Dr
PE13 . . . . **245** D3
Queen Emma Wlk CB6 . . **240** E6
Queenholme Way CB24 . . **209** C2
Queen Mary Cl PE26 . . . . **172** A6
Queensberry Rd CB8 . . . . **111** A3
Queens Cl
Balsham CB21 . . . . **52** F2
Harston CB22 . . . . **48** A3
St Ives PE27 . . . . **144** A5
Queen's Cl
Holme PE7 . . . . **176** F4
1 Over CB24 . . . . **208** D1
Queens' Coll CB3 . . . . **246** A2
Queens Dr
Eaton Socon PE19 . . . . **74** B3
7 Haverhill CB9 . . . . **23** E8
Queens Dr PE29 . . . . **141** F5
Queen's Dr
Mildenhall IP28 . . . . **239** B4
Wisbech PE14 . . . . **236** A3
Queen's Drive Inf Sch
PE1 . . . . **198** A5
Queen's Drive W PE1 . . . **198** A5
Queensgate Ctr PE1 . . . . **198** A2
Queens Gdns PE19 . . . . . . **74** B4
Queen's Gdns PE1 . . . . . . **198** A5
Queens' La CB2 . . . . **246** A2
Queen's Marlborough Coll
The CB2 . . . . **64** E7
Queen's Mdw CB1 . . . . **65** F7
Queens Rd
Littleport CB6 . . . . **242** B5
Peterborough PE2 . . . . **187** B7
Royston SG8 . . . . **5** D7
Somersham CB28 . . . . **215** C1
Wisbech PE13 . . . . **245** C4
Queen's Rd CB3 . . . . **64** C8
Queens St Cl PE15 . . . . . . **243** D6
Queens Sq CB9 . . . . **24** A8
Queens St
March PE15 . . . . **243** D6
Stamford PE9 . . . . **244** B6
Withersfield CB9 . . . . **38** C4
Queen St
Cowlinge CB8 . . . . **73** C1
Haverhill CB9 . . . . **23** E8
Newmarket CB8 . . . . **111** B3
2 Peterborough PE1 . . . . **198** A2

Queen St continued
Whittlesey PE7 . . . . **189** D7
Wisbech PE13 . . . . **245** C6
Yaxley PE7 . . . . **181** F6
Queens View CB8 . . . . **110** A8
Queensway
Cambridge CB2 . . . . **64** E6
Chatteris PE16 . . . . **241** D5
Exning CB8 . . . . **110** B8
Haverhill CB9 . . . . **23** E8
Mildenhall IP28 . . . . **239** B4
Royston SG8 . . . . **5** D7
Sawston CB22 . . . . **32** F8
Soham CB7 . . . . **212** B4
St Neots PE19 . . . . **74** F7
Queens Way SG24 . . . . . . **103** D6
Queens Wlk PE2 . . . . **186** F8
Queen's Wlk PE9 . . . . **244** A5
Quendon Pl CB9 . . . . **24** B8
Quickset Rd CB11 . . . . **9** B5
Quidditch La CB23 . . . . **79** A4
Quince Rd CB23 . . . . **81** A3
Quinion Cl PE7 . . . . **189** F6
Quinton Garth PE3 . . . . . . **197** C5
Quorn Cl PE6 . . . . **205** C8
Quy Ct CB25 . . . . **86** A6
Quy Rd CB25 . . . . **86** B8

R

Raceys Cl PE14 . . . . **236** D6
Racey's Cl PE14 . . . . **236** D6
Rachel Cl 1 CB5 . . . . **84** E4
Rackham CE Prim Sch The
CB6 . . . . **217** E1
Rackham Cl CB4 . . . . **83** C4
Radcliffe Cl 1 PE9 . . . . . . **244** B5
Radcliffe Rd CB5 . . . . **244** A5
Radegund Rd CB1 . . . . **65** B7
Radegunds CB22 . . . . **32** C5
Radford Cl PE8 . . . . **230** C1
Radwinter Rd CB10 . . . . . . **21** B1
RAF Molesworth PE28 . . **147** C8
RAF Witchford Display of
Memorabilia★ CB6 . . . **217** F1
RAF Wyton PE28 . . . . **143** A8
Ragdale Cl PE1 . . . . **198** E7
Railway Cl CB25 . . . . **109** B8
Railway La PE16 . . . . **241** D5
Railway Rd PE13 . . . . **245** C3
Railway St CB1 . . . . **65** F7
Railworld Ex Ctr & Mus★
PE2 . . . . **197** F1
Raine Ave CB9 . . . . **23** D8
Raleigh Cl PE19 . . . . **74** A2
Raleigh Way PE3 . . . . **197** B6
RALINGHAM HALL **229** C6
Ramnoth Jun Sch PE13 . **245** D4
Ramnoth Rd PE13 . . . . **245** D4
Rampart The CB6 . . . . **210** A6
Ramper Rd CB24 . . . . **123** A3
Rampley La PE19 . . . . **95** F2
Rampleys The PE28 . . . . . **143** D2
Ramply Cl PE19 . . . . **95** F1
RAMPTON **125** F4
Rampton Drift
Oakington/Longstanton
CB24 . . . . **124** B2
Westwick CB24 . . . . **103** A8
Rampton End CB24 . . . . . **209** A1
Rampton Rd
Cottenham CB24 . . . . **125** B4
Longstanton CB24 . . . . . . **124** A2
Oakington/Longstanton
CB24 . . . . **123** F1
Willingham CB24 . . . . **124** B7
Ramsden Sq CB4 . . . . **84** A7
RAMSEY **172** B6
Ramsey Abbey Gatehouse★
PE26 . . . . **172** C7
Ramsey Adult Ed Ctr
PE26 . . . . **172** C6
RAMSEY FORTY FOOT . . **221** C2
RAMSEY HEIGHTS **171** A7
Ramsey Hollow Dro
PE26 . . . . **173** B7
Ramsey Hts Nature Reserve★
PE26 . . . . **170** E6
Ramsey Jun Sch PE26 . . **172** A7
Ramsey Leisure Ctr
PE26 . . . . **172** D6
RAMSEY MERESIDE **221** A4
Ramsey Rd
Benwick PE15 . . . . **221** F4
Ely PE7 . . . . **240** E6
Kings Ripton PE28 . . . . . . **153** C5
Old Hurst PE28 . . . . **154** D6
Ramsey PE26 . . . . **221** C2
St Ives PE27 . . . . **143** F7
Upwood & The Raveleys
PE26 . . . . **171** D2
Warboys PE28 . . . . **164** E6
Whittlesey PE7 . . . . **220** E7
Ramsey Rural Mus★
PE26 . . . . **172** D7
RAMSEY ST MARY'S . . . **220** D3
Ramsey Way PE7 . . . . **187** F6
Ramshill Cotts PE6 . . . . . **203** A2
Randalls La CB24 . . . . **208** D1
Rangefield PE2 . . . . **185** E4
Range The PE7 . . . . **240** C4
Ransome's Cl PE14 . . . . . **236** E4
Ransonmoor Dro PE15 . . **222** D7
Ransonmoor Grange
PE15 . . . . **222** F8
Raptor Foundation The★
PE28 . . . . **155** E4

Rasen Ct 2 PE1 . . . . **198** D3
Ratcliffe Ct PE1 . . . . **198** D7
Ratfords Yd CB21 . . . . **68** A8
Rathmore Cl CB1 . . . . **65** A6
Rathmore Rd CB1 . . . . **65** A6
Ravel Cl PE9 . . . . **244** A6
Raveley Fen Rd PE28 . . . . **162** D8
Raveley Rd PE28 . . . . **161** F6
Raven Cl
Mildenhall IP28 . . . . **239** D4
St Neots PE19 . . . . **75** B7
Ravenhill Dr PE15 . . . . . . **243** C3
Ravenscourt 6 PE27 . . . . **208** A3
Ravenscroft PE16 . . . . **241** C6
Ravens Ct CB6 . . . . **240** C5
Ravensdale
Landbeach CB25 . . . . **105** D7
Stilton PE7 . . . . **175** F7
RAVENSTHORPE **197** C6
Ravensthorpe Prim Sch
PE3 . . . . **197** C7
Ravensworth Gdns CB1 . . **65** A7
Rawlyn Cl CB5 . . . . **84** D3
Rawlyn Ct CB5 . . . . **84** D3
Rawlyn Rd CB5 . . . . **84** D3
Rayes La CB8 . . . . **111** A4
Rayleigh Cl CB2 . . . . **64** E5
Raymond St 14 PE13 . . . . **245** C4
Rayner Ave PE2 . . . . **187** E5
Rayner's Cl SG8 . . . . **30** D1
Rays Ct PE15 . . . . **223** B6
Ray's Dro PE26 . . . . **220** B1
Rayson Way CB5 . . . . **84** D3
REACH **130** C1
Reach Dro PE7 . . . . **189** B5
Reaches The PE6 . . . . **232** C3
Reach Rd
Burwell CB25 . . . . **109** B8
Reach CB25 . . . . **129** F1
Read's St CB5 . . . . **210** F5
Ream Cl PE19 . . . . **74** E2
Recreation Cl CB24 . . . . . **105** C2
Recreation Ground Rd
PE9 . . . . **244** B6
Recreation Rd CB9 . . . . **23** F7
Recreation Way IP28 . . . . **239** C4
Rectors Way 3 PE4 . . . . . **204** F2
Rectory Cl
Brampton PE28 . . . . **140** E2
Great Paxton PE19 . . . . . . **96** E4
Oakington/Longstanton
CB24 . . . . **123** F1
Sawtry PE28 . . . . **168** C5
Rectory Dr PE15 . . . . **243** D1
Rectory Farm Cl PE28 . . . **162** C1
Rectory Farm Rd CB1 . . . . **86** F2
Rectory Fields CB6 . . . . . . **216** B3
Rectory Gdns
Glinton PE6 . . . . **203** E8
Godmanchester PE29 . . . **141** F2
Peterborough PE7 . . . . **187** B7
Wisbech PE13 . . . . **245** E6
Rectory La
Abbotts Ripton PE28 . . . . **152** B8
Ashdon CB10 . . . . **21** A1
Etton PE6 . . . . **231** E5
Fowlmere SG8 . . . . **15** E8
Glinton PE6 . . . . **203** E8
Kingston CB23 . . . . **61** B3
Peakirk PE6 . . . . **206** B2
Somersham PE28 . . . . **215** B1
Southoe & Midloe PE19 . . . **95** D6
St Ives PE28 . . . . **142** F5
Rectory Leys PE19 . . . . . . **117** F2
Rectory Rd
Bluntisham/Colne PE28 . . **208** D5
Duxford CB22 . . . . **17** E8
Newton PE13 . . . . **238** B5
Outwell PE14 . . . . **236** F2
Rectory Way PE7 . . . . **175** F7
Red Barn PE4 . . . . **204** A6
Redbridge PE4 . . . . **204** A6
Redcaps La CB8 . . . . **217** E6
Redcot Gdns 8 PE9 . . . . . **244** B6
Redcott Gdns PE9 . . . . **244** B5
Red Cross La CB2 . . . . **65** B3
Red Dock La CB8 . . . . **73** F1
Redbourne La PE26 . . . . . **171** F4
Red Fen Rd CB6 . . . . **210** F7
Redfern Cl CB4 . . . . **83** E6
Redgate Ct PE1 . . . . **198** E7
Redgate Rd
Girton CB3 . . . . **82** E8
Tydd St Giles PE13 . . . . . **238** C8
Red Hill Cl CB22 . . . . **48** E8
Red Hill La CB22 . . . . **48** E8
Redhouse Gdns 3 CB2 . . **212** B3
Redit La CB7 . . . . **211** E1
Redlands SG8 . . . . **8** E8
Redlands Rd CB23 . . . . . . **101** E5
Red Lion Cl PE18 . . . . **150** F4
Red Lion La 6 CB6 . . . . . **216** E1
Red Lion St 12 PE9 . . . . . **244** B5
RED LODGE **213** F1
Redman Cl PE7 . . . . **240** F7
Redmile Wlk PE1 . . . . **198** D8
Redmoor Bank PE14 . . . . **235** F4
Redmoor Ct PE27 . . . . **144** B7
Redmoor La PE14 . . . . **235** F5
Redroofs CB6 . . . . **211** B7
Red Roofs CB6 . . . . **210** B8
Redshank Cl
Haverhill CB9 . . . . **24** C7
6 Soham CB7 . . . . **212** A5
Whittlesey PE7 . . . . **201** A1
Redwell Cl PE27 . . . . **143** E5
Redwing Cl PE2 . . . . **187** D7

Redwing Dr
Royston SG8 . . . . **5** E8
5 Wisbech PE14 . . . . . . **245** D5
Redwing Pl 2 PE19 . . . . . . **75** B7
Redwing Rise SG8 . . . . **5** E8
Redwongs Way PE29 . . . **141** D7
Reed Cl
Cambridge CB2 . . . . **64** E1
Chatteris PE16 . . . . **241** C3
Reedland Way PE7 . . . . . . **186** C5
Reedmace Cl PE6 . . . . **205** C8
Reeds La CB9 . . . . **24** A8
Reed Way PE14 . . . . **236** A4
Reepham PE2 . . . . **185** D4
Reeve Hill SG8 . . . . **8** A6
Reeves Pightle SG8 . . . . **7** F3
Reeves Way PE1 . . . . **198** D5
Regal Dr CB7 . . . . **212** C3
Regal La CB7 . . . . **212** C3
Regal Pl PE2 . . . . **187** A8
Regal Rd PE13 . . . . **245** B2
Regatta Ct CB5 . . . . **84** B4
Regency Sq CB1 . . . . **65** A7
Regency Way PE3 . . . . **197** E1
Regent Ave PE15 . . . . **243** D5
Regent Cl PE19 . . . . **74** B4
Regent Pl 1 CB7 . . . . **212** B3
Regents Ct CB8 . . . . **110** F3
Regent St CB2 . . . . **246** B1
Regent Terr CB2 . . . . **246** B1
Reidy Gdns 2 PE7 . . . . . . **189** C8
Reilly Way CB1 . . . . **65** D8
Rembrandt Way PE27 . . . **144** A7
Renoir Cl PE27 . . . . **144** A7
Resbury Cl CB22 . . . . **50** A1
Retreat The 8 PE6 . . . . . **231** C7
Reubens Rd CB25 . . . . **105** C7
Reynolds Cl PE27 . . . . **144** A7
Reynolds Cl 6 PE19 . . . . . **74** D6
Reynolds Dr PE19 . . . . **95** F1
Reynolds' Dro CB24 . . . . **124** D3
Rhee Lake Dro PE28 . . . . **208** E8
Rhee Mdw CB22 . . . . **29** E7
Rhees The PE28 . . . . **208** D6
Rhine Ave PE2 . . . . **186** E8
Rhonda Pk PE15 . . . . **223** C2
Rhone Pl 3 PE13 . . . . **245** E3
Rhugarve Gdns CB21 . . . . **35** D2
Rhymers Gate PE28 . . . . **142** F5
Ribble Cl PE27 . . . . **144** B6
Ribe Ct CB6 . . . . **240** C4
Ribes Cl PE7 . . . . **186** D3
Ribston Way CB4 . . . . **84** C6
Richard Foster Rd CB2 . . . **64** F6
Richards Cl PE15 . . . . **243** B5
Richardson Way PE7 . . . . **189** E7
Richard Young Cl PE13 . . **245** C4
Richmond Ave
March PE15 . . . . **243** C3
Peterborough PE4 . . . . . . **204** C2
Richmond Cl
Huntingdon PE29 . . . . **141** D8
7 St Neots PE19 . . . . **74** F1
Richmond Ct PE13 . . . . . . **245** A4
Richmond Field PE13 . . . **237** E2
Richmond Rd CB4 . . . . **83** B4
Richmond Terr CB1 . . . . . **246** B4
Richmond Way 6 PE13 . . **238** B2
Rickard Cl CB1 . . . . **65** E6
Rickards CB22 . . . . **32** B4
Rickwood Cl CB6 . . . . **216** C5
Rickyard The SG7 . . . . **2** D3
Riddiford Cres PE27 . . . . **140** C2
Riddy Cl CB22 . . . . **48** B5
Riddy La CB23 . . . . **60** C5
Rideaway PE28 . . . . **119** F2
Ridgefield Prim Sch CB1 . **65** D1
Ridge The PE7 . . . . **186** D1
Ridgeway
Papworth Everard CB23 . . . **99** A4
Perry PE28 . . . . **115** D2
Peterborough PE2 . . . . **187** B8
St Neots PE19 . . . . **74** F7
Ridgeway The CB21 . . . . . . **35** E2
Ridley Hall Rd CB3 . . . . . . **64** C8
Rigg Cl PE13 . . . . **245** B3
Rightwell PE3 . . . . **197** A6
Rightwell E PE3 . . . . **197** A5
Rightwell W PE3 . . . . **197** A5
Riley Cl PE7 . . . . **181** D6
Ringers La PE13 . . . . **238** B2
Ring Fort Rd CB4 . . . . **83** D7
RING'S END. **234** F1
Ringstead Rd PE4 . . . . **204** F1
Ringwood PE3 . . . . **196** F3
Ringwood Cl PE26 . . . . . . **172** A4
Ripon Cl PE4 . . . . **204** B3
Rippons Dro PE6 . . . . **231** F7
Risby PE3 . . . . **197** B8
Riseholme PE2 . . . . **185** E3
Rivar Pl CB1 . . . . **84** A1
Rivendale PE4 . . . . **204** B2
River Bank CB7 . . . . **128** C6
Riverbank Cl
Guyhirn PE13 . . . . **234** F2
12 Market Deeping PE6 . **231** F8
River Cl
2 Benwick PE15 . . . . **222** A5
Little Paxton PE19 . . . . **95** F1
Mepal CB6 . . . . **216** E4
Riverdown PE15 . . . . **243** F5
River Dr PE15 . . . . **243** E4
River Dro PE7 . . . . **191** C5
River End PE8 . . . . **178** C4
Rivergate 3 PE1 . . . . **198** A3
Rivergate Sh Ctr PE1 . . . **198** A3

River La
Brampton PE28 . . . . 140 E1
Cambridge CB5 . . . . 84 A3
Elton PE8 . . . . 178 C8
Fordham CB7 . . . . 212 F1
Great Paxton PE19 . . . . . . 96 D3
Haslingfield CB23 . . . . 47 C5
Peterborough PE3 . . . . . . 197 F2
River Mdw PE28 . . . . 142 F3
Rivermill Gall★ PE19 . . . 74 C2
River Pl PE27 . . . . 144 A4
River Rd
Eaton Socon PE19 . . . . . . 74 C4
Kimbolton PE28 . . . . 114 B7
West Walton PE14 . . . . . . 238 D4
Riverside
Cambridge CB5 . . . . 84 B3
11 Market Deeping PE6 . 231 F8
Riverside Cl
Ely CB7 . . . . 219 B5
Mildenhall IP28 . . . . 239 B4
Whittlesey PE7 . . . . 189 D6
Riverside Ct CB1 . . . . 246 B4
Riverside Gdns
Parson Drove PE13 . . . . . 234 C7
Peterborough PE3 . . . . . . 197 D1
Riverside KS2 Ctr PE2 . . 186 D8
Riverside Mead PE2 . . . . 187 B8
Riverside Mid Sch IP28 . 239 A4
Riverside Pl CB5 . . . . 84 A3
Riverside Rd PE28 . . . . . 141 E4
Riverside Spinney PE8 . 194 A3
Riverside Way PE13 . . . . 245 B3
Riverside Wlk
Ely CB7 . . . . 240 E3
Moulton CB8 . . . . 112 F6
Riversmead PE19 . . . . . . 74 E6
River Terr
3 St Neots PE19 . . . . . . 74 E5
Wisbech PE13 . . . . 245 A8
Rivey Cl CB21 . . . . 35 D3
Rivey Way CB21 . . . . 35 D2
Roan Wlk 8 SG8 . . . . 5 E6
Robbs Wlk PE27 . . . . . . 144 A3
Robden Ct PE2 . . . . 197 E1
Robert Arkenstall Prim Sch
CB6 . . . . 210 A6
Robert Ave
Peterborough PE1 . . . . . . 197 F8
4 Somersham PE28 . . . . 215 C1
Robert Jennings Cl CB4 . . 84 A6
Robert May Cl CB1 . . . . . . 65 D7
Robert Rayner Cl PE2 . . 186 D6
Roberts Cl PE19 . . . . 74 B2
Robertson Cl PE28 . . . . . 152 E1
Robertson Way PE29 . . . 152 E1
Robin Cl
Bar Hill CB23 . . . . 102 C4
Haverhill CB9 . . . . 24 C7
Mildenhall IP28 . . . . 239 D4
Robingoodfellow's La
PE15 . . . . 243 C6
Robin Goodfellow's La
PE15 . . . . 243 D5
Robin Hood Cl PE3 . . . . . 196 F2
Robin Mews 4 PE14 . . . . 245 D2
Robins Cl
5 Ely CB6 . . . . 240 B5
8 Isleham CB7 . . . . 213 A5
Peterborough PE2 . . . . . . 186 E8
Robins Field PE28 . . . . . 194 A4
Robins' La CB23 . . . . 101 F5
Robinson Coll CB3 . . . . . . 83 B1
Robinson Ct CB2 . . . . 49 A4
Robinson Way CB2 . . . . . 65 A3
Robins Wood PE8 . . . . . 194 A4
Robshaw Cl 4 PE15 . . . . 243 E4
Rocester Way SG8 . . . . 5 D8
Rochford Wlk 5 PE13 . . 245 C4
Rochford Ave CB8 . . . . . 110 E5
Rockall Cl CB9 . . . . 24 D7
Rockingham Gr PE4 . . . . 204 C2
Rockingham Rd PE28 . . . 168 B3
Rockingham Yd CB8 . . . . . 90 D8
Rockmill End CB24 . . . . . 209 A1
Rock Rd
Cambridge CB1 . . . . 65 A6
Peterborough PE1 . . . . . . 197 F6
Royston SG8 . . . . 5 C8
Stamford PE9 . . . . 244 B5
Rodham Rd PE15 . . . . . . 228 F5
Rodings The CB5 . . . . 84 E4
Rodney Rd PE29 . . . . . . 142 A6
Roedeer Cl CB1 . . . . 66 A7
Roe Gn PE19 . . . . 74 B5
Roe's Cl CB22 . . . . 32 F8
Roger's Cl CB23 . . . . 100 B4
Rogers End CB10 . . . . 21 B1
Rogers Rd CB25 . . . . 108 E6
Rogues La CB23 . . . . 99 D5
Roland Cl CB4 . . . . 83 E5
Rolfe Cl IP28 . . . . 213 C7
Rolleston Garth PE1 . . . 198 C8
Rolls Cl PE7 . . . . 181 E7
Rollys La SG7 . . . . 2 D4
Roman Bank
Newton PE13 . . . . 238 B4
Stamford PE9 . . . . 244 A4
Roman Cl
Burwell CB25 . . . . 130 A2
Whittlesey PE7 . . . . 189 F8
Roman Courts CB4 . . . . . . 83 E8
Roman Dr PE28 . . . . 194 D2
Roman Drift CB23 . . . . . . 80 C1
Roman Hill CB23 . . . . 63 C4
Roman Way
Godmanchester PE29 . . . 142 A1
Haverhill CB9 . . . . 24 D7

Roman Way *continued*
March PE15 . . . . 243 E6
Perry PE28 . . . . 115 D2
Stilton PE7 . . . . 176 A8
Roman Way Fst Sch SG8 . . 5 D8
Romany Gdns PE2 . . . . . 187 D5
Romney Cl PE27 . . . . . . 144 A7
Romney Ct 2 PE19 . . . . . 74 C5
Romsey Mews CB1 . . . . . . 65 B7
Romsey Rd CB1 . . . . 65 C8
Romsey Terr CB1 . . . . 65 B7
ROMSEY TOWN 65 B8
Ronaldsway 5 PE15 . . . . 222 F5
Ronalds Way PE16 . . . . . 241 C5
Rookery Cl
Great Chesterford CB10 . . . 18 D3
St Ives PE27 . . . . 144 C4
Waterbeach CB25 . . . . . . 106 A8
Rookery Pl PE28 . . . . . . 121 C5
Rookery Rd PE19 . . . . 74 A1
Rookery The
Balsham CB21 . . . . 53 A2
Little Paxton PE19 . . . . . . 95 F2
8 Newmarket CB8 . . . . 111 A3
Peterborough PE2 . . . . . . 185 C7
Yaxley PE7 . . . . 181 D5
Rookery Way PE28 . . . . . 121 B5
Rook Gr CB24 . . . . 209 A4
Rooks St CB24 . . . . 125 E4
Rookswood Rd PE15 . . . . 243 C4
Rookwood Way CB9 . . . . . 24 A6
Rosary The CB24 . . . . . . 121 F5
Rose Ave PE2 . . . . 187 C6
Rosebay Gdns 6 CB7 . . . 212 B5
Roseberry Rd PE14 . . . . . 236 B5
Rosebery Way CB8 . . . . . 110 E5
Rose Cres CB2 . . . . 246 A3
Rose Croft PE28 . . . . 115 E2
Rose & Crown Rd CB24 . . 122 C3
Rose & Crown Yd 10
CB24 . . . . 209 A1
Rose Ct PE7 . . . . 181 F7
Rosedale PE14 . . . . 236 E8
Rosedene Dr PE15 . . . . . 243 D3
Rosefinch Cl CB9 . . . . 24 C7
Roseford Rd CB4 . . . . 83 D6
Rose Gn La 10 IP28 . . . . 213 F8
Rose Hill CB9 . . . . 38 D5
Rose La
4 Elm PE14 . . . . 236 A5
Great Chesterford CB10 . . . 18 E2
Melbourn SG8 . . . . 14 C6
Roselea CB24 . . . . 104 C3
Rosemary Cl 7 IP28 . . . 214 A1
Rosemary Gdns PE1 . . . . 197 F8
Rosemary Greene Cl
CB23 . . . . 78 E2
Rosemary La
Cambridge CB1 . . . . 65 E7
Chatteris PE16 . . . . 241 B4
Sutton CB6 . . . . 216 C1
Rosemary Rd CB25 . . . . . 106 B7
Rosemeadows 4 PE28 . . 208 B8
Rose's Cl PE15 . . . . 243 D2
Rose Wlk
Royston SG8 . . . . 5 C7
Wisbech PE13 . . . . 245 A6
Wittering PE8 . . . . 230 B1
Rosewood Cl PE7 . . . . . . 181 E5
Rosie Maternity Hospl
CB2 . . . . 65 A3
Ross Cl CB9 . . . . 24 D6
Ross Peers Sports Ctr
CB7 . . . . 212 B3
Ross St CB1 . . . . 65 B8
Roswell View CB7 . . . . . . 240 E5
Rosyth Ave PE2 . . . . 185 D3
Rotherby Gr 4 PE1 . . . . 198 D7
Rotherwick Way CB1 . . . . 65 C3
Rothleigh Rd 2 CB1 . . . . 65 D5
Rothwell Way PE2 . . . . . 186 C7
Round Church St CB2 . . . 246 A3
Roundhills View PE28 . . . 167 E8
Round Hills Way PE28 . . 168 A5
Roundhouse Cl PE1 . . . . 198 D3
Round House Cl CB23 . . . . 80 C2
Round House Com Prim Sch
The PE19 . . . . 75 C6
Roundhouse Dr PE28 . . . 115 D3
Round House Dro PE28 . . 222 A1
Rous Rd CB8 . . . . 111 B3
Rowan Ave
Peterborough PE1 . . . . . . 198 C6
Sawston CB22 . . . . 32 F6
Rowan Cl
Bottisham CB25 . . . . 86 F6
Haddenham CB6 . . . . . . 210 A5
Hanchet End CB9 . . . . 38 E1
Huntingdon PE29 . . . . . . 141 C5
Wisbech PE13 . . . . 245 F7
Rowans The
2 Doddington/Wimblington
PE15 . . . . 223 A6
Milton CB24 . . . . 105 C1
Rowan Wlk IP28 . . . . . . 239 E5
Rowe Ave PE2 . . . . 186 D7
Rowell Cl
Haverhill CB9 . . . . 39 A2
Newborough PE6 . . . . . . 207 C1
Rowells The CB24 . . . . . 125 C3
Rowell Wlk PE26 . . . . . . 172 A4
Rowland Ct PE4 . . . . 204 B5
Rowlands Cl CB22 . . . . . . 30 C5
Rowles Way CB24 . . . . . . 101 D3
Rowley Ct
Newmarket CB8 . . . . 110 E3
1 Sturmer CB9 . . . . 24 E5

Rowley Dr CB8 . . . . 110 F4
Rowley Gdns CB25 . . . . . . 86 E6
Rowley Rd PE19 . . . . 75 B7
Rowlinson Way CB4 . . . . . 84 B3
Rows The CB8 . . . . 110 F3
Row The CB6 . . . . 216 E1
Roxburgh Rd CB4 . . . . . . 83 E7
Royal Anglian Regiment Mus
The★ CB22 . . . . 16 F8
Royal Ct 2 PE19 . . . . 74 B4
Royal Oak La PE27 . . . . . 143 A2
Royal Palace Cl CB8 . . . . 110 D7
Royal Pl 2 PE13 . . . . . . 245 C4
Royce Cl PE7 . . . . 181 E6
Royce Ct PE27 . . . . 144 B7
Royce Rd
Alwalton PE7 . . . . 185 A4
Eastfield PE1 . . . . 198 D3
Royle Cl PE2 . . . . 186 C5
Royse Gr SG8 . . . . 5 D4
Roysia Mid Sch SG8 . . . . . 5 D8
ROYSTON 5 B6
Royston Ave
Peterborough PE2 . . . . . . 186 C6
Spaldwick PE28 . . . . 137 F6
Royston & District Mus★
SG8 . . . . 5 C6
Royston Hospl SG8 . . . . . . 5 D4
Royston La
Comberton CB23 . . . . 62 C3
Elmdon CB11 . . . . 9 C6
Royston Rd
Barley SG8 . . . . 6 F3
Caxton CB23 . . . . 59 F7
Duxford CB22 . . . . 32 D3
Foxton CB22 . . . . 30 A5
Harston CB22 . . . . 47 D1
Litlington SG8 . . . . 12 B1
Royston Sta SG8 . . . . 5 C7
Rubens Way PE27 . . . . . 144 A7
Ruddles La PE28 . . . . . . 142 E6
Rudlands Cl 3 CB7 . . . . . 213 A5
Rudyard Gr PE4 . . . . 204 E3
Ruffles Rd CB9 . . . . 24 C7
Rupert Brooke Mus★ CB2 64 A3
Rushbrook Cl CB23 . . . . . . 59 F7
Rush Gr CB1 . . . . 66 A8
Rushington Cl PE27 . . . . 144 B5
Rushmere PE2 . . . . 185 F6
Rushmere Cl PE26 . . . . . 171 B1
Rushton Ave PE4 . . . . . . 204 A4
Ruskin Cl 2 PE19 . . . . . . 74 B4
Russel Ct PE26 . . . . 172 A8
Russell Ave PE15 . . . . . . 243 B6
Russell Cl
Steeple Morden SG8 . . . . . 11 B2
7 Thorney PE6 . . . . . . 233 A3
Russell Ct
Cambridge CB2 . . . . 64 E7
St Neots PE19 . . . . 74 F6
Russell Dr PE14 . . . . 236 F2
Russell Hill PE8 . . . . 193 F6
Russell St
Cambridge CB2 . . . . 246 C1
Peterborough PE1 . . . . . . 197 F3
St Neots PE19 . . . . 74 E6
Wisbech PE13 . . . . 245 C6
Russet Cl PE27 . . . . 144 B5
Russets The PE14 . . . . . 236 E2
Russett Ave PE27 . . . . . . 208 A2
Russet Way SG8 . . . . 14 C8
Russet Wlk 3 CB23 . . . . . 81 A3
Rustat Ave CB1 . . . . 65 A7
Rustat Cl CB1 . . . . 65 A6
Rustat Rd CB1 . . . . 65 A6
Ruster Way PE7 . . . . 186 B2
Ruston Ct PE16 . . . . 241 D4
Rustons Rd PE14 . . . . . . 236 F7
Rustons The CB22 . . . . . . 32 D1
Rusts La PE28 . . . . 150 F4
Ruther Cl PE2 . . . . 186 D8
Rutherford Rd CB2 . . . . . 64 E4
Rutland Cl
Cambridge CB4 . . . . 83 D6
St Ives PE27 . . . . 143 F7
Rutland Ct 5 CB9 . . . . . . 23 E7
Rutland Gn PE28 . . . . . . 120 B1
Rutland Rd PE9 . . . . 244 D7
Rutland Terr PE9 . . . . . . 244 A4
Rutland Way PE15 . . . . . 224 B4
Rutner Cl PE2 . . . . 186 D8
Rycroft Ave
3 Deeping St James
PE6 . . . . 231 F8
St Neots PE19 . . . . 74 E6
Rydal Cl PE29 . . . . 141 B6
Rydal Ct PE4 . . . . 204 E3
Rye Cl
Littleport CB6 . . . . 242 C3
4 St Neots PE19 . . . . . . 74 F1
Rye Ct 10 PE9 . . . . 23 E7
Rye Gdns CB6 . . . . 218 A6
Ryhall Rd PE9 . . . . 244 D6

S

Saberton Cl CB25 . . . . . . 106 B8
Sable Cl CB1 . . . . 66 A7
Sackville Cl CB4 . . . . 83 E7
Sackville St CB8 . . . . 111 B4
Sackville Way CB23 . . . . . 79 C4
Sacred Heart RC Prim Sch
PE3 . . . . 197 A5
Sacrewell Farm & Ctry Ctr★
PE8 . . . . 194 C5

Saddle Ct PE4 . . . . 197 E8
Saddlers Cl PE6 . . . . 203 E8
Saddlers Pl SG8 . . . . 5 C7
Saddlers Way 1 PE16 . . . 241 D5
Sadlers Cl
Coton CB23 . . . . 82 B2
Hardwick CB23 . . . . 81 A1
Sadlers Way PE28 . . . . . 143 D1
Saffron Cl CB1 . . . . 242 C2
Saffron Piece 3 CB6 . . . . 216 E1
Saffron Rd
Histon CB24 . . . . 104 B3
Sawston CB22 . . . . 33 A8
Saffron St SG8 . . . . 5 B5
Sage's La PE4 . . . . 197 C8
Saggers Cl SG8 . . . . 12 C6
Sainfoin Cl CB22 . . . . 33 A8
Sainsfoins CB22 . . . . 48 F1
St Albans CB8 . . . . 111 A6
St Alban's Dr 20 PE6 . . . . 232 A1
St Albans RC Prim Sch
CB2 . . . . 246 B1
St Albans Rd CB4 . . . . 83 D6
St Andrew CB8 . . . . 111 A4
St Andrew's CE Prim Sch
CB7 . . . . 212 B3
St Andrews Cl
1 Isleham CB7 . . . . 213 A5
Sutton CB6 . . . . 216 E2
St Andrew's Cl CB22 . . . . . 49 C4
St Andrews Hill CB25 . . . 106 B7
St Andrew's Hill CB25 . . . 106 B7
St Andrews La 2 PE28 . . . 113 F4
St Andrews Pk 15 CB7 . . . 212 B4
St Andrew's Pk CB24 . . . 104 B5
St Andrew's Pl PE7 . . . . . 189 D6
St Andrew's Rd 4 PE6 . . . 231 F7
St Andrew's Rd CB4 . . . . . 84 A3
St Andrew's St
Cambridge CB2 . . . . 246 B2
Mildenhall IP28 . . . . 239 C4
St Andrews Way
Histon CB24 . . . . 104 A4
Sawtry PE28 . . . . 168 C4
St Andrew's Way CB6 . . . 240 B6
St Annes CE Prim Sch
PE29 . . . . 118 F8
St Anns Dr IP28 . . . . 239 B4
St Ann's La PE27 . . . . . . 141 F1
St Anselm Pl 1 PE19 . . . . 74 E5
St Anthony 2 CB8 . . . . . . 111 A4
St Anthonys Wlk CB2 . . . . 64 E7
St Audleys PE27 . . . . 144 A5
St Audrey Cl
Peterborough PE2 . . . . . . 187 D6
St Ives PE27 . . . . 144 B5
Saint Audrey La PE27 . . . 144 A5
St Audrey's Cl CB24 . . . . 104 A4
St Audrey's Way CB6 . . . 240 D6
St Augustines CE Jun Sch
PE2 . . . . 186 B6
St Augustines RC (Aided)
Prim Sch PE9 . . . . 244 C7
St Augustines Rd PE13 . . 245 C5
St Augustine's Wlk PE2 . 186 E8
St Barnabas Ct 3 PE29 . . 141 F7
St Barnabas Rd CB1 . . . . . 65 A8
St Barnabus Ct CB1 . . . . . 65 A8
St Bartholomew's Ct CB5 . 84 B3
St Bede's Cres CB1 . . . . . . 65 A8
St Bede's Gdns CB1 . . . . . 65 A8
St Bede's Inter Church Comp
Sch CB1 . . . . 65 D6
St Bee's Dr 18 PE6 . . . . . 232 A1
St Benedict's Cl PE6 . . . . 203 F7
St Benedicts Ct 10 PE29 . 141 D4
St Benedict's Ct PE29 . . . 141 D4
St Benet's Gdns 5 PE6 . . 232 A1
St Botolph La PE6 . . . . . 186 C6
St Botolphs CE Prim Sch
PE2 . . . . 186 B6
St Botolph's Gn PE8 . . . . 178 E7
St Botolph's Pl CB23 . . . . . 23 E7
St Botolph's Way
Haverhill CB9 . . . . 23 F8
Thorney PE6 . . . . 233 A2
St Catharines Coll CB2 . . 246 A2
St Catharines Hall CB23 . . 82 C2
St Catharines Sq
Arbury CB4 . . . . 83 C7
7 Kings Hedges CB4 . . . 83 D7
St Catherine's Cl CB5 . . . 240 C5
St Catherine's Cl IP28 . . . 239 D6
St Catherines Ct SG8 . . . . 11 F2
St Catherines Prep Sch
CB2 . . . . 64 E7
St Christophers Ave 2
CB4 . . . . 83 C4
St Clement Cl PE14 . . . . . 236 F2
St Clement's PE9 . . . . . . 244 A5
St Clements Gdns CB1 . . 246 A3
St Clements Pas PE2 . . . . 141 E4
St Colettes Prep Sch CB1 . 64 F7
St David CB8 . . . . 111 A4
St David's Sq PE1 . . . . . . 198 D1
St David's Way PE28 . . . . 168 C4
St Denys CB8 . . . . 111 A4
St Edmunds Coll CB3 . . . . 83 C3
St Edmunds Dr PE14 . . . 236 D5
St Edwards Pas 4 CB1 . . 246 A2
St Ethelwolds Cl CB6 . . . 240 B4
St Fabians Cl CB8 . . . . . . 110 F5
St Faith's Sch CB2 . . . . . . 64 E6
St Felix CE VC Mid Sch
CB8 . . . . 110 F6
St Felix Cl CB7 . . . . 212 B5
St Felix RC Prim Sch CB9 . 23 D7

St Felix Rd PE26 . . . . . . 221 C2
St Francis Dr 2 PE16 . . . . 241 D5
St George 1 CB8 . . . . . . 111 A4
St George Ave PE2 . . . . . 187 E6
St Georges Ave PE9 . . . . 244 C5
St Georges CE Prim Sch
PE9 . . . . 244 C7
St Georges Cl PE28 . . . . 140 E1
St Georges Ct 3 PE29 . . . 141 D4
St George's Rd
St Ives PE27 . . . . 144 A4
14 Wittering PE8 . . . . . . 230 B1
St George's Sq 5 PE9 . . . 244 C5
St George's St PE9 . . . . . 244 C5
St Georges Way CB24 . . . 104 E4
St Germain PE29 . . . . . . 141 D4
St Germain Walk Sh Ctr
PE29 . . . . 141 E4
St Germain Wlk 8 PE29 . 141 D4
St Gilberts CE Prim Sch
PE9 . . . . 244 B5
St Giles Cl PE7 . . . . 176 F4
St Giles Gr PE14 . . . . . . 236 B5
St Goerges Ct CB24 . . . . 104 E4
St Helena Farm IP28 . . . 239 F6
St Helena Wlk IP28 . . . . 239 C7
St Helens Prim Sch
PE28 . . . . 208 D6
St Hugh's Rd PE19 . . . . . 117 A4
ST IVES 143 E7
St Ives Rd
Eltisley PE19 . . . . 77 E6
Hemingford Grey PE28 . . 143 D2
Old Hurst PE28 . . . . 154 D6
Papworth Everard CB23 . . 98 F2
Somersham PE28 . . . . . . 208 A8
St Ives PE28 . . . . 143 A5
St Ivo Leisure Ctr PE27 . . 143 F6
St Ivo Sch PE27 . . . . 143 F5
St James CB8 . . . . 111 A4
St James Ave PE1 . . . . . . 197 F7
St James Cl
Newton PE13 . . . . 238 A5
3 Stretham CB6 . . . . . . 210 F5
St James Ct 9 CB9 . . . . . . 23 E8
St James Rd PE19 . . . . . . 95 F3
St John Fisher RC Sch
PE1 . . . . 198 C4
St johns SG8 . . . . 14 C5
St Johns Ave CB8 . . . . . . 111 A1
St Johns Bsns Pk PE29 . . 141 D7
St John's CE Prim Sch
PE29 . . . . 141 E7
St John's Chase PE15 . . . 243 D5
St Johns Church Sch
PE2 . . . . 185 E3
St Johns Cl PE28 . . . . . . 155 B5
St John's Cl
Mildenhall IP28 . . . . 239 D6
7 Needingworth PE27 . . 208 A3
Waterbeach CB25 . . . . . . 106 B7
St Johns Coll CB2 . . . . . . 246 A3
St Johns Coll Sch CB3 . . . 83 C2
St John's Innovation Ctr
CB4 . . . . 84 C8
St Johns La CB23 . . . . 99 B2
St John's La CB25 . . . . . . 106 A2
St Johns Mews PE19 . . . . 96 E4
St John's Pl
Cambridge CB4 . . . . 83 C3
Wistow PE28 . . . . 163 F7
St Johns Prim CE Sch
PE1 . . . . 187 C7
St Johns Rd
Cambridge CB5 . . . . 246 A4
Peterborough PE2 . . . . . . 187 B7
St John's Rd
Coton CB23 . . . . 82 B2
Ely CB6 . . . . 240 A4
March PE15 . . . . 243 D5
13 Wittering PE8 . . . . . . 230 B1
St Johns St PE29 . . . . . . 141 D5
St John's St
Beck Row, Holywell Row &
Kenny Hill PE28 . . . . . . 214 A8
Cambridge CB2 . . . . 246 A3
Duxford CB22 . . . . 32 D1
Mildenhall IP28 . . . . 213 F8
Peterborough PE1 . . . . . . 198 B2
St Johns Way CB23 . . . . . 79 A4
St Judith's La PE28 . . . . 160 B6
St Katherines Mews PE7 186 C6
St Kilda Ave CB4 . . . . 84 A7
St Kyneburgha Cl PE5 . . . 195 C2
St Laurence Rd CB22 . . . . 30 C5
St Laurences RC Prim Sch
CB4 . . . . 83 D7
St Lawrence Way 2 PE9 . 230 F7
St Leger Dr CB8 . . . . 110 F7
St Leonard's Rd 2 PE13 . 238 D2
St Leonard's St 4 PE9 . . 244 C5
St Louis RC Prim Sch
CB8 . . . . 111 A4
St Lukes CE Prim Sch
CB4 . . . . 83 C4
St Lukes Cl PE29 . . . . . . 141 D5
St Lukes Mews CB4 . . . . . 83 C4
St Lukes St CB4 . . . . 246 A4
St Margarets Pl PE2 . . . . 186 F6
St Margarets Rd PE2 . . . 186 F6
St Margaret's Rd CB3 . . . . 82 F6
St Margaret's Sq CB1 . . . . 65 B5
St Margarets Way PE29 . . 141 C6
St Marks Ct CB3 . . . . 64 C8
St Mark's Ct 3 PE1 . . . . . 198 A3

St Marks Rd PE13 . . . . . . 237 E3
St Marks St PE1 . . . . 198 A3
St Martin's Cl
  Chatteris PE16 . . . . 241 D5
  Exning CB8 . . . . 110 C7
  Stamford PE9 . . . . 244 C4
St Martin's Rd
  Chatteris PE16 . . . . 241 D4
  Newborough PE6 . . . . . . 205 B8
  Wisbech PE13 . . . . 245 E7
St Martin's St PE1 . . . . . 197 F5
St Martins Wlk CB7 . . . . 240 D5
St Mary's
  Earith PE28 . . . . 208 E6
  Gamlingay SG19 . . . . . . 41 E5
St Mary's Ave PE8 . . . . . 230 B1
St Marys CE Prim Sch
  Mildenhall IP28 . . . . 239 C5
  St Neots PE19 . . . . 75 A5
St Marys Cl CB6 . . . . . . 216 E3
St Mary's Cl
  Bainton PE9 . . . . 230 F6
  Bluntisham PE28 . . . . . . 208 D5
  Farcet PE7 . . . . 187 C2
  Mildenhall IP28 . . . . 239 C4
  Peterborough PE1 . . . . . 198 B4
  Thorney PE6 . . . . 233 A2
  Wisbech St Mary PE13 . . 235 C7
St Marys Ct
  Ely CB7 . . . . 240 C4
  Peterborough PE1 . . . . . 198 B2
St Mary's Dr
  March PE15 . . . . 243 C5
  Peterborough PE2 . . . . . 185 F4
St Mary's Gn PE28 . . . . . 164 E6
St Mary's Hill 9 PE9 . . . 244 C5
St Marys Pas CB1 . . . . . 246 A2
St Mary's Pas 2 CB1 . . . 246 A2
St Marys Pk SG8 . . . . . . 5 D6
St Mary's RC JMI Sch SG8. 5 D7
St Mary's Rd
  Bluntisham/Colne PE28 . . 208 C5
  Ramsey PE26 . . . . 220 C3
  Sawston CB22 . . . . 33 A7
  Stilton PE7 . . . . 175 F8
  West Walton PE14 . . . . . 238 E4
St Marys Sen Sch CB2 . . 64 E7
St Marys Sq 7 CB8 . . . . 111 A3
St Marys St 5 PE29 . . . . 141 D6
St Mary's St
  1 Cambridge CB1 . . . . . 246 A2
  Ely CB7 . . . . 240 C4
  Farcet PE7 . . . . 187 C2
  Stamford PE9 . . . . 244 C5
  St Neots PE19 . . . . 74 E4
  Whittlesey PE7 . . . . 189 D6
St Mary's View CB25 . . . 130 C1
St Mary's Wlk
  Everton SG19 . . . . 40 C3
  Fowlmere SG8 . . . . 15 E8
St Matthew's Ct 5 CB1. . 84 A4
St Matthew's Gdns 6 CB1. 84 A4
St Matthews Prim Sch
  CB1 . . . . 246 C2
St Matthew's St CB1 . . . 84 A2
St Michaels CB24 . . . . . 103 A8
St Michael's Ave PE13. . . 245 C7
St Michael's Gate PE1 . . 198 F7
St Michaels La
  Longstanton CB24 . . . . . 124 A1
  Oakington/Longstanton
  CB24. . . . . 103 A8
St Michael's Rd 12 PE8 . 230 B1
ST NEOTS 74 E4
St Neots Com Coll PE19 . 74 E4
St Neots Comm Nature
  Reserve ★ PE19 . . . . . . 74 E7
St Neots Leisure Ctr PE19 74 E2
St Neots Mus ★ PE19 . . . 74 E5
St Neots Rd
  Abbotsley PE19 . . . . . . 57 A7
  Comberton CB23 . . . . . . 81 D3
  Coton CB23 . . . . 82 B3
  Eaton Socon PE19 . . . . . 74 C4
  Eltisley PE19 . . . . 77 D4
  Hardwick CB23 . . . . 80 E4
  Knapwell CB23. . . . . . . 79 D5
  Madingley CB23 . . . . . . 81 F3
St Neots Sta PE19. . . . . 75 B6
St Olave's Dr 19 PE6 . . . 232 A1
St Ovins Gn CB6 . . . . . . 240 B5
St Patrick 4 CB8 . . . . . 111 A4
St Paul's CE Prim Sch
  CB2. . . . . 246 B1
St Paul's Cl
  Gorefield PE13. . . . . . . 237 E2
  5 Wisbech PE13. . . . . . 245 C4
St Pauls Dr PE16 . . . . . 241 D6
St Paul's Rd
  Cambridge CB1 . . . . 246 C1
  Peterborough PE1 . . . . . 197 F7
St Paul's St PE9. . . . . . 244 C5
St Pauls Wlk CB1 . . . . . 246 C1
St Pega's Rd PE6 . . . . . 204 A8
St Peters Ave CB8. . . . . 112 F4
St Peter's CE Jun Sch
  PE13 . . . . 245 E6
St Peters Cl CB8 . . . . . . 112 F5
St Peter's Cl 9 PE9 . . . . 244 B5
St Peters Dr PE16 . . . . . 241 D5
St Peter's Dr 10 PE15. . . 223 B7
St Peter's Field CB25 . . . 86 E5
St Peter's Hill 8 PE9 . . . 244 B5
St Peters Pl CB7 . . . . . . 212 C4

St Peters Rd
  Outwell PE14 . . . . 236 E1
  Peterborough PE1 . . . . . 198 A2
St Peter's Rd
  Coton CB23 . . . . 82 B2
  Huntingdon PE29 . . . . . . 141 D7
  March PE15 . . . . 243 D3
  4 Wisbech PE13. . . . . . 245 C4
St Peters Sch PE29 . . . . 141 D6
St Peter's St
  Cambridge CB3 . . . . 83 C3
  Caxton CB23 . . . . 59 E8
  Duxford CB22 . . . . 17 D8
  Stamford PE9. . . . . 244 B4
St Peters Terr CB1 . . . . . 246 B1
St Peter's Vale PE9 . . . . 244 B4
St Peter's Way
  Ellington PE28 . . . . 139 A4
  Thorney PE6. . . . . 233 A2
St Philips CE Prim Sch
  CB1 . . . . 84 C1
St Philips Rd
  Cambridge CB1 . . . . 65 C8
  Newmarket CB8 . . . . . . 110 E4
St Philip's Rd CB1. . . . . 65 B8
St Regis CB4. . . . . 83 F4
St Stephen's Dr PE16 . . . 241 C6
St Stephen's Pl 1 CB4 . . 83 C4
St Thomas PE19 . . . . . . 77 E4
St Thomas Cl CB23 . . . . 62 D6
St Thomas Dr PE15 . . . . 243 C7
St Thomas Moore RC Prim
  Sch PE13 . . . . 198 D4
St Thomas' Pl CB7 . . . . . 240 C2
St Thomas's Sq CB1. . . . 65 D6
St Tibb's Row CB2 . . . . . 246 B2
St Vigor's Rd CB21 . . . . 66 F4
St Vincent's Cl CB3 . . . . 82 E8
St Wendreda's Dr PE15. . 243 C1
St Wendred's Way CB8 . . 110 B7
Salcott Dr PE13 . . . . . . 245 E5
Salem Ct PE16 . . . . 241 C4
Salgasson Wlk CB23 . . . 79 B2
Salisbury Cl PE27 . . . . . 143 F8
Salisbury Cl 1 CB9 . . . . 23 F7
Salisbury Rd PE4. . . . . . 204 B3
Salisbury Villas CB1. . . . 64 F7
Salk Rd PE7 . . . . 186 B2
Sallowbush Rd PE29 . . . . 141 D6
Sallows PE28 . . . . 121 C6
Sallows Rd PE1 . . . . 198 B6
Salmon La CB1 . . . . 246 C3
Salon Way PE29. . . . . . . 141 B7
Saltergate PE1. . . . . . . 198 E7
Saltersgate PE1. . . . . . 198 F7
Salters Way
  Sawtry PE28 . . . . 168 B5
  Wisbech PE13 . . . . 245 A2
Saltmarsh PE2. . . . . . . 186 C4
Salts Rd PE14 . . . . 238 F4
Sambar Cl 3 PE19 . . . . 74 B5
Sames Ct CB24 . . . . . . 125 E5
Samian Cl CB23 . . . . . . 80 C2
Samuel Pepys Sch PE19 . 75 A4
Samuels Cl PE28 . . . . . . 164 E4
Samuels Way CB6. . . . . 240 C4
Samuel Ward Art & Tech Coll
  CB9 . . . . 39 B1
Samworths Cl PE5 . . . . . 195 F2
Sancton Wood Sch CB1 . 246 C1
Sand Acre Cl IP28 . . . . . 239 D5
Sandall Rd PE13 . . . . . . 245 C5
Sand Bank PE13 . . . . . . 235 A7
Sand Dro CB25. . . . . . . 127 C8
Sanderling Cl IP28. . . . . 239 D4
Sanderlings The PE6 . . . . 206 B1
Sanders Cl PE28 . . . . . . 151 D3
Sanders La CB21 . . . . . . 67 A4
Sandfields Rd PE19 . . . . 74 F4
Sandford PE3. . . . . 197 B5
SANDHILL 242 E3
Sandhill CB6. . . . . 242 F3
Sandhurst Rd PE7. . . . . 186 C1
Sandown Rd PE13. . . . . 245 A2
Sandpiper Cl
  Haverhill CB9 . . . . 24 B7
  St Neots PE19 . . . . 74 B1
  Whittlesey PE7 . . . . 190 A8
Sandpiper Dr PE2. . . . . 187 E6
Sandpit Rd PE6 . . . . . . 233 A3
Sand Rd SG19 . . . . 58 F5
Sandringham Ave PE13. . 245 D6
Sandringham Cl PE28 . . . 141 E7
Sandringham Dr PE26. . . 221 C2
Sandringham Rd PE14. . . 237 A7
Sand Road Ind Est SG19 . 58 F5
Sand St CB7 . . . . 212 B3
Sandwich Cl
  Huntingdon PE29 . . . . . . 141 E7
  St Ives PE27 . . . . 143 F6
Sandwich Rd
  Brampton PE28 . . . . 140 D1
  St Neots PE19 . . . . 75 A5
Sandwick Cl 2 CB4 . . . . 83 E8
Sandy Dro IP28. . . . . . . 214 D3
Sandy Gate PE12. . . . . . 237 A7
Sandy La
  Cambridge CB4 . . . . 83 F4
  Kimbolton PE28 . . . . . . 113 C6
  Tydd St Giles PE13. . . . . 238 B7
  Wisbech PE13 . . . . 245 F4
Sandyland PE13. . . . . . 245 B5
Sandy Rd
  Everton SG19 . . . . 40 B2
  Lode CB25. . . . . 107 C6
Sandys Cres CB6. . . . . . 242 E3
Sanfoin Cl 5 IP28 . . . . . 214 A1

Sapcote Way PE28 . . . . . 168 B3
SAPLEY 141 F8
Sapley Pk PE29 . . . . 141 F8
Sapley Rd PE29 . . . . 152 F1
Sapley Spinneys Nature
  Reserve ★ PE28 . . . . . . 152 E1
Sapley Sq PE29 . . . . 141 E7
Sapperton PE4. . . . . . . 204 B6
Saracen Way PE1 . . . . . 198 F4
Sarah Ct CB9 . . . . 24 A5
Sargent's Ct PE9 . . . . . . 244 A6
Sassoon Cl CB8 . . . . . . 111 A4
Saunders Cl
  Huntingdon PE29 . . . . . . 141 E6
  Peterborough PE2 . . . . . 186 E8
Saunders Ct CB23 . . . . . 79 B3
Savile's Cl PE19. . . . . . 74 D7
Savile Way SG8 . . . . . . 15 E8
Saville Rd PE3 . . . . 197 D5
Saville Road Ind Est PE3 197 D5
Savory Rd PE13 . . . . . . 245 B7
Sawpit La PE28 . . . . . . 159 A4
SAWSTON 33 A7
Sawston Rd CB22 . . . . . 33 D8
Sawston Village Coll
  CB22. . . . . 32 E8
SAWTRY 168 C4
Sawtry Com Coll PE28. . . 168 C4
Sawtry Jun & Inf Sch
  PE28 . . . . 168 B3
Sawtry Leisure Ctr PE28. 168 B3
Sawtry Rd
  Conington PE28 . . . . . . 167 F8
  Sawtry PE28 . . . . 168 A6
Sawtry Roughs PE28 . . . 168 F2
Sawtry Way PE28 . . . . . 153 E2
Sawtry Way Cotts PE28. . 143 C6
Saxby Gdns PE1. . . . . . 198 C8
Saxham Ct CB9 . . . . . . 38 B1
Saxon Cl
  Ely CB6 . . . . 240 C5
  Exning CB8. . . . . 110 D8
  Godmanchester PE29 . . . 141 F1
  Oakington CB24 . . . . . . 103 D6
  Sawtry PE28 . . . . 168 C3
Saxon Dr CB25. . . . . . . 130 B1
Saxongate Com Learning Ctr
  PE29. . . . . 141 C4
Saxon Pl PE19 . . . . 74 F4
Saxon Rd
  5 Barnack PE9. . . . . . . 230 D3
  Cambridge CB5 . . . . 84 A3
  Peterborough PE1. . . . . 198 C4
  Whittlesey PE7 . . . . 189 C7
Saxon St Rd CB8 . . . . . . 91 D4
Saxon St CB22 . . . . 246 B1
SAXON STREET 91 B3
Saxon Way
  Bar Hill CB23. . . . . 102 B2
  Knights End PE15 . . . . . 228 B1
  Melbourn SG8 . . . . 14 C4
  3 Waterbeach CB25. . . . 106 A7
  Willingham CB24 . . . . . . 209 A1
Sayer Ct PE2. . . . . 185 F2
Sayers Ct PE28 . . . . . . 208 C5
Sayer St PE29. . . . . 141 C5
Scaldgate PE7 . . . . 189 E6
Scalford Dr PE1. . . . . . . 198 C8
Scaltback Cl CB8. . . . . . 110 E6
Scaltback Mid Sch CB8. . 110 E5
Scarfield La PE14 . . . . . 236 C6
Scargell's La PE15 . . . . . 243 D3
Scarlett's La CB21 . . . . . 53 D4
Scarsdale Cl CB4 . . . . . 84 B6
Sch of Clinical Medicine
  CB2 . . . . 65 B3
Scholars Ave CB23 . . . . 141 C4
Scholars Cl PE15 . . . . . . 224 B4
Schole Rd CB24 . . . . . . 209 A1
School Cl
  Cheveley CB8. . . . . 91 C6
  Gamlingay SG19 . . . . . . 41 D5
  5 Maxey PE6 . . . . 231 C7
  Peterborough PE3 . . . . . 197 A5
School Dro PE26 . . . . . . 171 F4
School Farm Dro PE26 . . 171 E8
School Hill CB24 . . . . . . 104 B4
School La
  Alconbury PE28 . . . . . . 150 F5
  Barley SG8. . . . . 7 A1
  Barton CB23 . . . . 63 B4
  Bourn CB23 . . . . 79 B3
  Boxworth CB23 . . . . . . 101 B5
  Buckden PE19 . . . . 117 B4
  Burwell CB25 . . . . 130 B1
  Bythorn & Keyston PE28. . 146 D4
  Conington CB23 . . . . . . 121 C1
  Coveney CB6 . . . . 217 D5
  Downham CB6 . . . . 218 A7
  Eaton Socon PE19 . . . . . 74 C2
  Elton PE8 . . . . 178 D8
  Fenstanton PE28 . . . . . . 121 B6
  Fulbourn CB21 . . . . . . 66 F4
  Glinton PE6 . . . . 203 E8
  Haslingfield CB23 . . . . . 47 B5
  Haverhill CB9 . . . . 23 D8
  Histon CB24 . . . . 104 C3
  Kings Ripton PE28 . . . . . 153 C6
  Little Paxton PE19 . . . . . 96 A2
  Longstanton CB24 . . . . . 123 F1
  Longstowe CB23 . . . . . . 60 A3
  Manea PE15. . . . . 224 B4
  4 Maxey PE6 . . . . 231 C7
  Mepal CB6. . . . . 216 E3
  Pymoor CB6. . . . . 224 D1
  Ramsey PE26 . . . . 172 B7

School La continued
  St Neots PE19 . . . . 74 E4
  Swavesey SG24 . . . . . . 122 E6
  Thriplow SG8. . . . . 31 B2
  Toft CB23 . . . . 61 D4
  3 Uffington PE9 . . . . . . 230 C6
  Warmington PE8 . . . . . . 178 B3
  Waterbeach CB25 . . . . . 127 B8
  Wilburton CB6 . . . . 210 C5
  1 Wisbech PE13. . . . . . 245 C5
School Rd
  5 Barnack PE9. . . . . . . 230 D4
  Broughton PE28. . . . . . . 153 F8
  Earith PE28 . . . . 208 E6
  Great Wratting CB9 . . . . 39 E5
  Moulton CB8 . . . . 112 F6
  Newborough PE6 . . . . . . 205 D8
  Outwell PE14 . . . . 229 D8
  Warboys PE28 . . . . 164 F5
  West Walton PE14 . . . . . 238 E4
  Wooddition CB8 . . . . . . 91 A3
School St CB10 . . . . 18 D2
School Wlk CB23 . . . . . . 99 A3
Scolding Dro PE6 . . . . . 233 E5
Scorney PE28. . . . . 121 C6
Scotendon PE2 . . . . 185 E3
Scotenoon PE2 . . . . 185 E3
Scotgate PE9 . . . . 244 A5
Scotland Cl CB4 . . . . . . 84 B5
Scotland End CB7 . . . . . 213 C1
Scotland Rd
  Cambridge CB4 . . . . 84 A5
  Dry Drayton CB23 . . . . . 81 A6
Scotney St PE1 . . . . 197 E7
Scotney Way PE28 . . . . . 168 C3
Scotred Cl CB25 . . . . . . 109 B8
Scotsdowne Rd CB2. . . . 64 D3
Scott Ave IP28 . . . . 239 C5
Scott Cl
  Peterborough PE2 . . . . . 187 E6
  Royston SG8 . . . . 13 D1
Scotts Cl PE28 . . . . 120 B1
Scotts Cres PE28. . . . . . 120 B1
Scotts Gdns CB22 . . . . . 32 C5
Scotts Rd PE6 . . . . 203 F8
Scott's Rd PE14. . . . . . . 229 C2
Scotts Yd CB23 . . . . 47 B5
Scrolans PE27 . . . . 143 E6
Seabank Rd PE13 . . . . . 245 F6
SEADYKE 234 F6
Seadyke Bank PE13 . . . . 235 A7
Seadyke Rd PE13 . . . . . 234 F6
Seafield Rd 7 PE13 . . . . 238 B2
Sealey's La PE13. . . . . . 234 D8
Sealodes Rd CB7. . . . . . 211 E5
Seargeants Cl PE6 . . . . . 207 C1
Searjeant St PE1. . . . . . 197 E5
Searles Ct PE7 . . . . 189 D8
Searles Mdw CB23 . . . . 102 B1
Searle St CB4 . . . . 83 D4
Sears Cl PE28 . . . . 118 F8
Searson Cl PE9 . . . . 230 F7
Seathwaite PE29 . . . . . . 141 B6
Seaton Cl PE7 . . . . 181 D6
Sebrights Way PE3. . . . . 196 F3
Second Ave
  Warboys PE28 . . . . 164 E6
  Wisbech PE13 . . . . 245 D4
Second Broadpool Dro
  PE28. . . . . 165 F8
Second Drift PE9 . . . . . . 244 B2
Second Dro
  Downham CB6 . . . . 218 A8
  Ely CB7 . . . . 218 F5
  Littleport CB6 . . . . 225 B1
  Peterborough PE1 . . . . . 198 D1
  St Ives PE27 . . . . 144 C2
Second Drove Ind Est
  PE1. . . . . 198 D1
Second Marsh Rd PE14. . 238 C3
Sedge Fen Rd PE38 . . . . 226 E7
Sedge Way CB6. . . . . . . 217 D2
Sedgwick Mus of Earth
  Sciences ★ CB2 . . . . . . 246 B2
Sedgwick St CB1. . . . . . 65 B8
Sedley Taylor Rd CB2 . . . 64 F4
Sefton Ave PE13 . . . . . . 245 E6
Sefton Cl CB2. . . . . 64 D3
Sefton Way CB8 . . . . . . 110 D5
Selby Ct 2 PE29 . . . . . . 141 F7
Sellers Grange PE2 . . . . 186 B4
Selsingen Way CB22 . . . 32 F7
Selwyn Cl
  Great Shelford CB22 . . . . 49 A5
  Mildenhall IP28 . . . . 239 D6
  Newmarket CB8 . . . . . . 111 A1
Selwyn Coll CB3 . . . . . . 64 B8
Selwyn Gdns CB3 . . . . . 64 B8
Selwyn Rd
  Cambridge CB3 . . . . 64 B7
  Stamford PE9. . . . . 244 A7
Senate House Hill 6
  CB2 . . . . 246 A2
Senate House Pas CB2 . . 246 A2
Senes Calls 9 PE27 . . . . 208 A3
Sennitt Way PE28 . . . . . 210 F5
Seppings Cl 2 CB6 . . . . 210 C6
Serby Ave PE6 . . . . 5 C8
Serjeants Cl PE26 . . . . . 172 A6
Serlby Gdns PE3 . . . . . . 197 B3
Serpentine Green Sh Ctr
  PE7 . . . . 186 D3
Setchel 11 PE19 . . . . . . 74 C6
Setchel Dro CB24 . . . . . 125 F7
Setchell Cl PE19 . . . . . . 97 F5
Setchfield Pl PE7 . . . . . 186 F7
Sevenacres PE2. . . . . . 185 E5
Seven Rides SG8 . . . . . . 5 D3

Seventh Ave PE13 . . . . . 245 E4
Seventh Dro CB6. . . . . . 225 A3
SEVERALS THE 111 B5
Severn Cl PE4 . . . . 204 E1
Severn Pl CB1 . . . . 84 A2
SEWELL'S BARN. 138 A2
Seymore Dr CB9 . . . . . . 23 D7
Seymour Cl CB8 . . . . . . 111 C3
Seymour Cl CB1 . . . . . . 65 C8
Seymour Pl PE4. . . . . . . 205 B2
Seymour St CB1. . . . . . . 65 C8
Seynory Dro PE7. . . . . . 177 E7
Shade The CB7 . . . . 212 A5
Shadowbush Cl 2 CB9 . . 38 F1
Shady Wlk 2 PE19. . . . . 74 F5
Shaftenhoe End Rd SG8 . . 7 A1
Shaftesbury Ave
  March PE15 . . . . 243 E5
  St Neots PE19 . . . . 74 F5
Shaftesbury Ct 17 CB21. . 23 E7
Shaftesbury Rd CB2. . . . 64 F6
Shaftesbury Way SG8 . . . 5 F8
Shaftsbury Ct PE15. . . . 243 E3
Shakespeare SG8 . . . . . 5 D8
Shakespeare Ave PE1 . . . 197 F7
Shakespeare Rd
  Eaton Socon PE19 . . . . . 74 C3
  St Ives PE27 . . . . 143 F6
Shamrock Cl PE2 . . . . . . 187 C7
Shannon Cl CB9 . . . . . . 24 D7
Shardlow Cl 1 CB9 . . . . 38 C1
Sharma Leas PE4 . . . . . 204 A3
Sharman's Rd CB7 . . . . . 212 E1
Sharnbrook Ave PE7 . . . . 186 C1
Sharp Cl PE27 . . . . 143 E9
Sharps La PE28 . . . . . . 150 F3
Shaw Dr PE15 . . . . 243 C3
Shawley Rd PE28 . . . . . 168 A4
Shearling Dr CB23 . . . . . 79 A4
Shearwater PE2 . . . . . . 185 D6
Sheepfold La CB23 . . . . 79 B5
Sheep Mkt
  6 Stamford PE9. . . . . . . 244 C3
  St Ives PE27 . . . . 144 B3
Sheep St PE28 . . . . 148 D3
Sheepwalk PE4 . . . . . . 205 A1
Sheepwash Way CB24 . . 123 E2
Sheldrick's Rd CB7. . . . . 213 B5
Shelford Mill CB22 . . . . 48 F4
Shelford Park Ave CB22 . 49 A5
Shelford Rd
  Cambridge CB22 . . . . . . 48 E8
  Fulbourn CB21 . . . . 66 C3
  Harston CB22 . . . . 48 C3
  Whittlesford CB22 . . . . . 32 A6
Shelford Sta CB22 . . . . . 49 B5
Shelley Cl
  Huntingdon PE29 . . . . . . 141 F6
  Peterborough PE1 . . . . . 197 E8
  Royston SG8 . . . . 13 D1
Shelley Pl 5 PE19 . . . . . 74 D6
Shelly Gdn CB3 . . . . . . 83 C3
Shelly Row 4 CB3 . . . . . 83 C3
Shelton Rd PE2 . . . . 187 D6
Shepherd Cl SG8. . . . . . 5 E5
Shepherd Dr PE19 . . . . . 74 E2
Shepherds Cl PE4 . . . . . 204 C4
Shepherd's Cl
  Cambridge CB1 . . . . 66 A6
  Fen Ditton CB5. . . . . . . 84 F5
Shepherds Ct 9 CB9 . . . 23 E7
Shepherd's Dro CB7 . . . . 226 B2
Sheppard's Dro CB6 . . . . 232 D8
Sheppard Way CB1. . . . . 85 B1
Sheppersons Gr PE15 243 E4
SHEPRETH 29 F5
Shepreth L-Moor Nature
  Reserve ★ 29 D3
Shepreth Rd
  Barrington CB22 . . . . . . 29 C3
  Foxton CB22. . . . . 30 A4
  Shepreth SG8. . . . . 30 B3
Shepreth Sta SG8 . . . . . 29 E5
Shepreth Wildlife Pk ★
  SG8. . . . . 29 E5
Sheralds Croft La SG8. . . 31 A2
Sherborne Rd PE1 . . . . . 198 D6
Sherbourne Cl CB4 . . . . 84 B6
Sherbrooke Cl PE15 . . . . 243 D1
Sheridan Rd PE1. . . . . . 197 F8
Sheriffs Ct CB8 . . . . . . 70 F3
Sheringham Way PE2 . . . 186 C6
Sherlock Cl CB3 . . . . . . 83 B4
Sherlock Ct CB3 . . . . . . 83 B4
Sherlock Rd CB3 . . . . . . 83 B5
Sherwood Ave
  4 Peterborough PE2 . . . 186 F7
  Wisbech PE13 . . . . 245 D7
Shetland Rd CB9 . . . . . . 24 D8
Shillow Hill PE26. . . . . . 172 B1
SHINGAY 26 F2
Shingay La CB22 . . . . . . 32 F7
Ship Gdns IP28 . . . . 239 B3
Ship La CB7 . . . . 240 D3
Shippea Hill Rd IP28 . . . 213 E8
Shirdley Rd PE19 . . . . . 74 F4
Shire Ct 7 CB9 . . . . 23 E7
Shire Gr PE1. . . . . 198 C5
Shires The
  Bluntisham/Colne PE28. . 208 C5
  March PE15 . . . . 243 E2
  Royston SG8 . . . . 5 E6
Shirley Cl CB4 . . . . 105 E2
Shirley Gr CB4 . . . . 84 B5
Shirley Inf Sch CB4 . . . . 84 B5
Shirley Rd CB24. . . . . . . 104 B3
Shooter's Hollow PE19 . . 116 D3

hores Cl IP28 . . . . 213 C3
hore View PE7 . . . . 186 C2
hortacres Rd PE2 . . . . . . 186 F7
hort Cl PE8 . . . . 178 B3
hort Cswy CB6 . . . . 217 C4
hort Dr PE15 . . . . 224 B5
Short Dro
  Cottenham CB24 . . . . . . 125 F2
  Downham PE28 . . . . 224 F3
  Earith PE28 . . . . 208 F6
  Holme PE7 . . . . 177 A4
  Little Downham CB6 . . . 217 F5
  Pymore CB6 . . . . 217 C8
  Ramsey PE26 . . . . 221 A4
  Somersham PE28 . . . . . 215 D3
hortfen PE2 . . . . 186 C4
Short La
  Bluntisham/Colne PE28 . 208 C5
  Coveney CB6 . . . . 217 C4
  Papworth Village Settlement
   CB23 . . . . 99 A2
  Willingham CB24 . . . . . 209 A1
  Wisbech PE13 . . . . 238 A1
hortland 6 PE28 . . . . . . 215 C1
hort Nightlayer's Dro
  PE16 . . . . 241 C6
hort North Dro CB6 . . . . 216 B4
Short Rd
  Exning CB8 . . . . 131 F2
  Snailwell CB8 . . . . 132 A3
  Stretham CB6 . . . . 210 E5
hortsands Yd 3 PE19 . . . 75 A5
Short St
  Bourn CB23 . . . . 60 C5
  Cambridge CB1 . . . . . . 246 B3
hrewsbury Ave PE2 . . . . . 186 D5
hropshire Pl PE1 . . . . . . 198 C2
hrubberies The CB6 . . . . 111 D1
hrubbery Gr SG8 . . . . 5 D1
hrubbery The PE6 . . . . . 241 D4
hrub House Cl IP28 . . . . 213 F8
hrublands IP28 . . . . 239 C4
hrub Rd PE7 . . . . 186 C1
hubbery The PE29 . . . . . 140 F5
HUDY CAMPS 22 B5
hudy Camps Pk CB21 . . . 22 C6
IBSON 183 E8
ibson Aerodrome PE8 . . . 183 E6
idgwick Ave CB3 . . . . 64 C8
iding Dro PE28 . . . . 215 C5
idings The PE26 . . . . . . 172 B6
idney Farm Rd CB1 . . . . . 65 E6
idney Gdns CB23 . . . . 47 B6
idney St CB2 . . . . 246 A3
idney Sussex Coll CB1 . . 246 B3
iggin's La CB1 . . . . 20 D6
ignal Rd PE26 . . . . 172 B6
ilhalls Cl CB8 . . . . 91 F7
ilt Rd
  Littleport CB6 . . . . 242 D5
  March PE15 . . . . 243 F4
  Upwell PE14 . . . . 229 F5
ilvan Cl PE19 . . . . 95 E1
ilver Birch Ave PE27 . . . 143 F6
ilver Birch Cl PE29 . . . . 141 E7
ilver Ct SG7 . . . . 2 D4
ilverdale Ave PE2 . . . . . . 82 B2
ilverdale Cl CB23 . . . . . . 82 A2
ilver Hill PE7 . . . . 186 D3
ilver La PE27 . . . . 208 A3
ilverley Way CB8 . . . . . . 91 F7
ilver Lodge IP28 . . . . . . 239 F3
ilvers Cl CB7 . . . . 212 B5
ilver's La PE13 . . . . 234 E7
ilver St
  Ashwell SG7 . . . . 2 D4
  Buckden PE19 . . . . 117 B4
  Burwell CB25 . . . . 130 B4
  Cambridge CB3 . . . . . . 246 A1
  Ely CB7 . . . . 240 C4
  Godmanchester PE29 . . 118 E8
  Guilden Morden SG8 . . . 10 F4
  Litlington SG8 . . . . 12 A2
  March PE15 . . . . 243 C7
  Peterborough PE2 . . . . 186 F7
  Ramsey PE26 . . . . 172 B7
  St Neots PE19 . . . . 74 E4
  Willingham CB24 . . . . . 209 A1
  Wisbech PE13 . . . . 245 C6
  Witcham CB6 . . . . 217 A2
  Withersfield CB9 . . . . . 38 A4
ilverweed PE19 . . . . 74 C5
ilverwood Cl CB1 . . . . . . 84 B2
ilverwood Rd PE1 . . . . . 197 F5
ilvester Rd PE5 . . . . 195 E2
imeon Cl CB6 . . . . 240 F7
immer Piece PE28 . . . . . 121 C5
impkin Cl PE19 . . . . 74 B2
ingerfire Rd PE5 . . . . . . 195 D2
ir Harry Smith Com Coll
  PE7 . . . . 189 F7
ir James Black Rd CB7 . . 240 C2
iskin Cl SG8 . . . . 5 E8
issley PE2 . . . . 185 E2
itch Rd CB23 . . . . 79 C2
ix Bells 14 PE28 . . . . . . 215 C1
IX MILE BOTTOM 68 F7
ix Mile Bottom Rd CB21 . 69 C5
ixteen Foot Bank
  Christchurch PE14 . . . . 229 C4
  Wimblington PE15 . . . . 223 E5
ixth Ave CB4 . . . . 83 D8
ix Mile Rd CB23 . . . . . . 245 E4
keaping Cl CB8 . . . . 111 A4
keels Ct PE29 . . . . 141 F7
keggles Cl PE29 . . . . . . 141 B5
keifs Row 4 PE15 . . . . . . 222 A5
kelton Pl PE27 . . . . 144 B5

Skelton's Dro IP28 . . . . . 213 F8
Skipper's La
  West Wickham CB21 . . . 37 F8
  West Wratting CB21 . . . . 54 E1
  Withersfield CB9 . . . . . 38 A5
Skiver Cl CB22 . . . . 32 F6
Skylark Pl 9 SG8 . . . . 5 E8
Skylarks Cl PE7 . . . . 186 D3
Slade Cl PE26 . . . . 172 A7
SLADE FIELD 241 B7
Slade Mews PE26 . . . . . . 172 A7
Slade The
  Witcham CB6 . . . . 217 A2
  Wrestlingworth & Cockayne
   Hatley SG19 . . . . 25 B3
Slade Way PE16 . . . . 241 C5
Slatebarn Dro PE7 . . . . . 221 C8
Slaters Dr CB7 . . . . 38 E2
Sleaford St CB1 . . . . 84 A1
Sleford Cl CB1 . . . . 53 B2
Sleights Dr 4 PE14 . . . . . 238 F1
Slid La CB22 . . . . 29 F8
Slipe Cotts PE28 . . . . . . 146 A6
Small Lode PE14 . . . . . . 236 F1
Smallwood PE3 . . . . 197 B5
Smeefield PE28 . . . . 99 B8
Smeeth Rd
  Emneth PE14 . . . . 236 E6
  Marshland St James PE14 236 F7
Smith Dr PE19 . . . . 117 B3
Smithy Fen Engine Dro
  CB24 . . . . 209 E2
Smithfield PE6 . . . . 233 B3
Smiths Chase PE15 . . . . 243 B5
Smith's Dr PE15 . . . . . . 243 F3
Smith's Dro CB8 . . . . . . 226 F4
Smith's End La SG8 . . . . . 6 F1
Smith St CB23 . . . . 100 A4
Smiths Yd PE19 . . . . 94 A6
Smithy Way CB23 . . . . . . 79 C4
Snail Croft PE13 . . . . . . 238 A2
SNAILWELL 133 B4
Snailwell Rd
  Fordham CB8 . . . . 131 F5
  Newmarket CB8 . . . . . . 111 A6
Snailwell Short Rd CB8 . . 131 E1
Snoots Rd PE7 . . . . 189 B7
Snowberry Way 3 PE2 . . 212 B5
Snowden Cl 1 PE6 . . . . . 232 C8
Snowdon Cl 9 CB9 . . . . . 23 E6
Snowdonia Way PE29 . . . 141 A4
Snowley Pk PE7 . . . . 189 B8
Snowy Way PE29 . . . . . . 142 B6
Sobrite Way PE4 . . . . . . 204 B7
SOHAM 212 B4
SOHAM COTES 211 F5
Soham Mere CB7 . . . . . . 211 F4
Soham Rd
  Ely CB7 . . . . 211 D8
  Fordham CB7 . . . . 212 D2
Soham Village Coll CB7 . 212 B3
Sokemans Way PE28 . . . . 117 D8
Soke Parkway PE3 . . . . . 197 A3
Soke Rd PE6 . . . . 207 B1
Somerby Cl PE9 . . . . 244 A7
Somerby Garth 1 PE1 . . 198 D7
Somers Rd PE13 . . . . . . 245 B4
Somervell Ct 5 CB4 . . . . 83 E7
Somerville PE4 . . . . 204 A5
Somerville Rd 1 PE9 . . . 244 A6
Somes Cl 1 PE9 . . . . . . 230 C6
Sorbus Cl PE7 . . . . 186 D3
Sorrel Cl SG8 . . . . 5 F5
Sorrell Cl SG8 . . . . 5 F5
Sorrel Wlk CB9 . . . . 38 D1
Southacre Cl CB2 . . . . . . 64 E6
Southacre Dr CB2 . . . . . . 64 E6
Southampton Pl PE16 . . 241 C3
South Brink
  Elm PE14 . . . . 235 B4
  Wisbech PE13 . . . . 245 A3
Southbrooke Cl 2 CB2 . . 64 E6
Southbrook Field CB23 . . 99 A2
South Cl SG8 . . . . 5 B7
Southcourts CB22 . . . . . . 48 F3
Southdown Rd PE7 . . . . . 181 F5
South Dr
  March PE15 . . . . 243 E4
  Newmarket CB8 . . . . . . 110 F4
South End SG8 . . . . 12 E3
Southerns The 7 CB6 . . . 216 E1
Southey Wood ★ PE9 . . . 231 A1
Southfield CB10 . . . . 18 A3
Southfields Ave PE2 . . . . 187 D5
Southfields Cl
  Newmarket CB8 . . . . . . 110 E4
  Wisbech PE13 . . . . 245 A3
Southfields Dr PE2 . . . . 187 D6
Southfields Jun & Inf school
  PE2 . . . . 187 D5
Southgate Ave IP28 . . . . 239 D7
Southgate Way PE2 . . . . 185 C2
SOUTH GREEN 190 F7
South Green Rd CB3 . . . . 64 C7

South La 3 CB23 . . . . . . 62 C5
Southlands Ave PE1 . . . . 198 A6
SOUTHOE 95 E5
Southoe Rd PE7 . . . . 187 D2
SOUTHORPE 230 D2
Southorpe Meadow Nature
  Reserve ★ PE9 . . . . . . 230 D2
Southorpe Paddock Nature
  Reserve ★ PE9 . . . . . . 230 E1
South Par PE3 . . . . 197 E3
South Park Dr CB3 . . . . . 99 B1
South Park St PE16 . . . . 241 C4
South Rd
  Brampton PE28 . . . . . . 117 D8
  Great Abington CB21 . . . 33 F4
  Histon CB24 . . . . 104 B1
Southside Ct CB4 . . . . . . 84 A5
South St
  Comberton CB23 . . . . . 62 C4
  Great Chesterford CB10 . 18 D2
  Huntingdon PE29 . . . . . 141 F5
  Litlington SG8 . . . . 12 A2
  Peterborough PE1 . . . . 198 B2
  St Neots PE19 . . . . 74 E5
  Woodhurst PE28 . . . . . 155 A4
South Terr CB22 . . . . 32 F5
South View PE7 . . . . 186 F7
South View Rd PE4 . . . . . 197 D8
Southwell Ave PE4 . . . . . 204 A4
Southwell Cl PE15 . . . . . 243 C6
Southwell Rd CB4 . . . . . . 245 C8
Southwick Cl 5 PE4 . . . . 204 F1
Sovereign Cl PE13 . . . . . 245 A6
Sovereign Ct PE29 . . . . . 141 B8
Sovereign Pl PE3 . . . . . . 197 E2
Sovereign Way CB24 . . . 125 E3
Spaldings La CB25 . . . . . 105 D7
Spalding Way CB1 . . . . . . 65 D4
SPALDWICK 137 F6
Spaldwick Prim Sch
  PE28 . . . . 137 F5
Spaldwick Rd PE28 . . . . 137 C3
Spar Cl CB23 . . . . 79 A4
Sparkes Cl 2 CB7 . . . . . 213 A5
Sparrow Cl PE29 . . . . . . 141 E5
Sparrow Dr PE28 . . . . . . 150 E4
Sparrowgate Rd PE14 . . 238 F1
Sparrowhawk Way PE29 . 142 B7
Sparrow Rd 2 PE7 . . . . . 186 D1
Sparrows Cl PE28 . . . . . 117 D8
Sparrow Way PE28 . . . . . 120 B1
Spartan Cl
  Haverhill CB9 . . . . 23 C8
  Wisbech PE13 . . . . 245 E2
Speechley Rd PE7 . . . . . 181 F6
Speechley's Dro PE6 . . . 207 F2
Speed La CB7 . . . . 212 B4
Speedwell Cl CB1 . . . . . . 66 A6
Spencer Ave PE2 . . . . . . 187 D5
Spencer Cl
  3 Eaton Socon PE19 . . . 74 D6
  West Walton PE14 . . . . 238 E4
Spencer Croft CB7 . . . . . 240 E6
Spencer Dr
  Melbourn SG8 . . . . 14 D6
  St Ives PE27 . . . . 144 A7
Spencer Dro
  Guyhirn PE13 . . . . 235 A2
  Soham CB7 . . . . 212 A4
Spencer Rd CB10 . . . . . . 18 D3
Spens Ave CB3 . . . . 64 B8
Spenser Cl SG8 . . . . 13 D1
Sperling Dr CB9 . . . . 38 F2
Speyside 1 PE2 . . . . 185 D4
Spicer's Cl CB21 . . . . . . 53 F4
Spiggots Cl SG24 . . . . . . 123 E2
Spindle Rd CB9 . . . . 38 D1
Spinney Abbey CB7 . . . . 211 D2
Spinney Cl
  Warboys PE28 . . . . 164 F5
  Warmington PE8 . . . . . 178 E6
Spinney CP Sch The CB1 . 65 E6
Spinney Dr CB22 . . . . . . 49 A4
Spinney Field CB22 . . . . 138 F3
Spinney Fields PE7 . . . . 176 F4
Spinney La PE29 . . . . . . 150 F5
Spinney The
  Bar Hill CB23 . . . . 102 B3
  Cottenham CB24 . . . . . 125 E5
  Huntingdon PE29 . . . . . 142 B6
Spinney Way
  5 Needingworth PE27 . . 208 A3
  St Ives PE27 . . . . 144 A6
Spinning Inf Sch PE26 . . 172 B7
Spires End PE28 . . . . . . 150 D6
Spitfire Cl PE29 . . . . . . 141 B8
Spittals Way
  Huntingdon PE29 . . . . . 141 C7
  The Stukeleys PE29 . . . 152 C1
Splash La
  Castor PE5 . . . . 184 E8
  St Ives PE27 . . . . 142 F6
Split Dro CB25 . . . . 129 A4
Spong Dro CB24 . . . . . . 209 B1
Spooners Cl CB8 . . . . . . 70 F8
Spignall PE3 . . . . 196 F4
Sprigs Rd PE7 . . . . 186 B2
Spring Ave PE7 . . . . 186 B1
Springbrook PE19 . . . . . 74 F4
Spring Cl
  Burwell CB25 . . . . 130 B1
  Histon CB24 . . . . 104 A1
  Huntingdon PE29 . . . . . 141 C6
Spring Comm Sch PE29 . 141 F6
Spring Dr PE7 . . . . 187 B2
Springfield
  Huntingdon PE29 . . . . . 141 E5

Springfield continued
  Peterborough PE2 . . . . 187 A7
  Somersham PE28 . . . . . 215 C1
Springfield Ave PE15 . . . 243 C2
Springfield Cl
  Buckden PE19 . . . . 117 A3
  Great Cambourne CB23 . 79 C2
  2 St Neots PE19 . . . . . . 75 A5
Springfield Rd
  Alconbury Weston PE28 . 150 D5
  Cambridge CB4 . . . . . . 83 E4
  1 Parson Drove PE13 . . 234 D7
  Peterborough PE1 . . . . 197 F5
  Sawston CB22 . . . . 32 F5
  Yaxley PE7 . . . . 181 F5
Springfields PE7 . . . . . . 190 C7
Springfield Terr 1 CB4 . . 83 E4
Springhead SG7 . . . . 2 D4
Springhead La CB7 . . . . 240 E5
Spring Hill MK44 . . . . . . 93 A3
Springhill Rd CB24 . . . . 121 E6
Spring La
  Bassingbourn SG8 . . . . 12 F3
  Bottisham CB25 . . . . . . 86 F6
Spring Meadow Inf Sch
  CB7 . . . . 240 E6
Spring Pl PE19 . . . . 95 A1
Spruce Dr PE28 . . . . 151 E2
Spurgeons Cl CB8 . . . . . 106 B8
Spurgeon's Cl CB1 . . . . . 85 B1
Spurling Cl CB8 . . . . 91 C5
Square The
  6 Barnack PE9 . . . . . . 230 D4
  Stow cum Quy CB25 . . . 86 A6
Squires Cl 17 PE28 . . . . 215 C1
Squires Cl
  5 Eaton Socon PE19 . . . 74 B4
  Haverhill CB9 . . . . 23 E7
Squire's Dr PE14 . . . . . . 229 F7
Squire's Field The CB21 . 67 F7
Squires Gate PE4 . . . . . . 204 F1
Squires The PE2 . . . . . . 186 F8
Stables Cl PE13 . . . . 238 B2
Stables The PE7 . . . . 189 C7
Stable Yd PE13 . . . . 79 B3
Stackyard The
  Ickleton CB10 . . . . 18 A3
  Peterborough PE2 . . . . 185 E5
Stafford Rd PE7 . . . . 189 F6
Staffordshire Gdns 8
  CB1 . . . . 84 A1
Staffordshire St CB1 . . . 84 A2
Stagsden PE2 . . . . 185 F4
Stagshaw Dr PE2 . . . . . . 187 B8
STAGS HOLT 228 D7
Stained Glass Mus ★
  CB7 . . . . 240 D4
Staithe Rd PE13 . . . . . . 245 E5
Stake Piece Rd SG8 . . . . 5 C5
Stakings PE22 . . . . 32 D7
Stallebrass Cl PE2 . . . . . 187 E5
STAMFORD 244 D4
Stamford Arts Ctr ★ PE9 . 244 C5
Stamford Ave SG8 . . . . . 5 D7
Stamford Cl SG8 . . . . 5 D7
Stamford Coll PE9 . . . . . 244 D6
Stamford Ct SG8 . . . . 5 D7
Stamford High Sch PE9 . 244 C4
Stamford Jun Sch PE9 . . 244 D3
Stamford La PE8 . . . . . . 178 B3
Stamford Leisure Ctr
  PE9 . . . . 244 D6
Stamford Lodge Rd PE6 . 196 D4
Stamford Mus ★ PE9 . . . 244 C5
Stamford Rd
  Barnack PE9 . . . . 230 C4
  Easton on the Hill PE9 . 244 A1
  Helpston PE6 . . . . 231 C1
  Marholm PE6 . . . . 203 B2
  Market Deeping PE6 . . . 231 D8
  Tallington PE9 . . . . 231 A8
Stamford Ret Pk PE9 . . . 244 D6
Stamford & Rutland Hospl
  PE9 . . . . 244 D6
Stamford Sch PE9 . . . . . 244 C5
Stamford St 3 CB8 . . . . 111 B2
Stamford Sta PE9 . . . . . 244 B4
Stamford Theatre ★ 14
  PE9 . . . . 244 C5
Stamford Wlk 11 PE9 . . . 244 C5
Stamford Yd SG8 . . . . . . 5 C6
Stamper St PE3 . . . . 196 F3
Stanbury Cl CB5 . . . . 84 E6
Stanch Hill Rd PE28 . . . 168 C3
Standish Ct PE2 . . . . . . 186 D8
Stanegate 3 PE28 . . . . . 168 C2
Stanesfield Rd CB5 . . . . 84 D3
Stanford Bus Pk PE9 . . . 244 D7
Stanford Wlk PE3 . . . . . 197 C7
Stangate Hill PE28 . . . . 160 E5
STANGROUND 187 C5
Stanground Coll PE7 . . . 187 C5
Stanground Newt Ponds
  Nature Reserve ★ PE7 . 187 C4
Stanground Wash Nature
  Reserve ★ PE7 . . . . . . 187 D7
Staniland Way PE4 . . . . . 204 B5
Stanley Ave CB4 . . . . 83 D8
Stanley Ct CB5 . . . . 84 B3
Stanley Rd
  Cambridge CB5 . . . . . . 84 B3
  Great Chesterford CB10 . 18 E3
  Newmarket CB8 . . . . . . 111 C3
  Peterborough PE1 . . . . 198 A3
Stanley St PE9 . . . . 244 C5
Stanley Webb Cl CB22 . . 33 A8
Stanpoint Way PE27 . . . . 144 A5
Stan Rowing Ct PE2 . . . . 187 C7

Stansfield Gdns CB21 . . . 66 F5
Stansgate Ave CB2 . . . . . 65 B3
Stanton Mere Way CB24 . 124 A6
Stantons CB21 . . . . 35 B2
Stanton Sq PE7 . . . . 186 D2
Stanwick Ct PE3 . . . . . . 197 F2
Stapledon Rd PE2 . . . . . 185 D2
Staploe Way PE1 . . . . . . 198 F6
STAPLEFORD 49 C4
Stapleford Com Prim Sch
  CB22 . . . . 49 C4
Staples La CB7 . . . . 212 B3
Staploe Mews 16 CB7 . . 212 B4
Star Cl PE1 . . . . 198 C3
Star & Garter La CB8 . . . 91 C7
Stargoose Cl CB23 . . . . . 80 B1
Star La
  Ramsey PE26 . . . . 172 A5
  Stamford PE9 . . . . 244 C5
Starling Cl
  Alconbury PE28 . . . . . . 150 E4
  Milton CB24 . . . . 105 D3
Starlock Cl CB6 . . . . 210 E4
Star Mews PE1 . . . . 198 C2
Star Rd PE1 . . . . 198 C2
Stathern Rd PE1 . . . . . . 198 D7
Station App
  March PE15 . . . . 243 C6
  Newmarket CB8 . . . . . . 111 A2
  Somersham PE28 . . . . . 208 C8
Station Ave PE13 . . . . . . 234 D5
Station Dr
  Wisbech PE13 . . . . 245 C4
  Wisbech St Mary PE13 . 235 C7
Station Gate CB25 . . . . . 109 B8
Station Gdns PE26 . . . . . 172 A8
Station La PE19 . . . . 117 F3
Station Rd
  Abbots Ripton PE28 . . . 162 B1
  Ailsworth PE5 . . . . 184 C8
  Ashwell SG7 . . . . 2 E4
  Barnack PE9 . . . . 230 E4
  Bluntisham PE28 . . . . . 208 C4
  Cambridge CB1 . . . . . . 64 F7
  Catworth PE28 . . . . . . 136 D5
  Chatteris PE16 . . . . . . 241 C4
  Deeping St James PE6 . 206 E6
  Dullingham CB8 . . . . . . 89 C2
  Elm PE14 . . . . 235 C2
  Ely CB7 . . . . 240 D3
  Fordham CB8 . . . . 131 A8
  Foxton CB22 . . . . 30 B6
  Fulbourn CB21 . . . . . . 67 A5
  Gamlingay SG19 . . . . . 41 E5
  Gedney Hill PE12 . . . . . 233 F8
  Great Shelford CB22 . . . 49 A5
  Haddenham CB6 . . . . . 210 A6
  Harston CB22 . . . . 47 F2
  Haverhill CB9 . . . . 24 A8
  Histon CB24 . . . . 104 C3
  Holme PE7 . . . . 177 A4
  Isleham CB7 . . . . 213 A4
  Kennett CB8 . . . . 133 F5
  Kimbolton PE28 . . . . . . 113 F5
  Linton CB21 . . . . 35 B2
  Littleport CB6 . . . . 242 E4
  Lode CB25 . . . . 107 C2
  Longstanton CB24 . . . . 123 F4
  Manea PE15 . . . . 224 B5
  March PE15 . . . . 243 D5
  Meldreth SG8 . . . . 14 B6
  Mildenhall IP28 . . . . . . 239 B3
  Oakington & Westwick
   CB24 . . . . 103 D7
  Over CB24 . . . . 122 F8
  Pampisford CB21 . . . . . 33 F6
  Peterborough PE3 . . . . 197 F2
  Ramsey PE26 . . . . 172 A7
  Shepreth SG8 . . . . 29 E5
  Soham CB7 . . . . 212 B4
  Stamford PE9 . . . . 244 B4
  Steeple Morden SG8 . . . 3 B7
  St Ives PE27 . . . . 144 B3
  St Neots PE19 . . . . 75 B5
  Stow cum Quy CB25 . . . 106 E1
  Sutton CB6 . . . . 216 F1
  Swaffham Bulbeck CB25 . 108 A2
  Swaffham Prior CB25 . . 108 C5
  Swavesey CB24 . . . . . . 122 E7
  Thorney PE6 . . . . 233 A4
  Tilbrook PE28 . . . . 113 B7
  Walsoken PE14 . . . . . . 236 E8
  Warboys PE28 . . . . 164 F7
  Waterbeach CB25 . . . . . 106 B7
  Whittlesey PE7 . . . . . . 189 C5
  Wilburton CB6 . . . . 210 C7
  Willingham CB24 . . . . . 124 A4
  Wisbech St Mary PE13 . 235 C7
  Yaxley PE7 . . . . 182 A7
Station Road E CB22 . . . 32 E3
Station Road W CB22 . . . 32 E3
Station St PE16 . . . . 241 B4
Station Yd IP28 . . . . 239 B3
STAUGHTON GREEN . . . 93 F7
STAUGHTON HIGHWAY . 94 A5
Staughton Pl 2 PE19 . . . 74 C4
Staunch Hill PE28 . . . . . 148 C3
Staverton Rd PE4 . . . . . . 204 A3
Staxton Cl PE6 . . . . 203 C1
Stearne's Yd CB23 . . . . . 47 B5
Steel Cl PE19 . . . . 74 B2
STEEPLE GIDDING 159 B7
STEEPLE MORDEN 11 A1
Steeple Morden CE Prim Sch
  SG8 . . . . 11 B2

Steeple Row 13 CB7 . . . . 240 D4
Steeple View
  March PE15 . . . . 243 C1
  Wisbech PE13 . . . . 245 F7
Stephen Cl PE15 . . . . 23 F8
Stephenson Cl
  1 March PE15 . . . . 243 D1
  Royston SG8 . . . . 5 B7
  Yaxley PE7 . . . . 181 D6
Stephenson Ct PE1 . . . . 198 B2
Stephenson Rd PE7 . . . . . . 144 B6
Stephens Way 15 PE6 . . . . 231 F8
Stepping Stones PE28 . . . 143 D1
Stermyn St 14 PE13 . . . . . . 245 C5
Sterndale Cl CB3 . . . . 82 E8
Sterne Cl CB1 . . . . 65 B6
Sternes Way CB22 . . . . 49 C4
STETCHWORTH 90 A2
STETCHWORTH LEY 71 B7
Stetchworth Rd
  Dullingham CB8 . . . . 70 F8
  Stetchworth CB8 . . . . 71 C8
Stevens Cl CB24 . . . . 125 D4
Stevenson Ct
  Cambridge CB5 . . . . 84 A3
  Eaton Socon PE19 . . . . 74 A3
Stevensons Rd CB24 . . . . . 123 E2
Stevens Way PE15 . . . . 243 D6
STEVENTON END 21 C2
Steward Cl CB7 . . . . 211 D8
Stewards Field 16 CB7 . . . 212 E1
Steward's La CB8 . . . . 216 E1
Stewart Cl PE28 . . . . 140 C2
Steynings The PE4 . . . . 204 C3
STIBBINGTON 194 C2
Stickle Cl PE29 . . . . 141 B7
Stile Plantation SG8 . . . . . . 5 E6
Stiles The PE29 . . . . 141 F1
Still The PE13 . . . . 238 B1
STILTON 176 A7
Stilton CE Prim Sch PE7 175 F7
Stirling Cl
  Beck Row, Holywell Row &
    Kenny Hill IP28 . . . . 213 D6
  Cambridge CB4 . . . . 84 A3
  Warboys PE28 . . . . 164 F4
Stirling Ct PE29 . . . . 23 E8
Stirling Gdns CB8 . . . . 110 E4
Stirling Rd PE27 . . . . 144 A7
Stirling Way
  Papworth Village CB23 . . . . 99 C1
  Peterborough PE3 . . . . 204 A1
  10 Sutton CB6 . . . . 216 E2
  Witchford CB6 . . . . 217 F1
STIRTLOE 118 B2
Stirtloe La PE19 . . . . 117 A2
Stitch The PE14 . . . . 236 B4
Stocker Way 2 PE19 . . . . . . 74 E2
Stocking Ct PE28 . . . . 161 C4
Stocking Dro
  Chatteris PE16 . . . . 241 B1
  Ferry Hill PE16 . . . . 215 E6
Stocking Fen Rd PE26 . . . 221 A1
Stocking La
  Nuthampstead SG8 . . . . 1 A2
  Spaldwick PE28 . . . . 114 E8
Stockley Cl CB4 . . . . 24 C7
Stocks Bridge Way PE27 144 C5
Stocks Cl CB24 . . . . 86 E5
Stocks Hill PE5 . . . . 195 F1
Stocks La
  Gamlingay SG19 . . . . 41 D4
  Orwell SG8 . . . . 45 E1
Stockwell St CB1 . . . . 65 B8
Stokesay Ct PE3 . . . . 197 B1
Stokes Cl CB24 . . . . 123 F1
Stonald Ave PE7 . . . . 189 C8
Stonald Rd PE7 . . . . 189 C8
Stonea Camp ★ PE15 . . . . 223 E8
Stonebridge PE2 . . . . 186 C5
Stonebridge La PE21 . . . . . 67 A4
Stonebridge Lea PE2 . . . . 186 C5
Stonecross Way PE15 . . . 243 D3
Stone Field CB23 . . . . 102 A3
Stonehill
  Huntingdon PE29 . . . . . . 141 C7
  St Neots PE19 . . . . 75 C5
Stonehill Rd CB22 . . . . 48 E7
Stonehouse Rd
  Upwell PE14 . . . . 236 E1
  Yaxley PE7 . . . . 181 E5
Stone La
  Meldreth SG8 . . . . 29 C3
  Peterborough PE2 . . . . . . 197 F5
Stoneleigh Ct PE3 . . . . 197 B2
STONELY 115 B3
Stonely Rd PE28 . . . . 138 B3
Stone St CB1 . . . . 84 B1
Stone Terr CB1 . . . . 84 B1
Stoney Cl PE29 . . . . 141 F8
Storbeck Rd 2 PE13 . . . . . 245 D7
Storers Wlk PE7 . . . . 190 C6
Stores Hill CB8 . . . . 92 E8
Storey's Bar Rd PE6 . . . . . 199 A3
Storey's Way CB3 . . . . 83 B3
Storrington Way PE4 . . . . 204 C3
Stott Gdns CB4 . . . . 84 A6
Stott St CB23 . . . . 99 A2
STOURBRIDGE COMMON . . 84 B4
Stourbridge Gr CB1 . . . . . . 84 C1
Stour Cl PE27 . . . . 144 A6
Stour Gn PE26 . . . . 240 D6
Stour Valley Rd CB9 . . . . . . 24 B7
STOW CUM QUY 86 A6
Stowehill Rd PE4 . . . . 204 F2

Stowgate Rd PE6 . . . . 206 B7
Stow Gdns PE13 . . . . 245 E4
Stow La PE13 . . . . 245 E4
STOW LONGA 137 C2
Stow Rd
  Kimbolton PE28 . . . . 113 F5
  Spaldwick PE28 . . . . 137 F6
  Stow cum Quy CB25 . . . . . 85 F5
  Wisbech PE13 . . . . 245 F5
Straight Dro
  Bury PE26 . . . . 172 D3
  Coveney CB6 . . . . 217 C7
  Farcet PE7 . . . . 187 B1
  Sawtry PE28 . . . . 168 D3
  Wistow PE28 . . . . 172 D3
Straight Furlong CB6 . . . . 224 E2
Straight Rd PE15 . . . . 224 B3
Strangeways Rd CB1 . . . . . 65 D4
Strasbourg Sq 6 CB9 . . . . 24 B8
Stratfield Cl CB4 . . . . 83 B5
Stratford PI PE19 . . . . 74 C3
Strathcarron Ct CB4 . . . . . . 83 E7
Strawberry Cl PE13 . . . . . . 245 A6
Strawberry Fields CB9 . . . . 23 D7
STREETLY END 37 A5
Streetly End CB21 . . . . 37 B5
Street The
  Barton Mills IP28 . . . . 239 E2
  Beck Row, Holywell Row & Kenny
    Hill IP28 . . . . 214 A8
  Dalham CB8 . . . . 92 E8
  Freckenham CB8 . . . . 213 C3
  Great Bradley CB8 . . . . 55 F7
  Great Wratting CB9 . . . . . . 39 E6
  Kirtling CB8 . . . . 72 D6
  Lidgate CB8 . . . . 73 D8
  Mildenhall IP28 . . . . 213 E8
  Moulton CB8 . . . . 112 F5
  Snailwell CB8 . . . . 132 A4
  Westley Waterless CB8 . . . . 70 C5
  Woodditton CB8 . . . . 91 B2
  Worlington IP28 . . . . 213 F4
Streetways CB8 . . . . 68 E7
STRETHALL 9 F4
STRETHAM 210 E5
Stretham Com Prim Sch
  CB6 . . . . 210 F5
Stretham Old Engine ★
  CB6 . . . . 210 F4
Stretham Rd
  Wicken CB7 . . . . 211 D2
  Wilburton CB6 . . . . 210 D5
Stretten Ave CB4 . . . . 83 D4
Stretton Ave CB8 . . . . 111 B2
Stricklands Dr 5 PE6 . . . . 232 B8
Strollers Way CB8 . . . . 90 A2
Stroud Hill PE28 . . . . 165 E2
Strympole Way CB23 . . . . . 80 B1
Stuart Cl
  Godmanchester PE29 . . . . 142 A1
  Peterborough PE2 . . . . . . 187 C6
Stuart Ct PE1 . . . . 198 B4
Stuart Dr SG8 . . . . 5 D8
Stubbs Cl
  3 Haverhill CB9 . . . . 38 D1
  St Ives PE27 . . . . 144 A7
Studland Ret Pk CB8 . . . . 110 F7
STUDLANDS PARK 110 F8
Studlands Park Ave CB8 110 D6
Studlands Rise SG8 . . . . . . 5 E6
Studlands Rise Fst Sch
  SG8 . . . . 5 E5
STUKELEY 141 B6
Stukeley Cl
  Cambridge CB3 . . . . 64 A8
  Peterborough PE2 . . . . . . 187 D5
Stukeley Meadows Com Prim
  Sch PE29 . . . . 141 C6
Stukeley Meadows Ind Est
  PE29 . . . . 141 C6
Stukeley Pk PE29 . . . . 152 A2
Stukeley Rd PE29 . . . . 141 C6
Stulp Field Rd CB3 . . . . 64 A4
Stumpacre PE3 . . . . 197 A4
Stumpcross 4 PE28 . . . . . 168 C2
Stump Cross CB10 . . . . 18 D5
STUNTNEY 218 D1
Stuntney Cswy CB7 . . . . . 240 E2
STURMER 24 F4
Sturmer Cl 6 CB4 . . . . 83 C7
Sturmer Rd CB9 . . . . 24 C6
Sturmer Road Ind Est
  CB9 . . . . 24 C6
Sturrock Way PE3 . . . . 197 C8
Sturton St CB1 . . . . 84 A1
Sudbury Ct
  Peterborough PE7 . . . . . . 187 F5
  Whittlesey PE7 . . . . 189 D8
Sudeley Gr CB23 . . . . 81 A3
Suet Hills Dro PE7 . . . . . . 188 E1
Suez Rd CB1 . . . . 65 C7
Suffolk Cl
  5 Ely CB6 . . . . 240 A3
  Huntingdon PE29 . . . . . . 141 F6
  Peterborough PE3 . . . . . . 197 B2
  St Ives PE27 . . . . 144 A8
Suffolk Rd 5 SG8 . . . . 5 E6
Suffolk Way
  March PE15 . . . . 243 E2
  Newmarket CB8 . . . . 110 E5
Sugar Way PE2 . . . . 186 C5
Sulehay Rd PE8 . . . . 193 C1
Sumerling Way PE28 . . . . 208 C6
Summerfield CB3 . . . . 64 C8
Summerfield Cl
  Burwell CB25 . . . . 130 C1
  Wisbech PE13 . . . . 245 A6
Summerfield Rd PE1 . . . . 197 F4

Summerhayes 1 CB7 . . . . 240 F6
Sunderland Ave CB22 . . . . 33 A8
Sundew Cl PE19 . . . . 74 B6
Sunfield Rd PE26 . . . . 172 A4
Sunflower St CB4 . . . . 83 D7
Sun Hill SG8 . . . . 5 C5
Sun La 6 CB8 . . . . 111 A3
Sunmead Wlk CB1 . . . . 66 A6
Sunningdale PE2 . . . . 185 E6
Sunningdale Ave IP28 . . . 239 B4
Sunningdale Cvn Pk CB4 . 84 D6
Sunnybank 1 PE19 . . . . . . 75 A5
Sunnymead 1 PE4 . . . . . . 204 A6
Sunnymead Orch SG7 . . . . 3 A3
Sunnyside CB5 . . . . 84 E2
Sunnyville Rd PE7 . . . . 190 F8
Sunset Gdns PE13 . . . . . . 245 E2
Sunset Sq 2 CB4 . . . . 83 D7
Sun St
  1 Cambridge CB1 . . . . 84 A2
  Isleham CB7 . . . . 213 A5
Surrey Rd PE29 . . . . 141 E8
Sussex Rd
  Stamford PE9 . . . . 244 B6
  Wyton Airfield PE28 . . . . 143 B8
Sussex St CB2 . . . . 246 B3
Sutcliffe Rd PE8 . . . . 193 D8
SUTTON
  Ailsworth 194 F2
  Ely 216 E2
Sutton CE Prim Sch CB6 216 E1
Sutton Cl CB24 . . . . 105 D3
Sutton Ct 6 CB6 . . . . 216 E2
Sutton Gate PE12 . . . . 237 D8
SUTTON GAULT 216 C2
Sutton Heath Rd PE9 . . . . 194 D7
Sutton Mdws PE13 . . . . . . 245 A8
Sutton Pk CB6 . . . . 216 E2
Sutton Rd
  Eyeworth SG19 . . . . 10 A8
  Haddenham CB6 . . . . 210 A8
  Mepal CB6 . . . . 216 E3
  Newton CB6 . . . . 238 B6
  Wentworth CB6 . . . . 217 C1
  Wisbech PE13 . . . . 245 A7
  Witchford CB6 . . . . 217 C1
Suttons Cl PE14 . . . . 236 F2
Sutton's La PE6 . . . . 231 E8
Sutton Way 1 PE15 . . . . . 223 A5
Svenskaby PE2 . . . . 185 C6
SWAFFHAM BULBECK . . . 108 B1
Swaffham Bulbeck CE Prim
  Sch CB25 . . . . 108 B1
Swaffham Heath Rd
  CB25 . . . . 108 C1
SWAFFHAM PRIOR 108 E4
Swaffham Prior CE Prim Sch
  CB25 . . . . 108 D5
Swaffham Rd
  Bottisham CB25 . . . . 107 E1
  Burwell CB25 . . . . 109 A7
  Reach CB25 . . . . 108 A5
Swain Ct PE2 . . . . 186 F8
Swain's Dro PE13 . . . . 238 C8
Swale Ave PE4 . . . . 204 E1
Swallow Cl PE7 . . . . 201 A1
Swallow Ct
  Manea PE15 . . . . 224 B4
  3 St Neots PE19 . . . . 75 B6
Swallowfield PE4 . . . . 204 A4
Swallow La PE13 . . . . 238 B8
Swallow Way PE15 . . . . . . 243 F5
Swan Cl
  St Ives PE27 . . . . 143 F7
  Whittlesey PE7 . . . . 189 F8
Swan Ct PE15 . . . . 243 D6
Swan Dr PE16 . . . . 241 D5
Swan End PE19 . . . . 117 B4
Swan Gdns
  Fenstanton PE28 . . . . 121 B5
  Parson Drove PE13 . . . . . 234 C7
  Peterborough PE1 . . . . . . 198 E6
Swan Gr CB3 . . . . 110 B8
Swanhill PE8 . . . . 194 A4
Swan La
  Exning CB8 . . . . 110 B8
  Guilden Morden SG8 . . . . . 10 F4
  Haverhill CB9 . . . . 24 A8
Swann Rd CB5 . . . . 84 C4
Swann's Cl SG8 . . . . 26 A3
Swann's Rd CB5 . . . . 84 B4
Swann's Terr 4 CB1 . . . . . . 65 A8
Swan Rd
  Fenstanton PE28 . . . . 121 B5
  Whittlesey PE7 . . . . 189 F8
Swansley La CB23 . . . . 79 A4
Swanspool PE3 . . . . 197 B6
Swan St SG7 . . . . 2 D4
Swanton Cl PE15 . . . . 243 D7
Swasedale Dro CB7 . . . . . 219 A5
SWAVESEY 123 E6
Swavesey Prim Sch
  CB24 . . . . 122 C6
Swavesey Rd CB24 . . . . . . 122 A4
Swavesey Village Coll
  CB24 . . . . 122 E6
Swayne's La CB23 . . . . 62 C5
Sweetbriar La PE4 . . . . . . 204 B6
Sweetentree Way 3
  CB23 . . . . 79 A4
Sweeting Ave PE19 . . . . . . 95 F1
Sweetings Rd PE29 . . . . . 118 F8
Swift Cl
  March PE15 . . . . 243 F5
  Market Deeping PE6 . . . . 231 E8
  Royston SG8 . . . . 13 D1
  St Neots PE19 . . . . 75 B6
Swifts Cnr CB21 . . . . 66 F5

Swinburne Cl SG8 . . . . 13 D1
SWINGBROW 222 D3
Swinnell Cl SG8 . . . . 13 A5
Sybil Rd PE13 . . . . 245 C6
Sycamore Ave PE1 . . . . . . 198 C6
Sycamore Cl
  4 Cambridge CB1 . . . . . . 65 D5
  March PE15 . . . . 243 C3
Sycamore Dr PE29 . . . . . . 141 E8
Sycamore La CB7 . . . . 240 F5
Sycamore PI CB6 . . . . 242 D4
Sycamore Rd PE7 . . . . 189 F6
Sycamores The
  Bluntisham/Colne PE28 . . 208 C6
  Little Paxton PE19 . . . . . . 95 F2
  Milton CB24 . . . . 105 C2
Sydney Rd PE2 . . . . 187 D5
Syers La PE7 . . . . 189 D7
Sylton Cl PE29 . . . . 141 F1
Sylvden Dr PE13 . . . . 245 F6
Sylvester Rd CB3 . . . . 83 B1
Symington Cl PE2 . . . . 186 B3
Symonds Cl CB24 . . . . 104 B4
Symonds La
  Grantchester CB3 . . . . 64 A4
  Linton CB21 . . . . 35 B3
Sywell Gr 5 PE14 . . . . 236 A5

T

Tabor Ct PE7 . . . . 186 D2
Tabrum Cl CB23 . . . . 63 F4
TADLOW 26 A3
Tadlow Rd SG19 . . . . 25 C3
Tait Cl PE1 . . . . 198 C5
Talbot Ave PE2 . . . . 186 D6
Talbot Cl PE7 . . . . 175 F8
TALLINGTON 230 E7
Tallington Dry Ski Slope
  PE9 . . . . 230 F8
Tallington Lakes Leisure
  Pk ★ PE9 . . . . 231 A8
Tallington Rd PE9 . . . . 230 F5
Tall's La PE28 . . . . 121 B6
Tall Trees 3 SG8 . . . . 5 E6
Tamar Cl PE27 . . . . 144 B6
Tamarin Gdns CB1 . . . . 66 A6
Tanglewood
  Alconbury Weston PE28 . . 150 E6
  Peterborough PE4 . . . . . . 204 B6
Tanhouse PE2 . . . . 186 C5
Tan House La CB25 . . . . . . 109 B8
Tannersfield Way CB8 . . . 110 F4
Tanners La CB7 . . . . 212 B3
Tanners Cl SG8 . . . . 5 C6
Tannery Drift Fst Sch SG8 . 5 C6
Tannery Rd CB22 . . . . 32 F6
Tansor Garth PE3 . . . . 197 C5
Tansor Grange PE8 . . . . . . 178 A1
Tansur Cr PE19 . . . . 74 E8
Tansy Cl 2 PE19 . . . . 74 B5
Tantallon Ct PE3 . . . . 197 B1
Tanyard The SG8 . . . . 12 E4
Tan Yd PE19 . . . . 74 E5
Tarrant PE4 . . . . 204 A6
Taskers Field CB23 . . . . . . 78 E2
Tasman Rd CB9 . . . . 24 C7
Tates Field
  Caxton CB23 . . . . 78 E1
  Great Grandsen CB23 . . . . 59 E8
Tatwin Dr 8 PE6 . . . . 232 B8
Taunton Cl CB1 . . . . 65 D7
Taverners Dr PE26 . . . . . . 171 F5
Taverners Rd PE1 . . . . 197 F4
Tavistock Cl 8 PE6 . . . . . . 233 A3
Tavistock Rd
  Cambridge CB4 . . . . 83 C6
  Wisbech PE13 . . . . 245 D5
Tawny Cres PE29 . . . . 142 B7
Tay Cl PE27 . . . . 144 B7
Taylor's Dro PE12 . . . . 237 C8
Taylor's Field CB8 . . . . 70 F8
Taylors Gn PE8 . . . . 178 A2
Taylors La PE19 . . . . 116 F5
Taylor's La CB24 . . . . 122 D6
Taymor PE14 . . . . 225 A8
Teachers Cl PE15 . . . . 224 B4
Tea Kettle La CB8 . . . . 89 F1
Teal Ave CB7 . . . . 212 A5
Teal Cl
  Chatteris PE16 . . . . 241 C6
  St Ives PE27 . . . . 143 F7
Teal Rd PE7 . . . . 189 F6
Teanby Ct PE3 . . . . 196 F3
Teasdale Cl SG8 . . . . 13 C1
Teasel Cl
  15 Eaton Socon PE19 . . . . 74 C6
  5 Haverhill CB9 . . . . 38 D1
  2 Royston SG8 . . . . 5 E5
Teasel Dr CB6 . . . . 240 E5
Teasel Way CB1 . . . . 66 A5
Tebbutts Rd PE19 . . . . 74 E5
Tedder Way CB4 . . . . 83 C6
Telegraph St CB24 . . . . . . 125 E4
Telford Dr PE7 . . . . 181 D6
Templars Ct CB9 . . . . 23 E7
Temple Cl
  Duxford CB22 . . . . 32 D1
  Huntingdon PE29 . . . . . . 141 E4
Temple Ct 4 CB4 . . . . 83 E7
TEMPLE END 55 D2
Temple End
  Great Wilbraham CB21 . . . 68 A8
  Little Thurlow CB9 . . . . . . 55 F2
Temple Grange PE4 . . . . . 204 B6
Templemore Cl CB1 . . . . . . 65 B4

Temple PI PE29 . . . . 141 E?
Temple Rd CB7 . . . . 212 A?
Temples Ct PE6 . . . . 231 B?
Tempsford Rd SG19 . . . . . . 40 A?
Ten Acre Dro PE7 . . . . 220 C?
Ten Bell La 6 CB7 . . . . . . 212 B?
Tenby Cl CB1 . . . . 66 A?
Tenby Way 6 PE19 . . . . . . 74 F?
Tenison Ave CB1 . . . . 64 F?
Tenison Manor CB24 . . . . 125 D?
Tenison Rd CB1 . . . . 65 A?
Ten Mile Bank CB7 . . . . . 225 F?
Tennis Court Ave PE29 . . 141 E?
Tennis Court Rd CB2 . . . . 246 A?
Tennis Court Terr CB2 . . . 246 A?
Tennyson Ave PE27 . . . . . 143 F?
Tennyson Cl
  Huntingdon PE29 . . . . . . 141 F?
  Royston SG8 . . . . 13 D?
Tennyson PI
  Eaton Socon PE19 . . . . . . 74 D?
  Ely CB6 . . . . 240 A?
Tennyson Rd PE1 . . . . 197 F?
Tenter La PE9 . . . . 244 C?
Tenterleas PE27 . . . . 144 B?
Tern Cl CB9 . . . . 24 C?
Tern Gdns PE16 . . . . 241 C?
Tern Rd PE7 . . . . 186 C?
Tern Way 4 PE19 . . . . 75 B?
Terrill Cl PE29 . . . . 141 C?
Terrington Cl PE14 . . . . . . 236 D?
Terr The
  Little Shelford CB22 . . . . . 48 E?
  Newmarket CB8 . . . . 111 A?
TETWORTH . . . . 40 F?
Tetworth Hill SG19 . . . . . . 41 A?
TEVERSHAM . . . . 85 C?
Teversham CE Prim Sch
  CB1 . . . . 85 B?
Teversham Drift CB1 . . . . . 66 A?
Teversham Rd CB1 . . . . . . 66 A?
Teversham Way CB22 . . . . 50 A?
Texas PE28 . . . . 151 E?
Teynham Cl CB1 . . . . 65 D?
Thackeray Cl SG8 . . . . 13 D?
Thackers Cl PE8 . . . . 194 A?
Thackray Cl PE29 . . . . 141 E?
Thames Rd PE29 . . . . 141 F?
Tharp Way CB7 . . . . 213 C?
Thatchers Cl
  Ramsey PE26 . . . . 171 B?
  Yelling PE19 . . . . 98 B?
Thatcher Stanfords Cl
  SG8 . . . . 14 C?
Thatchers Wood CB24 . . . 123 F?
Thatchwood Ave PE14 . . . 236 C?
Thetford Cnr CB6 . . . . 211 A?
Thetford Rd IP28 . . . . 239 E?
Thetford Terr CB5 . . . . 84 E?
Thicket Rd PE28 . . . . 143 B?
Thickwillow 2 PE29 . . . . . 118 F?
Thimble Cl PE28 . . . . 208 D?
Third Ave
  Warboys PE28 . . . . 164 C?
  Wisbech PE13 . . . . 245 E?
Third Dro
  Downham CB6 . . . . 225 ?
  Peterborough PE1 . . . . . . 198 E?
Third Marsh Rd PE14 . . . . 238 C?
Thirlby Gdns CB7 . . . . 240 E?
Thirleby Cl CB4 . . . . 83 D?
Thirlemere Gdns PE4 . . . 204 E?
Thirlmere PE29 . . . . 141 B?
Thirlmere Gdns 3 PE4 . . 204 E?
Thirlwall Dr CB7 . . . . 213 A?
Thistle Cnr CB7 . . . . 218 D?
Thistledown PE15 . . . . . . 222 F?
Thistle Dr PE2 . . . . 187 C?
Thistle Gn CB24 . . . . 122 E?
Thistlemoor Rd PE1 . . . . . 197 E?
THISTLEY GREEN . . . . . . 213 C?
Thodays Cl CB24 . . . . 209 A?
Thoday St CB1 . . . . 65 B?
THOLOMAS DROVE . . . . . 235 A?
Thomas Christian Way
  CB25 . . . . 86 B?
Thomas Cl PE3 . . . . 196 F?
Thomas Clarkson Com Coll
  PE13 . . . . 245 C?
Thomas Deacon Acad
  PE1 . . . . 198 B?
Thomas Eaton Prim Sch The
  PE15 . . . . 223 B?
Thomas King Dr PE29 . . . 141 E?
Thomas Parsons Sq CB7. 240 C?
Thomas Rd CB21 . . . . 66 D?
Thomas Way SG8 . . . . 13 D?
Thomas Wlk CB11 . . . . 9 F?
Thompsons Gd PE7 . . . . . 186 D?
Thompson's La CB24 . . . . 246 A?
Thompsons Mdw SG8 . . . . 11 A?
Thongsley PE29 . . . . 141 D?
Thongsley Fields Prim Sch
  PE29 . . . . 141 F?
Thorby Ave PE15 . . . . 243 A?
Thorley Cres PE2 . . . . 186 D?
Thorleye Rd CB5 . . . . 84 C?
Thornbury CB23 . . . . 62 D?
Thorn Cl 9 CB7 . . . . 212 A?
Thorndown Cl PE27 . . . . . 143 F?
Thorndown Inf Sch PE27 143 F?
Thorndown Jun Sch
  PE27 . . . . 143 F?
THORNEY . . . . 233 A?
Thorney Dyke PE6 . . . . . . 201 C?
Thorney Heritage Mus ★
  PE6 . . . . 233 A?

Thorney Rd
Eye PE6 . . . . **232** B1
Newborough PE6 . . . . **206** E2
Wisbech St Mary PE13 . . **234** C2
THORNEY TOLL **234** A3
Thornham Way PE7 . . . . . **190** C6
THORNHAUGH **193** F5
Thornhill Pl CB24 . . . . **123** F2
Thornleigh Dr PE2 . . . . . . **186** C6
Thornmead PE4 . . . . **204** D4
Thorn Rd PE7 . . . . **186** C2
Thornton Cl
Girton CB3 . . . . **82** F6
Peterborough PE4 . . . . . **204** E3
Thornton Rd
Girton CB3 . . . . **82** F7
March PE15 . . . . **243** D6
Thornton Way CB3 . . . . . . **83** A6
Thorolds Way PE5 . . . . . . **195** D2
Thoroughfare La CB7 . . . **218** F1
Thoroughfare Way CB6 . . **242** E4
Thorpe Ave PE3 . . . . **197** C2
Thorpe Lea Rd PE3 . . . . . . **197** F1
Thorpe Mdws PE3 . . . . . . **197** D1
Thorpe Park Rd PE3 . . . . . **197** C3
Thorpe Prim Sch PE3 . . . **197** B3
Thorpe Rd PE3 . . . . **197** B1
Thorpe The PE28 . . . . **143** B1
Thorpe Way CB5 . . . . **84** F4
Thorpe Wood PE3 . . . . . . **196** F1
Thorpe Wood Nature
Reserve★ PE3 . . . . **196** F1
Thorseby Rd PE3 . . . . **197** B3
Thrapston Rd
Brampton PE28 . . . . **140** B4
Catworth PE28 . . . . **147** C2
Ellington PE28 . . . . **139** A4
Kimbolton PE28 . . . . **113** F5
Spaldwick PE28 . . . . **137** F6
Three Cups Wlk CB7 . . . **240** D4
Three Hills CB1 . . . . **21** A7
THREE HOLES **229** E2
Three Shires Way PE28 . . **135** E4
Thrifts Wlk CB4 . . . . **84** A4
THRIPLOW **31** C2
Thriplow CE Prim Sch
SG8 . . . . **31** B2
Thriplow Rd SG8 . . . . **30** F1
THROCKENHOLT **234** B8
Throckmorton PE28 . . . . . **164** E5
Throckmorton Rd PE28 . . **117** D8
Throstlenest PE7 . . . . **187** C3
Thruffle Way CB23 . . . . . . **102** C3
Thulborn Cl CB1 . . . . **85** B1
Thurland's Dro PE14 . . . **229** C8
Thurlaston Cl PE3 . . . . **197** B2
Thurley Cl PE19 . . . . **95** E5
Thurloe Cl PE13 . . . . **245** C2
Thurlow Rd
Great Wratting CB9 . . . . . **39** C6
Withersfield CB9 . . . . **38** D4
Thurnall Ave CB5 . . . . **5** D5
Thurning Ave PE2 . . . . . . **187** C6
Thurning Rd PE28 . . . . . . **157** F7
Thuro Gr PE2 . . . . **186** A3
Thursfield PE4 . . . . **204** C4
Thurston Gate PE3 . . . . . . **197** A1
Tiberius Cl CB9 . . . . **24** D7
TILBROOK **114** B7
Tilbrook Mill MK44 . . . . . . **113** A7
Tilbrook Rd PE28 . . . . . . **113** D6
Tillbrooks Hill CB8 . . . . . . **73** C1
Tilling Way CB6 . . . . **242** C4
Tillyard Way CB1 . . . . **65** C7
Tilton Ct PE1 . . . . **198** C8
Tindall Cl PE13 . . . . **245** C4
Tinker's Dro PE13 . . . . . . **245** D8
Tinkers La PE28 . . . . **168** B4
Tinker's La CB23 . . . . **61** C2
Tintagel Ct
Peterborough PE3 . . . . . **197** B1
2 St Neots PE19 . . . . **74** F2
Tintern Rise 3 PE6 . . . . . **232** A1
Tinus Ave PE7 . . . . **186** C1
Tinwell Rd PE9 . . . . **244** A4
Tinwell Rd La PE9 . . . . . . **244** A4
Tipplers' Rd CB24 . . . . . . **122** E2
TIPPS END **229** F2
Tiptree Cl CB5 . . . . **84** F4
Tirrington PE3 . . . . **197** A3
Titchmarsh Cl SG8 . . . . . . **5** D7
Tithe Ave IP28 . . . . **213** F8
Tithe Cl PE28 . . . . **120** B2
Tithe Rd PE16 . . . . **241** C2
Tithe Way CB23 . . . . **79** C3
Tiverton Rd PE3 . . . . **197** C3
Tiverton Way CB1 . . . . **65** C7
Toates Cl CB6 . . . . **210** C6
TOFT **61** E4
Toft La CB21 . . . . **67** F7
Toftland PE2 . . . . **186** D5
Tointons Rd PE14 . . . . . . **229** F8
Tolethorpe Sq 4 PE9 . . . **244** B6
Toll Bar La PE28 . . . . **146** B5
Toll Dro PE15 . . . . **224** A3
Tollfield PE28 . . . . **113** F4
Tollgate PE3 . . . . **197** A5
Toll House Rd PE2 . . . . . . **186** C7
Toll Rd PE7 . . . . **188** A5
Tom Jennings Cl CB8 . . . **110** F5
Tomlins Cl SG8 . . . . **6** F1
Tomlinson Ct PE29 . . . . . **141** F8
Toneham La PE6 . . . . **232** F1
Topcliffe Way CB1 . . . . . . **65** C3
TOP END **93** B1
Topham Cres 9 PE6 . . . . **233** A3
Topham Ct PE19 . . . . **74** F7
Topham Way CB4 . . . . **83** D6

Top La PE19 . . . . **57** B5
Topmoor Way PE4 . . . . . . **204** F1
Topper St CB4 . . . . **83** E8
Top St CB6 . . . . **210** F5
Torkington Gdns 3 PE9 . **244** B5
Torold Dr PE7 . . . . **186** E2
Torpel Way 2 PE6 . . . . . . **231** C7
Tort Hill PE28 . . . . **168** C5
TOSELAND **97** D2
Toseland Rd PE19 . . . . **97** E4
Tothill Rd CB25 . . . . **108** D4
Touthill Cl PE1 . . . . **198** A2
Tower Cl
Bassingbourn SG8 . . . . . . **12** F5
Cottenham CB24 . . . . . . **125** D3
Huntingdon PE29 . . . . . . **141** D8
11 Over CB24 . . . . **208** D1
Ramsey PE26 . . . . **172** C7
Whittlesey PE7 . . . . **189** B8
Tower Ct
Ely CB6 . . . . **240** B3
Haverhill CB9 . . . . **23** E7
Peterborough PE2 . . . . . **186** F8
Tower Rd
Downham CB6 . . . . **217** F7
Elm PE14 . . . . **236** A3
Ely CB7 . . . . **240** B3
Sawston CB22 . . . . **33** A8
Sutton CB6 . . . . **216** E2
Tower Sq PE29 . . . . **152** D1
Tower St PE2 . . . . **186** F8
Tower View CB21 . . . . **35** D3
Towgood Way PE19 . . . . . . **96** D4
Towler St PE1 . . . . **198** A3
Town Bridge PE13 . . . . . . **245** B5
Town Cl CB22 . . . . **32** C5
TOWN END **243** D1
Town End PE15 . . . . **243** D1
Town End Cl CB9 . . . . **38** F1
Towne Rd SG8 . . . . **5** D5
Town Farm Cl SG8 . . . . **10** F4
Town Green Rd SG8 . . . . . . **28** D8
Town La CB22 . . . . **33** B5
Townley Cl PE14 . . . . **236** E1
Town Orch PE19 . . . . **95** E5
Townsend
Little Downham CB6 . . . . **217** F6
Soham CB7 . . . . **212** A5
Townsend Cl CB24 . . . . . . **105** C3
Townsend Rd
Needingworth PE27 . . . . **208** A3
Upwell PE14 . . . . **229** E7
Wittering PE8 . . . . **230** B1
Townsend Way PE7 . . . . . **175** D8
Townshend Rd PE13 . . . . **245** D6
Town St
Newton CB22 . . . . **31** B7
Outwell PE14 . . . . **236** E1
Town The PE19 . . . . **93** E6
Toyse Cl CB25 . . . . **130** C4
Toyse La CB25 . . . . **130** B4
Trafalgar Rd
Cambridge CB4 . . . . **246** A4
Eaton Socon PE19 . . . . . . **74** C5
Trafalgar St CB4 . . . . **246** B4
Trafalgar Terr PE9 . . . . . . **244** B6
Trafalgar Way CB23 . . . . . **102** B5
Trafford Est PE14 . . . . . . **238** F4
Trafford Pk 1 PE13 . . . . . **245** E6
Trafford Rd PE13 . . . . **245** D5
Tramar Dr 7 CB6 . . . . **216** E2
Tram Station La PE14 . . . **236** B6
Tramway The PE14 . . . . . **236** F2
Trap Rd SG8 . . . . **11** A4
Treading Bank PE13 . . . . **237** C4
Treading Field PE13 . . . . **237** C4
Tredegar Cl CB4 . . . . **83** E6
Treeway PE13 . . . . **241** B5
Trefoil Ct 2 CB9 . . . . **23** F7
Trent Cl PE27 . . . . **144** A7
Trent Rd PE8 . . . . **193** D8
Tresham Rd PE2 . . . . **185** D3
Trevone Pl CB1 . . . . **65** D7
Tribune Cl PE16 . . . . **241** D3
Tribune Ct CB4 . . . . **83** E7
Trienna PE2 . . . . **186** B5
Trigg Way SG8 . . . . **14** D6
Trinity Ave IP28 . . . . **239** C5
Trinity Cl
Balsham CB21 . . . . **53** B2
Bottisham CB25 . . . . **86** F6
Ely CB6 . . . . **240** C5
Fordham CB7 . . . . **212** F1
Great Paxton PE19 . . . . . . **96** E4
Haslingfield CB23 . . . . . . **47** B5
Trinity Coll CB2 . . . . **246** A3
Trinity Dr CB8 . . . . **111** B2
Trinity La CB2 . . . . **246** A2
Trinity Link CB9 . . . . **39** A1
Trinity Pl PE29 . . . . **141** E4
Trinity Rd
Stamford PE9 . . . . **244** A6
Wisbech PE13 . . . . **245** E6
Trinity St
Cambridge CB2 . . . . **246** A2
3 Peterborough PE1 . . . **198** A2
Triplow Meadows Nature
Reserve★ SG8 . . . . **31** B2
Trotwood Mews PE13 . . . **245** D3
Troughton Way 12 PE13 . **238** B2
Troutbeck Cl PE4 . . . . **204** F3
Truman Ave PE15 . . . . . . **243** A5
TRUMPINGTON **64** C2
Trumpington High St CB2 **64** D3
Trumpington Rd CB2 . . . . . **64** E5
Trumpington St CB2 . . . . **246** A2

Trundle Mere PE7 . . . . . . **182** B2
Trundle The PE28 . . . . . . **215** C1
Trundley Cl CB9 . . . . **38** F1
Tuckers Nook 1 PE6 . . . **231** C7
Tucker's Yd PE2 . . . . **187** C7
Tuck's Yd PE15 . . . . **224** B4
TUDDENHAM **214** D2
Tuddenham CE Prim Sch
IP28 . . . . **214** E2
Tuddenham Rd IP28 . . . . **239** F2
Tudor Ave PE7 . . . . **186** C1
Tudor Cl PE4 . . . . **204** E2
Tudor Ct
Bassingbourn cum Kneesworth
SG8 . . . . **13** B4
Kimbolton PE28 . . . . **113** F5
Tudor Rd PE29 . . . . **141** F2
Tulyar Wlk CB8 . . . . **110** E8
Tunbridge Cl
Bottisham CB25 . . . . **86** E6
Burwell CB25 . . . . **130** B2
Tunbridge La CB25 . . . . . . **86** E6
Tunkers La PE26 . . . . **171** F4
Tunwells Cl CB22 . . . . **49** A5
Tunwells La CB22 . . . . **49** A5
Turberville Ct PE28 . . . . . **143** C1
Turf Dro PE7 . . . . **191** C5
Turf Fen La PE15 . . . . **222** F5
Turf Fen Rd PE26 . . . . . . **170** F3
Turf Lot Dro PE14 . . . . . . **229** C5
Turf Maze★ PE28 . . . . . . **120** C1
Turnbull Rd PE15 . . . . . . **243** B5
Turner Cl CB9 . . . . **38** D1
Turner Rd
Eaton Socon PE19 . . . . . . **74** C5
St Ives PE27 . . . . **144** A7
Turners La PE7 . . . . **189** D6
Turningtree Rd PE7 . . . . . **190** A3
Turnover Bank PE13 . . . . **237** D2
Turnpike Cl 2 PE13 . . . . . **245** E6
Turnpike La IP28 . . . . **133** E8
Turnpike Hill CB9 . . . . **38** C4
Turnpike Rd IP28 . . . . **133** E8
Turnpike The CB7 . . . . . . **240** B3
Turnpole Cl PE9 . . . . **244** D7
Turnstone Cl IP28 . . . . . . **239** D4
Turnstone Way PE2 . . . . . **187** D7
Turpin's Ride
4 Royston SG8 . . . . **5** D5
Stilton PE7 . . . . **176** A3
Turpyn Ct CB4 . . . . **83** E6
Turvers La PE26 . . . . **172** B7
TURVES **191** F6
Turves Rd PE6 . . . . **232** A2
Tuyar Wlk CB8 . . . . **110** E8
Tweedale CB1 . . . . **65** F5
Twelvetree Ave PE4 . . . . **204** A5
Twenty Foot Rd PE15 . . . **227** F8
Twenty Pence Rd
Cottenham CB24 . . . . . . **125** F6
Wilburton CB6 . . . . **210** B3
Two Pole Dro
Farcet PE7 . . . . **187** F1
Soham CB7 . . . . **211** E7
Two Tree Hundred Dro
PE15 . . . . **228** A6
Twyford Gdns PE1 . . . . . . **198** D2
TYDD ST GILES **237** F7
Tydd St Giles Golf & Leisure
Ctr PE13 . . . . **238** A7
Tyesdale PE3 . . . . **197** A4
Tylers Mews PE4 . . . . **204** B3
Tyrrell Pk PE1 . . . . **198** D2
Tythe Piece PE28 . . . . . . **121** C5

U

Uffen Way CB22 . . . . **32** E8
UFFINGTON **230** C6
Uffington CE (Cont) Prim
Sch PE9 . . . . **230** C6
Uffington Rd
1 Barnack PE9 . . . . **230** D4
Stamford PE9 . . . . **244** D5
UFFORD **230** F3
Ufford Pl 1 CB9 . . . . **24** B8
Ugg Mere Ct Rd PE26 . . **220** D1
Uldale Way PE4 . . . . **204** F2
Ullswater PE29 . . . . **141** C5
Ullswater Ave PE4 . . . . . . **204** D2
Underwood Cl PE7 . . . . . . **190** D7
Union La CB4 . . . . **83** F5
Union Pl 12 PE13 . . . . **245** C5
Union Rd CB2 . . . . **246** B1
Union St 4 PE13 . . . . **245** C5
Univ Arts Sch CB2 . . . . . . **246** A2
University Concert Hall
CB3 . . . . **83** C1
University Music Sch CB3 **83** C1
Univ Mus of Zoology★
CB2 . . . . **246** B2
Univ of Cambridge
Cambridge CB1 . . . . **84** A2
Cambridge CB2 . . . . **246** B2
Madingley CB23 . . . . **81** E6
Univ of Cambridge
Biotechnology Ctr CB3 . . **82** D7
Univ of the 3rd Age in
Cambridge CB2 . . . . **246** A3
Unwin's La 13 CB24 . . . . . **208** D1
UPEND **92** A1
UPEND GREEN **91** F2
Uphall Rd CB1 . . . . **84** D1
Upherd's La CB6 . . . . **240** C5
Uplands PE4 . . . . **204** C5
Upper Delph Dro CB6 . . . **209** A5
Upper Gatley End SG8 . . . . **3** D6

Upper Gwydir St 1 CB1 . . **84** A1
UPTON
Ailsworth **195** B6
Alconbury **160** C1
Upton Cl
Longthorpe PE3 . . . . **197** A2
Stanground PE2 . . . . **187** C5
Upton Hill PE28 . . . . **160** C1
Upton La CB6 . . . . **242** D4
Upton Pl CB6 . . . . **242** C4
UPWARE **211** B1
Upware Rd
Swaffham Prior CB7 . . . . **128** D8
Wicken CB7 . . . . **211** C1
UPWELL **236** D1
Upwell Pk CB25 . . . . **243** F3
Upwell Prim Sch PE14 . . **229** D8
Upwell Rd
Christchurch PE14 . . . . . **229** C4
March PE15 . . . . **243** E3
UPWOOD **171** C2
Upwood Airfield PE26 . . . **171** D4
Upwood Meadows National
Nature Reserve★ PE26 . **171** A2
Upwood Prim Sch PE26 . **171** D3
Upwood Rd PE26 . . . . **171** B5
Utah PE28 . . . . **151** F4

V

Valarian Cl 14 PE19 . . . . . **74** C6
Vale Dr PE7 . . . . **186** C1
Valence Rd PE2 . . . . **185** F4
Valerian Ct CB1 . . . . **66** A5
Vale The PE29 . . . . **140** F5
Valiant Rd PE27 . . . . **143** F7
Valiant Sq PE26 . . . . **171** F3
Valley Rise SG8 . . . . **5** E6
Valley The CB23 . . . . **62** D6
Valley Way CB8 . . . . **110** E4
Valparaiso Univ CB3 . . . . . **83** C3
Van Diemans Way PE28 . **116** A7
Van Dyke Pl PE27 . . . . . . **144** A7
Vange Pl CB9 . . . . **24** B8
Vanners Rd CB9 . . . . **24** A7
Varrier Jones Dr CB23 . . . . **99** A3
Varrier Jones Pl CB23 . . . . **99** A3
Vars Rd PE2 . . . . **186** B2
Veasey Rd PE29 . . . . **142** A7
Velos Wlk CB5 . . . . **84** E4
Vence Cl PE7 . . . . **244** A5
Ventress Cl CB1 . . . . **65** D5
Ventress Farm Ct CB1 . . . . **65** E5
Verdun Rd PE13 . . . . **245** D5
Vere Rd PE1 . . . . **197** F7
Vergette Rd PE6 . . . . **203** F8
Vergette St PE1 . . . . **198** B4
Vermont Gr PE3 . . . . **197** E1
Vermuyden PE28 . . . . **208** E6
Vermuyden Gdns 5 CB6 . **216** E2
Vermuyden Way CB4 . . . . **121** C5
Verulam Way CB4 . . . . **83** D6
Vester's Hill Dro PE26 . . . **171** B7
Vetchfield PE2 . . . . **185** E5
Vetch Wlk CB9 . . . . **38** D1
Vicarage Ave CB22 . . . . . . **32** F7
Vicarage Cl
Chatteris PE16 . . . . **241** D5
Dullingham CB8 . . . . **89** C1
Holme PE7 . . . . **177** A4
Melbourn SG8 . . . . **14** C6
Oakington/Longstanton
CB24 . . . . **103** D6
Swaffham Bulbeck CB25 . **108** A1
Waterbeach CB25 . . . . . **106** A7
Vicarage Dr CB3 . . . . **64** A3
Vicarage Farm Rd 5
PE1 . . . . **197** F8
Vicarage Farm Yd PE19 . . **57** B6
Vicarage Gdns
Mildenhall IP28 . . . . **239** B4
6 St Neots PE19 . . . . . . **74** B3
Vicarage La
Swaffham Prior CB25 . . . **108** D4
Whittlesford CB22 . . . . . . **32** B5
Wooddittion CB8 . . . . **90** D3
Vicarage Rd
Newmarket CB8 . . . . **111** B3
Waresley SG19 . . . . **58** A2
Vicarage Terr CB1 . . . . **84** A1
Vicarage Way PE7 . . . . . . **181** D5
Vicarage Wlk PE19 . . . . . . **93** F6
Viceroy Cl PE19 . . . . **74** A3
Victor Cl PE27 . . . . **144** A7
Victoria Ave CB5 . . . . **246** B3
Victoria Cres
Royston SG8 . . . . **5** D7
St Ives PE28 . . . . **143** A5
Victoria Gdns CB6 . . . . . . **242** D4
Victoria Gn 3 CB6 . . . . . . **217** D1
Victoria Pk CB4 . . . . **83** D4
Victoria Pl
Peterborough PE1 . . . . . **197** F4
Sutton CB6 . . . . **216** D1
16 Wisbech PE13 . . . . . **245** C4
Victoria Rd
Cambridge CB4 . . . . **83** D4
Haverhill CB9 . . . . **23** D7
Stamford PE9 . . . . **244** B6
Wisbech PE13 . . . . **245** C4
Victoria Sq PE29 . . . . **141** E4
Victoria St
Cambridge CB1 . . . . **246** B2
Chatteris PE16 . . . . **241** C4
Ely CB7 . . . . **240** D3
Littleport CB6 . . . . **242** E4

Victoria St continued
Old Fetton PE6 . . . . **186** F6
Peterborough PE1 . . . . . **198** A5
Victoria View CB24 . . . . . **125** F7
Victoria Way
Melbourn SG8 . . . . **14** D5
Newmarket CB8 . . . . **110** E3
Victor St PE28 . . . . **154** A1
Victory Ave PE7 . . . . **189** F7
Victory Rd PE13 . . . . **245** B3
Victory Way CB24 . . . . . . **125** D4
Victory Wlk 7 SG8 . . . . **5** E5
Viersen Platz PE1 . . . . . . **198** A1
Viking Cl CB21 . . . . **53** C5
Viking Way
Bar Hill CB23 . . . . **102** B4
Whittlesey PE7 . . . . **189** E8
Villa Ct CB4 . . . . **83** E8
Village The PE2 . . . . **186** B5
Village Way SG7 . . . . **3** A3
Villa Pl CB24 . . . . **104** C2
Villa Rd CB24 . . . . **104** C2
Vincent Cl CB8 . . . . **110** E7
Vinces Ct CB6 . . . . **240** C4
Vine Cl
Great Shelford CB22 . . . . **49** C4
Hemingford Grey PE27 . . **143** E2
Vinegar Hill PE15 . . . . . . **150** E7
Vine Inter-Church Prim Sch
The CB23 . . . . **79** E3
Vinery Pk CB1 . . . . **84** C1
Vinery Rd CB1 . . . . **65** C8
Vinery Way CB1 . . . . **84** C1
Vine St PE9 . . . . **244** C5
Vine Wlk PE3 . . . . **197** B4
Vineyard Rd PE1 . . . . **198** B2
Vineyards The CB7 . . . . . **240** D4
Vineyard The PE28 . . . . . **208** D7
Vineyard Way
Buckden PE19 . . . . **117** B3
Ely CB7 . . . . **240** E5
Vineyard Wlk CB25 . . . . . . **86** C3
Viney Cl PE1 . . . . **198** D5
Vintner Ct CB23 . . . . **99** A3
Vintners Cl PE13 . . . . **197** D3
Violet Cl CB1 . . . . **66** A5
Violet Way PE7 . . . . **182** A7
Virginia Cl PE3 . . . . **197** A2
Virginia Rd IP28 . . . . **213** E8
Virginia Way PE27 . . . . . . **143** E6
Viscount Ct PE19 . . . . **74** B3
Viscount Rd PE2 . . . . **187** A6
Vixen Cl PE7 . . . . **181** F6
Vokes St PE2 . . . . **186** D8
Voyager Sch PE4 . . . . **204** C1
Vulcan Way PE19 . . . . **74** B1

W

Waddelow Rd CB25 . . . . . **106** A8
Wade Park Ave 4 PE6 . . . **231** E8
Wadloes Rd CB5 . . . . **84** D4
Waggoners Way 15 PE15 **223** B7
Wagstaff Cl CB4 . . . . **83** F7
Wainman Rd PE2 . . . . **186** D5
Wainwright PE4 . . . . **204** A5
Waits The PE27 . . . . **144** A3
Wake Ave PE28 . . . . **239** C5
Wakefield Cl CB10 . . . . **18** D3
Wakelyn Rd PE7 . . . . **189** C7
Wake Rd
March PE15 . . . . **243** D6
Peterborough PE1 . . . . . **198** B2
Wakerley Dr PE2 . . . . **186** C7
Walcot Rd PE9 . . . . **230** E2
Walcot Wlk PE3 . . . . **197** B3
Walden Cl 17 PE15 . . . . . **223** A5
Walden Gr PE29 . . . . **141** D4
Walden Rd
Great Chesterford CB10 . . **18** E3
Hadstock CB21 . . . . **20** B6
Huntingdon PE29 . . . . . . **141** D4
Walden Way CB22 . . . . **48** F6
Wales Bank PE14 . . . . . . **236** A5
Walgrave PE2 . . . . **186** B4
Walkden's SG7 . . . . **2** E4
Walker Ct CB4 . . . . **83** E6
Walker Rd PE6 . . . . **203** F7
Walkers Way PE3 . . . . **196** F3
Walkling Way CB24 . . . . . **105** D1
Walks E The 7 PE29 . . . . **141** D4
Walks N The PE29 . . . . . . **141** D4
Wallace Ct PE29 . . . . **142** A8
Wallace's Dro PE6 . . . . . . **233** D4
Waller's Cl SG8 . . . . **7** F2
Wallman's La CB24 . . . . . **122** E6
Walnut Cl
Milton CB24 . . . . **105** C2
Newborough PE6 . . . . . . **205** C8
Royston SG8 . . . . **5** D6
Wisbech St Mary PE13 . . **235** B6
Walnut Dr CB22 . . . . **48** E7
Walnut Gr
Gunthorpe PE4 . . . . **204** D2
Worlington IP28 . . . . **213** E4
Walnut Tree Ave CB5 . . . . **84** A3
Walnut Tree Cl
Bassingbourn SG8 . . . . . . **12** E5
Little Downham CB6 . . . . **218** A6
8 Stretham CB6 . . . . . . **210** F5
Walnut Tree Cres PE28 . . **121** B5
Walnut Tree Dr PE29 . . . . **141** C6

Walnut Tree Gr PE28....**140** D3
Walnut Tree Way CB4...**83** C7
Walnut Way PE7........**175** F7
Walpole Bank PE14.....**238** F7
Walpole Ct PE14.......**240** C4
WALPOLE MARSH........**238** F8
Walpole Rd CB31.......**65** D6
Walsham Rd PE7........**181** D8
Walsingham Ct PE13....**245** A7
Walsingham Way
  Ely CB6..............**240** B5
  🔟 Eye PE6...........**232** A1
WALSOKEN..............**245** F6
Walsoken Rd PE14......**236** E7
Waltham Cl PE1........**198** D8
WALTON................**204** D1
Walton Cl CB7.........**212** E1
WALTON DAM............**238** D4
WALTON HIGHWAY........**238** F4
Walton Hill PE6.......**161** D5
Walton Pk PE4.........**204** C1
Walton Prim Sch PE4...**204** C1
Walton Rd
  🔟 Leverington PE13...**238** B2
  Marholm PE6..........**203** E1
  Wisbech PE13.........**245** E7
Waltons CB10..........**21** C3
Wamil Rd IP28.........**213** F5
Wamil Way IP28........**239** B4
Wandlebury Ctry Pk★
  CB22................**50** B8
WANSFORD..............**194** A4
Wansford Pasture Nature
  Reserve★ PE8........**193** F3
Wansford Rd
  Elton PE8............**183** D5
  Wansford PE8.........**194** A3
  Yarwell PE8..........**193** F2
Wantage Gdns PE19....**96** A2
Warbon Ave PE1........**197** F7
WARBOYS...............**165** A5
Warboys Airfield Ind Est
  PE28................**164** D2
Warboys Cl PE28.......**61** D5
Warboys CP Sch PE28...**164** E5
Warboys Rd
  Bury PE26............**172** B4
  Old Hurst PE28.......**154** D8
  Pidley cum Fenton PE28..**155** E8
Ward Cl
  Peterborough PE1.....**198** B3
  Ramsey PE26..........**172** A4
  St Ives PE28.........**143** A5
Warden Hill SG19......**40** C3
Ward Rd CB1...........**65** D6
Ward Way CB6..........**217** D1
WARDY HILL............**217** B4
Ware La PE28..........**142** F5
Wareley Rd PE2........**197** F1
Ware Rd PE19..........**74** E6
WARESLEY..............**57** E2
Waresley & Gransden Woods
  Nature Reserve★ SG19..**58** C2
Waresley Rd
  Gamlingay SG19.......**41** D6
  Great Gransden SG19..**58** B3
Warkworth St CB1......**246** C1
Warkworth Terr CB1....**246** C2
WARMINGTON............**178** A3
Warmington Sch PE8....**178** B3
Warner's Dro
  Pidley cum Fenton PE28..**215** B3
  Somersham PE28.......**215** C2
Warners Gr PE27.......**144** A4
Warren Cl
  St Ives PE28.........**142** F6
  Wilburton CB6........**210** C5
Warren Croft PE28.....**168** B5
Warren Ct 🔲 CB9......**23** E7
Warren La
  Bythorn & Keyston PE28..**146** D4
  Titchmarsh PE28......**156** F1
Warrenne Keep PE9.....**244** B4
Warren Pl CB8.........**111** F5
Warren Rd
  Cambridge CB4........**84** A6
  Herringswell CB8.....**134** A7
  Red Lodge IP28.......**214** A1
  St Ives PE27.........**144** B4
  Wothorpe PE9.........**244** B1
Warren The
  🔳 Royston SG8.......**5** D5
  St Neots PE19........**75** C5
  Witchford CB6........**217** E1
Warren Twrs CB8.......**111** E4
Warrington St CB8.....**111** A2
Warwick Ct
  Eaton Socon PE19.....**74** C3
  🔲 Haverhill CB9.....**23** E8
Warwick Dr CB6........**240** A3
Warwick Rd
  Cambridge CB4........**83** C5
  Peterborough PE4.....**204** C1
Wasdale Gdns PE19.....**205** A2
Washbank Rd PE19......**74** E4
Washingley La PE7.....**175** B7
Washingley Rd
  Folksworth PE7.......**175** D8
  The Stukeleys PE7....**141** C8
Washington Cl CB6.....**242** D5
Washington St IP28....**213** E8
Wash La PE7...........**189** E8
Washpit La CB23.......**46** D7
Washpit Rd CB3........**82** C8
Wash Rd PE14..........**225** B8

Wastwater PE29........**141** B6
WATERBEACH............**106** C7
Waterbeach CP Sch
  CB25................**106** B8
Waterbeach Rd CB25....**105** C7
Waterbeach Sta CB25...**106** C6
Watercourse The CB8...**111** A4
WATER END.............**25** B3
Water End
  Alwalton PE7.........**185** A5
  Marholm PE6..........**203** D1
  Peterborough PE3.....**197** D2
  Wrestlingworth SG19..**25** B3
Waterfall Gdns PE6....**207** C1
Waterfields PE16......**241** B3
Waterfurlong PE9......**244** A4
Watergall PE3.........**197** B8
Watergall Prim Sch PE3..**197** A8
Water Gdns The PE13...**245** A5
Watergrove La CB23....**79** C5
Water La
  Bourn CB23...........**60** D6
  Cambridge CB4........**84** B5
  Castor PE5...........**195** F1
  Cottenham CB24.......**126** A7
  Great Bradley CB8....**55** F8
  Histon CB24..........**104** C3
  Oakington/Longstanton
    CB24...............**103** C5
  Sturmer CB9..........**24** F5
Waterlees Rd 🔲 PE13..**245** E7
Waterloo Cl
  Brampton PE28........**140** D3
  Newmarket CB8.......**110** D8
Waterloo Dr 🔳 PE19...**74** F3
Waterloo Rd PE1.......**198** A5
Watermead CB23........**102** C3
Watermead Cres CB23...**79** A3
WATER NEWTON..........**184** C7
WATERSIDE.............**213** A6
Waterside
  Ely CB7..............**240** E4
  Isleham CB7..........**213** A5
Waterside Gdns
  March PE15...........**243** E6
  Whittlesey PE7.......**189** D8
Waterslade Rd PE7.....**181** C4
Watersmead PE19.......**117** E3
Waters Meet PE29......**141** D3
Water St
  Cambridge CB4........**84** B4
  Stamford PE9.........**244** C4
Waterton Cl 🔲 PE6....**231** F8
Waterwick Hill CB11...**1** F1
Waterworks La PE6.....**203** D6
Waterworks Rd IP28....**213** E8
Watsons La 🔲 CB6......**211** B7
Watt Cl PE4...........**204** E2
Wattle Cl CB23........**79** A4
Wavell Way CB4........**83** E6
Waveney Dr PE15.......**243** B5
Waveney Gr PE4........**204** E2
Waveney Rd PE27.......**144** A7
Waveney Terr CB9......**24** B7
Waverley Cl PE13......**235** A3
Waverley Gdns 🔳 PE9..**244** A6
Wayford Cl PE3........**197** A2
WAY HEAD..............**217** C6
Way Head Dro CB6......**217** C6
Way La
  Waterbeach CB25......**106** B8
  Wicken CB7...........**211** D2
WAYSIDE...............**138** C5
Way The SG8...........**30** E1
WEALD.................**76** B4
Weasenham La 🔲 PE13..**245** D2
Weatheralls Cl 🔳 CB7..**212** B4
Weatheralls Prim Sch The
  CB7.................**212** B4
Weatherthorn PE2......**186** C5
Weavers Field CB3.....**82** E7
Webbs Mdw SG19.......**58** D4
Webb's Rd CB21........**36** F5
Websters Cl PE6.......**203** F8
Webster's Way CB24....**208** D1
Wedgewood Cl CB1......**65** F6
Wedgwood Dr PE13......**245** D5
Weedon Cl 🔲 PE4......**204** F1
Weir Cl
  Buckden PE19.........**117** A3
  Hemingford Grey PE28..**143** D1
Weir Rd PE28..........**143** D1
Weirs Dro CB25........**129** F1
Welbeck Rd PE13.......**245** E4
Welbeck Way PE2.......**186** D7
Welbourne PE4.........**204** C4
Welbourne Prim Sch
  PE4.................**204** C4
Welby Cl PE28.........**115** D3
WELCHES DAM...........**224** A1
Welches Dam Visitor Ctr★
  CB6.................**217** A8
Welland Bank PE6......**207** D7
Welland Cl
  Peterborough PE1.....**198** A7
  St Ives PE27.........**144** A7
Welland Ct 🔳 PE19....**74** C4
Welland Mews PE9......**244** C4
Welland Pl CB6........**240** D6
Welland Prim Sch PE1..**198** C8
Welland Rd
  Peterborough PE1.....**198** B8
  Wittering PE8........**230** B1
Welland Way 🔳 PE6....**231** F8
Well Bottom CB8.......**112** B8
Wellbrook Way CB3.....**82** F7

Wellcome Trust Genome
  Campus CB10..........**18** B6
Well Creek Rd PE14....**236** F2
Well End PE14.........**236** A3
Wellingly Ct CB23.....**79** A3
Wellington Ave PE27...**143** F7
Wellington Cl
  Old Hurst PE28.......**154** E7
  Thistley Green IP28..**213** D6
  Warboys PE28.........**164** F4
  Waterbeach CB25......**106** B7
Wellington Ct 🔳 CB1..**84** A2
Wellington Pl SG8.....**13** B5
Wellington Rd
  Ely CB6..............**217** F1
  Mildenhall IP28......**213** E8
Wellington St
  🔳 Cambridge CB1....**84** A2
  Littleport CB6.......**242** D4
  🔳 Newmarket CB8....**111** A3
  Peterborough PE1.....**198** B2
  St Ives PE27.........**144** A3
Wellington Terr
  🔳 Haverhill CB9.....**23** E7
  🔳 Wisbech PE13......**245** C5
Wellington Way PE28...**154** A1
Well Rd PE14..........**236** D4
Wells Bridge PE26.....**221** C3
Wells Cl
  Haslingfield CB23....**47** A3
  Peterborough PE4.....**204** B3
Wells Ct
  Mildenhall IP28......**239** B5
  Peterborough PE2.....**187** D6
Wellsfield PE29.......**141** E6
Wells Way PE7.........**177** A5
Wellum Cl 🔳 CB9......**23** E7
Welmore Rd PE6........**203** F8
WELNEY................**225** B8
Welstead Rd CB1.......**66** A6
WENDY.................**27** C4
WENNINGTON............**162** D4
Wenny Ct PE16.........**241** C4
Wenny Est PE16........**241** D3
Wenny Rd PE16.........**241** C4
Wenny Severals PE16...**216** B7
Wensum CP PE27........**144** B6
WENTWORTH.............**217** B1
Wentworth Dr IP28.....**239** B4
Wentworth Rd CB4......**83** C4
Wentworth St 🔲 PE1...**198** A1
Wentworth Terr 🔲 CB9..**23** E8
Wenvoe Cl CB1.........**65** F6
WERRINGTON............**204** B4
Werrington Bridge Rd
  PE6.................**204** C4
Werrington Ctr PE4....**204** B5
Werrington Gr PE4.....**204** B2
Werrington Grove Cvn Pk
  PE4.................**204** B2
Werrington Mews 🔳
  PE4.................**204** C3
Werrington Park Ave 🔳
  PE4.................**204** C3
Werrington Parkway
  PE6.................**203** E5
Werrington Prim Sch
  PE4.................**204** C4
Werrington Sports & Recn
  Ctr PE4.............**204** B4
Wertheim Way PE29.....**141** B6
Wesleyan Rd PE1.......**198** A7
Wesley Dr PE16........**241** D5
Wesley House CB5......**246** B3
Wessex Cl PE2.........**187** D7
West Ave PE26.........**171** F6
Westberry Ct CB3......**64** B8
Westbourne Cl PE16....**241** B3
Westbourne Dr PE6.....**203** E8
Westbourne Rd PE16....**241** B4
West Brook PE28.......**120** B2
Westbrook Ave 🔲 PE2..**186** F7
Westbrook Cl
  🔲 Brampton PE28....**140** C3
  Steeple Morden SG8..**3** B8
West Brook Rd PE28....**120** B2
Westbrook Park Cl 🔳
  PE2.................**186** F7
Westbrook Park Rd PE2..**186** F7
Westbury Rd PE27......**143** F4
West Cl
  Alconbury Weston PE28..**150** D6
  March PE15...........**243** B6
  Waresley SG19........**57** F2
Westcombe Sq PE1......**198** D4
WESTCOTE..............**211** F6
Westcott House Theological
  Coll CB1............**246** B3
Westcroft 🔲 CB23.....**62** B4
WEST DEEPING..........**231** B8
West Delph PE7........**189** D8
West Dr
  Friday Bridge PE14...**236** A4
  Highfields CB23......**80** C2
  March PE15...........**243** B6
  Mildenhall IP28......**239** B4
  Soham CB7............**212** B4
West Drive Cres CB7...**212** A4
West Drive Gdns CB7...**212** A4
West Drove S PE12.....**233** E8
WEST END..............**155** A5
West End
  Ashwell SG7..........**2** C3
  Brampton PE28........**140** C3
  Ely CB6..............**240** C4
  Gorefield PE13.......**237** E3
  Haddenham CB6........**209** F6

West End continued
  March PE15...........**243** B4
  Somersham PE28.......**208** B8
  Whittlesey PE7.......**189** C7
  Whittlesford CB22....**32** B4
  Wilburton CB6........**210** B5
  Woodditton CB8.......**71** D8
  Yaxley PE7...........**181** D4
West End Cl PE16......**241** B4
West End La CB9.......**38** E8
West End Rd
  Fenstanton PE28......**121** A5
  Maxey PE6............**231** C7
West End Villas PE6...**244** A5
Westering The CB5.....**84** E2
Westerley Cl PE3......**197** C4
Westerman Cl PE28.....**168** B5
Western Ave
  Haverhill CB9........**38** E1
  Peterborough PE1.....**198** D4
West Fen Dro
  Downham CB6.........**218** A6
  March PE7............**227** A1
  Whittlesey PE7.......**191** F3
West Fen Rd
  Coveney CB6..........**217** E4
  Ely CB6..............**240** B5
  Willingham CB24......**208** F2
  Witchford CB6........**218** A3
Westfield CB24........**124** A6
West Field CB21.......**34** B7
Westfield Com Prim Sch
  CB9.................**24** B7
Westfield Jun Sch PE27..**144** A4
Westfield La CB3......**83** C4
Westfield Rd
  Fowlmere SG8.........**15** D8
  Great Shelford CB22..**48** E7
  Newton PE13..........**237** F5
  Peterborough PE3.....**197** E4
  Ramsey PE26..........**171** F7
  Sawtry PE28..........**168** B4
  Wisbech PE13.........**245** E2
  Yaxley PE7...........**181** D5
West Field Rd PE15....**224** A3
Westfields CB23.......**99** A2
Westgate
  Cambridge CB1........**65** E5
  Peterborough PE1.....**197** F2
Westgate Arc PE1......**198** A2
West Gn CB22..........**29** D7
Westhawe PE3..........**196** F7
West Hill Rd CB22.....**30** B4
Westhorpe CB25........**130** B4
Westlake Ave PE7......**186** C1
Westlands
  Comberton CB23.......**62** B4
  Littleport CB6.......**225** B3
WESTLEY BOTTOM........**69** C7
Westley Bottom Rd CB8..**69** B4
West Leys PE27........**143** F4
West Lodge La CB6.....**216** D1
Westmead Ave PE13.....**245** E4
Westmeadow CB24.......**208** F1
West Meadowgate PE14..**245** D4
Westminster & Cheshunt
  Colleges CB3........**83** C3
Westminster Gdns 🔟
  PE6.................**232** A1
Westminster Pl PE1....**198** F5
West Moor Ave CB22....**32** E8
Westmoor Comm CB6....**217** E8
Westmoor Dro
  Chatteris PE16.......**222** D2
  Littleport CB6.......**225** D1
Westmoreland Gdns PE1..**198** B2
Westmorland Ave PE28..**143** A8
West Newlands 🔳 PE28..**208** B8
Weston Ave SG8........**5** C7
Weston Cl PE19........**95** A1
Weston Colville CB8...**70** D1
Weston Colville Rd CB8..**70** D1
Weston Ct PE19........**74** C4
WESTON DITCH.........**213** C7
Weston Gr CB21........**66** E5
WESTON GREEN.........**54** D5
Weston Miller Dr PE13..**245** C3
Weston Rd PE13........**245** C3
Weston Way CB8........**110** F6
West Par
  Peterborough PE3.....**197** D3
  Wisbech PE13.........**245** B7
West Park St PE16.....**241** C4
WEST PERRY............**116** D2
West Perry PE19.......**115** D2
West Rd
  Cambridge CB3........**83** C1
  Gamlingay SG19.......**41** C4
  Histon CB24..........**104** B3
  🔳 Tallington PE9...**230** F7
  Tydd St Giles PE13...**238** B8
WEST ROW.............**213** D6
West Row Com Prim Sch
  IP28................**213** D6
West Row Rd
  Beck Row, Holywell Row &
    Kenny Hill IP28....**213** F6
  Mildenhall IP28......**239** A5
WESTRY...............**227** F5
Westry Ave PE15.......**243** B4
Westry Cl 🔳 PE1......**198** D4
West St Gdns PE9......**244** A4
West St
  Chatteris PE16.......**241** B3
  Godmanchester PE29...**141** E1
  Great Gransden SG19..**58** D4
  Helpston PE6.........**231** B4

West St continued
  Huntingdon PE29......**141** E5
  Isleham CB7..........**212** F5
  Over CB24............**123** A8
  Stamford PE9.........**244** B4
  St Ives PE27.........**144** A4
  St Neots PE19........**74** E5
  Toft CB23............**62** B5
  Wisbech PE13.........**245** C4
West Stonebridge PE2..**186** C5
West Town Prim Sch
  PE3.................**197** E3
West View
  Cambridge CB3........**64** C7
  Little Stukeley PE28..**151** F1
WEST WALTON..........**238** E4
WEST WALTON CHURCH
  END.................**238** D5
West Water Cres PE7...**186** C1
West Way
  Meldreth SG8.........**28** F1
  Sawston CB22.........**50** A1
Westway Pl CB6........**217** A2
WESTWICK..............**103** E7
WEST WICKHAM.........**37** B7
West Wickham Rd
  Balsham CB21.........**53** C1
  Horseheath CB21......**37** A3
West Wlk CB25.........**86** F6
WESTWOOD.............**197** B6
Westwood PE3.........**197** C6
Westwood Ave PE15....**243** C5
Westwood Com Jun Sch
  PE15................**243** C5
Westwood Ind Est PE3..**197** C3
Westwood Park Cl PE3..**197** C3
Westwood Park Rd PE3..**197** C2
Westwood Rd PE27.....**144** A4
WEST WRATTING........**53** E8
West Wratting Rd CB21..**53** B2
Wetenhall Rd CB1......**65** B8
Wetherby Way 🔲 PE1...**198** C3
Wether Rd CB23........**79** C2
Weymouth Way PE1.....**198** C6
WHADDON..............**28** C1
Whaddon Gap SG8......**28** A1
Whaddon Rd SG8.......**28** E2
Whaddons The PE29....**141** F6
Whalley St PE1........**198** B3
Wharf Rd PE9.........**244** C4
Wheat Croft PE21.....**35** D3
Wheatdole PE2........**186** B4
Wheatfield Cres 🔳 SG8..**5** E6
Wheatfield Dr PE26....**171** F5
Wheatfields PE27......**144** A6
Wheatfields Prim Sch
  PE27................**144** A6
Wheatley Bank PE14...**238** F2
Wheatley Cres PE28...**208** C6
Wheats Cl 🔲 CB6......**217** D1
Wheatsheaf 🔲 CB6....**240** A3
Wheatsheaf Dro PE14..**229** C2
Wheatsheaf Rd
  Alconbury Weston PE28..**150** D6
  Eaton Socon PE19.....**74** C3
  Woodhurst PE28......**155** D4
Wheatsheaf Way CB21..**35** D3
Wheatsheaves 🔳 PE28..**168** C2
Wheel Ctr The PE15...**243** D4
Wheelers CB22........**49** B6
Wheeler's Cl CB23.....**46** A7
Wheeler St CB2........**246** A2
Wheeler's Way CB23....**46** A7
Wheelwright Way CB25..**86** A5
Wheel Yd PE1.........**198** A2
Wellams Yd PE26......**172** C2
Wherry Cl PE15.......**243** D4
Whetstone Cl 🔳 PE1..**198** D7
Whetstone Way PE14...**236** E2
Whichcote Rd PE6.....**206** E6
Whincups Yd PE9......**244** C4
Whines La CB24.......**123** A6
Whinfell Cl PE29.....**141** A7
Whipple Mus of the History
  of Science★ CB1....**246** A2
Whippletree Rd CB22..**32** A3
Whiskins CB22........**32** C5
Whistler Rd 🔳 PE19..**74** C4
Whistlers The PE27...**144** A7
Whiston Cl
  Peterborough PE4.....**204** F2
  🔲 Somersham PE28..**208** C8
Whitacre PE1.........**198** E6
Whitby St 🔳 PE13....**245** C5
Whitebeam Cl 🔳 PE7..**186** D3
White Caville CB9....**23** C8
Whitecroft Rd SG8....**14** A8
Whitecross PE7.......**144** A4
White Cross PE3......**197** B6
White Cross Hill CB6..**210** D6
White Cross Rd CB6...**210** E7
White Droveway PE15..**108** A3
White Fen Droveway
  CB25................**107** B5
White Field Way CB22..**32** C8
Whitefriars CB4......**84** B5
Whitegate Cl
  Girton CB3...........**82** E8
  Swavesey CB24.......**122** D6
Whitegates CB8.......**111** C3
WHITE HALL...........**235** E6
White Hall Cl 🔳 PE28..**215** C7
Whitehall Gdns CB22..**31** E1
Whitehall Rd PE28....**115** D2
Whitehall Sch PE28...**215** B1
Whitehall Wlk PE19...**74** F4
White Hart Ct PE27...**144** A7

White Hart Dr **5** PE15. . .222 A5
White Hart La
  Godmanchester PE29 . . . . .142 A1
  6 Littleport CB6. . . . . . . .242 D4
  13 Soham CB7. . . . . .212 B4
  St Ives PE27 . . . . .144 A3
Whitehill Cl CB1 . . . . .84 D2
Whitehill Rd CB5. . . . . .84 C2
White Horse Gdns PE15 .243 C4
White Horse La 218 A6
Whitehouse La CB3 . . . . . . .83 A5
Whitehouse Rd PE28 . . . . .168 A4
White House Rd CB7 . . . . .226 C5
White Lion Cl **1** PE15. . . .243 D2
Whitemill Rd PE16 . . . . . . .241 C3
Whitemoor Rd PE15. . . . . .227 C4
Whitepost Rd
  Borough Fen PE6. . . . . . .207 F1
  Newborough PE6. . . . . . .205 F6
White Rose Wlk **5** CB4. . .83 D7
Whiteway Dro CB25 . . . . . .107 F8
White Wr PE2. . . . . .185 D6
Whitfield Cl CB4 . . . . .83 E7
Whitgift Rd CB1 . . . . .85 B1
Whitlocks CB2 . . . . .64 D2
Whitman Cl **7** PE9. . . . . .230 D3
Whitmore St PE7 . . . . .189 D7
Whitmore Way CB25 . . . . .106 B6
Whitsed Rd PE6. . . . . .207 D1
Whitsed St PE1 . . . . .198 B3
Whittets Cl SG19. . . . . .58 D4
Whittington PE1 . . . . .198 E2
WHITTLESEY. 189 D5
Whittlesey Mus★ PE7 .189 D7
Whittlesey Rd
  Benwick PE15 . . . . .221 C6
  March PE15. . . . . .243 A5
  Peterborough PE2 . . . . . .187 B7
  Thorney PE6. . . . . .200 F7
WHITTLESFORD. 32 B5
Whittlesford Rd
  Little Shelford CB22. . . . .48 F2
  Newton CB22. . . . . .31 D7
Whittlesford Sta CB22. . . .32 E3
Whitton Cl CB24 . . . . .122 E5
Whitwell Way CB23 . . . . . . .82 A2
Whybrows La PE28. . . . . . .208 E6
Whydale Rd **4** SG8. . . . . .5 C8
Whytefield Rd PE26. . . . . .172 A7
Whytford Cl CB4 . . . . .84 A3
WICKEN. 211 F1
Wicken Fen National Nature
  Reserve★ CB7. . . . . . . .211 D1
Wicken Rd CB7 . . . . .212 B1
Wicken Way PE3. . . . . .197 C6
Wickfield Ct PE13. . . . . . . .245 D4
Wick Rd PE7. . . . . .186 B2
Widgham Gn CB8. . . . . .71 D7
WIGGENS GREEN. 23 E1
Wiggin Cl IP28. . . . . .239 D2
Wigmore Cl PE29 . . . . .141 E1
Wigmore Dr PE7. . . . . .187 F5
Wigsted Cl CB23. . . . . .99 C2
Wigstone's Rd PE15. . . . . .243 E6
Wilberforce Rd
  Cambridge CB3 . . . . .83 B2
  Peterborough PE1. . . . . . .197 E7
  Wisbech PE13 . . . . .245 D5
Wilbraham Rd
  Bottisham CB1. . . . . .86 F3
  Fulbourn CB21. . . . . .67 C7
Wilbraham Temple CB21. .68 A8
WILBURTON. 210 B5
Wilburton CE Prim Sch
  CB6. . . . . .210 C6
Wilburton Rd CB6. . . . . . . .210 A6
Wild Acres CB23 . . . . .130 B1
Wildber Cl PE19 . . . . .74 F4
Wilderness The PE27. . . . .144 B3
Wilderspin Cl CB3 . . . . .82 F6
Wild Goose Leys PE28. . . .152 D5
Wilding Wlk CB4. . . . . .84 A5
Wildlake PE2 . . . . .186 C5
Wildmere La IP28. . . . . . . .214 A8
Wiles Cl
  Cambridge CB4 . . . . .84 A7
  Waterbeach CB25 . . . . . .106 A4
Wilff Cl PE29 . . . . .152 E1
Wilford Dr CB7 . . . . .240 E6
Wilford Furlong CB24. . . . .209 A1
Wilfred Sherman Cl **7**
  CB8. . . . . .111 A4
Wilkinson Cl
  Eaton Socon PE19 . . . . . . .74 B3
  March PE15. . . . . .243 E5
Wilkinson Pl CB2 . . . . .64 E5
Wilkins Rd PE14 . . . . .236 D7
Wilkin St **1** CB1. . . . . . . .65 A8
Willan Ct PE2. . . . . .186 F8
Willesden Ave PE4 . . . . . . .197 D8
William Blake Ct CB9 . . . . .38 E1
William Ct PE9. . . . . .244 A7
William de Yaxley CE Jun
  Sch PE7. . . . . .181 E6
William Dr **8** PE19. . . . . .74 F4
William Law CE Prim Sch
  PE4. . . . . .204 B5
William Rd PE13 . . . . .245 C5
Williams Cl
  Brampton PE28. . . . . .140 C3
  Ely CB6. . . . . .240 E7
  Great Gransden SG19. . . . .58 E4
  Newborough PE6. . . . . . .207 C1
William Smith Cl CB1. . . . . .65 A7
Williamson Ave PE3. . . . . .197 E3
Williams Way PE15. . . . . . .224 B4

William's Way IP28 . . . . .213 D6
William Westley CE Prim Sch
  CB22. . . . . .32 D5
Willie Snaith Rd CB8 . . . . .110 F6
WILLINGHAM. 209 B1
WILLINGHAM GREEN. 54 D8
Willingham Green Rd
  CB8 . . . . .54 D8
Willingham Prim Sch
  CB24. . . . . .209 A1
Willingham Rd CB24 . . . . .208 E1
Willis Rd CB1. . . . . .246 C2
Willmott Rd SG8. . . . . .12 F5
Willonholt PE3. . . . . .197 C7
Willoughby Ct PE1 . . . . . . .198 E8
Willoughby Rd PE9. . . . . . .244 C7
Willow Ave PE1. . . . . .198 B7
Willowbrook Dr PE7 . . . . . .201 F1
Willow Cl
  Beck Row, Holywell Row &
    Kenny Hill IP28. . . . . . .214 A8
  Brampton PE28 . . . . .140 C2
  Doddington PE15. . . . . . .222 A5
  Haverhill CB9. . . . . .38 D1
  Little Paxton PE19. . . . . . .95 F1
  Stilton PE7 . . . . .175 F7
  St Neots PE19 . . . . .74 F3
Willow Cres
  Milton CB24. . . . . .105 D2
  Newmarket CB8. . . . . . . .111 B2
Willow Ct CB6 . . . . .242 E4
Willow Dr
  Manea PE15. . . . . .224 C5
  March PE15. . . . . .243 B3
Willow Dro PE6. . . . . .207 D4
Willow End PE28. . . . . . . .150 F4
Willow Farm Cl PE28. . . . .150 C2
Willow Gate PE6. . . . . .198 D6
Willow Gn PE27. . . . . .208 A3
Willow Gr
  Ely CB7. . . . . .240 E4
  Lode CB25 . . . . .107 C2
Willow Hall La PE6. . . . . . .199 D6
Willow Holt PE7 . . . . .186 C3
Willow La CB23 . . . . .79 C3
Willow Rd PE7. . . . . .182 A6
Willow Row Farms CB6. . . .226 A5
Willowside Way SG8 . . . . . .5 C8
Willows The
  Glinton PE6. . . . . .203 F8
  Great Chesterford CB10. . .18 D3
  Highfields CB23. . . . . .80 C3
  Mildenhall IP28. . . . . . . .239 B3
Willow Tree Cl PE16 . . . . .241 B4
Willow Way
  Bottisham CB25. . . . . .86 F6
  Hauxton CB22. . . . . .48 B4
  Ramsey PE26. . . . . .172 B7
  St Ives PE27 . . . . .144 C4
  Wisbech PE13 . . . . .245 D3
Willow Wlk
  Cambridge CB1 . . . . .246 B3
  Ely CB6. . . . . .240 E4
Wilson Cl CB4 . . . . .84 A7
Wilsons La SG7 . . . . .2 C4
Wilson's Rd CB24 . . . . . . .103 A8
Wilson Way
  Brampton PE28. . . . . .117 E8
  Milton CB24. . . . . .105 D2
Wilthorne CB6. . . . . .165 A5
Wilton Cl PE3. . . . . .197 C4
Wilton Dr PE3. . . . . .197 C4
Wilton Gdns CB6. . . . . . . .216 E3
Wiltshire Rd PE28. . . . . . .154 B1
Wimbish Rd CB23 . . . . .99 A2
WIMBLINGTON. 223 A6
Wimblington Rd
  Doddington/Wimblington
    PE15. . . . . .223 A5
  March PE15. . . . . .243 C1
  Wimblington PE15. . . . . .223 C6
Wimborne Dr PE1. . . . . . . .198 E7
Wimbridge Cl SG8. . . . . . . .27 F6
WIMPOLE. 128 B8
Wimpole Hall★ SG8. . . . . .44 F3
Wimpole Home Farm★
  SG8. . . . . .44 F3
Wimpole Pk★ SG8 . . . . . . .44 E3
Wimpole Rd
  Barton CB23 . . . . .63 A2
  Great Eversden CB23 . . . . .45 E7
Wimpole St PE16 . . . . .241 B4
Winchester Way PE3 . . . . .197 E1
Winchfield Cl SG19. . . . . . . .58 E5
Winchmore Dr CB2 . . . . . . .64 C3
Windermere Cl CB1. . . . . . .66 A7
Windermere PE29. . . . . . . .141 B6
Windermere Way PE4 . . . . .204 E3
Winders La CB24. . . . . . . .104 B5
Windgate Way PE8. . . . . . .194 A6
Windlesham Cl CB4 . . . . . . .83 E6
Windmill Cl
  Ellington PE28. . . . . .138 F4
  2 Ely CB6. . . . . .240 B3
  Sawston CB22. . . . . .32 F8
  Soham CB7 . . . . .212 C2
Windmill Hill CB8. . . . . . . .110 C8
Windmill La
  Fulbourn CB21. . . . . .66 E4
  Histon CB24. . . . . .104 B4
  8 Sutton CB6. . . . . . . .216 E1
Windmill St
  Peterborough PE1. . . . . . .197 F5
  Whittlesey PE7 . . . . .189 D8
Windmill Wlk CB6. . . . . . . .216 E1
Windover Rd PE29 . . . . . . .141 D7
Windrush Dr PE4 . . . . .204 F1

Windsor Ave PE4 . . . . . . .197 C8
Windsor Cl
  Chatteris PE16. . . . . .241 E5
  Stamford PE9. . . . . .244 B7
  St Ives PE27 . . . . .143 F8
  10 St Neots PE19 . . . . . .74 F2
Windsor Dr
  March PE15. . . . . .243 B5
  Peterborough PE2. . . . . . .187 D6
  Ramsey PE26. . . . . .221 D2
  Wisbech PE13 . . . . .245 D8
Windsor Gdns **9** PE28. . .208 C8
Windsor Pl PE7 . . . . .190 A7
Windsor Rd
  Cambridge CB4 . . . . .83 C5
  Godmanchester PE29 . . . .142 A1
  Newmarket CB8. . . . . . . .110 E4
  Royston SG8 . . . . .5 F6
  Sawtry PE7. . . . . .168 B3
  Yaxley PE7. . . . . .181 F6
Windsors The PE15. . . . . .243 A5
Windsor Terr CB9. . . . . .23 D8
Winfold Rd CB25. . . . . . . .106 A8
Wingate Cl CB2 . . . . .64 D3
Wingate Way CB2 . . . . .64 D3
Wingfield PE2. . . . . .185 F3
Winhills Prim Sch PE19. . .75 A4
Winship Rd CB24. . . . . . . .105 C1
Winslow Rd PE3. . . . . .197 C3
Winston Way PE7 . . . . .187 C2
WINTRINGHAM. 75 F4
Wintringham Rd **8** PE19 .74 F5
WINWICK. 158 B6
Winwick Pl PE3. . . . . .197 C5
Winwick Rd PE28 . . . . . . .158 B8
Winyates PE2. . . . . .185 F3
Winyates Prim Sch PE2 .186 A3
WISBECH. 245 A6
Wisbech Castle★ PE13 . .245 C4
Wisbech & Fenland Mus★
  PE13. . . . . .245 C4
Wisbech Gram Sch PE13 .245 B5
Wisbech Rd
  Lakes End PE14. . . . . . . .229 F3
  Littleport CB6. . . . . .242 A6
  Manea PE15. . . . . .224 C5
  March PE15. . . . . .243 D8
  Outwell PE14. . . . . .236 F3
  Thorney PE6. . . . . .233 A4
  Walsoken PE13. . . . . . . .245 E8
  Welney PE14 . . . . .229 E2
  Whittlesey PE7 . . . . .191 C8
  Wisbech St Mary PE13 . . .234 A2
WISBECH ST MARY 235 C6
Wisbech St Mary Prim Sch
  PE13. . . . . .235 B7
Wisbey's Yd CB23 . . . . .47 B5
Wissey Way CB6 . . . . .240 C6
Wistaria Rd PE13. . . . . . . .245 F7
Wisteria Rd PE7 . . . . .181 D4
WISTOW. 163 F6
Wistow Ct **3** PE19. . . . . .74 C6
Wistow Fen Dro PE28 . . . .173 B4
Wistow Fen La PE28. . . . . .164 C8
Wistow Way PE2. . . . . .185 D6
Wistow Wood Nature
  Reserve★ PE2. . . . . . . .172 D1
WITCHAM. 217 A2
Witcham Bridge Dro
  CB6. . . . . .217 A4
Witcham Rd CB6. . . . . . . .216 E3
WITCHFORD. 217 D1
Witchford Rd
  Ely CB6. . . . . .240 A3
  Witchford CB6. . . . . .217 F1
Witchford Village Coll
  CB6. . . . . .217 E2
Witham Cl PE9. . . . . .244 C6
Witham Way PE4 . . . . .204 F1
WITHERSFIELD. 38 C4
Withersfield Rd
  Haverhill CB9. . . . . .38 E1
  Withersfield CB9 . . . . .38 F7
Withers Pl CB7 . . . . .212 E1
WITTERING. 230 C1
Wittering Airfield PE8. . . .230 A2
Wittering Ford Rd PE9 . . .230 C2
Wittering Prim Sch PE8. . .230 B1
Wittering Rd PE9 . . . . .230 D3
Woburn Cl
  Cambridge CB4 . . . . .83 E7
  Peterborough PE3. . . . . . .197 A1
Woburn Ct PE7 . . . . .176 A7
Woburn Dr PE6. . . . . .233 A2
Woburn Pl PE2 . . . . .31 F1
Wolf Cl PE28. . . . . .152 E1
Wolf La
  Gorefield PE13. . . . . .237 F1
  Wisbech PE13 . . . . .235 C8
Wolfson Coll CB3 . . . . .64 B8
Wollaston Rd
  Cambridge CB4 . . . . .246 C1
  Peterborough PE3. . . . . . .197 C6
Wolseley Pl PE7 . . . . .181 E6
Wolsey Gdns PE19 . . . . . . .117 A5
Wolsey Way CB1. . . . . .65 F7
Woodbine St PE2 . . . . .187 A8
Woodbrook Cl CB23. . . . . . .99 B2
Woodbyth Rd PE1. . . . . . . .198 A6
Woodcock Cl
  Haverhill CB9. . . . . .24 C7
  Histon CB24. . . . . .104 D3
Woodcock Rd **10** SG8. . . .6 E7
Woodcote Cl PE1 . . . . .198 A7
Woodcote Pk PE13. . . . . . .245 A4
Woodcroft Castle★ PE6 .203 C5
Woodcroft Rd
  Etton PE6 . . . . .203 B7

Woodcroft Rd continued
  Glinton PE6. . . . . .203 C3
  Marholm PE6 . . . . .203 D1
WOODDITTON. 90 E3
Woodditton Rd
  Kirtling CB8 . . . . .72 B5
  Newmarket CB8. . . . . . . .111 A1
  Woodditton CB8. . . . . . . .90 B8
Wood End
  Bluntisham/Colne PE28. . .208 C6
  Pertenhall MK44 . . . . . . .113 D1
Woodfen Rd CB6. . . . . . . .242 A4
Woodfield Ave PE26. . . . . .172 A4
Woodfield Dr PE28. . . . . . .168 A3
Woodfield La CB23. . . . . . . .79 A3
Woodfield Rd PE3 . . . . .197 D3
Woodforde Cl SG7. . . . . . . .2 E4
Woodgate CB6 . . . . .231 C4
Woodgate La PE6. . . . . . . .231 D5
Woodgate Rd **8** PE13. . .238 B2
Wood Green Animal Ctr★
  PE29. . . . . .119 C5
Woodhall La CB21 . . . . .53 A1
Woodhall Rise PE4. . . . . . .204 B6
Woodhead Dr CB4 . . . . .83 F6
Woodhead Pl CB23. . . . . . . .99 B3
Woodhouse Way CB4 . . . . . .84 A7
WOODHURST. 155 B4
Woodhurst Rd PE2. . . . . . .187 D6
Wood La
  Abbots Ripton PE28 . . . . .162 E2
  Broughton PE28. . . . . . . .163 A2
  Papworth Everard CB23 . . .99 A4
  Ramsey PE26. . . . . .172 C8
  Stretham CB6 . . . . .210 F5
WOODLAND GREEN. 24 E7
Woodland Lea PE6. . . . . . .231 B4
Woodland Rd CB22. . . . . . . .32 F8
Woodlands
  1 Royston SG8. . . . . . . .5 E6
  St Neots PE19 . . . . .75 A7
  Stukeley PE29 . . . . .140 F7
  Warboys PE28. . . . . .164 F5
Woodlands Ave PE15. . . . .243 D2
Woodlands Cl
  Girton CB3. . . . . .103 D1
  Great Shelford CB22. . . . . .49 A4
Woodlands Ct PE13 . . . . . .245 F7
Woodlands Dr SG8. . . . . . . .14 B8
Woodlands Pk CB3. . . . . . .103 D1
Woodlands Rd CB22. . . . . . .49 A4
Woodlands The
  Linton CB21. . . . . .35 B4
  Peterborough PE1. . . . . . .198 D5
Woodlands Way IP28 . . . . .239 F5
Woodland Wlk **2** CB23. . .79 C3
Woodlark Dr CB24 . . . . . . .125 D4
Woodlark Rd CB3. . . . . .83 B5
Woodmans Way CB24 . . . . .105 D2
Woodpecker Way CB23. . . . .79 C3
Woodroffe Rd PE8 . . . . . . .193 D8
Woods Cl CB9 . . . . .24 E5
Woodside
  Chatteris PE16. . . . . .241 C4
  Oakington/Longstanton
    CB24. . . . . .123 F1
Woodside Way PE27 . . . . . .144 B5
Wood St
  Chatteris PE16. . . . . .241 C4
  Doddington/Wimblington
    PE15. . . . . .223 A6
  Huntingdon PE29 . . . . . . .141 E4
  Wisbech PE13 . . . . .245 B6
WOODSTON. 186 E7
Woodstone Gate PE2. . . . .186 D6
Woodston Ind Est PE2. . . .186 E6
Woodston Prim Sch PE2 .186 E7
Wood View PE28. . . . . . . .140 B4
WOOD WALTON. 161 E6
Woodwalton Fen National
  Nature Reserve★ PE26 .170 B6
Woodwalton Marsh Nature
  Reserve★ PE26. . . . . . .161 E2
Woodward Cl PE7. . . . . . . .176 A8
Woodysfield **2** PE15. . . .223 B7
Woolcroft Cl PE13. . . . . . .238 A1
Woolfellhill Rd PE6. . . . . . .205 F3
Woolgard PE3. . . . . .197 A3
Woollards La CB22. . . . . . . .49 A4
WOOLLEY. 149 E1
Woolley Cl PE28 . . . . .140 D3
Woolley Hill PE28. . . . . . . .138 D6
Woolley Rd PE28. . . . . . . .149 B3
Woolpack La
  St Ives PE27 . . . . .144 A3
  2 Whittlesey PE7 . . . . .189 D6
Woolpack Way SG8 . . . . . . .29 B1
Woolthwaite La CB23 . . . . . .79 A4
Wooton Field SG19. . . . . . .41 D4
Wootons Ave PE2 . . . . .186 F6
Wootton Way CB3. . . . . . . .64 A8
Worboys Ct SG8 . . . . .10 F5
Worcester Ave CB23 . . . . . .81 A4
Worcester Cres **2** PE9. . .244 B6
Worcester Rd PE13 . . . . . .245 C7
Worcester Way SG8. . . . . . .14 E6
Wordsworth Ave PE19. . . . . .74 C5
Wordsworth Cl
  Peterborough PE4. . . . . . .197 A8
  Royston SG8 . . . . .13 D1
Wordsworth Gr CB3. . . . . . .64 C8
Workhouse La PE14 . . . . . .229 D8
WORLINGTON. 213 E4
Worlington Rd
  Barton Mills IP28 . . . . . . .214 C3
  Worlington IP28. . . . . . . .239 A3

Worsley PE2. . . . . .186 A4
Worsley Chase PE15 . . . . .243 D2
WORSTED LODGE 51 B4
Wortham Pl **2** CB9 . . . . .24 A8
Wortham Rd SG8. . . . . .5 E4
Worthington Cl PE7. . . . . .176 A7
Worts' Cswy CB1. . . . . .65 C2
WOTHORPE. 244 B2
Wothorpe Hill PE9 . . . . . . .244 A1
Wothorpe Mews **5** PE9 .244 B4
Wothorpe Rd PE9 . . . . . . .244 B4
Wragg Dr CB8 . . . . .111 A6
Wratting Rd
  Great Thurlow CB9 . . . . . .39 B8
  Haverhill CB9. . . . . .24 A8
Wren Cl
  Little Stukeley PE28. . . . .150 E4
  Mildenhall IP28 . . . . .239 D6
Wren Pk CB22. . . . . .32 B4
Wrens Cl CB6. . . . . .240 B5
WRESTLINGWORTH. 25 C4
Wrestlingworth Lower Sch
  SG19 . . . . .25 B3
Wrexham Terr **4** SG8. . . . .5 D7
Wright Ave PE2. . . . . .187 D5
Wright's Cl CB5. . . . . .84 E6
Wrights Dro PE7 . . . . .220 B3
Wright's Dro PE6 . . . . .232 B7
Wrights Gr CB21. . . . . .66 F4
Wrights Way PE28 . . . . . . .140 E2
Wroe The PE14 . . . . .236 C5
Wulfric Sq PE3 . . . . .197 C8
Wulfstan Ct CB1 . . . . .65 C4
Wulfstan Way CB1. . . . . . . .65 C4
Wyatt Cl PE26. . . . . .172 B6
Wyboston Ct **1** PE19. . . .74 C4
Wycliffe Gr PE4. . . . . .204 A5
Wycliffe Rd CB1 . . . . .65 C8
Wydham Pk PE2 . . . . .185 D6
Wye Pl PE4. . . . . .204 E1
Wye Valley Rd PE2 . . . . . . .186 E8
Wykes Dr **3** PE13. . . . . .235 B7
Wykes Rd PE7. . . . . .181 D4
Wyman Way PE2 . . . . .185 F5
Wynborne Cl CB4 . . . . .83 E5
Wyndham Way CB8 . . . . . .111 A6
Wynemares CB22. . . . . .32 E7
Wynford Way CB4. . . . . . . .83 F7
Wype Dro PE7 . . . . .191 A5
Wype Rd PE7 . . . . .190 C7
Wysing Arts Ctr★ CB23. . .60 C3
Wytches The CB6 . . . . .211 A7
WYTON. 142 F5
Wyton Airfield PE28. . . . . .153 F2
Wyton Prim Sch PE28 . . . .143 B8
Wyvern The PE28 . . . . .116 A7

Y

Yardy Cl PE15. . . . . .243 B4
Yarmouth Pl **1** CB9. . . . . .24 A8
Yarrow Cl PE15 . . . . .243 B5
Yarrow Rd CB1 . . . . .66 A5
YARWELL. 183 A8
Yarwell Cl PE2. . . . . .186 D7
Yarwells Headlands PE7 .189 D8
Yarwells Wlk PE7. . . . . . . .189 D8
YAXLEY. 181 F4
Yaxley Inf Sch PE7 . . . . . .181 E4
Yaxley Rd PE7 . . . . .177 B4
Yeats Cl CB1. . . . . .13 D1
Yeldham Pl CB9. . . . . .24 A8
YELLING. 98 C1
Yellowgate Rd PE28 . . . . . .154 A1
Yeomans Cl PE28 . . . . .136 D7
Yerril Gdn **3** CB9. . . . . . .23 E7
Yew Tree Wlk PE4 . . . . . . .197 A2
Yokine Gdns PE13. . . . . . .235 A3
York Cl
  Godmanchester PE29 . . . .141 F1
  Mildenhall IP28 . . . . .213 D8
Yorke Way CB6 . . . . .240 B3
York Gdns PE13. . . . . .245 D6
York Rd
  Chatteris PE16. . . . . .241 C4
  Haverhill CB9. . . . . .23 E7
  Peterborough PE1. . . . . . .197 F6
  9 Stamford PE9. . . . . . .244 B6
  Sutton CB6. . . . . .216 D1
  Wisbech PE13 . . . . .245 D6
York Row **23** PE13. . . . . .245 C5
York Sq PE13 . . . . .143 B8
York St CB1 . . . . .84 A1
York Terr
  Cambridge CB1 . . . . .84 A1
  Wisbech PE13 . . . . .245 C6
York Way
  Royston SG8 . . . . .5 B8
  St Ives PE27 . . . . .144 A8
Youngman Ave CB24 . . . . .104 C5
Youngman Cl CB24. . . . . . .104 C5
Young St CB1. . . . . .84 A2

Z

Zara Ct PE9. . . . . .244 B6
Zetland Wlk CB1. . . . . .65 D7

Addresses

Name and Address	Telephone	Page	Grid reference